FROMMER'S
COMPREHENSIVE TRAVEL GUIDE
CALIFORNIA & LAS VEGAS '91

by Mary Rakauskas

PRENTICE
HALL
PRESS

NEW YORK • LONDON • TORONTO • SYDNEY • TOKYO • SINGAPORE

FROMMER BOOKS

Published by Prentice Hall Press
A division of Simon & Schuster Inc.
15 Columbus Circle
New York, NY 10023

ISBN 0-13-333212-8
ISSN 1044-2146

Manufactured in the United States of America

CONTENTS

MAPS

Inflation Alert

It is hardly a secret that costs will rise regardless of the level of inflation. The author of this book has spent laborious hours attempting to ensure the accuracy of prices appearing in this guide. As we got to press, I believe we have obtained the most reliable data possible. Nonetheless, in the lifetime of this edition—particularly as it approaches 1992—the wise traveler will add 15% to 20% to the prices quoted throughout these pages.

A Disclaimer

Readers are advised that prices fluctuate in the course of time and travel information changes under the impact of the varied and volatile factors that affect the travel industry. The author and publisher cannot be held responsible for the experiences of the reader while traveling. Readers are invited to write the publisher with ideas, comments, and suggestions for future editions.

CALIFORNIA

California has the world's seventh-largest economy and is the home of the aerospace industry. It has the largest population of the 50 United States and possesses a bloc of volatile voters capable of affecting the election or rejection of a presidential candidate. Inexplicably to some, its 28 million inhabitants live with (and for the most part accept) the incredible natural forces unleashed by earthquakes.

Eureka! (I have found it!) is the motto of the State of California—and people have been echoing that sentiment since 1542, when navigator Juan Rodríguez Cabrillo in fact did find it. The first permanent white settlers were the Franciscan friars who came from Spain to convert and control the Native Americans as part of Spain's plan to colonize California. They erected a chain of 21 missions extending almost 600 miles from San Diego to Sonoma. The famous Mission Trail, begun in 1769 with the San Diego Mission, grew into El Camino Real (The Royal Road), which can be followed to this day.

It was almost a century later that the next wave of immigrants found their way to California—half a million forty-niners from clear around the world lured by the cry of "Gold!" Many of those who came for gold stayed to find their fortunes farming the millions of acres of virgin soil.

With the planting of orchards and vineyards—first sown by the mission padres—came great numbers of Mexican, Chinese, and Japanese laborers to tend them. Still more immigrants arrived from distant shores with the discovery of oil in the 1890s. And in the 1930s it was dreams of a land of milk and honey that prompted "Okies" by the thousands to leave their dust-storm-ravaged lands behind and head for California.

By this time, of course, the movie industry (itself a New York emigrant) was firmly rooted on West Coast soil, and Hollywood hopefuls were flocking to California to pursue glittering stardom.

Of course, not everyone who came to California found the rainbow's end. Very few of the prospectors of 1849 unearthed a gold mine (the daily profit of the average speculator was about $1). Only a relatively small number of aspirants ever struck oil, achieved stardom, or found the Promised Land. But that reality has not daunted California's incredible growth: One out of every 10 Americans lives here. Following a deep-rooted American tradition, people are still heading west to the Golden State—tourists and settlers, dreamers and speculators, spiritual seekers and political idealists—all lured by the sunshine, by the laid-back, free-and-easy life-style, and most of all, by California's magical ability to assume the shape of any dream.

FROM THE REDWOOD FORESTS TO THE L.A. FREEWAYS

Pack up your own dreams, and I can guarantee you'll run no risk of disappointment. California is a tourist mecca overflowing with attractions sufficient to satisfy and surprise the most jaded of visitors.

A land of almost excessive natural beauty, it contains Mount Whitney, at 14,500 feet the tallest mountain in the contiguous 48 United States. Death Valley, not far away in the Mojave Desert, is the lowest point in the entire Western

Hemisphere—almost 300 feet below sea level. Some 400 miles of towering trees make up the majestic "Redwood Empire." Visitors can marvel at the picturesque vineyard regions of the Napa Valley and Sonoma, explore quaint, historic towns like Monterey and Carmel, discover delightful beach resorts from Santa Cruz to Santa Barbara—and still not have seen the greater part of California.

There are more miles of coastline—1,264 to be exact—than in any other state except Alaska. Perhaps the most breathtakingly beautiful vista in the world is from the road (the famous Calif. 1) that winds along the Big Sur coast, yet it's only one of the many awe-inspiring California sights.

The results of human effort in California are equally impressive—and as diverse. Los Angeles and San Francisco are both "typical" of California, yet they share no apparent similarities—nor do they wish to.

Los Angeles presents a glamorous, sometimes bawdy, often ostentatious face. Crisscrossed by an astonishing number of freeways, it sprawls on seemingly forever. It's the home of the stars, stamping ground of wealthy jet-setters, right wingers, and every faction of the lunatic fringe—a colossal Technicolor ode to modernity, chic, sophistication, and success.

About 400 miles up the coast and a world away is mist-enshrouded San Francisco, draped delicately over steep hillsides—small, enchanting, elegant, independent, yet still a trifle zany. It's almost a conglomerate of tiny self-contained cities squeezed into a small area superficially shaped like a compressed accordion.

San Diego resembles neither of the above and is proud of it. The largest county and second most populous city in California, it has an ideal climate, a marvelous zoo, and somewhat less air pollution than Los Angeles (as of this writing). It also has more U.S. Navy personnel, more golf courses, and possibly more retirees than either Los Angeles or San Francisco, but it does not appear to be seeking increases in any of these categories, with the possible exception of the golfing facilities.

Sporting enthusiasts in particular will find there's too much to do in just one trip to California. Facilities abound for everything from skiing to hang-gliding—the wide spectrum encompassing fishing, boating, white-water rafting, golf, tennis, surfing hiking, scuba diving, snorkeling, horseback riding, mountain climbing, camping, even skateboarding.

Then, of course, there are the "special" attractions of California. They range from Disneyland (one of scores of amusement-park extravaganzas) to Hearst Castle to across-the-Nevada-border gambling centers at South Lake Tahoe, Reno, and Las Vegas (Reno is not included in this book).

All of this, along with much, much more, is why so many tourists come to California—and why so many consistently return or never leave.

ABOUT THIS BOOK

In brief, this is a guidebook giving specific, practical details (including prices) about hotels, restaurants, nightlife, sightseeing attractions, and other tourist-related activities throughout California and Las Vegas. I've tried to open up some new realms for you to explore, to give you the data you need to make a vacation into an adventure. Establishments in all price ranges have been described, from the luxurious Beverly Hills Hotel in (you guessed it) Beverly Hills to a little bath-in-the-hall budget hostelry in San Francisco. No restaurant, hotel, or other establishment has paid to be included in this book. What you read are entirely personal recommendations, carefully checked out and judged by the strict yardstick of value. If they measured up—gave good value for the money—they were included, regardless of price range.

You'll find that the majority of listings are geared neither to the super-rich nor to the best-things-in-life-are-free contingent. Rather, the book is aimed at the dollarwise middle-income traveler who wants occasionally to splurge and occasionally to save, but always to get maximum value for his or her dollar.

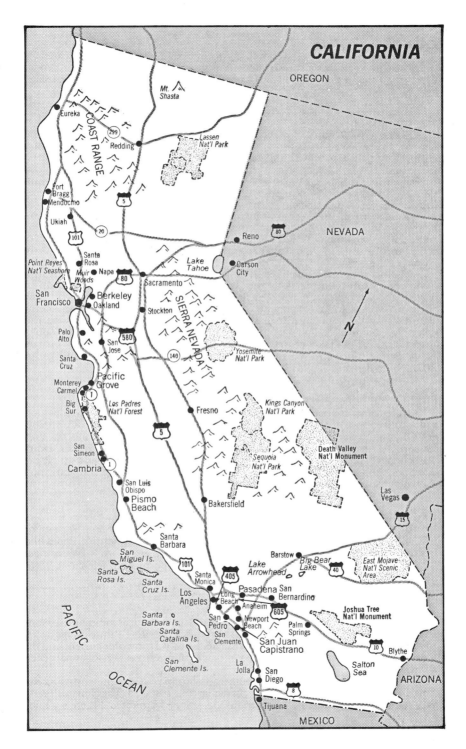

CALIFORNIA HOTELS

As a state that yearly receives millions of visitors, California is well prepared for the onslaught with the best accommodations situation I've ever seen. In just about every city, I found a good selection of hotels, motels, and inns in every price range and category.

For the Frugal

I've covered all kinds of hotels, but I want to make a special recommendation here for the traveler who is on a particularly tight budget. The no-frills **Motel 6** chain, charging $20 to $37 for a single room, $26 to $43 for a double, depending on locale and season, has motels in over 90 key California locations, including Anaheim, South Lake Tahoe, Monterey, Napa, Palo Alto, San Diego, San Jose, San Luis Obispo, Santa Barbara—even posh Palm Springs. All units have air conditioning and shower baths, most locations have swimming pools, and they're almost all centrally located, frequently near some luxury hotel in whose plush coffee shop you can enjoy your morning bacon and eggs. And they now have free TVs and phones in the rooms, with free local calls. For a listing of all Motel 6 locations, write to Motel 6, Inc., 14651 Dallas Pkwy., Dallas, TX 75240. It's best to make reservations as far in advance as possible.

Another excellent budget-saving choice is **Allstar Inns,** of which there are over 50 in convenient California locations, including Fullerton (near Disneyland), La Mesa (San Diego), Long Beach, Rancho Mirage (Palm Springs), Carpinteria (Santa Barbara), Salinas (near Monterey), San Luis Obispo, and Vallejo (near Marine World Africa USA). All units are air-conditioned and have full tubs and showers, free color TVs, and free local phone calls. Their singles range from $23 to $29, doubles from $29 to $35, and they charge $6 for each additional person. Most locations have pools. For a listing of Allstar Inn locations, write to Allstar Inns, L. P., P.O. Box 3070, Santa Barbara, CA 93130.

First Come is *Not* First Served

To reiterate, tourists flock like lemmings to California shores. I've seen enormous conventions of Shriners, Rosicrucians, and once even (shudder!) IRS employees fill an entire city of hotel rooms. You're taking a big chance, and certainly lessening your options, if you don't book ahead, particularly in summer. Don't waste hours of precious vacation time hunting down hotel rooms when a simple call or two in advance will take care of business. Be a smart lemming and you won't drown in a sea of tourists and conventioneers.

CALIFORNIA CAMPING

If you prefer roughing it, California has a terrific state park system. For a guide to California's parks, you can write to the **California Department of Parks and Recreation,** Publications Unit, P.O. Box 942896, Sacramento, CA 94296. Enclose $2 for the guide, postage, and handling. For more information, telephone 916/322-7000.

CALIFORNIA CLIMATE

The two words "California climate" create a phrase about as meaningless as any I've ever heard. Climate here varies from the summer's sizzling Palm Springs desert to the cool mountain regions, and factors like the cold Humboldt current and the warm Japanese current swirling about don't make things any easier. Regional generalizations follow.

As far as weather is concerned, Southern California (an area encompassing San Luis Obispo to San Diego) has no one particular tourist season. The climate doesn't vary too much, although the summer months are the warmest and there is a rainy

Average Monthly Temperatures (°F)

Los Angeles		San Francisco	
January	55.8	January	50.7
February	57.1	February	53.0
March	59.4	March	54.7
April	61.8	April	55.7
May	64.8	May	57.4
June	68.0	June	59.1
July	73.0	July	58.8
August	73.1	August	59.4
September	71.9	September	62.0
October	67.4	October	61.4
November	62.7	November	57.4
December	58.2	December	52.5

season (except in San Diego) from January to May. After that, don't even bother packing your umbrella. When it rains in summer, Southern Californians go outside to look at the novelty. Be warned that when the sun goes down the air is considerably cooler, so pack some warmer apparel for nocturnal adventures. The Los Angeles monthly temperature chart in the box will give you a fair indication for the entire region.

Up north, the climate is even trickier. In San Francisco, for instance, the mercury rarely dips below 40°F or rises above 70°. When the latter occurs, Bay Area residents go into a tropical stupor and mutter darkly about a "heat wave," while astonished New York tourists consider the weather balmy. Anyway, San Francisco seldom gets more than a few hottish days every summer, and a warm jacket or coat is a *must*—much more important than your bathing suit. Coastal regions north as far as Mendocino and south to about Santa Cruz are fairly close to San Francisco in climate, give or take a few degrees. Once again, check the chart for average monthly temperatures in San Francisco.

Areas farther east of the coast get progressively warmer, unless they're in the mountains—like South Lake Tahoe, where, for instance, April temperatures will be anywhere between 1°F and 74° and you may encounter a snowstorm in June!

In the coastal area between San Luis Obispo and Santa Cruz, things might vary in either direction.

In summation: When you go to sunny California, take some warm clothes along.

CALIFORNIA LANGUAGE

It is now law in the State of California that English (or for those who are sticklers, American) is the official language of the state, though it may not always seem so.

AN INVITATION TO READERS

Like all the Frommer Guides, *Frommer's California and Las Vegas* hopes to maintain a continuing dialogue between its writer and its readers. All of us share a common aim to travel as widely and as well as possible, at the best value for our money. And in achieving that goal, your comments and suggestions can be of tremendous help. Therefore, if you come across a particularly appealing hotel, restaurant, store, even sightseeing attraction, please don't keep it to yourself. And the solicitation of letters applies not only to new establishments but also to hotels or restaurants already recommended in this guide. The fact that a listing appears in this edition doesn't give it squatter's rights in future publications. If its services have deteriorated, its chef grown stale, its prices risen unfairly, whatever, these failings should be known. Even if you enjoyed every place and found every description accurate—that, too, is good to know. Send your comments to Frommer Books, Prentice Hall Travel, 15 Columbus Circle, New York, NY 10023.

Other Prentice Hall Travel Guides to California and Las Vegas

In addition to the guide you are now reading, Prentice Hall publishes six other guides that cover California and Las Vegas. Each provides information for travelers with particular needs.

Frommer's California with Kids is a must for parents traveling in California. It provides key information on selecting the best accommodations, restaurants, and sightseeing for the particular needs of the family, whether the kids are toddlers, school-age, preteens, or teens.

Frommer's San Francisco, Frommer's Los Angeles, and **Frommer's Las Vegas** are pocket-sized guides to hotels, restaurants, nightspots, and sightseeing attractions covering all price ranges.

Gault Millau Los Angeles and **Gault Millau San Francisco** are irreverent, savvy, and comprehensive guides with candid reviews of over 1,000 restaurants, hotels, shops, nightspots, museums, and sights.

For order forms with which to order these and all the Prentice Hall travel guides, as well as information on the **Frommer's Dollarwise Travel Club,** turn to the last four pages of this book.

GETTING THERE

1. TRAVELING TO CALIFORNIA
2. TRAVELING WITHIN CALIFORNIA
3. CALIFORNIA FAST FACTS

How you get to the Golden State and how you get around it obviously depend on where you're coming from, how much you want to spend, how much time you have, and similar considerations. What follows is information on the various options.

1. Traveling to California

BY AIR
TWA, United, Delta, Pan Am, and **American Airlines** connect most major American cities with San Francisco and Los Angeles.

Your best bet is to consult a travel agent (it's free), who can tell you the latest developments and newest fares. Make your arrangements as soon as you know your departure date, since some budget fares depend on advance purchase and can be substantially lower than regular coach fares.

Package Tours
All the above-mentioned airlines, and many others, offer packages that include land arrangements—car rental, tours, hotel, etc.—along with airfare. If you're interested in a package, it's once again advisable to discuss the many options with a travel agent, who can find the plan that most perfectly fits your needs.

BY BUS
The **Greyhound/Trailways** system encompasses every major American city and many less-than-major cities in its vast transportation network. The line offers excellent excursion sales. For instance, the regular New York to Los Angeles or San Francisco round-trip fare is $230, or $120 if you pay 30 days in advance of departure and depart Monday through Thursday.

Depending on how you take to bus travel, and how many places you want to visit, the Greyhound/Trailways **Ameripass** can provide terrific savings. These passes offer unlimited travel between *all* route cities for a fixed price during a given time period. Prices are $189 for 7 days, $249 for 14 days, and $349 for 30 days. It's also a good idea to ask if any special rates are in effect.

BY TRAIN

Amtrak, the nation's most complete long-distance passenger railroad network, connects about 500 American cities, over 30 of them in California.

By train, in coach, round trip between New York and San Francisco, and New York and Los Angeles, is $340. However, as with bus travel, special rates may be available, so be sure to ask. This is a 45-day excursion rate allowing three stopovers.

Amtrak also has family plans, tours, and other money-saving fares. And often they offer good value to and from cities other than New York. Call them for details and further information (tel. toll free 800/USA-RAIL).

---

2. Traveling Within California

BY CAR

In every chapter of this book, easy-to-follow driving instructions have been provided. Within this chapter as well those on San Francisco, Los Angeles, and Las Vegas, there are data on car rentals. Of course, you'll want to pick up a good map of the state before you start your trip and keep it handy in the glove compartment. In addition, a glance at the boxed mileage chart will give you a quick idea of distances between various California cities.

My first two words of advice on car rentals are *plan ahead*. If you intend to rent a car during your vacation, check your policy and call your insurance agent to determine the limits of your coverage before you leave home. Does your insurance cover collision damage to the rented car? If not, you may want to pay the added cost for the collision- or loss-damage waiver. As of this writing, most rental firms make customers liable for damage up to the total value of the car. The waiver currently averages $10 to $12 per day.

It's becoming increasingly difficult to keep up with the changes many car-rental companies are making. One such change is the shift of responsibility for theft of vehicles or damage caused by vandalism (previously covered by the company) to

---

Distances (in miles) by Car from San Francisco to:

Oakland	13	Avenue of the Giants	240
Muir Woods	17	Yosemite	193
Tiburon	18	South Lake Tahoe	209
Napa Valley	46	Monterey	130
Sonoma	45	Big Sur	156
Marriott's Great America	45	San Simeon	224
San Jose	48	San Luis Obispo	266
Santa Cruz	74	Santa Barbara	332
Mendocino	125	Los Angeles	460
Fort Bragg	166	Palm Springs	565

From Los Angeles to:

San Diego	125	Las Vegas	298

renters. To avoid liability for damage or theft, as well as collision damage, renters must buy what is now called the loss-damage waiver (formerly the collision-damage waiver). Some of the major credit-card companies provide most, if not all, of the above coverage if you charge your car rental using their cards. Be sure to check this out in advance.

First, let's say that if you rent from one of the well-established companies, large or small, the odds are that the car won't be a clunker. You're obviously going to check the cost (daily or weekly) and the charge for mileage, as well as optional insurance and taxes. And since not all rental companies are located at the airport, ask about pickup and delivery—you may need a taxi (heaven forbid) or shuttle-bus ride to or from the terminal. Those are the basics.

If you plan to pick up the car at one location and return it to another, ask about the drop-off charge, if any. And if you rent the car at a weekly rate and decide to return it early, you may be charged at the much higher daily rate. *Ask!*

Then before you drive away, check the registration—make certain it's still in effect. Finally, find out if the company has its own emergency phone number and one for emergency road service.

BY AIR

National airlines, as well as local airlines, provide service to San Francisco, Los Angeles, San Diego, and Las Vegas. The airlines serving these points are listed under the "Getting There" sections in the chapters covering each of these cities.

BUS AND TRAIN

Once again, **Greyhound/Trailways** can provide bus service to just about anywhere you want to go in California, plus Las Vegas. The merger of Greyhound and Trailways has resulted in the elimination of some of their former terminals. In some cities, as in San Francisco, the name Greyhound is still the only designation for the merged bus system. Its terminal there is located at the Transbay Terminal, at First and Mission streets. The main Greyhound/Trailways terminal in Los Angeles is downtown at 208 E. 6th St.; in San Diego, the terminal is at 120 W. Broadway.

Amtrak has trains serving over 30 California cities. Amtrak service from the San Francisco area to Los Angeles and Seattle operates out of Oakland. Regularly scheduled connecting buses leave San Francisco from the Transbay Terminal. From Los Angeles, Amtrak has service south to San Diego and north to Oakland, Seattle, and points in between. Amtrak also has daily service between Los Angeles and Las Vegas. **Southern Pacific** has train service from San Francisco to the towns of the Peninsula.

3. California Fast Facts

The information contained below is intended to arm you with facts suitable for coping with assorted general needs and contingencies. You'll find more detailed basic information for the larger cities under "Fast Facts" at the beginning of the chapters on San Francisco, Los Angeles, San Diego, and Las Vegas.

AIRLINES: Every major domestic carrier and most international carriers serve California; international flights arrive and depart via San Francisco International Airport (SFO) and Los Angeles International Airport (LAX), the two most heavily trafficked airports in the state.

AIRPORTS: See the "Getting There" sections of the chapters on individual cities.

AREA CODES: California has more area codes than any other state. This chart and its footnotes will help you sort them out.

California Telephone Area Codes

Anaheim	714	Palm Springs	619
Berkeley	415*	San Diego	619
Big Sur	408	San Fernando Valley	818
Buena Park	714	San Francisco	415
Burbank	818	San Jose	408
Carmel	408	San Luis Obispo	805
Fort Bragg	707	San Simeon	805
La Jolla	619	Santa Barbara	805
Los Angeles	213 or 818**	Santa Cruz	408
Monterey	408	Sausalito	415
Napa Valley	707	Sonoma	707
Newport Beach	714	South Lake Tahoe	916
Oakland	415*	Yosemite	209

Telephone numbers with 800 as the area code may be dialed toll free from anywhere in the U.S., unless otherwise indicated.
* Pacific Bell advises that as of October 7, 1991, Oakland and Berkeley will have the new area code of 510. The boundary for the new area code is San Francisco Bay. Alameda and Contra Costa counties will also be identified with the new area code.
** After February 1, 1992, parts of Los Angeles County will be identified with the new area code of 310. As of this writing, the new code will include Los Angeles International Airport (LAX); the western, coastal, southern, and eastern portions of the county; and communities such as West Los Angeles, San Pedro, and Whittier. The reason for the addition is that Pacific Bell is running out of telephone numbers in the Los Angeles area. And so it grows!

BANKS: As with most states, banks are generally open Monday through Friday from 10am to 3pm (some from 9am to 4pm and some on Saturday). However, if you need to cash a check, your hotel may be your best resource.

CHARGE CARDS: Please note that not all restaurants, stores, or shops in California accept all major credit cards, and some accept none. Therefore, check first if you expect to use plastic for a large expenditure; it can save annoyance and possible embarrassment. If you're visiting from another state, you may not know that in California you can charge package liquor purchases.

CLIMATE: See the "California Climate" section in the Introduction.

CRIME: As in all states with a considerable influx of tourists from within the U.S. and abroad, crime is always a problem in the larger cities. Whenever you're traveling in an unfamiliar city or country, stay alert. Be aware of your immediate surroundings. To avoid an unpleasant incident or an end to a pleasurable trip, use common sense. One practical option is to leave valuables in the hotel safe. Wear a moneybelt and don't sling your camera or purse over your shoulder; wear the strap diagonally across your body. This will minimize the possibility of your becoming a victim of crime. Every society has it criminals. It's your responsibility to be aware and alert, even in the most heavily touristed areas.

CURRENCY EXCHANGE: Foreign-currency exchange services are provided by the **Bank of America** in San Francisco and Los Angeles at both international airports; for other locations, it's best to check with the bank. Branches of **Deak International** also serve San Diego, San Francisco, and Los Angeles.

DENTISTS: Hotels usually have a list of dentists, should you need one, but they are always listed in the *Yellow Pages* as well. Or contact the local Dental Society for referrals.

DOCTORS: Here again, hotels usually have a list of doctors on call. For referrals, contact the local medical association.

DRIVING: For a start, California law requires buckling up seatbelts; this applies to both driver and passenger. Then be sure to carry registration and proof of insurance in the car, whether you're driving your own vehicle or a rented one. Pay attention to signs and arrows on the streets and roadways or you may find yourself in a lane that requires exiting or turning when you want to go straight on. You can turn right at a red light, unless otherwise indicated—but be sure to come to a stop first. Pedestrians always have the right-of-way; so stop if one steps into the street in front of you. And whatever your destination, if you are unfamiliar with the area, get a map and orient yourself before you're on the freeway. For some reason I've yet to determine, freeway signs frequently indicate direction by the name of a town (one you may never have heard of) rather than north, south, east, or west.

As for individual cities, driving in San Francisco is relatively easy if you have no hang-ups about stopping at the top of a hill and waiting for the light to change or negotiating your way through snug traffic. On-the-street parking is tough to find there, and garage parking is relatively expensive, especially if you expect to park for only an hour or two. And remember, cable cars—like pedestrians—always have the right-of-way; on wet days it's a good idea to avoid their slippery tracks. (See "Driving in San Francisco" in Section 3 of Chapter II.)

Driving in Los Angeles is a cross between an art form and a competitive sport. It poses few problems once you get the hang of the freeway system—where the freeways are and where they go. A good map, courage, and much patience, especially during the drive-to-and-from-work hours, will help. In fact, to save yourself much aggravation, it would be best to avoid driving during the usual commuting hours.

Driving in San Diego is a cinch compared to driving in Los Angeles, but here, too, a good map will help to work out the freeway system. And don't forget what I've said about getting the lay of the land before you plunge onto the freeways.

EARTHQUAKES: There will always be earthquakes in California—most of which you will never notice. However, in case of a significant earthquake, there are a few precautionary measures to take, whether you're inside a high-rise hotel, out driving, or just walking.

When you are inside a building, seek cover—do not run outside. Move away from windows in the direction of what would be the center of the building. Get under a large, sturdy piece of furniture (like a desk in an office, a bed in a hotel) or stand against a wall or under a doorway. When exiting the building, use stairwells, *not* elevators.

If you are in your car, pull over to the side of the road and stop, but not until you are away from bridges or overpasses, and telephone or power poles and lines. Stay in your car.

If you are out walking, stay outside and away from trees or power lines or the *sides* of buildings. If you are in an area with tall buildings, find a doorway to stand in.

EMERGENCIES: For police, fire, highway patrol, or life-threatening medical emergencies, dial **911.**

EVENTS AND FESTIVALS: See the "Fast Facts" sections of the chapters on individual cities.

FOOD: San Francisco and Los Angeles are cities with restaurants for everyone. There are over 100 Chinese restaurants and more Italian restaurants than you would believe could prosper just in San Francisco alone. Both cities also have Indian, American, Japanese, Moroccan, French, Greek, Basque, Czech, Jewish, Tuscan, Vietnamese, Lithuanian, Mexican, Salvadorean, old nouvelle, new nouvelle, and cuisines that combine several into one. Some of the most creative chefs in the country work in one or the other of these two cities. And the food ranges from good to superb. San Diego is working toward this stature.

And one further word about eating. Throughout California there are innumerable chains serving fast food, and not-so-fast food, best categorized as rather mediocre. There are three notable exceptions: **Denny's,** found throughout the state (and open 24 hours); **Chili's,** found in such places as Palo Alto and Las Vegas; and **La Salsa,** found primarily in Southern California, notably Los Angeles and San Diego. All serve excellent food at modest prices.

LIQUOR LAWS: In California, liquor and grocery stores, as well as some drugstores, can sell packaged alcoholic beverages between 6am and 2am. Most restaurants, nightclubs, and bars are licensed to serve alcoholic beverages during the same hours. The legal age for purchase and consumption is 21, and proof of age is required.

MEDICAL SERVICES: See "Dentists" and "Doctors," above.

PETS: Hotels and motels generally will not accept pets. If you're traveling with Rover or Katie the Cat, ask before making the reservations. Motel 6 will accept a pet (of a size within reason) in the room, but will not permit the animals to be left unattended.

POLICE: For emergency help, dial 911. I stress the word "emergency"—this does not include misplaced objects, flat tires, etc. However, theft, burglary, and other crimes should be reported immediately.

SPORTS (SPECTATOR): The three major cities in California all have baseball and football teams of note, though of varying degrees of proficiency. Two have top-notch basketball teams. You'll find more details on all of the teams and where you can view the action (or inaction, in some instances) under the "Fast Facts" for each city.

STORE HOURS: Stores are usually open Monday through Saturday from 10am to 6pm; most (except some malls and department stores) are closed Sunday.

TAXES: California state sales tax is 7¼%.

TIPPING: In most California restaurants, just follow the usual U.S. tipping practices: standard 15%, 20% if the service was excellent. However, in some California restaurants, 15% will automatically be added to the cost of the meal, in which case you will see it listed above the total.

If you're checking into a hotel with several bags, a tip of $5 is par for the course. Valet parking is a great convenience at many hotels. A tip of $1 is appropriate for the service, over and above the charge for parking. And when you're leaving the hotel, a tip of $1 per day for the period of your stay, left in your room, will be appreciated.

SAN FRANCISCO

What is the secret of San Francisco's continuing attraction? Ask anyone who has fallen in love—it's romantic, breathtaking, classy, bohemian, frequently unpredictable, a bit eccentric, exciting, gutsy, and very much a survivor.

Overlooking San Francisco's two major earthquakes—one in April 1906, the other in October 1989—would be like ignoring the tilt in the Leaning Tower of Pisa. The one in 1906 left much of the city in ruins. What happened, or rather what did not happen, to San Francisco on October 17, 1989, demonstrates what the city has learned in 83 years—structural techniques for survival—and what it has yet to improve. The force of the quake (7.1 on the Richter scale) collapsed whole sections of the Oakland Bay Bridge and tore at Interstate 880. Though hardworking construction crews quickly healed many wounds, you may still see tragedies sculpted in the fallen brick and torn metal of the Marina section and the scarring and devastation south in Santa Cruz, Los Gatos, and Watsonville.

The city of San Francisco has retained most of its beauty and allure, however. You'll find much that is exciting and unusual atop Nob Hill, along the waterfront, in North Beach, Chinatown, Union Square, the area known as South of Market, the Mission Street and Castro Street sections, Japantown, and Golden Gate Park.

There are thousands of quotable quotes about San Francisco, from Georges Pompidou's approbatory tribute—"Your city is remarkable not only for its beauty. It is also, of all the cities in the United States, the one whose name, the world over, conjures up the most visions and more than any other incites one to dream"—to the pithy praise of Francis Ford Coppola: "I kinda like this place."

Most people do. This 47-square-mile peninsular city exerts a compelling charm, composed of open-air fish markets at the Wharf, Victorian houses, exotic ethnic districts (from whence springs a lauded international cuisine), quaint, bell-clanking cable cars, and sudden, breathtaking glimpses of the ocean and Golden Gate Bridge from atop steep hills.

The hills at first seem of an impossible steepness (bring comfortable shoes), but you'll soon find yourself enjoying the exercise, the views, and the camaraderie of fellow mountaineers. And as someone once said, "When you get tired of walking around San Francisco, you can always lean against it."

---

1. Getting There

AIRLINES

Domestic carriers serving the San Francisco International Airport include **Air Cal** (tel. 415/433-2660), **Alaska Airlines,** (tel. 415/931-8888, or toll free 800/426-0333), **American** (tel. 415/398-4434, or toll free 800/433-7300), **Delta** (tel. 415/552-5700, or toll free 800/221-1212), **Northwest Airlines,** (tel. 415/392-2163, or toll free 800/225-2525), **Southwest** (tel. 415/885-1221, or toll free 800/531-5601), **TWA** (tel. toll free 800/221-2000), **United** (tel. 415/397-2100), and **USAir** (tel. 415/956-8636, or toll free 800/428-4322).

Domestic carriers serving the Oakland Airport are **Alaska Airlines, Alpha Air** (tel. toll free 800/421-9353), **America West** (tel. 415/839-1292, or toll free 800/247-5692), **American, Southwest, United,** and **USAir.**

AIRPORTS

The **San Francisco International Airport** has undergone massive rebuilding to accommodate increased traffic. Located on the bay, 15 miles south of the city on U.S. 101, it is at least a 45-minute ride from the city. **SFO Airporter** (tel. 415/673-2433) provides buses serving the downtown area near Union Square, with stops at the Grand Hyatt San Francisco on Union Square, the San Francisco Hilton, the Westin St. Francis, the Parc Fifty Five, and the Meridien San Francisco; the fare is $5 for adults, $2.50 for children under 17 accompanied by an adult. **SAM-TRANS buses** (tel. 415/761-7000) serve the downtown as well as the southern peninsula; the fare to downtown is $1. There's also a 24-hour **Super Shuttle** (tel. 415/558-8500) airport service that, with six hours' notice (minimum), will pick you up at your door (hotel or residence) and take you to the airport 45 to 60 minutes before departure. Or you can arrange to have them pick you up at the airport. The fare to downtown is $10. **Taxi** fare to downtown is about $28.

Oakland International Airport is about 5 miles south of downtown Oakland on Calif. 17 (I-880) at the Hegenberger Road exit. It primarily serves East Bay communities, though more and more San Francisco travelers do use it. There's lots of parking space, and bus service is available to and from various Bay Area locations. There is also **BART,** San Francisco's rail service. Shuttle buses to BART (signs say "Air BART") stop in front of terminals 1 and 2 near the signs for ground transportation; every 15 to 20 minutes one of the vans comes by to take passengers to the BART Coliseum station. The fare on the van is $1. The fare on BART varies according to your destination, but the fare to downtown San Francisco is about $2; the trip takes 45 minutes. **Taxi** fare will be approximately $28.

If you need to know the location of the airport terminal from which you will be departing, the *Smart Yellow Pages* of the San Francisco telephone directory gives a handy illustration at the front of the book under the "Airports" heading.

Other Airport Transportation

Another approach for getting to downtown San Francisco will make life easier, providing you plan in advance; it is also less costly than a taxi. The **AM/PM Airporter** (tel. 415/547-2155) will meet you any time of the day or night, with an advance reservation. Depending on the number of people, the cost from Oakland Airport generally is $35 or less; check it out when you call. The AM/PM Airporter (otherwise called "Al") will meet you at Terminal 2 or at the Information Desk (tel. 415/577-4015) at Oakland Airport and at the baggage claim at San Francisco International Airport.

TRAINS

Amtrak service to and from Los Angeles and Seattle operates out of Oakland. Regularly scheduled connecting buses leave San Francisco from the Transbay Terminal (tel. 415/982-8512).

BUSES

Greyhound Bus Lines serves San Francisco from most cities in California. Greyhound is located at the Transbay Terminal at First and Mission streets (tel. 415/558-6746). For general information and schedules, call your nearest ticket office.

2. Getting Your Bearings

San Francisco is a town to walk in. The hub of the city is **Union Square,** flanked by Geary, Post, Powell, and Stockton streets. Named for a series of violent pro-union demonstrations staged here in Civil War days, today it is an impeccably manicured 2.6-acre park, planted with palms, yews, boxwood, and flowers. You'd never know you were sitting atop a huge underground garage capable of housing over 1,000 automobiles. This compact area is the logical setting for many of San Francisco's hotels.

From Union Square it's an easy walk to the gateway of **Chinatown** at Bush Street and Grant Avenue.

Adjoining Chinatown is **North Beach** (where Columbus crosses Grant), home of San Francisco's Italian community and a slightly passé bohemian outpost similar to New York's Greenwich Village; the scene has moved elsewhere, but the atmosphere lingers on.

Keep going in the same direction and you come to the **Embarcadero,** one of the world's largest and busiest ports. Slightly to the west lie **Fisherman's Wharf** and **Aquatic Park.**

Union Square is equally convenient to the **Financial District,** to the northeast; and a few blocks south of Union Square is **Market Street,** the city's seemingly endless main artery.

South of Market Street is an area appropriately named **South of Market** and sensibly abbreviated to SOMA. A few blocks to the south of Market Street and paralleling same is Folsom Street, part industrial, part gay, part nightlife. Tracking south on Market takes you through some of **Haight** (you remember Haight-Ashbury) and through **Castro**—a focal point of the gay community that begins at the intersection of Castro, Market, and 17th.

GOLDEN GATE BRIDGE

No description of San Francisco would be near complete without mention of the Golden Gate Bridge, the most beautiful bridge in the world—a 1.7-mile-long span of spidery bracing cables and lofty red-orange towers—50 years old in 1987. As beautiful to look at as to look out from, the Golden Gate can be enjoyed from many vantage points of the city and can be crossed by bus, car, foot, or bicycle. Every year an average of 28 million vehicles cross it, and millions of pedestrians enjoy the terrific views.

Bridge-bound Golden Gate Transit buses depart every half hour during the day for **Marin County,** starting from the Transbay Terminal at Mission and 1st streets and making convenient stops at Market and 7th streets, at the Civic Center, and along Van Ness Avenue and Lombard Street. Call 415/332-6600 for schedule information.

SAN FRANCISCO–OAKLAND BAY BRIDGE

Less celebrated, but nonetheless important, this 8¼-mile silvery giant links San Francisco with **Oakland,** her neighbor across the bay. You can drive across the bridge (toll is $1 coming into the city, nothing going out). Or you can catch an AC Transit bus at the Transbay Terminal (Mission at 1st Street) and ride to downtown Oakland.

---

3. Getting Around

San Francisco is easier to get around than most large American cities. For one thing, most attractions are within walking distance of your hotel and of each other. And the public transportation is excellent, varied, and efficient.

Most of San Francisco's public transport is operated by the Municipal Railway, always referred to as the **MUNI.** Its streetcars and buses service an area of about 700 square miles. (For detailed information, call 415/673-MUNI or consult the bus map and routings at the front of the *Yellow Pages* in the San Francisco telephone book.) Fares are an extremely reasonable 85¢ on all buses and streetcars, $2 on cable cars (exact change only). Express buses, which stop at major intersections only, also charge 85¢. Transfers are free on all rides and are good in any direction for 1½ hours. San Francisco bus and streetcar drivers are usually cheerful, courteous, and helpful, but they're not equipped to make change—so have correct fare ready when you board.

San Francisco now offers a **transit pass** for unlimited rides on the public transportation system (including the cable cars). The San Francisco Municipal Railway Passport is $6 for one day, $10 for three consecutive days. With presentation of the pass, $1 discounts are available at the M. H. De Young Memorial Museum, the Asian Art Museum, the California Academy of Sciences, the California Palace of the Legion of Honor, the Maritime Museum and historic ships, the USS *Pampanito,* the SS *Jeremiah O'Brien,* the Exploratorium, and the San Francisco Zoo; discounts of 50¢ are given at Coit Tower and the Japanese Tea Garden. Among the places where you can purchase the pass are the Visitor Information Center at Hallidie Plaza (Powell and Market), the STBS ticket booth at Union Square, and the cable-car ticket booth at Pier 39.

STREETCARS

There are five lines, lettered, **J, K, L, M,** and **N,** and they all run up and down Market Street past the Civic Center, from whence they proceed in different directions. Streetcars are gradually being replaced by the MUNI metro, which will run alongside of and under BART in the downtown area.

BUSES

Some 70 different bus lines go to virtually every point on the San Francisco map, as well as to Marin County and Oakland. For information on city bus routes, call **MUNI** at 415/673-MUNI. Other bus information is available from **Golden Gate Transit** (tel. 415/332-6600) and **AC Transit** (tel. 415/839-2882).

TRAINS

Southern Pacific has train service from San Francisco to the towns on the Peninsula. The depot is at 700 4th St., at Townsend (tel. 415/541-1000).

CABLE CARS

A century-old San Francisco tradition, cable cars were named a national historic landmark in 1964. With no engines, cable cars are hoisted along by means of a steel cable permanently moving at a speed of 9½ miles an hour; it feels considerably faster, though, when you're slamming around curves on San Francisco terrain that turn this ride into a veritable roller coaster. About half the passengers at any given time are tourists aboard for the ride itself, which further enhances the amusement-park atmosphere.

A typical San Francisco sight is the crew manually reversing the cars on a turntable at Powell and Market streets—always with a crowd of willing helpers. And the cars' clanging bells are an essential part of the San Francisco experience.

The two types of cable cars in use hold a maximum of 90 to 100 passengers, in theory—in practice, it's as many as can grab on somewhere.

There are three lines in all. The **Powell-Mason line** leads from the corner of Powell and Market streets in the center of the shopping district up over Nob Hill and down again into the lively hubbub of Fisherman's Wharf. The **Powell-Hyde line** follows a scenic and exciting vertical and lateral zigzag course from the corner of Powell and Market streets over both Nob Hill and Russian Hill to a turntable at gaslit Victorian Square in front of Aquatic Park. Ghirardelli Square is less than a block away. And the **California Street line** stretches from the foot of California Street in the Financial District, cuts through Chinatown, and crests Nob Hill to Van Ness Avenue.

The cable-car fare is $2 for adults, but it's only $1 for students (ages 5 to 17) and 15¢ for seniors. Transfers are free.

Cable cars operate from about 6am to 12:30am. Call 415/673-MUNI for more information.

TAXIS

As everywhere else, this is an expensive way to get about: $2.90 for the first mile after the meter drops and $1.50 for each mile thereafter. It's about $28 from the airport to downtown. If you need one, though, it's not too hard to find a cab here. And if you call one, you pay no extra charge. Herewith, a few sample numbers:

Yellow Cab: 626-2345
Veteran's Cab: 552-1300
De Soto Cab: 673-1414
Luxor Cabs: 282-4141
Allied Taxi: 826-9494
City: 468-7200
Pacific: 986-7220

BART

I love to travel on BART (it stands for Bay Area Rapid Transit)—a supermodern, high-speed rapid-transit rail network that connects San Francisco with Oakland, Richmond, Concord, Daly City, and Fremont. Run by a system computerized right down to the ticket gate, BART offers a ride with the feel of a sci-fi adventure.

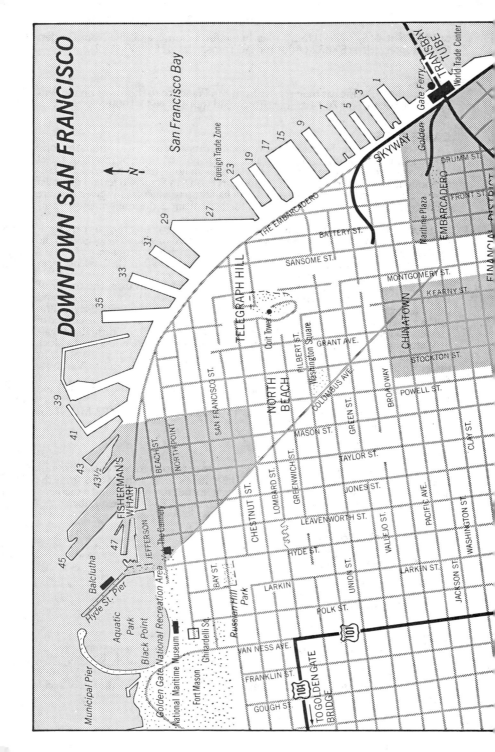

Its air-conditioned coaches are 70 feet long and come complete with such luxurious trappings as carpeted floors, tinted picture windows, and recessed lighting. The trains hit a top speed of 80 mph (average, including stops, is 42 mph), and the aforementioned computer system monitors and adjusts speeds and maintains safe spacing.

Minimum fare is 85¢ and extra costs depend on distance ($4 from Fremont to Daly City is the highest BART fare). Information boards at all stations show the fares to all other stations. And large maps in the stations and trains make this simple system extra easy to use.

If you're continuing your journey by local bus in the East Bay, get one free transfer to the AC Transit or MUNI bus system from the white machine in the station. Bus route and schedule information can be found in free *BART and Buses* folders in the stations.

BART operates Monday through Saturday from 6am to midnight and on Sunday from 9am to midnight. Children under 5 ride free; children 5 through 12 and handicapped persons can purchase a red ticket worth $16 for $1.60; at banks only, senior citizens can purchase a green ticket also worth $16 for $1.60. For information about BART routes and connections with other public transport, call 788-BART. You can pick up a copy of the *Fun Goes Farther on BART* brochure at any station. Or you can pick up the excellent *Regional Transit Guide,* which is sold in many bookstores throughout the city.

Even if you have no real reason to ride BART, you might want to try this computerized subway for the experience. It's like jumping into the 21st century.

DRIVING

Chapter I (see "Driving" in Section 3) provides you with an introduction to the fundamentals of getting around California and, to some extent, around the major cities. If you're a newcomer to driving in this state, read it—it can save a lot of wear and tear on all concerned.

As for San Francisco, first let's say that it's a profusion of one-way streets, which can create a few small problems in going around the block or in getting from point A to point B; however, most maps of the city indicate which way traffic flows. At the expense of repeating myself, remember that cable cars are like sailing ships—they *always* have the right-of-way. You may notice that they cannot change course. So don't argue with them; they're sturdy vehicles. On wet days their tracks tend to be slippery and are best avoided.

Note: When parking on a grade, engage the hand brake, put the car in gear, and *always* turn your wheels toward the curb when facing downhill; turn them away from the curb when facing uphill. In either case, you'll be using the curb as a block. This practice is law in San Francisco. Otherwise, your car may join the hundreds of yearly runaways, or at the least you'll get a parking ticket. And when driving downhill, always use low gear.

Street parking is a tough business (the local cops are the quickest tow-away lot I've ever seen). Parking lots abound in all the difficult-to-find-a-spot areas, but they're quite expensive. Where street parking is not metered, signs will tell you when you can park and for how long. Curb colors indicate reserved parking zones—red means don't stop, don't park—and they mean it. Blue is for the disabled with California-issued disabled plates or a placard. White is a five-minute limit. Yellow and yellow/black are for commercial vehicles. Once again, the San Francisco Police Department does not regard parking regulations lightly. Violate the law and you may be towed away, and that won't be cheap. In total, the tab to retrieve your car may be as much as $100 plus daily storage fees. So resist temptation and don't park at a bus stop or fire hydrant, and watch for street-cleaning signs. No matter how flush you are, parking in a garage is almost always cheaper and less stressful.

As long as I've brought up the topic of garages—short-term parking is expensive. It can run from $3.75 to as much as $5.25 ($1.75 for 20 minutes) for the first hour. For 24 hours, prices are more reasonable and usually range from $12 to $15. There are some exceptions, however, to the high cost of short-term garage parking.

In **Chinatown,** the best (and cheapest) place to park is the Portsmouth Square Garage at 733 Kearny (enter between Clay and Washington). Between 10:30am and 2:30pm you may wait in line to enter. The price is 75¢ for the first hour, $2 for two hours, $4 for three hours, $5.75 for four hours, on up to the maximum of $12.50 for 7 to 24 hours. At the **Civic Center,** try for the Civic Center Plaza at Taylor and O'Farrell, where parking starts at 75¢ per hour, $15 for 24 hours. **Downtown,** head for the Sutter-Stockton Garage at 330 Sutter, where it's 75¢ for the first hour, $14 for 24 hours. At **Fisherman's Wharf/Ghirardelli Square,** try the North Point Shopping Garage at 350 Bay, where the tab is $1 per half hour, $8.50 maximum; or the Ghirardelli Square Garage at 900 North Point, where they charge $1 per half hour, $6 maximum. On **Union Street,** in the area of high-traffic shopping, try for the Cow Hollow at 3060 Fillmore for $2 per hour, $10 maximum.

Car Rentals

If you ordinarily rent a car for business and the company pays for it, you may not need to know much about the subject. However, for those who are personally footing the bill, I've discussed the topic of car rentals in Chapter I under "Traveling Within California" (Section 2).

You don't need a car to explore most of San Francisco, and in crowded areas like Chinatown it's a handicap. But if you're going farther afield, you may want to utilize one of the many car-rental firms in the area.

Rentals of specific-size vehicles, including vans, are almost always easier to obtain from the big car-rental companies. Each of the companies I've mentioned below has an airport office at San Francisco International and at Oakland International, as well as more than one office in town.

Avis is at 675 Post St. (tel. 415/885-5011, or toll free 800/331-1212), at the San Francisco Airport (tel. 415/877-6780), and at the Oakland Airport (tel. 415/562-9000). **Budget Rent-A-Car** is at 321 Mason (Union Square) (tel. 415/775-5800, or toll free 800/527-0700), at the San Francisco Airport (tel. 415/875-6850), and at the Oakland Airport (tel. 415/568-7498). **Hertz** is at 433 Mason (tel. 415/771-2200, or toll free 800/654-3131), at the San Francisco Airport (tel. 415/877-1600), and at the Oakland Airport (tel. 415/568-1177). **National Car Rental** is at 550 O'Farrell St. (tel. 415/474-5300, or toll free 800/227-7368), at the San Francisco Airport (tel. 415/877-4745), and at the Oakland Airport (tel. 415/632-2225).

Whichever rental company you use, remember it's always a good idea to check out the car before you leave the lot.

4. San Francisco Fast Facts

This section organizes, in alphabetical order, some basic information intended to help make your trip as enjoyable and frustration-free as possible.

AREA CODE: The telephone area code for San Francisco is **415.** Pacific Bell advises that as of October 7, 1991, Oakland and Berkeley will have the new area code of **510.** The boundary for the new area code is San Francisco Bay. Alameda and Contra Costa counties will also be identified with the new area code.

BABY-SITTERS: If you're staying at one of the larger hotels, the concierge can usually recommend organizations to call. Be sure to check on the hourly cost (which may vary by day and time) as well as any additional expenses such as transportation and meals for the sitter. One such service is **Temporary Tot Tending** (tel. 415/355-

7377, 871-5790 after 6pm), which offers childcare by fully licensed teachers, by the hour or day, for children from infants on up. Open Monday through Friday from 6am to 9pm, except for conventions.

BANKS: As with most cities, banks are generally open Monday through Friday from 10am to 3pm (some from 9am to 4pm and some on Saturday). However, if you need to cash a check, your hotel may be your best resource, depending on the amount involved.

CHARGE CARDS: Please note that not all restaurants, stores, or shops in California accept all major credit cards, and some accept none. Therefore, check first if you expect to use plastic for a large expenditure—it can save annoyance and possibly some embarrassment. Purchases of package liquor can be charged in California.

CLIMATE: One major point to remember is that San Francisco has a cool marine climate year-round. There usually is morning and evening fog in the summer, a good deal of rain in the winter, and sun much of the remainder of the year. Women should take a light jacket or warm sweater or wear a suit. Men should wear light- to medium-weight suits or sports clothes. Bringing an all-weather coat is a good idea for both sexes. Lightweight summer clothes are rarely, if ever, useful. (See the "Average Monthly Temperature" chart on page 5.)

CRIME: As in all cities with a considerable influx of tourists from within the U.S. and abroad, crime is always a problem. San Francisco is no exception. To avoid an unhappy incident or an end to what might have been a pleasurable trip, use discretion and common sense. One sensible option is leaving valuables in the hotel safe, if you are staying at one of the larger hotels. It would also be wise to review the "Crime" section of "California Fast Facts" in Chapter I for more saftey tips.

CURRENCY EXCHANGE: Foreign-currency exchange services are provided by the **Bank of America** and **Deak International,** among others. Bank of America has offices at 345 Montgomery St. in the Financial District (tel. 415/622-2451), 1 Powell St. (tel. 415/622-4097), and 420 Post St. (tel. 415/622-2379), open Monday through Thursday from 9am to 3pm, on Friday to 5pm; and at the Central Terminal International Building, San Francisco International Airport (tel. 415/742-8079) for the convenience of incoming and outbound passengers, open daily (including holidays) from 7am to 11pm.

DENTISTS: Hotels usually have a list of dentists should you need one, but they are also listed in the *Yellow Pages.* The **San Francisco Dental Society** can be reached at 415/421-1435.

DOCTORS: Here again, hotels usually have a list of doctors on call. The **San Francisco Medical Society** number is 415/567-6234.

DRIVING: Driving in San Francisco is relatively easy if you have no hang-ups about stopping at the top of a hill and waiting for the light to change or negotiating your way through snug traffic. As I've pointed out, on-the-street parking is tough to find, and garage parking is relatively expensive. (See also "Driving" in Section 3 of this chapter.)

If you plan to drive very far outside of the city, you might want to call about **California road conditions** (tel. 415/557-3755) or **weather** (tel. 415/936-1212).

EARTHQUAKES: See the "California Fast Facts" section in Chapter I.

EMERGENCIES: For police, fire, highway patrol, or life-threatening medical emergencies, dial **911**. Otherwise, you can reach **ambulance** service at 415/931-3900; the nonemergency police number is 415/553-0123. To reach the **Poison Control Center,** call 415/476-6600.

EVENTS AND FESTIVALS: For a listing of annual events in advance of your trip, write to the **San Francisco Convention and Visitors Bureau,** P.O. Box 6977, San Francisco, CA 94101, and enclose a self-addressed stamped envelope. During your stay, you can pick up a copy of *Key* or the *San Francisco Guide*—two excellent free weekly publications, both found at most hotels. A third alternative for finding out what's going on in a given week is the pink "Date Book" section of the Sunday edition of the *San Francisco Examiner and Chronicle.*

FOOD: There are lots of places to eat in this city for less than $4; on the other hand, you can spend as much as $75 per person for a meal, without wine. This is a city with a restaurant for everyone—there are over 100 Chinese restaurants, more Italian restaurants than you could believe would prosper, plus Indian, American, Japanese, Moroccan, French, Greek, Basque, Czech, Jewish, Tuscan, Vietnamese, Lithuanian, Mexican, Salvadorean, etc. And the food ranges from good to superb. Those restaurants located in hotels are described in Section 3 of this chapter; the majority are listed in Section 4. I've tried to select some of the best in all price categories.

If you're planning to charge a meal, you might call ahead to see if the restaurant takes plastic. Not all of the better restaurants do, and not all of them take every major credit card.

HAIR SALONS: If your hotel does not have a hair salon on the premises, they're usually glad to make a recommendation.

HOLIDAYS: Obvious holiday occasions and dates of major conventions are not the times to try for reservations on short notice. While the city's many hotels can accommodate conventions of almost any size and scope, bear in mind that San Francisco hosts over eight million tourists, conventioneers, and travelers each year. So if you're not certain what events are in the offing and you have specific vacation dates in mind, send for the annual list—see "Events and Festivals" above.

HOSPITALS: **CliniCARE** at Saint Francis Memorial Hospital, 900 Hyde St., on Nob Hill (tel. 415/775-4321) provides drop-in outpatient services Monday through Friday from 8am to 5pm. No appointment is necessary. The hospital also has 24-hour emergency service.

INFORMATION: The **Visitor Information Center,** 900 Market St. (tel. 415/391-2000), is on the lower level of Hallidie Plaza at Market and Powell streets. Their multilingual staff is there to answer your questions weekdays from 9am to 5:30pm, on Saturday to 3pm, and on Sunday from 10am to 2pm.

A 24-hour **recorded announcement** (tel. 415/391-2001) lists daily events and activities. Similar recorded information is available in French (tel. 415/391-2003), in German (tel. 415/391-2004), in Spanish (tel. 415/391-2122), and in Japanese (tel. 415/391-2101).

It's well worth your while to write in advance of your trip: Send $1 to San Francisco Convention and Visitors Bureau, P.O. Box 6977, San Francisco, CA 94101, and they'll send you an invaluable packet of literature, including the *San Francisco Book,* with restaurant, shopping, sightseeing, events, and a "Lodging Guide." When in town, dial 391-2001 any time of the day for a recorded description of current cultural and sporting events.

Also worth a visit is the **Visitors Information Center of the Redwood Empire Association,** 785 Market St., 15th Floor, San Francisco, CA 94103 (tel. 415/543-8334). The walls are lined with racks of brochures, and the staff will help you plan tours of San Francisco and points north. Their invaluable free *Redwood Empire Visitor's Guide,* updated annually, is chock-full of detailed information on everything from Sonoma County farm trails to favored fishing areas in the entire northern region. There's also a guide to over 100 wineries north of San Francisco. (If you write for either guide, enclose $2 for postage and handling.) It's open Monday through Friday from 9am to 4:30pm.

Information on **gay and lesbian activities** is not totally organized, so let me give you some input on the best available resources. First, pick up copies of the *San Francisco Sentinel* and the *Bay Area Reporter.* Both weeklies are free and distributed on Thursday; they can be found stacked at the corner of 18th and Castro and at 9th and Harrison. The centerfold of the *Sentinel* has a map of San Francisco and lists gay and lesbian bars and restaurants, plus the clientele, entertainment, and dancing (if any). (See also "Some Gay Spots" in the "After Dark" section toward the end of this chapter.) The *Sentinel* also lists community and spiritual services, but it doesn't give phone numbers (check the phone directory). The *Bay Area Reporter*'s convenient and comprehensive "This Week" listing in its "Arts and Entertainment" section gives a weekly calendar of events for gays and lesbians, from social gatherings to art classes, sports events, and meetings of AIDS support groups.

And then there's a very special **walking tour** of the Castro area conducted by Ms. Trevor Hailey, who was an integral part of the growth of the Castro in the '70s. You'll find this informative and fascinating tour described under "Sights" (Section 7 of this chapter).

LIQUOR LAWS: Liquor and grocery stores, as well as some drugstores, can sell packaged alcoholic beverages between 6am and 2am. Most restaurants, nightclubs, and bars are licensed to serve alcoholic beverages during the same hours. The legal age for purchase and consumption is 21, and proof of age is required.

If you are in the Wine Country and decide to make some larger-than-usual purchases of a vintage or two, California (unlike many other states) permits you to purchase packaged liquor with a credit card. The store may also handle the shipment of wine and relieve you of what might otherwise be a weighty problem.

NEWSPAPERS: The *San Francisco Chronicle* and the *San Francisco Examiner* are widely distributed throughout the Bay Area. The Sunday edition of the *San Francisco Examiner and Chronicle* will fill you in on happenings in the upcoming week. There's also a good weekly—the *San Francisco Bay Guardian,* a freebie that will fill you in on a variety of happenings about town. And then there are the gay- and lesbian-oriented *San Francisco Sentinel* and *Bay Area Reporter,* both available free; you can usually pick up copies of the *Sentinel* and the *Reporter* at the corner of 18th and Castro and at 9th and Harrison. (For more about these two newspapers, see "Information," above.)

RELIGIOUS SERVICES: San Francisco has hundreds of churches and synagogues, and about 100 denominations. Your hotel desk can help direct you to the nearest church of almost any denomination. If not, the *Yellow Pages* can be helpful for the location and, frequently, the times of the services.

SPORTS (SPECTATOR): As of this writing, the Bay Area has two major-league baseball teams—the **San Francisco Giants** (tel. 415/392-7469 or 467-8000) and the **Oakland Athletics,** or "A's" (tel. 415/638-0500 or 638-4900); an NFL football team—the **San Francisco 49ers,** locally known simply as the "Niners" (tel. 415/468-2249 or 467-8000); and an NBA basketball team—the **Golden State Warriors** (tel. 415/638-6000). Both the Giants and the 49ers roost at Candlestick Park (where no one can hold a candle to the wind), located on Giants Drive at Gilman Avenue. The A's, the 1989 World Series champs, play at the Oakland Coliseum, at the 66th Avenue or Hegenberger Road exit from I-880 (Nimitz Freeway). The Warriors reside next door at the Oakland Coliseum Arena. You'll find a complete schedule of games at home and away under "Sports Schedules" at the front of the *Yellow Pages.*

And, finally, there's the sport of kings. The Bay Meadows **thoroughbred racing** season runs from August through the latter part of January. Quarter-horse racing is held February through April. The track is located at the intersection of Hillsdale Boulevard and Bayshore Freeway/U.S. 101 (San Mateo) (tel. 415/574-7223).

STORE HOURS: Stores are usually open Monday through Saturday from 10am to 6pm; most are closed Sunday. Stores in Chinatown are generally open daily from 10am to 10pm.

TRANSPORTATION: For information on transportation to and from San Francisco, see Section 1 of this chapter, "Getting There"; for information about transportation within San Francisco, see Section 3, "Getting Around."

USEFUL TELEPHONE NUMBERS: You can obtain **weather information** for San Francisco at 415/936-1212, **time** at 415/767-8900, information on **highway conditions** at 415/557-3755, and of course **directory assistance** at 411.

5. Hotels

One of the world's great hotel cities, San Francisco has over 48,000 rooms for visitors and is constantly adding more. The wide variety of high-quality facilities, however, is matched by the large volume of tourist and convention traffic (about three million visitors per year accommodated). Especially in peak season—from late May to late September—it's foolish not to make prior reservations.

A remarkable number of historic buildings large and small have been reconstituted, reworked, and refurbished (most successfully) into handsome new edifices, made into posh hotels with elegance (many with a European feel), beauty, and remarkably lovely tone.

San Francisco boasts over a dozen hotels in the international luxury class. A cross section of these, from the old-world traditional to the supermodern, comprises the first two categories in this section—deluxe and upper bracket—the latter a shade less expensive and luxurious than the former. The bulk of the selections fall in the moderately priced range, and the hotel section concludes with budget listings for those traveling on limited funds.

But all these hotels have one thing in common. They come up to an exacting standard of comfort, hospitality, and cleanliness. Most (although not all) are in the downtown area. There's something to suit just about every taste and pocketbook— read carefully and you'll find what you're looking for.

Remember: There is an 11% tax on all hotel bills in San Francisco, which must be added to the price.

THE DELUXE HOTELS

The **Four Seasons Clift Hotel,** Geary and Taylor streets, San Francisco, CA 94102 (tel. 415/775-4700, or toll free 800/332-3342), is a 329-room hotel emphasizing excellence of service, quiet but unimpeachable style, and total comfort, and it's the kind of place where the staff remains unchanged year after year and guests' names and preferences are remembered.

Its spacious accommodations are among the most elegant in town. A typical room might have peach rugs, bedspreads, and drapes, with pale-green and plum velvet furnishings. Beautiful artwork adorns the walls. All rooms have oversize beds and pillows, color TVs, clock radios, and bathrobes in the dressing rooms. What's more, there are computer hookups in the bedrooms and telephones in the baths. The Clift will also polish your shoes overnight if you leave them outside the door, loan you an umbrella should the gentle rains fall, and put a flower on your pillow to greet you when you go to bed.

Free newspapers and another flower come with your morning breakfast tray. Room service is available around the clock—offering most of the French Room menu (see below), as well as a special hors d'oeuvres menu from late afternoon through dinner—and a traditional English tea is served in the lobby every afternoon. For families, the Four Seasons Clift also has prepared a folder listing the many items the hotel can provide for children, from baby blankets to teddy bears, baseball cards, and coloring books.

There are two restaurants. In the prestigious French Room you dine beneath ornate 18th-century crystal chandeliers. The adjoining Redwood Room, designed by architect Albert Lansburgh in 1934 (he also did the War Memorial Opera House), is paneled in 2,000-year-old redwood burl. Art deco in style, its furnishings are upholstered in plush forest-green velvet. Both rooms serve breakfast, lunch, and dinner.

The French Room offers seasonal cuisine composed of the freshest ingredients available, and many of the dishes can be prepared as appetizers or entrees— whichever suits your fancy. At lunch, there may be pan-broiled Black Angus rib-eye steak with shoestring potatoes and onion rings, or poached Pacific salmon and scallops with dill yogurt sauce and mixed garden greens ($11 to $15). And there's always a full selection of hamburgers, salads, and sandwiches available. Dinner, served nightly, may feature such excellent dishes as grilled swordfish with roasted garlic sauce and warm marinated asparagus, and the traditional roast prime rib of beef with an English popover and creamed horseradish sauce. Entrees are in the $23 to $30 range. The French Room also offers appetizers and entrees reduced in calories, cholesterol, and sodium, presented in such toothsome dishes as roast loin of veal with smoked tomato orzo and braised fennel.

To live in quiet comfort away from the parvenus and the convention trade will cost you $170 to $250 for a single, $170 to $270 for a double; suites begin at $300.

Among the newer San Francisco luxury high-rise hostelries, the **Parc Fifty Five** (formerly the Ramada Renaissance), 55 Cyril Magnin St. (at Market and North 5th), San Francisco, CA 94102 (tel. 415/392-8000, or toll free 800/338-1338), is ideally situated in the heart of the city—two blocks from Union Square and a half block from the Powell Street cable car. Built at a cost of $130 million, the hotel is palatial in scope and appearance. It occupies an entire city block, has 1,005 rooms, and boasts all the extra services and conveniences even the most sophisticated traveler might expect.

As you enter the hotel, there is an imposing seven-panel bas-relief mural of the history of San Francisco by Ruth Asawa. Two stone lions hold court in the travertine marble lobby. Ahead is the main staircase, covered in a rich beige-pink-and-blue Tai Ping sculpted carpet woven in China. The second-floor lobby looks upward into a three-story atrium. Here you can enjoy a leisurely drink at the Piazza Lounge while listening to contemporary and classical music played on a grand piano, somehow fitting in a room this size.

Throughout the hotel, guest rooms reflect the same subdued elegance, from the beige carpeting and furnishings of bleached ash to the floral and city prints. Each room has a king-size bed, bathroom phones, well-lit makeup mirror, shower massage, even French-milled hand soap on the marble vanity, and window vents that open if you want fresh air! And there are rooms with special facilities for handicapped persons.

Should you need special cosseting, check into the Concierge Club, which occupies the top four floors and features personal check-in and concierge service, a Continental breakfast and afternoon hors d'oeuvres, and access to the health club. Guest rooms are supplied with terrycloth robes, hairdryers, the daily newspaper, and evening turndown service. Seven suites contain private whirlpool baths.

You will be pleased by the helpful staff and the number of services provided. You'd expect a concierge and bell captain, but there are also a foreign-language information desk, currency exchange, a tour desk, and, on request, acoustic couplers linking personal computers to off-site computers. And all guests are offered complimentary morning limousine service to the Financial District.

There are two areas for dining, both on the second floor—the Corintia Ristorante and the Veranda. The Corintia specializes in northern Italian cuisine. (I've covered the restaurant in more detail in Section 6.) The Veranda's menu features both traditional favorites and some innovative specialties for breakfast, lunch, and dinner. If you yearn for salsa piquante at breakfast, the guacamole omelet will satisfy your innermost craving. For Mexican-food urges at lunch, the tostada grande with chicken, avocado, tomato, cheese, and refried beans is delicious. For dinner, sautéed pork medallions with chanterelles are excellent; barbecued veal short ribs are always reliable too. Luncheon entrees range from $8 to $15; at dinner they run $12 to $20 (lobster, $30).

Single rooms at the Parc Fifty Five range from $150 to $195. Doubles run $175 to $220; suites, $325 to $475. Rates for the Concierge Level are $195 for a single, $225 for a double. One-bedroom suites run $425 to $750; two-bedroom suites, $700 to $990. The charge for an additional person is $25. If you're in town for a grand evening of theater or a personal celebration, the hotel has special packages you might want to check into. Some include complimentary champagne, Continental breakfast, even limousine service.

The **Stanford Court,** 905 California St. (at Powell Street), San Francisco, CA 94108 (tel. 415/989-3500, or toll free 800/468-3571), stands at the top of Nob Hill at the *only* cable-car crossing in San Francisco; all three cable-car lines pass these historic doors. Once the site of the Leland Stanford mansion and the luxurious Stanford Court Apartments, constructed in 1912 and considered a historic landmark, the eight-story building has been preserved on the outside; inside, however, the hotel has been updated at a cost of $17 million. A lofty stained-glass dome highlights the entrance, where you'll find the hotel's 1972 Rolls-Royce Phantom VI and Mercedes stretch limousines (available to transport guests to the Financial District, the theater, restaurants, or shops).

In each of the 402 guest rooms, a reproduction of a classic French armoire serves as a desk and a discreet hideaway for the remote-control color TV (there's a second TV and an additional phone in the bath/dressing-room area). The rooms also feature handcrafted bamboo furnishings, AM/FM clock radios, marble bedside tables, and original wall lithographs of early San Francisco scenes; rooms even have canopied beds. Other thoughtful touches include terrycloth robes in all rooms, complimentary newspaper and coffee or tea delivered at wake-up, twice-daily maid service, free overnight shoeshine, and 24-hour room service.

The Café Potpourri, a delightful dining area encompassing three intimate cafés, serves breakfast and lunch.

The hotel also houses a fine restaurant—Fournou's Ovens. Open for dinner nightly, Fournou's offers a warm French provincial ambience—floors of terra-cotta tile, walls and grilled balcony levels decorated with antiques, beamed ceilings of substantial mahogany—and both classic French and American cuisine. You might begin with bay shrimp in sour cream with mushrooms, or with a bowl of cream of artichoke soup with hazelnuts, then continue with one of the succulent specialties —such as roast rack of lamb—that emerge from the massive tiled coal-burning, open-hearth ovens. Oven-roasted potatoes and a fresh vegetable du jour are served with all entrees, which run $23 to $30. Dacquoise is a memorable Fournou's dessert. All desserts, in fact, as well as breads and pastries, are made in the Stanford Court's own pastry kitchen. The sourdough starter is kept on the hotel's roof to take advantage of San Francisco's fog (truly). And to accompany all the excellent food at Fournou's Ovens, the Stanford Court's wine cellar offers an inventory of some 21,000 bottles—one of the largest in the city.

Room rates are $180 to $270 for singles, $210 to $300 for doubles, with suites beginning at $425. An extra charge for a third person 18 or over is $30. Overnight valet parking is $17 for guests.

Another Nob Hill hostelry is the elegant **Mark Hopkins Inter-Continental,** 1 Nob Hill, San Francisco, CA 94108 (tel. 415/392-3434, or toll free 800/332-4246). It occupies the site of one of the most ornate and extravagant homes built by railroad tycoons in the 1870s, the gabled and turreted Mark Hopkins mansion. In its over half a century of operation the Mark has been headquarters for distinguished visitors and celebrities ranging from Prince Philip, King Hussein, and Eleanor Roosevelt to Frank Sinatra and Michael Jackson.

When the hotel opened its doors it was (at 19 stories) the highest point in San Francisco, with each room designed to offer an expansive view. All guest rooms are beautifully furnished and have sumptuous baths and huge closets. Thoughtful extras include hairdryers, bathrobes, makeup lights on bathroom mirrors, and proper hangers for all types of clothing. Some 29 of the suites offer the ultimate in luxury and comfort, as does the Jacuzzi Suite, which affords a view of the Golden Gate Bridge.

The hotel's warm, oak-paneled Nob Hill Restaurant serves breakfast, lunch, and dinner daily. The restaurant specializes in French and California cuisine, using the finest and freshest of ingredients. Dinner here might begin with an appetizer of sautéed escalope of goose foie gras with lentils, apple purée, and olive oil; continue with roast loin of lamb in a fresh herb coulis with garlic sauce and braised red cabbage; and conclude with a delectable crème brûlée. Entrees cost $20 to $35. The lobster bouillabaisse with fennel and orange, traditional rouille, and garlic croutons ($50 for two) is truly worth writing home about and requires a one-day advance order.

Afternoon or evening, there's a visual feast to be had at the Top of the Mark, a glass-walled room offering a panoramic 360° view of the city with your cocktails. (See "Cocktails in the Sky" in Section 8 of this chapter.)

Rates at the Mark Hopkins are $175 to $235 for a single, $205 to $265 for a double. Suites cost $385 to $1,100.

Just across the street is the magnificent stone-and-marble carriage entrance to the **Fairmont,** at California and Mason streets, San Francisco, CA 94106 (tel. 415/ 772-5000, or toll free 800/527-4727), a third Nob Hill hostelry where old-world luxury and graciousness are still alive and well. The historic main building with its opulent marble-walled and colonnaded lobby contains 340 rooms and 40 distinctive suites. The adjoining tower has 200 more rooms and 20 suites, all with bay views. Room decor is richly traditional, and guests are pampered with nightly turndown service. Extra pillows, electric shoe polishers, AM/FM clock radios, bathroom scales, makeup mirrors, oversize towels, and custom-made soap are among the other little conveniences.

There are four restaurants to choose from: the Tonga, offering dancing on a boat deck along with the Chinese and island specialties; the Crown Room—29 stories high and reached by an outdoor glass elevator—with its lavish buffet luncheons, dinners, and Sunday brunches; the Bella Voce Restaurant, featuring Italian cuisine and (as you might expect) the lovely voices of waiters and waitresses singing opera and operetta selections nightly; and the dome-ceilinged Squire Room, serving California cuisine. In addition, there's live music nightly in the New Orleans Room, as well as afternoon tea, cocktails, and piano music in the newly redecorated Cirque.

Rates in the Fairmont's main building are $150 to $210 for a single, $180 to $240 for a double or twin; suites start at $475. In the Tower, singles go for $210 to $260, doubles or twins cost $240 to $290, and suites are $500 and up.

Discreet Nob Hill elegance and old-world charm are the hallmarks of the **Huntington Hotel,** 1075 California St. (between Mason and Taylor), San Francisco, CA 94108 (tel. 415/474-5400, or toll free 800/227-4683, 800/652-1539 in California). The Huntington's beauty lies in its luxurious oversize accommodations. All offer views of either the city or the bay and overlook Huntington Park (the original site of the Huntington Mansion) and Grace Cathedral. From Irish linens and imported silks to Ming Dynasty treasures and signature artwork, each of the 140 rooms and suites is individually decorated and uniquely furnished with many antique and custom-made pieces, as well as all the modern amenities—color TVs, direct-dial phones, hairdryers, etc. A complimentary formal service of tea or sherry awaits you upon arrival in your room. And for your private dining pleasure, room service is from the prestigious Big Four restaurant.

There is also daily complimentary chauffeured service (one way) to the Financial District and Union Square from 8:30am to 4:30pm. (I'm not suggesting it as an optional mode of transportation, but there is a cable-car stop conveniently located at the hotel entrance.) Guests also have privileges at the Nob Hill Spa and Fitness Center. You can enjoy lunch and dinner in the Big Four, named for the railroad tycoons C. P. Huntington, Charles Crocker, Mark Hopkins, and Leland Stanford. It specializes in traditional American cuisine. Dinner entrees are in the $22.50 to $32 range.

Rates at the Huntington are $160 to $230 for a single, $180 to $255 for a double; suites run $270 to $680.

On opening night there was a spectacular star-studded party. An Indian guru blessed the place, and a ritual Victorian-style murder in the best Agatha Christie tradition was enacted, with "the body" tumbling down the grand staircase. The scene of these happenings: Bob Pritikin's poshly located **The Mansions,** a sprawling, twin-turreted Queen Anne house—yes, it *is* a mansion—at 2220 Sacramento St. (between Laguna and Buchanan streets), San Francisco—CA 94115 (tel. 415/929-9444). It's where hip young couples up for the weekend from L.A., the requisite sprinkling of celebs—like Barbra Streisand, Robin Williams, and Joan Baez—and in-the-know New Yorkers stay. You're received in the Grand Foyer by a host or hostess in Victorian attire who offers you a glass of sherry (note the strains of baroque music wafting from the music room), then conducts you up the exquisitely paneled grand staircase, its walls adorned—like those in most of the public areas—with murals of turn-of-the-century San Francisco.

But before I get to the rooms, just a note that in addition to the Victorian Cabaret Theater (wherein a live parrot, not to mention an ostensible ghost, resides, and concerts/magic shows take place several times weekly), the main floor also contains a game room. Also notable are the original set from Edward Albee's *Tiny Alice* and the largest number of Beniamino Bufano's works on display anywhere.

As for the 30 guest rooms: Each is dedicated to a historic San Francisco personality, and a mural on the wall tells his or her story. There is, of course, a Bufano Room, plus a Coit Room, a Huntington Room—even a Pritikin Room, which salutes The Mansions' eccentric owner (no doubt he will go down in San Francisco history). Most rooms look out over the rose garden or sculpture garden; from some, in season, you can reach out your window and pick a plum off a tree. Each room is different, but all have antique furnishings, velvet drapes, Victorian memorabilia, and brass beds with handmade quilts. There's nothing as vulgar as a TV, but you can have one brought to your room, and you do get a direct-dial phone. All rooms have private baths; towels are thick and luxurious. All rooms are abundantly charming as well, one with an antique sink, another with a marble fireplace, etc. The ultimate indulgence is the very French Empress Josephine Room, furnished in priceless antiques and renting at $220 a night.

Dinner is available to everyone. The Mansions has one of San Francisco's fine restaurants.

The price for returning to a bygone era: $75 to $150 for single occupancy, $90 to $200 for double occupancy. And these rates include a full breakfast, fresh flowers in your room, concerts, and the opportunity to experience whatever else is happening at the time. It's not just a place to stay, it's theater, and Pritikin's motto is "The Mansions is only as good as its last performance."

The **Hyatt Regency San Francisco,** 5 Embarcadero Center, San Francisco, CA 94111 (tel. 415/788-1234, or toll free 800/233-1234), takes us not only to another section of town from the above-mentioned listings but also to another century— the ultramodern 20th. Even if you don't stay here, you might want to come by to ogle this amazing seven-sided pyramid hotel and its spectacular atrium lobby, the setting for events from big-band ballroom dancing to a high-wire circus act. The centerpiece of the vast central court is an enormous aluminum sculpture—*Eclipse,* by Charles Perry—rising four stories over a huge reflecting waterfall pond. There are several restaurants, most of them located off the lobby, plus a nightclub and several cocktail lounges. The hotel's 16th floor houses the Regency Club, with 52 deluxe guest rooms, private bar and game room lounges, complimentary Continental breakfast, after-dinner cordials, and private concierge.

As for the rooms on all other floors, over two-thirds offer bay views. They're done in tranquil earth tones set off by splashes of royal burgundy. Custom-designed modern furnishings are softened by elm burl and cane accents, brushed-bronze hardware, and sheer draperies. Above the beds are abstract paintings. Each room has a dressing area with makeup and full-length mirrors, and there's a choice of six first-run movies on your color TV. Room service is available 24 hours.

Singles range from $185 to $238, and doubles run from $215 to $248; add $25 for each additional person. Rooms on the Regency Club floor cost $238 for singles, $268 for doubles. Parking in the plaza is $18 for 24 hours, with in-and-out privileges.

The **Grand Hyatt San Francisco on Union Square,** 345 Stockton St. (between Post and Sutter streets), San Francisco, CA 94108 (tel. 415/398-1234, or toll free 800/233-1234), is another member of the Hyatt chain, and although it's less space-age spectacular than the Regency, it is quite handsome and exceedingly well located. Inside, the ultramodern decor has an almost theatrical quality of hushed elegance. The 693 rooms, restaurants, many shops, and facilities are housed in a three-story forebuilding and a 40-story tower fronted by a lovely brick courtyard. Bedecked with potted trees and flowers, the old-world courtyard is the setting for Ruth Asawa's bronze fountain sculpture, the design of which imaginatively depicts the city's familiar landmarks.

Your room at the Hyatt will be spacious and contemporary, with sliding doors that open onto a railed parapet. The baths have marble floors and sinks, while the amenities in each room include a minibar, color TV (with first-run movies) in both the bedroom and bath, a telephone compatible with computer connection, and two robes for guests' use. The Hyatt now offers a full-service health club to its guests. Businesspeople will appreciate the free limousine service to the Financial District weekday mornings (and the early-morning limo to the jogging course at the Embarcadero Center) and the variety of secretarial and hi-tech services.

A good inexpensive restaurant, Napper's, Too, is on the ground floor. In the summer months it spills out onto the Plaza Deck to create the largest outdoor café in San Francisco. The Plaza Restaurant, also overlooking the courtyard, is another Hyatt dining choice. With floor-to-ceiling windows, bamboo furnishings, an abundance of potted palms—even a fountain—it's like dining in a delightful garden, and the Continental fare is quite good. The Plaza's hours are 6:30am to 10:30pm weekdays, from 7:30am on Saturday, and there is Sunday brunch from 10am to 2pm. You can also watch the sunset, enjoy cocktails, take lunch, dinner, or Sunday brunch at One-Up, 36 stories skyward. The One-Up Lounge is open daily for cocktails, served with piano music until 2am. Great view, very romantic. And Club 36, another spot for cocktails on the 36th floor, features jazz music in the evening.

Rates at the Hyatt are $190 to $245 for a single, $220 to $275 for a double. Suites cost from $550.

The **Westin St. Francis,** 335 Powell St. (centrally located at Union Square), San Francisco, CA 94102 (tel. 415/397-7000, or toll free 800/228-3000), has welcomed thousands of prominent guests, from royalty to theatrical luminaries. The addition of the 32-story tower (the view is spectacular!) brought room capacity to 1,200. Rooms throughout are quietly elegant, with very attractive furnishings and all modern appurtenances; those in the original building have unusually high ceilings. The tower is topped by the award-winning rooftop restaurant, Victor's, offering California cuisine and an extensive wine selection in posh surroundings. Oz, a leading San Francisco dance club, also occupies the 32nd floor. The oak-paneled English Grill, featuring fresh seafood, is another dining option, as are the Dutch Kitchen, a coffee shop, and Dewey's Union Square Bar and Monument Saloon. The Compass Rose, just off the lobby, serves a weekday lunch and high tea, but is most popular with locals for cocktails.

Rates are $160 to $280 for singles, $195 to $315 for doubles, $400 to $1,725 for suites. The St. Francis has its own garage, charging $19 for 24 hours with in-and-out privileges.

One of the most conveniently situated of San Francisco's deluxe hostelries— and with 1,900 rooms, it's among the largest hotels on the West Coast—is the **San Francisco Hilton (on Hilton Square),** 333 O'Farrell St. (at Mason Street), San Francisco, CA 94102 (tel. 415/771-1400, or toll free 800/445-8667). It is the complete luxury hotel, a city within a city, composed of three connecting, centrally located buildings. Hilton Square includes the original 19-story main building with 955 rooms, a 46-story 569-room tower topped by a panoramic restaurant, and a new 23-story landmark with an additional 386 luxurious rooms and suites.

There's a beautiful, sweeping grand entrance to the lobby on imported custom carpet. An elegant sidewalk café, Café on the Square, provides a lovely spot for spectators to eye the passing parade and the promenade of hotel shops. And at the 16th-floor level of the original tower, an inner courtyard is outfitted with a heated swimming pool and garden rooms. The heated 40-foot outdoor swimming pool has a resistance-swimming exerciser, while the complete state-of-the-art health facility boasts the latest in exercise equipment, including weight machines, exercise bikes, treadmills, stair-climbers, and rowers. All this exercise can be topped off with a dry sauna and shower. Professional massage is available by appointment.

Hilton Square offers several characteristically San Francisco restaurants to choose from. Cityscape, on the 46th floor, serves classic California cuisine in a breathtaking setting. The magnificent 360° view displays the Golden Gate Bridge and the Bay Bridge, Sausalito, Telegraph Hill, and the East Bay; the retractable skylight exposes the night sky in all its grandeur. Kiku of Tokyo presents authentic Japanese cuisine. And Phil Lehr's Steakery, a restaurant that has been a San Francisco tradition for over 40 years, offers prime cuts by the ounce.

All guest rooms are spacious and modern in typical Hilton style. Memorable floor-to-ceiling views are available from many of these spacious and grandly appointed rooms, each with color TV with first-run movies, minibar, radio, marble bathroom, and 24-hour room service to pamper each guest during her or his stay. Forty rooms are located poolside. Nonsmoking rooms are available, as are others specially equipped for the handicapped.

Room rates range from $155 to $215 for a single, $180 to $240 for a double; suites are $260 to $660. There is no charge for children, regardless of age, when occupying the same room as their parents. The Hilton has an internal parking system (there's a daily charge); however, there is space for about 250 cars only, though the hotel has almost 2,000 rooms, and parking is *not* restricted to hotel guests. Therefore, if you're arriving by car, you might ask the concierge about nearby garages, their hours, and their rates.

The **Meridien San Francisco,** 50 3rd St. (at Market), San Francisco, CA 94103 ·

(tel. 415/974-6400, or toll free 800/543-4300), came into national prominence shortly after its 1983 opening when it played host to the French president, François Mitterrand. Located near Union Square and the Moscone Convention Center, the Meridien attracts both businesspeople and tourists. There are 650 beautifully appointed rooms here and 26 suites on 36 floors. All are elegantly decorated in pastels, and there are luxuries galore. Rooms and suites have remote-control color TVs with in-house movies, minibars, nightly turndown service, direct-dial phones, air conditioning, expansive floor-to-ceiling windows, AM/FM clock radios, 24-hour room service, and—from the upper floors—breathtaking views of the city and bay.

The Meridien boasts two excellent restaurants: Café Justin, an informal dining room that serves three meals a day (open from 6am to 11pm); and Pierre at the Meridien, an elegant, intimate French restaurant open for dinner Tuesday through Sunday from 6:30 to 10:30pm.

Rooms at the Meridien cost $170 to $220 for a single, $243 to $253 for a double.

One of the smallest luxury hotels in town (126 rooms) is the **Campton Place Hotel,** 340 Stockton St. (between Post and Sutter), San Francisco, CA 94108 (tel. 415/781-5555, or toll free 800/647-4007, 800/235-4300 in California). But smaller is better, according to the management; it allows the staff to offer better and more personal service. The hotel's buildings—formerly occupied by the Drake-Wiltshire—were renovated to the tune of $25 million, and the results are spectacular.

Guest rooms are beautifully appointed, each with a king-size bed or two double beds, concealed color TV with remote control, AM/FM clock radio, direct-dial phone, air conditioning, and luxurious bathroom with marble floor, vanity and tub, brass fixtures, bathrobes, telephone, special soaps, shampoos, and bath gels. There's a concierge to arrange for theater tickets, restaurant reservations, and travel plans; and there are maids and butlers available to pack and unpack your luggage for you. On the premises is the Campton Place Restaurant, one of the "in" spots for breakfast, lunch, and dinner.

Rooms at the Campton Place rent for $200 to $300, single or double; suites begin at $450. Overnight parking is available for guests at $20.

Another luxury hotel in San Francisco is the **Donatello** (formerly the Pacific Plaza), 501 Post St. (at Mason Street), San Francisco, CA 94102 (tel. 415/441-7100, or toll free 800/227-3184, 800/792-9837 in California). The marble lobby is small but elegant, containing many antiques and a massive tapestry on one wall. Many of the rooms also have walls adorned with tapestries. They're very large and are decorated in subdued colors, live plants adding a homey touch. Amenities include extra-length beds, remote-control TVs, clock radios, and robes for each guest. Room service is available from 6pm to midnight.

Ristorante Donatello, the hotel restaurant, has gained a good reputation in the city; local patrons fill the place at breakfast, lunch, and dinner. The menu is à la carte and features classic northern Italian cuisine. Pasta is excellent here and can be enjoyed as an appetizer preceding entrees like quail and boneless squab. Entrees range from $20 to $28. Breakfast is served from 7 to 10:30am; lunch, from 11:30am to 2pm; dinner, from 6 to 11pm. Cocktails are served in the lounge daily from 11am to 1am.

Single rates range from $150 to $210, and doubles run from $165 to $210. Suites range from $300 to $460. Parking is available for $17 a day, with in-and-out privileges.

I'd be remiss if I neglected to mention the newest of the giant hotels, namely the **San Francisco Marriott,** 55 Fourth St., San Francisco, CA 94103 (tel. 415/896-1600, or toll free 800/228-9290). This is one of the largest buildings in San Francisco and has 1,500 rooms and suites to prove it. Located a block from the Moscone Convention Center and the Powell Street cable-car turnaround and a short stroll from Nordstrom, the Marriott has been variously described as a giant jukebox, a 40-story robot, and the world's biggest parking meter. All critical comments notwithstanding, it is the only hotel that can lay claim to opening its doors the week of the October 1989 quake.

A word of advice for those planning to stay at the Marriott: Despite the Market Street address, enter from 4th Street (between Market and Mission); otherwise, you'll find yourself with a very long trek to the registration area. Accommodations are light and comfortably furnished, offering the expected amenities of remote-control color TVs, phones, and plush baths. Rooms on the Concierge Level are more spacious and afford a lengthy list of complimentary services, such as Continental breakfast, mid- to late-afternoon light snacks and beverages, and evening hors d'oeuvres and canapés, all served in the attractive and comfortable lounge on the 18th floor, where there is also an honor bar for Concierge Level guests. The hotel's recreational facilities include an indoor pool and spa, a health club with men's and women's saunas, plus steam and massage rooms.

The San Francisco Marriott has a plethora of eating places and lounges. The Kinoko is an authentic Japanese teppanyaki restaurant with a sushi bar. The Garden Terrace, facing the hotel's central fountain, has a breakfast bar and two buffets that prepare made-to-order omelets, and serves a varied menu for lunch and dinner. On the other hand, there's the Fourth Street Oyster Bar & Deli for seafood and snacks. As for the lounge areas, the Terrace View Lounge is on the atrium level; the View Lounge, on the 39th floor, offers a truly spectacular vista of the bay and the Golden Gate Bridge (assuming no fog), as well as live entertainment; Treats serves refreshments in the Golden Gate Foyer; and then, of course, there's the serene Club Bar. And here's a stopwatch challenge that Marc Hoffman, director of food and beverage services, poses (per the *San Francisco Business Times*): The Marriott will pick up the tab for anyone waiting longer than 3 minutes for a drink (presumably other than water), 5 minutes for breakfast, 15 minutes for lunch, 25 minutes for dinner, or 35 minutes for room service. Now how's that for service!

Standard rooms range from $180 to $198, those on the Concierge Level from $218 to $275, and suites from $1,200 to $1,500.

THE UPPER BRACKET

The **Prescott Hotel,** at 545 Post St. (between Mason and Taylor), San Francisco, CA 94102 (tel. 415/563-0303, or toll free 800/283-7322), is an elegant beauty with a once-upon-a-time style of gracious living and courtesy almost forgotten these days. The Prescott, one block from Union Square, opened in 1989 following a complete renovation of the former Hotel Cecil, built in 1917. This prestigious first-class hotel is small—seven stories—but that's part of its charm. The aura of quiet luxury is apparent as soon as you enter the Prescott. The lobby, traversed by a long Oriental carpet, has two separate areas, the reception and concierge desks, and to the left of the lobby is the handsome "living room," with comfortable antique furniture, a large wood-burning hearth fireplace, plush carpeting, and wood paneling. It's a great place to relax, socialize, and enjoy the evening wine hour.

The Prescott has 109 soundproof, air-conditioned guest rooms, including 17 suites, each in a simple neoclassical design with custom-made cherry furnishings: beds with columned headboards, bow-front armoires housing the TV/minibar/ chest of drawers, black-granite-topped nightstands and dressers. In addition, each room has a stocked refrigerator/honor bar, a direct-dial telephone with call-waiting and an extra-long cord, color TV with remote control and complimentary HBO, and a digital clock radio. Bathrooms are in black and taupe, with marble-topped vanities and brass and pewter accents; terrycloth robes and hairdryers are provided. No-smoking rooms are available. Suites have an adjoining parlor with comfortable furniture, plus a VCR and a whirlpool bathtub. Here the bathroom also has a scale, should you be interested in measuring your pound-by-pound progress through San Francisco's many great restaurants.

Complimentary services include coffee and tea throughout the day, wine and hors d'oeuvres every evening in the library, and limousine service weekday mornings to the Financial District. The Prescott also provides concierge service, evening turndown, same-day valet/laundry service, and valet parking. And most important, there is full room service (breakfast, lunch, and dinner) from Wolfgang Puck's Postrio restaurant, adjoining the Prescott (Postrio is discussed in detail in Section 6 of this chapter). If you prefer to dine at Postrio, it would be wise to make a reservation at the same time you reserve your accommodations at the Prescott.

Room rates are $149 a night, single or double; one-bedroom suites are $199.

The **Inn at the Opera**, 333 Fulton St. (near Franklin), San Francisco, CA 94102 (tel. 415/863-8400, or toll free 800/325-2708, 800/423-9610 in California), is a unique part of San Francisco's cultural heritage. Originally built over 50 years ago to cater to visiting opera stars, the inn recently was transformed into a small (48 rooms) luxury hotel, a romantic beauty situated at the heart of San Francisco's creative center—only steps from the Opera House and Davies Hall. The inn still caters to many performing artists. It's an elegant celebrity hideaway.

Approaching the inn is like stepping into another, more gracious age: portico, flowerboxes, polished brass, curtained windows, and carpet to the door. The reception area is light and airy, with European furnishings, soft pastel colors, and a floral French area rug in warm, delicate browns, pinks, and greens. Each guest room reflects the same feeling of warmth. Subtle tones of green and beige complement finely checked drapes. There's a well-stocked refrigerator with wines, pâtés, and other gourmet items, and there are wine glasses on the wet bar. Other pleasant amenities are the terrycloth robes you'll find in the armoire and the chocolates placed on your pillow before you turn in. There is a complimentary overnight shoeshine, and light pressing is available if you feel a bit wrinkled. With the arrival of morning, expect a Continental breakfast to be delivered to your room along with the day's newspaper.

One of the true joys of the Inn at the Opera is the Act IV Lounge, whether you're dining or lounging. The plump throw cushions can induce you to spend the evening in total comfort on overstuffed sofas, unless you prefer sitting at the handsome mahogany bar. In the evening, the fireplace and the music of the pianist at the grand piano give the lounge a quiet intimacy. Act IV is open daily for breakfast from 7 to 10:30am, for lunch from 11:30am to 2pm, and for dinner from 5:30 to 10:30pm. The chef who put Donatello on the culinary map presents an Italian country menu, even to delicious boned quail stuffed with pancetta and sage. Luncheon entrees range from $6 to $12; dinner entrees from $12 to $21. And who knows, for dessert you may even view Mikhail B., Luciano, Betty White, Tony Bennett, Rita Moreno, Doc Severinsen, or one segment of the Modern Jazz Quartet—a few of the many celebrities who have stayed at the Inn at the Opera.

Guest rooms range from $110 to $155 for a single, from $120 to $165 for a double; suites are $165 to $195. Add $10 for each extra person. Rates include Continental breakfast. Valet parking (an excellent idea in this area) is $15 per night. The inn will obtain tickets to the opera, symphony, or ballet.

The Orchard, 562 Sutter St. (near Powell), San Francisco, CA 94102 (tel. 415/433-4434, or toll free 800/433-4343, 800/433-4434 in California), a meticulously reconstructed historic building, has 96 rooms, each with imported furnishings that reflect a luxurious, comfortable European ambience. Armoires and woods have rich dark-walnut tone, complemented by warm deep-rose carpeting and delicate rose-toned walls and draperies. As you might expect, all rooms have color TVs, and each has a minibar and an international direct-dial phone. The luxuriously appointed suites have large sitting rooms, bedrooms, and bathrooms with separate toilets and bidets. A concierge is available for information on the town and to make reservations.

The lobby lounge, with its magnificent Austrian crystal chandeliers, French furnishings, and delicate Oriental paintings, is a lovely relaxing spot from which to watch the passing parade. The lobby adjoins the Sutter Garden Restaurant (an art deco delight), which serves breakfast, lunch, dinner, and cocktails daily.

Rates range from $99 to $140, single or double; suites are $195. (Should you be traveling to Australia, there is also an Orchard Hotel in Perth, and reservations can be made through the hotel in San Francisco.) The Orchard is nicely situated near a number of fine galleries, theaters, and restaurants. It's just a half block to the Powell

Street cable car, one block to Union Square, four blocks to Chinatown and the Financial District.

A handsome four-story hotel, reminiscent of an English garden inn, the **White Swan Inn**, 845 Bush St. (between Taylor and Mason), San Francisco, CA 94108 (tel. 415/775-1755), has charm, serenity, and style, and it's geared to fill the needs of the most sophisticated traveler. The hotel was originally constructed in the early 1900s and recently renovated by Four Sisters, Inc. A handsome reception area boasts a cheery fireplace, a carousel horse (Sir Winston) with a handsome but nameless teddy bear astride, an antique oak breakfront, plants, soft chairs—all surrounded by rich warm woods.

There are 26 rather spacious rooms in all, each with its own teddy bear companion. Softly colored English wallpaper and floral-print bedspreads add to the feeling of warmth and comfort. As for the more utilitarian details, each room has a wet bar with a refrigerator, working fireplace (especially welcome on crisp San Francisco days), private bath with fluffy oversize towels, color TV, and bedside telephone. There is turndown service in the evening, a morning newspaper at your door when you arise, and if you put your shoes outside the door at night, you will wake to find them polished.

Each morning a generous breakfast is served in a lovely common room just off a tiny garden. Afternoon tea is also served, and includes hors d'oeuvres, sherry, wine, and home-baked pastries. You can have your sherry in front of the fireplace while you browse through the books in the library. The White Swan Inn will also arrange reservations for restaurants, theaters, sports, and special events, and for limousine service, if needed.

Rates are $145 to $160, double occupancy; $15 for an extra person. The Ashleigh Suite is $260 and offers a large separate sitting room in addition to the sleeping quarters. Valet parking can be arranged at $15 per day. Just 2½ blocks from Union Square, 2 blocks from Nob Hill, and 1½ blocks from the Powell Street cable car, the inn is excellently located.

On the scene for over half a century, the superbly located **Sir Francis Drake**, 450 Powell St. (right on Union Square at Sutter and Powell streets), San Francisco, CA 94102 (tel. 415/392-7755, or toll free 800/227-5480, 800/652-1668 in California), offers quality service and tasteful surroundings. The lobby sets the elegant tone, with richly carpeted marble floors, marble and mirrored walls, 30-foot-high vaulted ceilings with gold-leaf trim, and crystal chandeliers. Also handsomely appointed are the 415 guest rooms, each with an AM/FM clock radio and first-run movies available on the color TV.

Crusty's Café offers reasonably priced full dinners nightly. And there's also dancing nightly, as well as cocktails and complimentary hors d'oeurves served from 4pm, on the Starlite Roof, 21 stories up.

Single rooms are $120 to $180. Doubles and twins are $140 to $200; suites, $280 to $550.

Just across from the Drake is the excellent **Holiday Inn Union Square**, 480 Sutter St. (at Powell), San Francisco, CA 94108 (tel. 415/398-8900, or toll free 800/464-4329). The 400 rooms (mostly with two double beds or a king-size bed) are attractively decorated in muted earth tones and have large bay windows. Of course, all the expected conveniences are on tap, right down to an AM/FM clock radio and first-run movies on your color TV.

A rooftop cocktail lounge is seemingly a San Francisco hotel prerequisite; this one's on the 30th floor and is called S. Holmes Esquire. It features a private collection of Holmes memorabilia and a posh decor with backgammon tables, velvet-upholstered furnishings, and wood-burning fireplaces. There's a pubby eatery on the premises too, the White Elephant, complete with framed fox-hunting prints on the walls and items like prime rib on the menu.

Rates are $144 to $164 for a single, $164 to $184 for a double; children 18 and under stay free in their parents' room.

A unique kind of luxury accommodation is offered at the **Miyako Hotel**, 1625

Post St. (at Laguna, in Japan Center), San Francisco, CA 94115 (tel. 415/922-3200, or toll free 800/533-4567)—a first-class Japanese hotel, remodeled and refurbished in 1985, just a mile from the heart of downtown. Here your room, decorated in subtle pastel colors, will feature shoji screens, delicate watercolors, or scrolls, and a *tokonoma*—an alcove for flowers, a bowl, or perhaps a statue of the Buddha. Rooms also have direct-dial phones, clocks, AM/FM radios, color TVs, and whatever other accoutrements of modern living you might expect. Most of the bathrooms have Japanese sunken tubs, wherein you'll find instructions on how to take a Japanese bath. There are showers too, for those not in the mood for a ritual bath. Some accommodations also have built-in saunas, and most have balconies.

There are 10 luxury suites, 2 with their own private redwood saunas and deep-tub Japanese baths. The top floor of the Garden Wing has a comfortable, spacious lounge and 13 deluxe Club Floor rooms, which offer such elegant amenities as generous work/sitting areas and marble bathrooms with oversize whirlpool baths and yukata cotton kimonos (not for the taking), as well as a complimentary Continental breakfast in your room or in the hotel's Asuka Brasserie.

Four rooms and two suites are entirely Japanese in decor. Here you sleep on the floor on Japanese beds called *futons*—downy quilts laid on tatami mats. If you're in one of the suites, you'll even find a bamboo and rock garden. Ceilings are wood-paneled and there are fusuma screens and shoji panels. Most Japanese prefer the hotel's American-style accommodations, but I think the Japanese rooms are exquisite and romantic, as do many Westerners; if you want them, reserve far in advance. Four accommodations (two rooms and two suites) combine traditional American and Japanese styles and are ideal for families.

The Asuka Brasserie (opened in 1986) offers Continental-Japanese cuisine prepared and presented in a contemporary California garden setting. The restaurant serves breakfast ($3 to $10, or $12 to $14 for a Japanese breakfast), lunch, dinner (entrees at $15 to $30, served from 6:30 to 10:30pm), and Sunday brunch. The mezzanine cocktail lounge is open daily from 10am to 1am.

Rates are $105 to $200 for singles, $125 to $220 for doubles and twins; suites are $250 to $775. Children 18 and under may stay free of charge in their parents' room. Indoor parking is available beneath the hotel.

Although I've stressed the downtown area, many tourists prefer to stay near Fisherman's Wharf, a part of San Francisco chock-full of visitor attractions, because of which prices tend to be higher than those elsewhere. The upper-bracket hotel of choice in this part of town is the **Sheraton at Fisherman's Wharf,** 2500 Mason St. (at Beech Street), San Francisco, CA 94133 (tel. 415/362-5500, or toll free 800/325-3535), a modernistic stucco hostelry with tree-lined courtyards that looks ever so much like a Vail ski condominium. The interior, also ski-lodgey, sports a good deal of raw redwood paneling. Facilities include a glass-enclosed sidewalk café called Chanen's Windowbox; one lounge, Chanen's (a Victorian-style piano lounge with entertainment); the Mason Beach Grill restaurant, specializing in beef; shops; and an outdoor heated swimming pool with sun deck for the polar-bear set.

The 525 rooms are attractively done in soft pastel color schemes. Each has every accoutrement right down to in-room movies on the television and an AM/FM clock radio; in the bathroom you'll find extra-thick towels. There is 24-hour room service.

The rates are $120 to $220, single or double.

Every year in San Francisco a growing number of elegant old apartment buildings and Victorian dwellings are converted into inns, bed-and-breakfast hostelries, and small but luxurious hotels. Most are in the deluxe or upper-bracket category and are immensely popular. It's a trend I heartily commend, because it offers visitors an ever-increasing choice of attractive accommodations. One such enterprise is Bob and Marily Kavanaugh's **Bed & Breakfast Inn,** 4 Charlton Court (off Union Street, between Buchanan and Laguna), San Francisco, CA 94123 (tel. 415/921-9784). Their charming Victorian house is a European-style luxury pension with a country-inn feel. Each of the 10 rooms is charmingly decorated—perhaps in a *Casablanca* motif with rattan furnishings and an overhead ceiling fan, perhaps with cherished family antiques. Each is provided with fresh flowers and fruit, live plants, books and magazines, down pillows, a clock, and a thermos of ice water. Rooms with baths have color TVs and plug-in phones if desired, while the bathless accommodations open onto a lovely enclosed garden with Cinzano umbrella tables. The Kavanaughs are a friendly couple who delight in offering gracious service to their guests. Breakfast (fresh-baked croissants, orange juice, and coffee, fancy tea, or cocoa) is served in a sunny flower-bedecked dining room decorated with framed English prints; you can also have it brought to your room with the morning paper. Sherry is available at all times. There's also a library for guests, with a backgammon table and a writing desk.

Rooms with shared baths cost $70 to $90 a night, single or double, the higher prices for larger, more luxurious accommodations. Rooms with private baths are priced at $115 to $215, the latter for an entire flat with a complete kitchen, a private plant-filled latticed terrace, a bedroom up a spiral staircase, and a double-tub bath. Rates include breakfast.

San Francisco has some of the finest hotels in the United States, in all categories, but it excels when it comes to small inns. The **Petite Auberge,** 863 Bush St. (between Mason and Taylor), San Francisco, CA 94108 (tel. 415/928-6000), is the crème de la crème. It's a small place, with only 26 rooms of varying sizes, all decorated in French country style with floral wallpapers, antiques, quilts, and lacy throw pillows. Eighteen rooms have fireplaces and bathrooms with tubs; one of these is a suite with Jacuzzi tub, wet bar, private entry, and private deck. The other eight rooms (some of them quite small) have shower bathrooms. All rooms have direct-dial phones, plus cable color TVs concealed in armoires. Other amenities include a selection of shampoos, conditioners, and bath gels, a daily newspaper, shoeshine service, afternoon sherry and hors d'oeuvres, and a hearty breakfast consisting of eggs, cereals, muffins, croissants, breads, yogurts, fresh fruits and juices, coffee and tea. Coffee, tea, and soda are also available around the clock.

Rooms at the Petite Auberge cost $110 to $170, single or double; the suite rents for $205. An extra person pays $15. The Petite Auberge staff is friendly and always willing to help with reservations, plans, and even valet parking, available at a nearby security garage (for $15 a night).

Another of the fine European-style hotels—small, comfortable, beautifully done—is the **Juliana Hotel,** 590 Bush St. (at Stockton), San Francisco, CA 94108 (tel. 415/392-2540, or toll free 800/382-8800, 800/372-8800 in California), a charming haven located near the heart of San Francisco, close to Union Square. The lobby is quite the Continental beauty with its warm teal-and-rose upholstered armchairs and sofa and its handsome white-and-pink marble fireplace brightened with brass framing—cozy on those cool days. A walnut chest with a coffee urn smugly centered on top, brass lamps with opaque green shades, and a trim teal-and-white window seat complete the picture. Complimentary coffee and tea are served in the lobby during the day, and wine in the evening, around the fireplace. The Juliana also provides complimentary morning limousine service to the Financial District.

The 107 rooms are done beautifully with an elegant country air of delicate gray walls, white furnishings, striking pastel print and stripe drapes, spreads, and a comfortably upholstered chairs. Each room has a small stocked refrigerator, its own air conditioning and heat, remote-control TV with HBO, and direct-dial telephone. Other thoughtful touches are reflected in the bath, where you'll find large bulbs around a sizable mirror and a charming small-bird wicker basket that holds soap and other house toiletries.

Rates are $98 for all guest rooms, single or double occupancy; $115 for junior suites, $135 for deluxe suites. If you plan to visit San Francisco during the winter months, ask the hotel about special rates (based on availability and not including New Year's Eve).

The **Queen Anne Hotel,** just a mile from Union Square at 1590 Sutter St. (at Octavia), San Francisco, CA 94109 (tel. 415/441-2828, or toll free 800/227-

3970, 800/262-2663 in California), looks exactly like what it is—a handsomely restored Victorian mansion. At the turn of the century, in its first life, the building was Miss Mary Lake's School for Girls; later it became a private gentlemen's club, then returned to its original gender as the Girl's Friendly Society Lodge. After a complete renovation and restoration, it opened as the Queen Anne in 1981.

The English oak–paneled lobby is furnished in antiques, and 49 unique rooms manage to preserve a turn-of-the-century atmosphere while providing all modern conveniences. Each room has been individually decorated: Some have corner turret bay windows that look out on tree-lined streets, as well as separate parlor areas and wet bars; others have cozy reading nooks and fireplaces. All rooms have telephones (with bathroom extensions) and remote-control color TVs. The Queen Anne provides complimentary Continental breakfast, brought to your room along with the morning's newspaper. Complimentary afternoon tea and sherry are served in the parlor from 4 to 6pm.

Rates range from $99 to $135.

A converted 19th-century Edwardian home is the setting for Helen Stewart's **Union St. Inn,** 2229 Union St. (between Fillmore and Steiner), San Francisco, CA 94123 (tel. 415/346-0424). Ms. Stewart, a gracious hostess (one journalist described her as looking "as if she spent her life sipping tea in a velvet-walled drawing room"), treats guests like she might in her own home. The parlor here actually is velvet-walled (it also has a fireplace), and guests wandering into it are likely to be offered wine, hors d'oeuvres, even homemade pâté. Breakfast is served in the parlor, although you can also have it served in your room or out on a terrace overlooking a lovely garden of lemon and plum trees. The six exquisitely furnished rooms have brass or canopied beds, tasteful art and antiques, live plants, and fresh flowers. All have private baths. The newest room, the Carriage House, has a huge tub with a Jacuzzi. Some have multipaned bay windows overlooking the garden. There are phones, and TVs are available upon request.

Rates, which include a Continental breakfast (fresh-baked croissants, fresh-squeezed orange juice, fruit, homemade kiwi or plum jam, and coffee), are $135 to $225, single or double.

MODERATELY PRICED ACCOMMODATIONS

If the feeling of an English country inn, or breakfast with scones and crumpets, is your style, the small British-owned **Abigail Hotel,** at 246 McAllister St. (near Larkin), San Francisco, CA 94102 (tel. 415/861-9728, or toll free 800/243-6510, 800/553-5575 in California), may be your pot of tea. What the Abigail lacks in luxury it more than makes up for in charm. The hotel's handsome white exterior, with its canopy and polished brass, seems to have been plucked from London and set down two blocks from the San Francisco Opera. Enter and you'll find a small desk, Oriental area rugs, polished woods, ceiling-to-floor white drapes, and wicker straight-back chairs at red-clothed tables in the breakfast area, all reflecting a very English aura. However, don't be astounded at the hunting trophies in the lobby— they're less from India than from auction.

The 62 guest rooms carry out the English tone with blue floral drapes, white curtains, old prints, and an occasional antique table or lamp. Most rooms are quite light and quiet, though you might inquire when making your reservations. All have the usual amenities; pushbutton telephones, color TVs, and private baths. Valet service is available. J. A. Melon's Restaurant and Bar adjoins the hotel.

Single rooms are $62 to $72; doubles, $72 to $82; and suites, $160. There is an additional charge of $8 for an extra person.

The **Hotel Vintage Court,** 650 Bush St. (between Powell and Stockton), San Francisco, CA 94108 (tel. 415/392-4666, or toll free 800/654-1100, 800/654-7266 in California), is a handsome European-style hotel conveniently situated two blocks from Union Square and one-half block from the cable car. It's a relatively small establishment (106 rooms), which allows for the personal touch in service, and as you enter the hotel, the classically comfortable armchairs, lobby, fireplace, flowers, and warm tones of the furnishings create an intimate, cozy feeling. The decor of the rooms has the same character. Grape clusters embossed on custom-made bedspreads and drapes are complemented by impressionistic prints of the Wine Country. Each room has a private refrigerator and minibar stocked daily, as well as the usual color TVs, phones, and private bath. Complimentary tea and coffee are served through the day, and Napa Valley chardonnay in the evening.

As of 1989, a deluxe two-room penthouse suite had been added, featuring an original 1913 stained-glass skylight, a wood-burning fireplace, a whirlpool tub, and a magnificent view of the city. The suite has a French country theme—comfortable roll-arm furniture and tapestrylike fabrics in rich old-world colors—and for your in-the-room enjoyment, there is a complete entertainment center that includes a color TV, VCR, and stereo.

The charm and popularity of this hotel require that reservations be made at least two to three weeks in advance. Rates are $117 for all rooms—single or double. The penthouse suite is $259.

The famous Masa's restaurant (see Section 6 of this chapter) adjoins the hotel, but each is a separate operation.

It would be hard to find a more convenient place to stay than the **Villa Florence,** 225 Powell St. (near Geary), San Francisco, CA 94102 (tel. 415/397-7700, or toll free 800/553-4411, 800/243-5700 in California, 800/345-8455 in Canada). It's ideal for anyone who wants to be in beautifully appointed surroundings in the center of the downtown area, near Union Square.

Opened in May 1986, the Villa Florence is the superb result of a $6.5-million renovation of what once was the turn-of-the-century Manx Hotel. As soon as you enter the hotel, you'll have an idea of the magnificent refurbishing job done throughout: The arched entryway, graceful palms, marble columns, murals of Florence, huge marble fireplace, rich maroon upholstered chairs, Etruscan-style table lamps, giant urns on pedestals, fresh flowers, and maroon-and-tan floral carpet all reflect an aura of Italian grandeur.

The beautiful, elegant bedrooms feature pink-and-blue floral chintz drapes and matching spreads, as well as white furnishings that include very comfortable chairs. Though the rooms are a bit smaller than most, the decor and the high ceilings afford a feeling of airiness. All modern amenities grace the rooms—color TVs and pull-out writing tables concealed in the chests of drawers, direct-dial phones, and well-stocked refrigerator/honor bars. The bath has a makeup mirror lighting, overhead heat lamps, hand-milled soap—some of life's little pleasures for your convenience and comfort.

If there were nothing more to be said about the Villa Florence, its price and location would be enough to consider it an exceptional buy. However, as you enter the hotel, you'll notice a dining area to your left separated from the main body of the hotel by glass walls elegantly etched with simple shell designs. Beyond the dining area is Kuleto's, the northern Italian restaurant with specialties from Tuscany. See the "Restaurants" section of this chapter for details of this gem.

There are 177 rooms in all, including junior and deluxe suites. Rooms are $119, single or double occupancy. Junior suites are $139; deluxe suites, $189.

I suspect that Thomas Jefferson would have been pleased with the **Monticello Inn,** 127 Ellis St. (between Cyril Magnin and Powell), San Francisco, CA 94102 (tel. 415/392-8800, or toll free 800/669-7777). Opened in September 1987—a renovation of a 1906 building—it's a first-rate addition to the neighborhood. Certainly the only Early American influence near Union Square, it's attractive, beautifully decorated, and exceptionally reasonable. The spacious lobby is replete with colonial reproductions hanging on Williamsburg-blue walls, a Federal-period desk, a stately grandfather clock, fresh floral displays, and, to the rear, a charming parlor where you can enjoy a late-afternoon glass of sherry by the fireplace.

All the 91 rooms feature the country colonial luxury and elegance of canopied beds, with spreads in light-blue, pale-yellow, and peach floral prints, and upholstered chairs to match. Baths are spacious and afford all the amenities one expects in a fine hotel. And for the peace and quiet of a superb night's rest, the rooms are thoroughly soundproofed. There's also a stocked refrigerator/honor bar in each room, color TV with remote control, and digital clock/radio. In-room videos are available.

The inn provides complimentary Continental breakfast and evening wine service at the cozy fireplace in the parlor, as well as complimentary limousine service to the Financial District. Same-day laundry and valet service is available. For those with cars, the in-house parking is a real blessing in this part of town. Nondrivers will find the inn quite conveniently located—it's two blocks from Union Square and a half block from the Powell Street cable car.

Guest rates are $109 for a single, $119 for a double; suites are $139 to $189. Should you need information of any sort, the young, friendly staff will be very helpful.

The Corona Bar & Grill, adjacent to the hotel and at the corner of Ellis and Cyril Magnin, opened in November 1987. You will find this extraordinary restaurant discussed in the next section of this chapter; don't miss it.

Right in the center of everything, just one block from Union Square, cable cars, and shops, the **King George Hotel,** 334 Mason St. (near Geary), San Francisco, CA 94102 (tel. 415/781-5050, or toll free 800/288-6005), is another European-style renovation. Across from the stage door of the Geary Theater, the hotel is entered via a pleasant lobby with an air of elegance and charm following a recent renovation.

On the mezzanine above the lobby, the Bread & Honey Tearoom (also renovated) serves a bountiful light breakfast daily from 7 to 10am. Every afternoon from 3 to 6:30pm (except Sunday) a piano recital accompanies a proper high tea complete with scones, trifle, tea sandwiches, and assorted pastries. Remarkable as it may seem, there's a Japanese restaurant, Ichirin, on the premises; you'll find a detailed discussion of this excellent eatery in Section 6 of this chapter. The hotel also has a most comfortable cocktail lounge and nightly piano bar.

The 143 rooms have all been renovated in subtle pastel colors and equipped with color TVs, direct-dial phones, and private baths. Services include laundry, valet, and 24-hour room service. Parking is conveniently located directly across the street.

Rooms range from $87 for a single to $97 for a double.

The **Edward II Inn** (read "the Second"), 3155 Scott St. (at Lombard), San Francisco, CA 94123 (tel. 415/922-3000), in a building erected in 1914 for the Pan-Pacific Exposition, is among the least expensive of San Francisco's B&B inns. The decor of the 30 rooms and suites is simple and charming, with quilted bedspreads, antique and English country rattan dressers, and white plantation shutters. There are color TVs for those rooms with private baths, and black-and-white TVs in the rooms with shared bath facilities. All rooms have phones. Of the six luxuriously appointed suites, four have whirlpool Jacuzzi baths and wet bars. Two suites are located in the main house, two in the carriage house, and two in proximity to the main house.

Upstairs, a beautiful stained-glass skylight offers an aesthetic experience; downstairs, a stained-glass door leads to more down-to-earth delights in the inn's own Café Lily, where guests take their complimentary Continental breakfast. The café sells an impressive collection of calorie-rich pastries and muffins, as well as quiches, soups, salads, and sandwiches; hours are 7:30am to 3pm Sunday through Tuesday, to 6pm the balance of the week. Off the lobby is Bloomer's Pub, a quaint English-style pub offering a variety of English and other imported beers, wines, and traditional English pub fare; open daily from 4 to 11pm.

Rooms, either single or double occupancy, are $65 to $70 for shared bath, $86 to $96 for private bath. Suites range from $180 to $210 plus. Light sleepers should request rooms to the rear of the building. Limited overnight parking is available at $8 per night.

The centrally located **Commodore International,** 825 Sutter St. (at Jones, four blocks from Union Square), San Francisco, CA 94109 (tel. 415/923-6800, or toll free 800/327-9157), built in 1920, welcomes guests in a warmly old-fashioned lobby, replete with a ticking grandfather clock. Just off the lobby is a pleasant coffee shop-restaurant-cocktail lounge, open daily for breakfast and lunch. Some of the city's most famous restaurants are less than two blocks away.

The 113 rooms have all been redecorated and provided with full baths and large wardrobes, as well as direct-dial phones and color TVs.

Rates are $55 to $80 for a single; doubles and twins run $60 to $110.

Billing itself as San Francisco's "little elegant hotel," the **Raphael,** 386 Geary St. (at Mason, one block from Union Square), San Francisco, CA 94102 (tel. 415/986-2000, or toll free 800/821-5343), provides quite luxurious accommodations at moderate prices. Its 155 rooms occupy 12 stories, and the door to each is individually hand-painted, making for very cheerful hallways. Each interior is uniquely attractive. All rooms have two phones, color TVs with HBO, AM/FM radios, individually controlled air conditioning/heating, clocks, makeup mirrors, and 21-hour room service. Mama's restaurant and cocktail lounge adjoins. Of course, there are also hundreds of eateries within walking distance.

Singles are $79 to $100; doubles, $92 to $113.

I was attracted to the **Lombard Hotel,** 1015 Geary St. (at Polk Street), San Francisco, CA 94109 (tel. 415/673-5232). From the outside it resembles the kind of hostelry you might expect to find on a fashionable London street. The lobby houses a small restaurant, the Gray Derby, where delectable Continental meals (breakfast and lunch daily; dinner on Thursday, Friday, and Saturday; and champagne brunch on weekends) are served by waiters in formal attire. The other part of the marble-floored lobby, boasting a grand piano and fireplace, is the perfect setting for afternoon tea.

The 100 rooms are all newly decorated, and most feature king- or queen-size beds. All have color TVs, phones, and private baths with tubs and/or showers. The hotel is located about six blocks from Union Square and three blocks from the Civic Center.

The Lombard's rates are $74 to $91.

The **Andrews Hotel,** 624 Post St. (near Taylor), San Francisco, CA 94109 (tel. 415/563-6877, or toll free 800/227-4742, 800/622-0557 in California), just two blocks west of Union Square, offers 48 charming and newly redecorated rooms that evoke the casual atmosphere of an intimate European-style hotel. All the accommodations have custom-made pastel bedspreads with matching pillow shams, coordinated with a white enameled headboard; fresh white lace curtains add a light touch. Each room has a private bath with tub and/or shower, phone, and color TV. Kimberly Higgins is a warm and friendly manager, and the rest of the staff emulates her courtesy. The Post Street Bar and Café (see the "Restaurants" section of this chapter for details) adjoins the hotel.

Rates at the Andrews are $76 to $99 for a single or double and $105 for the Petite Suite. All include complimentary Continental breakfast and a glass of California wine in the evening.

An attractive establishment on the "motel strip" that stretches from the Golden Gate Bridge to Van Ness Avenue is the **Chelsea Motor Inn,** 2095 Lombard St. (at Fillmore), San Francisco, CA 94123 (tel. 415/563-5600). Opened in May 1982, this motor inn is perfectly located for a stroll along Union Street, and there are restaurants at almost every turn. The 60 rooms are very comfortable and pleasantly decorated in shades of rose, blue, or brown. Each is equipped with a color TV, tub/shower combination bath, and phone. Parking is free, and buses run regularly to almost every part of the city.

Rates are $70 to $85 for a single, $75 to $95 for a double.

Under the same ownership are the **Cow Hollow Motor Inn,** 2190 Lombard St. (at Steiner), San Francisco, CA 94123 (tel. 415/921-5800), and the **Coventry Motor Inn,** 1901 Lombard St. (at Buchanan), San Francisco, CA 94123 (tel. 415/567-1200). Accommodations and prices are similar to those at the Chelsea.

Among the more reasonable establishments near Union Square, the **Handlery Union Square Hotel,** 351 Geary St. (between Mason and Powell), San Francisco, CA 94102 (tel. 415/781-7800, or toll free 800/223-0888, 800/522-5455 in New York), is the product of a merger of two names (Hotel Stewart and Handlery

Motor Inn) and the completion of a $7.5-million renovation in 1988. All the guest rooms at the Hotel Stewart, now simply called the hotel section, were totally renovated and refurbished. Each guest room, in both the hotel and the club sections, contains a safe (no charge) for your use; and 100 of the rooms in the hotel section also have minibars.

What had been the Handlery Motor Inn is now the Handlery Club—the concierge section of the new hotel, which has managed to maintain reasonable rates although it now offers services one usually expects from a larger hotel. Rooms in the club are truly large and luxurious. They include such frills as bedside remote-control color TVs (with movies available), electric shoe polishers, coffee makers, dressing rooms with makeup mirrors, custom bathroom amenities, weight scales, luxurious bath towels, robes, hairdryers, and two telephones. The club section also provides a turndown service and a complimentary copy of the morning newspaper. The merged facilities still include a large, heated outdoor swimming pool and sauna. The shopping, theater, and financial districts are easily accessible from this location, which is half a block from Union Square. The hotel offers overnight valet parking, truly a bargain at $9.

Rates in the hotel section are $99 to $110 for singles, $109 to $120 for doubles. Rates in the club section are $130 for singles, $145 for doubles.

The **Phoenix Inn,** 601 Eddy St. (at Larkin), San Francisco, CA 94109 (tel. 415/885-3109), has been variously described as stylish, offbeat, funky, contemporary, and arts-oriented. It's all of the above, which undoubtedly accounts for much of its appeal. The Phoenix is a gathering place for visiting rock musicians, writers, filmmakers, etc., creative types like us—all reasonably peaceful folk. Or, to put it another way, it's like a small transplanted segment of Los Angeles.

The Phoenix is definitely not in the posh section of town—it is more of an island in the middle of a less than prosperous area. At the center of this oasis is a small heated outdoor pool set in a spacious courtyard and modern sculpture garden. Rooms are spacious (high ceilings), light, comfortable, and attractively decorated in pastels. Oversize furnishings and chairs are handmade of Philippine bamboo, and potted plants and original art add attractive touches. In addition to the usual amenities, the inn's own cable channel plays films made in or about San Francisco (e.g., *The Maltese Falcon, Vertigo, Foul Play*).

Rates for single rooms are $75 to $90, with doubles costing $85 to $99. Suites go for $110 to $120. Free parking is included.

Adjoining the Phoenix Inn is Miss Pearl's Jam House, another creation of superchef Julie Rings (who established Rings Restaurant and Julie's Supper Club). The restaurant serves breakfast, lunch, and dinner indoors and out (given clement weather). The cuisine is a happy mingling of Caribbean, Cajun, and Créole. Your starter at lunch or dinner might be black-eyed pea fritters or catfish fingers with Trinidadian pepper and cilantro pesto; your salad choice, hearts of palm and jicama or the calamari salad with ginger, chiles, lime, and peppers. Miss Pearl's dinner menu also includes a tasty selection of small plates ($7 to $13), great for combining into a large or small meal. The specialty of the house is seafood, though other options such as the peppered flank steak and the grilled duck breast may appear on the menu ($14 to $16). Miss Pearl's Jam House has a full bar and a limited but good selection of California wines. The restaurant is open daily from 8am to 10pm. Miss Pearl's does not take reservations.

Ironically, since it's located at the gateway to Chinatown, the **Beverly Plaza Hotel,** 342 Grant Ave. (at Bush Street), San Francisco, CA 94108 (tel. 415/781-3566, or toll free 800/227-3818), has made considerable effort to court Japanese visitors. Brochures and guidebooks in Japanese can be obtained in the lobby, and the Midori Restaurant has a Japanese menu, decor, and staff.

Rooms are decorated in shades of blue and green, with matching floral-print drapes and spreads, color TVs with movies available, and direct-dial phones color coordinated to your room decor. Other facilities include a handy electric map in the lobby (like the ones in the Paris Métro). The friendly staff and concerned management here are noteworthy.

Room rates—very good value for the money—are $66 to $71 for a single, $75 to $79 for a double or twin. Suites are $115 to $170.

Step into the lobby of the **Hotel Beresford,** 635 Sutter St. (at Mason), San Francisco, CA 94102 (tel. 415/673-9900), and you'll find yourself in a Victorian drawing room. This delightful European-style hostelry is the homiest in town, from the flowerboxes adorning the street windows to the friendly staff offering good old-fashioned service. There's a writing parlor off the lobby with wicker furniture, desks, a gilt-framed portrait of Lord Beresford, and a color TV. Rooms have white drapes, color-coordinated spreads and wallpaper, baths with tubs and/or showers, color TVs, refrigerator/honor bars, and direct-dial phones.

The White Horse Taverne, reputedly an authentic replica of an old English pub, contains an antique bedwarmer and an ancient crossbow hung over the fireplace. A congenial place, the White Horse offers home-cooked breakfasts and lunches; they use only fresh produce and fresh-caught fish.

If you like European charm—and who doesn't?—this well-located hotel is a good choice. Rates are $69 for a single, $79 to $90 for a double.

No room at the Beresford? Try the nearby **Beresford Arms,** 701 Post St. (at Jones), San Francisco, CA 94109 (tel. 415/673-2600), equally European in ambience and run in the same friendly way by the same owners. Many of the 87 rooms here have fully equipped kitchens; all are immaculate and homey, equipped with color TVs, direct-dial phones, and tub/shower baths. Renovation has produced several Jacuzzi suites featuring queen-size beds, baths with brass fixtures, and antique furnishings from the 18th and 19th centuries. Rates are the same as at the Beresford, except for the Jacuzzi suites, which also have kitchen units or wet bars and rent for $90. Parlor suites are $110.

Similarly charming and well situated is the **Cartwright Hotel,** 524 Sutter St. (at Powell Street), San Francisco, CA 94102 (tel. 415/421-2865, or toll free 800/227-3844), a cozy little place where the owners and management (the Adams family) take pride in its reputation for comfort and efficiency—a pride that is reflected in every nook and cranny. Rooms sparkle with cleanliness; each is unique in size, shape, decor, and antique furnishings. All are brightened with fresh flowers and have pretty matching spreads and drapes, private bathrooms with shower massage and thick fluffy towels, terrycloth robes, direct-dial phones, color TVs, and little extra touches that add to guests' comfort—a third sheet to insulate skin from the roughness of blankets, turndown service, and the availability of such items as irons, hairdryers, and large reading pillows. Complimentary tea and cakes are served in the lobby from 4 to 6pm. There's a little restaurant at the Cartwright too: the charming French-provincial Teddy's serves delicious breakfasts.

Singles at the Cartwright cost $85 to $95, doubles and twins run $95 to $100, and family suites accommodating up to four people cost $150 to $170. The Cartwright also offers discount garage parking a block away.

The **Hotel Savoy,** 580 Geary St. (between Taylor and Jones), San Francisco, CA 94102 (tel. 415/441-2700, or toll free 800/227-4223, 800/622-0553 in California), is a delightful little place just three blocks from Union Square. Rooms here have antique or antique-style furnishings and a variety of pastel color schemes. Corner rooms are especially nice; they have lots of windows and are light and airy. The little extras are in evidence here—full-length mirrors, triple sheets, turndown service—along with direct-dial phones (there is a charge for local calls), color TVs, and modern bathrooms. The Savoy has no restaurants; the complimentary Continental breakfast is served in the Savoy lounge. Other extra touches include complimentary late-afternoon tea and sherry, plus weekly newspapers. The staff is friendly and helpful, full of smiles for guests and visitors.

Singles at the Savoy rent for $69 to $90, doubles or twins for $79 to $99. Suites are available from $127.

Another charming hostelry is the **Bedford,** 761 Post St. (between Leavenworth and Jones), San Francisco, CA 94109 (tel. 415/673-6040, or toll free 800/227-5642, 800/652-1889 in California). The hotel is three blocks from Union Square on the southwest slope of Nob Hill. Each of its 144 redecorated rooms is brightly painted in shades of yellow, gray, and white, with color-coordinated drapes and skirted beds. All have color TVs, video tape players, fully stocked refrigerator/ honor bars, and direct-dial phones, and there are good views of the bay or the San Francisco skyline from the upper floors. In the white marble-floored lobby, the beautiful chandeliers of the past remain. Café Bedford, the elegant award-winning gourmet restaurant that serves breakfast and dinner, has open skylights, and six large ficus trees thrive in the sunlight that streams in. A multilingual staff, proficient in at least 10 languages, is on hand to serve you. Room service is available, as is valet parking for overnight guests.

Rooms at the Bedford cost $94 to $99 for a single or double; suites begin at $150.

Under the same management is the **Galleria Park Hotel,** 191 Sutter St. (at Kearny), San Francisco, CA 94104 (tel. 415/781-3060, or toll free 800/792-9639, 800/792-9855 in California). From its lobby, complete with fireplace, to its 177 beautifully appointed rooms and 15 suites, the Galleria Park has been totally restored in the art nouveau style of the time of its original construction. The hotel features a full-time concierge, room service, a bar, and a sundries shop. And the Galleria is the only hotel in San Francisco to have an outdoor running track and park. The hotel also features Bentley's Oyster Bar & Restaurant (under separate management), offering fresh seafood specialties, oysters at a grand-scale bar, and a diversity of other dishes.

Rooms at the Galleria Park let for $120 to $130, single or double. Suites begin at $160.

The **Hotel Union Square,** 114 Powell St. (at Ellis), San Francisco, CA 94102 (tel. 415/397-3000, or toll free 800/553-1900), located just a couple of blocks south of Union Square itself, dates from the early 20th century, when it was known as the Golden West. It's been renamed and renovated. There are 131 guest rooms with art deco decor and soft floral-print bedspreads and curtains. Shampoos, conditioners, bath gels, and soaps are supplied in the bathrooms. Each morning complimentary croissants and coffee are served in a small hall lounge on each floor, and each evening there is turndown service. Though the Union Square has no restaurant of its own, two neighboring establishments, Tad's and Les Joulins, offer room service daily from 7am to 11pm. And of course there are dozens of restaurants in the area. There's parking for guests' cars on the hotel property, at $12 a day.

Rates are $92 to $119, single or double. Penthouse suites with redwood decks and garden patios begin at $189.

A delightful example of the bed-and-breakfast inn in San Francisco is the **Albion House,** 135 Gough St. (at Lily), San Francisco, CA 94102 (tel. 415/621-0896). Built as a small hotel in 1907, it was remodeled under the aegis of innkeeper Richard Meyer. There are eight rooms here, including one two-room suite; each is decorated differently. Sonoma, for example, evokes the Wine Country with a double-size brass bed and floral prints; and Cypress, inspired by the Lone Cypress in Carmel, is decorated in tans and furnished with a queen-size bed. All rooms have telephones and private baths; some rooms have color TVs.

The heart of the Albion House is the common room, a large living room decorated in cool pinks with exposed redwood beams and a fireplace. Breakfast (included in the room prices) is served here every morning; you can feast on fresh-squeezed orange juice, croissants, eggs, and coffee.

Albion House is near Louise M. Davies Symphony Hall, the War Memorial Opera House, and the Civic Center, and it is convenient to the entire city via public transportation. If you come by car, there are inexpensive lots and garages nearby, as well as lots of overnight street parking.

Rooms at the Albion House rent for $65 to $85, single or double, and $120 for suites. A full breakfast is included in the rates.

The **Shannon Court,** 550 Geary St. (near Taylor), San Francisco, CA 94102 (tel. 415/775-5000, or toll free 800/821-0493, 800/228-8830 in California), formerly the El Cortez, has been the beneficiary of a multimillion-dollar refurbishment. The historic landmark building, constructed in 1925, has a distinctly Spanish flavor. The ambience of the original building with its white stucco walls and graceful curved arches has been retained, while the 174 spacious guest rooms have been updated with a comfortable contemporary look. All rooms have outside exposures and are equipped with color TVs and phones.

Adjoining the lobby is a French restaurant, La Mère Duquesne, offering some of the best buys to be found in the city. Luncheon entrees range from $5.50 to $10.95, dinner entrees from $12.50 to $16.25. An excellent prix-fixe dinner for $10 offers such choices as coq au vin, veal Marengo, or fish filets wrapped in layers of boursin cheese in puff pastry. After 9pm, an entree selection from the classic menu is offered for $9. Lunch is served weekdays, and dinner nightly.

The rates: Singles are $85 to $125; doubles or twins, $95 to $135; suites, $200 to $275. Ask for the holiday rates in the winter season.

BUDGET HOTELS

San Francisco has more than its share of small charming hotels born near the turn of the century. Among them is a real gem, the **Golden Gate Hotel,** 775 Bush St. (between Powell and Mason), San Francisco, CA 94108 (tel. 415/392-3702), just two blocks north of Union Square and two blocks down (literally) from the crest of Nob Hill. Part of the beauty and charm of the Golden Gate is that it is family-run by John and Renate Kenaston, delightful, hospitable innkeepers. In the nicest sense, it's rather like being part of a large family with European guests.

The lovely, immaculately clean accommodations have been individually decorated with handsome antique furnishings from the early 1900s and with floral-print draperies and spreads. Renate keeps fresh flowers in all of the rooms. The European-style rooms share a bath; those with queen-size or twin beds have private baths. The antique claw-foot tubs are great for long hot soaks. Each of the rooms has a color TV; most, but not all, have phones, so if you need one, request it when you make your reservation. Continental breakfast and afternoon tea are served in the parlor.

Concierge services are available and sightseeing tours can be arranged, with pickup at the hotel. You will find a member of the staff who is fluent in French, Spanish, and German, should you need a translator. Garage parking is available directly across the street at a reasonable price with in-and-out privileges.

Rooms with queen-size or twin beds and private baths are $79 to $89; European-style rooms, sharing a bath, are $50 to $55. Rates include Continental breakfast and afternoon tea. European-style rooms, sharing a bath, are $50.

The **Adelaide Inn,** 5 Isadora Duncan (off Taylor Street), San Francisco, CA 94102 (tel. 415/441-2261), as billed, evokes memories of a European pension and is run like one. The inn has 18 rooms on two floors above ground level and is situated on a tiny dead-end street conducive to peace and quiet. There is no emphasis on decor, but the travel and art prints make you feel as though you're on holiday in France. You may have to walk up a couple of flights to your room, but rest assured that all accommodations are clean, bright, and comfortable. There are no private baths, though all rooms have washing facilities and the shared baths are well kept. Sorry, TV is black-and-white, and while there are no phones in the rooms, the inn will take messages.

The Adelaide Inn is a relaxed, pleasant place where guests quickly become friends. The hosts, Serge and Mary, are gracious fonts of information on almost any topic relating to your stay in San Francisco. If hotel services are what you must have, however, this is not the place for you.

It's hard to beat the price: Singles are $32 to $38, and doubles run from $42 to $46, including Continental breakfast.

The **Cornell Hotel,** 715 Bush St. (near Mason), San Francisco, CA 94108 (tel. 415/421-3154), within walking distance of Union Square, is one of a number of small European-style hotels ideal for travelers who enjoy the personal attention and the relaxed air of a charming, unpretentious hostelry. As you enter you'll see a number of medieval prints opposite the desk. Each floor of the Cornell has an artist of its own—I rather like the Modigliani floor, where you'll see reproductions of a number of his better-known paintings along the hallways.

The hotel has 60 rooms, all simple, comfortable, and individually decorated. Draperies and spreads with floral patterns, attractive prints, and dark-toned maroon carpeting give the rooms a pleasant, warm feeling. All the rooms have baths, color TVs, and phones.

Rooms can be had by the day or week, with or without breakfast and dinner. Meals are prepared by a French chef and served in the adjoining restaurant, Jeanne d'Arc. Without meals, singles are $55 to $70; doubles, $60 to $75; and twins, $70 to $75. The Cornell also offers a special and very popular arrangement—a room for one week (seven successive nights), with seven breakfasts and five dinners, at $380 for a single, $455 for a double (make reservations at least three months in advance).

The location of the pleasant, recently renovated **Pacific Bay Inn,** 520 Jones St. (between Geary and O'Farrell), San Francisco, CA 94102 (tel. 415/673-4781, or toll free 800/445-2631, 800/343-0880 in California)—just three blocks west of Union Square and the Powell Street cable car—is good. This was once a rather frumpy neighborhood, and though it's still not Nob Hill, the area is rapidly improving by virtue of the expansion of some of its neighbors—the San Francisco Hilton Square and the very elegant Nikko Hotel.

As you approach the Pacific Bay Inn, it's easily identified by its blue-and-gold canopy resting on well-polished brass poles. The lobby has recently been given a comfortable hi-tech look.

The rooms are cozy, light (no view), and done in an airy peach color, with maroon floral-print spreads and maroon-and-gray carpeting. The rooms have showers only, no tubs. The inn has a 24-hour desk service. They also provide reduced-rate tickets for parking in the Taylor Street Garage, around the corner.

Singles are $60; doubles, $70. Rates include a Continental breakfast.

If you want a really inexpensive, hearty meal, it's hard to beat the Family Inn across the street, open from 6:30am to 6pm. The menu varies daily, but homemade soups are part of the fare at lunch, and how can you beat pot roast, mashed potatoes, a vegetable, bread, and dessert—all for $4.75?

The YWCA Hotel is no more. In its place is the **Sheehan,** 620 Sutter St. (near Mason), San Francisco, CA 94102 (tel. 415/775-6500). The location of the Sheehan (if you never stayed at the Y) is in an area convenient for students and families looking for low-cost facilities. It is close to restaurants, cable cars, buses, and BART, and you can easily walk to most places in the downtown area.

As with its predecessor, rooms at the Sheehan are comfortable, clean, and simple in terms of furnishings. The rooms are carpeted and each has a table, chairs, and one or more beds, depending on whether it's a single, double, or suite. The hotel has a heated Olympic-size swimming pool for the use of its guests, as well as a comfortable reading room.

Singles with shared baths are $37.50, $50 with private baths. Doubles without baths are $60; with baths they're $70. Suites with four twin beds and private baths are $80. Rates include a Continental breakfast. Only those rooms with baths also have phones. All rooms have color TVs, but reception is for local stations only (no cable). Weekly rates are available—if you stay for seven successive nights, you pay for six.

Unfortunately for those who always look for the economy and convenience of a **Motel 6,** there is not one to be found in San Francisco. However, don't despair: One is located in Palo Alto at 4301 El Camino Real, Palo Alto, CA 94306 (tel. 415/949-0833) near U.S. 101.

If you don't mind a dormitory, none of the budget accommodations in San Francisco can beat the **San Francisco International Hostel,** Building 240, Fort Mason, San Francisco, CA 94123 (tel. 415/771-7277)—$11 a night. From Bay Street and Van Ness Avenue, follow the hostel signs to the grounds of Fort Mason. Call for space from 7am to 2pm and from 4:30pm until midnight. Anyone can use the dormitory, regardless of age. The only limitation to your stay is time—at the end of three nights you must move on to new lodgings. For families or compatible couples, there are three rooms with four bunks each, obviously in great demand.

Kitchen facilities are available, as are lockers, laundry facilities, snack-vending machines, and several community rooms with fireplaces, stereo, piano, and a wide selection of books. You'll also find several bulletin boards with information on tours and places to go during your stay.

---

6. Restaurants

Only New York can surpass the quality, quantity, and ethnic variety of eateries in what Trader Vic (he lives here) once called "the city that knows chow" (a variation on President Taft's tribute to San Francisco—"the city that knows how").

What's your dining pleasure: Indonesian rijstaffel, Filipino chicken in adobo sauce, dim sum, gourmet pizza, Russian piroshki, or a chopped liver on rye? From acclaimed (and pricey) gourmet French cuisine to budget Basque, San Francisco has a place to please every palate. And the special savor of dining out in San Francisco is enhanced by California wines.

In the upcoming section I've selected over 50 of the city's 3,000-or-so restaurants and ranged them according to price bracket, subdivided by nationality. I could easily add another hundred worthy establishments, but that would fill the whole book. Be sure, too, to consider the hotel restaurants recommended throughout the previous section as well as those discussed here. Particularly worthy choices are **Ristorante Donatello** at the Donatello, the **French Room** at the Four Seasons Clift Hotel, and the new **Postrio,** adjoining the Prescott Hotel.

LUXURY ESTABLISHMENTS

Splurge at least once during your visit at one of the following venerables. Several are highly acclaimed internationally, and each provides a dining experience par excellence—a romantic and memorable evening made up of sumptuous cuisine, distinguished service, and ambience. If your budget doesn't stretch to dinner, try lunch—at one of those places that serve lunch—same chef, same dishes, lower prices. Also notice that in some spots you can go early and get a full set dinner for the price that one entree might cost on the à la carte menu served later.

A final word about prices. They're in a permanent state of one-way flux—upward. Here as elsewhere. So while you will find most of the listed rates models of accuracy, you may discover unannounced increases by the time you get here. Don't blame me, please. With or without high inflation, prices do rise.

Masa's, 648 Bush St., between Powell and Stockton (tel. 415/989-7154), was started by Masataka Kobayashi, who left New York City for Auberge du Soleil in the Napa Valley, and ultimately opened Masa's in San Francisco. After his death in 1984, there was some question about the restaurant's survival. There is none now. The cuisine has been polished to a brilliance surpassing even the talents of Masa by chef Julian Serrano. Masa's is now regarded as one of the country's great French restaurants.

As you enter Masa's you can't help but be impressed by its elegant simplicity. There's obviously no need for decor to compete with the food. The upholstery and carpeting are a quiet plum; the walls are buff; and small chandeliers are placed at useful and attractive intervals. You expect this to be the setting for great performances to come.

The prix-fixe dinner is $65—unquestionably expensive, but a memorable dining experience. Generally you may choose from among four appetizers, five entrees, plus a small salad with cheese, and three or four desserts. The menu changes daily. You might begin the evening with the fresh foie gras sautéed with a sauce created from the pan juices, cognac, and black truffles. The entree of medallions of venison, marinated for several days in zinfandel, sautéed and served with a superb rich brown sauce, is a glory and unlike any other you've ever tasted. Should any one of several game birds be available as entrees, take advantage of the occasion to order it. The dessert, whether sorbet, frozen soufflé, or a special combination of sorbets and mousse, will be among the best endings to any meal you've ever had. Masa's also has an à la carte menu if you prefer the extended list of choices.

As you might expect, Masa's wine list is selective and includes some excellent older French wines as well as an impressive group of California wines. You'll also be pleased to discover that the quality of the service happily matches that of the dinner.

Reservations are taken up to 21 days in advance. It may be difficult to get a weekend reservation if you wait until a day or two ahead of time; if you have your heart set on a Friday- or Saturday-night dinner, phone ahead from whatever city you're in. If you wonder whether Masa's is worth the price or the advance reservations date, it may be one of the very few restaurants in the country that is. For those who forget to call ahead, now and then there may be a last-minute cancellation.

Masa's is open for dinner only, Tuesday through Saturday from 6pm, with last seating at 9:30pm.

Another of San Francisco's prestigious and elegant restaurants, **Ernie's,** 847 Montgomery St., at Pacific (tel. 415/397-5969), proffers distinguished French fare in suitably plush surroundings. The decor is ornate Victorian, with champagne silk walls and intricate woodwork; it would be a shame not to enjoy a quiet drink before dinner at the massive mahogany and stained-glass bar. Many of the furnishings here originally adorned San Francisco's extravagant turn-of-the-century mansions.

The menu is à la carte, and every dish is excellent. I'd suggest a dinner starting with pheasant pâté en croûte with wild mushrooms, then baby greens with a walnut vinaigrette and duck crackling, followed by delicate fish quenelles on a bed of black pasta blessed with a delectable lobster sauce. Of course, you'll order one of Ernie's fine wines to complement your meal, and who could resist the sumptuous desserts, especially the feather-light Grand Marnier or chocolate soufflé. Entrees average $24 to $28, so expect your bill to be at least $100 for two—a worthy splurge. A prix-fixe menu that changes daily is offered at $40 per person. It includes a choice of three appetizers, three entrees, and two desserts.

In many restaurants in this category, the quality of the haute cuisine is matched only by the icy hauteur of the staff, but the maître d' and waiters at Ernie's are actually polite and friendly.

Dinner is served nightly from 6:30 to 10:30pm. Coats and ties are required for men; reservations are essential.

The lavish decor of the elegant **Fleur de Lys,** 777 Sutter St., between Taylor and Jones (tel. 415/673-7779), is a superb setting for dinner before an evening on the town. This downtown restaurant is a visual and gastronomic delight. The Fleur de Lys is one of the city's most romantic dining spots: the lovely interior was designed by the late Michael Taylor, who created a feeling of an immense garden tent set in the French countryside. The deep-red fabric, locally hand-printed with an autumnal design, creates a rustic mood enhanced by strategically placed floor-to-ceiling mirrors. Even the menu covers, quite probably the loveliest I've even seen, are a reflection of the outstanding cuisine.

One of the many joys of the Fleur de Lys is that co-owner and host Maurice Rouas has kept a watchful eye on service since 1970, assuring its continuing excellence for each guest. His partner and executive chef, Hubert Keller, is a master of his trade, having served under such great French chefs as Roger Verge, Paul Haeberlin, and Paul Bocuse.

As for the fare, it includes appetizers such as the American foie gras, presented in a black-pepper and herb gelée, and the thin-sliced Norwegian salmon in a tender corn pancake topped with golden caviar and watercress sauce; entrees (prices average $22 to $35) such as Maine lobster served with flageolets and black chanterelles accented with a cilantro broth, and veal loin rolled over roasted tricolor bell peppers and sweet onions with a shallot-thyme sauce; and for dessert, perhaps a fresh berry sabayon soufflé. Besides the impressive à la carte menu, a four- and five-course tasting menu is offered ($53 and $60, respectively). The dishes are representative of what is freshest in the market and therefore change daily. Fleur de Lys now offers espresso, caffè latte, and cappuccino (regular and decaffeinated). To complement your meal, there's an extensive wine list.

Open for dinner from 6 to 10pm; closed Sunday. Reservations are required.

EXPENSIVE RESTAURANTS

Just a shade less grandiose than the bastions of haute cuisine we've looked at up to now, the following restaurants are nonetheless elegant and delightful in every respect. In general, they offer meals in varying price brackets, and with a careful perusal of the menu you needn't spend a king's ransom. All offer superb cuisine and a suitable atmosphere in which to enjoy it. If your budget doesn't stretch to dinner, try lunch where it's available—same chef, same dishes, lower prices. Also, notice that some spots serve a full dinner early in the evening for the price of an entree later on.

American

Right about now, Wolfgang Puck is firmly entrenched in San Francisco. The internationally known chef/entrepreneur is the creator of two successful ventures in Los Angeles, Spago and Chinois on Main. Puck's newest venture, **Postrio,** is located at 545 Post St., between Mason and Taylor and adjacent to the new Prescott Hotel (tel. 415/776-7825). The name Postrio alludes to the combined talents of the three executive chefs—Wolfgang, and Anne and David Gingrass (both longtime chefs at Wolfgang's Spago restaurant)—and the restaurant's location on Post Street.

The design of Postrio is unique and dramatic. The restaurant functions on three levels with several ambiences, from that of the modern European bar area to the art-gallery look of the main dining room. The levels are beautifully tied together with a ribbon theme evident in the carpet and marble flooring, the wrought-iron handrails, and the custom lighting overhead. Your choice of seating is in comfortable booths and tables. Floral arrangements are spectacular and much greenery adds a lush air to the decor. There is far more to see than space allows—go and be amazed.

The Postrio menu is à la carte and each selection is made to order. You might begin the day with a choice of freshly made juices, followed by cinnamon raisin French toast with strawberry jam and maple syrup; or skip the juice and enjoy a warm fruit compote with scones. I opt for the grilled lamb and eggplant crêpinettes with sunshine eggs and tomato–red onion relish, or Postrio's delicious Hangtown Fry—a crisp oyster-and-pancetta omelet served with fresh salsa and delicate potato cakes. (If you aren't familiar with pancetta, it's Italian bacon that has been cured but not smoked.) Baked goods, breads, and desserts are made fresh daily on the premises. I particularly look forward to the whole-wheat pecan bread and the almond brioche.

Luncheon highlights are the home-smoked salmon with dill cream and toasted brioche, and braised veal shank on barley risotto. One dish that I particularly take to has sweet herb sausage with artichokes and fennel on pasta triangles. Postrio also has Annie's Favorite Lunch Sandwiches, including an interesting club sandwich with smoked lobster, arugula, and grilled bacon. A reservation is not needed to walk into the bar for one of several designer pizzas. They're $8.50; the Jewish Pizza, topped with smoked salmon, crème fraîche, and golden caviar, is $15.

Dinner specialties of the house include a number of exceptional choices. Among the appetizers are a Mediterranean fish soup with garlic croutons, and David's homemade salami. And lovers of pâté should try the terrine of American duck liver with grilled country bread. Postrio also offers several exceptional pasta dishes, including duck raviolis with sun-dried tomatoes. Highlights of the dinner menu are the lobster, roast Dungeness crab with spicy curry risotto and fried leeks, and the crispy Wolf Ranch quail with scallions and spicy pineapple sauce. Two of my choice selections are the crisply sautéed sweetbreads with arugula and sherry wine sauce, and the heavenly sand dabs with artichoke, tomato, and oregano sauce.

And now we come to the dessert specialties—life is full of difficult choices. Top of the list is the chocolate devil's-food cake with coconut and walnuts, served with mango sauce. The lemon cream tartlette with boysenberry sauce is difficult to resist, but the menu just happens to include a personal favorite—crème brûlée with seasonal berries. The wine list is exceptionally diversified, including offerings from California, France, and Italy (several of the California wines are available by the glass).

Breakfast at the Postrio will cost $4 to $10. Pastries, such as croissants, bagels, and pecan bread, are an added $2 to $3.50; beverages, $2.50; freshly made juices, $2 to $3. Luncheon prices are in the $9.50 to $17 range. Dinner appetizers and pastas cost $8 to $14; main courses, $18 to $23. Desserts are $5; beverages, $2.50.

Postrio is open seven days a week. Breakfast is served from 7 to 10:30am; lunch, from 11:30am to 2:30pm; dinner, from 5:30 to 10:30pm. The bar is open from 11:30am to midnight; it has a late-night menu that includes several of the gourmet pizzas. Reservations are necessary—for dinner, at least two weeks in advance.

Jack's, 615 Sacramento St., at Montgomery (tel. 415/986-9854), a venerated San Francisco institution, was founded in 1864 and proudly displays its One Hundred Year Club certificate awarded by the state. It has been run by the Redinger family (currently Jack Redinger, though the restaurant was not named for him) since 1902. Located deep in the Financial District, it has a fanatically faithful following among the financial wizards.

The wooden Thonet chairs, the unpretentious gold-embossed walls adorned with brass coathooks, the old tile floors, and the dignified waiters all look as they might have a century ago. Jack's specializes in rex sole, calves' head, and fowl dishes, but entrees (ranging in price from $11 to $22) run the gamut from cheese blintzes to roast turkey with dressing and cranberry sauce to a rack of spring lamb with potatoes boulangère. Desserts also cater to a wide variety of moods—anything from apple pie à la mode to zabaglione. Complete dinners, served from 5 to 9pm only, cost $21.50. Jack's accepts American Express.

Jack's is open Monday through Friday from 11:30am to 9:30pm, on Saturday and Sunday from 5 to 9:30pm. Reservations are advised, and jackets and ties are required for men.

Wherever else you may dine in San Francisco, persevere in finding **Splendido's** —it's worth the effort. It is in Embarcadero Four (Market between Clay and Drum) on the Podium Level, otherwise known as the Third Level (tel. 415/986-3222). You may find it difficult to believe that the aura of a small old-world Mediterranean village could be created within a building representing the ultimate in architectural sophistication, but restaurant designer Pat Kuleto has achieved just that with Splendido's—from the 200-year-old olivewood doors that form the entryway to the Moorish arches inside, the rustic French stone walls, Italian tiles, Spanish wrought-iron banisters, Greek grain thrashers, and Portuguese pewter–topped bar. The color scheme of blue, teal, mauve, sunset pink, and pomegranate enhances Splendido's warm country look. And when the weather is pleasant, you have the option of dining outside in the canopied patio area. An appetizer menu is available both here and in the handsome bar area. Splendido's also features a full display kitchen, with exhibition seating, an open grill, and a wood-burning pizza oven.

Ah yes, and then there is the food. The lunch and dinner menus offer excellent choices of what might be called first courses, but conceivably they could be combined to constitute a main meal. At lunch there may be the fish and shellfish soup; the pheasant, roasted wild mushroom, and pistachio terrine; the spinach salad with grilled red onion, Explorateur cheese, and pepper brioche; the ravioli of prosciutto, mascarpone, and shallots. Turning to the main courses, the grilled entrecote with toasted garlic sauce and a roasted fennel flan is perfectly done and beautifully seasoned. On the other hand, the pan-roasted chicken with saffron, tomato, and scalloped fennel potatoes, or the grilled shrimp with white beans, may better suit your taste of the moment.

For dinner Christophe Majer, formerly of San Francisco's Campton Place and New York's Quilted Giraffe, has created eminently satisfying dishes that blend a variety of textures, flavors, colors, and shapes. For a first course, you might begin with one of the small pizzas, such as that with grilled eggplant, roasted tomato, and gorgonzola, or an excellent roast squab with smoked ham duxelle, baby lettuce, and hazelnut oil. As for a main course, I was torn between the sautéed sweetbreads with pancetta vinaigrette, wild mushrooms, and chestnuts, and the grilled loin of lamb with white bean–garlic flan, fried shallots, tomatoes, and basil. Should you be oriented toward seafood, the choices are several. And for those who tend toward very hearty dishes, osso buco alla milanese with pecorino romano could be just the right choice.

Then there are the desserts—somewhere beyond the pearly gates they must be like this. These are the creations of pastry chef Maryanne ("Lulu") Young. The list may include polenta cake with fresh strawberry sauce; dried figs poached in port with crème fraîche; a frozen terrine of pear, chocolate, Armagnac, and prune; tiramisu with chocolate pinenut bark; or my favorite, pistachio crème brûlée. All desserts are made daily in the restaurant's on-the-premises bakery, as are the breads, baked goods, and pastas.

The menu is à la carte, with all selections made to order. Appetizers cost $4.75 to $9.75; entrees are $13 to $18; all are slightly less at lunch. Desserts will add another $5 to $6. As you might assume, the wine list offers excellent choices, including a good selection of wines by the glass.

The restaurant is open daily from 11:30am to 10pm, with the bar open to midnight. Reservations are necessary, though you may choose simply to have a light bite in the bar.

The charming little **Post Street Bar and Café,** 632 Post St., next to the Andrews Hotel (tel. 415/928-2080), is an outstanding example of the growing number of restaurants beginning to take full advantage of the tremendous quality and variety of foodstuffs grown or raised in Northern California. The basic philosophy is to serve the best and the freshest available, in a style that is perhaps not just Californian but truly American, and here chef Paula Linton does it admirably.

It's a small place adjoining the lobby of the Andrews Hotel. As you enter the café from the street, a grand and quite handsome mahogany bar leads you into the main dining area. High ceilings and arched windows of hand-poured glass give the room a light, open and airy feeling. In season, the brick fireplace gives a cheery touch of warmth. White tablecloths, fresh flowers, and original watercolors add charm and style. And completing the ambience is the jazz played softly in the background.

The Post Street Bar and Café's menu is seasonal, but at any time of the year you can expect delectable appetizers. The café also has daily pasta and fresh fish specials to satisfy the pickiest palate. The homemade spinach ravioli stuffed with rock prawns and sea scallops under a spicy saffron cream sauce should not be ignored. Meat eaters will wonder how they could have lived this long without tasting home-cured pork loin medallions with sweet-potato hash or the café's grilled chicken with roast-tomato garlic sauce.

To accompany your meal, the café has a nice selection of California wines, many of which you can enjoy by the glass. I found a fine choice to be the Edna Valley chardonnay, a lovely product of one of the several boutique wineries featured by the café. Be sure to save room for one of the homemade desserts. The apple-pear crisp and chocolate hazelnut cake are mouthwatering. Dinner entrees average $14 to $18; with an appetizer, add another $7.

You can also lunch at the Post Street Bar and Café: The menu offers a selection of delicious and surprising combinations. You might think a sandwich to be less than inspired until you've had the smoked bacon, sweet pepper, and lettuce; or the turkey breast sandwich with sun-dried tomato relish. Fresh fish, pasta, and salads are also available. Luncheon entrees range from $7 to $14.

Dining at the Post Street Bar and Café is an enjoyable experience you won't want to miss. Be sure to make reservations. It's open for lunch Monday through Friday from 11:30am to 2:30pm, and for dinner Tuesday through Saturday from 6 to 10pm.

For Dashiell Hammett and/or Sam Spade fans, **John's Grill,** 63 Ellis St., between Stockton and Powell (tel. 415/986-DASH), should be at the top of the "don't miss" list. The restaurant has been around since 1908; in the 1920s it was one of Hammett's hangouts. It's even one of the San Francisco landmarks that Hammett used to make *The Maltese Falcon* come to life. (Before setting out on a wild goose chase after the mysterious Brigid O'Shaughnessy, Sam Spade stops by John's Grill for a dinner of chops, baked potato, and sliced tomatoes.)

The restaurant works hard to preserve the Hammett/Spade legend. The main dining room and bar on the ground floor are decorated in wood and leather, with glass chandeliers and white-clothed tables. On the two upper floors are the Dashiell Hammett Room and the Maltese Falcon Room, used for spillover dining and banquets. John's Grill is headquarters for the Dashiell Hammett Society of San Francisco, which was founded in 1977 by William F. Nolan, who wrote a biographical study of Hammett, and Jack Kaplan, director of Pinkerton's. (Hammett was a Pinkerton detective during his early days in San Francisco.) A coincidence has even added an extra touch: The restaurant is owned by Gus Konstantinides; Charilaos Konstantinides is named in *The Maltese Falcon* as a Greek dealer who found the bird "in an obscure shop in Paris." (As far as is known, the two are not related.)

You can begin your experience at John's Grill with a Bloody Brigid—named after Spade's Miss O'Shaughnessy—consisting of sweet-and-sour vodka, soda, fresh pineapple, lime, grenadine, and other ingredients. It comes in a souvenir glass, which you can take home with you. (Souvenir glasses, copies of the art deco menu cover, *Maltese Falcon* ties, and a Dash Hammett mural are also available for purchase.) For dinner, there's Sam Spade's Chops, a re-creation of the detective's *Maltese Falcon* meal. You can also partake of several entrees recommended by *Gourmet* magazine: chicken à la Girard or chicken Jerusalem, with fresh artichokes and mushrooms and marsala or white wine; oysters Wellington; and filet of sole stuffed with crab and shrimp, baked in lemon and butter sauce. And then there's Jack La Lanne's favorite salad of crab, shrimp, avocado, mushrooms, chopped egg, tomato, and a very special dressing for $13. Dinner entrees are mostly in the $12 to $20 range. At lunch many of the same dishes are available for $9 to $18. There are also salads, omelets, and sandwiches for $7 to $14.

Reservations are strongly advised for lunch or dinner; the restaurant is popular with local businesspeople and reporters from both city newspapers, as well as mystery buffs and writers. Dining at John's Grill is a real San Francisco experience. It's open Monday through Saturday. Lunch is served from 11am to 4pm; dinner, from 4 to 10pm.

Chinese

With over 100 Chinese restaurants in San Francisco, one might wonder why there would be a need for another. **Harbor Village,** 4 Embarcadero Center, on the lobby level (tel. 415/781-8833), was opened in 1985 to introduce Imperial cuisine —the famous classical Cantonese cuisine of Hong Kong—to this country. It differs from most Chinese food served in American restaurants in its complexity and subtlety. Harbor Village has five chefs, each with a specialty, all of whom came from sister Hong Kong establishments. While most of the dishes are classical Cantonese, spicy Szechuan items and "northern" specialties such as crackling Peking duck are part of the restaurant's repertoire.

Harbor Village is impressive: Its atmosphere and decor represent a successful merger of nouveau California and Chinese influences. The attention to elegant detail reflects the belief that only the best will do: crystal chandeliers, place settings of the finest Chinese porcelain, delicate gleaming glassware, engraved chopsticks. Six opulent private dining rooms with Chinese antiquities and teak furnishings serve 9- to 15-course miniature Imperial feasts for parties of 10 to 300.

The "only-the-best-will-do" philosophy applies also to the quality and freshness of the ingredients the Harbor Village uses in preparation of its dishes. Near the kitchen entrance are two large fish tanks filled with what may be your fresh dinner swimming about.

Lunch affords two excellent options: It can be a toothsome dim sum affair from a lengthy list of choices at about $2.20 per dish; or, for $6 to $8, you might select one of the delicious rice and noodle dishes such as fried rice with mixed meats in a pineapple boat, seafood chow mein, or bean-vermicelli soup with shredded ham and chicken.

The extensive dinner menu offers a remarkable selection of appetizers, from pot stickers through elegant choices such as shredded spicy chicken, minced squab in lettuce cups, and roast duck. Soups, too, are unusual and exceptional—for example, the julienne duck with fish maw, the mushroom with eggflower, the shark's fin in supreme broth. There are some 30 seafood dishes, including four featuring braised abalone. A number of the entrees have a very delicate flavor, while others are more strongly seasoned—say, the fresh prawns stir-fried in garlic, or the sizzling beef in black-pepper sauce with vegetables. A very courteous professional staff can guide you through the menu or recommend dishes that do not appear on it.

Dinner entrees average $9 to $16 with some obvious exceptions: Abalone dishes are $22 to $24; crackling Peking duck, $28; shark's fin soup, $18. Prices vary for seasonal specialties such as the Dungeness crab, lobster, and the incredible selected shark fin with silky chicken, $60. Appetizers will add another $7 to $12; soups, apart from the exceptional items, are $6 to $10. Dinner for two can range from $50 to $100, without wine. The Harbor Village does have a respectable wine list, and the house chardonnay is quite good at $12.75 a bottle.

Harbor Village is open weekdays from 11am to 2:30pm and 5:30 to 9:30pm, and weekends from 10:30am. Harbor Village has free validated parking at all the Embarcadero Center garages, at the foot of Clay Street, after 5pm on weekdays and all day on weekends and holidays.

Located in the Woolen Mill Building, the **Mandarin,** 900 North Point in Ghirardelli Square (tel. 415/673-8812), is the domain of gracious owner/hostess Madame Cecilia Chiang. Her northern Chinese cuisine is among the best in town, the setting as elegant, I'm told, as her palatial childhood home in Peking. Reminiscent of an ancient Chinese temple, the rich interior is accented by quarry floor tiles, burnt-orange carpeting, and Mandarin furnishings. The focal point of the dining area is the Mongolian fire pit, where guests can barbecue their own dinners or have the chef do it for them. The ceiling is lined with haige twigs and supported by heavy rough-hewn beams. The walls are exposed brick or covered in gold silk; exquisite paintings, priceless antiques, and forbidden-stitch embroideries (using stitches allowed for the Imperial Court only) from Madame Chiang's home complete the decor. Some tables offer bay views.

A complete dinner for two including five dishes (about $22 to $25 per person) might include hot-and-sour soup, tangerine chicken, Mongolian beef, gourmet vegetables, ham fried rice, jasmine tea, and cookies. For each extra person taking part in the meal another dish is added. Mandarin specialties that require one-day advance notice for preparation include Peking duck (for four or more) and Beggar's Chicken—a whole chicken magnificently flavored, encased in clay, and baked.

If you're ordering à la carte, an appetizer of chiao tzu—grilled meat-filled dumplings served with vinegar and hot pepper oil—is heartily recommended, as is a cauldron of sizzling rice soup that serves four. Smoked tea duck, baked to crispness is special ovens over burning tea leaves, and Mongolian beef—slices of lamb or beef grilled quickly over the fire pit, served in hot Mandarin buns—are specialties. Or you might share minced squab or walnut chicken. These entrees and others cost $14 to $35. For a superb finish, try the Mandarin glazed apples or bananas, dipped in batter, glazed with candy syrup, and plunged into ice water at your table to crystallize the coating.

At lunch you can order a very good Mandarin chicken salad or sautéed shrimp with peas for $14 to $16, that price including soup, rice, and tea.

Open daily from noon to 11:30pm. Reservations are recommended.

For haute cuisine Cantonese style, the magnificent **Imperial Palace,** 919 Grant Ave., between Washington and Jackson (tel. 415/982-4440), is as elegant as the name implies. Entered via imposingly tall Chinese-red doors, the interior is papered in gold. Alternating panels frame ancient Chinese paintings, and a velvet-lined showcase displays Ch'ing Dynasty antiques. Large bouquets of flowers are judiciously placed, and red roses enhance the beautifully appointed tables. Soft lighting is provided from candle lamps and gold-and-crystal chandeliers above. Strains of Chinese music can be heard in the background.

As you enter you'll notice a wall lined with photos of prominent clients, of which there are many—John Travolta, Alex Haley, Francis Ford Coppola, Clint Eastwood, Barbra Streisand, James Caan, even Richard Nixon.

Prints of ancient Chinese paintings on rice paper adorn the elaborate menu. You might begin with a crabmeat puff—wrapped fillings of crabmeat and cheese, deep-fried. For your entree, which costs $16 to $22, you might choose the squab Macao style (marinated in wine and deep-fried), tossed chicken Imperial (shredded fried chicken with onions, parsley, chopped almonds, and spices), or fresh prawns in a crystal glaze sauce. Exotic desserts include flaming black leaf lichee and almond delight pudding. A complete dinner including soup, appetizer, two entrees, rice, tea, and cookies is $20 to $40 per person, and a comprehensive wine list is available. Prices are considerably reduced at lunch.

If you're part of a group, consider the following—for $375 per table you can partake of a banquet. Begin with stuffed clams baked on rock salt, honey-glazed spareribs, and bird's nest soup in fresh coconut (served individually); move on to Peking duck with lotus buns, flaming quails (served individually), fresh Maine lobster with ginger roots and green onions, filet of beef with roasted walnuts, sliced filet of rock cod on peach halves in Chinese fruit sauce, and triple mushrooms with seasonal greens; and finish with honey-glazed apples. Most assuredly it would be something to write home about, on more than a postcard.

Open daily: Sunday through Thursday from 11:30am to 1am, on Friday and Saturday to 2am. Reservations essential.

Indian

Be it in Bombay, New York, Delhi, San Francisco, Palo Alto, or Beverly Hills, **Gaylord's,** here at Ghirardelli Square (tel. 415/771-8822), is one of my favorite Indian restaurants. The candlelit setting is as exquisite as the authentic and subtly spiced northern Indian cuisine. Windows all around offer tranquil views of boats on the bay, there are cushiony banquettes covered in paisley cotton and handsome mahogany chairs to sit on, large potted plants here and there, napkins and tablecloths of dusty rose-pink linen, and Indian art on the walls. Ragas play softly in the background; all is lovely and peaceful.

Full dinners are priced from $22 to $26 for everything from an all-vegetarian meal to the maharaja feast: mulligatawny soup or dal, tandoori chicken or fish, two kinds of lamb kebab, chicken tikka, nan (an Indian bread), lamb in mildly spiced cream sauce with nuts, saffron-flavored rice with vegetables, vegetables with farmer's cheese in a spiced gravy, choice of exotic desserts, and tea or coffee. There's a wide selection of à la carte choices ranging from vegetable dishes to tandoori prawns. You can even choose from eight varieties of freshly oven-baked Indian breads. Gaylord's is the kind of place you'll want to visit again and again to try everything offered, then begin all over ordering favorites. Complete lunches are $14 to $18.

Open daily for lunch from noon to 2pm, and nightly for dinner from 5 to 10:45pm. Reservations suggested. There's another Gaylord's at 1 Embarcadero Center (tel. 415/397-7775).

Italian

When Lorenzo Petroni and chef Bruno Orsi started the **North Beach Restaurant,** 1512 Stockton St., between Union and Green (tel. 415/392-1587), they vowed to serve the finest *cucina toscana* possible. And they do! They prepare their own fresh pasta daily (highest honors to the fettuccine), use only fresh vegetables, hang and cure their own prosciutto hams, and serve fine California wines.

The decor is cheerful and unpretentious, with a certain unmistakable dignity, especially at night, when the white-clothed tables are candlelit. The ambience is flamboyantly Italian; women can expect frank ogling and admiration.

But it's the food one comes to revel in. Each entree is cooked to order. The specialties of the house (which should come as no surprise) are veal and pasta. Complete dinners include antipasto, mixed green salad, minestrone or soup du jour, pasta della casa with prosciutto sauce, fresh vegetable, dessert, and coffee, for $19 to $28, with a lengthy list of seafood, veal, beef and poultry choices. Entrees are also available à la carte. For dessert, zabaglione is a supreme joy. The North Beach is less expensive at lunch, though the menu is à la carte ($8 to $17).

Open daily from 11:30am to 11:45pm.

Moroccan

Marrakech, 419 O'Farrell St., between Taylor and Jones (tel. 415/776-6717), is a superb place to enjoy an evening of Arabian splendor. The interior of this regal palace is sumptuous. Once you pass the marble pool, you enter elegant dining areas where seating is on goatskin ottomans resting on rare Oriental rugs.

The meal is a ritual feast (don't eat all day in preparation!) served by waiters in kaftans. It begins when the server washes and dries your hands, as the entire meal is eaten with your hands—no plates or silverware are supplied! And to feast the eyes, a belly dancer weaves between the tables while Middle Eastern music plays.

Marrakech offers a choice of four dinners, award-winning menus, all under $22 per person. Two dinners include six dishes, with three main courses (I told you to come hungry); a third features a single main choice with appetizer; whereas the "theater special" omits the b'stila appetizer because of the time involved in preparation. All dinners begin with a piquant Moroccan salad scooped up with chunks of homemade bread. Then comes the b'stila, a pastrylike appetizer of chicken with egg and almonds, lovingly encased in filo. The six-course meals offers a choice either of chicken with lemons, and lamb with honey (wonderful); or lamb with onions, and hare with paprika. The third main course for either selection is a delicious couscous with vegetables, easily a meal in itself.

For the cowardly appetites in the group, Marrakech offers the salad and b'stila followed by a single main course chosen from the above dishes, or chicken with olives, lamb kebab, and couscous fassi (with lamb). End the meal with fresh fruit for dessert and mint tea. As you lounge, satiated, over tea or an after-dinner drink, your server once again washes your hands.

Marrakech is open for dinner nightly from 6 to 10pm, and reservations are essential.

Natural Foods

A longtime favorite in San Francisco is **Greens at Fort Mason,** Building A, Fort Mason Center (tel. 415/771-6222), an enterprise of the Tassajara Zen Center. It's located in an old warehouse building, though from the inside you'd never know it. It's open, light and airy, with a huge redwood burl sculpture near the entrance. The food is simple and natural, but it bears little resemblance to what most of us think of as "health food." Dinner on Friday and Saturday is a fixed-price multicourse meal costing around $32 per person. (Tuesday through Thursday dinner is à la carte.) The menu changes nightly; you might feast on a warm red-cabbage salad with apples, fire-dried walnuts, Sonoma goat cheese, and watercress; squash soup with crème fraîche and chives; or potato, leek, and celery-root gratin with Gruyère cheese, thyme, and cream, served with pepper relish, sautéed green and wax beans, and carrots. Your dessert might be chocolate applesauce cake with ice cream, chestnut ice cream with chocolate sauce, or a bosc pear puff-pastry tart with frangipan cream. There's an extensive wine list to select from.

Lunch is a simpler affair, though equally interesting, and entrees range from $8 to $9. Offerings include sandwiches, garden lettuce and radicchio salad, grilled tofu on potato bread, chili and soup, and specials like spinach frittata. For brunch (generally in the range of $8 to $10) you can order one of the various three-egg omelets, buttermilk pancakes, or an open-face sandwich with Stilton and cream cheese, apples, and chives. There are also lots of fresh muffins and homemade desserts.

Greens at Fort Mason is open for lunch Tuesday through Saturday from 11:30am to 2:30pm, and for the prix-fixe dinner on Friday and Saturday from 6 to 9:30pm (by reservation only; plan two weeks in advance). Sunday brunch is from 10am to 2pm. Tuesday through Thursday, dinner is served from 6 to 9pm. The Greens bakery is open Tuesday through Saturday from 9:30am to 4:30pm, on Sunday from 10am to 3pm.

Polynesian

At the San Francisco branch of **Trader Vic's,** 20 Cosmos Place, off Taylor Street between Post and Sutter (tel. 415/776-2232), the old trader himself, Victor Jules Bergeron, could sometimes be seen. Some quotes from the great man: "When I started the restaurant business, I did everything to keep customers. I sang and I even let them stick an ice pick in my wooden leg." On the South Seas decor: "It intrigues everyone. You think of beaches and moonlight and pretty girls without any clothes on. It is complete escape, relaxation." Indeed, Trader Vic's outdoes all others in creating an ambience of South Seas enchantment—lush jungle foilage, authentic tapa-covered walls, spears, lots of bamboo and rattan, even a palm-frond canoe overhead. It's a great place for people-watching and, strange as it seems, it is *the* society restaurant. Go once just for the experience.

The menu is enormous—order one of the potent rum concoctions to sip while you peruse at leisure (order a second and you won't care if they serve you a Big Mac). There are lots of hors d'oeuvres, including typically Polynesian caviar with blinis and sour cream. A more "conventional" start would be bongo bongo (cream of puréed oyster) soup. A whole page is devoted just to accompanying vegetables and salads. One hundred entrees, ranging in price from $15 to $35, include Malay peanut chicken, a wide variety of curries served with nine condiments, Trader Vic's special oysters flambé, Szechuan beef, roast Indonesian lamb, and breast of peach blossom duck. Save room for one of the 29 exotic desserts—perhaps rum ice cream with praline sauce. The luncheon menu, although extensive, is simpler and a bit less pricey.

Open for lunch weekdays from 11:30am to 2:30pm, for dinner nightly from 5 to 11pm, and for late supper Monday through Saturday to 12:30am. Reservations recommended. Jacket and tie are required for men.

Seafood

Established in 1849—along with the Gold Rush—the **Tadich Grill,** 240 California St., between Battery and Front (tel. 415/391-2373), is a venerated California institution. A mahogany bar and counter extends the entire length of the restaurant. On the wall is an old wooden clock with Roman numerals. Tables, draped in no-nonsense white linen and provided with big plates of sourdough bread and lemon wedges, are arranged along the wall, separated from the counter by a mahogany partition. There are also seven enclosed private booths. (I imagine discreet business deals are more frequent than romantic trysts in these compartments, more's the pity.) Lighting is provided by brass wall lamps and art deco fixtures.

The food is just fantastic. Seafood is the specialty. For a light meal you might try one of the delicious seafood salads, like shrimp or prawn Louis, with a glass of wine, fresh sourdough bread, and butter. Hot entrees include baked avocado with shrimp diablo, baked casserole of stuffed turbot with crab and shrimp Newburg, and charcoal (mesquite)–broiled petrale sole with butter sauce, a local favorite. The sand dabs, rex sole, and calamari steak are truly exceptional. Entrees cost $11 to $17, with broiled lobster at $25. A side order of big, tasty french fries is hard to resist, as is the homemade custard pudding for dessert, probably the best ever.

For your famous footnote file: Tadich's was the very first to broil seafood over mesquite hardwood coal back in the early 1920s. Then it was known simply as charcoal broiling.

The Tadich Grill is open Monday through Saturday from 11am to 9pm. *No credit cards are accepted.*

MODERATELY PRICED RESTAURANTS

The following choices are in the moderate price range that most of us prefer when dining out. Yet many offer a great deal of "atmosphere," along with affordable prices and first-rate cuisine.

American

One of San Francisco's best-kept dining secrets (and my source, Patricia Yakutis, would probably prefer that it remain so) is the **Symphony Restaurant,** 298 Gough St., at Fell (tel. 415/861-3388). As you might guess, it's conveniently located near Symphony Hall and the Opera House, beneath a maroon canopy.

The interior is beautifully simple and tastefully designed. Delicate pink walls are complemented by the light-gray ceiling, and blue-gray banquettes, beige café curtains and blinds cover the windows; and a charming group of small prints depict opera scenes, all reflected in a facing mirrored wall. As with most of the better restaurants I've found, the Symphony is relatively small—20 tables or so, meticulously finished. Bentwood chairs have very comfortable reed seats. Overhead lighting is from a unique circular chandelier surrounded with clear starburst plaques.

The chef (simply known as "Da," more formally as Pounarong Nimearm-On) is also the proprietor, trained and creatively imbued with the California/French touch. Rolls arrive hot; butter is sweet; service is expert, smooth, and thoughtful. A number of the entrees tend toward the light touch. There is always at least one special of the day—unfailingly delicious. If it happens to be the sautéed sole with capers, order it: The dish is superb and beautifully presented. There's also an exceptional bouillabaisse (otherwise known as cioppino, or fisherman's soup) graced with a deliciously serious touch of spice. Another dish I find difficult to pass by is the sautéed scallops meunière; at dinner, it's with a beurre-blanc sauce.

The Symphony serves more than seafood. There's an excellent minute steak shallot, or you might prefer the select aged New York steak. Chicken supreme Cordon Bleu and the marinated Cornish game hen bourguignon are choice alternatives. Luncheon entrees range from $7 to $14; for dinner, entrees are $9 to $14.

For dessert, the baked alaska or the cherries jubilee will turn your dinner into an event. But the Symphony also has one of my favorites—a simple but absolutely delectable and light caramel custard. The Symphony has a modest but good selection of California and French wines, reasonably priced. Several California wines are also available by the glass. Beer is also served.

The Symphony is open for lunch weekdays from 11:30am to 2pm, and for dinner Tuesday through Saturday from 5:30 to 9pm. Reservations are especially necessary on those days when the opera and symphony perform.

Of the many San Francisco restaurants in which I've had breakfast, there simply is none better than **Doidge's,** 2217 Union St. (tel. 415/921-2149). Doidge's began in 1971 with counter service and six tables. (The original mahogany counter is still a favorite spot for customers to watch their orders begin prepared.) Since that time, the restaurant has expanded to include an airy, comfortable dining room with a distinctly French look—cream walls, prints of Paris and the French countryside, fresh flowers on the tables, and oak sideboards.

Doidge's lays claim to serving the very best eggs Benedict in town, and they are right. But that's only the beginning. There are eggs Florentine with thinly sliced Motherlode ham, and then there are eggs with Motherlode bacon (honey-cured, thicker, no preservatives). The appetite of Paul Bunyan would be suitable for the breakfast casserole of ham or Italian sausage, potato, onion, tomato, baked with cheese and then topped with a poached egg, or for the corned beef hash supreme. The list of omelets includes enough variations to satisfy the choosiest diner. And for those who want to avoid eggs, there is French toast with a variety of fresh fruits; buttermilk pancakes (not served on Saturday or Sunday) are also available in a variety of options. Should you simply want fresh fruit, that too has several tasty accompaniments. Each entree is served with buttered toast and a choice of green salad, home fries, or sliced tomato.

As for lunch, sandwiches are served with the choice of a green salad, a cup of homemade soup, cottage cheese, or home fries. Homemade soup is also sold by the bowl with a warm roll, and with or without a salad. Salads are limited to a generous portion of fresh vegetables and garden greens, or a tuna salad centered into a tomato or avocado half.

Doidge's serves fresh-squeezed orange and grapefruit juice as well as the usual beverages, plus beer and wine (available by the glass). Without beverage, breakfast will cost from $4.25 to $9.50, lunch from $3.50 to $7.75, and you will relish every bite.

Doidge's is open daily for breakfast and lunch from 8am to 2pm. Reservations are definitely necessary for Saturday mornings.

Housed in an old brick building facing Sydney G. Walton Square, **MacArthur Park,** 607 Front St., at Jackson (tel. 415/398-5700), offers a garden ambience, plants and trees flourishing in the sunlight streaming in from skylights overhead. Long and L-shaped, the restaurant has exposed brick walls that are tastefully adorned with attractive original artwork. In the back is another comfortable room, this one with a wood-burning fireplace. Fresh flowers on white-clothed tables provide a cheerful note, and there's a long oak marble-topped bar behind which are racks containing some of the Park's extensive wine collection.

This is a good spot for dinner after the theater or lunch after a morning of exploring the historical district and the antiques shops of Jackson Square. MacArthur Park prides itself on serving great American food. You might wonder how exceptional a club sandwich or Cobb salad can be for lunch. Order either one and you'll know, since both include chicken and bacon smoked to perfection by the restaurant itself. There's also a magnificent smoked duck, apple, and Wehani rice salad with yogurt-curry dressing, not to mention an appetite-defying grilled double-decker five-cheese-and-tomato sandwich. Lunch will cost $4 to $11, top of the line being cold poached salmon. At any time, there are great baby back ribs and barbecued chicken, as well as a lengthy list of mesquite-broiled entrees. For dinner, add on about a dozen seafood choices done in several styles, plus the choice of a 1-pound or 1½-pound Maine lobster. For the meat lover, consider the braised short ribs with morel mushrooms or the 22-ounce porterhouse steak. Dinner entrees will cost about $10 to $25. For dessert, Judy's mud pie—a blend of coffee and chocolate ice creams in a chocolate cookie crust smothered with hot fudge sauce—is as good as it sounds. A very impressive wine list features many California wines available by the glass.

The restaurant schedule seems more like a listing of train times. It is open for breakfast weekdays from 7 to 10am, and for lunch from 11:30am to 2:30pm. Dinner is served Monday through Thursday from 5 to 10:30pm, on Friday and Saturday to 11pm, and on Sunday from 4:30 to 10pm. Reservations are essential at this deservedly popular restaurant.

Hard Rock Café, 1699 Van Ness, at Sacramento (tel. 415/885-1699). If standing in line with 18-year-olds is not your bag, go to the Hard Rock Café for lunch instead of dinner. But regardless of your age, or the time of day, the Hard Rock Café is fun, interesting, and noisy. It's a look back at the '50s and '60s. If you're a traveler, there's an HRC in Los Angeles, La Jolla (San Diego), New York City, Chicago, Houston, London, Stockholm, and Frankfurt.

This one is rather like a large hall (actually it's a former auto showroom) decorated with a candy-apple caddy hanging from the ceiling; gold records; front pages headlining the deaths of John Kennedy, Elvis, and John Lennon; Elvis Presley's cape, framed; photos of Presley; Beatles memorabilia; a cow at the door (no, not alive); and "Save the Planet" and "All is One" signs. It's rather like a family convention center with ceiling fans. The hub of activities is an oversize oblong oak bar. Surprisingly, the decibel level of the background music at midday doesn't inhibit conversation or eating, but it's period rock'n'roll.

If food is one of your objectives, there are booths, tables, and a counter with lots of elbow room. Food is reasonably good and moderately priced. At the high end of the price range are steak for $13 and baby back ribs for $11. Then you go down to grilled burgers for $6 and a bowl of homemade chili for $4.50. Salads and sandwiches are the usual assortment, and liquid refreshments are soft or hard, as you wish. Dessert options range from homemade apple pie or strawberry shortcake to thick shakes or your choice of floats, from $2.50 to $3.25.

It's open weekdays and Sunday from 11:30am to midnight, on Friday and Saturday to 1am.

Aptly located in the Wells Fargo Building, its decor evocative of Fargo's 19th-century heyday, the **Stagecoach Restaurant,** 44 Montgomery St., at Sutter (tel. 415/956-4650), is richly appointed, comfortable, and prosperous-looking. Seating is in plush tufted-leather booths and banquettes, complemented by white linen tablecloths. Candles, lamps, wall sconces, and wrought-iron chandeliers provide a soft amber light. The walls are adorned with stained-glass panels, framed mirrors, and oil paintings, the most notable of which is the original nude, *Stella,* from the 1893 World's Fair in Chicago. The menu offers a wide variety of choices, from light foods like sandwiches, salads, and omelets (for $5 to $11), to pastas and fish dishes like scallops or prawns sautéed with white wine and mushrooms, to filet mignon or New York steak (for $12 to $24).

The Stagecoach is open Monday through Thursday from 11am to 9pm, on Friday to midnight. On Saturday it is open from 7pm to 2am and serves a Russian prix-fixe dinner for $37.50, including such delicious goodies as piroshki and chicken Kiev; the price includes tax and tip. There's dancing with live band music to the 2am hour. Reservations are suggested for dinner and essential for lunch.

Hamburger Mary's is south of Market at 1582 Folsom St. (tel. 415/626-5767). You may think you've wandered into an industrial area and, in part, that's correct. But Folsom Street is in a state of transition and gradually becoming part of the city's afternoon and evening scene (straight and gay), especially on weekends. Dance clubs, supper clubs, and bars have begun to move into Hamburger Mary's territory, elbowing out a number of small industrial enterprises.

On any given evening or weekend, Hamburger Mary's can be an absolute madhouse and you may never have the opportunity to appreciate the tongue-in-cheek, tossed-together decor. All sorts of thrift-style floral wallpapers abound, plus photos of someone's relatives, garage-sale prints, stained glass, and generally glorious, happy funk, including some paintings Aunt Fanny from Des Moines would never have chosen. You enter the establishment by way of the narrow, comfortable, and busy bar, otherwise known as the Good Time Saloon, whose crowd typically represents every major and minor group in town. To the left and rear is the dining room (of sorts).

Hamburger Mary's serves some of the best (you guessed it) burgers in town in any number of forms, the tasty options including grilled mushrooms, avocado spread, salsa, blue cheese, a swamp of chili and cheese; all versions arrive with french or home fries. But the place also serves breakfast, lunch, and dinner. From the top, breakfast includes a choice of human-size or three-egg Fantasy Omelettes with home fries, banana bread or nine-grain toast, jam, and fruit garni. As for the "Fantasy," Hamburger Mary's offers a choice of 18 delectables (60¢ to $2.75 per delectable) to add to your basic omelet ($3.75). If you'd rather have french toast or Hawaiian toast, there's that too—as well as an industrial-size steak-and-egg breakfast. For lunch, in addition to the hamburger selection, there are old standbys such as BLT, tuna salad, club, and chicken sandwiches, served grilled or at room temperature on Giusto's nine-grain bread with a variety of spiced sauces and garnishes. Despite the name, the establishment also serves several styles of vegetarian sandwiches. All in all, breakfast averages $3.25 to $8.25; lunch and dinner, $3.50 to $9—top of the line being the steak dinner. A dessert of cream-cheese pie, carrot cake, etc., will add $3.

The restaurant is open daily from 10am to 1:15am.

Basque

Entered via a bar adorned with jai alai baskets, **Des Alpes,** 732 Broadway, between Stockton and Powell (tel. 415/391-4249 or 788-9900), has a homey Basque decor: brown-and-white-checked plastic tablecloths and wainscoted cream walls that are hung with travel posters and paintings of the French, Spanish, Alpine, and Basque countryside; note an early photo of the restaurant, which dates from 1908.

The cuisine is far from "haute"—it offers French family cooking of the kind you might have eaten once in some little "auberge" in the Midi and have been reminiscing about ever since. A single entree is offered each night—perhaps a choice of lamb stew, filet of sole, or roast beef. Your meal includes soup, stringbean salad, potatoes, green salad, coffee, and ice cream. The price: $9 to $12. A bottle of house wine with your dinner is easily affordable.

Des Alpes is open Tuesday through Saturday from 5:30 to 10pm, on Sunday from 5 to 9:30pm.

Chinese

The Castro Street section of town is usually noted for its gay population, but it's also home to several very good eating establishments. Outstanding on the list is a terrific Chinese restaurant that looks for all the world as though it had been transported from Paris. The **Metro**, 3600 16th St. (tel. 415/431-1655), is at the corner of Market and Noe, where everything intersects. Situated upstairs, it's a black beauty touched here and there with slim gold lines, looking part art deco, part Parisian Métro, with a classy touch of MOMA out of New York City.

The Metro does not take reservations except for a party of six or more. But this provides you with the pleasure of waiting in the attractive oval-shape bar, where small theatrical spots of light are strategically placed over beautifully arranged fresh flowers.

The two-level dining area is relatively small, done simply but handsomely in gray and charcoal. Among the beef and lamb dishes, there are a first-rate hot braised beef and a delicious lamb curry. The list of seafood choices is lengthy, primarily including shrimp and scallop dishes; one of my choices for the evening was the scallops with black mushrooms. But if you want a dish with flourish, there are several iron-platter choices that arrive sizzling on same; the garlic prawns are truly exceptional. The hot braised bean curd, garlic-braised eggplant, and black mushrooms in oyster sauce are great whether or not you are a vegetable afficionado. All in all, entrees average a moderate $6.50 to $10; vegetables dishes, $5 to $7; appetizers and soups, $3 to $7.

The Metro restaurant is open daily from 5 to 11:30pm; the bar is open from 11am to 3am.

So popular was the delicious and reasonably priced Mandarin fare at **Yet Wah,** 1829 Clement St., at 19th Avenue (tel. 415/751-1231), that the restaurant sprouted another Clement Street location at no. 2140 (tel. 415/387-8040). (The latter is open daily from 11am to 9pm.) The 1829 Clement Yet Wah is elegant in decor, with gold bamboo-print wallpaper, Chinese lanterns overhead, and candlelit tables. It's really very pleasant—always lively and buzzing with conversation. The no. 2140 Yet Wah is larger and more luxurious and recently underwent extensive redecoration.

A $16-per-person dinner for two includes sizzling rice soup, su mi (deep-fried wonton), Mandarin beef, almond pressed duck in sweet-and-sour sauce, phoenix and dragon (a shrimp and chicken dish with mushrooms and snow peas), rice, tea, and cookies. Ordering à la carte, you might begin your meal with an order of kuo teh (six crispy pot stickers) or su mi. Entrees, averaging $9 to $15, include kubla lamb (lamb slices in spicy Szechuan brown-bean sauce and scallions), princess garden chicken salad (shredded chicken with lettuce, nuts, green onions, and Chinese parsley, served with fun see noodles), and fried duck with mandarin orange sauce. Everything sounds so good that it's difficult to decide what to order; best to go with a bunch of friends and sample a wide choice of entrees. Domestic and Chinese wines and beers are available to complement your meal.

Open daily from 11am to 11pm. There's yet another branch of Yet Wah at the Pier 39 complex (tel. 415/434-4430), open weekdays from 11:30am to 10pm, weekends to 11pm.

The **Hunan Restaurant,** 853 Kearny St., off Columbus (tel. 415/397-8718), is an insignificant-looking place, but it has drawn praise from the likes of Craig Claiborne, former food editor of the *New York Times*, who called it the "hottest Hunan restaurant" in the West. The food is hot indeed and free of MSG. The onion cakes and dim sum (called pot stickers at most other San Francisco Chinese restaurants) are de rigueur as appetizers. The hot-and-sour soup and the cold bean-sprout and cucumber salad are also great. The special chicken, shrimp, and scallops with hot black-bean sauce is a favorite entree, and there are smoked specialties and vegetarian items to choose from. Some dishes, the menu claims, are "spicy but not hot," like the diced chicken with fresh garlic sauce and the sliced beef with green onions. Dinner entrees cost $6 to $10. The lunch menu is more limited and even less expensive —most items cost less than $6.

The Hunan Restaurant is open daily from 11:30am to 9:30pm. There's a second location, larger and fancier, at 924 Sansome St., near Broadway (tel. 415/956-7727), with the same hours as above.

Not to be confused with the above is **Hunan Shaolin on Polk,** 1150 Polk St., between Sutter and Post (tel. 415/771-6888), another Hunan eatery, located a short distance from Chinatown in "Polk Gulch." There's not much decor to speak of, but the food is wonderful, and the service is friendly and efficient. You can begin your meal with the standards—pot stickers (dim sum) and onion cakes—which are terrific here. So is the hot-and-sour soup. There are lots and lots of entrees to choose from; my favorites are the iron-platter specials like sizzling prawns, as well as the delicious Manchu beef (it's not on the menu, but you can ask for it). Most dishes here are spicy-hot, but you can ask to have them mild if that's your preference. Dinner entrees cost $5 to $8; at lunch you can order any of 20 entrees for about $6. Peking Duck (order it a day in advance) is $20.

Hunan Shaolin on Polk is open Monday through Saturday from 11:30am to 9:30pm, on Sunday from 4 to 9:30pm. Reservations are accepted only on weekends for large parties. In the evening there's valet parking, a bonus in this area of scarce parking spaces.

I've been advocating the ordering of pot stickers for several paragraphs; this pleasantly modern Mandarin restaurant, actually called the **Pot Sticker,** 150 Waverly Place, off Washington Street (tel. 415/397-9985), specializes in them. A pot sticker, as it's no doubt time to explain, is a pan-fried thin-skinned dumpling stuffed with seasoned meat or vegetables—and it does, yes, tend to stick to the pot. Here you can order several varieties of the dumplings, as well as other delicious Mandarin dishes. The family dinner includes soup of the day, pot stickers, entrees like almond chicken or sweet-and-sour pork, steamed rice, cookies, and tea, for $8 to $11 per person. À la carte, you might order Szechuan prawns or other entrees for $6 to $9. You can also just gorge yourself on a variety of dumplings (about $2 to $3 a plate). Leave some room for yummy green-tea ice cream for dessert.

I especially like the decor—unusually spartan for a Chinese restaurant: exposed brick walls hung with attractive Chinese paintings and scrolls, live plants, and globe lights overhead.

Open daily for lunch from 11:30am to 4pm, and for dinner from 4:30 to 9:30pm. There's another Pot Sticker a bit below Haight-Ashbury at 335 Noe St., near 16th Street (tel. 415/861-6868). It's open daily from noon to 10pm.

Brandy Ho's Hunan Food, 217 Columbus, at Pacific (tel. 415/788-7527), sits at the intersection of Italian North Beach, the Financial District, and Chinatown. It has a simple but pleasant look—tables with granite tops, floors of black-and-gray ceramic tile throughout, and new designs on the Chinese lanterns to brighten the restaurant. Even with the newer look, Brandy Ho's is still the same down-to-earth place with great food. Don't miss the fried dumplings with sweet-and-sour sauce. Several uncommon soups are offered in addition to the traditional (and excellent) hot-and-sour variety: There's a moo shu soup with eggs, pork, vegetables, and tree-ear mushrooms, as well as a fishball soup with spinach, bamboo shoots, noodles, and other goodies.

Entrees are varied and tasty. I recommend a dish called Three Delicacies, a combination of scallops, shrimp, and chicken with onion, bell pepper, and bamboo shoots seasoned with ginger, garlic, and wine and served with black-bean sauce. The moo shu pork is also good. Most dishes here are quite hot and spicy; the kitchen will adjust the level to meet your specifications. Entrees average $7 to $12. Brandy Ho's has a small selection of wines and beers to accompany your meal, including plum wine and sake. To cool your tongue after your meal, there are the traditional lichees and ice cream.

Open weekdays and Sunday from 11:30am to 11pm, on Friday and Saturday to midnight. There is a new, elegant Brandy Ho's at 450-452 Broadway (tel. 415/362-6268), still with great food but a significantly expanded menu and full bar service. Entrees average $9 to $13. It's open daily from 11:30am to midnight.

Crêpes and Quiches

Large and airy, with one wall of windows overlooking a garden courtyard, the **Magic Pan,** 341 Sutter St., between Grant and Stockton streets (tel. 415/788-7397), is one of the prettiest branches of this well-known chain. Like the others, the decor here is French provincial, with parquet floors, antique cupboards, oak tables, framed French prints on the walls, and pots of hanging ferns. Up front is a spacious bar with comfortable couches, very popular at cocktail hour when free hors d'oeuvres are served.

The Magic Pan specializes in crêpes stuffed with a variety of delicious fillings: chicken or seafood with ratatouille; Cordon Bleu with layers of ham, turkey, Swiss and herbed cheeses; and mixed vegetables, to name a few. Crêpe dinners ($9.50 to $12) give you combinations such as the chicken divan crêpe complemented by a European-blend vegetable crêpe. If you're traveling with a nothing-but-steak eater, don't despair. The Magic Pan has all bases covered with filet mignon, New York strip steak, peppercorn steak, and veal in a variety of dishes ($12.50 to $18). Pasta, chicken, seafood, and several stir-fry dishes ($9.50 to $14) complete the extensive menu. All crêpe entrees are served with salad or soup. Dessert crêpes are tantalizing, including the likes of a Chantilly crêpe with banana slices in apricot sauce, with whipped cream and toasted almond slivers.

The reasonably priced Magic Pan is popular for lunch and Saturday or Sunday brunch, serving a variety of omelets, gourmet egg dishes, etc. The restaurant is open Monday through Thursday from 11am to 10pm, on Friday and Saturday to 11pm, and on Sunday to 9pm. There's another Magic Pan at 900 North Point (tel. 415/474-6733) in Ghirardelli Square.

Situated in the heart of the theater district and flanked by Jewish delis, **Salmagundi,** 442 Geary St., between Mason and Taylor (tel. 415/441-0894), offers a chic alternative to chopped liver and pastrami. Contemporary/country French in decor, it's furnished with bentwood chairs, matte white tables, an occasional high table with rattan stools, lots of plants, wicker baskets, antiques, and framed woodcuts on the walls. In the back there's a Spanish-tile fountain, and windows look out on a garden. There's always good background music—light jazz, classical, or whatever. Crowded at lunch and dinner, bustling with excitement after theater, Salmagundi takes on a casual coffeehouse ambience during off-hours—people hang out drinking wine or cappuccino, playing backgammon, writing letters, or perusing scripts.

Every day three different choices of soup and one kind of quiche are offered. Among the soups, the changing daily menu might list Hungarian goulash, Barbary Coast bouillabaisse, Ukrainian beef borscht, or English country cheddar. As for the quiches, you might find a simple quiche Lorraine listed, but more often it's bedecked with shrimp, broccoli, and cheddar cheese, or onion and zucchini. Soups, salads, or quiches alone cost $3 to $4.50. Wine and beer are available, as are homemade desserts.

Open daily: weekdays from 8am to 11pm, weekends from 11am to 11:30pm. Other branches are at 2 Embarcadero Center (tel. 415/982-5603) and at 1236 Market St. (tel. 415/431-7337) in the Civic Center.

There is only one quiche Lorraine, say the owners of **La Quiche,** 550 Taylor St., between Post and Geary (tel. 415/441-2711), and this pure and classic quiche is the only one they serve. La Quiche is a charming little bistro such as you might find on a

Paris side street. The 20 or so tables are draped with pink cloths. Hanging copper pots and a shelf of decorative plates adorn the beamed walls, and there are lace curtains in the windows.

Meals are accompanied by crusty loaves of French bread (the authentic baguette) and fresh butter in little ceramic pots. The quiche (exceptional—the lightest crust ever) with salad, a glass of wine, homemade chocolate mousse with real crème Chantilly, and a pot of espresso makes an excellent lunch or dinner. Eight delicious crêpes with scrumptious fillings, plus four dessert crêpes, are also available at both meals. Quiche or crêpes cost $7 to $9. Dinner entrees, served with soup or salad and French bread, might feature boeuf bourguignon or chicken sautéed in Riesling wine, for $11 to $14. At lunch, entrees served with soup, salad, and French bread include chicken in cream and mushrooms, and a very tasty seafood salad for $7 to $10. There are three specials daily for lunch and dinner.

Open for lunch Monday through Saturday from 11:30am to 2:30pm and for dinner nightly from 5:30 to 10pm. La Quiche is a must.

Czechoslovakian

Run by Vlasta and Frank Kucera and their son, John, **Vlasta's Czechoslovakian Restaurant,** 2420 Lombard St., between Scott and Divisadero (tel. 415/931-7533), is a homey establishment, cozy and intimate. Wood-paneled walls are hung with framed oil paintings, tables are covered with starched white linen, a plant-lined divider creates two dining areas, and soft lighting is achieved by chandeliers overhead and wall sconces. The motherly Vlasta presides in the kitchen, and the entire family makes diners feel like welcome guests.

Dinners include soup of the day and salad. The house specialty is herbed roast duck with red cabbage and Bohemian dumplings. Viennese schnitzel is also on the menu, as are chicken paprika and goulash topped with sour cream and served with dumplings or potatoes. Entrees, which range from $10 to $14, change daily; the above were among the choices on my last visit. Try some of Vlasta's homemade apple strudel for dessert.

Open Tuesday through Sunday from 5:30 to 11pm. Reservations are essential.

French

Le Central, 453 Bush St., between Kearny and Grant (tel. 415/391-2233), is San Francisco's version of a classic Parisian bistro, with a truly elegant bar for waiting. It sports a red "Tabac" sign, and the rows of banquettes, mirrored walls, racks of Gauloises and Gitânes behind the gleaming copper-topped bar are all perfectly typical of the genre. Ditto the gauzy white curtains in the window, the chalkboard menu, and baskets of fruit and flowers. The ambience is convivial, chic, and cosmopolitan, enhanced at night by background music. Herb Caen and various political types are frequent customers. It's a place to see and be seen.

The cassoulet—a stew rich with chunks of lamb, duck, sausage, and pork, clove-studded onions, beans, etc.—is a house specialty; they started it cooking when the restaurant opened and have been adding to it ever since. Returned expatriates will be thrilled to find an authentic steak pommes frites or choucroûte alsacienne (sauerkraut cooked in white wine, studded with juniper berries, and arranged with bacon, ham, pork loin, Viennese sausage, and Dijon mustard). Entrees cost $12 to $18. Appetizer choices are equally apropos: saucisson chaud, escargots de Bourgogne, onion soup gratinée, etc.

Le Central is open Monday through Saturday from 11:45am to 3pm and 6 to 10:30pm.

Hungarian

Paprikás Fono, 900 North Point, at Ghirardelli Square (tel. 415/441-1223), has a charming country-inn setting with provincial Hungarian antiques and folk-art pieces. The hand-painted chairs are copies of those designed for King Ferdinand of Hungary's hunting lodge at the turn of the century. Walls are hung with farm implements, big bunches of dried flowers, baskets, pottery, etc. And in the center of the room is a hearth with a large copper kettle used to cook goulash soup. An especially pleasant dining area is the glassed-in balcony overlooking the bay.

Whatever you order, ask for the fried peasant bread—it's delicious. Among the entree choices are chicken paprikás, veal Tokany, gypsy steaks, fish paprikás, fresh seafood of the day, and pasta specials, for $12 to $20. The dessert strudels and palacsintas are irresistible. Luncheon entrees are mostly in the $7 to $11 range.

Paprikás Fono is open Monday through Saturday from 11:30am to 11pm, on Sunday to 10:30pm. Reservations are advised.

Italian

Circolo Restaurant & Champagneria, 161 Sutter St. (tel. 415/362-0404), is at the border of the Crocker Galleria. When you leave San Francisco you may have trouble remembering the location of Circolo, but assuredly you won't forget the name of the restaurant or its superb Italian food. When you enter under the canopy that spells out Circolo, straight ahead is an elevator. There may be an element of confusion as to whether you push the button to go up or down, until you notice the well-thumbed "Dining Room" button—a bit hard to read, but that's the "open sesame."

If you've been to elegantly designed restaurants in San Francisco, you'll notice a pleasantly familiar feeling from the decor at Circolo. Brown bentwood chairs have beige-and-maroon cushioning. White cloths and starched napery stand distinct against the rosy-beige walls and mirroring. Fresh flowers are on each table, and the total effect is completed by the immaculate black-and-white attire of the waiters.

Circolo is one of those places where a creative chef marries ingredients to produce an outstanding dish, now and then an original, at a price still in the real world. If you think that the quality of lasagne, in whatever form, is all much the same, that at Circolo will surprise you. The veal lasagne (the lasagne special changes daily) is absolutely beautiful to the eye, and the pasta has a delicacy more like that found in a Chinese dim sum. If you can manage an appetizer and an entree, there is an excellent antipasto selection, most for about $4. Two of my favorite choices are the mozzarella e pomodoro (mozzarella with beefsteak tomato and fresh basil) and the melanzane alla griglia (paper-thin eggplant with three cheeses and tomato sauce). Salads range from the simple baby lettuce with beefsteak tomato and raspberry vinaigrette to grilled breast of chicken with mixed greens and balsamic vinaigrette. There's sufficient variety in the selection of pasta dishes to please almost every palate, like pasta with fresh vegetables, gulf shrimp, or bay scallops, or the agnolotti filled with fresh chard and ricotta cheese. A choice of individual pizzas (around $8) includes those with a somewhat familiar ring, as well as the more exotic calzone with Roquefort, mozzarella, cheddar, pasilla, pepper, tomato, and basil.

The list of entrees also offers a delicious variety. The choice of fresh fish changes daily, or you might prefer the jumbo prawns with basil-butter sauce. The grilled veal chops are bound to be the delight of the meat eater in the group, though it's not an easy choice versus the marinated rabbit, among other excellent offerings, all in the range of $10 to $15. And so we come to dessert and a chocoholic's ecstasy: semisweet chocolate with pecan crust served with caramel sauce. Other offerings include somewhat less addicting substances such as the fresh berries or the cheesecake with berry sauce, any one of which will add on about $3 to $4. Should you choose to have wine, by the glass or the bottle, the selection is good and the prices within reason.

Circolo Restaurant & Champagneria is open weekdays from 11:30am to 11pm, on Saturday from 5 to 11pm. I strongly advise reservations.

Even with more than 100 Italian restaurants for competition, **Kuleto's,** 221 Powell St., at Geary (tel. 415/397-7720), is a tough act to follow. It has chefs who create exceptionally delicious, out-of-the-ordinary dishes, in an extraordinary setting and at moderate prices. The same extensive northern Italian menu with Tuscan specialties is offered for lunch and dinner.

Enter through the bar on Powell Street to get the full impact of this delightful and relaxing place: the years-gone-by high ceilings, black-and-white marble-tile floors, strings of dried peppers and garlic hanging over a magnificent long mahogany bar. Kuleto's has the familiar, friendly air of a restaurant you've known for years: small circular tables with tall bar chairs, dark-wood booths with gray-green cushions, a huge open kitchen with black hood and copper trim housing a group of hardworking chefs—all compose a homey picture.

Reviewing the menu from the top, the antipasti are sufficiently varied to satisfy most every taste, from the roasted garlic or the grilled radicchio and pancetta to the calamari fritti or the crostini with fresh mozzarella. For the traditionalists, there's always the antipasto platter. As for the second course, there's nothing commonplace about the soup or such salads as the Mediterranean chicken salad with olives, cucumbers, aged ricotta, and oregano.

Every entree I ordered was excellent, from the least expensive pasta dish on up the list. You can't go wrong with the risotto Zafferano, with saffron risotto, prawns, scallops, and sun-dried tomatoes. The selection of fresh fish, grilled over hardwoods, changes daily. The veal piccata consists of medallions served with lemon, artichokes, and capers. There's a New York steak grilled with onion-and-pepper compote, or the Panini grilled sirloin sandwich with mozzarella, tomato, onion, and peppers. On this deliciously diverse menu, entree prices range from $7.50 to $17. Desserts, from the Chocolate Decadence to the tiramisu, are just as unforgettable as the rest of your meal. The wine list does justice to this fine restaurant, ranging from a choice selection of California and imported wines to some fine champagnes. Kuleto's also offers a dozen first-quality beers, domestic and imported.

The restaurant is open daily from 7am to 10:30am for breakfast, and from 11:30am on through to 11pm for lunch and dinner. It's wise to make reservations at this deservedly popular place.

Corintia Ristorante is in the Parc Fifty Five (formerly the Ramada Renaissance), 55 Cyril Magnin St., at Market and North 5th (tel. 415/392-8000). One of San Francisco's finest restaurants, Corintia offers northern Italian cuisine prepared for the most discriminating palate. The restaurant presents a magnificent deep-blue (almost midnight-blue) setting with brass pedestals, handsome etched-glass panels, and mirrors overhead. Attentive and knowledgeable waiters in sparkling white bistro aprons serve you to background music ranging from Sinatra to Pavarotti.

The Corintia's menu features a delectable choice of distinctive entrees. You might begin with one of the excellent antipasti such as the baked brie and roasted garlic bulb, or the zucchini stuffed with prawns. Or go directly to one of several salad selections—say, the insalata Ilsa with arugula, spinach, butter lettuce, and wild mushrooms. Then on to the entrees: Among the pasta dishes is a superb veal and wild mushroom cannelloni in cream, parmigiana. If you yearn for beef, the Corintia has created exceptional tournedos of beef tenderloin with a sweet roasted garlic sauce. But don't overlook the sautéed veal filet with fresh tarragon sauce or the baked jumbo prawns with shallots. Fresh fish is also available each day, and the specialty changes with market availability. Entrees range from $12 to $20.

Some marvelous extra touches make dining at the Corintia very pleasureable. Fresh-baked breads and grissini are presented with virgin olive oil and individual cheese graters. A well-stocked wine cart is brought to each table with a large selection of wines by the glass, and you're given complimentary samples to help you make your choice. The wine list features only Italian wines (ah, but what wines!) that have been carefully selected from the principal regions to complement the menu. For those who prefer California selections or wines from other European regions, the full hotel list is also available. Most wines are reasonably priced below $20 a bottle.

To conclude your evening, the cordial cart presents a full selection of Italian liqueurs and grappas, as well as the traditional cognacs. For those who prefer more solid finales, look for the pastry cart, which should include one of my favorites, the chocolate cassata Siciliana with ricotta and fruits.

Dinner is served nightly from 6 to 11:30pm. Reservations are necessary.

Heralded by white awnings and a small red neon sign in the window, **Ciao**, 230 Jackson St., near Front Street (tel. 415/982-9500), features a functionalist Milano decor: white rubber flooring, gleaming brass railings, white enamel lamps and fans overhead, and creamy white walls hung with Jasper Johns prints and Wayne Thiebaud posters. You can watch the chef at work in an exhibition pasta kitchen and peruse Italian charcuterie in glass display cases, behind which are shelves of colorful biscotti tins. Tables, simply adorned with vases of red carnations, are set on a raised platform.

The same menu is in effect at lunch and dinner. An order of Ciao salad—lettuce, mushrooms, tomatoes, cheese, onions, chickpeas, and salami—makes a good beginning to either meal, as do the thin slices of raw steak in mustard sauce and the fisherman's salad. Does it come as a surprise that the specialty here is pasta? Homemade fettuccine is prepared in a variety of ways—with four different cheeses; with seafood, wine, tomatoes, and spice; with cream, butter, and cheese; etc. A charbroiled mixed grill (pork, sausage, beef, chicken, and quail) is served with fresh vegetables, and a brochette can be ordered with shrimp or sea scallops. Entrees cost $13 to $20, with pasta dishes at the lower end of the scale. Toasted garlic bread with parmesan cheese spread is served with all entrees. Desserts include cheesecake, chocolate fudge cake with marzipan filling, and Italian chocolate torte.

Ciao is open Monday through Saturday from 11am to midnight, on Sunday from 5pm. Reservations essential.

Tommaso's, 1042 Kearny St., between Broadway and Pacific (tel. 415/398-9696), is a boisterous and utterly delightful Italian trattoria. There's a long row of tables down the center with partitioned dining areas on either side; oil murals of Neapolitan scenes decorate the walls. But the center of attention is Mama Crotti, expertly tossing huge hunks of garlic and mozzarella onto the pizzas and sliding them into a brick oak-burning oven with a long wooden spatula. The pizza's great! Try the superdeluxe version: mushrooms, anchovies, peppers, ham, cheese, sausage, basil, and garlic. Less jaded palates will be satisfied with any of 18 other varieties ($10 to $17). A basket of hot homemade bread accompanies entrees like veal scaloppine alla marsala and chicken cacciatore—also oven-baked. Homemade manicotti with a side order of chilled broccoli salad makes an excellent meal. Pasta dishes are $8 to $12; meat entrees average $12 to $14. Of course, you need at least a half bottle of Soave with such a feast, and you'd do well to order homemade cannoli and a pot of Italian roast coffee for dessert.

Open Tuesday through Saturday from 5 to 10:45pm, on Sunday from 4 to 9:45pm.

Decorative plates, plants, sausages, trinkets, dolls, flags, mirrors, and other such oddments (many varnished to a high gloss) are hung from the ceiling and glued to the walls to create a decor best described in *New West* magazine as "a masterpiece of contemporary Sicilian rococo." The **Caffè Sport,** 574 Green St., between Grant and Columbus avenues (tel. 415/981-1251), is a great favorite of Italians, bohemians, neighborhood folk, visitors, and celebrities who revel in the lusty Sicilian ambience and the hearty free-hand-with-the-garlic cookery. Those with delicate appetites, temperaments, or digestive systems should read no further; the rest may proceed with gusto.

Sauces are laced with chunks of raw garlic, and portions are immense and delicious. When you are seated at your table, you'll be offered the restaurant's only menu for perusal. No matter what you order, though, your waiter will undoubtedly suggest some choices of his own. (Somehow, everyone seems to end up with the same dishes each meal!) Go along with him; you won't be disappointed. Among the more-than-ample dishes you might get: the calamari, prawns, and clams sautéed in garlic and olive oil and laced with white wine, or the pasta rustica alla Carrettiera—hollow rigatoni noodles al dente, smothered in parmesan cheese, cream, small bay shrimp, and thick tomato sauce. Fresh crusty bread and butter come with all entrees, which cost $13 to $29. Lunches are lighter and less expensive, at $10 to $14. If you aren't full to bursting, you can finish your meal with cannoli.

Open Tuesday through Saturday from noon to 2pm and 6:30 to 10:30pm. Caffè Sport is a real experience and worth the wait to get in (reservations are accepted only for parties of four or more). Bring a huge appetite, but above all, don't be late if you have a reservation.

By now a tradition in the North Beach area is the **Little City Restaurant and Antipasti Bar,** 673 Union St., at Powell (tel. 415/434-2900). Colorful prints and paintings line the exposed-brick walls, and brass fans whir slowly overhead. Burgundy café curtains frame the windows, white linen covers heavy dark-wood tables, and there's a huge oak bar up front. Somehow it all adds up to an unmistakably San Francisco decor.

The menu offers a wide and changing selection of excellent appetizers that can be ordered all day. Among these choices are grilled sausage and polenta, baked brie with roasted garlic, Manila clams, and prawns borracho (marinated in tequila, chiles, garlic, and lime), all in the $5 to $8 range. Soups and salads are also available.

After 6pm or for lunch, pasta specials include fettuccine with gorgonzola, walnuts, and sun-dried tomatoes, and spaghetti with wild mushrooms. Daily entrees offer a delicious variety of choices—fresh sea bass, tuna and sea scallops, pot roast, osso buco, stuffed chicken breasts, even a New York steak. Entrees run $12 to $15 (the steak is $16). But save room for dessert. The tiramisu is superb—chilled rum-soaked sponge cake topped with marscapone and shaved chocolate ($3.50, and worth every bite)—as are the crème caramel ($2.75) and other daily specials. There is a limited but excellent wine list, and specials offered by the glass, featuring local wines.

Little City is open daily from 11:30am to midnight, and the bar stays open until 2am.

A light and airy trattoria, **Prego,** 2000 Union St., at Buchanan (tel. 415/563-3305), is pretty and pleasant with a garden of seasonal flowers in the window. Crisp, crusty pizza emerges from oak-fired ovens, and a variety of antipasti ($5 to $11), as well as marvelous homemade pastas ($7 to $12), are available. While pasta is the specialty of the house, there's nothing commonplace about the meat and fowl dishes ($10 to $18). You'll always find fresh fish on the menu, but also keep an eye out for the flavorful aged T-bone steak served with white beans; pounded duck breasts prepared with balsamic vinegar, mint, and rosemary and served with fresh vegetables; or pork chops served with roasted garlic sauce and potatoes. Prego's also has a good selection of wines (domestic and imported) to accompany your choice. Desserts have always been my downfall, and the semifreddo al caffe—white-chocolate ice cream, espresso, and whipped cream—made me decide to eat now, diet later.

Prego is open daily from 11:30am to midnight. Reservations are available at lunch, but be prepared to wait during evening hours, as this very popular eatery takes dinner reservations for parties of six or more only.

"Rain or shine there's always a line" is the motto at **Little Joe's** (Baby Joe's on Broadway), 523 Broadway, near Columbus (tel. 415/433-4343). It's the truth as well (or very near it)—no reservations are accepted, and the place is popular enough that customers are willing to wait (sometimes as much as an hour) for a table. At Little Joe's, even queuing up is an experience: You can sip a drink, peruse the menu, and work up an appetite watching the cooks whip up the food and the customers devour it.

Specialties here are veal and pasta. For $9 to $13 you can dig into veal piccata, scaloppine, saltimbocca, ravioli, cannelloni, or rigatoni. (At lunch, everything's about $1 less.) Or you can enjoy an omelet or a sandwich on French bread for $5 to $7. There are daily specials as well—beef stew, roast chicken and gnocchi, roast lamb—for $8 to $10. And of course there are desserts, like flan or spumoni ice cream.

Little Joe's is open Monday through Thursday from 11am to 10:30pm, on Friday and Saturday to 11pm, and on Sunday from noon to 10pm. *No credit cards.*

Japanese

There are three great advantages to dining at **Ichirin,** 330 Mason St. (tel. 415/956-6085), adjacent to the King George Hotel. First, its location is excellent for a night on the town—just around the corner from Theater Row and across from a large garage with all-night parking. Second, Ichirin has a menu with considerable variety. Third, the food and service are first-rate.

The simplicity of the main dining room—decorated in subtle green, mauve, and beige, with relatively plain tables and booths—sets off the beautiful and colorful kimonos worn by the Japanese women who prepare and serve food at the table. Should the size of your party warrant it, or if you simply enjoy the privacy they afford, tatami rooms are available. And on each floor of the restaurant you can watch sushi chefs preparing delights.

Ichirin has some 28 special appetizers, ranging from such standards as pot stickers (gyoza) and deep-fried chicken wings (teba kara-age) to the exotic. Other excellent choices are the deep-fried eggplant served with a special teriyaki-type sauce (nasu shigi age) and the fish cakes with Japanese horseradish (itawasa). The sushi bar offers assortments, combination rolls, and chirashi—the chef's choice of fresh filets of fish served over sushi rice with seaweed. There's also a "beginner's sushi plate"— the shrimp, egg cake, barbecued eel, and two pieces of futomaki roll will be certain to make sushi converts.

Then there are the delicious nabe dishes, cooked at the table for two or more: shabu-shabu—thinly sliced beef, vegetables, and tofu, cooked in a tasty broth and served with two special sauces; a marvelous ishikari nabe—salmon and vegetables cooked in a soybean-based broth; and chanko nabe—fresh seafood, tender chicken, and crisp vegetables in broth (said to be the most popular nabe among the sumo wrestlers). Other entrees include tempuras, teriyaki dishes, and a multitude of udon (flour) and soba (buckwheat) noodle dishes.

If you have the kiddies in tow, Ichirin serves a complete luncheon plate for them, including broiled and deep-fried items, vegetables, plus fruit for dessert.

Dinner appetizers cost $2.50 to $8, though most are in the $4 range. Entrees are $10 to $14; the Ichirin dinner box with the chef's choices of the day is $19. At lunch, donburi dishes (served over a bowl of rice) are $6 to $10, and bento (combination lunch box) range from $7 to $14. Dinner plates for the kids are $6; lunch plates, $5.50.

Ichirin ("Single Flower") is open daily from 7am to 10am, 11:30am to 2pm, and 5 to 10pm. There is a cocktail lounge on the premises.

An unpretentious little restaurant, **Sanppo**, 1702 Post St., near Laguna, almost across from the Miyako Hotel (tel. 415/346-3486), is always filled with a friendly mix of Nihonmachi (Japantown) locals, businesspeople, and tourists. The small room has lots of small tables as well as a square counter area in the center of the room. It is rare to have a private table here, but the food is so good I just don't care.

Sashimi, teriyaki, tempura, sushi, and donburi (dinner in a bowl) all sell for about $5 to $12. Two of my favorite meals here are gyoza (seasoned, ground pork wrapped in pastry and fried) and soba (wheat noodles in broth with tanuki, fried dough). Combination meals—tempura, sashimi, and gyoza or tempura and teriyaki—come with rice, miso soup, and pickled vegetables for $10 to $17.

Sanppo is open Tuesday through Saturday from 11:45am to 10pm, on Sunday from 3 to 10pm.

Jewish

If you're craving an authentic pastrami on rye, you don't have to hop the next plane to New York. Just head on over to **David's**, 480 Geary St., at Taylor (tel. 415/771-1600), where a lively crowd of theater-goers will be taking apart the evening's performance over the blintzes.

A complete dinner—including appetizer, soup, entree, dessert, and coffee—is a good buy for the truly hungry at about $16. Such a meal might consist of chopped liver, matzoh-ball soup, chicken paprikás, and a napoleon. À la carte entrees include cheese blintzes smothered in sour cream and laced with jam, and sweet-and-sour stuffed cabbage with potatoes, for $7 to $10. Don't overlook the appetizers: herring in cream sauce, gefilte fish with matzoh or challah, chicken liver in schmaltz. Sandwiches come on rye or Siberian soldier's bread and include a traditional hot pastrami, for under $8. Desserts are homemade.

Open daily from 8am to 1am.

Mexican

Some people perpetually research good French restaurants; my passion has been to discover really great Mexican restaurants this side of the border. I didn't expect to find one as far north as San Francisco, but there it was, all new and shiny as of November 1987—the **Corona Bar & Grill,** 88 Cyril Magnin, at the corner of Ellis and Cyril Magnin (tel. 415/392-5500), where entrepreneur Bill Kimpton brought together the restaurant-designing talents of Pat Kuleto, the creative California-Mexican cuisine of chef Robert Helstrom, and the management skills of Sarah Graves.

Handcrafted Mexican masks, some as old as 100 years, and a large mural of a coastal sunset help make this a warm, comfortable place in which to relax and enjoy the superb margaritas and creative food. Part of the Corona's stunning effect lies in the way it incorporates the basic beauty of food and its preparation into the decor. A 90-foot-long cherrywood bar with an open cooking line stretches across much of the restaurant's length. At the end of the open kitchen, in a continuing state of creative activity, a large glass-front frige contains an attractive display of oysters and clams on ice.

A variety of appetizers are available from the bar and regular menu. "Bowls and salads" are great for diners with medium-size appetites or those who would like to try several dishes; entrees are of larger than standard proportions but you'll love every bite. My first order was a Fresh Oyster Shooter with peppered Cuervo 1800 from the bar appetizers: It came in a small, attractive square glass (about jigger size) with the sauce of Cuervo on top, and it turned out to be a tantalizing introduction for the good things to come. Among the appetizer highlights are the quesadilla with shiitake mushrooms and Roquefort, scallop ceviche, the black-bean cake and grilled prawns, the duck tamale with orange barbeque sauce (absolutely delicious), and the chile relleno with goat cheese and wild mushrooms. As for the entrees, the exceptional choices include a superb roast duck with pumpkin-seed sauce and shoestring yams, a fresh green-corn tamale with chicken breast or sirloin and black beans, and roast rack of lamb with a piñon-nut crust and light mole sauce. The food presentation is itself a work of art, and the servers are knowledgeable, friendly, and well turned out in white shirts, string ties, and black trousers.

The bar appetizer menu ranges from $1.50 for my Fresh Oyster Shooter to $8.50 for a marinated chicken salad. Appetizers are $5 to $7.50; bowls and salads, $4 to $9; and entrees, $10 to $20, the top price being for the roast rack of lamb. There is a good selection of domestic wines by the bottle and premium wines by the glass, as well as eight varieties of cerveza mexicana, some gringo beers, magnificent margaritas, and even agua—Calistoga and Penafiel.

The Corona Bar & Grill is open daily for lunch and dinner from 11:30am to 11pm; the bar serves to midnight. I would suggest that you make a reservation.

Seafood

Pacific Heights Bar & Grill, 2001 Fillmore St., at the corner of Pine Street (tel. 415/567-3337), is the setting for some of the best seafood in the city. It's handsome and spacious and has a warmth typical of the neighborhood. As you enter under the burgundy canopy, the look of the long oak bar on your right, the comfortable lounge chairs arranged around cocktail tables, create a feeling of ease—a place to relax, visit a while, and listen to the soft jazz in the background. The high ceilings and cream-colored walls add to the room's airiness. Tables in the dining area and the banquettes are a rich plum color, as is the carpeting. A huge frosted-glass seascape framed in oak separates the entryway from the inner dining area. A broad expanse of window dominates the room—great for people-watching and viewing the neighborhood activity. Sea-gray prints decorate one wall.

For lunch or dinner, oysters of at least 12 to 16 varieties, including Belons, jumbo Blue Points, and Portuguese, are available individually or by the half dozen. Clams and mussels can also be had on the half shell. Prices average 90¢ to $1.30

each, or $5.25 to $7 for six. Fresh fish, from amberjack to sturgeon, is the specialty of the house, followed by seafood stews, paella, and cioppino. The selection of oysters and fresh fish, as well as the sauces and specialty dishes, changes daily so that you're always assured of having the freshest and best of what is available that day. Lunch prices range from $6.50 to $11. If fish is not your choice, never fear—you won't be disappointed in either the quality or quantity of their other fare. The mesquite-grilled burger is a meal in itself for $7, or try the delectable spinach pasta with spicy Italian sausage, fried zucchini, and tomato sauce for $8.50. Dinner at Pacific Heights Bar & Grill will cost $16 to $22 without your favorite oysters. A good selection of California wines is available by the glass.

Open Monday through Thursday from 11:30am to 9:30pm, on Friday to 11pm, on Saturday from 3 to 11pm, and on Sunday from 10:30am to 9:30pm. Reservations are recommended for dinner.

Very similar in style to the previously described Tadich Grill, **Sam's Grill and Seafood Restaurant,** 374 Bush St., near Kearny (tel. 415/421-0594), also has an old mahogany bar, intimate booths separated by mahogany partitions (although here there's even a curtain you can draw for greater privacy), schoolroom lights overhead, and big plates of lemon wedges on every table. Maybe they copied the idea; newcomer Sam's came on the scene almost 20 years after Tadich's—in 1867.

Entrees at Sam's (priced at $7 to $26) include fresh charcoal-broiled salmon, fried deep-sea scallops with tartar sauce, rex sole, and deviled crab à la Sam—a specialty. There are many nonseafood offerings as well: half a broiled chicken, for example. Accompanying side dishes might include creamed spinach and/or potatoes au gratin. A glass of house wine can be ordered, and there's a considerable choice of desserts. What to choose? A wedge of Camembert, French pancakes with lemon and sugar, or perhaps the traditional homemade cheesecake.

Open Monday through Friday from 11am to 8:30pm.

Steak

For over 40 years **Phil Lehr's Steakery,** in the Hilton Hotel, at Taylor and Ellis streets (tel. 415/673-6800), has been one of San Francisco's most popular restaurants. Lehr himself is almost always on the scene making sure the food (every recipe is his own creation) is up to standard and the service faultless.

Flambé dishes are a specialty here, and they're cooked on flameless Fasar ranges (a Lehr creation) using magnetic induction to create evenly distributed heat; you don't have to understand it, just enjoy the results. Lehr also pioneered the pay-by-the-ounce concept of steak service so that people didn't have to order more than they could eat. Options available (from $16 to $28): 7 ounces of New York steak, top sirloin, rib-eye, or filet mignon; 16 ounces of T-bone; 18 ounces of porterhouse. All dinners come with a relish tray, salad, stuffed baked potato with sour cream, chives, butter, beef bacon (it's delicious), deep-fried onion rings, and sourdough bread and butter. Excellent beef, chicken, salmon, or lamb rack Wellington can also be ordered. Nothing is cooked in advance, and everything is fresh. Although flambé desserts are featured, you can also get cheesecake or a hot fudge sundae.

The Steakery is open nightly from 5pm to midnight. Reservations suggested.

BUDGET MEALS

The following are for those of you who haven't got too many coins jingling in your jeans. Nothing prosaic, these low-cost eateries range from American to Vietnamese and are worth investigating even by better-heeled travelers.

American

On the outside, **Tommy's Joynt,** 1109 Geary St., at the corner of Van Ness Avenue (tel. 415/775-4216), is carnivalesque with brightly painted walls depicting oversize edibles, signs proclaiming world-famous sandwiches, and 22 purely deco-rative flags. Inside it's funk-and-junk time: old hockey sticks, a statue of a lion guz-zling Löwenbräu, stuffed birds, a Santa Claus mask—and a TV going full blast during big games to add lots of noise to the general confusion.

The food is cafeteria style and high in quality. Buffalo stew, stronger and gamier than beef stew, is a specialty; a platter of barbecued beef with potatoes or a big turkey leg is also served. Entrees like this cost $5 to $9. You can also order from a variety of salads; and cheesecake is available for dessert. Beer comes in 78 varieties, listed alpha-betically by national origin—from Australia to Switzerland. Average price is $2.50 a bottle.

Open daily from 11am to 2am. The bar opens at 10am.

Sears Fine Foods, 439 Powell St., between Sutter and Post (tel. 415/986-1160), is a San Francisco tradition, this time for breakfast on the way to work, or lunch to sustain a downtown shopping foray. Located across the street from the Sir Francis Drake hotel, it's famous locally for its luscious dark-brown waffles, light sourdough French toast, and pancakes. Two specialties I enjoy are the 18 Swedish pancakes (count 'em!) served with whipped butter and warm maple syrup, also avail-able with smoky Canadian bacon or link sausages; and the strawberry waffle with fresh berries and whipped cream. These and other breakfast entrees cost $4 to $8. At lunch you can't beat the turkey with dressing and cranberry sauce, fresh vegetables, potatoes, and roll and butter. Full lunches or lighter meals run $6 to $9.

The restaurant is a pleasant place, decorated in browns and golds with framed oil paintings on the walls and pillars, and a choice of counter or table seating. Be prepared for a short wait before you get your seat.

Sears is open Wednesday through Sunday from 7am to 2:30pm.

Chinese

Sam Wo, 813 Washington St., off Grant Avenue (tel. 415/982-0596), is a Chinatown institution and one of the handiest spots to know, since it's open for anything from midnight snacks to predawn repasts. Whatever you feel about appear-ances, don't be put off by the look downstairs. The establishment consists of two tiny dining rooms piled on top of each other on the second and third floors—you have to walk past the kitchen on the first floor and up the stairs to reach the dining areas. The rooms are bare and usually packed, and you almost invariably have to share a table.

The specialty of the house is jook (known as congee in its native Hong Kong)—a thick, wonderfully tasty rice gruel flavored with fish, shrimp, chicken, beef, or pork, and costing $3 to $4. Equally famous is the marinated raw-fish salad. I guarantee that you've never seen many of these great-tasting dishes on the menu of your local Chinese restaurant—steelhead fish with greens over rice, sweet-and-sour pork rice, wonton soup with duck, and roast pork rice noodle roll. Chinese dough-nuts go for 45¢ per hole. Sam's is for mingling almost as much as for eating.

Hours are 11am to 3am six days a week; closed Sunday.

CHINESE TEA LUNCH   The Chinese call it dim sum. Literally translated, dim sum is "a delight of the heart." Gastronomically, it is a delight to the palate. Small, succulent dumplings with skins made of wheat flour or rice dough, dim sum are filled with tasty concoctions of pork, beef, fish, or vegetables. This cuisine is not limited to the dumpling format, however—it also includes dishes such as congees (porridges), stuffed lotus leaves, spareribs, stuffed crab claws, scallion pancakes, shrimp balls, pork buns, and egg custard tarts. At a dim sum meal, you pick these tidbits either from a menu or, more often, from a cart wheeled from the kitchen to the customers. It's not necessary to select all the dishes for your meal on the first pass of the cart—carts come by quite regularly. The bill depends on how many dishes you choose, and this, in turn, is usually calculated by the number of serving dishes that have piled up on your table by the end of the meal. The more people in your party, the more fun this ritual is; a large group can go on sharing dim sum for hours. What's more, it's very economical.

Traditionally, dim sum has been served in teahouses—large, good-natured restaurants where families and friends sit around circular tables talking, eating, and drinking pots and pots of steaming Chinese tea. About 15 or so Chinatown restaurants, and some not in Chinatown, serve dim sum from 11am to 3pm.

Yank Sing has two locations in the Financial District, at 427 Battery (tel. 362-1640) and at 49 Stevenson (tel. 495-4510). Yank Sing on Battery is open weekdays from 11am to 3pm, weekends and holidays from 10am to 4pm; the Stevenson branch is open weekdays only, same hours.

Yank Sing serves award-winning dim sum in a modern setting. As with most such restaurants, it is bustling and noisy—something like a Chinese version of a Brueghel feast. Yank Sing offers over 60 varieties of fresh delicacies (with some variations from day to day). There's no menu, but the best part about dim sum (exclusive of the joy of eating) is that you can see all of the goodies coming by on carts before ordering. Most plates cost around $2, and you get two or three of the same item per plate.

The specialties on any given day might include crab claws in a golden batter; shrimp dumplings shaped like goldfish and rabbits; cream cheese and curry wonton; spring rolls; Mandarin dumplings with chives; Peking duck by the slice (a Yank Sing exclusive). Save room for some dessert dim sum—perhaps coconut cream rolls, sesame balls, or egg-custard tarts. The average bill comes to about $9 to $12. Soft drinks, beer, and wine are available (there's a full bar at the 427 Battery location).

Hang Ah Tea Room, 1 Pagoda Plaza, off Sacramento near Stockton (tel. 415/982-5686), is another good spot for dim sum meals as well as Mandarin specialties. Tucked into a Chinatown alleyway, it's a pleasant, well-lit, and unpretentious little place with linoleum tile floors, tables covered with white plastic, and pale-yellow walls adorned with Chinese embroideries. Some 25 varieties of tea-lunch delicacies are available, among them fried beef or pork wonton, bean-curd rolls, spareribs in black-bean sauce, and a sesame ball filled with sweet bean paste and coconut. Most plates cost $1.50.

Hang Ah is open daily from 10am to 9pm.

Mexican

La Victoria, 2937 24th St., at the corner of Alabama (tel. 415/550-9309), is the most authentic and least costly of San Francisco's Mexican eateries. Entered via an aromatic bakery-cum-grocery where fresh-from-the-oven breads and pastries, plantains, chiles, cactus leaves, chayote, mangoes, hot sauces, and the like are attractively displayed, it consists of two small rooms divided by an open kitchen with hanging plants over the counter. Mexican travel posters and a plaque of the Virgin adorn red walls, the floor is covered in ginger linoleum, and the tables are brown Formica. During the day it's bright and sunny.

The menu is in Spanish only, and entrees are $7 or less. Among the offerings: two burritos, tacos, or enchiladas with rice and frijoles (beans); orden birria (an order of lamb stew marinated in chili sauce, hearty and thick, served with fresh chopped onions and cilantro); and menudo grande (a large serving of hunks of tripe with fresh lemon, chopped onions, fresh oregano, and red chili). Another specialty is fried pork skin with chile verde. Have a bakery-fresh pan dulce with your coffee and homemade flan for dessert.

Open daily from 10am to 10pm.

Salvadorean

La Santaneca, 3781 Mission St., at Richland (tel. 415/648-1034), is a small storefront place with simple decor—wood-grain paneling, Formica-topped tables, wooden chairs, hanging plants. It's run by a brother and sister, Oscar and Nena Carcamo, who've been at it for over a decade.

If you aren't familiar with Salvadorean food, Nena will graciously help you make your selections. There are soups, like beef tripe or prawn. For $2.50 to $6 you can order any of a number of typical dishes. A plate of papusas (corn tortillas with cheese or pork stuffing) and another of plantains and beans with sour cream make a wonderful light lunch or supper. They can also serve as prelude to an entree like chile relleno, Salvadorean-style chicken, or a combination platter of steak, prawns, rice, french fries, and salad. Such Mexican classics as tostadas, chorizo (sausage), tacos, and burritos are also available. Entrees, which cost $6 to $8, are served with rice, beans, and a spicy-hot Salvadorean "coleslaw" of cabbage, carrots, vinegar, and chiles. No liquor is served at La Santaneca, but there are coffee and tea as well as tropical fruit juices and a delicious Salvadorean drink made of rice, milk, peanuts, sesame, cinnamon, and other spices, with the consistency and color of light chocolate milk, called horchata.

La Santaneca is open Tuesday through Thursday from 10:30am to midnight, Friday through Sunday to 3am. A bit off the beaten track, it's well worth seeking out. It's easy to get to by car, and can also be reached on the no. 14/Mission bus or by BART (it's a short walk from the Glen Park stop).

Vietnamese

With the proliferation of Vietnamese in San Francisco, there's been a rash of Vietnamese restaurants. The best, in my opinion, is **Mai's,** 1838 Union St., at Laguna (tel. 415/921-2861). It's a pleasant, intimate place, with only small touches of Asia: prints on the wall, soft Vietnamese music playing in the background. While you peruse the menu, you can order a drink from the fully stocked bar. Be sure to start with the Imperial or Vietnamese rolls. (The former are like traditional eggrolls, while the latter are made of shredded pork and lettuce wrapped in rice paper—both delicious.) Don't miss the hot-and-sour soup; it's quite different from the Chinese variety, with a clear broth, crisp vegetables like tomatoes, bean sprouts, celery, and chives, and lots of cilantro. Entrees include lots of pork, chicken, beef, seafood, and vegetarian dishes, priced from $5 to $9. You can also order a complete dinner of soup, appetizer, selected entree, and rice for about $10. Jasmine tea accompanies any meal. And for dessert, you can order flan, lichees, or tropical fruit.

Mai's is open weekdays from 11am to 10pm, weekends from noon to 11pm. There is another Mai's at 316 Clement St., between Fourth and Fifth avenues (tel. 415/221-3046), open the same hours as above.

And in Conclusion

The perfect finale for a meal or a restaurant-listings section, **Just Desserts,** 3735 Buchanan St., between Marina Boulevard and Beach Street, across from the Marina Green (tel. 415/922-8675), is a delightful place for a late-night espresso or to indulge in a slice of Chocolate Velvet—layers of light- and dark-chocolate mousse on gâteau au chocolat—or a piece of cherry pie. Just Desserts has been baking some of San Francisco's finest desserts, from scratch, since 1974. There are more than 30 delectable calorie-laden choices, from danish, muffins, and croissants to cookies, cakes, pies, and tarts. The chocolate fudge cake, made with seven varieties of chocolate, has been called the best in San Francisco. Prices range from $1.75 to $5. Fresh-ground coffee, a large variety of teas, and the full espresso bar complement the dessert menu. Just Desserts—light and airy, with lots of windows, a garden room, and patio—is also the perfect spot to start your day with a fresh-baked muffin or croissant.

Open Monday through Thursday from 7:30am to 11pm, on Friday to midnight, and on Saturday and Sunday from 8:30am to midnight. There are four other Just Desserts: at 248 Church St., between Market and 15th; at 835 Irving, between

9th and 10th; at 3 Embarcadero Center; and inside the Plaza Foods Complex at Fulton and Masonic. They have slightly different hours.

7. Sights and Shops

San Francisco is chockablock with sightseeing adventures, many of which can best be enjoyed on foot—but in very comfortable walking shoes and if you're in good shape. Chinatown, Japantown, Fisherman's Wharf, the Cannery, Ghirardelli Square, Pier 39, and the like make San Francisco a stroller's paradise, and while you're checking out these attractions you can savor the unique and charming atmosphere of the city.

As long as we're on the topic of walking excursions, you should know that volunteers sponsored by the Friends of the San Francisco Public Library (tel. 415/558-3857) conduct **free tours of historic areas** within the city's neighborhoods, generally from May through October. If you want to know the schedule of tours the day you're in town, get the taped message (tel. 415/558-3981). Tours usually take about 1½ hours; reservations are not required. There are tours of City Hall, Coit Tower, Gold Rush City, North Beach, Victorian Houses of Pacific Heights, and Cathedral Hill and Japantown.

In the upcoming pages, I've detailed daytime activities, including those mentioned above, as well as parks, museums, and excursions. Let's begin with an area of major importance in the San Francisco tourism picture:

CHINATOWN

Head for Grant Avenue at Bush Street, where an ornamental green-tiled archway, crowned by a symbolic dragon, marks the entrance to the biggest Chinese stronghold this side of Taiwan. Here begins an eight-block-long, three-block-wide labyrinthine array of pagoda-roofed buildings, dragon-entwined lampposts, exotic shops and food markets, renowned restaurants, temples, and museums; here Kuangchou dialect is the mother tongue.

The early-comers from Canton reached San Francisco during the Gold Rush in 1849. They called the city Gum Sum Dai Fow—"Great City of the Golden Hill." (Today their numbers have swollen to an estimated 80,000, although some local Chinese sources set the figure at more than 100,000.) Banding together in one tiny area of the city was not totally a clannish choice of these immigrants. They were partly forced into it by anti-Asian prejudice. It became, as ghettos will, ridden with vice, and until the earthquake of 1906 Grant Avenue (San Francisco's oldest artery, then Dupont Street) had an unsavory reputation as "the wickedest thoroughfare in the States." Only after devastation swept away the bordellos, gambling dens, and opium parlors was it given a new name—and a new image.

Along with vice, the earthquake swept away another old Chinatown symbol—the Tong hatchet men, so named because they actually dispatched their victims with an ax. Originally formed as protective societies, because "pigtail baiting" was a favorite pastime of San Francisco hoodlums, the Tongs evolved into criminal gangs. Today, however, the Tongs are gone, and, in fact, Chinatown is one of the safest neighborhoods in America. It's packed with interesting sights, which I've detailed below. And while you're here, have a meal or a dim sum feast in one of the restaurants suggested in the previous section.

At the corner of Grant Avenue and California Street, having survived the earthquake and fire in 1906, is **Old St. Mary's Church.** The city's first cathedral, it was erected in 1854 of brick brought around Cape Horn and a granite cornerstone cut in China. Above the clock dial, its red-brick façade bears this warning: "Son, Observe the Time and Fly from Evil." Diagonally across is **St. Mary's Square,** a tranquil, flower-filled retreat over which an imposing 12-foot statue of Sun Yat-sen, by sculptor Beniamino Bufano, presides.

The tiny **Chinese Historical Society of America,** 650 Commercial St. (tel.

415/391-1188), open Wednesday through Sunday from 12 to 4pm, houses a collection of regional Chinese artifacts. The society was started in 1962 to record the history of the Chinese in America; in 1963 the first exhibit of historical artifacts was held at the local Chinese YMCA. The contents of the old, often-battered trunks Chinese pioneers left for safekeeping but never claimed formed the basis of the exhibit. Later a fire destroyed this priceless collection of Chinatown memorabilia. Currently you'll view scores of sepia-toned photographs of early arrivals, tiny slippers for the bound feet of aristocratic ladies, a Chinese religious altar built in 1880, a wedding headdress, herb store paraphernalia, a shrimp winnower, mining artifacts, and gadgets and pipes used in opium dens. And, as in the original collection, there is a trunk full of personal effects that was checked but never claimed. What kept the owner from coming back for his trunk?

In 1969 the society's current home was provided by the Shoong Foundation. That same year the society conducted a seminar on the history of the Chinese in California. Subsequently a 90-page syllabus was produced (now in its sixth printing) covering the arrival of the Chinese, their culture and language, and their contributions to various industries in California. Admission to the museum is free, but a generous donation is very much in order.

At 838 Grant Ave., you'll come to the **China Trade Center,** an arcade of shops and restaurants, which is fun to visit.

If you've had your fill of bustling crowds, exotic wares, mountains of souvenirs, etc., you might want to take a break and stop in at a Chinese movie. Most of the theaters are on Mason and Jackson streets off Grant Avenue, and many have English subtitles. There's usually a double feature—a classical costume drama and a very Hollywood-style epic, or at least some Hong Kong studio's idea of one. Both are highly entertaining.

Chinese New Year

Chinese New Year occurs sometime in February or March, depending on the fullness of the moon. The merrymaking lasts a full week, and celebrations spill onto the streets of Chinatown, transforming them into noisy and exciting fairgrounds. There's a Miss Chinatown USA pageant parade, as well as marching bands, floats, barrages of fireworks, 10-foot-tall Taoist deities, blocklong dragons, and celestial lions. According to the Chinese lunar calendar, 1991 (or 4689 in Chinese dating) is the Year of the Ram; 1992 will be the Year of the Monkey and 1993 the Year of the Rooster.

Guided Tours

For an unforgettable Chinatown walking tour that takes you along paths and into the nooks and crannies not usually seen by the Occidental tourist, contact the **Wok Wiz,** P.O. Box 1583, Pacifica, CA 94044 (tel. 415/981-5588 or 415/355-9657). Its founder is Shirley Fong-Torres, a warm whirlwind of an author, TV personality, cooking instructor, and restaurant critic, whose staff of guides (plus Shirley) escorts groups through Chinatown. Each guide is Chinese and speaks fluent Cantonese and/or Mandarin and, of course, English. You'll learn about such things as dim sum and the Chinese tea ceremony, meet a Chinese herbalist, stop at a Chinese pastry shop to watch Chinese rice noodles being made, watch the delicate brush painting by the famous Chinese artist Y. K. Lau, visit a breakfast house and learn about jook, stop in at a fortune cookie factory, and visit a Chinese produce market and learn about the very unusual vegetables you may never identify at lunch or dinner.

The Wok Wiz walking tour is conducted daily, beginning at 9:30am and finishing by 1pm. The tour originates in the lobby of the Chinatown Holiday Inn, 750 Kearny St. (between Washington and Clay). Groups are generally held to a maximum of 12; reservations are essential. The cost is $30 per person and includes a complete lunch. Private tours, from 2 people to over 150, can be arranged. Multilingual interpreters are available on request.

Gray Line (tel. 415/558-9400) also offers a Chinatown by Night tour that takes you first on a bus ride to Ghirardelli Square, the Cannery, and Fisherman's Wharf, and then on a bus tour through Chinatown, followed by a walking tour of the area. The price of this outing is $22.50 (half price for children 5 to 11). If you sign on for the Chinatown Dinner Tour, a multicourse dinner is included with the walking tour and ride through the city at night. Prices with dinner are $35 for adults, half price for children.

JAPANTOWN/JAPAN CENTER

Set in and around Japan Center, a multimillion-dollar showcase completed in 1968, **Nihonmachi** (Japantown) is as slickly modern as Chinatown is ancient and exotic. The focal point of the city's Japanese business and cultural activities, the area abounds in Japanese art galleries, bookstores, restaurants, hotels, and shops displaying a fascinating array of products from Japan. The five-acre complex, designed by one of America's outstanding architects, Minoru Yamasaki, occupies three blocks bounded by Laguna, Fillmore, Geary, and Post streets. It is a mile west of Union Square.

Many of the shops and facilities here—including an academy that teaches flower arranging, a doll-making school, and a shiatsu school—are housed in three commercial buildings with staircases built around beautifully landscaped gardens. Two of these buildings are linked by the **Webster Street Bridge,** 135 feet long and lined with shops, a restaurant, and art galleries—including one that exhibits works from the Avery Brundage Collection of Asian Art.

The **Miyako Hotel** (see my hotel recommendations, above) offers traditional Japanese accommodations.

Kabuki Hot Spring, 1750 Geary Blvd. (tel. 415/922-6000), acquaints visitors with the pleasures of the traditional Japanese bath (individual or communal) and shiatsu massage. Facilities include the *furo* (hot bath), *mizoburo* (cold bath), dry-heat saunas, steam room, steam cabinets, and Japanese-style sit-down showers, as well as the familiar Western-style showers. Appointments are necessary.

The hub of Japan Center is the 30,000-square-foot **Peace Plaza,** landscaped with Japanese gardens and reflecting pools. A graceful *yagura* (wooden drum tower) spans the entrance to the plaza, and its focal point is the five-tiered, 100-foot-high **Peace Pagoda.** Designed by world-famous Japanese architect Yoshiro Taniguchi, the pagoda was a gift of friendship and goodwill from the children of Japan. Atop the highest tier is the *kurin,* a nine-ringed spire symbolizing great virtue. The pagoda is illuminated at night.

Buchanan Street between Post and Sutter streets is another mall area. Here shops and flowering plum and cherry trees line a cobblestoned walkway designed to resemble a meandering stream. The mall is graced with two fountains by Ruth Asawa.

Nihonmachi is also the scene of numerous Japanese festivals and events. These include: **Sakura Matsuri** (Cherry Blossom Festival), held for about nine days in April; **Aki Matsuri** (Fall Festival), held in late September; **Tanabata** (Star Festival), held the weekend closest to July 7; **Bon Festival,** a Buddhist celebration held one or two days in mid-July, its high point being a community dance with hundreds of costumed dancers; and the **Mochi-Pounding Ceremony,** held one Sunday in the latter part of December, an unusual event that culminates in the making of rice cakes. Colorful occasions, these are often beautifully costumed affairs with music, dance, demonstrations of everything from martial arts to doll making and flower arranging, calligraphy, origami, and exhibits ranging from bonsai trees to dog shows.

In addition to festivals, programs featuring traditional Japanese entertainment and activities are held most Saturday afternoons from June through September.

CASTRO STREET

There's a fascinating, friendly, fun, and historically informative tour of this remarkable community, the gay quarter of San Francisco. What more can I say except that **Cruisin' the Castro Tours** may give you new insight into the contributions of the gay community to the growth, beauty, and political maturity of San Francisco.

Tours are personally conducted by Ms. Trevor Hailey, a longtime resident of the gay community and active in the development of the Castro during the '70s. She knew Harvey Milk, the first openly gay politician elected to office in the United States. You'll learn about Harvey Milk's rise from shopkeeper to city supervisor, and visit Harvey Milk Plaza, from which most marches, rallies, and protests have begun. Then there are the beautifully resurrected Victorian homes on the side streets of the Castro area, the unusual gift shops, bookstores, restaurants, and businesses—with not a single hill to climb.

Daily tours (by reservation only) begin at 10am at Harvey Milk Plaza, atop the Castro Street MUNI station, and finish at 1:30pm. The price of the tour is $25 per person and includes a meal at a popular Castro restaurant—lunch during the week, breakfast on weekends. For reservations, call 415/550-8110 (preferably between 5 and 8pm), or write to Cruisin' the Castro, 375 Lexington St., San Francisco, CA 94110.

FISHERMAN'S WHARF AND VICINITY

When the cable cars are running, you can take the Hyde and Beach cable car from Powell and Market streets to the end of the line. Disembark at **Victorian Plaza,** a gaslit replica of a turn-of-the-century park that is the center of ocean-oriented activities stretching from the Maritime Museum and Hyde Street Pier at the western edge of Aquatic Park to Pier 43.

You can go out on sports-fishing boats from the Wharf. **Easy Rider Sportfishing,** 561 Prentiss St. (tel. 415/285-2000), takes out singles or groups for salmon or deep-sea fishing and offers special group rates, with or without tackle. Call for information, rates, or reservations from 9am to 9pm. For the salmon-fishing report, call 468-5463.

People jam the area, browsing through the street stalls selling handmade jewelry and craft items, and there are any number of street musicians, puppet shows, magicians, and ventriloquists. There are even bocci ball courts on the west side of the Maritime Museum.

At around 6am every day, and during the summer at around 3pm also, the fishing fleet sails out through the Golden Gate—a picturesque sight that has diminished but is not much changed since the Italian immigrants of 90 years ago earned their livelihood the same way. Even before the turn of the century the Italians had established a Little Italy fishing village in San Francisco. From there, the idea of seafood restaurants was an obvious step. At first the restaurants were really just sidewalk kitchens, but word of the delicious meals spread, and over the years the tiny counters evolved into the larger eateries of today's Wharf. On Taylor Street north of Jefferson Street, however, is a long row of seafood grottos still offering paper cups of crab and shrimp cocktails.

But eateries are just part of the Wharf's attractions. Here are some others you won't want to miss:

Ripley's Believe It or Not® Museum

This unlikely compilation of 2,000-or-so exhibits from the Ripley arsenal, at 175 Jefferson St., includes the world's smallest violin, among many other miniatures; a shrunken head from Ecuador; a replica of the Man of Chains (an ascetic who, clothed in 670 pounds of chains, dragged himself through the streets of Lahore, Pakistan, as an act of self-mortification); the Lord's Prayer on a grain of rice; and so on. Open in summer daily from 9am to midnight; the rest of the year, Sunday through Thursday from 10am to 10pm, on Friday and Saturday from 10am to midnight. Admission is $8 for adults, $7 for juniors 13 to 17, $4.75 for children 12 and under.

Guinness Museum of World Records

This Wharf attraction at 235 Jefferson St. (tel. 415/771-9890) deals in superlatives. You might even get to meet a record-holder like Sandy Allen, at 7 feet 7 inches the world's tallest woman. Otherwise, you can content yourself with trying to put your arms around a replica of the world's fattest (1,069 pounds!) man. There are exhibits, displays, and videotapes of record-breaking events, even a participation area where you can re-create world records.

The Guinness Museum is open daily from 9am to 11pm in summer; the rest of the year, Monday through Thursday from 10am to 10pm, on Friday and Saturday to midnight. Admission is $6 for adults, $4.75 for students, $2.75 for children 5 to 12 (under 5, free).

Maritime Museum

Walking west along the shore from Victorian Park, in the opposite direction from the Wharf, you come to a modernistic building that looks like a huge ship at dock. Built in 1939 as a "Palace for the Public," a huge bathing casino, it now houses the sailing, whaling, and fishing exhibits of the National Park Service's Maritime Museum (tel. 415/556-2904).

In addition to the finest collection of marine photography on the Pacific—over 250,000 pictures covering the whole subject of West Coast shipping from the Gold Rush to present day—the museum also has wonderful ship models, including a huge one of the *Preussen,* the largest wind-powered ship ever built. Lining the walls are the wooden figureheads favored by the old windjammers, wrought-iron caps, truss bows, and other examples of the shipsmith's craft.

A gallery of changing exhibits on the second floor showcases art and artifacts from the museum's rarely exhibited collections. Exhibits have illustrated West Coast whaling, the Gold Rush of '49, ferryboats on the Delta, and much more—all extremely interesting.

The museum is open Wednesday through Sunday from 10am to 5pm; in summer, daily to 6pm.

Hyde Street Pier

Five of the Maritime Museum's collection of historic ships are moored at the Hyde Street Pier (tel. 556-6435), a half block east of the museum exhibit building. They include the British-built *Balclutha,* a square-rigged Cape Horn sailing ship; the *C. A. Thayer,* a wooden-hulled steam schooner designed and built to bring lumber to rapidly developing turn-of-the-century California cities; the *Eureka,* a 100-year-old paddlewheel ferryboat; the *Alma,* the last sailing San Francisco Bay scow schooner; and the *Eppleton Hall,* a sidewheeled tugboat built in 1914 to operate on the Tyne River in England. The *Balclutha, Thayer,* and *Eureka* can all be boarded. Ranger-led tours and films are regularly scheduled. The pier is open daily from 10am to 5pm, to 6pm in summer. Admission to the museum and ships is $2 for adults, free to children under 16.

The huge oceangoing steam tug *Hercules,* temporarily moored at Pier 1, Fort Mason Center, is undergoing restoration to steaming condition and is not open to the public while work is under way. The 200-foot steam schooner *Wapama* is berthed in Sausalito at the U.S. Army Corps of Engineers Bay Model Visitor Center dock while undergoing extensive preservation treatment.

Balclutha

The *Balclutha* is a typical merchant ship of the late Victorian period. Launched in Scotland in 1886, the *Balclutha*'s maiden voyage was around Cape Horn to San Francisco. During her early trading years she rounded Cape Horn 17 times carrying rice, wine, hardware, nitrate, and wool. In 1899 she was put under the Hawaiian flag carrying lumber from Australia and coal from Newcastle, and in 1902, under the Stars and Stripes, began a new career in the Alaska salmon trade.

Wrecked in 1904, she was refitted and renamed the *Star of Alaska.* By 1930, when she made her final voyage north, she was the last square-rigger left in the salmon trade. From here the old girl went Hollywood—renamed the *Pacific Queen* and used as a background for motion pictures. But by 1954 she had had it. Plans were afoot to dismantle the old vessel, when she was bought by the San Francisco Mari-

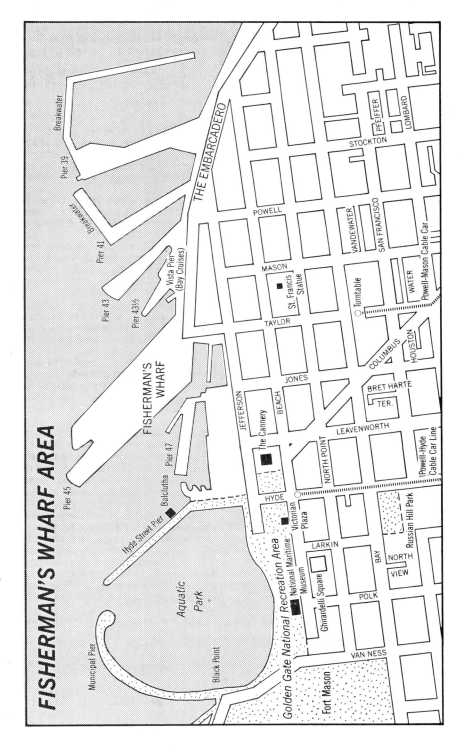

time Museum Association and restored to her original name and state. As of June 1978 the *Balclutha* and the Maritime Museum became part of the national park system's Golden Gate National Recreation Area.

Today she enjoys yet another incarnation as a playground for nautical-minded youngsters, who can spin her wheel, squint at the compass, and climb into the fo'c'sle.

The Wax Museum

This collection of over 275 wax figures of the famous and infamous is at 145 Jefferson St. (tel. 415/885-4975). All the residents were created to look as lifelike as possible. They have real human hair, and the men are given complete beards or, if clean-shaven, a very faint stubble. There is a wax reproduction of just about the entire King Tut show that traveled around the country a few years ago. So if you missed it at the art museums and can't afford a trip to Egypt, this may be your big chance. Other tableaux deal with royalty (including Prince Charles and Princess Diana), great humanitarians, celebs (Boy George and Michael Jackson), wicked ladies, world religions, and fairytale figures. And as in every wax museum, there's a chamber of horrors.

Admission is $9 for adults, $5 for children 6 to 12, $7 for seniors; under 6, free. Summer hours are 9am to 11pm Sunday through Thursday, to midnight on Friday and Saturday. The rest of the year the hours are 10am to 10pm Sunday through Thursday, to midnight on Friday and Saturday.

The Haunted Gold Mine

The same folks also operate the Haunted Gold Mine at Mason and Jefferson streets, a haunted funhouse with an abandoned-mine theme. There are mazes, a hall of mirrors, spatial disorientation areas, an electric chair, wind tunnels, and such. It's just the right degree of scary, and kids love it.

Hours during summer are 9am to 11pm Sunday through Thursday, to midnight on Friday and Saturday; the rest of the year, 10am to 10pm Sunday through Thursday, to midnight on Friday and Saturday. Admission is $5 for adults, $4 for seniors, $3 for children 6 to 12; under 6, free.

Bay Cruises from the Wharf

One of the best ways to see San Francisco is to leave it—just for a while—to enjoy a short cruise around the bay. The following leave from Fisherman's Wharf:

The **Red and White Fleet** (tel. 415/546-2896) runs a 45-minute tour, starting from Pier 41 or 43½, aboard deluxe sightseeing vessels with a passenger capacity of 400 to 500. There are open-air decks and glass-enclosed lower decks, and a snack bar dispenses hot dogs, sandwiches, and coffee. The round trip steers close to Alcatraz and passes under the Golden Gate Bridge.

Frequent departures begin at 10am year-round (weather permitting). Adults pay $13; ages 12 to 17 and 65 or over, $10; children 5 to 11, $8; under 5, free.

Frequent daily departures year-round from Pier 39's west marina are offered by the **Blue and Gold Fleet** (tel. 415/781-7877). Their 400-passenger sightseeing boats go under both bridges, come within yards of Alcatraz, and sail past Sausalito, Tiburon, Angel Island, and other points of interest. There are food and beverage facilities on board. The 1¼-hour narrated cruise costs $13 for adults, $6.50 for those 5 to 18 and seniors; under 5, free. Departures begin at 10am (at 11am December through February).

During the winter and spring there are whale-watching cruises on the catamaran *Gold Rush*.

ALCATRAZ ISLAND

A mile and a half out from Fisherman's Wharf, the bay's once-grim bastion, the Rock, has emerged from over a century of isolation. Its history dates from 1775, when the island was discovered by a Spanish explorer who christened the place Isla de los Alcatraces (Island of the Pelicans) after its original inhabitants. When the

Americans came, they drove off the birds and transformed the rock into a fortress, later an army prison.

The final transformation came in the '30s—America's gangster era—when the likes of John Dillinger and "Pretty Boy" Floyd seemed to bust out of ordinary jails with toothpicks. An alarmed public demanded an escape-proof citadel, and the federal government chose Alcatraz Island on which to erect it.

It seemed an ideal choice. The Rock was surrounded by freezing-cold water, with currents strong enough to defeat even the strongest swimmers. At a cost of $260,000 the old army cages were transformed into tiers of tiny, tool-proof, one-man cells, guarded by machine-gun towers, heavy walls, steel panels, and electronic metal detectors. Stern prison rules included no talking, no canteen, no playing cards, no privileged trustees or inducements to good behavior. One of the prisoners said it was like living in a tomb. Into that "tomb" went Al Capone, "Machine Gun" Kelly, "Doc" Barker, "Creepy" Karpis, and other big-time criminals. All were broken by Alcatraz, except those who died trying to escape.

But even though Alcatraz was successful in its intended purpose, in many ways it created as many problems as it solved. Its cells were intended to hold 300 convicts, and—happily—there simply weren't that many incorrigible heavies around. So more and more small fry (ordinary car thieves, burglars, forgers, etc.) were sent up just to maintain the population—petty crooks who could just as well have been sent elsewhere at a fraction of the cost. For the expense of maintaining Alcatraz was immense; by the 1950s the money required to keep a single inmate on the Rock could have housed him in a luxury hotel suite. So when three inmates seemed to stage a successful escape, tunneling out with sharpened spoons (no trace of them was ever found, and likely as not they drowned), the federal government took the opportunity to order the prison "phased out." On March 21, 1963, the Rock's last inmates— 27 pale men in wrist and leg shackles—were transferred to other federal penal institutions.

For the next ten years the Rock remained empty, inhabited only by a caretaker, his wife, and an assistant. And for a while, in 1969, a protest group of Native Americans took it over with the intention of establishing a Native American cultural center. They left in 1971.

Then in 1973 the National Park Service opened it to the public, running conducted tours from the San Francisco waterfront. Today great numbers of visitors flock to explore the main prison block with its steel bars, the claustrophobic (nine-by-five) cells, mess hall, library, and "dark holes" where recalcitrants languished in inky blackness. If you've ever had an urge to experience instant hysteria, the "deep six" is the place. Just ask the guide to close one of the steel-plated doors behind you. Displays of photographs further enhance the experience.

To take the tour with the **Red and White Fleet** (tel. 415/546-2896), purchase tickets at Pier 41 or through Ticketron (tel. 415/392-7469) as far in advance as possible. Only 150 people are taken on each tour, and there are always large groups of disconsolate standbys waiting on the windy pier. The ferry leaves Pier 41 about every hour between 8:45am and 5pm in summer (to 2:45pm only, the rest of the year), bound for the 1½-hour guided walking tour of the Rock.

Important note: Wear comfortable shoes and a heavy sweater or windbreaker— it can be very cold. And make sure the kids hit the restrooms on the ferry going over; the only restrooms on the island are at the landing, and once you start out on your 1½-hour hike, that's it. The visit involves a steep rise and some flights of stairs to climb. The National Park Service advises those with heart or respiratory conditions to reconsider taking the tour if climbing stairs leaves them short of breath. They can either stay at the ranger station and amble through the small museum or, as an alternative, take the trip around Alcatraz described below.

The ranger-guided outdoor walking tour on Alcatraz is free; however, it does not include a look into the cell house, so if you want the details on how unpleasant confinement can be, you'll have to pay $9.50 for the audio tour ($7.25 for children 5 to 11), including ferry fare. Round-trip fare is $7 for all over 12, $5 for those 5 to 11, and $6 for seniors; under 5, free.

For those who want to see Alcatraz without all the hiking, the Red and White Fleet also offers a 45-minute boat trip (summer only) around the island, leaving from Pier 41. You don't experience the eeriness firsthand, but you don't exhaust yourself either. The tour is narrated by a former Alcatraz prison guard. There are five departures each Wednesday through Sunday between 11:15am and 3:45pm, from Memorial Day through Labor Day. Tickets cost $9 for adults, $8.50 for seniors, $6.50 for kids 5 to 11.

THE 49-MILE SCENIC DRIVE

If you want a self-guided tour of the scenic and historic spots of San Francisco and have access to a car, there is no better way to see the city than to follow the blue-and-white seagull signs of the beautiful 49-Mile Scenic Drive (actually more like 51 miles). Virtually all the best-known sights are on this tour, as well as some great views of the bay and ocean. The drive covers a majority of the sights listed in this chapter, and more.

In theory, this mini-excursion can be done in half a day, but if you stop to walk across the Golden Gate Bridge or have tea in the Japanese Tea Garden in Golden Gate Park, or enjoy many of the panoramic views, you'll spend the better part of a day. And of course you can break up the drive to extend this interesting trip to more than one day.

The **Visitors Information Center** at Powell and Market streets can supply you with a map of the route. The blue-and-white seagull signs along the way will direct you counterclockwise, but the map will be especially useful. It's also a good idea to take someone along to help navigate. And for your sake, as well as the commuters', avoid the downtown area during the weekday rush hours, from 7 to 9am and 4 to 6pm.

VICTORIAN HOUSES

San Francisco is a Victorian city (architecturally speaking) as much as it is a modern one. The city has thousands of "painted ladies" dating from the early 20th century, many of them beautifully restored and maintained. The best place to view them is in a large area bordered by Baker, Franklin, Union, and Post streets. Some of the most renowned are: the **Octagon House,** 2645 Gough St., at Union (tel. 415/441-7512); the **Haas-Lillienthal House,** 2007 Franklin St., at Washington (tel. 415/441-3004); and the **Whittier Mansion,** 2090 Jackson St., at Laguna (tel. 415/567-1848). All three are open occasionally for tours; be sure to call ahead for days, times, and admission prices.

The most famous view of San Francisco is to be found at **Alamo Square,** where from the Hayes Street side of the park you can see a row of gorgeous Victorians on Steiner Street with the downtown skyline in the background. It's quite a view, as the proliferation of postcards containing it has proven.

LOMBARD STREET

It's a rare visitor to the City by the Bay who misses the "crookedest street in the world"—Lombard Street. There's one block (between Hyde and Leavenworth) that's so steep that the road curves back and forth like a snake. Needless to say, it's a one-way block—downhill in low gear (be sure your brakes are solid). It's fun to drive it, or just to watch as others do. If you're brave, you can climb the stairs along one side. Lombard is also one of the prettiest streets in the city, with its flowers, cobblestones, and charming homes.

GHIRARDELLI SQUARE

On the north waterfront, between Fisherman's Wharf and the Golden Gate entrance to San Francisco Bay, is Ghirardelli Square—a streamlined architecture-award–winning complex of terraces, shops, theaters, restaurants, cafés, and other diversions.

Originally a chocolate and spice factory built by an Italian immigrant, Domin-

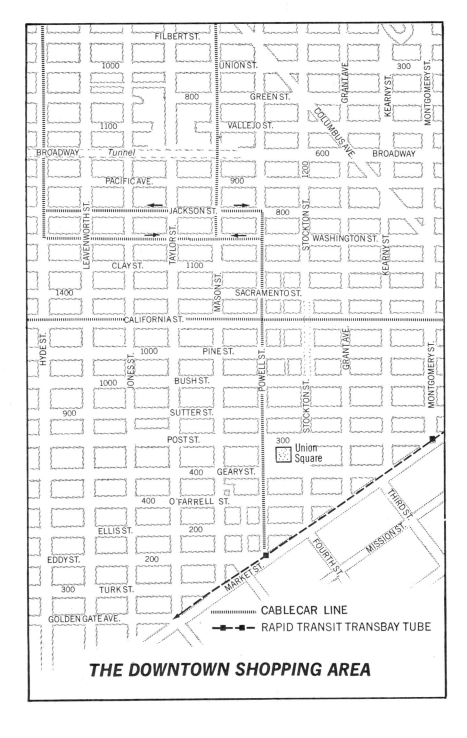

THE DOWNTOWN SHOPPING AREA

go Ghirardelli, the property was set on 21.2 acres that included the old Woolen Mill Building (dating back to 1864). When, in the early '60s, the chocolate company decided to sell the plant and relocate, a group of prominent San Franciscans, fearing the site might be acquired for high-rise office buildings, purchased the property with the idea of converting the fine old buildings to a contemporary use. A talented group of architects, landscape artists, and designers was hired to restore and transform the factory to the entertainment center that it is today.

There are 9 eateries in the complex (plus another 10 spots for noshables), among them an authentic Delhi/Bombay-based Indian establishment **(Gaylord's)**, as well as excellent Chinese **(Mandarin)**, Hungarian **(Paprikás Fono)**, and seafood **(Pacific Café)** restaurants. A San Francisco branch of New York's once-chic (now defunct) **Maxwell's Plum** is also here. Of all the waterfront complexes, Ghirardelli has by far the best restaurants, the above-mentioned all being especially recommendable. If you're exploring the Wharf–Cannery–Pier 39–Ghirardelli area, plan on dining here. At the **Ghirardelli Chocolate Manufactory,** a candy store and soda fountain, you can watch chocolate being made and purchase the rich results. The soda fountain dispenses irresistible and gooey sundaes—like the Golden Gate Banana Split, which has a base of three flavors of ice cream topped by three syrups and a banana bridge rising above great gobs of whipped cream.

Here, too, there are a cinema, a Japanese art gallery, and over 50 shops where you can buy or browse through Persian rugs, Dutch imports, kites of all nations, handmade Greek pottery, hand-sculptured glass items, music boxes, Japanese cultured pearls, and much more. There's something for everyone. And as at the Wharf, street entertainers are out in profusion.

Pick up a free copy of the *Don't-Miss-a-Thing Walking Tour of Ghirardelli Square* at the Information Center, in the middle of the central plaza. It's a complete map and guide to all Ghirardelli shops, eateries, and attractions.

During the summer Ghirardelli Square is open Monday through Saturday from 10am to 9pm, on Sunday from 11am to 6pm. The rest of the year it's open Monday through Thursday from 10:30am to 6:30pm, on Friday and Saturday to 9pm, and on Sunday from 11am to 6pm.

Want some more of the same? Proceed to another version of the above formula, known as—

THE CANNERY

The defunct Del Monte produce plant (circa 1894), two blocks to the east of Ghirardelli Square, made an equally dramatic comeback as the Cannery in 1967. Attorney Leonard V. Martin, obviously inspired by what could be done with a chocolate factory, acquired the pre-earthquake Del Monte cannery at the foot of Columbus Avenue in 1962 and gave it a multimillion-dollar facelift. A great effort was made to preserve the Cannery's early San Francisco exterior of weathered sienna brick with arched entrances and windows. A flower-filled courtyard with gnarled olive trees was landscaped and remodeled, and this became the setting for much entertainment, both organized and impromptu. Indeed, the centerpiece of this three-story compound is the open plaza where musicians, jugglers, and magicians entertain. Of course, there are the requisite number of boutiques and restaurants packed into the complex.

PIER 39

This $54-million, 45-acre specialty shopping center and pleasure ground is an ostensible re-creation of turn-of-the-century San Francisco. It has a multitude of shops and restaurants, but if you expect to experience maritime life, you'd do better with one of the ferry trips. There are two marinas that accommodate over 350 boats, including the Blue and Gold sightseeing fleet. Ongoing nautical events—boat races, etc.—add a special excitement to the Pier, as does the availability of sailing and sportfishing. The continuing flow of free entertainment alone can keep you busy for hours watching jugglers, mimes, musicians, and other street performers.

As for the shops, Pier 39 has over 100 of them, selling everything from games, toys, and teddy bears to costume and gold jewelry, San Francisco mementos, Christmas decorations year-round, everything for left-handers, and kites of the world. After all the to-ing and fro-ing, you'll probably be hungry. To please the palate, there are 10 restaurants of varying ambience and price, some with great views of the bay, and 17 nosheries with everything from hot pretzels to Mexican pastry. Although I still maintain that many of the best waterfront-complex eateries are over at Ghirardelli, the ones at Pier 39 offer the best water views.

There's also the **San Francisco Experience** (tel. 415/982-7394; for showtimes, 982-7550), a multimedia program that gives you the sights, sounds, and even the feel of the city. The city's history is reviewed, from its founding to the present day, in a rapid-fire presentation using three movie projectors, 32 slide projectors, and a 70- by 35-foot screen (with many surprises thrown in). The show, 27 minutes in length, is presented every half hour daily from 10am to 9:30pm. Tickets cost $5.50 for adults, $3 for those under 16.

The Pier has parking for 1,000 cars, and you can also easily catch a cab out front. Its restaurants are open daily from 11:30am to 11:30pm; cocktail lounges, to 2am; shops, from 10:30am to 8:30pm. To inquire about Pier 39 events, marina activities, shops, or restaurants, call 981-PIER.

EMBARCADERO CENTER

Yet another area for leisurely strolling and browsing is the Embarcadero Center, a "total living environment" designed by famed architect John Portman and situated in the Financial District on 8½ bayside acres between Wall Street West and the Ferry Building. The hub of activity is just outside the **Hyatt Regency San Francisco** (be sure to check out the lobby while you're here). Noon is the best time to go—that's when all the street merchants have their stalls set up on the Justin Herman Plaza.

The first three levels of each building (there are four) are a shopping area housing about 175 shops and a wide range of restaurants offering everything from yogurt and sprouts to McDonald's.

You can also stop at the Hyatt's outdoor café (the Market Place) for rest and refreshment. Then continue strolling about and take in the **Vaillancourt Fountain** (made of 100 concrete boxes), as well as the many sculptures scattered throughout the area. These range from a three-foot Bufano bear to works by Louise Nevelson and Willi Gutmann. Many Bufano animals are situated on the open deck of the **Alcoa Building,** from whence you can cross one of the pedestrian bridges to the **Golden Gateway,** a $150-million waterfront renewal program of town houses, apartments, shops, courtyards, and fountains.

GOLDEN GATE PROMENADE

Opened in 1973, this 3½-mile shoreline footpath, providing access to the Presidio and Fort Mason, has been called the most spectacular walk in the United States. Approach is from **Fort Point** (tel. 415/556-2857)—built in 1863 to protect San Francisco from the Confederate Army (made quite a success of it too!). Now it's a military museum, open daily from 10am to 5pm, and free guided tours are offered.

From Fort Point you meander along a rocky beach, past the fishermen at Fort Point dock, past the Coast Guard lifesaving station, and on to a sandy beach beside Crissy Field Landing Strip. Farther along are the decorative waterfront plaza of the municipal water-treatment plant, the St. Francis Yacht and Marina breakwater, Fort Mason, and, finally, **Aquatic Park.**

En route you might consider exploring the **Presidio Army Museum** (tel. 415/561-4115; open Tuesday through Sunday from 10am to 4pm), established in s a Spanish garrison. Now the Presidio is a 1,500-acre headquarters for the xth Army. The museum serves as a center of historical research, housing arti-ᵣₐᵤₛ ₐᵤd memorabilia from the Presidio's past. A second detour might be the **Palace of Fine Arts,** with its Exploratorium (details coming up).

The easiest way to begin this walk is to board a Golden Gate transit bus from Market and 7th streets, or from one of its stops along Van Ness Avenue, and get off at the bridge toll-gate plaza.

GOLDEN GATE PARK

Now the largest artificial park in the world (3 miles long and a half mile wide), Golden Gate is a far cry from the windswept wasteland of rolling sand dunes acquired by San Francisco back in 1868. The original plan was for a great public park to compare with the one then being developed in New York by Frederick Law Olmsted. Olmsted was invited to look at the proposed site and he declared it hopeless. But year after year, park superintendent John McLaren (an indomitable horticulturist and forester whose motto was "Trees and more trees") continued planting trees and shrubs, gradually taming the shifting sands. When he died in 1943, after 56 years of service, the park was an unbroken expanse of forest and glen, green lawns, bridle paths, lakes, and flowers.

You reach Golden Gate Park (tel. 415/666-7107) by taking a no. 38 bus on Geary Street to Tenth Avenue, then changing to a no. 10, which lets you off at the **Music Concourse,** where band concerts are held nearly every Sunday and holiday afternoon. Other musical events—Broadway shows, jazz, country music, operas, ballets, etc.—take place on summer Sunday afternoons at 2pm at the **Stern Grove Music Festival,** on Sloat Boulevard near 19th Avenue (tel. 415/398-6551); admission is free.

Free guided walking tours of the park are offered every weekend from May through October by Friends of Recreation and Parks (tel. 415/221-1311).

Not far from the Concourse is the **Japanese Tea Garden** (tel. 415/666-7100), created in 1894 for the California Midwinter International Exposition and kept on as a permanent attraction. Entered through a hand-carved gateway, it's an enchanting 5-acre Oriental garden of bamboo-railed paths, bonsai trees, rock creations, reflecting pools filled with goldfish, pagodas, torii statues, and Japanese art objects (including a bronze Buddha that dates from 1790). The garden is open daily from 8am to 6:30pm; admission is $2 for adults, $1 for seniors and children 12 and over. There's a Japanese tea house where kimono-clad waitresses serve aromatic blended teas. If you come in late March to early April, you'll see the cherry blossoms in bloom, not just in the Tea Garden but throughout the park; a few years ago Japan donated 700 cherry trees to Golden Gate Park as a Bicentennial gift.

Nearby is **Stow Lake,** where Tuesday through Sunday (9am to 4pm) you can rent a rowboat or paddleboat (tel. 415/752-0347) for a leisurely ride to the island in the center of the lake. The area near the lake is ideal for picnicking.

Other notable park features include the following:

The **Conservatory of Flowers,** Kennedy Drive near Third Avenue (tel. 415/666-7017), has tropical plants and a continuous flower show in bloom, open daily from 9am to 5pm October to April, to 6pm in other months. Admission is $1.50 for adults, 75¢ for seniors and children 5 to 12; under 5, free. It's the oldest building in Golden Gate Park.

The **Strybing Arboretum & Botanical Gardens,** Lincoln Way at Ninth Avenue (tel. 415/661-1316), covers almost 70 acres and has in its collection over 6,000 species of plants, trees, and shrubs. Open weekdays from 8am to 4:30pm, weekends and holidays from 10am to 5pm.

At this point, should hunger set in, you can go out of the park onto Ninth Avenue, walk a half block up, and stop at Gordo's Taqueria, 1233 Ninth Ave. (tel. 415/566-6011). It's small and there are a few tables, or you might want to take your order back to the park and dine surrounded by nature's elegance. Gordo's has some of the biggest burritos I've ever seen or attempted to eat—choose among bean and cheese,

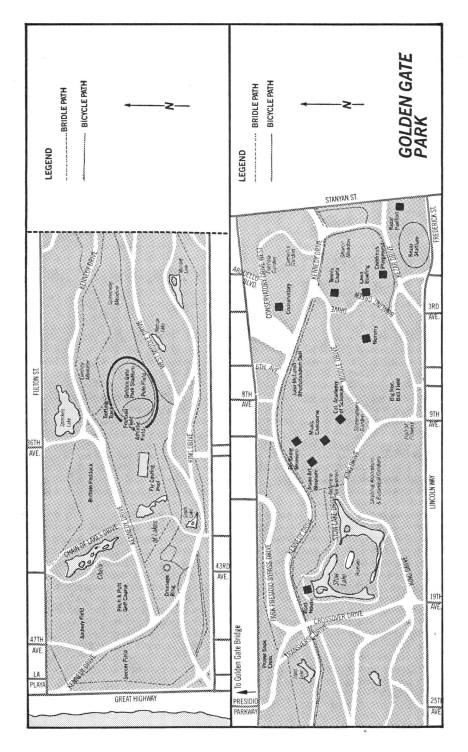

GOLDEN GATE PARK

LEGEND

━━━━━ BRIDLE PATH

------- BICYCLE PATH

N

chicken, carnitas (pork), or beef ($2.25 to $2.65). The super burritos ($2.85 to $3.35) are large enough for a man and small boy. As you might expect, there are tacos ($1.90 to $2.10) and appetizers such as guacamole, which is sold by the quarter or half pint ($1 and $1.80). Gordo's is open daily from 10am to 9pm.

The **M. H. De Young Memorial Museum,** the **California Academy of Sciences,** and the **Asian Art Museum** are all detailed below.

The **Golf Course** at 47th Avenue and Fulton Street, next to the archery field (tel. 415/751-8987), is a nine-hole course with a short and tricky layout. Greens fees are $7 weekends, $4 weekdays.

And then there are football and baseball fields; soccer pitches; bowling greens; tennis, handball, and basketball courts; horseshoe pits; bicycle, equestrian, and hiking trails; track facilities—even a vast enclosed pasture (near John F. Kennedy Drive) where a herd of buffalo roams. What's more, you can picnic anywhere in the park.

The best way to navigate the park is on a bicycle; you can rent one at shops on Stanyan Street. Some of these shops also rent roller skates, as do vans on Fulton Street and Lincoln Way on Sunday.

MISSION DOLORES

Founded in 1776, this was the 6th of the original 21 missions established throughout California by Father Junípero Serra. Mission Dolores (believed to be the oldest structure in San Francisco) was erected in what was then wilderness, the city later growing up around it. The name was taken from a nearby lake (Laguna de los Dolores—"Lake of Sorrows"), long since filled. The architecture combines Moorish, Mission, and Corinthian styles; the altar and decorations are from Spain and Mexico. Its adobe walls are 4 feet thick, its hewn roof timbers lashed with rawhide. There's a statue of Father Serra in the mission garden, where many pioneers and 5,000 Native Americans are buried.

Open daily from 9am to 4:30pm (to 4pm in the winter). A voluntary donation of $1 is requested. You can reach the mission by taking the J streetcar up Market Street to the corner of Church and 16th streets, then walking back one block to Dolores Street.

SAN FRANCISCO ZOOLOGICAL GARDENS AND CHILDREN'S ZOO

Take the L train on the MUNI Metro from downtown Market Street to the end of the line, and you'll come to one of the great zoos in the United States. Entrances are located on Sloat Boulevard at 45th Avenue and on Herbst Road off Skyline Boulevard.

It all began with a grizzly bear named Monarch, donated in 1889 by the *San Francisco Examiner.* As it evolved at its present site, the San Francisco Zoo was patterned after the pioneering Hagenbeck Zoo near Hamburg, Germany. It now takes up 65 of 125 acres of land. The rest of the park is to be developed in the coming decade under the Zoo 2000 plan.

Most of the animals in the San Francisco Zoo are kept in wonderfully realistic landscaped enclosures guarded by cunningly concealed moats. Construction of Wolf Woods, Gorilla World, and Musk Ox Meadow (described below) began the renaissance of the zoo, replacing small enclosures with open naturalistic habitats. You can see 38 species currently classified as endangered or threatened.

With the record-breaking Giant Panda Exhibition and the opening of the Primate Discovery Center and Koala Crossing, the zoo's attendance has grown to over a million visitors per year. The zoo boasts close to 1,000 animals and birds and 6,000 specimens of insects, including a hissing cockroach (those living in New York City haven't evolved to that stage yet) that can be found in the remarkable Insect Zoo, which I'll get to in a minute.

The innovative Primate Discovery Center (we, too, are primates, though not yet rare) exhibits 13 rare and endangered species in naturalistic settings, from soaring outdoor atriums and meadows to a midnight world for exotic nocturnal primates. This is where you'll find a Senegal bush baby that bounces as it walks, sometimes jumping 4 feet straight up though it's only 6 inches tall; and the Patas monkey, one of the fastest primates—it can run up to 35 miles per hour.

Other highlights include the Koala Crossing, patterned after an Australian outback station; Gorilla World, one of the world's largest naturalistic exhibits of these gentle giants; Wolf Woods, offering a chance to learn about the remarkably sophisticated social behavior of the North American timber wolf; Musk Ox Meadow, a 2.5-acre habitat for a herd of rare white-fronted musk oxen brought from Alaska; the Lion House, home to four species of cats, including Prince Charles, a rare white tiger (you can watch them being fed daily except Monday at 2pm); and Penguin Island, with its colony of about 50 Magellanic penguins from Chile.

The Children's Zoo, adjacent to the main zoo, is a special place for everyone to get close to animals and watch zoo babies being tended in the Nursery. You'll have a tough time tearing the children away from the barnyard, alive with strokable, sniffing, cuddlesome baby animals. And there's the fascinating Insect Zoo—the only one in the western U.S. and one of only three such exhibits in the country. You'll see velvet ants, honey bees, scorpions, and the marvelous hissing cockroaches I mentioned earlier. On weekends, at 2:30pm, you can see the popular Amazing Insects in Action, which gives an intimate look at live insects via the Insect Zoo's new macrovideo system. The Children's Zoo is open daily from 11am to 4pm. Admission is $1.50 for everyone (kids under 2 are free).

A free informal walking tour of the zoo leaves from Koala Crossing at 12:30 and 2:30pm on weekends. The Zebra Zephyr tour train takes visitors on a 20-minute safari tour of the zoo, daily except in winter, when it runs only on weekends. The tour is $3 for adults, $1.50 for children 15 and under.

The main zoo is open daily from 10am to 5pm. Admission is $6 for adults, $3 for a quarterly pass for seniors, free for children 12 and under if accompanied by an adult. For recorded information, call 415/753-7083; otherwise, 415/753-7080.

WELLS FARGO HISTORY MUSEUM

In a ground-floor area of the bank's headquarters, the History Museum houses hundreds of relics and photographs from the Wells Fargo's whip–and–six-shooter days. The centerpiece is the Concord stagecoach, proudly identified as the Wells Fargo Overland Stage—the 2,500-pound vehicle that opened the West as surely as did the Winchester rifle and the Iron Horse. There are samples of the treasure Wells Fargo carried—to wit, gold nuggets from the Sierra Nevada mines—and mementos of the men who were after it, men like "Black Bart," who single-handedly robbed 27 stagecoaches. There's a gold balance scale so sensitive it could, miners claimed, register the weight of a pencil mark on a piece of paper. This is where you can send off a telegraph message in code, using a telegraph key and the codebooks just the way the Wells Fargo agents did over a century ago.

On the mezzanine you can take an imaginary ride in the replica stagecoach. Those visitors interested in mail of the early days can also browse through the Wiltsee Collection of western stamps and postal franks.

The museum is open Monday through Friday from 9am to 5pm. The bank is located at 420 Montgomery St., at California (tel. 415/396-2619). Free admission.

THE EXPLORATORIUM

This unique do-it-yourself museum is organized around the theme of perception. *Scientific American* has called it the "best science museum in the world." The Exploratorium is a mind-boggling place. You can't really call it a museum, an exhibit, or a display, because you participate with your senses and stretch them to new dimensions. Plan to spend at least an hour here with the kids.

You'll find this experience in San Francisco's rococo old Palace of Fine Arts, 3601 Lyon St., at Marina Boulevard (tel. 415/563-7337, or 561-0363 for recorded information); take the no. 30 bus on Stockton Street. This is the only building left standing from the Panama-Pacific Exposition of 1915, which celebrated the opening of the Panama Canal. Almost torn down to make way for real estate developments, it was restored in the mid-1960s because a local millionaire, Walter Johnson, shamed local government by putting up millions of his own money, which the voters supplemented.

There are over 650 exhibits dealing with everything from color theory to Einstein's theory of relativity. It's an *Alice in Wonderland* world. Optics are demonstrated in booths where you can see a bust of a statue in three dimensions, but when you try to touch it, it isn't there. The same thing happens with an image of yourself where, as you stretch your hand forward, a hand comes out toward you and the two hands pass in midair. Every exhibit is designed for participation—"Do Not Touch" signs are nowhere to be seen.

Kids make up their own tours here and will spend as much time as you allow them without grumbling or asking, "What's next?" And if they're surfeited with things scientific, you can take them out to the adjoining lagoon and let them feed the ducks, swans, and seagulls that mooch there.

The Exploratorium is open on Wednesday from 10am to 9:30pm and Thursday through Sunday from 10am to 5pm. Admission is free the first Wednesday of each month, and other Wednesdays after 6pm; otherwise, adults pay $6; seniors pay $3; those 6 to 17 pay $1.50; under 6, it's free.

THE CALIFORNIA ACADEMY OF SCIENCES

At this famous complex of buildings, located on the Music Concourse in Golden Gate Park, you can view a Fijian cannibal fork, weigh yourself on the moon, or join an Arctic Eskimo on a seal hunt. It's actually a cluster of widely differing museums. Taking them one by one, we have first:

The **Steinhart Aquarium,** home to more than 14,500 specimens of fish from all over the globe, as well as invertebrates, amphibians, reptiles, and aquatic mammals. A big attraction here is the Fish Roundabout, which allows visitors to view—without getting wet—marine life from a ramp *inside* a 100,000-gallon doughnut-shape tank; it's like a midocean deep-sea dive. The aquarium also has a hands-on area where children can pick up starfish and sea urchins. And this is where you can see a living coral reef—the largest display of its kind in the country and the only one in the West.

Morrison Planetarium, presenting seven different shows a year, explores black holes, neutron stars, quasars, pulsars, UFOs, and other puzzles of the universe. Exhibits in the **Earth and Space Hall** further probe cosmic mysteries.

In the **Wattis Hall of Man** the concept of ecological anthropology—how human societies have related and adapted to their environments—is explored. Exhibits deal with evolutionary history and creative responses of man to each of several environmental situations (arctic, temperate, tropical, and desert), and displays range from gems, insects, birds, and mammals native to North America and Africa, to pre-Columbian art and gastroliths from the stomachs of dinosaurs.

New to the Natural History Museum is Wild California, seen in the renovated **Meyer Hall.** Wild California is devoted to the biodiversity of the Golden State. There are 13 exciting exhibits, including a 14,000-gallon aquarium and seabird rookery, life-size battling elephant seals, and two larger-than-life views of microscopic life forms.

In June 1990, the museum's **McBean-Peterson Hall** opened Life Through Time: The Evidence for Evolution. This massive exhibit takes you on a walk through 375 million years and shows you how body structures evolved. It begins with the age of the dinosaurs and goes on through the age of dinosaurs and mammals. You'll even see some highly animated creatures of the Coal Forest. This is an opportunity to discover how our amazing planet has changed over time and how the earth's past affects our world today; the exhibit also allows you to test your knowledge of evolution on an interactive computer program.

The California Academy of Sciences is open daily from 10am to 5pm (to 7pm in summer). Admission is $5 for adults aged 18 to 64, $2.50 for senior citizens and those 12 to 17, and $1.25 for those 6 to 11. Everyone gets in free the first Wednesday of every month. Planetarium shows are $3 for adults, $1.50 for persons under 17. For further information and show times, call 415/750-7145.

M. H. DE YOUNG MEMORIAL MUSEUM

The granddaddy of California museums, the M. H. De Young Memorial Museum had its origin in the California Midwinter International Exposition of 1894. At the end of the exposition, the Fine Arts Building was turned over to De Young, a newspaper publisher who had served as director-general of the fair, for the purpose of establishing a permanent museum.

Located on the Music Concourse of Golden Gate Park, the museum features an outstanding presentation of American art from colonial times into the 20th century, including the John D. Rockefeller III Collection; paintings, sculpture, furniture, and decorative arts by such artists as Paul Revere, Winslow Homer, Albert Bierstadt, James McNeill Whistler, and John Singer Sargent. Also on view are important collections of ancient art from Egypt, Greece, and Rome; arts of Africa, Oceania, and the Americas; British art by Gainsborough, Reynolds, Lawrence, Raeburn, and others; as well as costumes and textiles, including rugs from Central Asia and the Near East.

There's a café on the premises with a garden for al fresco dining, open from 10am to 4pm. Wine and beer are served.

The museum is open from Wednesday through Sunday 10am to 5pm (to 8:45pm the first Wednesday of the month). Admission is $5 for adults, $3 for seniors; those 18 and under get in free. The same fee also admits you to the Asian Art Museum and the California Palace of the Legion of Honor. The first Wednesday of the month (all day) and every Saturday from 10am to noon, admission is free. Guided tours are offered daily. For further information, call 415/863-3330.

ASIAN ART MUSEUM

Located in Golden Gate Park adjacent to the Japanese Tea Garden, the Asian Art Museum (tel. 415/668-8921) houses the world-famous Avery Brundage Collection of over 10,000 Oriental art treasures. The scope of the exhibits is dazzling, spanning over 6,000 years of Asian history and prehistory. The entire first floor is devoted to the arts of China, beginning with Neolithic ceramics and the earliest Chinese bronzes and surveying all the great ages of Chinese art through the 20th century. A high point is the Chinese jade display. One of the greatest Chinese lacquer collections is now owned by the museum. Arts of India, Central and Southeast Asia, Japan, Korea, the Himalayan region, and Middle East are also well represented on the second floor. Special temporary exhibits are held regularly.

Conducted tours are given daily and provide highly informative background information on the arts of Asia in the museum's collections. Open Wednesday through Sunday from 10am to 5pm. Entrance is through the De Young Museum. Admission is free on Saturday from 10am to noon and on the first Wednesday of each month. One admission lets you into the Asian Art Museum, the M. H. De Young Memorial Museum, and the California Palace of the Legion of Honor.

MUSEUM OF MODERN ART

The San Francisco Museum of Modern Art, 401 Van Ness Ave., at McAllister (tel. 415/863-8800), opened in 1935 and quickly established itself as an adventurous and dynamic repository of 20th-century art. Through its intensive program of temporary exhibitions and increasingly substantial permanent collection, it retains that position today. The museum's collection is distinguished by major works from the American abstract expressionist school of painters—Clyfford Still, Jackson Pollock, Mark Rothko, and Willem de Kooning—and by unique holdings in contemporary photography. It also has strengths in German expressionism (Max Beckmann, Max Pechstein), postimpressionism (Henri Matisse), Mexican painting (José de Rivera, José Orozco), and in the art of the San Francisco area.

A portion of the gallery space displays its permanent collection, but the museum also hosts important traveling exhibitions. Past shows have included Against Nature: Japanese Art in the Eighties, The Drawings of Richard Diebenkorn, and A History of Photography from California Collections. In fact, the museum was one of the first to recognize photography as an art form. Today its collection of 20th-century photography includes holdings of works by Americans such as Alfred Stieglitz, Ansel Adams, and Edward Weston, the German avant-garde artists of the 1920s, and the European surrealists of the 1930s.

The museum organizes special artistic events, lectures, concerts, dance performances, poetry readings, conceptual-art events, films, and many activities for children. There's a great gift, book, and art shop in the museum, one of the best I've seen outside Manhattan.

Admission is $4 for adults, $1.50 for seniors and children under 16; children under 6 are admitted free. Hours are 10am to 5pm on Tuesday, Wednesday, and Friday, to 9pm on Thursday (admission reduced 5 to 9pm—$2 for adults, $1 for seniors and those under 16); 11am to 5pm on weekends. The museum is closed Monday and holidays.

CALIFORNIA PALACE OF THE LEGION OF HONOR

Intended as a memorial for California's fallen of World War I, this beautiful museum is a replica of the Legion of Honor Palace in Paris, including the inscription "Honneur et Patrie" above the portal. Rising classically white and pillared from a hilltop, the building is neoclassic in architecture, and the collection housed within is European. Among the artists represented are El Greco, Rembrandt, Rubens, Manet, David, Renoir, and Degas. Also featured is one of the finest Rodin sculpture collections in the world, as well as continually changing exhibitions drawn from the museum's extensive collection of prints and drawings, the largest graphics collection in the western states.

To add to the beauty throughout, the museum runs a series of auxiliary attractions, such as pipe organ concerts on Saturday and Sunday afternoons.

Location is in Lincoln Park off 34th Avenue and Clement Street (tel. 415/750-3614, or 863-3330 for recorded information). On a clear day the view of the Pacific is magnificent. To get there, take a no. 38 Geary bus from Union Square to 33rd and Geary, then transfer to the no. 18 bus into the park. Admission is $4 for adults, $2 for seniors 65 and over and those 12 to 17, free for those under 12. Your ticket is also good for the Asian Art Museum and the M. H. De Young Memorial Museum in Golden Gate Park if you visit on the same day. Open Wednesday through Sunday from 10am to 5pm. All three museums are free the first Wednesday of the month.

SHOPPING AROUND

As long as you're traipsing around taking in the sights, it's time that you discover, if you haven't already, that San Francisco is an exciting and fun place to shop—or at least to look. And the delightful part is that wherever you choose to shop, you will find great places to eat. You won't find much in the way of shopping bargains, but what you will discover is much of what you won't find elsewhere. San Francisco is also home to what I've found to be the most pleasant, helpful, civilized department store in the country—**Nordstrom** on Market Street. They even offer sustenance at four excellent restaurants on the premises.

Shopping in San Francisco can be broken down by area. Downtown, in the vicinity of Union Square, you'll find the name boutiques. This is also where you'll have a chance to review the city's department stores, plus a goodly collection of its more expensive and elegant specialty shops. You'll recognize the names: **Polo/ Ralph Lauren, Mark Cross, A. Sulka & Company, Brooks Brothers, Eddie Bauer, Cartier, Gump's, Jaeger, Alfred Dunhill of London,** and **Gucci.** You'll also find some exceptional shops that can solve the gift-back-home problems, such as the **Napa Valley Winery Exchange,** 415 Taylor St.—a convenient place to shop at very reasonable prices for California wines and champagnes from the various regions in the state (about 250 different wineries).

Or if you'd like to take a really unique gift home, Chinatown offers some remarkable possibilities. The **New Unique Company,** 838 Grant Ave., carries a wide selection of carved stones used as seals; they'll carve one to order. If calligraphy happens to be your hobby, this is where you'll find supplies. **Art of China,** 839-843 Grant Ave., has an extensive collection of netsukes—small decorative carvings of animals and figurines, originally used in Japan as counterweights on sashes. And at **I-Chong Co.,** 661 Jackson St., you will find the lovely brush paintings of Mr. Y. K. Lau. For a very personal gift, Mr. Lau may be able to paint your given name (phonetically) in Chinese and have it framed in the shop.

Union Street between Van Ness and Steiner is another street of hard-to-resist treasures. This is where you'll find—to name just a few of my favorites—a crystal ball (just the thing for your friendly stockbroker or your favorite politician), at the **Enchanted Crystal,** 1771 Union St.; Native American masks, at **Images of the North,** 1782 Union; American folk-art carvings and handmade collector teddy bears, at **Yankee Doodle Dandy,** 1974 Union; and really neat knickknacks at **H. P. Corwith Ltd.,** 1833 Union.

Fisherman's Wharf has a plethora of shops at Ghirardelli Square, and if you run out of ideas, hie yourself over to **Cost Plus Imports,** 2552 Taylor St., at the cable-car turntable, where you could spend the day. The Cannery, 2801 Leavenworth, has a score of shops, including a gourmet market; Pier 39 is another galaxy of spots for spending; and then there's the Anchorage, bounded by Leavenworth, Beach, Jones, and Jefferson, with over 40 boutiques.

Finally, if you want a shop that specializes in everything and some of the most interesting knickknacks you've ever seen, try **Headlines,** 838 Market St., near Nordstrom.

8. After Dark

The Bay City is a great town for bars—plush bars, laid-back hangout bars, singles bars, Latin bars, gay bars, and neighborhood bars. Discos come in the same categories, and more.

There are enough quality theatrical, concert, ballet, and operatic productions to sustain the most culturally minded visitor. And enough bare pulchritude on one North Beach block to sustain the most salacious. Everything, in fact, for everyone. One special note—don't miss *Beach Blanket Babylon* (about which more later).

The best guide to San Francisco cultural and nightlife is the pink section (called the "Datebook") of the Sunday *San Francisco Examiner and Chronicle.* You can also refer to a small but very handy free publication called *Key,* which appears weekly and can be found in hotel lobbies and at newsstands.

TICKETS

The **San Francisco Ticket Box Office Service (STBS),** patterned after New York's TKTS, provides tickets at half price for day-of-performance sale to all types of performing arts—plays, concerts, operas, and dance events—in the major theaters and concert halls. In addition, STBS handles advance, full-price tickets for neighborhood and outlying performing companies, sporting events, concerts, and clubs, as a convenience to the public (tel. 415/433-STBS). Half-price ticket information is not available by phone.

Things to remember about STBS: Sales of half-price tickets are cash only or traveler's checks; tickets are not available for every attraction, but there will always be something available; no telephone reservations accepted, only in-person sales. A service charge is added to all tickets, ranging from $1 to $3 per ticket, based on the full price of the ticket. VISA and MasterCard are accepted for full-price tickets. Half-price tickets for Sunday and Monday events, if available, are sold on Saturday. However, STBS cannot predict what tickets will be available at half price on a given day.

STBS is located on Stockton Street between Geary and Post, on the east side of Union Square opposite Maiden Lane. Hours are noon to 7:30pm Tuesday through Thursday, to 8pm on Friday and Saturday (hours subject to change).

THEATER

The **American Conservatory Theater (ACT),** which made its San Francisco debut in 1966, has been heaped with praise—and even compared to the British National Theatre and the Comédie-Française. ACT offers solid, well-staged, and brilliantly acted productions, with some emphasis on the classics, but offering a sufficient number of new and experimental works to keep its repertoire exciting and contemporary. Some of the more recent productions have included *A Christmas Carol, 'night, Mother, Opéra Comique,* Shaw's *You Never Can Tell,* and Sondheim's *Sunday in the Park with George.*

Classic and contemporary plays are performed in repertory from October through May at the new **Stage Door Theatre,** 440 Mason St. (at Geary). Reservations can be made by calling 415/749-2228. Tickets range from $10 to $32.

The **Curran Theater,** another Theater Row resident at 445 Geary St. (tel. 415/474-3800), features Broadway musicals and comedies coming from or going to New York, usually with major stars—like *Les Misérables,* Judd Hirsch in *I'm Not Rappaport,* James Earl Jones in *Fences,* and Lily Tomlin in *The Search for Signs of Intelligent Life in the Universe.* Tickets range from $17.50 to $55. Monday is dark.

Under the same auspices as the Curran, and offering an identical Broadway musical format, is the **Golden Gate Theater,** 25 Taylor St., at Market Street and Golden Gate Avenue (tel. 415/474-3800). Built in 1922 and since restored to its original grandeur, the Golden Gate is impressively lavish, with marble floors, rococo ceilings, and gilt trimmings. Since its opening in 1979 with a 10-week run of *A Chorus Line,* it has presented Dick Van Dyke in *The Music Man,* Alexis Smith in *The Best Little Whorehouse in Texas,* Rex Harrison in *My Fair Lady,* and Richard Burton in *Camelot. La Cage aux Folles, My One and Only,* and *Me and My Girl* were recent offerings. They also stage expansive limited engagements, such as the Ukrainian State Dance Company. There are matinees every Wednesday, Saturday, and Sunday, and evening performances Tuesday through Saturday. Ticket prices are generally in the $20 to $45 range.

Fans would as soon go to India and skip the Taj Mahal as pass up a chance to see a production of *Beach Blanket Babylon* at the **Club Fugazi,** 678 Green St., near Columbus Avenue (tel. 415/421-4222), in San Francisco. This incredible revue is the magical creation of impresario Steve Silver (Cyril Magnin calls him the Flo Ziegfeld of the '80s). It grew out of his Rent-a-Freak service, a group of extraordinary party entertainers who hired themselves out with fabulous gags, props, and costumes. The first production moved to the Savoy-Tivoli in 1974, but the audiences soon grew too large for the facility. A devoted mass following (consisting of almost everyone who has ever seen the show) includes people like Beverly Sills ("I wish I lived in San Francisco so I could see it more"). The first Fugazi production, *Beach Blanket Babylon Goes Bananas* played for three years to an SRO crowd. And the latest evolution, *Beach Blanket Babylon Goes Around the World,* has been wildly successful. Skip the trip to Alcatraz, miss Chinatown, but don't miss *Beach Blanket Babylon.* What's all the excitement about? Whimsical costumes and 12-foot-high, 40-pound Carmen

Miranda hats, dancing palm trees, singing rainbows, and flights of imagination that have to be seen to be believed.

Performances are at 8pm on Wednesday and Thursday, at 8 and 10:30pm on Friday and Saturday, at 3 and 7:30pm on Sunday. Consider that this show has consistently sold out over 5,000 performances since 1974. Persons under 21 are welcome at Sunday matinees at 3pm, when no alcohol is served. Photo ID is required for the evening performance. Prices are $16 to $30, depending on the day, seat location, and time of the performance. If you know what date you're going to be in town, it's wise to write for tickets at least three weeks in advance of that time, or obtain them through STBS.

Note: The club now seats 393. When you purchase tickets, they will be within a specific section, depending on price. However, seating is still first-come, first-seated within that section.

The **Orpheum,** 1192 Market St., at Hyde (tel. 415/474-3800), has been handsomely refurbished, and the shows presented here have been terrific. Productions have included *On Your Toes, Singin' in the Rain, Fiddler on the Roof,* and *Sweet Charity.* There are performances Tuesday through Saturday evenings, and Wednesday, Saturday, and Sunday afternoons. Tickets cost $20 to $45. Call for performance times.

The **Eureka Theater,** 2730 16th St., at Harrison, south of Market (tel. 415/558-9898), a 200-seat facility, offers contemporary and classical plays dealing with political and social issues. Eureka has produced a number of outstanding, award-winning plays such as *The Colored Museum, Cloud Nine,* and *The Kiss of the Spider Woman.* Evening performances begin at 8pm Wednesday through Saturday, 7:30pm on Sunday. Matinees on Sunday begin at 2pm. Seats are $14 to $17.

The **Magic Theater,** Building D, Fort Mason, Laguna Street at Marina Boulevard (tel. 415/441-8822), while somewhat removed from the downtown area, offers interesting and often controversial works of new and established playwrights. Sam Shepard's Pulitzer Prize–winning play *Buried Child* premiered here. More recent productions have included Samuel Beckett's *Happy Days* and José Rivera's *The Promise.* Evening performances are at 8:30pm Wednesday through Saturday, 7:30pm on Sunday. Sunday matinees are at 2pm. Seats are $11 to $19.

OPERA, SYMPHONY, AND BALLET

San Francisco's magnificent **War Memorial Opera House,** built in 1932, is the focal point for most of the city's opera and ballet productions, and the quality of the performances is on a par with the world's greatest companies. The 14-week opera season begins in September. It's a good idea to get your name on the mailing list before your trip and order tickets in advance; they're hard to get. To do this, write to Opera Box Office, War Memorial Opera House, San Francisco, CA 94102. For phone reservations, dial 415/864-3330. (There are 300 standee places for opera sold two hours before curtain time.)

The San Francisco Opera Association

Under the direction of Lotfi Mansouri, this is actually a multifaceted conglomerate (tel. 415/864-3330), with each branch offering something a little different from the others. They include:

The **San Francisco Opera Company** features celebrated stars like Kiri Te Kanawa, Marilyn Horne, Plácido Domingo, and Luciano Pavarotti. Staging and direction are a wonderful blend of the traditional and the avant-garde. The company has presented 18 U.S. premieres by composers such as Richard Strauss, Britten, and Shostakovich, and provided American opera debuts for the likes of Birgit Nilsson and Renata Tebaldi.

Single (nonsubscription) tickets go on sale at the box office in August. There are performances each evening (except Monday), with matinees on Saturday and Sunday. Prices range from $15 to $85. Standing-room tickets ($7) go on sale two hours prior to the performance. The box office (tel. 415/864-3330) is open from Monday through Saturday from 10am to 6pm. If you'd like to get on the opera's mailing list, simply write to San Francisco Opera, War Memorial Opera House, 301 Van Ness Ave., San Francisco, CA 94102.

Western Opera Theater offers top-quality opera in English (plus educational programs and workshops) to communities around the country—a feat made possible by the mobility of its specially designed portable stage and lighting equipment.

The **Brown Bag Opera** offers 40-minute noontime productions geared to the typical lunch hour of office and factory workers. Audiences are encouraged to bring a lunch (or purchase one at the auditorium) and eat during the performance. The series is designed to offer opera at a minimal cost. Performances are held in varying locales—sometimes right on the street.

Another part of the San Francisco Opera Company is the **Merola Opera Program,** which selects 15 to 20 national audition finalists to participate in a 10-week period of performance and study, including two full-scale performances during the summer.

Finally, there's the **San Francisco Opera Center Showcase** every spring featuring exciting young performers in innovative repertoire.

The San Francisco Pocket Opera

Among the glories of San Francisco's theater and arts season is the unique Pocket Opera, 25 Taylor St. (tel. 415/346-2780)—don't miss it if you're in town any time from April through July.

With anywhere from 3 to 16 singers, the Pocket Opera treats you to a lively, entertaining operatic work on an intimate, intelligible level—in English, so no libretto is necessary. The rich repertoire ranges from the familiar *(The Merry Widow, Così Fan Tutte, Orpheus in the Underworld)* to the forgotten (Wagner's *Liebesverbot* and operas by Schubert, Telemann and Pergolesi), and from the baroque (Haydn's *Apothecary*) to the "popular" (Gershwin's *Oh! Kay!* and Jerome Kern's *Oh! Boy!).* There are no formal costumes or sets to impede your enjoyment or imagination. Translating and rescoring (nine instruments) are the products of Donald Pippin, artistic director and creator of the Pocket Opera, who also provides witty commentary. If you've never enjoyed opera before, the Pocket Opera will surely convert you.

Performances are at the Waterfront Theatre in Ghirardelli Square, 900 North Point, on Thursday and Saturday evenings at 8pm; and at the Florence Gould Theater, on Sunday at 2pm. However, I suggest that you call to check the schedule and times. Single performance tickets are $15 to $18. To get to the Florence Gould Theater, go west on Geary Boulevard to 34th Avenue, turn right into Lincoln Park, continue on almost to the end. On your left in the middle of the golf course is the Palace of the Legion of Honor, which contains the Florence Gould Theater.

The San Francisco Ballet

The San Francisco Ballet troupe is the oldest in the United States. Its artistic director is Helgi Tomasson. It performs from January to May at the War Memorial Opera House, although the season actually begins with the annual December performance of *The Nutcracker Suite.* Call 415/621-3838 for ticket information.

The San Francisco Symphony Orchestra

A cornerstone of the Bay City's cultural life, the San Francisco Symphony Orchestra, led by music director Herbert Blomstedt, is currently in its 78th annual season. The orchestra is headquartered in Louise M. Davies Symphony Hall, and its season lasts from September to May, featuring many internationally acclaimed guest artists and visiting orchestras. Known the world over by way of its touring and recordings, the orchestra has also built a widespread reputation for its New and Unusual Music series. Summer activities for the symphony include a Beethoven Festival, a Summer Pops series, and an annual presentation of the Joffrey Ballet.

Tickets can be obtained at Louise M. Davies Symphony Hall, Van Ness Avenue and Grove Street (tel. 415/431-5400).

COCKTAILS IN THE SKY

A good place to "get high" prior to an evening on the town, or after one, is at any of the city's plush skyline bars. Most stay open till about 2am.

The loftiest is the **Carnelian Room** (a "must see"), 779 feet up on the 52nd floor of the Bank of America Building, 555 California St. (tel. 415/433-7500). It's open for a Sunset Dinner from 6 to 7pm (about $28) and cocktails nightly, and neither hills nor high-rises interfere with its glorious outlook. After 7pm there's a prixfixe dinner for $37. The average drink is $6. Dinner reservations are essential. Jacket and tie are required for gentlemen.

The plushest, however, is the Fairmont Hotel's **Crown Room** (tel. 415/772-5131), on the 24th floor of the hotel, at California and Mason. It's reached by the Skylift, a glass-enclosed elevator that glides up and down the tower's east side. (Acrophobics can avail themselves of an inside lift.) Comfortably seated in tufted gold-leather banquettes, you can enjoy the panoramic backdrop. International buffet lunches ($18) and dinners ($25) and Sunday brunches are served here. Drinks average $6. It's open for cocktails Sunday through Thursday from 11am to 1am, on Friday and Saturday to 2am.

Originally a private penthouse on the 19th floor of the Hotel Mark Hopkins, 1 Nob Hill, the world-famous **Top of the Mark** (tel. 415/392-3434) is a popular rendezvous spot for San Francisco's well-heeled denizens. It's open daily for cocktails from 4pm to 1:30am. There's brunch ($25) on Sunday from 10am to 2pm. Libations average $6.

The **Starlite Roof,** 21 stories skyward at the Sir Francis Drake, 450 Powell St. (tel. 415/392-7755), throws in dancing to a combo along with the view. You can trip the light fantastic from 9pm to 1am. Drinks—even the nonalcoholic ones—cost $6.50 each. A facelift here a few years back expanded the view by replacing the northwest wall with glass.

Cityscape (tel. 415/776-0215), atop Hilton Tower I on the 46th floor—that is, at 333 O'Farrell St., at Mason—has a band and a marble dance floor as well. The dance combo swings into action Tuesday through Saturday at 8pm; a glass roof allows for dancing under the stars. It's very elegant. Drinks average $5 to $6.

Finally, there's **S. Holmes Esquire** (tel. 415/398-8900), on the 30th floor of the Holiday Inn Union Square, and the revolving **Equinox,** at the Hyatt Regency San Francisco, 5 Embarcadero Center (tel. 415/788-1234).

DANCING TO LIVE MUSIC

For dinner, dancing, and your first tango in San Francisco, head for the **Tonga Room** in the Fairmont Hotel, at California and Mason (tel. 415/772-5000). Built around what used to be the hotel's swimming pool, the Tonga Room has a South Seas decor complete with thatch-roofed tables and a tropical storm bursting over the pool at random intervals. The band plays in the middle of a lagoon on a roofed barge, and dancing is on what was once the quarterdeck of a three-masted schooner. There's a cover charge of $5 on Friday and Saturday, $4 other nights. The Tonga Room is closed Sunday and Monday. Dancing is from 9pm weekends, 8pm weeknights.

DISCOTHEQUES AND DANCE BARS

They come and go, and the "in" places certainly change with each edition of this book. San Francisco caught "Saturday Night Fever" with a vengeance a few years ago. As a result the entire Bay Area mushroomed with an immense crop of discotheques, ranging from heavenly to hideous, catering to every financial bracket and to a much wider age group than is generally assumed. A handful of the more interesting places are described below.

Considerably more sophisticated than most is **Oz,** on the 32nd floor of the Westin St. Francis, on Powell Street between Geary and Post (tel. 774-0116). No one is allowed in wearing jeans, sneakers, or casual attire. Disco jockeys are supplied by Juliana's of London, a discotheque consulting firm with a chic clientele. Reached via a glass elevator, Oz evokes a lush forest glade complete with trees and ferns—a rather unusual forest glade perhaps, with Tivoli lights moving to the beat of the music and a superb lighting system. The accoutrements are rather plush—a marble bar, cushioned bamboo armchairs and comfortable sofas, even backgammon and chess tables. The music: Top 40, contemporary dance music, both European and American. Oz is actually a private club, but nonmembers can enter by paying a cover of $8 Sunday through Thursday, $15 on Friday and Saturday. There's disco Sunday through Thursday from 9:30pm to 1:30am, on Friday and Saturday to 2:30am (hors d'oeuvres are served nightly to 11pm). The average drink is $6.

I-Beam, 1748 Haight St., at Cole (tel. 415/668-6006 for a recorded message), large and stylishly done, is the spot for rock. Lasers go, and go, and go. It's the home of the floor-quake, with a different vibration each night. Monday brings on line the local and national bands; Tuesday through Saturday the I-Beam moves with rock dancing, video, and laser shows from 9pm to 2am. Weekends attract the Bay Area crowd. Sunday is Gays' Night—there's a tea dance, not like any other you may have attended, which begins at 5pm and goes on to 2am. Video screens feature the latest releases. Admission is $3 to $15 depending on the night and the performers. Drinks are $3 to $5.

Club DV8, 540 Howard St., between 1st and 2nd streets (tel. 415/957-1730), has three huge dance floors, with two DJs playing on different levels. The decor is a spectacular mix of trompe l'oeil, pop art, candelabras, mirrors, and some extraordinary Dali-esque props. Several rooms have been set apart for just talking over a drink or an espresso. The club is open on Wednesday and Thursday from 10pm to 2am, on Friday and Saturday from 9pm to 4am. Drinks average $5 to $6.

The youth of the city gravitate, in part, to **City Nights,** 715 Harrison St., at 3rd (tel. 415/546-7774). The establishment has the largest dance floor in the city, large-screen videos, a laser-light spectacular, and music to fit almost any taste. Come have lunch during the day. But nightlife begins on Wednesday with a great modern music format; Thursday through Saturday are Top 40 nights, beginning at 9:30pm and going on through 2am. Those 18 and over are admitted every night. Cover charge is $7 on Wednesday, $8 on Thursday and Friday, and $10 on Saturday. Drinks average $3.50.

Then there's **Firehouse 7,** 3160 16th St., at Guerrero (tel. 415/621-1617), once (you guessed it) a firehouse, now a great disco. If you've always known that you were a friendly soul oriented toward the art, music, and film set, Firehouse 7 is your disco destiny. A good local rock or reggae band usually inhabits the premises every Friday, and there's DJ dance music nightly except Monday, which is Film Showcase night, when experimental films are screened. And don't miss (as though you could) the display of oversize artworks. Firehouse 7 is open daily from noon to 2am. Drink prices are reasonable—about $3.50. Firehouse 7 requires that you be over 21 and have appropriate ID for proof of age.

SOME GAY SPOTS

As I mentioned before, there's a gay bar for every style, with male clientele ranging from cowboy to leather to the three-piece suit. The greatest density of bars and dance establishments is to be found in the Castro, South of Market, and Mission sections of town. As to where to find a comprehensive listing of bars, dance/bars, restaurants, and brief descriptions of the clientele, see "Information" in Section 4 of Chapter II. The majority of the bars and dance establishments have a male clientele, and now and then a smattering of women. Comparatively speaking, the number of lesbian bars is quite small.

Below I've listed a few of the gay establishments where almost anyone, with the possible exception of Aunt Minnie from Duluth, would feel comfortable. You won't find the "fake ID crowd" of childlike yuppies, nor will you get a watered-down drink. What's more, the person at the door will have more the personality of a pleasant barkeep than a hostile bouncer.

Among the gay dancing and social establishments, **The Stud,** 399 9th St., at Harrison (tel. 415/863-6623), is one of San Francisco's classics. Contrary to the intensely aggressive sound of its name, The Stud is really rather relaxed and comfortable. The interior has an antiques-shop look, with a miniature train circling overhead above the dance floor and the bar; a pool table shares the bar's premises.

The crowd at The Stud is primarily male, though there may be a few women about, and dress is casual but neat. The dance style is whatever you want, the music a mix of old and new hits. If you want to glow in the dim dance-floor light, wear white so the ultraviolet light can pick you out; there's a wall of mirrors that reflects the glow-in-the-dark crowd.

(*Note:* If you must use the restroom facilities and want privacy, a friend advises that you use the women's facility.)

The Stud is open nightly from 8pm to 2am. Drink prices average $2.50. Friday and Saturday, there's a $2 charge for admission. You must be 21 or older and the doorman will check your ID.

Rawhide II, 280 7th St., off Folsom (tel. 415/621-1197), is perhaps the town's top country-and-western dance bar, albeit it's mostly gay. Rawhide II is a friendly place and you will find a few women there. Dress is mostly western: cowboy hats, western buckles, and neat jeans with or without chaps. Whether you plan to socialize, drink, or whatever, it's fun to watch—even more fun to participate in—the country-and-western dancing. For the most part it's waltzing in twos, otherwise stylized dancing in large groups—a bit like clogging. The music is classic country. For those who'd like to learn country and western dancing, there are free lessons Monday through Thursday from 7:30 to 9:30pm.

Rawhide II is open nightly for dancing and socializing from 7:30pm to 2am. Drinks average $2.25. There's no doorman and no charge for admission.

The **Twin Peaks Tavern,** 401 Castro, is right at the intersection of Castro, 17th, and Market (tel. 415/864-9470). It's one of the Castro's most famous hangouts. It's also one of the few gay bars with windows so you can look in and decide if it's your scene. Twin Peaks has an older, relaxed crowd and a pleasant men's-bar style. The place is relatively small, and on weekends it's generally packed by about 8pm.

Twin Peaks is open daily from noon to 2am. Drinks average $2.

The **I-Beam** is described above in the "Discotheques and Dance Bars" section. It's a super dance bar, and Sunday is Gays' Night.

PUBS AND BARS

To begin with the unusual, there's **Edinburgh Castle,** 950 Geary St., near Polk (tel. 415/885-4074), a Scottish pub complete with live bagpipe music on Saturday nights. Scottish coats-of-arms hang from the ceilings, the bartender is from Dundee, and the jukebox is heavy on Scottish airs. Of course there's a dart board, and the fare is the likes of fish and chips with Scottish draft beer to wash it down. It's lots of fun, and stays open to 1am Sunday through Thursday, to 2am on Friday and Saturday.

For sardine-packed singles action, there's no place like **Perry's,** 1944 Union St., at Buchanan (tel. 415/922-9022). The clientele includes many over-30s and tends to the yuppie class—successful lawyers, businesspeople, stewardesses—what New Yorkers would call an Upper East Side crowd. There are several dining areas (the bar action is up front), all very charming with such accoutrements as blue-and-white-checked tablecloths, candlelight, ivy climbing the walls, and hanging plants. Posted menus list simple fare like hamburgers (they're good), along with a wide selection of fresh fish, grilled steaks, and salads. On the walls are framed newspaper clippings of events like the moonwalk, movie posters, and other memorabilia. Drinks average $2.50 to $3.50. If you don't meet anyone, you can always browse through magazine-rack periodicals like the *Village Voice, The New Yorker,* or even the *New York Times.* Open nightly till 2am.

Laid-back and comfortable, **Specs,** 12 Saroyan Place, near the intersection of Broadway and Columbus (tel. 415/421-4112), is more or less a poets' and acting-types' bar. (Once Adler Place, the street name was changed in honor of William Saroyan, whose play *The Time of Your Life* was set in a bar in the area.) More or less, because the clientele is diverse, including white-collar conservatives, aging hippies, and seamen. Glass-fronted cupboards are filled with San Francisco memorabilia, scrimshaw, and other items given to Specs (who is usually behind the bar, by the way) by seamen who frequent the place. Entertainment is varied: You might catch a session by a musician from Ireland, Scotland, or Australia, or listen in as a local poet declaims. Unpredictability is the greatest asset of an evening here. Hours are from 4:30pm weekdays (from 5pm weekends) to 2am nightly. Drinks range up from $2.50; beer and wine run $1.50 to $2.50; cheese and crackers, $2.

Vesuvio Café, at 255 Columbus Ave., near Broadway (tel. 415/362-3370), across the newly renamed Jack Kerouac Alley from City Lights Bookstore, is one of those rare North Beach bars that has endured the '50s, the beatnik and hippie years, and maintained its character even into the current "me" years. Vesuvio is a neighborhood hangout for writers and poets, artists and songsters, longshoremen, seamen, cabdrivers and yuppies, not to mention domestic and imported tourists. The decor consists largely of biweekly exhibits by local painters and photographers of nudes; to add to the atmosphere, an antique slide machine projects photographs of women caught on film in the early years of this century. Vesuvio features espresso and cappuccino, well drinks at $2.50, and an abundance of reasonably priced mixed drinks. San Francisco–brewed Anchor Steam beer is served on draft. Wines ($1.75 and up) are sold by the glass. Vesuvio doesn't serve food, but customers can bring their own sandwiches or whatever. Vesuvio is open from 6am to 2am, 365 days a year. No credit cards are accepted.

For ambience, you can't beat the **Rusty Scupper,** 1800 Montgomery St. at Francisco, just a few blocks from Fisherman's Wharf (tel. 415/986-1180). With its raw-redwood exterior, raw-fir interior, and knotty-pine ceilings, the Scupper looks like a posh ski lodge. Candles glow on tables of ceramic tile or highly polished maple, leafy greenery abounds in the way of hanging and potted plants (there are even trees), and a few very fine rugs and patchwork quilts adorn the walls. The Scupper occupies two floors; upstairs areas are more intimate, with banquettes arranged in little alcoves. It's a lovely place for drinking, dining (anything from cheeseburgers to Chinese shrimp scampi on this unique menu), and relaxed hanging out. Open weekdays for lunch from 11:30am to 2pm, and for dinner nightly, from 5:30 to 9pm weekdays and 5 to 10pm weekends.

MOSTLY FOR MUSIC

Entertainment at the **Last Day Saloon,** 406 Clement St., between Fifth and Sixth avenues (tel. 415/387-6343), runs the gamut of rock 'n' roll, country rock, blues, jazz-rock, and Cajun, with dancing nightly. It's a pretty, two-level place with shag-carpeted floors, barnwood walls, large pots of hanging plants, and flowers on the rough wood tables. The cover charge ranges from $4 to $8, and there's always a one-drink minimum. (Drinks average $3 to $4). There's music daily from 9pm to 2am.

Sarah Vaughan, Wynton Marsalis, Joan Baez, B. B. King, Maynard Ferguson, and Herbie Mann are just a few of the performers who have played at the **Great American Music Hall,** 859 O'Farrell St., between Polk and Larkin. Other nights you may find new *a cappella* groups, satirical comedy, or a folk troubadour. The interior of this turn-of-the-century building is a great open square under carved plaster cupids on the ceiling, with gilded mezzanine boxes supported by huge marble pillars. There also are evenings of music for dancing, usually on weekends, with a wide range of music—from the classic '20s and '30s jazz sounds to the '60s rhythm and blues. The cover usually runs between $10 and $22, depending on who's appearing. Snack food is available, and drinks average $3 to $4. The hall is open two to seven nights a week; call 415/885-0750 to find out who's appearing.

Right across the street from Louise M. Davies Symphony Hall and the War Memorial Opera House is **Kimball's,** 300 Grove St., at Franklin (tel. 415/861-5585 or 861-5555), a handsome old brick building converted to a good-looking, comfortable two-level restaurant and jazz club. It's a great stop for a nightcap. There's live music featuring some of the top world-class performers on the jazz scene. What's more, the food's good. Lunch is served from 11am to 2pm. Kimball's is open Tuesday through Saturday to 1am; however, closing time depends on whether or not there is a show. Cover is $3 to $15, depending on the performer. It's best to call.

Milestones, 376 5th St., at Harrison (tel. 415/777-9997), became part of the San Francisco jazz scene just five years ago. Since that time it has made a name as one of the top jazz clubs in town. It books headliners as well as the best of local talent into its elegant and award-winning listening scene. The tone here is intimate, in contrast to a few of the larger, cooler establishments. If you enjoy soft lights and warm jazz, you'll like Milestones. The cover is $5 for evening performances. The club is open Monday through Friday from 4pm to 2am, on Saturday from 6pm to 2am, and on Sunday to 1am. There's a jazz matinee on Sunday from 5 to 9:30pm.

The **New Orleans Room** is located in the Fairmont Hotel, 950 Mason St., at California (tel. 415/772-5259). It's the new home of Don Neely's Royal Society Six, playing some of the purest '30s and '40s swing to be heard on the West Coast. The group performs every Tuesday through Saturday from 9:30pm to 1:30am. Jimmy Price and Friends take the stage on Sunday and Monday. The New Orleans Room is open nightly from 6pm. Cover is $5.

COMEDY

For all those who especially enjoy stand-up comedy, there's a great treat in store during August: the annual stand-up comedy competition—once a helping hand to the careers of Robin Williams, Marsha Warfield, and Dana Carvey (Roseanne Barr didn't make it to the semifinals in 1984!). Competitors are chosen from 500 applicants, preliminary rounds taking place throughout the Bay Area; major networks send scouts to the finals. Admission varies from $9 to $18. Performances generally start at 8:30 or 9pm. For detailed information on places and times, call Underground Comedy at 415/383-8394.

Holy City Zoo, 408 Clement St., between Fifth and Sixth avenues (tel. 415/386-4242), is a warm and woody place that offers a comedy format seven nights a week. Local and visiting headliners present a professional showcase Wednesday through Saturday. Sunday and Tuesday are "open-mike" nights, when amateurs and professionals drop in to try out new routines on the audience. Monday highlights the All-Pro Comedy Showcase. Usually three professionals entertain on Friday and Saturday nights. An improvisational group called Papaya Juice once played here, and one alumnus of that group made it big playing an alien on television. (You guessed right—Robin Williams.) There's a nightly cover charge ranging from $4 to $10 and a two-drink minimum Wednesday through Sunday. It is best to call ahead because showtimes do vary. Nonetheless, there's usually a 9pm show, plus one at 11pm on Friday and Saturday.

Punch Line, 444 Battery St., between Washington and Clay (tel. 415/397-7573), upstairs on the plaza level, is the largest comedy nightclub in the city. It has been San Francisco's premiere comedy club since 1978, showcasing top talent plus up-and-coming comedians. Three-person shows with top national and local talent are featured Tuesday through Saturday. Showcase night is on Sunday, with 15 to 20 up-and-comers, and there's an all-star showcase, or a special event, on Monday night. Showtime is 9pm Sunday through Thursday, plus 11pm on Friday; there are three shows on Saturday, at 7, 9, and 11:30pm. The usual cover is $4 on Sunday, $6 on Monday through Thursday, $8 on Friday and Saturday, with a two-drink minimum; drinks start at $2.50. You must be 18 or over, and ID is required. Major credit cards are accepted at the Punch Line. It's advisable to buy tickets ahead of time if you don't want to wait on line. Advance tickets are available through BASS outlets (tel. 415/762-2277).

Cobb's Comedy Club, 2801 Leavenworth, at Beach (tel. 415/928-4320), is in the very handsome Cannery at Fisherman's Wharf. The club gathers an upscale family audience by presenting national headliners such as Bob Saget, Paula Poundstone, Rick Overton, and Bobby Slayton. Kevin Nealon, Rita Rudner, Kevin Pollak, Jim Carrey, and Larry Miller have also performed.

There is comedy every night, including a 13-comedian All-Pro Monday Showcase (a three- to four-hour laugh marathon) for $5. Ticket prices the rest of the week are $7 to $10. There is also a two-drink minimum per person. Drinks average $2.50 to $4.50. Showtimes are 8pm on Monday, 9pm Tuesday through Sunday, plus an 11pm performance on Friday and Saturday. Cobb's is open to those 18 and over, and those 13 to 17 accompanied by a parent or legal guardian. The club is a short walk from most major Wharf-area hotels; however, if you're driving, Cobb's offers three-hour validated parking at the nearby Anchorage Garage, 500 Beach St.

San Francisco has been the launching pad for many movements, causes, trends, fads, politicians, and an assortment of creative types. It's also home to the **Improvisation** (known to one and all as the **Improv**), the original comedy showcase, which has featured a remarkable galaxy of superstars, not the least of which is Robin Williams. The Improvisation is at 401 Mason St., at the corner of Geary (tel. 415/441-7787). Every night three nationally known comedians are featured. Recent top billing has gone to Karen Anderson, Rob Becker, Rick Corso, Geoff Bolt, etc. Shows are presented Sunday through Thursday at 9pm, on Friday and Saturday at 9 and 11pm. Admission is $6 weekdays, $8 weekends. Drinks range from $2.50 to $5, and there is a full bar. No one under 21 is admitted.

POTPOURRI

The following are places where the entertainment is too varied to be categorized elsewhere.

It's hard to define **Harry's,** 2020 Fillmore St., at California (tel. 415/921-1000). There's jazz piano nightly in this crowded, friendly saloon where Harry Denton holds sway and mingles with politicians, local hoi polloi—young and well beyond the legal drinking age. If for no other reason than to observe the local fauna, or rich blue walls and the huge antique mahogany bar, or just to sit and listen to the music after the ballet or the opera, Harry's is a fun place to be. There's a small but satisfying menu. Harry's is open nightly from 4pm to 2am.

At the **Cow Palace,** Geneva and Santos streets, about 10 miles from downtown near Daly City (tel. 415/469-6000), you're likely to catch anything from the San Francisco Sports and Boat Show to the Golden Gate Kennel Club Dog Show to major entertainers like Lynyrd Skynyrd, The Cult, Neil Diamond, Prince, Aerosmith, and Randy Travis. The Cow Palace has also presented Olga Korbut; is used annually for the Grand National Rodeo, the Horse and Stock Show (October), and Ringling Bros. & Barnum and Bailey Circus; and has hosted two Republican National Conventions (an interesting juxtaposition). Check out the goings on at this 14,500-seat facility. Ticket prices for entertainers vary widely. Tickets are available through BASS/Ticketmaster, Ticketron, major ticket outlets, or the Cow Palace box office.

PIANO LOUNGES

The **Piazza,** in the Parc Fifty Five, 55 Cyril Magnin St., at Market and North 5th streets (tel. 415/392-8000), has one of the most comfortable places in which to relax in handsome plush-velvet chairs and listen to old and new melodies played on a magnificent grand piano. The three-story atrium surrounding the room provides an elegant background for the music, played from noon to 2am.

One of the nicest places in town for piano music is the conservatory-style **Fournou's Bar** at another hotel, the Stanford Court, 905 California St., at Powell (tel. 415/989-3500). In an extremely luxurious (not to say romantic) setting, windows all around provide splendid views in every direction, including the bay.

The Mark Hopkins, just up the street at 1 Nob Hill (tel. 415/392-3434), also has a pianist entertaining nightly, in a delightfully intimate room with hand-painted murals—the skylighted **Lower Bar,** just off the lobby. It's another very simpatico environment in which to enjoy drinks and music.

And if you're in a quiet, romantic mood, the intimacy of the **Act IV Lounge** at the Inn at the Opera, 333 Fulton St., near Franklin (tel. 415/863-8400), is a delight. The pianist at the grand plays melodies that soothe the spirit as comfortably as the throw cushions on the handsome green-velvet chairs, the fireplace, and the overstuffed sofas. The lounge is open to 1:30am.

AROUND SAN FRANCISCO BAY

With San Francisco as your base, you can explore nearby areas that range from the vineyards of Napa Valley to the ancient redwood forests, to sun-drenched missions (why does this sound like the lyrics to a song?) and one of America's greatest universities. All these destinations—and many more—can be seen in day trips from San Francisco and are reached in a few hours at most, by car or public transport. We'll begin with some fascinating forays in and around San Francisco Bay, traveling counterclockwise. In the next chapter, we'll investigate the Wine Country, and in Chapter V, we'll see what's to the south. First, then, a short and delightful excursion to:

1. Angel Island

This 730-acre island is a state park (tel. 415/435-1915), popular for bicycling, hiking, fishing, and picnicking. The park is open from 8am to sunset.

GETTING THERE
The **Red and White Fleet** (tel. 415/546-2896) sails from San Francisco's Pier 43½ to Angel Island. Round-trip fares, including admission to the park, are $8 for adults, $5 for children 5 to 11, free for younger ones. For year-round transportation, you can take the **Tiburon–Angel Island Ferry** (tel. 415/435-2131). From June to Labor Day (weekdays 10am to 4pm, weekends to 6pm) the ferry runs daily; the rest of the year it operates on weekends and holidays only (10am to 4pm). Round-trip

fares are $5 for adults, $3 for children 5 to 11. There's a $1 charge for bringing a bike. You can catch the ferry directly behind Christopher's Restaurant in Tiburon.

WHAT TO SEE AND DO

To explore the island, you can bring a bike or just hike along the many trails. There are picnic sites with tables, benches, barbecues, and restrooms at **Ayala Cove,** where you land, and at **West Garrison.** If you like hiking, 12 miles of trails lead you around the island and to the peak of **Mount Caroline Livermore,** 776 feet above the bay.

One more possible activity: If you feel like digging in the dirt, know that it's rumored pirates and smugglers once hid treasures on the shores of Angel Island.

---

2. Oakland

The name Oakland derives from the oak groves in which the city's first homes were constructed in the mid-19th century. Today a sprawling industrial port town of about 330,000 (the largest East Bay city), Oakland is no longer a few homes in the forest. But what the city lacks in charm is made up for in its several outstanding attractions.

GETTING THERE

To get to Oakland, you can drive over the Oakland Bay Bridge, take a direct bus from the Transbay Terminal (Mission and 1st streets) for $2 ($3 round trip), or take BART from Powell Street to Oakland City Center for $1.65.

WHAT TO SEE AND DO

For maps and detailed information on Oakland's attractions, stop in at the **Oakland Convention & Visitors Bureau,** 1000 Broadway (tel. 415/839-9000). It's open weekdays from 8:30am to 5pm.

First and most central, in the heart of downtown, is **Lake Merritt,** a 155-acre body of salt water (the largest natural tidal body of salt water wholly within an American city) that is Oakland's favorite recreation spot. Part of the lake is a refuge for wild ducks and other waterfowl; in winter the bird count sometimes goes as high as 5,000, and birds banded here have been traced as far away as Siberia.

The lake is encircled by Lakeside Park, off Grand Avenue, which is the setting for **Children's Fairyland** (tel. 415/452-2259). Entered via the home of the "Old Woman Who Lived in a Shoe," Fairyland features over 60 nursery-rhyme attractions, plus magic shows, live animals, clowns, dancers, musicians, and storytellers. Puppet shows are held at 11am and 2 and 4pm. In summer it's open daily from 10am to 4:30pm; in spring and fall, Wednesday through Sunday from 10am to 4:30pm; and in winter, weekends and holidays from 10am to 4:30pm.

On the west shore of Lake Merritt you can rent rowboats, sailboats, and canoes. Adjacent to Lake Merritt, the **Oakland Museum,** 1000 Oak St. (tel. 273-3401, or 834-2413 for recorded information), is five blocks east of I-880. As of this writing, you can still get there on 880 if you are going north. Another option for driving is taking Hwy. 580 to 980 and getting off at Jackson Street. But far and away the easiest way to get there is to take the BART and get off at the Lake Merritt station, which is one block from the museum.

The Oakland Museum is more appropriately called the Museum of California because it is just that—including just about everything you would want to know about the state, its people, history, culture, geology, art, environment, and ecology. And it has all been assembled within the award-winning architectural design of Kevin Roche (once a member of the Eero Saarinen group). It's a graceful building quietly nestled in the heart of the city and set down among the beauties of sweeping gardens and terraces designed by landscape architect Don Kiley. It's actually three museums in one and a great introduction to California's richness and diversity. The museum's collections boast the work of California artists, from Bierstadt to Diebenkorn; artifacts from California's history, from Pomo basketry to Country Joe McDonald's guitar; and re-creation of California habitats, from the coast to the White Mountains.

From time to time the museum has major shows devoted to California artists. Currently being assembled and scheduled to open in 1992 is a large show of California arts and crafts from 1890 to 1930. As the time approaches, you might call the museum for a specific date.

The Natural Sciences Gallery's recently completed Walk Across California cuts a swath from the coast to the Sierras, exhibiting the many-faceted nature of the terrain and its inhabitants. New aquatic exhibits are being added to the gallery's side bays.

The museum, in fact, is in a constant state of evolution. Interactive exhibits are being planned for completion by the end of 1991 for the Cowell Hall of California History. Visitors will then be able to call up a screenful of information about any object in the gallery.

Forty-five-minute guided tours leave the gallery information desks on each level of the museum at 2pm on weekdays and, on request, at gallery entrances on weekends. A simulated trek across California is offered in the Hall of California Ecology at 1:30pm each Saturday and Sunday. On the first and third Sundays of the month, a tour of highlights in the galleries and gardens starts from the first level of the main lobby.

To further your interest and knowledge about this magnificent state, the museum's History, Natural Sciences, and Art Guilds offer some great one-day and weekend tours to history-laden places. The sites vary throughout the year. There may be a discovery trip to Half Moon Bay, following the old stagecoach trail; a visit to some very exceptional homes—one by architect Willis Polk, two designed by Frank Lloyd Wright; a walk around San Francisco's three famous hills—Nob, Russian, and Telegraph; etc. There is a fee, and groups are limited in size. For information about current tours by the Guilds, call the main museum number (above).

There's a fine museum café, inexpensive parking, and a gallery (tel. 834-2296) that sells works by California artists. An interesting place to browse is the book and gift shop (tel. 834-2129), where you'll find not only books and posters but attractive jewelry and wearable art by California artists.

Admission to the museum is free. It is open Wednesday through Saturday from 10am to 5pm, on Sunday from noon to 7pm; closed Christmas, New Year's Day, and July 4. The snack bar (tel. 834-2329) is open Wednesday through Saturday from 10am to 4pm, on Sunday from noon to 5pm. The garage is open on Saturday from 8am to 5pm and on Sunday from noon to 7pm; the rate is 40¢ per hour for the first three hours, then 50¢ per hour; entrances are on Oak and 12th streets. The primary wheelchair-accessible entrance to the museum is through the garage off Oak Street.

At the end of Oakland's Broadway lies **Jack London Square,** dedicated to the writer, a bust of whom overlooks the scene. At the foot of Webster Street, about a block away, stands the **First and Last Chance Saloon,** 56 Jack London Square, built about a half century ago from the remnants of an old whaling ship. London did some of his writing and much of his drinking here (Robert Louis Stevenson is also supposed to have been a habitué). The corner table London used has remained as it was over 70 years ago, and his photos and other memorabilia abound.

Oakland is also home to hundreds of birds, reptiles, and mammals that roam in the 500-acre **Oakland Zoo** in Knowland Park. For an overall view take the 1,250-foot-long Jungle Lift, which takes you high up over the African Veldt, where animals graze in a natural setting. A train will take you around the zoo. There's also a **Child-**

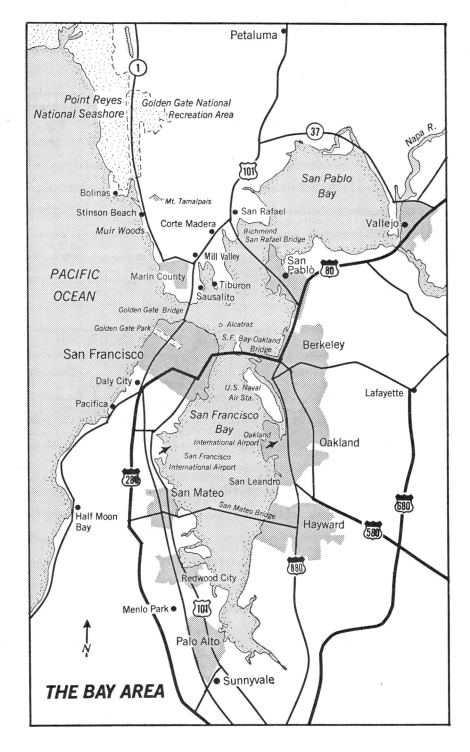

THE BAY AREA

ren's Petting Zoo where children can feed and pet friendly animals. It's open every day except Christmas from 10am to 4pm. Admission is $2.50 for adults, $1.50 for seniors and children 2 to 14. Parking is $2 per car, $6 per bus.

WHERE TO STAY

If you care to stay overnight in the Oakland/Berkeley area, there's a superb hotel choice that is a convenient sightseeing base for both areas (it's just 20 minutes from San Francisco) and a pleasure to stay at even if you never leave the grounds. The **Claremont Resort,** Ashby and Domingo avenues, Oakland, CA 94623 (tel. 415/843-3000), set amid 22 hillside acres, offers every facility, including free airport transfers, a beautiful restaurant, 10 tennis courts, an Olympic-size heated swimming pool, a new European health spa—not to mention very posh digs. And to top it all, there's a spectacular view of the bay. It's something like being a guest at a European castle. Rates are $140 to $220 for a single, $160 to $240 for a double. Suites are $295 to $700.

If you're looking for comfortable, inexpensive shelter, it's hard to beat a **Motel 6.** And there is one at 4919 Coliseum Way, Oakland, CA 94601 (tel. 415/261-7414), located near the I-880 freeway. However, this motel is located in an industrial warehouse district, adjacent to a neighborhood not exactly suited to evening strolls. What's more, you will need to drive a fair distance to a comfortable restaurant. For the same basic rate, consider the Motel 6 at 4301 El Camino Real, Palo Alto, CA 94306 (tel. 415/949-0833), which is about the same drive time to the city, just off U.S. 101, and 4 miles from Stanford University. Rates are $32 for a single, $38 for a double.

---

3. Berkeley

The complete college town, as well as retirement colony for the under-30 set, Berkeley is home to about 30,000 students and probably an equal number of folk who thrive on the campus energy but are enrolled only in the school of life. It has produced 10 Nobel Prize winners and, in the turbulent '60s, countless activists. The only student "town" that matches it in excitement is the St-Michel area of Paris. Berkeley is forever the city of commitment. It's still one of the few towns where, given the right time and the right year, you will see election posters everywhere.

GETTING THERE

To get to Berkeley from San Francisco by car, take the San Francisco–Oakland Bay Bridge (U.S. 80), keep left and turn off onto Ashby Avenue. Or you can simply take the bus from the Transbay Terminal (fare is $2; round trip is $3); it leaves every 15 minutes and goes right to the university. BART will also take you to Berkeley for a fare of $1.80.

If you plan on surveying the area near the campus (it is a bizarre experience), count on walking from some distance away because chances are that you won't find a place to park nearby. There are public parking lots, but you'll need much patience while you wait in line to enter.

WHAT TO SEE AND DO

The hub of student activities is where Telegraph Avenue runs into the university campus at **Bancroft Way.** Here, and all along Telegraph Avenue, you'll find stalls selling jewelry, falafel, tarot card readings, craft items, or whatever. Right across from you is the **Student Union.** Go to the visitor information desk on the second floor and get yourself a map of Berkeley, a local paper, and a brochure outlining a campus walking tour, which you can take on your own or with a guide at 1pm Monday through Friday; it's free and takes a little over 1½ hours.

Other than university-related activities, which can easily fill an entire day, you might want to visit the **Berkeley Marina Yacht Harbor,** a $2-million aquatic sports development on the Berkeley shore of San Francisco Bay, where several hundred private boats and yachts are anchored. The fishing pier extends 3,000 feet into the bay; it's open 24 hours daily, free to the public, with no license required. There are sandy beaches, picnic areas, play areas for children, trails, and lookout points—mostly it's a lovely, tranquil place to be.

WHERE TO STAY

Near the university, the most pleasant place is **Gramma's,** 2740 Telegraph Ave. (four blocks north of Ashby), Berkeley, CA 94705 (tel. 415/549-2145). These charming restored Tudor houses (a main house, carriage house, garden house, and Fay house) have 30 guest rooms altogether, all furnished in period style with antiques, floral-print wallpapers, and pretty patchwork quilts on the beds. All have private baths, phones, and TVs, and larger rooms have sitting areas. Accommodations in the restored carriage house overlook a garden and have fireplaces. Guests are served a complimentary breakfast in the downstairs dining room or on the deck overlooking the garden. Sunday brunch, not included in rates, is also an option.

Rates: $85 to $175, single or double occupancy.

Just one block from the university is the very pleasant **Hotel Durant,** 2600 Durant Ave. (near Bowditch), Berkeley, CA 94704 (tel. 415/845-8981). Built in 1928, it's the only full-service hotel this close to the university. New ownership restored it nicely to keep the best of its earlier days while providing conveniences now expected by vacationers and travelers. The rooms are tastefully furnished; most are quite light, done in pastels, and all have cable TVs, movies, radios, and phones. Some of the rooms can be connected for family groups. Henry's Publick House and Grille is on the premises and serves complimentary breakfast for hotel guests each morning from 7 to 9:30am. Henry's is also open for lunch and dinner.

Rates are $75 to $88 for singles, $88 to $96 for doubles.

On the other hand, if Gallic contemporary is more your cup of tea, Berkeley has that too, at the **French Hotel,** 1538 Shattuck Ave. (directly across from Chez Panisse), Berkeley, CA 94709 (tel. 415/548-9930). It's small, relatively new 18-room establishment with a charming café attached. Guest rooms, all with phones and color TVs, are light, airy, done in quiet grays and blues with warm maroon carpeting. The furnishings are attractive and practical—blue downy comforters and floral-pattern throw-cushions. Stacked sliding white baskets are for your personal things (lessening the possibility of leaving something). The café next door is casual, as you might guess from the exposed-brick walls, rust-colored cement floor, and outdoor tables for enjoying the espresso, croissants, and fresh orange juice. It's a relaxed gathering spot for locals.

Rates at the French Hotel range from $75 to $125, single or double occupancy. Senior citizen, university, and group rates are available by calling the above number.

WHERE TO DINE

If you really want to get the feel of student life, you can eat on campus in the building directly behind the Student Union Building. There are quite a few choices: on Upper Sproul Plaza, the **Terrace** and the **Golden Bear;** on the Lower Sproul Plaza, the **Cafeteria,** the adjacent **Bear's Lair Pub and Coffee House,** and a largish establishment that houses the **Deli** and the **Ice Creamery.** You can check them all out and choose your favorite in a matter of minutes; all offer low-priced food and indoor or al fresco dining.

The main drag here is **Telegraph Avenue,** lined with coffee shops, a wide variety of eateries, bookstores, record stores, head shops, and the like. Currently, the most popular student hangouts (subject to change any minute) are Larry Blake's and Spats.

Larry Blake's R&B Café, 2367 Telegraph Ave., off Durant (tel. 415/848-0886), was a mom-and-pop operation run by Larry and Leona Blake for 45 years. It has become a U.C. Berkeley tradition. A few years ago several employees took it over and made it into *the* place to go in Berkeley. Larry Blake's R&B Café now is one of the hottest blues clubs on the West Coast.

What's more, the restaurant is first-rate. Though the menu primarily reflects traditional American café table fare, the weekly specials are exceptional. To cite a couple: fresh broiled salmon with a fresh-fruit salsa and broiled breast of duck with a luscious raspberry sauce—products of the highly talented chef/owner, Joseph Zahner. The café also has an impressive selection of hamburgers made from freshly ground sirloin, sandwiches, salads, pasta, and such longtime American standards as a broiled top sirloin, ribs, and southern fried chicken. Among a list of "others," the café offers a favorite of mine—"Cajun popcorn"—made with bay shrimp sprinkled with Cajun spices, dipped in beer batter, and fried golden brown. Menu prices range from $4 to $12. As for beverages, Larry Blake's serves 5 varieties of tea, espresso, cappuccino, and 14 varieties of beer, including one by the pitcher. The café has a full bar, and wine is available by the glass.

There are three levels of fun and food at Larry Blake's: the main-floor dining room, the second-floor cocktail lounge for drinks and appetizers, and the subterranean nightclub for live music (blues is the specialty) Monday through Saturday nights, with a jukebox going between sets. Larry Blake's is open Monday through Saturday from 11am to 2am, on Sunday to 10pm.

Spats, 1974 Shattuck Ave., near University (tel. 415/841-7225), abounds in Victorian funk and junk—overstuffed couches, antiques, musical instruments, and not just a mounted elk head but a whole stuffed elk. There's a garden room under a skylight ceiling in back, its walls painted with a psychedelic jungle scene. Exotic drinks—such as the Company Z's Mai Tai, described as "a fishbowl full of rums, fruit brandies, and fruit juices, garnished like a Hawaiian wedding"—are featured. You can also dine here on fare ranging from moussaka to veal scallopine to quiche with salad and fruit, for $8 to $14. Open for lunch Monday through Friday from 11:30am to 4pm; hours on Saturday and Sunday are 4pm to 2am.

Alice Waters' **Chez Panisse,** 1517 Shattuck Ave., between Cedar and Vine (tel. 415/548-5525), has been acclaimed as one of the most innovative restaurants in the state. Or to put it another way, if you have never heard of this restaurant and its creator, surely you've been on another planet. California cuisine is so much a product of Waters' genius that all other restaurants, west and east, following in her wake should be dated "A.A.W." (after Alice Waters). A redwood cottage, it's sheltered from the bustle of the street by a lovely garden and patio where guests may sip wine while waiting for tables. There are two separate dining areas—the upstairs café and the downstairs restaurant—and both offer a Mediterranean-inspired cuisine.

The upstairs café has displays of pastries and fruit and large bouquets of fresh flowers on an oak bar. The menu changes daily, according to the best and freshest ingredients, and is posted out front; luncheon entrees are à la carte. Offerings might include a delicately smoked gravlax or a roasted eggplant soup with pesto, followed by an entree of lamb ragoût garnished with apricots, onions, and spices, served with couscous. Your luncheon tab will average $14 to $18, including the gratuity and tax. A glass of wine will usually add another $4. At night there's a brick-oven pizza, as well as salads and other entrees similar to those offered at lunch; other delights might include a fabulous calzone, stuffed with mozzarella, goat cheese, and prosciutto. The homemade pastas are just as exceptional. Lunch is served Monday through Thursday from 11:30am to 3pm, on Friday and Saturday to 4pm. Dinner is served Monday through Saturday from 5 to 11:30pm. Reservations for lunch may be made the same day, starting at 9am. Dinner reservations are not taken for the café, so your wait may be lengthy; but allow for the time—the food is superb.

In the cozy downstairs restaurant, only one prix-fixe five-course gourmet dinner is served each night, though there are four seatings: 6, 6:30, 8:30, and 9:15pm. The menu has changed daily since the restaurant opened in 1971 and is posted for each day of the week on Saturday (outside the restaurant). The dining area, paneled in redwood, has a working fireplace, art deco lamps, and big bouquets of fresh flowers everywhere. A typical dinner here might include pan-fried oysters with Chino Ranch curly endive, spinach-and-fennel soup, veal saltimbocca, straw potatoes, salad, and blood-orange ice cream in almond-cookie cups. The prix-fixe dinner is $55 *plus* gratuity and tax, which brings us up to about $150 for two, without wine. Is this expensive? Of course. Is it worth it? Absolutely. The wine list ($20 to $200) is excellent, as you might expect. The downstairs restaurant is open Tuesday through Saturday, and reservations are absolutely essential; they are taken up to one month in advance.

Note: There is no smoking in either dining area, but you may smoke in the bar area.

For Berkeley breakfasts I like **Smokey Joe's Café,** 1620 Shattuck Ave., between Cedar and Lincoln (tel. 415/548-4616), a traditional Berkeley hangout with walls plastered with protest posters, leaflets, and messages. It's a small place with pale-yellow walls and seating at the counter or tables. For those who insist on absolute tidiness, or who must have meat with breakfast or lunch, this is *not* the place to dine. But for those who enjoy out-of-this-world omelets, or scrambled eggs assembled with creative joy (rather like a tossed salad), or light multigrain pancakes with optional blueberries or bananas, etc., this is the unbeatable place for a hearty breakfast. On weekends you can try the homemade waffles. Smokey Joe's also features fresh-squeezed orange and grapefruit juice (heavenly!).

If by some chance you're more in the mood for lunch, there's the Big Mama Mushroom Sandwich, with egg and melted cheese served on whole wheat bread and topped with a bit of salad; the Holy Mole Frijole Bowl, a sort of do-it-yourself burrito; or El Amigo Cheese Torta Supreme, translated as a crusty base of bread smothered in refried beans, cheese, potatoes, onions, and mole sauce—all heaped with salad and topped with sour cream. Imported beers are available. Prices average about $4 to $7.

Open daily from 8am to 3pm.

Should your sweet tooth act up in Berkeley, head for **Cocolat,** a chocoholic's paradise over at 1481 Shattuck, near Vine (tel. 415/843-3265). You simply can't believe that heaven comes in so many forms of chocolate indulgence. Handmade truffles from an old French recipe are the specialty here, made fresh every day. Then there are chocolates filled with eau de vie (pear, raspberry, quince, kiwi, or Kirsch) that burst as you bite into them. Tortes and cakes are also available. You might indulge in Tricolor Mousse—three chocolate mousses in one—or in Chocolate Decadence, caressed by whipped cream and slices of truffle surrounded by raspberry sauce. Cocolat also has mail-order gifts to delight the heart of any chocoholic. Many of their spectaculars do travel well.

They're open Monday through Saturday from 10am to 6pm, on Sunday from 11am to 5pm. Cocolat now has a second East Bay location, at 3945 Piedmont Ave., in Oakland (tel. 415/653-3676). Pastries are served at table at four of Cocolat's closest locations—the two East Bay locations noted and in San Francisco at 4106 24th St. (tel. 415/647-3855) and 2119 Fillmore St. (tel. 415/567-1223), both open daily. A third store in San Francisco is at 655 Montgomery St. (tel. 415/788-5778), open weekdays from 8am to 6pm.

Just around the corner at 2122 Vine is **Delicktables,** where gelato (Italian ice cream) can be obtained. They also serve soup, sandwiches, cappuccino, espresso, and other desserts. Summer hours are 10am to 11pm Sunday through Thursday, to midnight on Friday and Saturday. During the winter the shop closes an hour earlier.

4. Muir Woods

One of the best things about San Francisco is that just a half-hour drive away is a 500-acre redwood forest, Muir Woods, one of the most impressive sights in America. It's rumored that even the late Charles de Gaulle was reduced to silence when he viewed these trees.

The redwood trees (or *Sequoia sempervirens*) you'll see here, among the tallest trees on the planet, are also among its longer-lived inhabitants. At the entrance to Muir Woods a cross section of a fallen tree shows growth rings attesting to its birth before the Normans conquered England.

This magnificent forest was almost lost to advancing civilization in the early 1900s when a water company wanted to dam up Redwood Creek, which gives life to the 300-foot spires. But William Kent, a nearby landowner, persuaded President Theodore Roosevelt to proclaim the area a national monument and name it for the great Scottish-American naturalist, John Muir.

GETTING THERE

To reach Muir Woods, take U.S. 101 north; signs will tell you where to turn off. Admission is free; the gate opens at 8am and closes at sunset. Go during the week if you can and avoid the weekend crowds. There are a visitor center, gift shop, and snack bar; however, I suggest that you have a bite to eat before heading up to Muir Woods.

Be advised that in driving to (and from) Muir Woods the secondary road is a steep series of S curves with very few places to pull over. Be sure to start with ample gas, firm brakes, and good tires. This is not the place to get a flat.

WHAT TO SEE AND DO

There are several trails to follow. A needle-carpeted nature trail will take you to the **Cathedral Grove,** where a group of redwoods rises skyward as if they were chapel walls. Another highlight is the **Family Circle,** where you can see how redwoods reproduce, younger trees forming a circle around the fire-scarred stump of a parent. Hikers may also follow a trail up the slopes of 2,600-foot **Mount Tamalpais.** On all the trails, trailside exhibits, signs, and markers will help guide your way, and picnic areas are provided.

But more impressive than the fact and figures as to height, width, age, etc., are the entrancing beauty and tranquility that pervade the forest, the feelings of peace, awe, and reverence that it inspires. One easily understands the sentiment expressed by Joseph B. Strauss, the builder of the Golden Gate Bridge, in his poem "The Redwoods":

> To be like these, straight, true and fine,
> To make our world, like theirs, a shrine;
> Sink down, Oh, traveler, on your knees,
> God stands before you in these trees.

5. Tiburon

This quaint little town grew up around a railroad settlement, wood-burning locomotives pulling the first trains into Point Tiburon in 1884. (If you really want to go back, though, Miwok Indians lived here in 100 B.C.)

GETTING THERE

You can drive the 18 miles from San Francisco via the Golden Gate Bridge and U.S. 101 (get off at the Tiburon Boulevard exit and take Calif. 131), but it's faster and more pleasant to go by boat. The **Red and White Fleet** (tel. 415/546-2896) ferries leave from Pier 43½ at Fisherman's Wharf several times a day, and the crossing costs $9 round trip for adults, $4.50 for children. You can also catch a ferry to Angel Island from here (see Section 1 on Angel Island, above).

A word of advice about parking in Tiburon. The designation of time limits painted on the curbs on Main Street may be rather faint, and it may be a federal or state holiday, but those who write up tickets hold to the time limit. While the price of the ticket may not break you, it's a nuisance. Therefore if you plan to have lunch, to shop, or just to sightsee, consider using the parking lot on the right just beyond the curve at the end of Main Street. A number of restaurants and shops will validate your parking chit, so ask.

WHAT TO SEE AND DO

The depot where passengers waited for trains, as well as the big ferryboats that met the trains, is still here, now the **Peter Donahue Building.** Today the town is a yacht-club suburb—home to several hundred upper-bracket businesspeople who commute daily to San Francisco offices. The bay view is bewitching, the hill setting glorious, and the living expensive. But the view of the San Francisco Skyline and the islands in the bay almost makes it worth the price. The pace of this seacoast village is sleepy, with whatever action there is centering on **Main Street,** which is lined with ramshackle old frame buildings that house chic boutiques, expensive antique shops, art galleries, and water-view restaurants.

WHERE TO DINE

Virtually all the restaurants listed below have magnificent views of the bay and San Francisco, and that makes for tough competition if your business is situated away from the water. Nevertheless, directly opposite Main Street and Tiburon Boulevard (on Paradise Drive) is a handsome and quite posh plaza with wood-shingled buildings and brick walkways and its own small body of water. You might want to ignore the fitness club, but there is a Chinese restaurant, the Dynasty, the Egret Landing ("an American eatery"), a health-food bar, a bakery, and a small gourmet food market.

One of the most attractive restaurants is **Christopher's** (formerly Sabella's), at 9 Main St. (tel. 415/435-4600). The elegant interior is carpeted in rich blue and gold, the walls paneled in unfinished redwood. There are many beautiful ship models around, including a large one of the *Flying Cloud,* fastest clipper ship of the 19th century. The upstairs dining room, with window walls overlooking the water and San Francisco skyline, is especially lovely. As you might expect, seafood is the specialty of the house. Dinner entrees, costing $13 to $27, range from a superb calamari steak to a filet-mignon/lobster-tail combination. At lunch, when prices are lower, you might try the seafood crêpe with shrimp, scallops, and mushrooms. Open for dining Monday through Thursday from 11:30am to 9pm, Friday through Sunday to 10pm; the bar is open to 1 or 2am, depending on the action.

You can step right off the Red and White ferry, which leaves from Pier 43½ in San Francisco, walk about 10 paces on the landing, and be at **Guaymas Restaurante,** 5 Main St. (behind the Sierra Galleries) (tel. 415/435-6300). You might even make an excursion day of it and, after lunch, take the ferry from the same dock to Angel Island and back.

Guaymas is quite probably the only restaurant in the Bay Area offering the delicious combination of authentic Mexican regional dishes and a spectacular panoramic view of San Francisco and the bay. In clement weather, dining at either of the two outdoor patios adds to this special treat. Guaymas has a beautiful adobe dining room with a beamed ceiling, simple cement flooring sectioned with wood, and a shoulder-high stucco wall—topped with seasonal arrangements and a cactus or two—that comfortably breaks up the dining areas. It's all very attractive and warm.

Guaymas is named after a Mexican fishing village on the Sea of Cortez famous for its harvest of camarones (giant shrimp). The restaurant features a number of dishes prepared with these giant shrimp, as well as specialties such as ceviche; handmade tamales; charcoal-grilled beef, seafood, and fowl; and a variety of regional dishes not usually seen north of the Mexican border. The ceviche appetizer is prepared from fresh fish marinated in lime and lemon juices with chopped onions, tomatoes, jalapeño chiles, cilantro, and avocado. Tamales are made with corn husks, fresh corn masa, chicken or several other stuffings, and red- and green-chile sauces. If they all sound delicious, you can order an assortment of them. Other favorites include the half chicken, prepared with a sauce of chocolate, chiles, fruits, and spices; a delicious roast half duck with pumpkin-seed sauce; and a slowly roasted pork sirloin served with tomatoes, chopped onions, cilantro, serrano chiles, and hot tortillas. The excellent grilled entrees include giant shrimp marinated in lime juice and cilantro (one of my favorites), and a changing selection of spit-roasted meats and fowl. Entrees cost from $9 to $17.50. Several of the appetizers can be ordered in *chica* or *grande* size, depending on your capacity, but in general prices are $3 to $8.

Save room for dessert. Among the tempting choices there's an outrageously delicious fritter with "drunken" bananas and vanilla ice cream ($4.25), or you might opt for the white-chocolate mousse with fresh strawberry sauce ($4). There are margaritas shaken to order, an exceptional selection of tequilas and Mexican beers, mineral waters with fruit flavors, as well as a variety of unusual waters flavored with flowers, grains, or fruits. The restaurant also has a good selection of California wines.

Guaymas is open daily: Monday through Friday from 11:30am to 10pm, on Saturday to 11pm, and on Sunday from 10:30am to 10pm.

Tiburon is liveliest on Sunday afternoons, when weekend boatmen tie up at the open docks of the waterside restaurants and there is much singing, laughter, and general conviviality. For over 60 years now, the traditional place to tie up has been **Sam's Anchor Café** at 27 Main St. (tel. 415/435-4527), a tavern with two 110-foot piers and a large outdoor wooden deck that is filled to overflowing with blithe Sunday spirits from early on; it's laid-back Tiburon's version of the neighborhood bar. Sam's specials are cioppino and fresh seafood items like red snapper piccata with lemon and capers, for $8 to $13; everything is served with sourdough French bread and butter. Open weekdays from 11am, on Saturday from 10am, and on Sunday from 9:30am, closing nightly about 2am.

There's a small place on Main Street without a view, but with pleasant, friendly service, and most important, good food. The name is **Mangia**, 15 Main St. (tel. 415/435-3440), and it's about as unpretentious as a good restaurant can get. The fare at lunch has some standard pizzas, but also some unusual and delicious salads, sandwiches, and house specialties. There's an excellent grilled chicken salad, an outstanding Mangia burger, homemade minestrone with garlic bread and salad, fried calamari, and delicious chicken parmigiana. Lunch can range from $6 to $13, the higher price for a large pizza.

The dinner menu sparkles with house specials. Special pizzas are prepared in individual eight-inch sizes and in a number of exotic combinations, such as prawns and mozzarella, or sautéed calamari, and all are caressed by a marvelous spicy marinara sauce. But it's hard to resist the prosciutto-and-broccoli pizza with basil, oregano, plus mozzarella, parmesan, and romano cheeses—and that's just the start of the special list. Special pizzas range in price from $10 to $14; the standard combinations, for those with more prosaic tastes, from $7 to $13.

Mangia offers pasta in many forms and with many accompaniments: fettuccine Alfredo, carbonara, or with any number of vegetables; linguine simply prepared with garlic, basil, and oil, as well as several other choices. There's always a fish of the day as well as mixed seafood, calamari fried or sautéed, and hot spicy scallops. Among the specialties of the house are an eggplant parmigiana made to order and a steak of the day grilled and finished with garlic butter. Dinner entrees range from $9 to $16 and are served with vegetable garnish and pasta. Mangia serves house wine by the glass or the liter and a good selection of beers.

Mangia is open daily. Lunch is served Monday through Friday from 11:30am to 3pm; dinner, Monday through Friday from 5 to 10:30pm, on Saturday and Sunday from 4 to 10:30pm.

Sweden House Bakery-Café, 35 Main St. (tel. 415/435-9767), has a plant-filled outdoor terrace overlooking the bay for al fresco dining. Inside, the walls are done in yellow-and-white-checked gingham and hung with copper pots and pans, rolling pins, neat little prints, and tapestries. There are fresh flowers on every table and café curtains on the windows. Full breakfasts are served daily, and not just the usual, run-of-the-mill variety. You can have scrambled eggs with a choice of green onions, tomatoes, cheese, mushrooms, shrimp, or slices of smoked salmon. And combination vegetable omelets are offered too. All are served with the restaurant's own toasted Swedish limpa bread. At lunch, there are open-face sandwiches like avocado and bacon with sprouts, or delicious asparagus tips rolled in Danish ham; you can also order such American standards as chicken salad. Garden salads are also an option, and you can have a soup-of-the-day-with-salad combination. Look for the daily luncheon specials too. If you're not up to breakfast or lunch, you can simply sit on the terrace, sip espresso, and enjoy a home-baked Swedish pastry, such as the raspberry-iced, cream-filled napoleon. Everything is very well prepared; prices range from $4 to $8.

Sweden House is open Monday through Friday from 8am to 5pm, on Saturday and Sunday from 8:30am to 7pm. Beer and wine are available.

FINAL LIBATIONS

After a leisurely browse down Main Street and a relaxed meal at one of the above establishments, head over to the **Windsor Vineyards,** around the corner at 72 Main St. (tel. 415/435-3113). This century-old frame building with its twisting spiral staircase is an outlet for the premium estate-grown wines produced by Windsor Vineyards in Sonoma County. Their Victorian tasting room dates to 1888. You may choose from over 30 fine Windsor Vineyards wines for complimentary sampling, including many award winners. Windsor has been awarded more than 180 medals at prestigious wine-tasting competitions since 1987—the list is impressive. Windsor Vineyards also carries a good selection of wine accessories and gifts— glasses, cork pullers, gourmet sauces, posters, maps, etc. Carry-packs are available (they hold six bottles); as of now, only California, New York and New Mexico residents can have their wines shipped home for them. Ask about personalized labels for your own selections. The shop is open Sunday through Thursday from 10am to 6pm, on Friday and Saturday to 7pm. If you drive to Tiburon, they will validate your parking ticket for one hour in the Main Street parking lot next door.

---

6. Sausalito

Even more "consciously quaint" than Tiburon—and making no attempt to hide it—Sausalito is a picturesque seacoast village just 8 miles from downtown San Francisco. Its lovely harbor is filled with vessels of all shapes and sizes, and its streets are lined with restaurants, art galleries, hip boutiques, and shops wherein the arts of candle making, pottery, glassblowing, and scrimshaw are practiced. What other little town can boast eight goldsmiths? But one forgives Sausalito its pretensions.

A slightly bohemian, completely nonchalant, and very relaxed adjunct to San Francisco, Sausalito has scenery and sunshine and lots of very real charm, both because of, and in spite of, its efforts in that direction. It also has a fascinating community of houseboats just north of the village (that's where I left my heart).

GETTING THERE

The village can be reached most gloriously by ferry: both the **Red and White Fleet** (tel. 415/546-2815), for $8 round trip, and **Golden Gate Transit** (tel. 415/ 982-8834 or 457-3110), for $7 round trip, offer service to Sausalito. Or you can travel more prosaically by **Golden Gate bus** (tel. 415/332-6600) for $1.85 one way (have exact fare).

WHAT TO SEE AND DO

Watching the Bay at Work

Don't miss a fascinating exhibit at the **Bay Model Visitors Center,** 2100 Bridgeway (tel. 415/332-3871). Here, in a 1.5-acre model of San Francisco Bay and Delta, the Army Corps of Engineers can make water behave as it does in nature. It's a scientific tool used by engineers, scientists, and planners to analyze problems that can't be resolved through textbooks, experience, or mathematical models alone. It reproduces (in scale) the rise and fall of the tide, the various currents, the mixing of fresh and salt water, and indicates trends in sediment movement.

An introductory film that lasts about 10 minutes orients visitors to the purpose and operation of the Bay Model. You can see the impact of pollution, view the Sacramento and San Joaquin rivers flowing into the bay, and even see the swift current around Alcatraz. Rangers are usually available to answer questions, and the center now also has a 30-minute tour on tape in English, Japanese, German, French, and Spanish. Guided tours are available by reservation for groups of 10 or more. Admission and the taped tour are free. In winter (Labor Day to Memorial Day) the center is open Tuesday through Saturday from 9am to 4pm; in summer (Memorial Day to Labor Day), Tuesday through Friday 9am to 4pm, on Saturday and Sunday from 10am to 6pm.

Note: The model is most interesting when it's actually in operation, and that happens only when a test is being conducted. It pays to call before you go.

Shopping

What everyone does in Sausalito is shop, stroll, and browse. The town's main street, running along the water, is **Bridgeway;** this, along with Princess Street and Caledonia Street, is where most of the action is. The **Village Fair,** 777 Bridgeway, a complex of 30 shops (from a rug-making store to a bath boutique) and restaurants, is a logical place to begin your explorations.

Pegasus Women's Store, 30 Princess St. (tel. 415/332-5624), and **Pegasus Men's Store,** 28 Princess St. (tel. 415/332-1718), just off Bridgeway, are vendors of beautiful leather clothing. In the women's store some of the leathers are so soft they seem to be made of flowing fabric, and their colors are sure to add excitement to a wardrobe. For the fall Pegasus also features beautiful Italian shearling coats and, as always, carries an extensive accessories collection. Along with jackets, coats, and even leather blouses, there are handsome leather belts and purses. Pegasus for men offers ruggedly good-looking jackets in award-winning designs, including a shearling jacket by a California designer, as well as a fine selection of leather briefcases, belts, hats, and wallets. In addition to their off-the-rack items, the people at Pegasus offer their styles customized to ensure a perfect fit. Both shops are open daily from 10am to 5:30pm.

WHERE TO STAY

If you care to spend the night, one of the best places in town is the **Casa Madrona,** 801 Bridgeway, Sausalito, CA 94965 (tel. 415/332-0502). It's a delightful mix of the old and the new: The original building is an 1885 mansion constructed by a lumber baron (madrona is a type of wood), and there's a large new section connecting the mansion with the lower street. The hotel's 32 rooms, cottages, and suites vary widely. Some rooms in the old house are bathless; others have bathrooms with Jacuzzis. The 16 newest rooms—those that range down the hill—are each decorated by a local designer. Lord Ashley's Lookout is decorated in hunter green, camel, and brass with oak trim, in 19th-century style; Le Petit Boudoir is a Victorian hideaway complete with a rose-colored chandelier. There are cottages as well, including the English Gate House, a four-room English cottage with a harbor view. Amenities in the rooms include quilts, telephones, and baskets of luxury shampoos, bath gels, etc. TVs and radios are available on request. Many rooms have bay views and fireplaces.

On the premises is the excellent Casa Madrona Restaurant (tel. 415/331-5888), which offers American cuisine for lunch and dinner daily; there's also Sunday brunch. The wine list is excellent, including a very good selection of French wines. The restaurant serves a complimentary breakfast daily for guests only.

Rates are $90 to $195, single or double occupancy, and the Madrona Villa, a three-room suite, rents for $300. Extra persons pay $10. There's a two-night minimum stay on weekends.

The **Sausalito Hotel,** 16 El Portal, Sausalito, CA 94965 (tel. 415/332-4155), is a charmer located in the heart of the shopping and restaurant area, set between Bridgeway and the bay shore, and conveniently adjacent to the Red and White Fleet dock. All the 15 rooms (8 with private baths) are furnished with pieces that antiques lovers among you will ache to own: beds with massive wooden carved headboards, great wooden dressers, delicate flowered glass lamps, period armchairs. For all this Victorian lushness, the rooms are remarkably uncluttered, their restfulness enhanced by views of the park or bay; some of them open onto public areas, however, and can get noisy on weekend nights. All accommodations have color TVs and phones. The largest, and one of the two most expensive rooms, is the Marquis of Queensbury—the only room with a fireplace, and containing a bed and an ornately carved dresser once owned by Ulysses S. Grant.

Bathless rooms cost $70 to $80; rooms with private bathrooms rent for $95 to $160. An ample Continental breakfast, served informally in the small lobby (it can also be taken to your room), and validated parking are included in the rates. All rooms are on the second floor (no elevator or porter), so leave the steamer trunk at home.

WHERE TO DINE AND DRINK

Sausalito has an abundance of dining choices, from snack bars and coffee shops to swank gourmet restaurants.

Boasting one of the best "bayscapes" in town is **Ondine,** 558 Bridgeway (tel. 415/332-0791). Enter via imposing white doors, and then proceed up a gold-carpeted stairway to a dining area with elegantly appointed tables. The expansive and spectacular view provides most of the decor and creates a delightfully tranquil ambience. A specialty here is roast pheasant Vladimir with vodka and sour cream sauce. If you come before 7pm, a complete dinner, including potage du jour, salad, dessert, coffee, and an entree like broiled salmon or lobster casserole, costs $18 to $25. Ondine is open daily for lunch from 11:30am to 3pm, for dinner from 5:30 to 11pm. Reservations are essential and jackets are required for men.

More terrific views from all directions at the **Spinnaker,** 100 Spinnaker Dr. (tel. 415/332-1500), just off Bridgeway near the ferry landing. Diners sit on comfortable tufted-leather banquettes or chairs facing 14-foot-high picture windows overlooking the bay (the Spinnaker is actually out on the bay). Cork-lined ceilings and fir-trunk columns add a natural note to the elegant decor. Dinner, served from 5 to 10pm daily (from 2pm on Sunday), includes soup or salad, ice cream or sherbet, and coffee. Prices vary from $12 to $20 according to the entree you select. Your choice might include the likes of rex sole meunière, New York steak, or scallops sauté. You can also order à la carte from a more extensive menu at lunch or dinner. Open daily from 11am to 11pm.

One of Sausalito's prettiest on-the-bay eateries is **Scoma's,** 588 Bridgeway (tel. 415/332-9551), with boxes of geraniums lining the entranceway, gray wood-paneled walls, and extremely well-selected antique furnishings. A scrumptious cioppino and linguine with clam sauce are among the Italian-style seafood entrees at this very charming establishment. A la carte menu prices are from $10 to $18, most including a vegetable and rice or pasta. Open for lunch and dinner on Friday and Saturday from 11:30am to 10:30pm, on Sunday to 9:30pm, and on Monday to 10:30pm. Tuesday through Thursday, open for dinner only, from 5:30 to 10:30pm.

A bit farther out of town (about a mile from the main shopping area) is **Guernica,** 2009 Bridgeway (tel. 415/332-1512). It's a delightful, homey place, under the aegis of owner Roger Minhondo, a French Basque. The cuisine is—of course—French Basque as well. It's popular with locals and San Franciscans alike, and justifiably so, for both food and ambience. The dining room is small and cozy, with wood and leatherette booths, and white-clothed tables with flowers and candles; a print of *Guernica* (by Pablo Picasso) adorns one wall. Dinner entrees (costing $12 to $21) come with a soup, salad, and warm crispy rolls. You can choose from delicious dishes like medallions of veal with mustard sauce, paella, rack of lamb, and daily fresh fish specials. Try not to skip dessert; there are chocolate mousse, peach Melba, and (in season) a delicious strawberry tart. Guernica is open Monday through Thursday from 5 to 10pm, on Friday and Saturday to 10:30pm, and on Sunday to 9:30pm. Reservations are advised.

Some of the best Chinese food I've tasted outside of San Francisco is served at the **Feng Nian Chinese Restaurant,** 2650 Bridgeway (tel. 415/331-5300). Feng Nian lies at the south end of a mall near the intersection of Bridgeway and Harbor Drive, well before you get to the main activity in Sausalito (look for the orange awning). A Chinese screen and tall green plants separate the entry area from the dining room and help to reduce the sense of ballroom space when you enter. Glass-covered tabletops, vinyl-covered cushions, paper napkins (even at lunch) always bother me in a good restaurant, but in this case the quality of the food more than makes up for these details.

Feng Nian has such a wide selection of appetizers ($4 to $6.50) that a combination of several would make a delicious meal in itself. The crispy roast duck served with cabbage pickle is a personal preference, but if you'd like an assortment of appetizers, Feng Nian has a flaming combination (enough for two) that includes eggroll, fried prawns, paper-wrapped chicken, barbecued ribs, fried chicken, and teriyaki ($9.50). Should you decide to follow your appetizer with soup, there are nine to choose from, including a sizzling-rice soup with sliced chicken, prawns, mushrooms, and snow peas on a golden rice crust.

As for a choice from the entrees list, the selection isn't easy. At the upper end of the chef's suggestions is the Peking duck, which requires half an hour preparation time, but it's always a superb dish. If you enjoy seafood, try the Twice Sizzling Seafood with prawns, scallops, squid, and fresh vegetables in oyster sauce, prepared at your table. Another dish prepared at table is the sizzling beef with shredded vegetables and a special house sauce. Beef comes in almost every concievable style—Mongolian, Szechuan, Hunan, Mandarin, with ginger, curry, and broccoli, just to name a few of the choices. Feng Nian offers over 90 main dishes, including a select number of entrees for vegetarians. Beef, pork, poultry, and vegetable entrees are in the $6 to $8 range, with the obvious exception of Peking duck ($25). Seafood dishes are $9 to $16, though most are about $9. The luncheon special also offers many choices ($4 to $5.50) with appetizer, soup, and fried rice, served from 11:30am to 2:30pm on Monday, and Wednesday through Friday. Feng Nian offers sake, wine, and several Oriental and domestic beers.

Feng Nian is open Monday, and Wednesday through Friday from 11:30am to 9:30pm, on Saturday and Sunday to 10pm; the restaurant is closed Tuesday.

For a drink and conversation, stop in at the local hangout—the **Bar with no name,** 757 Bridgeway (tel. 415/332-1392), a great-looking tavern, easy to overlook, with oak wainscoting, comfortable cushioned chairs, and stained-glass panels in the front door. It's now owned by two Englishmen, formerly by a cat named Cinderella. It was originally started by four partners who couldn't agree on a name. It's a very low-key kind of place—reminds you of the White Horse Tavern in New York's Greenwich Village. There's always good taped music playing, plus a shelf of books to read and a game of Scrabble or backgammon in progress. Live classic jazz is heard Wednesday through Saturday nights from 9pm to 1am and on Sunday from 3 to 7pm; no cover. In the delightful garden out back you can relax amid vines and plants hanging from a slatted wood arbor. The bar attracts local artists, yacht skippers, poets, and (of course) tourists. Drinks start at about $2.75. A Ramos Fizz is the house specialty, as are ports and sherrys. Hours are 10am to 2am daily.

7. Marine World Africa USA

GETTING THERE

About 10 miles south of the Napa wine country, and a bit less than 30 miles northeast of San Francisco off I-80 (exit at Calif. 37), is the new 160-acre Marine

World Africa USA, 1000 Fairgrounds Dr. in Vallejo (tel. 707/643-ORCA for a recorded announcement). It's less than an hour's drive up I-80, or you can have the fun of taking the **Red and White Fleet** high-speed catamaran from Pier 41 at Fisherman's Wharf (tel. 415/546-2896, or toll free 800/445-8880 in California), past Alcatraz and the Golden Gate Bridge, and be there in 55 minutes, including a brief bus ride. The round trip, including admission, is $37 for adults, $30 for seniors over 60 and juniors 13 to 18, $20 for kids 4 to 12.

WHAT TO SEE AND DO

Marine World Africa USA features animals of land and air in spectacular shows and innovative habitats; some even stroll the park with their trainers, meeting visitors face to face. Count on participation in the shows—it's a big part of your enjoyment and education as a visitor. Throughout the day a variety of events are scheduled. There's a **Killer Whale/Dolphin Show** where seven rows of wet-area seats are saved for guests who want a thorough drenching. In the **Sea Lion Show** you can be a recipient of one of the many kisses handed out by some of the oldest and largest performers in the country.

When you cross the bridge over the waterfalls, through the trees, and past the flamingos, you enter Africa. At the **Elephant and Chimpanzee Show** the young elephants kick beachballs to the spectators. The **Parrot and Predatory Bird Show** is remarkable in its beauty and in the skill of the birds, as is the incredible **Butterfly World**. And the **Wildlife Show** at the **Ecology Theater** teaches us what a precarious foothold wildlife has on the earth. Then there's the beautiful **Magic of Animals** at the **Showcase Theater.** You'll leave the **Tiger and Lion Show** with a new understanding of what's required to work with 14 lions and tigers as a group. **The African Animal Exhibit** is another spot you don't want to miss in the **Tiger Island/Cove.** In the **Small Animal Petting Corral,** you can make a friend of a llama for a handful of food you can buy there. Or if the spirit of adventure is in your soul, take a ride on an Asian elephant or a dromedary camel.

You may be sorry you're not a child again when you see the unique playground, the **Gentle Jungle,** which combines education, fun, and adventure. It's one of the most innovative play areas of its type. Among other things, children can crawl through burrows in the prairie dog village and pop up into Plexiglas domes so they learn to see the world through the eyes of these cute little animals.

And finally, there's a 55-acre lake (once a golf course) that is the stage for a **Water Ski and Boat Show.** Daredevil athletes jump, spin, and even hang-glide while wearing waterskis.

A wide variety of fast food is available at the restaurant plaza—everything from burgers and pizza to nachos and chicken. Prices are moderate, averaging about $6 to $7 in total. A sit-down restaurant completes the food choices. Or you can bring your own food—there are also barbecue facilities on the grounds.

Marine World Africa USA (tel. 707/643-6722) is open daily during the summer (Memorial Day through Labor Day) from 9:30am to 6pm; it's open Wednesday through Sunday for the balance of the year, with hours to 5:30pm during the spring and fall, to 5pm during the winter. Admission is $19 for adults, $14 for children 4 to 12, $15 for seniors over 60, and free for under-4s. Credit cards are accepted. The price covers all shows: dromedary/camel and elephant rides will add $4. Tickets to Marine World Africa USA are available through Ticketron. All shows and attractions are handicapped-accessible except the elephant and dromedary rides and the Whale-of-a-Time Playground. Some pathways are too steep for easy access, but alternative routes are available.

Note: The best way to cope with the full schedule of shows is to get there early, make up your own itinerary from the leaflet and map given you at the entrance, and then stick to it. Otherwise, you'll find yourself missing parts of each presentation and feeling frustrated.

THE WINE COUNTRY

You're about to enter the Wine Country, one of the most uniquely lovely and fascinating areas of California. Some of the wineries date back to the days of the Franciscan fathers, who planted the first vines as they built their missions. Of course, in those days all the wine was—ostensibly—for sacramental use. Today the many wineries of this picturesque district are giving stiff competition to those in France. A drive through the Wine Country, stopping for tours here and there, and a picnic lunch en route, is one of the most delightful outings I can imagine.

A similarly enjoyable day can be spent exploring historic Sonoma, which sprang up around the last of the missions. More wineries here too, if you've not yet quenched your thirst. Then take a slight detour west from Sonoma and visit Fort Ross, founded by the Russians in 1812 (did you know that the Russians once occupied parts of California?).

Before you head into the Wine Country, you may want to visit the **Wine Institute,** 425 Market St., Suite 1000, San Francisco, CA 94105 (tel. 415/512-0151), for a free copy of *California Is Wine Country,* which tells about wineries throughout the state. If you write for it, please enclose a stamped, self-addressed no. 10 envelope. Once in the Wine Country, you can also pick up a free copy of the *Wine Country Review,* a weekly newspaper full of information on every aspect of Napa, Sonoma, and the other wine regions.

There's also a guide to over 100 wineries north of San Francisco available from the **Visitors Information Center of the Redwood Empire Association,** 185 Market St., 15th Floor, San Francisco, CA 94103 (tel. 415/543-8334); they are open Monday through Friday from 9am to 4:30pm. If you write for the guide, enclose $1 for postage and handling.

1. The Napa Valley

Nestled in the coastal mountain range some 50 miles north of San Francisco, this fertile valley has close to 31,000 acres of vineyards, and it produces most of California's superior wines.

GETTING THERE

To get there from San Francisco, head north on U.S. 101, turn east at Calif. 37, and proceed to Calif. 29, where the greatest concentration of wineries open to visitors is located. The **Napa Chamber of Commerce**, 1556 1st St., in downtown Napa (tel. 707/226-7455), will provide you with a list of lodgings, recreational facilities, rides of every kind, antiques dealers, picnic facilities, bike routes, etc. They also have maps and brochures for sale. It's open weekdays from 9am to 5pm, weekends from 11am to 3pm.

WHAT TO SEE AND DO

The best and busiest time to visit Napa is during September and October, when the grapes are being harvested. But any time of year the very air seems intoxicating in this area of unparalleled scenic beauty. As you drive along Calif. 29, you'll see welcoming signs beckoning you to one winery or another. Almost all offer free tours and samples of their product, most free. Two or three tours are the most you'll want to take, and I've recommended the ones that are more intriguing or picturesque. If you find the lecturers at these a little pedantic, be assured that the situation is much the same or worse at the other vineyards. The tours are nonetheless interesting, and the tasting is lots of fun. There are a number of interesting events that go on each year in the Napa Valley. A small sampling would include the **Napa Valley Wine Auction,** sponsored by the Napa Valley Vintners Association and usually held in June. This is the most important annual auction, one a wine connoisseur would not want to miss. In July, Calistoga holds the old-fashioned **Napa County Fair,** complete with rides, food, etc. At the end of July or the beginning of August, there's the **Napa Town & Country Fair** at the Napa Fairgrounds. Let's just say that there's always much to see and do in the valley throughout the year. The Napa Chamber of Commerce will be glad to answer any questions you might have or to send you a calendar of events for the month or the year.

Napa Valley now has about 150 wineries and an exceptional selection of fine restaurants and hostelries at all price levels. It's a good idea to plan on spending more than one day if you'd like to tour even a small segment of the valley and its wineries. And if you do spend a weekend, or better yet a week, plan in advance and bear in mind that the summer is quite busy.

For the most part, we'll saunter (by car) north along Calif. 29, though a few of the Napa Valley vineyards I've included are a bit off the main road. But you'll enjoy the diversion—the beauty of the valley is striking whatever the time of year, and especially in the fall season. Throughout Napa, Yountville, St. Helena, and Calistoga, the colors are breathtaking as the leaves on the vines change to gold, rust brown, deep maroon—all in preparation for the next season of grapes. And while November and the rest of the winter months are a bit cooler, each has its own beauty. It's the time of the year when the rain in Napa has its own soft-spoken love affair with the hills, where the mists lie softly and lovingly.

One of the nicest treats you can afford yourself is a trip on the **Napa Valley Wine Train,** based at 1275 McKinstry St. in Napa, just off 1st and Socolo (tel. 707/253-2111, or toll free 800/522-4142). In 1989 the train began offering excursions and gourmet dining in its vintage 1915 parlor cars, beautifully refurbished to recreate the opulence and sophistication of the '20s and '30s. Luxurious Pullman and dining cars are finished with polished Honduran mahogany paneling, brass accents, etched-glass partitions, and fine fabrics. Two cars are fitted as 50-passenger lounge cars with 26 individual cushioned chairs and 6 four-person booths for surveying the countryside and vineyards. The Wine Train affords a deliciously relaxing 36-mile trip through the Napa wine region, with stops at Napa, Yountville, Oakville, Rutherford and St. Helena.

Should you choose to dine, there are all the accoutrements of gracious living—damask linen, bone china, silver flatware, and etched crystal. Each dish—at lunch, for instance, filet of Norwegian salmon poached in court bouillon and presented with saffron sauce, or Black Angus filet mignon served with a cabernet and Roquefort sauce—is prepared to order. There is a full bar and an extensive wine list.

From March through December, there are brunch trips on Saturday, Sunday, and holidays, as well as luncheon and dinner sojourns Tuesday through Sunday. During January and February the train runs only from Thursday through Sunday. The fare for the three-hour trip, including a prix-fixe lunch, beverages, and service charge, is about $45. For dinner the total is about $70. At this time, for $25 you can make the train trip on Saturday or Sunday without subscribing to lunch or dinner. Complete beverage service is available in both the lounge and dining cars during all trips. And every Saturday there is a Family Special Train, leaving at 9am, with one car reserved for families with children. Train fare for children under 14 is $8; kiddies under 4 ride free. Optional Continental breakfast is available. All departures are from the Napa Valley Wine Train main depot at the above address. Reservations are required.

The Wineries

Napa Valley's fame began with cabernet sauvignon and, except for the white chardonnay, more acreage is devoted to the growth of this grape than any other.

Most of the wineries en route conduct their tours daily from 10am to 5pm. And there's considerably more to them than merely open vineyards. There are the huge presses and an elaborate system of pipes and vats through which the wines flow and are blended before mellowing in giant casks in the deep cellars. Most wineries instruct as to proper tasting procedure: Begin with the lightest white wines, go on to the rosés, reds, and finally sherries and dessert wines—sparkling wines come last.

We'll begin in Napa with **Stag's Leap Wine Cellars,** 5766 Silverado Trail, Napa, CA 94558 (tel. 707/944-2020). For the most part, the Silverado Trail parallels Calif. 29 and you can get there by going east on Trances Street or Oak Knoll Avenue, then north to Stag's Leap Wine Cellars. The man who has guided the destiny of this now famous winery and attracted the attention of France's noted wine experts is Warren Winiarski. A hill hides the group of buildings at its foot that comprise Stag's Leap. The first building, which once housed the entire operation, still offers a summary view of wine making from start to finish. Undoubtedly one of the best-known wines is the Cabernet Sauvignon Cask 23, under Winiarski's distinguished Stag's Leap Vineyard label. (Winiarski also offers good-value wines under the Hawk Crest label.) Sales hours are 10am to 4pm daily. You can taste selected current releases too. Tours are by appointment.

Now back to Calif. 29 and its intersection with California Drive, where you'll find **Domaine Chandon,** California Drive, Yountville, CA 94599 (tel. 707/944-2280). The firm produces about 500,000 cases annually of *méthode-champenoise* California sparkling wines. Founded in 1968, this is a very modern winery; its parent company in France is Moët et Chandon. ("Champagne" properly refers only to wines from the province of Champagne in France.) In the winery's cool gallery, there's an informative exhibit on the history of sparkling wines, from champagne's "inventor," Friar Dom Pérignon, to the present.

The tour, offered from 11am to 5pm, led by very informed and witty guides, goes past sample vines and into the cool, damp cellar, where the wines are aged, past the machinery that prepares the wines for market. (On weekdays you can see them in operation.) At the end of the tour you can stop in at Le Salon, for a taste of Domaine Chandon's products. There are no free samples, but you can purchase a glass of sparkling wine for about $3. Free hors d'oeuvres come with your drink. There's also a small shop where you can purchase wines, wine paraphernalia, and souvenirs. From May to October the winery is open daily and lunch is served in the adjoining restaurant; dinner is served Wednesday through Sunday. During the winter (November through April) the winery and restaurant are closed Monday and Tuesday.

Continuing on Calif. 29 up to Oakville, you'll arrive at the **Robert Mondavi Winery,** 7801 St. Helena Hwy. (Calif. 29), Oakville, CA 94562 (tel. 707/963-9611). This is the ultimate hi-tech Napa Valley winery, housed in a magnificent mission-style facility. Almost every conceivable processing variable in their wine making is computer-controlled—fascinating, especially if you've never watched the procedure before. Sales hours are 9am to 5pm daily. After you've taken the guided tour, you can taste the results of all this attention to detail with selected current wines. The Vineyard Room usually features an art show, and you'll find some exceptional antiques in the reception hall. In summer the winery has some great outdoor jazz concerts.

Farther north on Calif. 29, you'll reach Rutherford and the **Inglenook–Napa Valley Winery,** 1991 St. Helena Hwy. (Calif. 29, opposite Rutherford Cross Road), Rutherford, CA 94573 (tel. 707/967-3362). Inglenook's history dates back to 1879, when the vineyards were bought by Gustave Niebaum. The original winery, designed and built by Captain McIntyre, the architect of several neighboring wineries, is now the tasting room and starting point for tours. Sales hours are 10am to 5pm daily, during which time you can taste current releases. Guided tours are available.

A bit farther on is the **Beaulieu Vineyard,** at 1960 St. Helena Hwy. (Calif. 29), Rutherford, CA (tel. 707/963-2411), founded by a Frenchman named De Latour. During Prohibition this clever Frenchman built up a nationwide business in altar wines while other establishments were forced to close. When Repeal came, he was one of the fortunate few with well-aged wines on hand. In 1938 De Latour brought over a young Russian enologist (wine scientist), who helped him to produce a sensational cabernet sauvignon, a wine for which Beaulieu is still famous. This winery offers one of the most comprehensive tours—daily from 11am to 3pm. The tour takes about 30 minutes, after which you can sample selected current products in the tasting room and purchase some if you so desire.

The **Flora Springs Wine Co.** is at the end of West Zinfandel Lane, off Calif. 29 at 1978 W. Zinfandel Lane, St. Helena, CA 94574 (tel. 707/963-5711). While this handsome stone winery dates back to Napa Valley's early days, the Flora Springs label first appeared in 1978. The owners, the Komes family, have vineyards throughout Napa Valley and select choice lots for their own label. They are known especially for their sauvignon blanc and barrel-fermented chardonnay, as well as cabernet sauvignon.

Flora Springs offers an excellent two-hour "familiarization seminar" that almost everyone interested in wines would enjoy. And best of all, it's tailored to all levels of enophiles. Limited to 10 participants, the course is held on the second and fourth Saturdays of each month at 10am, or on days when requested by groups. The program begins in the vineyards, where you'll see a good-growing vine and taste the grapes. While the grapes are being crushed, you taste the must (just-pressed juice) and ultimately see how it becomes a beautiful, clear wine. Then you are taught how to evaluate wines; you'll blind-taste different ones and learn to distinguish between them, trying an older and a younger wine, for example, to see what happens with aging. You will also learn to pair wines with different foods. There is a fee of $25 to cover the wines that are part of the eight-wine tasting. The two hours will be among the most interesting and enjoyable you'll ever spend. Make reservations by calling Fritz Draeger (tel. 707/963-5711), or by writing to him at the above address.

Be sure to stop at **Beringer Vineyards,** 2000 Main St. (Calif. 29, just north of the business district), St. Helena, CA 94574 (tel. 707/963-7115), if only to look at this remarkable Rhine House and view the hand-dug tunnels carved out of the mountainside, the site of the original winery. Beringer Vineyards was founded in 1876 by the brothers Jacob and Frederick. The family owned it until 1971, when it was purchased by the Swiss firm of Nestlé, Inc. In true Swiss fashion, the business has prospered. It is the oldest *continuously* operating winery in the Napa Valley.

What about Prohibition? you might ask. Beringer made "sacramental" wines during the dry years.

The modern working winery on the opposite side of the road is not open to the public, but you can get a general look at it from the Rhine House. Sales hours are 9:30am to 5pm daily. Tasting of current products is conducted during sales hours in the Rhine House. Tasting of reserve wines is available in the Founders' Room (upstairs in the Rhine House) during sales hours. A modest fee is charged per taste. Tours are conducted by very knowledgeable guides.

Just beyond the Beringer Vineyards, still on the same side of the road at the north end of St. Helena, is the showplace of the **Christian Brothers,** 2555 Main St. (P.O. Box 552), St. Helena, CA 94574 (tel. 707/963-0763). In 1987 the Christian Brothers resurrected the body and soul of what has been known as Greystone Cellars—originally built at the turn of the century to be the largest stone winery in the world. Greystone now has a very detailed and informative visitors' tour through a portion of the first floor of this splendid building; it covers many aspects of wine making, from cooperage to wine aging, discussing the vines at Greystone and pointing out the subtleties of tastings. Sales and tour hours at Greystone are Monday to Thursday from 10am to 4pm and Friday to Sunday from 10am to 4:45pm. Tasting of selected products is offered after the tour.

Practically next door is **Charles Krug,** 2800 Main St., St. Helena, CA 94574 (tel. 707/963-2761 or 963-5057). The winery was founded in 1861—a classic old Napa estate set in a shady grove of oak trees on beautifully landscaped grounds. Krug was one of the first California wine makers to produce wines by other than the primitive Spanish methods introduced by Father Junípero Serra. Two of his original stone buildings remain the core of the present winery, and the one-time coachhouse holds a small cooperage for aging select wines. Since 1943 the winery has belonged to the Mondavi family. Winemaker Peter Mondavi believes that the human element is as important as modern equipment: "The oldtimers believed the quality of the man's wine depended on his own quality and character. A little bit of himself goes into every bottle. To gain lasting fame a winemaker must be a poet, a philosopher, an honorable man, as well as a master craftsman." Krug's ably led winery tour shows you the crushers, fermenters, tanks (both redwood and steel), aging cellars, and bottling lines, ending up in the tasting room. Tours are given at regular intervals daily from 10am to 4pm.

Spring Mountain Vineyards, 2805 Spring Mountain Rd. (about 1½ miles west off Calif. 29 via Madrona Avenue and Spring Mountain Road), St. Helena, CA 94574 (tel. 707/963-5233), has probably the most unique claim to fame of any Napa Valley vineyard—it was the setting for the TV program "Falcon Crest." While the grand house was built in the late 19th century, Spring Mountain Vineyards as a working winery is housed in a new structure. The cellars were built in the early 1970s, though the label goes back to 1968. The free winery tours are by appointment, 10:30am daily, 2:30pm weekdays; however, if you're a "Falcon Crest" fan who would like to take a guided tour of the grounds around the house, there is a fee. Grounds tours are on the hour from 11am to 4pm. Sales hours, during which there are tastings, are 10am to 5pm daily.

Sterling Vineyards, at 1111 Dunaweal Lane, Calistoga, CA 94515 (tel. 707/942-5151), is just south of the town of Calistoga and approximately half a mile east of Calif. 29. Sterling Vineyards is probably more startling in appearance than any of its neighbors. Perched on top of an island of rock, it looks much more like a Greek or even an Italian mountaintop monastery. Reaching this isolated facility is relatively easy—just take the aerial gondola (there's a $5-per-person visitor fee). However, if you have any infirmity that makes walking or climbing difficult, this is not your cup of tea, or glass of wine. Gravity moves the wine and the visitors. You will go downstairs to the fermentors, then down to the aging cellar; you'll climb farther down to the final aging cellar, then up to the reserve cellar, and finally up to the top of the rocky perch, where you'll be rewarded in the tasting room. The very informative tour is guided by signs, not humans, so you can set your own pace. The winery has

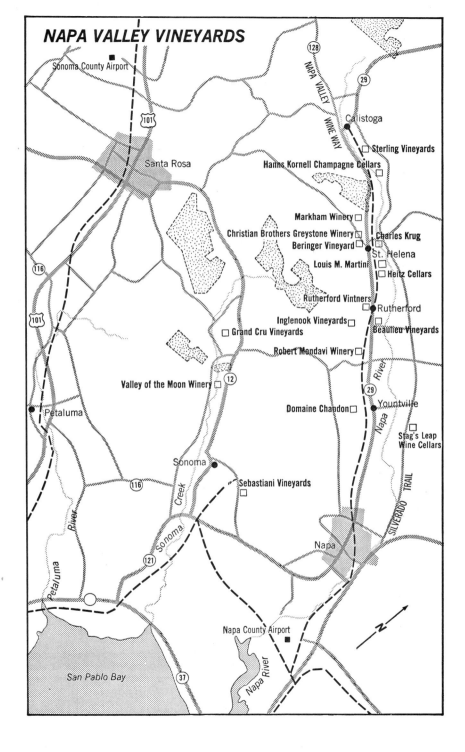

changed hands more than once since its founding in 1969; its current owner is the Seagram Classics Wine Company, which produces over 200,000 cases per year. Sales hours and tasting times are 10:30am to 4:30pm daily.

Other Things To Do

While you're in the area, there are a few other activities you can take in while sobering up for the drive back to San Francisco.

You'll find a variety of interesting choices discussed under the town headings. In Yountville, there's the **Vintage 1870 Complex,** originally a brick winery that can keep you occupied for at least a couple of hours. In St. Helena, you'll find **Vintners' Village,** the **Hurd Candle Factory** (actually more of a country store), and the **Silverado Museum,** which is devoted to Robert Louis Stevenson. And Calistoga offers for entertainment **Old Faithful Geyser of California** and the **Petrified Forest,** plus a collection of spas, mud baths, and other facilities.

And for those of us irresistibly attracted to acres of grass with now-and-then patches of sand, water, and an occasional rock (otherwise termed golf courses), there are some interesting spots to spend a few hours, as described below.

Chardonnay Club, 2555 Jamieson Canyon Rd., just off Calif. 12 (1¼ miles east of Calif. 29) and south of Napa, is a country-club-for-a-day built to seduce the golf addicts of this world. Its course is classy, stunning, mean, beautiful, challenging —all the qualities that describe the great ones. But its attraction only begins there, because Chardonnay Club is a 27-hole land-links golf complex with first-class service. It is not surrounded by condominiums, and there are no tennis courts or swimming pools. It's beautiful championship golf—just that.

Chardonnay is brand-new, but evolved with much thought given to the existing lay of the land—it's very European in its style, ambling through and around 120 acres of vineyards. Hills, creeks, canyons, and rock ridges remain, while mounds were added to raise flat terrain and sand bunkers were strategically placed to deceive the best of course managers. Greens are intricately shaped for interesting pin placements; several have two tiers. The 13th green is a beauty—21,000 square feet that slopes from left to right with three separate flags. Take your pick before teeing up.

There are three nines of similar challenge, all leaving from the clubhouse, so that you can play the 18 of your choice. Five sets of tees provide you with a course measuring from 5,300 yards to a healthy 7,400. You pay only one fee for a day's membership, which includes the use of a golf cart, the practice range (including a bucket of balls), and services usually found only at a private club. The day I played, a snack cart came by on the course with a full complement of sandwiches and soft drinks. And at the end of the round my clubs were cleaned.

Chardonnay Village services include the golf shop, locker rooms, and a restaurant and grill. The course is open year-round. The greens fee is $40 daily, including your cart (mandatory) and practice balls. Starting times can be reserved up to two weeks in advance (tel. 707/257-8950). The club also offers some great packages for tournament groups.

Another golfing option is the **Napa Municipal Golf Course,** right alongside Calif. 121 next to Napa Junior College (tel. 707/255-4333). This is an 18-hole course with lots of water, sand, and a few tricky elevated greens. Weekdays the greens fee for 18 holes is $11; weekends, $17. Carts are available ($15).

About other courses in Napa, if you're staying at the **Silverado Country Club & Resort,** you don't need me to tell you that Silverado has two 18-hole golf courses. If you're not staying at Silverado, these courses can be played only if you belong to a private country club with a reciprocal-play agreement.

2. Napa

If you're touring the Wine Country, you might want to take as your base its commercial center, the town of Napa. The gateway to the valley, Napa rose at the juncture of two streams; it was served by ferries and steamboats as early as the mid-1800s, and later by the Napa Valley Railroad. The valley is just 35 miles long, so if you stay in Napa and want to dine, wine, shop, or sightsee in Yountville, Rutherford, or St. Helena, you won't have very far to travel.

WHERE TO STAY

To go the way of elegance in Napa is to stay at the **Silverado Country Club & Resort,** 1600 Atlas Peak Rd., Napa, CA 94558 (tel. 707/257-0200, or toll free 800/532-0500). It's north on Calif. 29 to Trancas Street, and east to Atlas Peak Road. Silverado is a 1,200-acre resort lavishly arranged at the foot of the hills. The resort has 280 spacious accommodations ranging from very large studios with king-size beds, kitchenettes, and roomy, well-appointed baths, to one-, two-, or three-bedroom cottage suites, each with a wood-burning fireplace. The setting is superb: The cottage suites are in private, low-rise groupings, each sharing tucked-away court-yards and peaceful walkways. This arrangement allows for a feeling of privacy and comfort despite the size of the resort.

The main building and center of the resort looks more like an old southern mansion, pillars and all, than a California country resort. Lace curtains, white bent-wood chairs, white tables, and gray carpeting complete the picture. Silverado offers exceptional resort services, including eight swimming pools and the largest tennis complex in Northern California: 20 superlative Plexi-paved courts with a mini-clubhouse, canvas-topped review decks, and sport shop. You say you don't play tennis anymore but have switched to golf? Silverado has two 18-hole courses, occupying some 360 acres, very cleverly designed by Robert Trent Jones, Jr. The South Course is 6,500 yards, with a dozen water crossings (how many balls do you plan to take?); the North Course is 6,700 yards—somewhat longer but a bit more forgiving. Obviously, there is a staff of pros on hand. Use of the courses is restricted to guests staying at the Silverado or those belonging to a private country club with a reciprocal-play agreement. The greens fee is $70 for 18 holes on either course, including a mandatory cart.

Silverado has three restaurants to accommodate your every taste (well, almost). The Royal Oak is the quintessential steak restaurant, with high-back chairs, carved-wood tables, and exposed beams and brickwork. Vintner's Court offers superb California cuisine in a chandeliered salon with a view of the surrounding eucalyptus and beautifully groomed flowerbeds. The Silverado Bar & Grill is a large indoor terrace/bar and outdoor deck that overlooks the North Course and serves breakfast, lunch, and cocktails. Room service is also available.

Rates at Silverado range from $145 for a studio to $215 for a one-bedroom suite, single or double occupancy. Two- to three-bedroom suites are $310 to $465. Special packages are in effect at various times of the year, so be sure to ask.

The **Château Hotel,** 4195 Solano Ave., Napa, CA 94558 (tel. 707/253-9300, or toll free 800/253-6272 in California), is located virtually at the entrance to the Napa Valley wine region, just west of Calif. 29 and north of Trower Avenue. The hotel has the charm of a country inn combined with the amenities of a contemporary city hotel. The traditional decor in the lobby typifies that throughout the Château. Settees and chairs are upholstered in a rich, dark blue with a small floral pattern, which contrasts attractively with the light woods and color of the walls. The spacious rooms have exceptionally large baths, plus separate vanity-dressing areas. All rooms have color TVs with complimentary in-room movies, and all have phones, but there is a 25¢ charge per call. Included in the rates are a European-style breakfast buffet, the daily newspaper, and a wine social hour each evening. If you're used to a daily swim, the Château has a heated pool and an in-ground Jacuzzi. On the other hand, if you'd prefer golf, tennis, bicycling, or even hot-air ballooning, the staff can arrange it.

Winter rates (November through March) throughout the week are $75 for singles, $81 for doubles. The balance of the year, singles are $85 and doubles run $95.

For those who really want or need a home away from home, there is **Tall Timbers Chalets,** 1012 Darms Lane, Napa, CA 94558 (tel. 707/252-7810), located just south of Yountville. (While the Tall Timbers Chalets is not particularly difficult to find, be sure to ask for specific directions.) Tall Timbers is a group of eight white-washed, very roomy cottages surrounded by pines and eucalyptus and sheltered away from the east side of Hwy. 29. It's certainly one of the best buys in the Napa Valley; after all, where can you get an entire house at these rates and one as conveniently located? Its close proximity to Yountville makes it ideal for sightseeing and shopping, as well as dining at Yountville's excellent restaurants. It's also a good starting point for trips through the surrounding countryside and up to Calistoga. The Newlan vineyards are located next door, and Domaine Chandon is well within walking distance.

Each of the cottages is well furnished and nicely decorated, and each has a breakfast nook with refrigerator (stocked with breakfast treats), toaster oven, and coffee maker (no stove)—plus a basket of fresh fruit and complimentary bottle of champagne on your arrival. There are color TVs in the cottages, but no phones apart from the one in the main office. Each cottage can sleep four—there's a bedroom plus a queen-size sofa bed in the living room. Most of the cottages have full tubs and shower baths; two have showers only. Several of the cottages also have decks for outdoor lolling around—and for watching the colorful hot-air balloons as they float over in the morning.

November through April, rates Sunday through Thursday are $60 to $75; May through October, $80 to $95. On Friday, Saturday, and holidays, rates are $95 to $105. All of the above are based on double occupancy; there is a $10 charge for each additional person over 6 years of age.

And now let's look at an even less costly place to stay—the ever-handy **Motel 6,** at 3380 Solano Ave., Napa, CA 94558 (tel. 707/257-6111). From Calif. 29, turn west on the Redwood Road turnoff and go one block to Solano Avenue, then half a block south and there you'll find Motel 6. It's location is excellent, since you are close to Calif. 29 and just across the street from a pleasant minimall. Rooms are simple, comfortable, and clean. Free TV and feature movies are included in the rates, and now every Motel 6 room has both air conditioning and a phone. Local calls are free. There is a small pool. Rates are $33 for one person and $6 for each additional adult. One other important feature: The managers of this Motel 6 are pleasant, helpful, and chock-full of useful information (but then I found that to be true of most people in the Napa Valley—it must be the air).

---

3. Yountville

Yountville is casual nouveau posh (and advancing on chichi) but undoubtedly the most charming village along Calif. 29. Of less historic interest than St. Helena or Calistoga, it is nonetheless an interesting jumping-off point for a wineries tour or for the simple enjoyment of the beauties of the valley. What's more, it has several lovely places to stay, interesting places to shop, and excellent to superb restaurants at various price levels. And Yountville is walkable—you can easily take a very enjoyable stroll from one end of town to the other.

WHAT TO SEE AND DO

At the center of the village is **Vintage 1870** (tel. 707/944-2451), once a winery (from 1871 to 1955) and now a gallery with specialty shops featuring art, antiques, wine accessories, country treasures and collectibles, gifts, contemporary furnishings, linens, clothing, music boxes, pastries, noshes, and chocolates. It is also home to three restaurants and to the Keith Rosenthal Theater and gallery, where for 15 minutes you can absorb a multi-image film presentation of the valley's four seasons and see the interior of Spring Mountain's famous "Falcon Crest" mansion. The *San Francisco Examiner* has called photographer Keith Rosenthal "the Ansel Adams of the Wine Country." Admission to see the film is $3 for adults, $2.50 for seniors, and $1 for children under 12. One of the most intriguing shops I found in the complex was the **Basket Bazaar,** where you'll also find lamps, vine and sorghum wreaths, and wicker chairs, chests, baskets, and rockers. And then there's **Gami's** for Scandinavian imports—Copenhagen figurines, jewelry, and a troll or two to bring along. Before you leave, be sure to stop in at **Gerhard's Sausage Kitchen,** purveyors of absolutely delicious sausages (chicken apple, Syrian lamb, Lyonnaise brand with pistachio nuts, etc.) and real beef jerky made from scratch (so to speak).

And if you've always wanted to try real hot-air ballooning, this may be the place to indulge your airy whim. **Adventures Aloft** (tel. 707/255-8688) is located at Vintage 1870 and is Napa Valley's oldest hot-air balloon company with full-time professional pilots. Groups are small, and the flight will last about an hour. If you're a late sleeper, this may not be your bag, since Adventures Aloft flies in the early sunrise hours; it's then that the winds are gentle and the air is cool, which makes for an especially enjoyable trip. If you need reassurance about flying, be advised that modern balloons are operated by licensed pilots under the supervision of the Federal Aviation Administration. The flight is $175 per person, which includes a preflight Continental breakfast, a champagne brunch after the flight, and a framed "First Flight" certificate attesting to your voyage aloft.

WHERE TO STAY

In Yountville, there are four notable choices. The **Vintage Inn,** 6541 Washington St., Yountville, CA 94599 (tel. 707/944-1112, or toll free 800/982-5539, 800/351-1133 in California), built on an old winery estate in the center of town, is very much the contemporary luxury country inn. The exterior is a brick-and-board construction; the reception lounge has a cathedral ceiling with exposed beams, brick fireplace, lavender couches, and shuttered windows, giving a sense of the handsome, warm look of the guest rooms. Each room has a fireplace, an armoire concealing the TV, oversize beds, a Jacuzzi, wine bar, refrigerator, and either a patio or veranda. The inn also provides nightly turndown service. If you insist on exercise other than walking through the lovely village and its shops, the inn has a 60-foot pool heated year-round, an outdoor heated whirlpool, and tennis courts reserved for the use of the guests. A California-Continental (cereals, yogurt, pastries, fruit, etc.) champagne breakfast is included with your stay and served daily in the Vintage Club, as well as afternoon tea.

November through April, rates for singles range from $119 to $149; doubles, $129 to $159; minisuites, $169 to $179. May through October, singles are $139 to $179; doubles, $149 to $189; minisuites, $199 to $219. The extra-person charge is $10 per night.

Just up the road a bit is the **Bordeaux House,** 6600 Washington St., Yountville, CA 94599 (tel. 707/944-2855). Accommodations here are surprisingly contemporary (definitely not French wine country), with grasspaper-covered walls, Lucite furnishings, and beds on carpeted platforms. Amenities are also more up-to-date: Your room will have a private bath, a TV, and a lovely wood-burning fireplace. There is an elaborate complimentary Continental breakfast, and evening wine (always available) is served in the attractive lobby. Rates range from $95 to $125.

The **Burgundy House Country Inn,** 6711 Washington St., P.O. Box 3156, Yountville, CA 94599 (tel. 707/944-0889), is a charming bed-and-breakfast place, distinctly French country in feel. Built of local fieldstone and river rock, the Burgundy House has had a remarkable history—originally a brandy distillery, then (successively) a winery, a hotel, and an antiques warehouse. The structure is impressive, with 20-inch-thick walls and hand-hewn beams, and the interior boasts handsome antique country furniture. Each of the five cozy guest rooms has colorful quilted spreads, comfortable beds, and its own private bath. Though there are no TVs or phones, all rooms are air-conditioned; delightful touches include fresh flowers and a complimentary decanter of local white wine. A full breakfast is served in the "distillery," though you might prefer to enjoy it outdoors in the inn's garden.

Rates are $95 for singles, $110 for doubles, both including breakfast.

And then there's the **Magnolia Hotel,** 6529 Yount St., Yountville, CA 94599 (tel. 707/944-2056), with 12 rooms in a beautifully restored old building (from 1873) and in the newly restored wing (the latter with fireplaces and sun decks). All rooms are individually decorated in Victorian motif with floral carpeting, and all have private baths but no phones or TVs. If you need to compensate for any such perceived disadvantages, a decanter of complimentary port is in each room. On-premises facilities include a large swimming pool, heated from May through October, and a Jacuzzi.

Rates—including a full hot breakfast daily—are $89 to $169, single or double occupancy. A secluded suite overlooking the pool and garden (suitable for four) is $288. No smoking is allowed indoors.

WHERE TO DINE

There are several excellent choices in Yountville. The ambience at **The Diner** (legendary food), 6476 Washington St. (tel. 707/944-2626), is friendly, warm, and unpretentious. Done in shell pink, with track lighting overhead, the restaurant features a functioning Morso stove (pleasantly warming in the cool months), a collection of vintage diner water pitchers, as well as some interesting black-and-white photos by a local artist. The Diner's art exhibit changes about every month. Seating is at the counter or in wooden booths.

For breakfast and lunch, everything I tried on the extensive menu was delicious and the portions were huge. House specialties range from huevos rancheros served with fried potatoes, and a breakfast burrito with eggs scrambled with homemade chorizo, garlic, jalapeños, and cream cheese, to the less exotic, but equally delicious, french toast and a wide range of eggs and pancakes. Fresh fruit with yogurt or cottage cheese is also available. The Diner's selection of natural, baked-on-premises breads usually includes raisin-walnut, whole wheat, cottage dill, and sourdough rye (with a starter descended from San Francisco's famous Larraburu Bakery, circa 1873). If you're not told, be sure to ask about the breakfast specials—usually some exceptionally delicious omelet.

Luncheon specialties include a superior carne asada, as well as several other toothsome Mexican dishes. For more staid tastes, there is quite an assortment of hamburgers, sandwiches, salads, and homemade soups. Sundaes, espresso, cappuccino, and a variety of drinks from fresh-squeezed orange juice and natural-fruit sodas to domestic and imported beer and wine by the glass are all available.

Dinners are exceptional variations on the Mexican theme. Don't pass by the enchiladas with chicken, green chiles, and cream cheese, topped with crème fraîche and Jack cheese. And the Tostada Grande—heaped with beans, cheese, lettuce, avocado, turkey breast, tomatoes, sour cream, and salsa—defies any appetite. Burgers, homemade soups, and salads are available at dinner too. If you still have room for dessert, flan, chocolate torte, and New York cheesecake are among the offerings (price range: $2 to $3.25). Service at The Diner is attentive, helpful, and friendly—indeed characteristic of all Napa Valley restaurants and inns.

Breakfast is served from 8am to 3pm; lunch, from 11am to 3pm; dinner, from 5:30 to 9pm. Prices at breakfast range from $3.50 to $6; lunch, $3.25 to $8; dinner, $5 to $11. Open daily except Monday.

Now the setting for the talents of chef Sally Schmitt and her creative American menu, the **French Laundry,** 6640 Washington St., at Creek Street (tel. 707/944-2380), was in truth once a laundry. There is no sign to indicate that this historic old building might be anything but a country home, nor is an address visible, so my advice is to look closely for the very small sign that indicates the cross street. At the French Laundry you'll feel as though you are an honored guest in a private home. Infinite care has been taken with every detail of cuisine and decor, from the perfectly arranged flowers, to the inviting lovely fabric tablecloths, to still-life paintings and historical prints.

A different five-course prix-fixe dinner (about $46 per person) is offered at the French Laundry each evening. It is difficult to get a reservation, but if you succeed, you're here for a relaxing evening. Your meal begins with a choice of three appetizers —perhaps sautéed sweetbreads and shiitake mushrooms in lemon cream, artichokes with garlic mayonnaise, or smoked trout with red-onion compote. In the late summer you can opt for the simple vine-ripe tomato, basil, and bread appetizer. Next comes a soup course, followed by an entree such as suprême of chicken with rosemary and orange, or pork loin with mustard-caper sauce, or the duckling with a curry glaze served with the French Laundry's own apricot chutney and a stir-fry of baby bok choy and shiitake mushrooms. A simple green salad with a selection of perfectly ripe cheeses at room temperature follows. The meal is capped by a choice of at least three desserts. Sally Schmitt specializes in fruit desserts: a fall favorite of mine is warm poached figs with ginger ice cream served with a sprig of cinnamon basil, or the simple but elegant apple clafouti (somewhat like a tart and absolutely delicious) served with hot cider sauce. The coffee is a special house blend, and as you might expect, there's an extensive and well-chosen wine list.

Dinner is served Wednesday through Sunday (there's only one seating, but times of arrival are spread from 7 to 8:30pm). Remember, reservations are essential. A meal at the French Laundry is an experience you'll savor.

A favorite hangout of local winemakers and growers, just north of the village of Yountville, is **Mustards Grill,** 7399 St. Helena Hwy. (tel. 707/944-2424). As a close relative of the Fog City Diner in San Francisco, Tra Vigne in St. Helena, and Rio Grill in Carmel, you might expect the restaurant to be successful—and indeed it has been. Look for the amusing bronze sculpture of a gentleman in bowler on the west side of the road. As you enter a barnlike structure, you'll see beamed cathedral ceilings, a black-and-white tile floor, track lighting, and a small bar. The main dining room is on two levels, and there's an airy glass-enclosed outer dining area for a simulated al fresco experience. The atmosphere is light, festive, and relaxed, as you might expect it to be in the Wine Country. The blue-jeaned, white-shirted servers are friendly and very knowledgeable. Specials of the day are listed on a blackboard along with featured local wines ranging from $4 to $5 by the glass. You can bring your own bottle of wine, as many diners seem to do, but the restaurant does charge a $5 corkage fee. I'd guess that more wine per table is consumed here than in any San Francisco restaurant.

While you review the dining possibilities, half of a sliced, warm, crusty baguette arrives with sweet butter. Among the starters are such gems as a cornmeal pancake with Tobiko caviar and sour cream; warm goat cheese with sun-dried tomatoes and chives; and Chinese chicken salad. Sandwiches, apart from a sizable hamburger or cheeseburger, also include a rib-eye steak with horseradish cream, and smoked ham and Jarlsberg cheese grilled with tomato chutney. Entrees are reasonably priced and range from wood-burning-oven specialties—barbecued baby back ribs, pork chops with Thai marinade, quail—to such items from the grill as Sonoma rabbit, New York steak with shiitake mushroom ragoût, gulf prawns, lamb chops with braised eggplant, and fresh fish. For dessert, the chocolate-pecan cake with chocolate sauce is a chocoholic's delight. I found the caramel custard with pistachios and cream irresistible. And Mustards has some of the best coffee I've ever tasted.

Back to basics: Entree prices range from $11 to $19; appetizers and sandwiches, from $5 to $9. Dessert will add another $3 to $4. Open daily from 11:30am to 10pm; at lunch, you can dine at the bar. Reservations are necessary for both lunch and dinner.

Backtrack a bit on Calif. 29 to California Drive, just south of the Yountville Cross Road, turn west into California Drive, and there you will find **Domaine Chandon** (tel. 707/944-2892), one of California's most pleasing restaurants. It forsakes the usual old-fashioned Wine Country quaintness for understated modern elegance—the keynote of the decor. It is one of the most dramatic and beautiful settings in the region. Multitiered, it has arched fir-paneled ceilings, big picture windows, dark-green chairs at white-clothed tables, and rows of plants and trees at each level.

At lunch, which can also be enjoyed al fresco, you might begin with a salad of arugula with prosciutto, parmesan cheese, truffle oil, plus home-baked Calimyrna fig bread. Entrees cost $13 to $19 and change daily, but might include lamb shank braised in chardonnay and herbs, served with garden vegetables. There are superb desserts ($4.50 to $7), including such mouthwatering choices as the hot chocolate soufflé served with a white-chocolate sauce, and the espresso and mascarpone ice-cream terrine with a crunchy peanut-butter layer and bittersweet chocolate sauce.

Dinner might start with fish and shellfish soup, discretely seasoned with garlic, fresh thyme, and red pepper rouille, and continue with roast California quail with chanterelles, soft polenta, and acorn squash, or sweetbreads with shallot-prosciutto butter and truffle juice, for $22 to $28. Need I say, the wine list is impeccable and includes some outstanding dessert wines and cognacs.

From November to April, Domaine Chandon is open Wednesday through Sunday for lunch from 11:30am to 2:30pm and for dinner from 6 to 9pm; the same hours daily from May through October. Reservations are essential; you can phone them in daily between 10am and 5pm, no more than two weeks in advance of your visit. The restaurant is closed the first three weeks in January.

4. Oakville

One of the outstanding culinary attractions in Napa Valley is located on St. Helena Highway (Calif. 29) in Oakville, at the Oakville Cross Road. There you will find the **Oakville Grocery Co., 7856 St. Helena Hwy., Oakville, CA 94562 (tel. 707/944-8802).** Its name, its location, and its exterior disguise one of the finest gourmet food stores this side of Dean and DeLuca in New York City. It's here that you can obtain provisions for a memorable picnic, or for a very special custom gift basket. You'll find the best of breads, the choicest selection of cheeses in the North Bay area, pâtés, fresh foie gras (domestic and French, seasonally), smoked Norwegian salmon, smoked sturgeon and smoked pheasant (by special order), fresh caviar (Beluga, Sevruga, Osetra), and an exceptional selection of California wines, including hard-to-find vintages. If you find the wine decision difficult, there are sampler sets to help you along. Special selections are available, but in limited quantities. The Oakville Grocery can ship wines by the case to anywhere in the United States, Canada, and Europe. Remember, you can charge liquor purchases in California; major charge cards are accepted here.

The Oakville Grocery Co. will prepare a picnic-basket lunch for you if you give them 24-hour advance notice. Delivery service is available to some areas. The Oakville Grocery Co. is open daily from 10am to 6pm. Oakville Grocery Co. has a branch in Palo Alto in the Stanford Shopping Center, where a larger assortment of imported wines is available, plus a greater selection of prepared foods to take out.

5. Rutherford

WHERE TO STAY AND DINE

For those of you on Calif. 29 (St. Helena Hwy.), take the Oakville Cross Road (at Oakville, of course) east to the Silverado Trail; turn north to Rutherford Hill Road, then east on up the hillside to the French gem of Napa Valley—the **Auberge du Soleil,** 180 Rutherford Hill Rd., Rutherford, CA 94573 (tel. 707/963-1211). This elegant hideaway with its glorious French country restaurant is nestled in a hill-side olive grove overlooking the lovely valley. It's a peaceful spot, air fragrant with eucalyptus, to rest and to eat brilliant classic French and California nouvelle cuisine. A magnificent fireplace (large enough to roast a whole pig), huge wood pillars, banquettes with rainbow-striped cushions, white tablecloths, and fresh flowers combine to create an elegantly rustic—or is that rustically elegant?—ambience. Light opera plays in a room that opens out to a wisteria-decked terrace with white umbrellas, pink-clothed tables, and attractive carved-wood chairs.

At lunch the appetizers may include, among several difficult choices, sautéed sea scallops and warm asparagus with cilantro pesto, capers, chopped eggs, and croutons; and carpaccio of beef, with parmesan and sun-dried tomatoes and a mustard-caper sauce. Ask about the soup of the day too. Among the lunch entrees are such excellent seafood dishes as grilled marinated prawns with black-bean cake and cranberry-lime chutney, and escalope of salmon with a Pinot noir sauce, as well as roasted quail with Basmati aquavit rice, pimento, and oregano coulis. The desserts are superb: My choice was a delicious Florentine fruit crêpe with sorbet and raspberry sauce, though it's difficult to pass up the almond-chocolate mousse cake with orange-cognac sauce. Luncheon entrees average $14 to $18; appetizers, $6 to $11; desserts, $7 to $8.

Dinner at the Auberge du Soleil is a four-course prix-fixe affair ($52). You might begin with the quail with Napa greens and truffle vinaigrette, the fresh goose liver with apple-and-ginger compote, or the artichoke heart filled with lobster, wild mushrooms, and touched with a lobster glaze. The soup of the day is followed by an enticing list of entrees. I find it difficult to pass over the squab with bordelaise sauce and truffle risotto, or the roast range chicken with crayfish port sauce (if you've never had range chicken as it's prepared in a fine restaurant, this may be your golden opportunity).

Each dish, at lunch or dinner, is a work of art. Reservations are necessary, and weekends are often booked a month in advance. The restaurant is open daily for lunch from 11:30am to 2pm, and for dinner from 6 to 9pm.

The Auberge du Soleil has 48 rooms, probably the most elegant in the valley, each with fireplace, TV, wet bar, and deck overlooking Napa Valley. One-bedroom rooms and suites range from $240 to $440; two-bedroom suites are $660. Room rates include a Continental breakfast and the use of swimming, spa, and tennis facilities. Even if you are staying at the inn, it is suggested that lunch and dinner reservations at the auberge restaurant be made in advance of your arrival.

Note: If staying at Auberge du Soleil would strain the budget, consider at least treating yourself to lunch: It's a modest indulgence and worth every luscious bite.

---

6. St. Helena

Reminiscent in some ways of the south of France, with its tall plane trees arching over the roads, St. Helena also suggests feudal England, with its mansions overseeing the vineyards and valleys from hillside perches. Many of the buildings in the main part of town date back to the 1800s; the modern wares in a variety of shops are also worth a look. It's a friendly place, with some excellent restaurants and inns.

WHAT TO SEE

Literary buffs won't want to miss the **Silverado Museum,** 1490 Library Lane in St. Helena (tel. 707/963-3757), devoted to the life and works of Robert Louis Stevenson, author of *Treasure Island, Kidnapped,* etc. It was here that Stevenson honeymooned in 1880, at the abandoned Silverado Mine. Over 8,000 items include original manuscripts, letters, photographs, portraits of the writer, and the desk he used in Samoa. Open daily (except Monday and holidays) from noon to 4pm. No admission charge.

There's also a small and quite charming complex—the Freemark Abbey, where you'll find the **Hurd Beeswax Candle Factory,** 3020 St. Helena Hwy. (Calif. 29) (tel. 707/963-7211). The candle factory has an open workshop where the public can observe a demonstration hive and the actual handcrafting of beeswax candles into a variety of lovely and intricate shapes. The candles, as well as wine, food items, and books about the area, can also be purchased here—it's sort of a country store. Hours are 8:30am to 5pm weekdays, 10am to 5:30pm weekends.

WHERE TO STAY

The **Wine Country Inn,** 1152 Lodi Lane, St. Helena, CA 94574 (tel. 707/ 963-7077), 2 miles north of the center of St. Helena, is a handsome hostelry. Set on a hillside overlooking the vineyards, it has 25 rooms decorated in New England–inn style. Many have fireplaces (for use mid-October to mid-April), balconies or patios, and though all have private baths, there are no TVs. The rooms are exquisitely furnished in country antiques. The owner's mother and grandmother made patchwork quilts for the beds and stichery hangings for the walls. To add to the aura of quiet relaxation, the inn now has an elegant pool and a Jacuzzi.

A buffet-style Continental breakfast—with homemade breads—is included in the rates—$87 to $181, single or double occupancy.

WHERE TO DINE

A spot that you don't want to miss is Vintners' Village and the **Vines Restaurant and Café,** 3111 N. St. Helena Hwy. (which as you already know is Calif. 29) (tel. 707/963-8991). The village is a bit north of St. Helena, on the east side of the highway, marked with a large sign. The entry to Vines is from within the village. The interior is huge, airy, light, and very comfortably decorated. Downstairs, mauve carpeting quietly precedes your entry onto a well-polished parquet floor. There's a long, friendly-looking wood bar to your left. A huge, cathedral-size window on the first floor gives diners (or drinkers) a peaceful view of the greenery and trees at the village center. Each table is appropriately graced with white cloths and nappery, and a bottle of California wine. The upstairs dining area offers a spectacular view of the valley and vineyards. There's also an outdoor patio for dining in pleasant weather.

Lunch and dinner menus change seasonally, since Vines features locally grown produce. The food is beautifully prepared, and the quality noteworthy. At lunch the mesquite-grilled and rotisserie-smoked sandwiches, including the delicious, thinly sliced Black Angus steak, are all served with fresh avocado salsa. Breads are freshly baked—wood-oven-baked brown bread, whole-grain wheat bread, brown-and-black combination rye, crisp sourdough, and special Napa Valley regional breads—and they are good! Vines also has crisp-crust pizzettes from its wood-fired oven. If you enjoy mushrooms, try the exceptional pizzette with smoked provolone cheese, earthy wild mushrooms, and fresh thyme. And there's nothing commonplace about the soups, salads, and fresh hand-carved sandwiches. Soups, sandwiches, and salads will cost $4 to $7; pizzettes are $8.

Dinner expands the menu with a number of exceptional entrees. On the list of fresh pasta dishes is a delectable fettuccine prepared with smoked duck and a madeira-cream sauce. Or if you have a taste for seafood, a fresh catch is always available; you might consider cappellini (angel hair) with sautéed Tiger prawns, basil, plum tomatoes, and St. Helena olive oil. For hearties requiring the sustenance of beef, a mesquite-grilled Black Angus steak and a rotisseried prime rib are on the list. Vines has range-fed Sonoma chicken brochette with a lemon-tarragon sauce. Dinner entrees are in the $7 to $18 range.

Vines also has a Sunday brunch served with complimentary champagne. There are, of course, soups and salads as well as such toothsome choices as french toast made with bread baked that morning. Try the herbed scrambled eggs served with Napa Valley honey-cured bacon and a wood-oven-baked apple. There's also a quiche of the day. Sunday brunch can be had for $5 to $8, including the complimentary champagne; the rib-eye steak with eggs is $12.50.

As for dessert, the list changes daily but the choices are always mouthwatering —ask your server. Vines also offers a fine selection of wines by the glass, and a good choice of beers. The quality of the service measures up to that of the food served. It's attentive, pleasant, and very helpful.

Monday through Saturday, lunch is served from 11:30am to 2:30pm; Sunday brunch is from 10:30am to 3pm. Monday through Wednesday, dinner is from 5:30pm to 7pm; Thursday through Saturday, to 9pm. On Sunday, Vines is closed for dinner.

---

7. Calistoga

Sam Brannan became California's first millionaire by building a hotel and spa to take advantage of the area's geothermal springs. His entrepreneurial instincts combined "California" with the name of a popular East Coast resort, "Saratoga": Calistoga was born in 1859 and incorporated in 1886, attracting the newly wealthy from San Francisco. Today Calistoga still has a main street about six blocks long, with no building higher than two stories; it looks for all the world like a set for a somewhat updated western. At the northern end of the lush Wine Country, near the Old Faithful Geyser and the Petrified Forest, the town remains popular. Calistoga is a delightfully simple place in which to relax and indulge in mineral waters, mud baths, sulfur steambaths, Jacuzzis, massages—and, of course, wines.

If you've never had a **mud bath** before, you might well wonder what it is and how it feels. Although mud baths are not recommended for people with high blood pressure or for pregnant women, all others may enjoy their benefits. The bath is composed of local volcanic ash, imported peat, and naturally boiling mineral hot springs water, all mulled together to produce a thick mud at a temperature of about 90° to 100°F. Once you overcome the hurdle of deciding how best to place your naked body into the stone tub full of mud, the rest is pure relaxation—you are in the mud bath, surprisingly buoyant, for about 10 to 12 minutes. A warm mineral-water shower, a mineral-water whirlpool bath, and a mineral-water steam-room visit are followed by a relaxing blanket wrap to cool your delighted body down slowly. All of this takes about 1½ hours; with a massage, add another half hour. The outcome is a rejuvenated, revitalized, squeaky-clean you.

In addition to Dr. Wilkinson's Hot Springs (discussed below), other spas providing similar services are the **Lincoln Avenue Spa,** 1339 Lincoln Ave. (tel. 707/942-5296); **Golden Haven Hot Springs Spa,** 1713 Lake St. (tel. 707/942-6793); and the **Calistoga Spa Hot Springs,** 1006 Washington St. (tel. 707/942-6269). All spas offer a variety of other treatments such as hand and foot massage, herbal wraps, acupressure facelift, skin rubs, and herbal facials. Appointments are necessary for all of the above services, and you should phone at least a week in advance.

WHAT TO SEE AND DO

Before you head off to see the Old Faithful Geyser and Petrified Forest, stop at the **Calistoga Depot,** 1458 Lincoln Ave. (tel. 707/942-6225), which houses a variety of shops, a restaurant, and the Calistoga Chamber of Commerce. The depot occupies the site of the original railroad station built in 1868; alongside it sit six restored passenger cars dating from 1916 to the 1920s that also house some enticing shops.

The **Old Faithful Geyser of California,** 1299 Tubbs Lane (tel. 707/942-6463), has been blowing off steam for as long as anyone can remember. It's one of the few geysers in the world that perform at regular intervals. The hot (350°F) water spews out every 40 minutes (on the yearly average), day and night, the performance varying with barometric pressure, the tides, the moon, and earth tectonic stress; it lasts about three minutes and you'll learn a lot about the origins of geothermal steam. You can bring a picnic lunch with you and catch the show as many times as you wish. Old Faithful is situated between Calif. 29 and Calif. 128 (there are signs directing you to it from downtown Calistoga). Admission is $3 for adults, $2 for children under 12, free for those under 6. The geyser area is open year-round: from 9am to 6pm in summer, to 5pm the rest of the year.

Also in Calistoga, off Calif. 128 at 4100 Petrified Forest Rd., is the **Petrified Forest** (tel. 707/942-6667). Don't expect to see thousands of trees turned into stone; however, you can see many interesting specimens of redwoods that have become petrified through the infiltration of silicas and other minerals in the volcanic ash that covered them after the eruption of Mount St. Helena 1.3 million years ago. Earlier specimens—petrified seashells, clams, and marine life—indicate that water covered the area before the redwood forest. Admission is $3 for adults, $1 for children 4 to 11 years, free for those under 4. The Petrified Forest is open daily: from 10am to 6pm in summer, from 10am to 5pm the rest of the year.

WHERE TO STAY

The **Mount View Hotel**, 1457 Lincoln Ave. (near Fairway), Calistoga, CA 94515 (tel. 707/942-6877), offers 25 art deco rooms and 9 glamorous suites named after movie idols of the past—like the Carole Lombard (it has peach-colored walls and light-green carpeting) and the western-themed Tom Mix. Amenities include private baths and phones in all rooms; no TVs. Facilities also include a heated swimming pool and Jacuzzi.

A Continental/nouvelle cuisine restaurant on the premises serves breakfast, lunch, dinner, and Sunday brunch, and the food is excellent. Typical dinner entrees here are rack of lamb with whole-grain mustard, and several fresh fish specials of the day, for $10 to $22. A prix-fixe dinner is $30. There's an extensive California wine list, reasonably priced and well balanced for any menu. A cocktail lounge (the scene of nightly piano music) adjoins.

Rates are $55 to $110 a night for singles or doubles, and $100 to $110 for suites, including a full American breakfast. A special package—"The Suite Life"— includes a suite for two evenings, champagne, and a dinner for two for $225.

Another Calistoga choice, oriented more toward the mud bath/mineral water/massage born-again set, is **Dr. Wilkinson's Hot Springs,** 1507 Lincoln Ave., Calistoga, CA 94515 (tel. 707/942-4102). It's a typical motel with 42 rooms, mostly distinguished by the mud baths on the premises. A mud-bath treatment takes about two hours. This rejuvenating process costs $36; it's $17 additional if you include a half-hour massage. Dr. Wilkinson's has any number of packages, from the "Stress-Stopper" through "Magical Morning," "Stay the Day," "Salon Sampler," and "The Works" ($49 to $170). The Salon includes facial treatments for men and women, acupressure facelifts, treatments for hands and feet, and an earth-and-sea body treatment on up to makeup application (for women). Prices range from $22 to $55. There's also a hot spring on the premises, and none of these healthful facilities is limited to guests. Be sure to reserve your spa visit four to six weeks in advance. Motel rooms at Dr. Wilkinson's have color TVs, phones, and drip coffee makers. Rates are $48 to $79 singles, $53 to $90 doubles, some with kitchens. Lower weekly rates are also available. Facilities include two outdoor pools and one indoor pool.

WHERE TO DINE

Apart from the fine food at the Mount View Hotel or making the short trip to St. Helena for dining at Tra Vigne, a delightful meal in a combination deli and treasurehouse of wines may be enjoyed at the **All Seasons Market,** 1400 Lincoln Ave. (tel. 707/942-9111). You may choose to eat in or gather provisions for a picnic. However, don't overlook the luncheon and dinner specials here and the fresh desserts. Recent luncheon entrees included a mesquite-grilled chicken sandwich served with homemade bread and salad, and fettuccine with prawns served with cucumber, bell peppers, and tomatoes in virgin olive oil and white wine. Entrees range from $6 to $9. The menu also includes homemade soup and an appetizer and salad of the day.

The All Seasons Market is open Thursday through Monday from 9am to 4pm and 5 to 9pm; Tuesday, from 9am to 4pm; closed Wednesday. They serve breakfast, lunch, and dinner Thursday through Monday; breakfast and lunch on Tuesday.

8. Sonoma

Although not far from Napa Valley, Sonoma, 45 miles north of San Francisco, is of sufficient historical interest to warrant a day's sightseeing all its own.

The look and style of the town of Sonoma is a cross, if you can imagine it, between early California Mission and western Victorian—a pleasant gaggle of architectural styles.

Centuries before Europeans colonized the area, it was inhabited by the Pomo and Miwok peoples. It wasn't until the 19th century that world powers—Spain, Mexico, Russia, and the United States—began to converge in the Sonoma region. During the 1830s and 1840s one man, Gen. Mariano Guadalupe Vallejo—a brilliant Mexican army officer—was given 44,000 acres in nearby Petaluma Valley and charge of the mission of Sonoma. Vallejo's far-reaching civil and military powers brought him immense wealth and undisputed rule of the area as long as California was in Mexican hands. By 1846 he had increased his personal holdings to 175,000 acres; in that same year, however, American frontiersmen under John C. Frémont captured the area and arrested him. He was soon released, and he later served as mayor of Sonoma in 1852 and 1860.

Many aspects of the town, including the approach via a wide boulevard, Broadway, and the central plaza, are still here as Vallejo laid them out originally. He left his mark everywhere, as you'll see when you explore Sonoma's major attractions, all of which center around the **plaza**—today a lovely city park, the largest town square in California, and the setting for City Hall. The plaza is also the location of the **Bear Flag Monument,** which stands adjacent to the exact site where a band of adventurers raised the crude Bear Flag; symbolizing the end of Mexican rule, the Bear Flag was later to become the state standard. There are a multitude of shops around the plaza offering everything from food, wines, and excellent sourdough bread to clothing and books. (See "Shopping," below.)

The last Spanish mission is here, northernmost in the Franciscan chain, as is California's first winery, founded in 1857. It was not until the 1970s that Sonoma arrived at the production of vintage-dated and varietal wines characteristic of California wine making. Chardonnay is the single white variety for which Sonoma is noted and represents almost one-quarter of the acreage in vines.

GETTING THERE

To get there, just take U.S. 101 north, making a right at Calif. 37, a left at Calif. 121, then head north on Broadway, following the signs.

WHAT TO SEE AND DO

Sonoma has moved into the world of good restaurants (some quite exceptional), boutiques, galleries, and gift shops. It even has a spa bearing a pink resemblance to the Beverly Hills Hotel. Major historical landmarks and attractions are detailed below. For a complete listing, an easy-to-read map, and information on wineries, restaurants, farm trails, and antiques shops in the area, make your first stop the **Sonoma Valley Visitors Bureau,** conveniently located at 453 1st St. East (in the plaza), Sonoma, CA 95476 (tel. 707/996-1090). The bureau is open daily from 9am to 5pm.

For an extraordinarily scenic trip with touches of local history, call the **Sonoma Cattle Company** (tel. 707/996-8566) for information regarding their guided tours on horseback offered from April through October. Dates for the guided tours hinge on the weather—there are no rides during the rainy season. You'll ride through the landscape where Jack London once rode—passing through London's eucalyptus grove, past his wood-frame cottage, on up to the top of Mount Sonoma for magnificent views of the countryside. You can also rent horses at the Jack London Park or Sugarloaf Ridge State Park. Rides are for one hour ($16 per person) or two hours ($26 per person).

And if you happen to be in the vicinity of the Russian River with fishing rod in hand, you'll find plenty of steelhead trout, shad, and smallmouth bass. State regulations and fishing licenses are available in most tackle shops and sporting goods establishments. *Note:* Ask before you cast.

There are a great variety of activities for anyone heading toward the northern end of Sonoma County, including historical attractions, more wine tours than you would believe, walking tours, farm tours and markets, a miniature horse ranch, carriage rides, hot-air ballooning, swimming, fishing, boating, bicycling, camping, rock climbing, you name it. For a detailed rundown on these activities and all the marvels of Sonoma County, write to the **Sonoma County Convention and Visitors Bureau,** 10 4th St. (Railroad Square), Santa Rosa, CA 95401 (tel. 707/575-1191).

Sonoma State Historical Park

All the historical landmarks described below, with the exception of the Swiss Hotel and the Nash-Patton Adobe, are part of the Sonoma State Historic Park, 20 E. Spain St., Sonoma, CA 95476 (tel. 707/938-1519). Tickets to the landmarks can be purchased at any one of them and are good for admission to all on the same day. Fees are $1 per adult, 50¢ per child 6 to 17. All Sonoma State Historic Park landmarks described below are open daily from 10am to 5pm.

CASA GRANDE General Vallejo's first home, this Mexican-style adobe was one of the grandest residences in California when it was built in 1836. In its heyday this Spain Street house was the center of social and diplomatic life north of San Francisco. Eleven Vallejo children were born here, and it was here that Vallejo was arrested in 1846. Unfortunately, the main wing of the building was destroyed by fire in 1867, and only the Indian servants' wing remains today.

VALLEJO HOME In 1850 Vallejo purchased some additional property about a half mile northwest of the plaza on which to build another estate, called, in Latin, **Lachryma Montis** ("Mountain Tear"). Grapevines, a wide assortment of fruit trees, and other foliage and shrubbery were planted, and the quarter-mile driveway was lined with roses and cottonwood trees. An arbor-shaded pathway encircled a pool, and a number of fountains further enhanced the carefully tended grounds. The Victorian-style house went up in 1852, its interior decorated with crystal chandeliers, lace curtains, and elaborate furnishings imported from Europe. General Vallejo and his wife lived here for over 35 years. Today the buildings, grounds, and interior—furnished with many of Vallejo's personal effects—are maintained as closely as possible to the original.

SONOMA BARRACKS Erected in 1836 by (you guessed it) General Vallejo, on Spain Street facing the plaza, this wide-balconied, two-story adobe was built to house the Mexican army troops. In the years 1835 to 1846, over 100 military expeditions set out from Sonoma, most with the aim of subduing hostile Indians. Following the military takeover by the Bear Flag party, and the subsequent raising of the Stars and Stripes, Sonoma continued to be an important U.S. Army post. In still later years the building served as a winery, store, law office, and private residence, until it was purchased in 1958 by the state and partially restored.

MISSION SAN FRANCISCO SOLANO DE SONOMA Founded in 1823, this was the last of the 21 missions founded in California by Father Junípero Serra. It was the only one founded under Mexican rule. The first building was a temporary wooden structure; later a low adobe wing was added for living quarters. This latter building, which stands east of the chapel, is the oldest in Sonoma. The mission reached peak prosper-

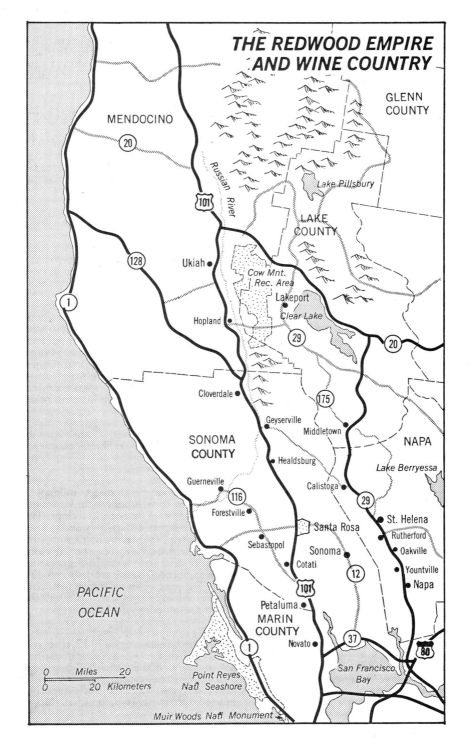

ity in 1832, when nearly 1,000 Indian converts were in residence. The present chapel was constructed in 1840 and furnished by Vallejo as a parish church. After later incarnations as a hay barn, winery, and blacksmith shop, the mission became a state monument in 1903 and was restored. It houses many mission artifacts as well as watercolors of mission scenes throughout California by Virgil Jorgensen.

SWISS HOTEL Over at 18 W. Spain St. (tel. 707/938-2884), facing the plaza, this adobe provided yet more living space for Don Salvador Vallejo. Later it was used as a hotel and restaurant, and meals are served here to this day. The furnishings are Eastlake, and the decor is of the ye-olde-inn variety. A menu on the wall from 1936 proffers a full dinner from appetizer to dessert for just $1. Full-course dinners today are considerably more expensive. Dinner is served Wednesday through Saturday from 5 to 9pm, on Sunday from 4pm. Weekdays the bar opens at 4pm; weekends, at 10am. Closed Monday and Tuesday.

BLUE WING INN This 1840 hostelry, at 133 E. Spain St., was erected by General Vallejo to accommodate travelers and emigrants who needed a place to stay while they built their Sonoma homes. It was purchased during Gold Rush days by two retired seafaring men who operated it as a hotel and store. Notable guests included John Frémont, Kit Carson, and Ulysses S. Grant; notorious guests included the bandit Murieta and "Three-fingered Jack." The inn itself is not open to the public. It now houses an antiques shop and folk-art shop, which are open Wednesday through Sunday from noon to 5pm.

TOSCANO HOTEL Among the most interesting sights in the plaza area, this wood-frame building next to the barracks looks almost as if the guests and staff just walked out suddenly one day leaving everything behind. In the parlor downstairs a game of cards in progress is laid out on the table. Bedrooms upstairs have period furnishings, rag rugs, lovely quilts, shaving stands, pitcher and bowl for washing up, and antique tortoiseshell dresser sets that include button hooks. On exhibit are some teensy clothes that were traveling salesmen's samples. Free docent-guided tours are given on Saturday and Sunday from 11am to 4pm. You'll also get to see the Toscano kitchen, furnished in the same period.

NASH-PATTON ADOBE This house, built in 1847, is where one John H. Nash was taken prisoner for refusing to surrender his post as alcade (mayor). The adobe was restored in 1931.

Train Town

The best-developed scale-model railroad in this country is located a mile south of the town square on Broadway. Everything at Train Town is built to the same one-quarter scale, including a depot, freight office, and other business buildings. The train runs a 1½-mile track through a manmade landscape of cedars, hills, and valleys, and around a lake. About midway in the 19-minute trip, a stop is made at a miniature Old West town, Lakeview. Passengers can get off the train and explore, peeking into the windows of a Wells Fargo express office, depot, Victorian bungalow, stores, fire station, and newspaper office. There's even a petting zoo. Trains leave daily every 20 minutes between 11am and 5pm from June 17 through Labor Day; on Saturday, Sunday, and holidays, weather permitting, the rest of the year. Fare is $2.50 for adults, $2 for seniors and those aged 1 to 17; those under age 1 ride free.

Jack London State Park

A ride to nearby Glen Ellen, about 7 miles northwest along Calif. 12, takes you to Jack London State Park (tel. 707/938-5216), where the famed author lived until his death at the age of 40 in 1916. Here you can see the cottage, ranch buildings, and the ruins of **Wolf House,** which London planned but never occupied—a magnificent rustic home of natural wood and stone. On August 22, 1913, a few weeks before the Londons were to move in, the house mysteriously burned down. **Happy**

Walls, where London's wife, Charmian, lived for many years after his death, is now a veritable London museum, filled with the author's possessions, mementos, and artifacts the couple brought back from their travels in the South Seas. A room on the first floor is fitted out as London's office used to be, with his desk, typewriter, and other items. Not far away, under a huge red lava boulder on a wooded knoll, are London's ashes.

The park is open daily from 8am to sundown or the closing hour posted at the station entrance; the museum, from 10am to 5pm. The park also includes London's ranch buildings, a lake, and hiking trails. There's a $3-per-car entrance fee.

Wineries

If I had the opportunity to see no more than three wineries in the Sonoma area, I'd choose Sebastiani, Buena Vista, and Chateau St. Jean. Sebastiani has a most interesting and informative guided tour and its place in the development of the region is unique. Buena Vista, after all, is the patriarch of California wineries. And Chateau St. Jean must be included for the exceptional beauty of its buildings, magnificent grounds, and its tasting room, once part of an impressive country estate.

Sonoma, like the Napa Valley, is Wine Country. It produces some of the finest wines in the States, including outstanding chardonnays. Sonoma's vineyards produce only about 4% of California's total, as does neighboring Napa. Nearly all the operations are small or medium-size, frequently family-owned (even families like the Smothers Brothers), and a far cry from the jug-wine business.

Vineyards, quite literally, are everywhere in Sonoma County, from the edges of industry up into the rugged hills that border the county. As you head north out of Sonoma on Calif. 12, the scenery evolves from an untidy backyard finish into the rough-hewn look of ranch country. You won't see the polished, city-bred look of the Napa Valley. The terrain extending up to and beyond the Sonoma Valley varies by the mile, past fields and farmland, as you proceed north toward Santa Rosa. These variations effect small changes in the climate, which in turn create the differences in the wines.

Sebastiani and Buena Vista wineries are, for all practical purposes, within the town of Sonoma. The Chateau St. Jean winery is near Kenwood, about a 20-minute drive north from Sonoma.

Sebastiani, 389 4th St. East (tel. 707/938-5532), was founded in 1904 by Samuele Sebastiani, though the original mission vineyard was founded in 1825. The winery is a survivor of Prohibition and the Depression and is still one of the most successful enterprises in the Sonoma Valley. It is the only winery in Sonoma Valley to offer a guided tour and tasting from a full selection of wines, which have won 95 awards. The tour through the stone aging cellars containing over 300 carved casks is fascinating and well worth the time. You can see the original crusher and press, as well as the largest collection of oak-barrel carvings in the world. One tank here holds 59,666 gallons of wine—if you drank a bottle a day, it would last for 800 years! If you don't want to take the tour you can go straight to the tasting room, where you can sample from an extensive selection of wines. The tasting room also offers a large assortment of winery gifts, including condiments and accessories. It's open daily from 10am to 5pm. Tours are 25 minutes; the last one starts at 4:10pm.

Buena Vista, 18000 Old Winery Rd. (tel. 707/938-1266), is slightly northeast of Sonoma. It was founded in 1857 by Count Agoston Haraszthy, the Hungarian émigré who is called the father of the California wine industry. A close friend of General Vallejo, Haraszthy journeyed to Europe at his own expense in 1861 and returned with 100,000 of the finest cuttings from European vineyards, which he made available to all wine growers. An official California landmark, the historic cellars and the original massive stone buildings are open for a self-guided tour. (Wine making now takes place in an ultramodern facility outside of Sonoma.) Tasting takes place in the restored 1862 Press House. The Knights of the Vine Wine Museum is housed in the 1857 wine cellars. There's also an art gallery and gift shop. Picnic grounds adjoin. Open daily from 10am to 5pm.

It's worth every minute of the 20-minute drive to visit **Chateau St. Jean,** 8555

Sonoma Hwy. (Calif. 12), Kenwood, CA 95452 (tel. 707/833-4134), founded in 1973 by a family of grape growers. The winery is just north of Kenwood and east of Calif. 12 on a private drive. Chateau St. Jean is situated at the foot of Sugarloaf Ridge on what once was a private 250-acre country retreat, built in 1920. The elegant tasting room had been the living room of the estate. A meticulously maintained lawn is now a picnic ground where you can enjoy the day; or you can sit by the fountain surrounded by grass and benches. It's a joy.

There is a self-guided tour with detailed photographic descriptions of the winemaking process; hours are 10:30am to 4pm daily. At the end of the tour be sure to walk up to the top of the tower for a magnificent view of the valley. Then head back to the tasting room where you can sample a range of St. Jean's wines at no charge. From each vintage, Chateau St. Jean offers several chardonnays, fumé and Pinot blancs, as well as Johannisberg Riesling and Gewürztraminer. Since 1984 the winery has been part of the Suntory family of premium wineries. Tasting room hours are 10am to 4:30pm daily, except major holidays.

The Chateau St. Jean "wine line" (tel. toll free 800/332-WINE) gives recorded reports from the Sonoma Wine Country, including updated information on vineyard conditions, interviews with winemakers and growers, what's happening at the winery, and descriptions of currently available wines.

SHOPPING

There are some marvelous places in which to browse and buy around Sonoma's plaza. A group of shops with unusual wares is to be found clustered at **The Mercato,** 452 1st St. East. **Papyrus** has a vast collection of lovely paper products, and try **Vigil's Native American Galleries** for blankets, pottery, and some exceptional jewelry. One of the most intriguing shops of its kind is the **Wine Exchange,** again at 452 1st St. East (tel. 707/938-1794), a handsomely decorated establishment bearing a slight resemblance to a proper old pub. Up front you'll find an old grape press, and to the rear is a stack of casks behind a small tasting bar. Not only does the Wine Exchange have a remarkable selection of wines, including some French wines and champagnes, but the profound beer connoisseur will also find 209 beers from around the world. It's worth a stop just to see the packaging. The Wine Exchange has both wine and beer tastings daily. They also have a number of useful books on wines, guides to the Wine Country, and copies of *The Wine Spectator* and the *Wine Journal.* It's a great place to shop, and they'll ship anywhere in the U.S. via air freight. The Wine Exchange is open daily from 10am to 6pm.

A few doors away is the **Arts Guild of Sonoma,** 460 1st St. East (tel. 707/996-3115), a nonprofit organization run by its artist members. Since it was organized in 1977, the guild has provided local professional artists with a gallery to showcase their work; exhibits change frequently. Do step in and treat yourself to a view of some truly exceptional pieces: You may see exquisite paper masks with an origami look, family figurines, Native American fiber sculptures, contemporary jewelry designed in silver and gold, in addition to paintings in a variety of mediums. The guild also sponsors art shows, some of them international in scope. In spring and summer the Arts Guild gallery is open daily from 10am to 6pm; in fall and winter, to 5pm.

WHERE TO STAY

The **El Dorado Hotel,** 405 1st St. West, Sonoma, CA 95476 (tel. 707/996-3030, or toll free 800/289-3031), is a true California beauty. The entrance, facing the pleasant Sonoma plaza and park, has an inviting air that suggests comfort, warmth, and relaxed elegance. The spacious patio within the hotel's private courtyard, the nearby ancient fig tree, and the beautifully placed plantings add to the aura of a soothing romantic retreat. The patio is a lovely place to enjoy the El Dorado's complimentary Continental breakfast—fruit, freshly baked breads and pastries, and just-made coffee—should you choose to enjoy your morning's repast outdoors.

The 23 guest rooms on the second floor have expansive French windows and terraces, some with lovely views of the plaza, others overlooking the courtyard and heated pool. The decor combines light peach-tone walls, terra-cotta floors with wine-colored rugs, and good-looking pewter-tone four-poster beds. Amenities include phones, remote-control color TVs, and private baths with plush towels and thick terrycloth robes. There are four lovely rooms on the ground floor off the private courtyard, similarly decorated, with handicapped access; each has its own partially enclosed patio.

Lunch or dinner at the Ristorante Piatti is an excellent choice. The regional Italian cuisine is prepared in an open, wood-burning oven, and the list of entrees is mouthwatering. As you might expect, the wine list offers a variety of Sonoma and Napa choices. Ristorante Piatti is open daily. Monday through Friday, lunch is served from 11:30am to 2:30pm, dinner from 5 to 11pm. Saturday and Sunday hours are noon to 11pm. Reservations are recommended (tel. 707/996-2351).

Rates at the El Dorado Hotel range from $120 to $130 for a single or double. Room rates include Continental breakfast for two per bedroom. The El Dorado Hotel is a member of the Auberge Collection, which includes the Auberge du Soleil in Rutherford and the San Ysidro Ranch in Santa Barbara.

The **Sonoma Hotel,** 110 W. Spain St., Sonoma, CA 95476 (tel. 707/996-2996), is a small, classic, historical beauty. Its accommodations evoke feelings of a different time—warm, romantic, gracious. Each of its 17 rooms has the aura of early California—magnificent antique furnishings, beautiful woods, floral-print wallpapers—all with emphasis on European elegance and comfort. Some of the room features include a handsome American brass bed, a suite of carved rosewood previously owned by General Vallejo's family, inlaid parquets, and a five-piece suite topped with very rare orange marble. You may even choose to stay in no. 21, the room on the third floor where Maya Angelou wrote *Gather Together in My Name.*

Five of the seven rooms on the second floor have private baths. Rooms on the third floor, in European tradition, share immaculate bathing quarters and toilets off the hallway; all have private wash basins. If you are bound body and soul to TV and the telephone, you'll be disappointed because rooms at the Sonoma Hotel have neither. However, for your convenience there is a hall phone on the second floor, or you can make a call at the downstairs desk. Each evening there's turndown service; each morning there's a complimentary Continental breakfast with fresh-baked pastries.

In addition to the superior location, at the corner of the square, within walking distance of picnic spots, art galleries, and historic landmarks, the Sonoma Hotel has a superb dining room and saloon, both open daily. The food is something to write a long letter home about (you'll find it discussed in detail under "Where to Dine"). Whether or not you stay at the hotel, have at least one meal there.

Rooms at the Sonoma Hotel (single or double) range from $70 to $100 on the second floor; they're $60 on the third floor. For the summer season I'd suggest at least one month's lead time for reservations.

About an hour's drive north of San Francisco and 2 miles from the Sonoma plaza is the **Sonoma Mission Inn & Spa,** Calif. 12 (P.O. Box 1447), Sonoma, CA 95476 (tel. 707/938-9000, or toll free 800/358-9022, 800/358-9027, 800/862-4945 in California). The hostelry is off Calif. 12, set back to the west on eight acres of lush landscaping surrounded by a stucco wall. It's a sweeping, three-story pink structure with mission towers, beautifully groomed lawns, bougainvillea, pines, a eucalyptus tree, and a pink fountain near the entry. Entry to the Sonoma Mission Inn is every bit as impressive as the guest facilities and services. The lobby is huge, with a beamed ceiling that presents the touch of an old Spanish mission. Tall palms serve to break up the length of the room, as does the large fireplace. Tables are finished with gray-and-pink marble; love seats are upholstered in a delicate gray-and-pink floral pattern. All of this lends a soft, warm look to what otherwise might seem to be a convention-size lobby.

There is very little the Sonoma Mission Inn does not offer in the luxurious pampering of its guests, beginning with breakfast in bed and going on to an incredible array of spa services. Guest rooms are spacious and designed with elegance and taste, from the attractively framed watercolors to the simple styling of the ceiling fans. TV sets are enclosed in cabinets, and there are minirefrigerators. A complimentary bottle of the inn's select Sonoma Valley wine is in your room when you arrive.

The large bathroom is comfortably carpeted in pink and gray, the same tones found in the marbled sinktop, and there is a bathroom scale, a telephone, a hairdryer, oversize bath towels, and a supply of Mission Inn toiletries.

Now, about the spa services—there are five categories of massage, body wraps, body scrubs, hair and scalp treatments, back treatments, and beauty salon services beyond belief. You can try the exercise class, early-morning hike, picnic hike, or the tennis courts. Private tennis lessons, fitness training, nutritional consultation, and slimming meals are all available. The cost of individual spa and salon services ranges from $10 to $70. Complimentary services include the use (adults only) of the sauna, steam room, whirlpool, outdoor exercise pool, Olympic-size pool, and gym with exercise equipment.

After all the above, should you require superior sustenance, the Mission Inn offers excellent Wine Country cuisine in the Grille or on their outdoor Terrace Grille (weather permitting).

The inn has 170 guest rooms, many with fireplaces and some with small balconies. Mission Inn rooms—those close to the focal point of the inn—range from $125 to $210 from November through April, $140 to $225 from May through October. Wine Country rooms are $160 to $245 during the above late-fall and winter season, $205 to $290 in the spring and summer months. Suites are $330 to $525 year-round.

Low-cost lodgings in Sonoma are simply not that easy to come by. But if you prefer to stay in Sonoma proper, the **El Pueblo Motel,** 896 W. Napa St., Sonoma, CA 95476 (tel. 707/996-3651 or 996-3652), falls into the moderate category. The rooms are quite pleasant, having post-and-beam construction, exposed brick walls, and brown carpeting throughout. All have an Early American look—knotty-pine headboard and furnishings, knobby white bedspreads, and pine desk and chairs. All rooms have two double beds, full baths, color TVs, phones, and individually controlled heat and air conditioning. A nice touch for early risers is a drip coffee machine supplied with packets of coffee. Rates are $50 for one or two people Sunday through Thursday, $55 on Friday and Saturday. For Thanksgiving and Christmas, rates are increased to $60. I'd suggest that, if possible, reservations be made at least one month in advance during the spring and summer months.

WHERE TO DINE

When you want a quick breakfast with fresh-baked rolls, or bagels with whatever, **Home Grown Bagels,** 122 W. Napa St. (tel. 707/996-0166), is the place to go. Orders are eat-here or take-out; the latter may be wise due to the frequent line of locals. There are onion bagels, garlic bagels, bialys, sesame bagels, pumpernickel bagels, egg bagels, etc. Spaces between the sliced halves can be filled with such goodies as cream cheese and lox, or try pastrami, salami, BLT, and Canadian BLT. For a somewhat more fitting breakfast, there's ham and egg on a bagel. For Manhattanites, the selection extends to lox, egg, and onion; lox, egg, and onion with cheese (!); and much more. All these complex glories fall in the $4 to $4.75 range. Salads, veggies, and salad plates are always available ($2.75 to $5.50), and in addition to the usual hot beverages, you can have cold beer, wine, and soft drinks.

Home Grown Bagels is open Monday through Friday from 7am to 3pm, on Saturday and Sunday from 8am. On the breakfast circuit, it's a mob scene after 8:30am, so be prepared to wait or get there early. In either case, it's worth it.

The great new place to eat is appropriately called **The Feed Store Cafe and Bakery,** 529 1st St. West, at the corner of West Napa (tel. 707/938-2122). You'll first notice that The Feed Store is attractive, airy, and fresh, and that everyone's nice as can be. The interior space, with its high ceilings, is typical of turn-of-the-century feed stores. The open kitchen adds to the total look of spaciousness. During warm weather you might enjoy al fresco dining on the lovely rear patio, all beautifully done with lots of flowers and greenery and a genteel gurgling fountain. On the other hand, if you'd like only a cup of coffee or an ice cream, you might just want to settle outside on the front patio.

Whatever your choice of meals may be, you'll find food that is first-rate, reasonably priced, and plentiful. For breakfast, The Feed Store Cafe has more varieties of eggs and omelets than you could eat in a month's stay, including such delectables as the Sonoma Mission Scrambler on tortilla strips and huevos rancheros, and there is delicious special-recipe french toast. Breakfast ranges from $2.50 on up to $8 for exotic mix-and-match options. Lunch selections, from $3.75 to $8, are designed to match any appetite—from quesadillas to half-pound burgers, grilled-chicken-breast sandwiches, and choices from Roberto's Mexican Corner.

In the early afternoon the counter becomes a tapas bar (Spanish-style appetizers) where you can also enjoy Sonoma Valley wines. As for dinner, specials change daily, though the mainstays of the dinner menu are seafood and chicken, barbecued ribs and chicken ($8.50 to $12.50). Lighter choices are available from the restaurant's list of appetizers, burgers, sandwiches, baked goods, and pizzas (sold by the pie or by the piece). The Feed Store Cafe serves beer on tap or by the bottle, and wines both still and sparkling, including a fine selection from the Sonoma Valley. The Bakery section of The Feed Store Cafe bakes fresh goods daily for the restaurant, and for purchase at the counter should you feel the need for a mid-afternoon nosh or midnight snack in your room.

Open Tuesday through Saturday from 7am to 9pm, on Sunday and Monday to 3pm.

Whether or not you've had your fill of cheese and wine, a great place for a different sort of lunch is **Ma Stokeld's Village Pub,** in the Place des Pyrénées (about halfway down on the right) at 464 1st St. East (tel. 707/935-0660). It's owned and operated by Yorkshireman Chris Stokeld and his family, and they've created a small, pleasant place with the friendly look of an English pub, complete with flag, dart board, out chart, and all. One wall is half-paneled and has a knickknack shelf above with an empty of Old Navy Rum, pictures of the current queen, the Prince and Princess of Wales, the Duke and Duchess of York, and an interesting collection of decorative mugs. There's a community wood bench along the wall to supplement the straight-back chairs and wooden stools.

The Stokeld family makes English pasties (puff-pastry turnovers with various meat and vegetable fillings), meat pies, and bangers daily (no preservatives), using Yorkshire recipes handed down from a butcher uncle. There are breakfast pasties with egg, cheese, potato, and tomato filling; Cornish pasties with beef, potato, and onion; chicken pasties; and other delightful concoctions ($4.50 to $5.25). Try a ploughman's lunch, a pork pie with cheese, cole slaw, and pickled onion ($4.75). Or you might prefer a tasty steak pie with onion, gravy, and seasoning ($5.25). Not exactly the English equivalent of hot dogs, bangers are English-style pork sausages (homemade), served on a French roll with fried onions ($4.50). Any and all of the above can be put up for you to picnic with on the grass at Sonoma Square.

Ma Stokeld's could hardly be regarded as the likeness of a very proper English pub without serving Bass and Guinness on draft. There's also an assortment of other ales, and lagers, wines and soft drinks, including hot tea.

Ma Stokeld's Village Pub is open Tuesday through Sunday from 11am to 10pm, on Monday to 5pm.

Dining at the **Sonoma Hotel,** 110 W. Spain St. (tel. 707/996-2996), is truly a visual and gastronomic treat you don't want to pass up. The Sonoma is a respectful restoration of the original hotel dating back to the 1880s. The beauty of the furnishings and decor of that period is what you first notice as you enter the hotel's Saloon. There's a magnificent old bar of oak and mahogany softened by the warmth and patina of decades of comfortable use. The Saloon is a guileless charmer—an inviting, relaxed, comfortable spot out of another time—great for wine tasting, cocktails, conversation, waiting for your dinner partner, or for a pleasant after-dinner drink. The dining room follows with its antique oak tables, decorative panels of stained glass, fresh flowers, comfortable oak chairs, and simply superb food. The dinner menu changes every two weeks and specials are offered each evening. There are always great choices whether your taste that evening happens to be for an exceptional beef, seafood, veal, chicken, or pasta dish. And the chef always includes seasonal vegetables, herbs from the hotel's garden, and homemade ingredients or those produced locally. One evening I had two exquisite portions of broiled oysters with cilantro pesto and goat cheese, generally deemed an appetizer. Among the dinner entrees offered during my Sonoma stay were a grilled New York steak with a marsala and green-peppercorn sauce, a nicely finished sautéed veal porterhouse stuffed with blue cheese and topped with champagne-cream sauce and chantrelles, and fresh Bodega Bay steelhead trout with cashews and cilantro in a lime-butter sauce.

Dinners are three-course affairs including entree, soup du jour, and a green salad; most are $14 to $17.50. Suppers ($12) are two courses, including an entree and green salad; choices for supper may include fresh pasta, a beautifully prepared shepherd's chicken pie, even calamari steak. The service is excellent—friendly, knowledgeable, competent, and most helpful. The wine list is first-rate, and there's a good selection at $3 to $4.50 by the glass. Should you decide to bring a bottle you may have selected at one of the vineyards, the corkage charge is $7.

The Sonoma Hotel serves lunch daily from 11:30am to 2:30pm; Sunday brunch is from 10:45am. In good weather you can dine on the patio. Dinner is served Thursday through Tuesday from 5:45 to 8:30pm, to 9pm during the summer. The Sonoma is a favorite dining place for locals, so make reservations for dinner.

Just off Sonoma Square and across the street from the Mission San Francisco de Solano, **La Casa**, 121 E. Spain St. (tel. 707/996-3406), is just the place to satisfy a yen for enchiladas, burritos, chiles rellenos, fajitas, ceviche, or even chimichangitas, perhaps preceded by a lovely margarita. La Casa opens onto a lounge and bar, then down to a two-tiered softly lit dining area. There are straight-back chairs with leather seats, oak tables, hanging plants, old photos, dark-wood paneling, and beige walls as background for decorative Mexican platters and colorful sombreros.

First to arrive are the tortilla chips accompanied by a delicious homemade chunky salsa. Appetizers might include ceviche (as available) or fresh snapper marinated in lime juice and served on two crispy tortillas. If your appetite is light, among a number of delectables there's a savory tortilla soup made with a base of homemade chicken soup. The real treats are to be found among the specialties de la casa. Tamales freshly made in La Casa's kitchen are prepared with corn husks spread with corn masa, stuffed with chicken filling, and topped with mild red-chile sauce. Then there are the enchiladas suizas, deep-dish enchiladas with corn tortillas filled with chicken or ground beef. But if the fresh snapper Veracruz is available, that tops the menu. For dessert, La Casa's flan ($1.50), with a delicate coffee flavor and a texture more like that of mousse, is exceptional. But for a truly unusual finale, have a piece of the icebox cake ($2.50), composed of flour tortillas, layered with sour cream blended with vanilla and bittersweet Mexican chocolate. And with your meal, try one of six cold Mexican beers, or choose one of the domestics (including nonalcoholic beer). Sonoma County wines are also available by the bottle or glass. Specialties of the house for lunch or dinner range from $6 to $10. Burritos or enchilada/taco/chile relleno combinations are $5 to $9. Appetizers will add another $4 to $6.

La Casa is open daily from 11:30am to 9pm. Make reservations for dinner, especially on weekends and for any evening during the summer.

Les Arcades, 133 E. Napa St. (tel. 707/938-3723), just off Sonoma Square, is a small (10 tables) French beauty that presents superb food and faultless service in a most charming setting. Pink cloths and pink napkins are at table, accompanied by a small chimney-style lamp and fresh flowers. Overhead, chandelier lighting glows from soft-light bulbs within deep golden tulip-shaped cups. Against one wall is a fireplace with a distinguished marble face decorated with bunches of carved grapes that, for all the world, have a Gallic look about them.

Beginning with the hors d'oeuvres, hot and cold, there is nothing commonplace about anything offered. The mousse of fish with champagne sauce, sweetbreads sautéed crisp with lemon and capers, and a delicate salmon pâté are just a few of the excellent choices. As the list of entrees will enchant almost any taste. My choice was the boneless medallions of lamb with basil sauce, and the flavor was as spectacular as the presentation. Among other delectables are prawns with garlic, cream, and Pernod; breast of Sonoma duck with green peppercorns and port sauce;

steak au poivre, served with black peppercorns and flambé cognac. Vegetables are served with all entrees. Les Arcades also offers daily specials for your consideration. Dessert choices aren't easy. I'm a pushover for the crème brûlée, a smooth custard topped with crispy caramel. However, it's difficult to ignore the puff pastries filled with vanilla ice cream and covered with warm chocolate sauce, or the very rich chocolate mousse. Entrees range from $15 to $20; appetizers, from $2 to $9; desserts, from $4 to $9. Les Arcades has an excellent selection of California as well as French wines.

Les Arcades is open Wednesday through Sunday from 5 to 10pm. Reservations are essential (during the summer, I suggest at least one week in advance, preferably two; otherwise, a week in advance for weekends).

A narrow brick pathway guides you from the street up to the entrance of **Pasta Nostra,** 139 E. Napa St. (tel. 707/938-4166). As you may have guessed, fresh homemade pasta is the specialty of the house as an entree or tasty accompaniment to several styles of veal and chicken. The interior of Pasta Nostra is an easy and attractive blend of effects that leaves no doubt that it's an Italian restaurant, though quite contemporary in design (no hanging chianti bottles here). A slim Roman column and huge bouquet of flowers are on the left as you enter; ahead are stacks of wine bottles and a map of Italy. On a warm summer night you may choose to dine on the patio.

The menu changes nightly, but entrees basically consist of select milk-fed veal prepared in scaloppine, parmigiana, piccata, or milanese style. Baked chicken is offered à la siciliana, scaloppine, or parmigiana. Though all dishes are à la carte, chicken and veal dinners are served with fresh pasta. For the lover of seafood, "fruit of the sea" is prepared with scallops and prawns in a rich cream sauce. A choice alternative is the prawns scampi served in a tasty blend of lemon butter and garlic. Both seafood dishes are served with fettuccine. Homemade pasta (fettuccine or spaghetti) is offered in a variety of ways. The fettuccine carbonara with bacon, egg, and Asiago cheese is above reproach, as is the spaghetti al pomodoro, simply served with a specially prepared tomato sauce. But the highlight of the pasta events is the spaghetti "1492" with sun-dried tomatoes, prosciutto, Asiago cheese, garlic, fresh tomatoes, and herbs. Entrees cost $9 to $13. Soup or salad will add $2.75 to $3.25 to the total. The dessert selection changes daily. As a final touch to all, espresso is available in several variations ($1.50 to $2.50). Pasta Nostra offers beer by the bottle and select house wines by the glass. Should you decide to bring your own wine, the corkage charge is $7.50 per bottle.

Pastra Nostra is open nightly: Monday through Thursday from 5 to 9pm, on Friday and Saturday to 10pm, and on Sunday from 4:30 to 9pm.

The **Depot Hotel 1870 Restaurant,** 241 1st St. West (707/938-2980), is just one block from Sonoma Square. It's in a handsome historic stone building that has seen several lives. The original owners (back in 1870, as you might have guessed) opened up their living room as a bar, then added a lean-to kitchen and dining room to what had become the Depot Saloon. In 1900 eight hotel rooms were added to the second floor. With the advent of Prohibition, the house once again became a private residence, later a print shop; finally, it was abandoned. Restoration was begun in 1962 and the Depot Hotel 1870 was reopened as a restaurant and wine bar. Today the place has a comfortable country finish polished to a fresh glow. To the rear you overlook a fenced-in terra-cotta patio with lots of greenery and a small pool surrounded by tables for dining. The main dining room is an airy array of white linen over dark-blue cloths, with white walls, mirrors, dark-blue carpeting, and, above all, a lovely antique chandelier with droplets of crystal.

Chef Michael Ghilarducci has owned the restaurant since 1985. When he is able to get away, he travels throughout France and Italy acquiring new recipes and visiting his family near Florence. Ghilarducci has received the honor of Grand Master Chef of America and is listed in the National Registry of Master Chefs along with such well-known California names as Alice Waters, Wolfgang Puck, Jeremiah Towers, and Phillipe Jeanty of Napa's Domaine Chandon.

A number of dishes, though not all, are northern Italian in origin, designed by

Ghilarducci to feature locally produced meats, poultry, seafood, bread, cheeses, and vegetables. At lunch there's a delicious sandwich of prosciutto and Sonoma Jack cheese served on French bread. On the other hand, you might begin a complete meal with an appetizer of vitello tonnato: paper-thin veal slices and capers touched with a delicate lemon and mayonnaise sauce. For those whose eyes gleam at the thought of a creamy pasta (and who have a hearty appetite), the tortellini supreme—stuffed with ricotta, veal, and chicken, touched with a delicate cream sauce and freshly grated parmesan cheese—is a path to sheer joy at lunch or dinner. Other entrees may include veal scaloppine, chicken and Italian sausage with polenta, the chef's selection of fresh seafood of the day, prawns bordelaise, bistecca alla fiorentina, calamari steak sautéed with white wine, shallots, and lemon. All entrees are served with a choice of salad or soup of the day. As for dessert, the tiramisu is a bestseller—here, sponge cake layered with freshly grated chocolate and mascarpone (an imported Italian cream cheese) and sprinkled with espresso and rum. For those lacking a sweet tooth, there is always fresh fruit and cheese.

Lunch entrees range from $6 to $12. Add another $5 for an appetizer. Dinner ranges from $7 for pasta dishes to $16 for main courses, and $5 to $7.25 for a selection from the appetizer list.

The Depot Hotel 1870 Restaurant is open for lunch Wednesday through Friday from 11:30am to 2pm. Dinner is served Wednesday through Sunday from 5 to 9pm. Reservations are suggested for both lunch and dinner.

Al Fresco

The eight-acre park surrounding the plaza is a lovely place for picnicking (how often have you picnicked in a national landmark?), and provisions are available directly across the street.

For gastronomical rather than historical intake, stop in at the **Sonoma Cheese Factory,** 2 Spain St. (tel. 707/996-1000), a bustling grocery/deli where a long display case is filled with every variety of Italian meat imaginable, 101 kinds of cheese, plus caviar, gourmet salads, pâté, and the Sonoma Jack cheese they make. They'll be happy to put whatever you choose into a crusty French bread sandwich, which, along with a small bottle of wine, will make a great picnic lunch. Picnic tables can be found in the plaza park. The Cheese Factory also has its own outdoor tables. And while you're here you can see a free narrated slide show about cheese making.

Open daily from 9:30am to 5:30pm.

Another special spot for picnicking supplies if you're given to the beauties of a superb cheese lunch is the **Vella Cheese Company,** 315 2nd St. East, one block north of East Spain Street (tel. 707/938-3232, or toll free 800/848-0505). This is where they make and sell the original dry Jack cheese, the carefully aged perfect accompaniment for wines. Vella Cheese also makes a rich, buttery Monterey Jack, naturally seasoned Jack, and a superb sharp white cheddar. The company has also become famous for the Oregon blue, a rich, spreadable blue cheese made at their factory in southern Oregon, one of the few great blues produced in this country. Any one of these fine handmade, all-natural cheeses can be purchased to take on your picnic or to be shipped. If you give it as a gift, you'll make a friend for life.

The Vella Cheese Company is open Monday through Saturday from 9am to 6pm, and on Sunday from 10am to 5pm.

Then there's the **Sonoma Sausage Co.,** 453 1st St. West, also on the plaza (tel. 707/938-8200). The fragrance is heavenly—smoked sausage, cooked sausage, Louisiana-style sausage, dry sausage, smoked meats, pâtés, lunch meats. In fact, there are more than 85 delicious varieties of sausages and lunch meats. All of the smoked sausages are fully cooked, so it's just a matter of heating them. On the other hand, for noshing or preparing later, you might pick up some smoked turkey breast, Sonoma ham, Westphalian ham, Sonoma hot salami, German bologna (all right, so it's a contradiction), Bierwurst, or liverwurst. It's encouraging to know that Sonoma sausages are made with 100% pure meat and contain no cereals, soy concentrates, or other fillers. Sonoma Sausage Co. will supply you with descriptive material about its various sausages—how to prepare or serve them, cooked or not—and some excellent recipes. The products are an accurate representation of the awards the company has won over the past several years. Sonoma Sausage Co. will ship orders to any state except Alaska or Hawaii. Gift packages are available for Christmas only.

9. Fort Ross

Now a state historic park, Fort Ross, 11 miles north of Jenner on Calif. 1, was once a North American outpost of the Russian empire. It was over 150 years ago, during the "fur rush" days, that Fort Ross was dedicated by the Russian-American Fur Company on the name-day of Czar Alexander I.

The history of Russian imperialistic designs on California (which helped prompt the Monroe Doctrine) actually dates back to 1740, when Russian explorer Vitus Bering brought news that Alaska was teeming with sea otters, for whose pelts the Chinese Mandarins would pay handsomely. Enter the Russian-American Company. By 1799 the Russians had taken possession of Alaska. They soon decimated the otter herds of Alaska, and sent ships southward for supplies and to scout out new sources of prey. One of these expeditions, headed by manager Ivan Kuskof, landed at Fort Ross in 1812. In two years they shipped home 200,000 otter skins from the area.

California at the time was more or less administered by Mexico. The Russians conveniently disregarded Mexican rule, trading blankets and beads with the peaceful Pomo coastal tribe in exchange for land. At first Fort Ross prospered. So highly did the czar value this California outpost that in 1821 he issued an imperial order denying the coast north of San Francisco to all except Russian ships. Mexico rose from apathy and sent one of its officers, Mariano Guadalupe Vallejo, up to the area with a few soldiers and orders to contain the Russians. Two years later President James Monroe promulgated his historic doctrine forbidding the American continent to foreign nations.

But it was neither the Americans nor the Mexicans who caused Alexander's minions to pull back. It was, rather, the work of the otter and the gopher. The "limitless" herds of otter, indiscriminately slaughtered, were just about extinct by the 1830s. And to make matters worse, gophers (described by the Russians as "hordes of underground rats") began to destroy crops. Fort Ross was fast becoming a liability. That same year Capt. Johann Sutter paid $30,000 for the land and the buildings and the Muscovites sailed home, putting an end to Russia's colonial expansion in the U.S.

In 1906 the State of California acquired the much-crumbled fort and a few acres around it and restorations were performed in the 1910s through the 1920s. Following documents and descriptions, the chapel (since burned down and rebuilt a second time), stockade, commandant's house, and blockhouses were carefully recreated.

The park is open daily from 10am to 4:30pm (except Christmas, New Year's Day, and Thanksgiving); a parking area ($3 per vehicle, $2 if you're 62 or older) and picnic grounds are on the premises. There's a **Visitors Center** on the grounds at 19005 Coast Hwy. (Calif. 1), where you can stop for information, as well as view slide presentations and artifacts; it also houses a gift shop.

Fort Ross' Reef, a campground, has been opened about 1½ miles south of the fort. There are 20 sites ($11 per night, $4 per extra vehicle), no hookups, no dogs allowed. For more information, call 707/847-3286.

DAY TRIPS SOUTH FROM SAN FRANCISCO

1. GREAT AMERICA
2. SAN JOSE
3. SANTA CRUZ

Up to this point we've been heading, roughly, north from San Francisco. Now round up the kids and head south, where an abundance of fun-for-the-family day trips awaits you. A tour of California's myriad amusement and theme parks (many located in Southern California) might begin with the old-fashioned boardwalk amusement park in Santa Cruz, and Great America, a Disneyland-esque 200-acre theme park complete with costumed characters, in Santa Clara. Little-known but eerily intriguing attractions like Winchester House and the Mystery Spot add their own excitement—and that's not the half of it. All this fun is just an hour or two from San Francisco.

1. Great America

South along U.S. 101, 45 miles below San Francisco, in Santa Clara (get off at the Great America exit), is a 100-acre theme park with 31 major rides, as well as shows and special attractions, a cinema housing the world's largest motion-picture screen, games, arcades, and plenty more for a full day's entertainment.

Great America has several theme areas: a 1920s rural American town, a replica of the legendary Klondike in the 1890s Gold Rush days, an 18th-century New England seaport, a turn-of-the-century county fair and midway, and a romantic 1850s version of the New Orleans French Quarter.

Attracting great hordes of daredevil San Franciscans, the ride-freak's favorite is the Demon, the only roller coaster in California to turn you upside down four times, speed through steaming tunnels, and plunge into a blood-red waterfall. But for pure hysteria, try the gigantic wooden roller coaster, the Grizzly, and more thrills on the Tidal Wave. This mechanical giant is one of the world's tallest coasters (142½ feet) and has a 76-foot-diameter loop that riders spin through forward and backward. You can get a great view of the proceedings from the top of the Sky Whirl, a triple-armed Ferris wheel; from the cable cars of the Delta Flyer skyride; or from the 20-story Sky Tower. And there's Rip Roaring Rapids, a $5-million white-water-raft ride—you're sure to get wet as you brave the quarter mile of churning water. It's wild and fun, but not scary. For the total coward (I'm one), Great America has just the thing—they've refurbished my favorite ride, the Columbia, the tallest carousel in the world and certainly one of the handsomest. Or you can share the kiddies' Blue Streak roller coaster. Among all Great America's terrific rides, you're sure to find one to match your level of courage.

There are over 100 varied show times daily, with entertainment ranging from dolphin and animal shows to puppet shows, Smurf Woods, to a comical stage show featuring Bugs Bunny and his *Looney Tunes* buddies live onstage. And strolling through the park, you'll see Fred Flintstone, Yogi Bear, Huckleberry Hound, Barney Rubble, and George Jetson and his faithful dog, Astro. In addition to the regularly scheduled acts, there are marching bands, barbershop quartets, parades, concerts, special events in spring and fall, fireworks, and other happenings.

If all the activity doesn't unsettle your tummy, there are 23 low-priced eateries to choose from, serving everything from hamburgers (4,500 are wolfed down every day) to fried chicken. After lunch you can browse through any one of 32 shops and boutiques, watch craftspeople (including totem pole carvers) at work, or test your skill at arcade games.

Guests pay a one-price admission that includes everything except food, games, and gifts. The price is $19 for all those over 7; under-7s get in free. For further information, phone 408/988-1800 (recording) or 408/988-1776. Parking is $4 per vehicle.

Great America usually opens about mid-March and closes in October. During the spring and fall it's open only on weekends and holidays from 10am to about 6pm. From May 31 through Labor Day, Great America is open daily from 10am to about 9pm.

---

2. San Jose

This is the town that Burt Bacharach immortalized some years back with the musical question: "Do you know the way to San Jose?" The answer: Just keep going south for 48 miles on U.S. 101, and you'll find yourself in a city that houses seven universities and colleges and an abundance of visitor attractions.

WHAT TO SEE AND DO

Winchester House
Most intriguing of all the local sights is the Winchester Mystery House, a 160-room Victorian mansion at 525 S. Winchester Blvd., at the intersection of I-880 and I-280 (tel. 408/247-2101), built by Sarah L. Winchester, widow of the son of the famous rifle magnate. Convinced by a spiritualist that the lives of her husband and baby daughter had been taken by the spirits of those killed with Winchester repeaters, she was told that she, too, would share their fate . . . unless, that is, she began to build a mansion on which work could *never* stop. Whether the medium had a strange sense of humor or a husband in the contracting business, no one knows. Maybe she was right—Sarah Winchester followed her instructions and lived to be 82. Starting with an eight-room house, a fortune of $20 million, and an income of $1,000 a day at her disposal, she proceeded to base her life on the medium's advice. At night passersby heard strange ghostly music wafting from the mansion, and a bell in the belfry tolled regularly at midnight to warn off evil spirits and summon good ones to protect her.

Her first move was to hire 22 carpenters and seven Japanese gardeners, the latter to keep the towering hedge thick enough to shut out all view of the premises from the road. None of them ever saw her, nor did the servants, except for the Chinese butler who served her meals on the Winchester $30,000 gold dinner service. All orders were issued by Miss Margaret Merriam, niece, secretary, and finally heiress to the fortune. The work went on seven days a week, 24 hours per day(!), 365 days a year, even on Christmas. (And you thought Howard Hughes was peculiar.)

Several rooms have been restored and furnished with period pieces. There are exquisite gold and silver chandeliers, doors inlaid with German silver and bronze, Tiffany stained-glass windows valued at $10,000 each, beautiful wood paneling, intricate parquet floors, windowpanes of French beveled plate glass, mantels of Japanese tile and hand-picked bamboo—I could fill pages describing the treasures within. But equally, if not more, interesting are Mrs. Winchester's bizarre constructions to foil the vengeful ghosts—particularly the ghosts of Native Americans, many of whom were dispatched to the Happy Hunting Grounds via Winchester repeaters. Doors lead to nowhere. Some staircases ascend to the ceiling, and others contain steps just 2 inches high, and go up, down, and up to climb to a height of about 7 feet. Such schemes were supposed to confound spirits, particularly those of the "simple redskins" she feared the most. And the number 13 comes up often—13 bathrooms, 13 windows in a room, 13 palms lining the main driveway—and many multiples of 13, such as 52 skylights.

Informative guided tours of this fascinating house take place daily between 9am and 5:30pm in summer, till 4:30pm in spring and fall, and till 4pm in winter. Admission to the Winchester estate is $11 for adults, $9 for seniors 60 and older, $6 for children 6 to 12, and free for those under 6. Included in the price is admission to the garden and outlying buildings, plus the Winchester Rifle and Antique Products Museums. The Winchester Rifle Museum obviously has a large collection of Winchesters, but as its name suggests, it also displays many rifles, some dating back to the 1800s. A number of these are from other countries, including some beautiful pieces with exquisitely designed stocks from the Middle East. The Antique Products Museum has on display many items made by the Winchester company in the early 1900s—knives, roller skates, fishing tackle, tools, flashlights—products not commonly associated with the name of Winchester. Allow at least 1½ to 2 hours for your visit.

Rosicrucian Park and Other Sights

Almost as unusual as Winchester House is Rosicrucian Park and the various museums on its grounds. Inside the imposing **Administration Building,** which copies the design of the Great Temple of Rameses III, members of the ancient order, with titles like Grand Master and Supreme Secretary, are doing the organization's work. In the **Egyptian Museum,** thousands of original and rare Egyptian, Assyrian, and Babylonian antiquities are on display: statuary, textiles, jewelry, and paintings; mummified high priests, animals, and birds; toys entombed with a child 5,000 years ago; a full-size reproduction of an Egyptian limestone tomb, sarcophagi, etc. The **Art Gallery** exhibits an eclectic variety of works of famous local, national, and international artists.

The Egyptian Museum and Art Gallery are open Tuesday through Sunday from 9am to 5pm. Admission is $3 for adults, $1 for those under 18.

The **Science Museum and Planetarium** deal with subjects ranging from seismography to space travel, demonstrating how fundamental laws of the physical sciences elucidate nature's mysteries. And if you should be interested in the Rosicrucian Order, there's much literature about, as well as people who can answer your questions. Admission to the Science Museum is free.

The Planetarium is open daily from 1 to 4:45pm. It's closed on Thanksgiving, Christmas, and New Year's Day. Different shows are presented yearly. Adults pay $2; seniors, $1.50; those 7 to 17, $1; under 7, free. There's no charge to see the science exhibits.

San Jose visitors can also take a stroll through **Kelley Park,** 1300 Senter Rd. (tel. 408/295-8383), one of San Jose's most unique and popular attractions. At the northern end of the park complex is **Happy Hollow Park and Zoo.** It's a creative children's park with play areas, puppet and marionette shows, and an exotic animal and petting zoo. In the center of the park is the **Japanese Friendship Garden,** modeled after the beautiful Korakuen Garden, a serene symbol of goodwill between the sister cities of San Jose and Okayama, Japan. At the southern end of the park is the **San Jose Historical Museum**, 1600 Senter Rd. (tel. 408/287-2290), with exhibits on local history in a city setting of over 21 buildings, including restored homes, stables, a firehouse, the Bank of Italy, a print shop, and a trolley barn. The museum is open daily: weekdays from 10am to 4:30pm, weekends from noon. Admission is $2 for adults, $1.50 for seniors, and $1 for children 6 to 17. There are food concessions throughout the park.

WHERE TO DINE

A convenient place for lunch following your exploration of Winchester House is the **Magic Pan**, 335 S. Winchester Blvd. (tel. 408/247-9970). Like the rest of the chain, this restaurant serves a variety of reasonably priced crêpe specialties as well as steaks, seafood, and pasta dishes in a French country setting. It's open daily for lunch and dinner, plus Sunday brunch.

3. Santa Cruz

When San Franciscans feel like a day at the beach, they willingly drive the 74 miles south along Calif. 1 to Santa Cruz, one of the few northern coastal locations where the water is actually warm enough to swim in—at any rate Northern Californians think it's warm. Whether you do or not, you'll find plenty of ways to amuse yourself. This despite the fact that some commercial areas are still under repair due to the October 1989 quake.

WHAT TO SEE AND DO

The Boardwalk

The hub of beach activities from May through mid-September and weekends the rest of the year is the old-fashioned Boardwalk. You can spend the morning digging your toes into the sand, surfing, sunbathing, and swimming; later take a walk on the Boardwalk, as the card says. There are over 20 rides, including a roller coaster, log flume, haunted castle, bumper cars, and a hand-carved merry-go-round (just about my speed). There are two big penny arcades, miniature golf, and of course, food concessions where you can buy hot dogs, corn on the cob, cotton candy, and other classic Boardwalk edibles, so to speak. If you continue your ramble west along the Boardwalk you'll get to—

Municipal Wharf

And a very nice fisherman's wharf it is, with picturesque shops, fish markets, and seafood restaurants. You can bring or rent tackle, buy bait, and fish off the wharf or in a rented boat. Deep-sea fishing trips depart daily from about February 1 to November 15, and on weekends during December and January, weather permitting.

Among the seafood restaurants is **Malio's** (tel. 408/423-5200), overlooking the water and serving seasonally fresh seafood dinners daily. It's a pretty place, with plank-wood walls and ceilings, cream-colored walls, and blue-and-white-checked tablecloths set with royal-blue napkins to add a splash of color. A bit pricey, but the food is good and the service is friendly. Malio's is also open for lunch on weekends only, from noon to 3:30pm.

Farther along the wharf is **Miramar** (tel. 408/423-4441), a little fancier than Malio's, with green wallpaper, carpeting, and large windows overlooking Monterey Bay. Luncheons here are a good buy: priced at $7 to $11 according to entree, they including soup or salad and rice or french fries. Sample entrees include broiled salmon, sole amandine, and scallops (each for $8). At dinner, similar meals average $11 to $14, also including soup or salad, and fresh vegetables. Open Tuesday through Sunday for lunch and dinner.

No need for fancy dining, however; you can stop in any of numerous shops and snack bars and get shrimp cups and other tasty edibles—seating and view are free on the wharf. By the way, there's lots of metered parking at the wharf.

Shopping and Browsing

Going north from the beach or wharf along Pacific Avenue, you'll come to the **Pacific Garden Mall** (a free shuttle operates from the beach to the mall and back daily in summer every 20 minutes). Scene of frequent craft fairs and festivities, the mall has a wide variety of shops to explore, including the **Cooper House,** a restaurant-shopping complex that was formerly the County Courthouse. Short rambles up side streets from the mall will reveal Victorian and Edwardian mansions, as well as other architectural landmarks, including the **Mission Santa Cruz,** 126 High St. A brochure detailing four historic walking tours will greatly enhance such an architecture stroll—pick one up at the **Conference and Visitors Council,** Cooper and Front streets (tel. 408/423-1111).

Mystery Spot

Situated in a redwood forest, 2½ miles north of Santa Cruz at 1953 Branciforte Dr. (tel. 408/423-8897; just follow the signs—getting there is no mystery), the "spot" is a section of woodlands, 150 feet in diameter, where the laws of gravity seem to have gone haywire. Wildlife avoids the area and birds will not nest here; instruments on planes flying overhead go dead; even the trees grow aslant. It's all due, we are told, to some mysterious, unexplainable, eerie "force."

There are some theories about what happens here: Perhaps there's a trace gas seeping from the earth that disorients visitors; maybe a meteor, minerals, or a magnet are buried deep underground, exerting a magnetic force or distorting the sun's rays. But such explanations don't satisfy scientists or sufficiently explain the phenomenon. The owners of the land have done a fine job of protecting the woodland setting and arranging excellent guided tours for visitors (wear rubber-soled shoes). A series of demonstrations allows you to experience the force for yourself: A ball set down on a slanted plank rolls uphill (skeptics can place the ball themselves or try another object like a lipstick). As you climb the hillside, you'll find that you're walking as straight-legged as you would on level ground. A tilted wooden house, used for demonstration purposes, makes the change in perspective most obvious. Ever walk up a wall? You can here, and it's easy. For one of the most amazing demonstrations, the guide places two people on either side of a level block (tested with a carpenter's level) and one seems to shrink while the other grows. It's an interesting diversion, even for skeptics.

The Mystery Spot is open daily from 9:30am to 5pm. Adults pay $3; kids 5 to 11 pay $2. Youngsters adore the Mystery Spot.

RC&BTNGRR

That mess of letters stands for **Roaring Camp and Big Trees Narrow-Gauge Railroad,** a major Santa Cruz–area attraction nestled in the Santa Cruz Mountains near Felton (off Calif. 17) on Graham Hill Road. America's last steam-powered passenger railroad offering daily scheduled runs, the RC&BTNGRR is a colorful reminder of Gold Rush days, operating authentic 1880 and 1890 equipment on a 6½-mile, 75-minute round trip through magnificent redwood forests. Passengers board trains from the old-fashioned depot at Roaring Camp. The train chugs through forests of trees towering hundreds of feet overhead, past such quaint station points as Big Trees, Indian Creek, Grizzly Flats, and Deer Valley en route to the summit of Bear Mountain. Passengers may detrain here for hiking or picnicking to return on a later train. On spring, summer, and fall weekends there's live country music. You can take this delightful ride any day during summer, on weekends and holidays the rest of the year. Departures are daily every hour and a quarter from 11am to 4pm in summer; from the end of October to the third week of March, trains depart on Saturday, Sunday, and holidays at noon, 1:30pm, and 3pm (only at noon on weekdays); from late March until early June, departures take place weekends and holidays every hour and a quarter from 11am to 4pm and weekdays at noon. Regular fare is $11 round trip, $8 for ages 3 to 17; under 3, free. For further information, call 408/335-4484.

HIGHLIGHTS OF NORTHERN CALIFORNIA

The previous two chapters dealt with areas that could be easily explored in day trips from San Francisco. The following are a bit farther along; you might still use San Francisco as a base, but plan to spend at least a night or two away. We'll begin by heading north.

1. Little River

Take a leisurely drive up the coast, maybe stopping along the way at historic Fort Ross, where for 40 years Russians dominated Northern California (see Chapter IV, Section 9). When you've traveled 123 miles north along Calif. 1, you'll come to Little River (in the vicinity of Mendocino), where the mountainous seascape has the look of a Renaissance painting backdrop, and quaint old inns welcome north-coast travelers. Advance reservations are a must at any of these accommodations.

Such a one is **Heritage House,** 5200 N. Hwy. 1, Little River, CA 95456 (tel. 707/937-5885), an ivy-covered New England–style inn on the sea side of the road (most rooms have ocean views, with perhaps the best views on the northern coast-line). Its main building used to be a farmhouse, built in 1877 by forebears of the present owners. The play *Same Time Next Year* was inspired by this idyllic retreat, and in less tranquil days, "Baby Face" Nelson used the then-abandoned farmhouse as a hideout. Cottages, inspired by old-fashioned institutions and buildings, have names like Scott's Opera House, Country Store, Bonnet Shop, and Ice Cream Parlor. Many antiques from old houses in the area have been used in furnishing rooms here. Heritage House operates on the Modified American Plan (rooms with breakfast and dinner); rates are $115 to $290 for a single and $150 to $375 for a double, with those meals included. Rooms have baths but no phones or TVs.

Even if you don't stay at Heritage House, you must stop by for a leisurely dinner; the dining room here is the long-sought country restaurant of everyone's dreams. Windows overlook the ocean or lush greenery, the interior decor achieves perfect elegance, and there are even outdoor tables (for cocktails) on a terrace bordered by pots of geraniums. Dinner is prix-fixe and ranges from $24 to $26. The choice of main courses is excellent: roast prime rib, pork ribs with orange glaze, fresh Pacific red snapper, etc. On one visit it included clam chowder, salad, roast chicken with plum glaze, two vegetables, homemade biscuits, cream puffs with hot fudge, fruit, cheese, and coffee. There's an outstanding wine list. Men are requested to wear jackets and reservations are essential.

2. Mendocino

A few miles farther along is Mendocino, its mixture of 19th-century charm and beauty, weathered barns, old mansions, deep-green forests, blue sea, and white surf providing the backdrop for a major center for the arts on California's northern coast.

Originally known as Meiggsville, the town was so named after one Harry Meiggs, who came to Big River in search of a wrecked cargo of Chinese silk. He didn't find the silk, but he did find another treasure in giant redwoods. He built the area's first sawmill and began shipping cargoes of lumber back to fast-growing San Francisco. He later went to South America, where he built the first railroad across the Andes, but his legacy in California was a lumber boom that lasted over 50 years in Mendocino. The New England woodsmen who followed him to California built a New England–style town at Big River, thus accounting for the misplaced architecture still seen today. Steeply pitched roofs are slanted to shed snow—which, of course, never falls in Mendocino—and many old houses even have widow's walks.

As the port grew in importance, coastal ships from Seattle and San Francisco made regular calls at Mendocino. In the height of the logging boom residents numbered 3,500, and eight hotels went up along with 17 saloons and 15 or 20 bordellos. Today Mendocino is populated by about 1,000 people, some still employed in the lumber and fishing industries, many of them artists and artisans. The entire town has been declared a historic monument, and although the brothels are, as far as I know, gone, and the saloons fewer, it still looks like a western movie set—much as it looked in an 1890 photo. Mendocino is one of the world's Shangri-las, a serene, romantic, away-from-it-all dream retreat. Don't miss it.

WHAT TO SEE AND DO

There's a tremendous amount to do in and around Mendocino—every kind of land and water sport, art galleries and antique shops to explore, fairs, wine tasting, etc. For a rundown on what's available, stop in at the **Fort Bragg/Mendocino Coast Chamber of Commerce,** 332 N. Main St. (tel. 707/964-3153) in Fort Bragg (about which more below), or send your request to them at P.O. Box 1141, Fort Bragg, CA 95437.

Mendocino is also a great place to do nothing but gaze at the blue sea and white surf, stroll through hushed redwood forests, stroll along miles of deserted sandy beach strewn with driftwood, and enjoy the brilliant flowers blooming amid weathered barns and old picket fences. It's a place to replenish the spirit and bask in nature's bounty.

Just a couple of miles up the coast there is the **Point Cabrillo Lighthouse,** built in 1909. It's open to the public in March, during the whale festival, when the entire area celebrates the migration of these marvels of the sea.

Mendocino Art Center

Headquarters for much Mendocino cultural activity, as well as the coast's artistic renaissance, is the Mendocino Art Center, 45200 Little Lake Rd. (tel. 707/937-5818). The center offers classes and workshops covering a broad range of artistic disciplines, including a year-round ceramics program and a three-year certificate program in textiles. Founded in 1959, it was the creation of William Zacha, a painter, and his wife, Jenny, who had long dreamed of establishing a unique art school in an area of great beauty and creative energy.

In addition to classes, the Art Center offers a Sunday-afternoon concert series, two galleries, and shops displaying local fine arts and crafts for sale. And two art fairs (Thanksgiving and summer) yearly draw visitors from around the country and serve as a showcase for local and outside artists, musicians, and craftspeople. They also publish a free monthly magazine called *Arts and Entertainment* that announces upcoming Mendocino and Art Center events and features interviews with local artists, short stories, poems, etc.

Botanical Gardens

Six miles north of Mendocino at 18220 North Calif. 1 in Fort Bragg (about 2 miles south of town), you'll come to the **Mendocino Coast Botanical Gardens** (tel. 707/964-4352), a charming cliff-top public garden among the pines along the rugged coast. The gardens were fashioned by a retired nurseryman who spent years reclaiming wilderness and nurturing rhododendrons, fuchsias, azaleas, and a multitude of flowering shrubs. The area contains trails for easy walking, bridges, streams, canyons, dells, and picnic areas. Daily hours are from 9am to 5pm from March through October, 10am to 4pm the rest of the year. The gardens charge $5 admission for adults, $4 for seniors (60 plus), $3 for ages 13 to 17, free for children 12 and under accompanied by their parents.

WHERE TO STAY AND DINE

The accommodation of choice in Mendocino is **MacCallum House,** Albion Street (P.O. Box 206), Mendocino, CA 95460 (tel. 707/937-0289), a 15-room historic Victorian gingerbread mansion constructed in 1882 by pioneer lumberman William H. Kelly as a wedding present to his daughter Daisy, and her husband, Alexander MacCallum. Alexander died in 1908, but strong-willed Daisy lived to the ripe old age of 93 and became the town matriarch. She started the town's fire department, and like the well-bred Victorian lady she was, kept busy teaching, studying botany and horticulture, traveling, enlarging her residence, and playing a leading role in community affairs. She died in 1953, but her son occupied the house until 1970, making so few changes that when Bill and Sue Norris bought the place in 1974, they said it looked as if she had gone out to walk the dog.

The Norrises, a young couple with know-how and reverence for authenticity, did a first-rate job with MacCallum House. I think Daisy would have approved. They were fortunate enough to purchase the mansion with all its invaluable original furnishings and contents. Every nook and cranny here reveals some delightful secret. Exploring the public areas, you might come across Daisy's books of pressed flowers, her scrapbooks full of Christmas cards and other mementos, or her 4,000 books and countless magazines—the former still lining the dining room walls, the latter used to paper the attic. Here and there is an original Tiffany lamp or real Persian carpet.

Each guest room is unique, exquisitely papered and furnished, for the most part, with Daisy's old pieces. Your room might have a Franklin stove, handmade quilt, cushioned rocking chair, bed with high headboard, old sewing dummy, or child's cradle. Without a doubt these are the most charming rooms in town. Most have sinks and share common large baths, and there are no radios, TVs, or phones to disturb the tranquil atmosphere. Room rates range from $65 to $185 per night, double occupancy; luxurious barn suites with stone fireplaces are at the top of that range, the latter big enough to accommodate six people. A generous Continental breakfast is included in the price.

You may not be staying at the MacCallum House, but if you're anywhere in the vicinity, don't miss the opportunity to have dinner at the **MacCallum House Restaurant** (tel. 707/937-5763), or at the very least a light meal at the adjoining Grey Whale Bar & Cafe. Owner Rob Ferrero oversees a very professional staff, and the outstanding food is served in a delightful setting: beautiful woods, wainscoted walls lined with bookcases, antique built-in sideboard, and huge old cobblestoned fireplaces. Recently it has all been lightened with accompanying floral draperies.

Everything is made "from scratch"—and from the very freshest ingredients (local products whenever they are available). For a first course, my choice is the fresh oysters broiled with garlic basil butter, herbed bread crumbs, and aged Asiago. The second course may be an outstanding seafood dish such as local ling cod braised in a fresh fennel tomato fume; perhaps the grilled chicken, which has been marinated in herbs, garlic, and olive oil; or the pan-broiled tenderloin filet steak served with shiitake mushrooms. Desserts are all homemade and irresistible, whether you're inclined toward a seasonal fruit tart, chocolate nut torte, or puff pastry. First courses are priced at $3 to $7.50, entrees at $10 to $17. Reservations are suggested.

The establishment is open weekends from mid-February to late March, and every night from April through December. The restaurant's hours are 5:30 to 10pm. The Bar & Parlor Cafe is open for food from 4:30 to 10pm, offering everything on the restaurant dinner menu, plus assorted appetizers. *Note:* No credit cards.

Right on the town's Main Street is the **Mendocino Hotel,** Mendocino, CA 95460 (tel. 707/937-0511, or toll free 800/548-0513), a wood structure that dates from 1878 and is entered via beautiful beveled-glass doors. The lobby and public areas evoke the Victorian opulence of Gold Rush days, and furnishings in both the rooms and the public areas utilize a harmonious combination of antiques and reproductions. The oak reception desk comes from a bank in Kansas. The 50 rooms all have hand-painted French porcelain sinks with floral designs, quaint wallpapers, and old-fashioned beds and armoires, cable TVs, and phones; 38 have bathrooms.

About half the 50 rooms are located just across the road in four small handsome buildings, one of which is called the Heeser House, built in 1852 by one of Mendocino's pioneer families. Each room contains photographs and memorabilia reflecting the history of the town and its founders, and 22 of the 25 rooms have fireplaces. A lovely English country garden surrounds the buildings. The hotel offers room service, and there is a nightly turndown accompanied by homemade chocolates. And there's an excellent restaurant on the premises for lunch in the garden ($4 to $7) or dinner (entrees from $13 to $19). Don't miss the olallieberry deep-dish pie for dessert. Rooms range from $65 to $225 (for suites), single or double; lower rates are for those rooms without a private bath.

Making no attempt at quaintness, but relaxed, unpretentious, and homey nonetheless, the **Sea Gull,** on Lansing Street, at Ukiah (tel. 707/937-2100), is a hub of Mendocino life day and night. On the premises is the Cellar Bar, ironically upstairs (it used to be in the cellar, but after a fire in 1976 it was moved), where residents gather nightly under a cathedral ceiling to drink, hang out, and listen to music; they always play good jazz, classical, rock, or whatever in the background, and often have live music. The comfy furnishings, woody decor, and very relaxed ambience make this the ideal spot to meet Mendocino's diverse and talented populace.

By day, the Sea Gull has to be the favorite breakfast spot in town, offering a complete breakfast menu with homemade breads from their new Bake Shoppe next door. Lunch features homemade soups and chili, along with gigantic sandwiches, fresh fish, and the very best cheeseburger in town. A hearty breakfast is about $3 to $8; lunch, $4 to $9.

Over the last couple of years, owners Jim and Rochelle Marquardt have created a veritable dining feast for the evening menu. The selection is excellent—fresh local seafood, chicken, and veal entrees, steaks, pasta—all at prices ranging from $7 to $16. Specialties of the house include their own Mendocino seafood gumbo and an excellent traditional cioppino. There's a full bar, plus an extensive wine list consisting of virtually all Mendocino County wines, many available by the glass.

The restaurant is open daily from 8am to 9pm; the Cellar Bar, from noon to midnight. *Note:* No credit cards are accepted.

Although Mendocino's hostelries all have fine dining rooms, there are also many restaurants in town worth checking out. None is more totally charming than the **Café Beaujolais,** 961 Ukiah St. (tel. 707/937-5614). Papered in Victorian reproduction wallpaper (the most beautiful pattern I've ever seen), this French country-style inn has oak floors, Victorian rose-colored carnival glass chandeliers suspended from a wood ceiling painted white, a wood-burning stove, spindle-back chairs, and substantial oak pedestal tables, each adorned with a posy of flowers. There's more seating on an outdoor deck overlooking the garden.

You couldn't find a more delightful place to begin the day, and here you can do so with homemade coffee cake and excellent coffee, or if the ocean air has given you a hearty appetite, with waffles in pure maple syrup or chicken-apple sausage and three scrambled eggs, all for under $8. The lunch menu changes daily and might offer anything from a terrific burger served with country fries to Mendocino fish stew or an extraordinary black-bean chili. Entrees are priced at $6 to $10. Breakfast and lunch are served daily from 8:30am to 2:30pm. Dinner is served on Thursday, Friday, Saturday, and Sunday evenings from 6:15 to 9:30pm during the spring through fall only (about April through December). Once again, the menu is constantly changing; on different visits I've enjoyed the chicken stuffed under the skin with eggplant and mushrooms, cheese, garlic, and fresh herbs, and roast filet of beef, for $12 to $24. Fresh salmon and roast leg of lamb are among the specialties of the house. "Decadent chocolate desserts" are worth the splurge. Reservations are necessary. *Note:* No credit cards.

The newest addition to Café Beaujolais is **The Brickery** next door, with its new wood-fired bread and pizza oven. This is where you can buy delicious crusty breads (baked daily) and pizzas to eat in or take out. And while you're there, avail yourself of a copy of the Café Beaujolais bakery catalog. Among the mouthwatering items listed are the chicken-apple sausages served in the café, dried tomatoes, and pear barbecue sauce—a rich, mildly spicy sauce with a natural fruity sweetness.

3. Fort Bragg

Continuing along the Mendocino coast another 10 miles, you'll come to Fort Bragg, the largest coastal city between San Francisco and Eureka. Its southern gateway is the harbor town of **Noyo,** sportfishing center of the county and locale of many gourmet seafood restaurants. Visit the **Noyo Store,** 32450 North Harbor (tel. 707/964-9138), to find out about fishing boats and to buy or rent tackle. It's in the heart of this small village.

WHAT TO SEE AND DO

From Fort Bragg you can foray into the ageless redwood groves in nearby parks, many of which have camping facilities (for details on camping and anything else in Fort Bragg, visit the Fort Bragg/Mendocino Coast Chamber of Commerce, listed above).

If you're in the area during whale-watching season, don't miss the opportunity to take one of the local boats and get a view of the gray whales. March sees Fort Bragg's annual **Whale Festival.**

One of the best ways to see the redwoods is to "ride the **Skunks"**—California Western Railroad's self-powered diesel trains. They were so nicknamed for their original gas engines; people used to say, "You can smell 'em before you can see 'em." The trains, boarded at the foot of Laurel Avenue in Fort Bragg (two blocks from the Grey Whale Inn), travel along the Redwood Hwy. (U.S. 101) to **Willits,** 40 miles inland—a journey through the very heart of the towering redwood forest along a spectacular route inaccessible by auto. With windows front and side, they're wonderful for sightseeing. The ride takes you across 31 bridges and trestles, and through two deep tunnels, its serpentine route encompassing changes of scenery from forest to sunlit fields of wildflowers, grazing cattle, and apple orchards.

The Skunks run all year, leaving Fort Bragg daily each morning. The round trip takes six to eight hours, which allows ample time for lunch in Willits before returning on the afternoon train. Half-day trips are offered only in summer from mid-June to early September, with daily Fort Bragg morning departures. The price of a roundtrip ticket is $22, $18 one way. Children 5 to 11 pay half price. For further information and a time schedule, phone 707/964-6371.

Another Fort Bragg attraction is the **Georgia-Pacific Corporation's Tree Nursery,** 275 N. Main St., at the junction of Calif. 1 and Walnut Street (tel. 707/ 964-5651). You can stop in from March to November, weekdays from 8:30am to 4:30pm, weekends from 10am to 4pm, for a free look at some 3 million trees. There are a picnic area and a self-guided nature trail, plus an interesting visitor center. They also operate a logging museum donated to the city of Fort Bragg on North Main Street near the Skunk depot; it's open Wednesday through Sunday from 8am to 4:30pm, and admission is free.

If it proves convenient, hit Fort Bragg on Labor Day Weekend, when crowds gather for **Paul Bunyan Days** activities: axe-throwing, pole-climbing, log-rolling, and the like.

WHERE TO STAY

You might consider staying overnight at the historic **Grey Whale Inn,** 615 N. Main St., Fort Bragg, CA 95437 (tel. 707/964-0640, or toll free 800/382-7244 in California), a handsome four-story redwood building—spacious, elegant, relaxed, and attractively furnished with some antiques and modern amenities such as a color TV with VCR in the Theater Room and a pool table in the recreation room. The Fireside Lounge is a great gathering place for guests. There are 14 guest rooms, all with private baths and all nonsmoking. Each room offers its own special features— one has an ocean view, or a fireplace, or whirlpool tub; another has a private deck or a shower with wheelchair access. The inn is just six blocks from the beach and two blocks from the Skunk Train depot. Rates—which include a buffet breakfast of homemade bread or coffeecake, juice or fresh fruit, and a selection of hot beverages, cereals, and brunch casseroles—are $55 to $120 for a single and $65 to $140 for a double. Off-season rates, November through March, are half price for the second consecutive night Monday through Thursday, holidays excluded.

More redwoods? Hop in the car again and head north to **Sylvandale,** 6 miles above Garberville on U.S. 101 (Calif. 1 and U.S. 101 converge at Leggett). Soon you'll come to a sign directing you to one of the most spectacular routes in the West, the—

---

4. Avenue of the Giants

Thirty-three miles long, this scenic avenue, roughly paralleling U.S. 101 (240 miles north of San Francisco), was left intact for sightseers when the freeway was built. Its giants are majestic coast redwoods—*Sequoia sempervirens*—over 50,000 acres of them making up the most outstanding display in the redwood belt. Their rough-bark columns climb 100 feet or more without a branch—some are taller than a football field is long and older than Christianity. The oldest dated coast redwood is over 2,200 years old.

WHAT TO DO AND SEE

Drive slowly, leaving your car occasionally for walks through the forest. En route you'll notice three public campgrounds: **Hidden Springs,** above Miranda; **Burlington,** 2 miles south of Weott; and **Albee Creek State Campground,** off to the left above Weott. You'll also come across picnic and swimming facilities, motels, resorts, restaurants, and numerous resting and parking areas.

The biggest attraction along the Avenue of the Giants is **The Chimney Tree,** where the hobbit lives. This living, hollow redwood is over 1,500 years old. Nearby there is a gift shop, as well as a round building that offers sustenance in the form of gourmet beef burgers.

At the south end of the Avenue is another extraordinary sight—the **One-Log House,** a small apartmentlike house built inside a log.

You can have lunch a few miles past the end of the road in Scotia (there are picnic areas and a grocery), where you can also take a tour of the **Pacific Lumber Company,** one of the world's largest mills. If you're so inclined, you can drive your car *through* a living redwood at **Myers Flat Midway,** along the Avenue of the Giants.

For more information, you can contact The Chimney Tree, Avenue of the Giants, P.O. Box 86, Phillipsville, CA 95559 (tel. 707/923-2265).

The village of **Ferndale,** 15 miles south of Eureka and in the northernmost part of the Avenue of the Giants, is a historic landmark. Ferndale is a fairytale spectacle of Victoriana—gables and gingerbread, Victorian homes, shops, a smithy, even a saddlery. Contemporarily, it has humor, a repertory company, artists, sculptors, dairy farms, hand-dipped chocolates, and the annual World Champion Kinetic Sculpture Race in May. What it does not have are some of the mean touches of uncivilization. There are no parking meters, no traffic lights, no mail deliveries. It's enchanted!

Part of Ferndale's enchantment is the **Gingerbread Mansion,** 400 Berding St. (P.O. Box 40), Ferndale, CA 95536 (tel. 707/786-4000), a well-reviewed, frequently photographed peach-and-yellow gabled inn with elaborately elegant trim. The mansion is beautifully furnished with antiques, in keeping with its Victorian heritage. It is a masterpiece, run by Wendy and Ken Torbert. You may never sleep in more comfortable beds or feel more pampered than you will at the Gingerbread Mansion. Attractive bathrobes are provided, extra-large thick towels, fresh flowers. Two of the second-floor baths are 200 square feet; one is framed with mirrors and has a clawfoot tub on a pedestal. Hanging plants are all about and light filters through a lovely stained-glass window. If you must, there is a shower. Beds are turned down for the night, and you will find chocolates on the nightstand. When you rise, there's morning coffee or tea outside your door, enough to sustain you until breakfast of fruit, cheese, muffins, breads, cakes, and hard-boiled eggs—all included in the rates, as is afternoon tea with cake.

The Torberts have yellow- and peach-colored bicycles available for use by the guests. Should it rain, they also have a supply of umbrellas and boots. There are nine large guest rooms, all with private baths and some with *two* old-fashioned clawfoot tubs for "his and her" bubble baths. Rates for two, including the breakfast and afternoon tea, are $85 to $175 for two people per room, $15 less for singles. For the comfort of others, smoking is permitted only on the verandas.

---

5. Yosemite National Park

You might call Yosemite National Park and Yosemite Valley breathtaking, spectacular, incredible, awesome, humbling—all of which are accurate and none of which even begins to describe the magnificence of this country and the many faces of its beauty. Yosemite Valley is a glacier-carved canyon with crashing waterfalls (come in May and June and see), dramatic domes, and sheer walls of granite extending thousands of feet upward from the valley's flat floor.

The evolution of Yosemite Valley began with glaciers moving through the canyon that the Merced River had carved with repeated geological rises of the Sierras. The ice worked its way through weak sections of granite, bypassing the solid portions—what you now see as El Capitan is a good example of such a rock mass—and substantially widening the canyon. When the glacier began to melt, the moraine (the accumulated earth and stones deposited by a glacier) dammed part of the Merced River to form Lake Yosemite in the new valley. Sediment ultimately filled in the lake, which accounts for the flat floor of Yosemite Valley. This same process, on a much smaller scale, is even now occurring with Mirror Lake at the base of Half Dome.

The Ahwahneechee had been living in the valley for several thousand years when their first contact was made with European people in the middle of the 19th century. Members of the Joseph Reddeford Walker party were probably the first non–Native Americans to see Yosemite Valley as they crossed over from the east side of the Sierra in 1833, though they did not come into contact with the Ahwahneechee. With the later encroachment of visitors and indiscriminate abuse of the environment and the threat of potential private exploitation (it was ever thus), President Lincoln granted Yosemite Valley and the Mariposa Grove of Giant Sequoias to California as a public trust. Federal legislation created Yosemite National Park in 1890. And by 1913 a different problem arose—the auto was permitted into Yosemite.

Still, with tender loving care, the valley has survived. It remains a sensual blend of open meadows, wildflowers (1,400 species), woodlands with Ponderosa pine, incense cedar, and Douglas fir. Wildlife from monarch butterflies and a world of birds (223 species) to mule deer and black bear flourish in the protected environment.

Today **Yosemite Valley** is a focal point of activities in one of America's most spectacular national parks, and the logical place to begin your visit. Though occupying only 7 of the 1,200 square miles that make up the park, the valley offers campgrounds, lodgings, shops, and restaurants. Visitors who are in the valley for the day only are encouraged to use the day-use parking at Curry Village. A free shuttle-bus system travels on a continuous loop through the eastern portion of the valley and is quite convenient for visiting any of the above amenities.

While the valley is the hub of everything that's happening, and contains many scenic features (Yosemite Falls, Bridal Veil Falls, Mirror Lake, Half Dome, Sentinel Rock, El Capitan, the Three Brothers, and Cathedral Rocks), you'll want to leave the valley to explore the park's other natural bounties. There are 800 miles of trails you can cover, by horse, mule, or foot only, many leading up north in the mountain meadowlands, blanketed in wildflowers, which are known as the **High Country** and are snowed-in seven months of the year. There are 360 miles of road that you can traverse by car (rangers will recommend tours). And many bus tours are offered by the Yosemite Transportation System. Things to see and do are suggested below, but first—

GETTING THERE

If you're traveling from San Francisco by car, take I-580, then I-5 to the Gustine off-ramp, and finally Calif. 140 to Yosemite Valley. Of the westerly approaches, Calif. 140 is less mountainous and tends to have less snowfall; 120 East (Tioga Pass) is open only in summer. In the winter, chains must always be kept in the car. You can also make the trip by air via American Eagle (tel. 209/722-1587) to Merced from San Francisco or Los Angeles. A direct connection in Merced with Amtrak trains is available through California Yosemite Tours (tel. 209/383-1563), and VIA Bus Lines (tel. 209/384-1315) links Yosemite with the Greyhound terminal in Merced.

ENTRANCE FEES

An entrance fee is charged at the park, but no one minds paying it after seeing how well the National Park Service keeps its end of the bargain. At each of the four entrances—**Calif. 120** on the northwest, **Calif. 140** toward the west, **Calif. 41** on the south, and **Calif. 120** on the northeast (open in summer only)—rangers are stationed to check you in and out. As of this writing, the entrance permit still costs only $5 per car (no charge for seniors 62 and over). If you plan to stay longer than seven days, it might be worth your while to purchase an annual Golden Eagle Passport—for $25 you get free entrance to all national parks that charge fees—or an annual Yosemite Passport for $15, which allows you to leave and enter the park at will for the year your permit is valid.

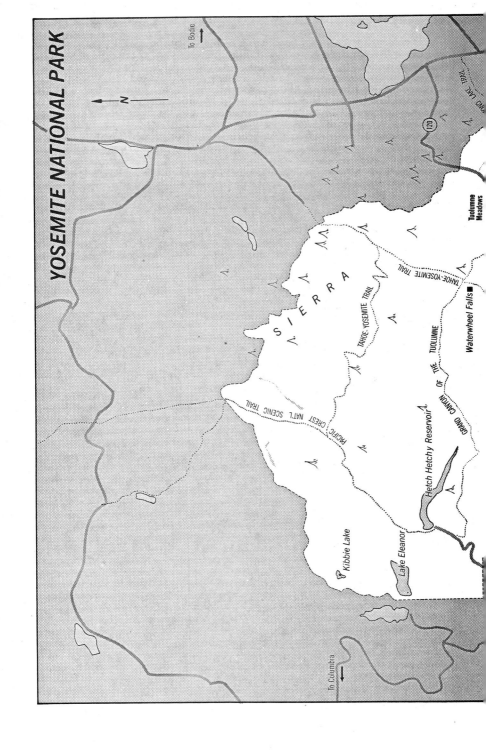

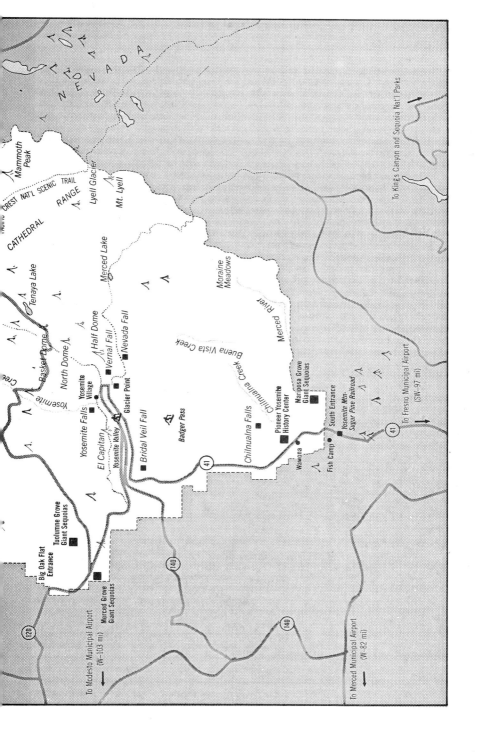

THINGS TO SEE

As soon as you reach the valley, stop at the **Visitor Center** (tel. 209/372-0299) in Yosemite Village to see the audiovisual programs and other exhibits and to pick up the *Yosemite Guide,* a free newsletter describing the week's activities, and a map for the Yosemite Valley free shuttle bus. Rangers are generally on duty here daily: from 9am to 6pm during April and May, 8am to 7pm in the summer, 8am to 6pm in September and October, and 9am to 5pm in the winter. They will provide you with information about park features, services, activities, and regulations. You'll want to know how to reach the museums, the sequoia groves, the inspiring granite summits, and the waterfall bases, and how to store food properly to avoid contact with wildlife.

Beginning each morning around 8:30am (sometimes earlier, sometimes later) and going till about 9pm, well over a dozen daily activities are offered. They might include lectures on photography, a 30-minute ranger-led fireside discussion on bears, a guided luncheon hike to a waterfall, a geological history tour, or a puppet show with an environmental theme. There are fewer activities off-season. You can also buy books and maps at the Visitor Center, which is open daily from 9am to 5pm during the winter, 8am to 8pm from Memorial Day to Labor Day (depending upon budgetary constraints).

There are 216 miles of paved road that you can traverse by car, and the rangers can give you a recommended road tour. You'll also want to know how to reach the museums, the sequoia groves, the inspiring granite summits, and the waterfall bases, plus what to do if a begging deer or squirrel approaches you for a handout (absolutely nothing). Although some of Yosemite's deer seem tame, they are wild and unpredictable and capable of inflicting serious injury with their antlers or hoofs.

Not to be missed are the following highlights:

Tuolumne Meadows

Gateway to the High Country, at an elevation of 8,600 feet, this is the largest alpine meadow in the High Sierras. Closed in winter, it's 55 miles from the valley by way of highly scenic Big Oak Flat and Tioga roads. A walk through this natural alpine garden makes a delightful day's excursion. In summer the park operates a large campground and conducts a full-scale naturalist program here.

Happy Isles Nature Center

Another gateway to the High Country, Happy Isles is also a trailhead for the John Muir Trail and for Vernal and Nevada Falls (the Mist Trail). Accessible by shuttle bus, the center is manned by ranger naturalists who provide information about traveling (or not) in the wildlands and **Mirror Lake.**

Mariposa Grove

One of three groves of giant sequoias, this is the largest, with hundreds of trees, over 200 of which measure 10 feet or more in diameter. Among them is the Grizzly Giant, largest and oldest tree in the park (it takes 27 fifth-graders to reach around it, but only 18 to reach around a school bus). Private vehicles can drive to the entrance of the grove; beyond that you can hike or board the free shuttle bus. There are stops where you can get off to hear nature talks, stroll around, take photos, or just absorb the peaceful atmosphere of the forest. The Mariposa Grove (not to be confused with the community of Mariposa) is 35 miles south of the valley; other redwood areas are Tuolumne and Merced Groves near Crane Flat.

Glacier Point

Offering a sweeping 180° panorama of the High Sierras and a breathtaking view from 3,200 feet above the valley, Glacier Point looks out over Nevada and Vernal Falls, Merced River, and the snowclad Sierra peaks of Yosemite's backcountry. The approach road from the Badger Pass intersection (closed in winter) winds through verdant red-fir and pine forest and meadow. Many fine trails lead back down to the valley floor.

Pioneer Yosemite History Center

Reached via a covered bridge constructed in 1858, the center, at Wawona, tells of man's history in the park. Exhibits include "living history" demonstrations, some of the early buildings and horse-drawn vehicles. In a similar category is the—

El Portal Travel Museum

At El Portal (Calif. 140), displays of old rail cars, a train station from Bagby, etc., tell the story of early-day rail and auto transportation in the Yosemite region.

Yosemite Indian Village

Behind the Visitor Center, during summer, you can watch Native Americans demonstrating traditional techniques of basket weaving, making arrowheads, and grinding acorns, among other things.

THINGS TO DO

A popular vacation destination in itself, Yosemite offers an exceptionally wide variety of visitor activities, from bicycling, backpacking, white-water trips, and mountaineering to the more rugged snow-related pursuits. Several are described in Chapter XIV.

Hiking and Backpacking

As I said before, over 800 miles of trails offer hiking possibilities to satisfy the hardy and the frail alike, as well as everyone in between. You can take anything from a leisurely stroll to a trip of a week or longer, on terrain ranging from plains to jagged mountains. If you wish to penetrate the less-traveled backcountry, a free wilderness permit is required. (Permits limit the traffic here to help keep the wilderness wild.) This can be obtained at any of the ranger stations or by writing to Wilderness Office, P.O. Box 577, Yosemite, CA 95389. Fifty percent of the permits are granted by reservation, by mail only; the other 50% are on a first-come, first-served basis.

Horseback Riding

Yosemite has excellent stable facilities, fully staffed with expert horsepeople. There are 30 miles of bridle paths in the valley, with all-day trips offered to the valley's rim. Stables—in **Yosemite Valley** near Curry Village, **Wawona, White Wolf,** and **Tuolumne Meadows**—are open in summer season only. Two-hour guided horseback rides leave several times daily for tours of their areas. There are also half-day guided mule trips: from the Valley Stables, the ride goes to Clark's Point and Nevada Falls; from Wawona, to Alder Creek or to Chilualna Falls. Full-day guided mule trips leave from all stables to such places as the base of Half Dome via Vernal and Nevada Falls, Glacier Point, the top of Yosemite Falls, or Mariposa Grove.

Several days a week four-day and six-day guided saddle trips leave the valley and tour the High Sierra camps, stopping at a different one each night. About 10 miles apart, the camps have dormitory tents equipped with mattresses, linens and blankets, hot showers, and central dining tents.

Burros, especially popular with kids, are also rentable. You might let the younger tots ride a burro while you hike along one of the scenic trails.

For information about saddle trips, contact the **Yosemite Park & Curry Co.,** High Sierra Desk, 5410 E. Home Ave., Fresno, CA 93727 (tel. 209/252-4848).

Swimming

Some accommodation facilities have swimming pools, but there are also the myriad sparkling streams, bracing rivers, and waterfalls to bathe in or under.

Bicycling

Why not see the sights on two wheels? Many trails are specially geared to cyclists, and you can rent a standard or multispeed bike from the Yosemite Lodge bike stand or the Curry Village bike stand.

Mountain Climbing

With vertical granite walls surrounding two-thirds of the valley, Yosemite is considered by experts to be one of the finest climbing areas in the Western world. And the **Yosemite Mountaineering School** at Curry Village has classes for beginning, intermediate, and advanced climbers. There are rock-climbing, ice-climbing, and natural-history trips, not to mention beginning and advanced survival trips. Inquire at the Visitor Center.

Skiing and Other Winter Sports

The oldest ski resort in California, **Badger Pass** (a 23-mile drive from the valley) opened to skiers in 1935. Facilities include one triple-chair lift, three double-chair lifts, one T-bar, and a rope tow for beginners. Other facilities include babysitting (for tots of 3 to 9 years) and a fast-food area. It's open through Easter (weather permitting), and the terrain is geared to the intermediate level, with about 35% for beginners and 15% for experts. An expert staff of ski instructors offers introductory and refresher courses, as well as children's ski lessons.

There are 90 miles of trails marked for **cross-country skiing,** with lessons scheduled daily. And 22 miles of machine-groomed track are set several times weekly from Badger Pass to Glacier Point. Skiers can stay overnight at the Glacier Point Ski Hut or at Ostrander Lake Ski Hut.

Winter-sports enthusiasts can also use an **outdoor ice rink** at Curry Village, open daily (weather permitting). Rental skates are available. In addition, you can rent cross-country ski equipment or snowshoes at Badger Pass. For nonskiers, Badger Pass offers a scenic Snow Cat ride to the top of the ski lifts.

For information on Yosemite ski facilities, contact Badger Pass, Yosemite National Park, CA 95389 (tel. 209/372-1330). For a daily update on ski, road, and weather conditions, dial the Badger Pass snow phone: 209/372-1338.

Fishing

Fishing licenses (required for anyone over 16) are easily obtainable at the Mountaineering School at Curry Village or at the Sports Shop in Yosemite Village. Beautiful High Country lakes, miles of rivers (the Merced and Tuolumne are especially popular), streams, and tributaries provide anglers with not only excellent fishing but unsurpassed views. Various kinds of trout are the main catch here.

And a Few Admonitions

The National Park Service and its rangers want you to have a marvelous time while you're in Yosemite. So here are a few common sources of trouble that can spoil the best vacation:

Streams in the Sierra Nevada can be dangerous, especially during the spring runoff when currents are fast, water is extremely cold, and rocks near the water are slippery. Supervise children closely.

Before you attempt to scramble or climb on Yosemite's walls, provide yourself with proper training and equipment and allow enough time.

Whenever possible, use only tap water for drinking. Water-borne *Giardia lamblia* may contaminate lakes and streams. Associated symptoms include diarrhea, abdominal cramps, bloating, and fatigue.

And pay special attention when driving—park roads are narrow, steep, and winding. If you want to view the scenery and wildlife, pull off the roadway into a safe turnout.

And need I remind you that park animals are wild—do not approach or feed them.

Note: National parks have toughened rules on drinking to cut down on drunk driving. New regulations outlaw open containers of alcoholic beverages in a car, specify a strict blood-alcohol level, and set penalties for anyone who refuses a Breathalyzer test. The regulations are being enforced by the local police and by the park service's 2,800 rangers.

WHERE TO STAY

From luxury hotel to woodland cabin to simple tent, Yosemite offers a wide choice of accommodations.

Camping

Yosemite has over 300 campsites for year-round use, and 2,324 open in summer. They all charge a $5 entrance fee and a $12 daily camping fee. Campsites are scattered over 20 different campgrounds in three categories. Type A campgrounds are the most elaborate, with well-defined roads, parking, drinking water, flush toilets, and, generally, a fireplace, table/bench combination, and tent space. Type B areas may be accessible by road or trail, and conveniences are limited to basic sanitary facilities and a smattering of fireplaces and tables. Type C areas don't concern us, as they are limited to groups (like Scout troops).

From June 1 to September 15, camping is limited to 7 days in the valley and 14 days in the rest of the park. Walk-in backpackers are limited to two nights *maximum* ($2 per person). The rest of the year the limit is 30 days throughout the park. Backcountry campers need a wilderness permit.

For more details on campgrounds, contact P.O. Box 577, Yosemite National Park, CA 95389 (tel. 209/372-0265 or 372-4845). Reservations must be made through Ticketron; check your local phone book, call 900/454-2100 (this is *not* a toll-free number), or write to the Ticketron Reservation Office, P.O. Box 62429, Virginia Beach, VA 23462. Reservations can be made no more than eight weeks in advance.

Other Accommodations

Reservations are advised at all times and especially in summer for all hotels, lodges, and cabins in the park.

Within walking distance of the valley is **Yosemite Lodge,** with attractive deluxe units, hotel rooms with or without bath, and redwood cabins with or without bath. Rates are the same for one or two people. Bathless hotel rooms are $43, bathless cabins are $40, cabins with bath run $52, and standard hotel rooms cost $75. (In season and during the holidays, reservations should be made one year in advance —it's that popular!) A coffee shop, lounge, two restaurants, and a cafeteria are on the premises, as are several shops.

Rustic **Curry Village** also charges the same rates for singles and doubles. Hotel rooms with bath are $68, cabins with bath are $52, and cabins without bath run $40. Tent cabins (wood platform floors with canvas sides and roofs) are about $27 per night.

There's less roughing-it at the **Wawona Hotel,** near the southern end of Yosemite. It offers such gracious accoutrements as a swimming pool, tennis court, and nine-hole golf course, as well as a dining room and nearby stables. Single or double hotel rooms are $74 with bath; bathless rooms cost $55.

Luxurious and very centrally located, **The Ahwahnee** in Yosemite Village has lovely dining facilities, a lounge, and a gift shop. Rooms and cottages are $185 for a single, $190 for a double; parlors are $366 for a single, $371 for a double. Midweek winter rates are substantially lower.

At any of the above, a deposit covering one night's lodging is required to confirm reservations, refundable if cancellation is received seven days before your arrival date. In season, or during the holidays, make your reservations for any of the above one year in advance to avoid being disappointed. Write to the **Yosemite Park & Curry Co.**, Reservation Department, 5410 E. Home Ave., Fresno, CA 93727 (tel. 209/252-4848).

---

6. South Lake Tahoe

"I ascended today the highest peak . . . from which we had a beautiful view of a mountain lake at our feet, about 15 miles in length, and so nearly surrounded by mountains that we could not discover an outlet." These are the words of John C. Frémont, the early California pioneer who discovered the "Lake of the Sky," set at 6,225 feet above sea level in the heavily timbered Sierra Nevada Mountains on the Nevada-California border.

Said by many to be the most beautiful lake in the world, Lake Tahoe is famous for its 99.7% pure water—a dinner plate at a depth of 100 feet is clearly visible from the surface, and divers claim visibility at 200 feet under. The dimensions of the lake belie its immense capacity; the average depth is 989 feet, which is sufficient water to cover the entire state of California with 14½ inches of water! It is the third-deepest lake in the world. More important to the visitor, though, the play of light during the day causes the color of the lake to change from dazzling emerald to blues and rich purples. And due to atmospheric conditions in the area, some of the most beautiful sunsets in the world are seen here.

The 72-mile circle around the lake is filled with recreational, historical, and scenic points of interest. In summer you can enjoy the crystal waters of Lake Tahoe for swimming (if you're hearty enough for some pretty cold water), fishing, boating, and water sports. Lakeside beaches, picnic areas, and campgrounds are plentiful. In winter Lake Tahoe becomes a popular ski resort. Year-round, there's glittering Vegas-style gambling and big-name entertainment on the Nevada border. And that's not the half of it.

GETTING THERE

Lake Tahoe can be reached by American Airlines (tel. toll free 800/433-7300) from San Francisco and Los Angeles. Most cities offer Greyhound bus connections. By car it's a fairly long drive—209 miles from San Francisco via I-80 and U.S. 50.

TAHOE ACTIVITIES

Make your first stop at the **South Lake Tahoe Chamber of Commerce,** 3066 U.S. 50 (P.O. Box 15090), South Lake Tahoe, CA 95706 (tel. 916/541-5255), 3 miles west of Stateline between Tallac and San Francisco avenues, where a knowledgeable and friendly staff has oodles of printed information about local activities. For vacation information and reservations, contact the **Lake Tahoe Visitors Authority,** P.O. Box 16299, South Lake Tahoe, CA 95706 (tel. 916/544-5050, or toll free 800/822-5922).

Skiing

Sierra snow is unique. It falls quickly, often quite unexpectedly, and in great quantities (20 feet the average winter) about one day in four from late November to mid-May, and its crystalline structure retains a powdery perfection on the slopes. It's also unusually reflective, so skiers should beware of getting a bad sunburn.

Since the weather affects not only the slopes but also the roads to them, you'll want to call 916/577-3550 for driving conditions before setting out—and hope that conditions don't change on your way up. (Many roads require chains in the winter, and I've found that it's always wise to take them, even in late spring or early summer.)

About 25 ski resorts are clustered within 50 miles of the city. The largest and most famous are actually to the northwest of the lake near Tahoe City. Right in South Lake Tahoe, however, is one of America's largest ski areas—

HEAVENLY VALLEY   This vast two-state complex, with the world's largest snowmaking system, covers over 20 square miles of High Sierra ski terrain encompassing nine mountain peaks. About 25% of the slopes are geared to beginners, 50% to intermediates, and 25% to advanced and expert skiers, including Mott Canyon for the super-expert. Ability levels and directions are carefully marked. An aerial tram and 23 other lifts convey 31,000 skiers an hour to the slope of their choice.

Both the Main Lodge on the California side and the two Nevada base facilities offer half- and full-day passes for adults for $25 and $40, respectively.

A full line of high-quality ski equipment can be rented at all three base facilities. Ditto ski lessons, using the ATM method and geared to various levels of ability, under the auspices of John Darby, who heads an expert staff of genial young American and European instructors, many of whom speak several languages. Private lessons are $45 an hour, $28 for each extra person. A full day of beginner group instruction (morning and afternoon sessions) is $30, $20 for a half day. First-time beginners do not need a lift ticket (for obvious reasons). Heavenly Valley ski season is mid-November through mid-May. The Heavenly Valley Tram operates year-round for sightseeing; fares are $15 for adults, $10 for children.

For further information about Heavenly Valley facilities, accommodations, package plans, etc., write to Heavenly Valley, P.O. Box 2180, Lake Tahoe, NV 89449 (tel. 916/541-1330 for information, 702/588-4584 for lodging and lift reservations).

SQUAW VALLEY   Site of the 1960 Winter Olympics, Squaw Valley is located on Calif. 89 between Truckee and Tahoe City. Once an old mining camp, it is now an alpine resort offering winter sports from November to May. The 27 major lifts carry 39,380 people per hour to slopes offering a wide range of challenges to skiers at all levels of proficiency. Facilities include a snow school center for children from ages 3 to 5 ($40 for 8:30am to 4:30pm, including lunch and equipment, plus lessons; $28 for a half day with lessons and snacks). Also at Squaw Valley: a ski school teaching the American Method, lodge accommodations, ski rentals, eating places, and après-ski bars.

All-day lift tickets are $35; a half day is $25. Children 12 and under and seniors over 65 pay $5. The price goes down for tickets purchased for two to seven consecutive days.

The ski school offers a full day of instructions for $30. Private lessons are $45 an hour.

Squaw Valley also has day care, with exercise facilities for children 6 months to 3 years. A full day is $45; a half day is $31, with lunch and snacks.

Monday through Friday, during nonholiday periods, first-time beginners ski free; they receive a free lift ticket, free rentals, and a free lesson.

For further information about facilities, accommodations, ski clinics, and ski packages, contact Squaw Valley Ski Corporation, Squaw Valley USA, CA 95730 (tel. 916/583-6985 for general information and 916/583-5585 for reservations, or toll free 800/545-4350).

SIERRA SKI RANCH   While not as large as the above two ski areas, Sierra Ski Ranch is among the best Tahoe ski values and is growing by leaps and bounds. Sierra Ski Ranch is 12 miles west of South Lake Tahoe on U.S. 50 (P.O. Box 3501), Twin Bridges, CA 95735 (tel. 916/659-7453). It has free shuttle-bus service from throughout the South Shore and Stateline, bringing skiers to the mountain in the morning and returning them in the late afternoon.

Sierra Ski Ranch has 2,000 acres, 2,212 vertical feet, and nine chair lifts (six double, two triple, and one high-speed detachable quad) with a capacity of 12,600 per hour. Trails are 20% beginner, 60% intermediate, and 20% expert. All-day lift tickets cost $27 for adults, $13 for children 12 and under (a terrific buy for many families). The ski school has 85 instructors for all levels of ability. Private lessons are $35 per hour; beginner group instruction (same-day morning and afternoon sessions) is $27. Special instruction for children 3 to 6 years is offered as a full-day (including lunch) or half-day program; all equipment is included, plus lessons and indoor playtime. Instruction is designed for the youngster just beginning through advanced little skiers. The all-day program is $40; a half day costs $30, including lifts during class (at the instructor's discretion).

There are special events for all sorts of skiers ranging from the serious to the silly, including a day for friendly competition among California and Nevada lawmakers (categorize it as you will) known as the Annual Legislative Cup Ski Race.

The Main Lodge has shops, lockers, an information center, and three cafeterias with three large sun decks featuring barbecue lunches, weather permitting. There are also a mountaintop solar ranch house (with a great view), open from 10am to 4pm for lunch, snacks, pizza, etc., and another outdoor barbecue.

Sierra Ski Ranch also has lodging/lift packages with accommodations ranging from a cozy cabin to luxurious suites (call toll free 800/822-5922 for lodging information).

INFORMATION AND SKI PACKAGES The above are the major ski resorts in the area. Also popular are **Kirkwood,** 30 miles southwest of South Lake Tahoe on Calif. 88 (P.O. Box 1), Kirkwood, CA 95646 (tel. 209/258-6000), a rapidly expanding area, part of Ski Lake Tahoe, with the highest base elevation (7,800 feet) in Northern California; and **Echo Summit,** Tahoe's newest family-oriented resort, only 8 miles west of U.S. 50 (P.O. Box 8955), South Lake Tahoe, CA 95731 (tel. 916/659-7154).

You can consult the individual resorts and your travel agent about ski packages. Packages can give you savings on air fare, ski schools, car rentals, tennis, golf, or casino shows—there are lots of different ones.

Summer Recreation

Tahoe is more than just a little Las Vegas–cum–ski area. It's a year-round resort playground, probably offering more options to vacationers in one place than anywhere else in the world. There's enough to fill an entire book, but due to space limitations I can only skim the surface. In addition to what's been covered, there are countless historical sites around the lake and nearby. A tour around the lake, offered by major Stateline hotels, is a must—not to mention spectator sports, biking trips, sailing, waterskiing, antiquing, visits to ghost towns, backpacking, and even panning for gold. So to reiterate what was suggested earlier in this chapter—make your first stop the South Lake Tahoe Chamber of Commerce to discover the full range of activities available.

One such activity, very popular in this beautiful natural setting is—

CAMPING Most of the campgrounds inside the Tahoe Basin are government-run (federal or state), and although a few operate sites on a first-come, first-served basis, reservations are highly recommended and often necessary in season. All California state campground reservations can be conveniently obtained through Ticketron. Privately owned campgrounds, however, usually provide more of the modern conveniences. I recommend the following:

Camp Richardson is a private campground 2 miles north of South Lake Tahoe on Calif. 89 at Jameson Beach Road (P.O. Box 9028), South Lake Tahoe, CA 95731 (tel. 916/541-1801). Camp Richardson has a bed-and-breakfast lodge and beach motel with rooms on the lake ($39 to $69) and cabins with fireplaces that sleep six to eight people ($00 to $00 in winter, $500 to $900 per week in summer). There are 200 campsites for tent camping at $15 and 100 RV/trailer sites with full hookup at

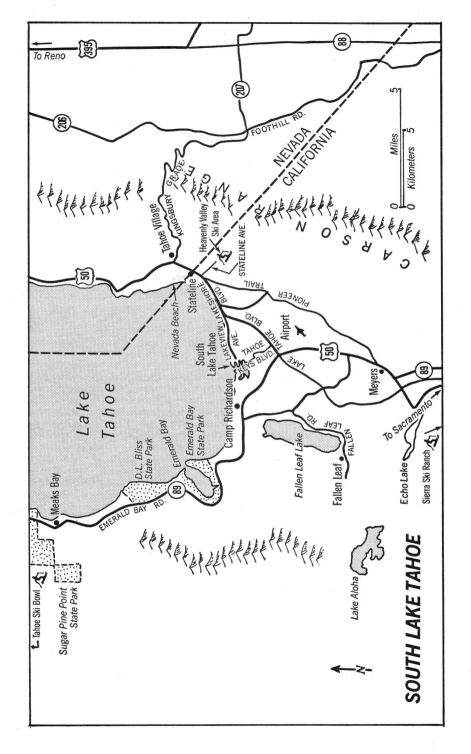

SOUTH LAKE TAHOE

$22 per night. Thirty RV/trailer sites with water and electricity only are available at $20 per night. Included in all rates for all sites is the use of toilets, showers, and beach and recreation facilities. Extra vehicles add to the basic price. Camp Richardson has a lodge, a full-service marina (including boat rentals), and the Beacon Restaurant and Bar. *Note:* No pets are allowed at Camp Richardson.

Campgrounds administered by California Land Management (tel. 916/544-0426) include: **Nevada Beach** in Nevada, off U.S. 50, 1 mile north of the state line ($10 per night); **Kaspian Walk-in Campground,** 4 miles south of Tahoe City ($4 per night); **William Kent Campground,** 2 miles south of Tahoe City ($8 per night); and **Meeks Bay,** 10 miles south of Tahoe City ($8 per night). For further information you can contact the U.S.D.A. Forest Service, P.O. Box 731002, South Lake Tahoe, CA 95731 (tel. 916/573-2600).

State park campgrounds include **Emerald Bay State Park** (tel. 916/525-7277), **D. L. Bliss State Park** (tel. 916/525-7277), and **Sugar Pine Point State Park** (tel. 916/525-7982), on Calif. 89 on the California side; and **Tahoe State Recreation Area** in Tahoe City on Calif. 28 (tel. 916/583-3074, summer only). Summer camping rates are $12 per night; day use is $4 per vehicle. Campsite reservations can be made through Mistix (tel. toll free 800/446-7275). During the winter, all parks are closed with the exception of Sugar Pine Point State Park where camping is $12 per night; for cross-country skiing, parking is $4 per vehicle. You can get further information on the above parks from the Sierra District State Parks, P.O. Drawer D, Tahoma, CA 95733 (tel. 916/525-7232).

GOLF AND TENNIS   Even the most dedicated craps shooters might want to get out of the casinos once in a while to breathe the fresh mountain air and get a little more exercise than that involved in tossing dice. Gambler golfers needn't go far; one of the best courses in town is the **Edgewood Tahoe Golf Course,** at Lake Parkway and U.S. 50 in Stateline, Nevada (tel. 702/588-3566), on the lake. Open May through mid-October, this 18-hole championship course offers challenges to every golfer. *Golf Digest* rates it as one of the top 100 courses in the country. What's more, it's a public course! Greens fees, including cart (mandatory), are $100. The course has a fleet of 94 golf carts, a modern driving range, three practice greens, a fully equipped pro shop, and a lovely clubhouse with the gourmet Terrace Restaurant open year-round. Clubs can be rented; tee time reservations are required.

As for **tennis,** the area has yet to develop facilities commensurate with this sport's popularity. You can, however, use the four resurfaced and lighted courts at the South Tahoe Intermediate School at U.S. 50 and Lyons Avenue or the six lighted courts at the South Tahoe High School, just off Lake Tahoe Boulevard, daily during the summer. The fee is $4 per hour for adults ($2 for those under 18 and seniors); reservations must be made in advance at the courts.

HIKING   A very big sport here, which is not surprising in this magnificent lake and woodland center. Both the South Lake Tahoe Chamber of Commerce and the **Visitor Center** (tel. 916/573-2674) operated by the U.S. Forest Service (off Calif. 89 just past Camp Richardson) can suggest guided and self-guided nature walks and trails for hikers of varying heartiness. One interesting trek that begins at the Visitor Center is along the Rainbow Trail to the **Stream Profile Chamber,** for underground viewing of aquatic life beneath the surface of a flowing mountain stream.

HORSEBACK RIDING   Tahoe has many stables and miles of good riding trails. There's **Camp Richardson Corral** (tel. 916/541-3113), on Emerald Bay Road (Calif. 89) in Camp Richardson, California (mailing address: P.O. Box 8335, South Lake Tahoe, CA 95731). Horses rent for $16 an hour for trail rides. Open May through October, daily from 8am to 5pm. In addition to trail rides, they feature steak rides, breakfast rides, overnight pack trips, and fishing trips. During the winter, there are sleigh rides daily from 10am to 5pm, at $11 per person.

FISHING   Within the Lake Tahoe Basin exists a great variety of opportunities for fishing enthusiasts. Should you need to obtain a fishing license while in California, the price is $21 for residents of California, $55.75 for nonresidents. A one-day license is $6.75 for both residents and nonresidents. Obviously, if you come to fish just over the one weekend, it would be cheaper to buy two or three one-day licenses. If you already have a fishing license from California or Nevada, it is good for South Lake Tahoe. Headquarters for fishing information, equipment, and licenses is **The Outdoorsman**, on U.S. 50 at the Truckee River (tel. 916/541-1660); they also sell sports clothing and equipment for tennis, golf, jogging, etc.

BOAT CRUISES If Lake Tahoe is too cold for swimming, non–polar bears can at least take a boat cruise on its waters. **Lake Tahoe Cruises** (tel. 916/541-3364, or toll free 800/238-2463) is at Ski Run Boulevard, operating out of the Ski Run Marina (next to Heavenly Valley). It offers daily cruises year-round on a genuine 500-passenger Mississippi stern-wheeler (don't ask how they got it up the mountain). There usually are four trips daily: 11am, 1:30pm, 3:55pm, and 7pm (June to October). The schedule is subject to change depending on the number of passengers, so I suggest that you call ahead to confirm the time. The 7pm trip is a dinner/dance voyage, with dinner optional. With the exception of the 7pm trip, adults pay $13.50; children 11 and under, $5.50. The dinner trip is $36 for adults, $27 for children 11 and under. The entree is usually prime rib or halibut, and the romantic aura is free. The winter schedule (October through May) is usually a trip at noon and the dinner trip at 6:30pm.

WHERE TO STAY

All the gambling action is just across Stateline (also known as the state line) in Nevada, and the closer you are to it, the more expensive are your accommodations. The four top choices are the big hotel/casino extravaganzas actually in Nevada, just a stone's throw from the California border. So popular is this multirecreational area that hotel rooms tend to get booked heavily in advance. Don't arrive without reservations or you may find yourself a reluctant camper.

Note: On weekends and holidays motel room rates tend to skyrocket in Tahoe; there seems to be a general philosophy of charging what the traffic will bear. If you're planning to come during one of these busy times, reserve especially far in advance, and try to get written confirmation of your room rate.

Harrah's, P.O. Box 8, U.S. 50 at Stateline, NV 89449 (tel. 702/588-6611, or toll free 800/648-3773), with 540 rooms and 18 stories, is a 24-hour hub of Lake Tahoe activity. It's one of Mobil's five-star hotels. Each of the posh rooms has a color TV with bedside remote control that also works the lights and radio, a small bar and refrigerator (you can order a choice of 14 drinks via a pushbutton mechanism), TV and phone in each of the two baths, and ice water on tap. In addition to all these little luxuries, the rooms, each decorated to reflect one of the four seasons, happen to be gorgeous.

Of course, the principal attraction at Harrah's is the casino, a biggie with 65,000 square feet of gaming area offering everything from baccarat to Bingo.

In the South Shore Room there's big-name entertainment—headliners like Bill Cosby, the Oak Ridge Boys, Billy Crystal, Engelbert Humperdinck, John Denver, Liza Minnelli, Tony Orlando, and Don Rickles. Prices for dinner shows range from $25 to $50, $20 to $40 for the late (11:30pm) show.

From 7pm on, you can also catch some pretty good acts at the Stateline Cabaret Lounge in the casino. No charge, just a two-drink minimum to see performers like Bill Medley and Tower of Power.

Harrah's chief dining facility is the very luxurious Summit Restaurant, with glass walls allowing panoramic views of the lake and surrounding mountains. Open for dinner, the Summit features live music nightly (except Sunday) till 11:30pm and Continental gourmet specialties such as chateaubriand bouquetière for two, quail, and roast Long Island duckling, for $22 to $42 per person. Tableside flambé preparations add drama to a meal at the Summit. Other options include breakfast with a special Sunday brunch, lunch and dinner buffets in the Forest Restaurant, a 24-hour coffee shop called the Sierra, and a steak house called Friday's Station; there are also six bars.

I'm not through yet. Harrah's has a geodesic-domed swimming pool, as well as superb health-club facilities with massage, sauna, gym, and whirlpool for men and women (men get steam too). The elaborately equipped dressing rooms have shampoo, deodorant, and cologne, even three-way mirrors and a scale to spur you on.

What does all this splendor cost? It depends on the season, but year-round the rates include free valet parking. During the summer, standard singles and doubles are $130 to $190; executive suites begin at $155. The rest of the year, standard rooms are $110 to $180; executive suites begin at $145. Larger suites begin at $500. An extra person pays $20 year-round.

Another Stateline operation is the **High Sierra Hotel/Casino,** P.O. Box C, U.S. 50 at Stateline, NV 89449 (tel. 702/588-6211, or toll free 800/648-3322). Rooms are luxurious and attractively modern, with full baths, direct-dial phones, and color TVs. They've been redecorated, in keeping with the hotel's western theme.

The main casino area is two city blocks in length and contains all the usual gaming action, including 1,000 slots.

The High Sierra's gourmet restaurant is Stetson's, a relaxed establishment with a classy western touch, complete with Stetson hat collection. The service is first-class, and the Continental cuisine excellent. Stetson's is open nightly from 5:30 to 11pm. Other dining choices here include a 24-hour coffee shop called the Four Seasons and the Chuckwagon for family dining.

The High Sierra has a big outdoor heated pool, hot tubs, barbershop and beauty salon, massage and sauna, shops, and free valet parking for guests.

Mid-June through August, rates are $98; the balance of the year, $76 to $116. All rates are for single or double occupancy; an additional adult pays $10, and children stay free with their parents.

Harvey's Resort Hotel/Casino, P.O. Box 128, Stateline, NV 89449 (tel. 702/588-2411, or toll free 800/648-3361), from humble beginnings has graduated to a Mobil four-star resort. Harvey's now towers 19 stories over the south shore of Lake Tahoe. The hotel/casino has 717 richly appointed rooms and suites, with spectacular lake and mountain views, and in-room amenities such as remote-control cable TVs, two phones, and (in many accommodations) minibars. There are six restaurants to satisfy most every taste, the 280-seat Emerald Cabaret, 10 cocktail lounges, a skilled concierge staff, a 1,500-car parking garage, an outdoor swimming pool and health spa, three tennis courts, and shopping services. The hotel's original handful of slot machines has multiplied to 2,300, and now there are 114 blackjack tables, as well as tables for baccarat, craps, poker, roulette, keno, and Oriental table games. In 1988 a Race and Sports Book was added to round out the gaming attractions.

You can dine at the Top of the Wheel, enjoying stunning lake views 12 stories up in a Polynesian setting. The decor reflects the cuisine—entrees (costing $16 to $25) like lobster Bali and chicken-breast teriyaki—although Continental fare is also served. Intoxicating rum concoctions are also a specialty here. Entertainment and dancing nightly. The Sage Room Steak House maintains its tradition of western elegance, specializing in steak and veal dishes ($17 to $30), prepared tableside. Or for seafood in its many variations, the Seafood Grotto has a netful of fresh fish and shellfish beautifully prepared, plus an authentic Chinese menu featuring seafood and Szechuan entrees ($6 to $33). For Mexican cuisine, there's the wrought-iron and leather ambience of El Vaquero ($7 to $14). The ambience is rustic; it still has the original Native American lighting fixtures, and framed western art prints adorn the rough-hewn walls. The El Dorado Buffet and Brunch has an "all-you-can-eat" dinner for $8.95.

Rates for singles or doubles are $95 to $165, depending on type of accommodations and time of year. Suites begin at $165.

The newest five-star resort at Lake Tahoe is the 15-story **Caesars Tahoe,** U.S. 50 at Stateline, P.O. Box 5800, Stateline, NV 89449 (tel. 702/588-3515, or toll free 800/648-3353). The resort hotel houses 446 large and luxurious guest rooms and suites. Rooms feature bathrooms with large sunken Roman tubs; suites have wide-screen TVs and wet bars. All accommodations are modern in decor and include amenities like two phones and two TVs (color in the bedroom, black-and-white in the bathroom).

The casino is one of the largest in the area, with blackjack, roulette, craps, pai gow, baccarat, keno, and poker. There are 1,000 slot machines, many with progressive slots, one of which paid the first $1-million jackpot, in 1981. The casino is also home to a large Race and Sports Book. Kids can try their luck in a video arcade stocked with all the latest games.

There are eight restaurants on the premises: Le Posh, a beauty with crystal, etched glass, plush booths, candlelight and gourmet dining; the Empress Court, for authentic Chinese food; the Broiler Room, for steaks, seafood, and Cajun offerings; the Café Roma, a 24-hour restaurant offering breakfast, lunch, and dinner; the Evergreen buffet, serving all-you-can-eat lunches and dinners; the Primavera, specializing in Italian cuisine; the Post-Time Deli, for snacks or a quick bite; and the Sweet Suite, with pies, pastries, ice cream, and yogurt.

Caesars has a major 1,700-seat showroom, the Cascade, featuring top-name entertainment: Julio Iglesias, Kenny Loggins, the Pointer Sisters, and Willie Nelson have all appeared here. The Crystal Cabaret is a 300-seat showcase for comedy, music, and revues.

And rounding out the facilities is the plush Caesars Spa. It features a lagoon-style pool with waterfalls; men's and women's spas, saunas, and massage rooms; a Nautilus weight and exercise room; two racquetball courts, four outdoor tennis courts, and a pro shop; and sun decks for total relaxation. And because there are always those who would rather shop than gamble, there is a host of shops featuring gifts from throughout the world, located in the shopping galleria.

Rates for singles or doubles are $110 to $165. Suites begin at $275.

As you get farther from Stateline, there are dozens of motels, and generally rates decrease as you go west on U.S. 50. Of course, if you're willing to stay even farther from Stateline, you can get both good rates and luxury accommodations. And all you really sacrifice is a few minutes' time getting back and forth to the casino area (even if you don't have a car), since there are shuttle buses running along U.S. 50 to and from the casinos throughout each day and into the night.

One of the most elegant properties in town is the **Inn by the Lake,** 3300 Lake Tahoe Blvd. (U.S. 50, between Fremont and Rufus Allen; P.O. Box 849), South Lake Tahoe, CA 95705 (tel. 916/542-0330, or toll free 800/822-5922), a Colony-managed resort just 2 miles from the casino action and 1½ miles from Heavenly Valley. It's a quiet, elegant place across the street from the lakeshore. The inn has 100 oversize rooms, all decorated in soothing neutral and pastel shades. Rooms at the front of the hotel have a breathtaking view of the lake and are furnished with king-size beds, refrigerators, and wet bars. Queen-size rooms and double-queens at the back look out on the mountains. Furnishings are plush and comfortable; amenities include pushbutton direct-dial phones, cable color TVs, and sparkling modern tub/shower baths. There is a year-round heated pool, hot tub, Jacuzzi, and redwood sauna. Complimentary coffee, juice, and croissants are served daily by the fireplace in the lobby lounge.

Rooms at the Inn by the Lake cost $80 to $120, single or double; suites begin $130. Seasonal rates apply.

Another pleasant property—this one directly on the lake—is the **Tahoe Marina Inn,** on Bijou Street off Lake Tahoe Boulevard (P.O. Box 871), South Lake Tahoe, CA 95705 (tel. 916/541-2180). There are 77 units here, all with floor-to-ceiling glass doors. The Tahoe Marina Inn has no restaurant, but there are several within walking distance. On the premises are a heated pool and a dry sauna; there's also a 500-foot-long beach. Rooms at the Tahoe Marina Inn are $89 to $120, single or double, in summer (June through October); lower during the rest of the year. Kitchen apartments are $120 to $160.

Now, continuing on the California side of town, within easy walking distance of all casino action (a shuttle bus is available in any case) is the **Forest Inn,** 1101 Park Ave. (P.O. Box 4300), South Lake Tahoe, CA 95729 (tel. 916/541-6655, or toll free 800/822-5950 in California). So close is this luxury resort to Stateline that it adjoins the side entrance of Harrah's casino. Set in 5 acres of garden and forest, it has 125 rooms housed in rustic buildings. There are three different types of accommodations. The first are regular motel units with all modern conveniences—color TVs, dressing areas, tub/shower baths, phones, alarm clocks, air conditioning, and heating. Then there are one- and two-bedroom suites, which in addition to the above also have fully equipped modern kitchens with dishwashers, living rooms, and dining areas. All the accommodations are well appointed and spacious, with attractive modern furnishings. Parking is included in the rates, and there are two large swimming pools with sunning areas, two whirlpools, and two sauna baths.

Motel units are $64 to $88, single or double; add $10 for an extra person. Kitchen units are $6 extra. Two-bedroom units are $110 and up, depending on the number of persons.

Also located near the casino action is the **Riviera Inn,** 890 Stateline Ave. (P.O. Box 4595), South Lake Tahoe, CA 95729 (tel. 916/544-3448). Year-round, the Riviera Inn has a whirlpool hot tub, and during the summer there's the use of a heated pool with a water slide. The inn is near the golf course and just one block from the beach and shopping. Kitchenette facilities are available. Rates are $55 to $90, single or double occupancy; add $10 for an extra person. Summer and ski packages are available.

The **Lucky Lodge Motel,** across the street from Harvey's, at 952 Stateline Ave. (P.O. Box 4385), South Lake Tahoe, CA 95729 (tel. 916/544-3369), offers standard accommodations at rates of $55 to $85, single or double occupancy.

Motel 6, 2375 Lake Tahoe Rd. (P.O. Box 7756), South Lake Tahoe, CA 95731 (tel. 916/542-1400), with 140 units and a small pool, has singles at $28 ($6 more for each additional adult). It's 3½ miles to the casinos. Need I tell you that you'll need reservations well in advance during the summer.

You can make reservations for these and many other hotels, motels, and vacation rentals through the **Lake Tahoe Visitors Authority,** P.O. Box 16299, South Lake Tahoe, CA 95706 (tel. toll free 800/822-5922). Call weekdays from 8am to 6pm (Pacific Time), or weekends from 9am to 5pm.

More Casino Action

The biggest casinos are in the first four hotels described above, but Tahoe also has some independent casinos. They're all popular, since few gamblers are content to lose all their money in one place, under the theory that prosperity and a winning keno ticket are just around the corner. One of the biggest of these nonhotel casinos is **Bill's** (tel. 702/588-2455), between Harrah's and Caesars. It's open 24 hours a day year-round; believe it or not, there's a McDonald's in the casino, and most Tahoe motels give out Bill's coupons for free games and discounts. Coupons are also distributed for **John's Tahoe Nugget** (tel. 702/588-6288), with the same hours; it's about three-quarters of a mile east of Stateline on U.S. 50.

The most important thing about Bill's and the Nugget is their year-round 24-hour free shuttle bus.

WHERE TO DINE

The most scenic choice is the **Top of the Tram,** at the end of Keller Road in Heavenly Valley (tel. 916/544-6263). The Governor's Room restaurant is open daily from Memorial Day, generally to the end of September, then daily for lunch only (11am to 2:30pm) during the ski season, Thanksgiving to April. Unless you're a hearty hiker, this restaurant can only be reached by car, which is left in the parking lot while you ascend 8,300 feet to the top of the mountain via cable car. The ride up is part of the fun, and the view from the restaurant is breathtaking. It's particularly exquisite in the early evening, when the magnificent Sierra sunset over the lake and mountains is yours to behold. There's an outdoor café area; inside, there are windows on three sides.

The restaurant is open Monday through Saturday from 10am to 10pm, on Sunday from 9am. Light fare is served at lunch/brunch and averages $6 to $9 for sandwiches, salads, pasta, etc. Dinner is served from 5pm, and the single price for any complete dinner includes the tram ride to get to the restaurant—$27 per person for prime rib, filet mignon, rack of lamb, breast of chicken Oscar, or the chefs selection. A child's dinner is $13. Reservations suggested. Should you choose to ride up simply for the incredible view, the tram trip costs $10 for adults, $6 for kids under 12.

One of the oldest and best-known restaurants in the area is the **Swiss Chalet, 4** miles on U.S. 50 west of Stateline near Sierra Boulevard (tel. 916/544-3304). It's one of the very few chef-owned and -operated restaurants (since 1957), which undoubtedly accounts for its high ratings by travel services. Cozy and candlelit, the Swiss Chalet is filled with beer steins, cuckoo clocks, paintings of the Alps, hanging copper pots, and large brass bells. It's really quite pretty, with more charm than kitsch, and the food is hearty and delicious. All entrees come with soup or salad, homemade rolls, and butter. Those entrees, priced at $13 to $24, include German sauerbraten with noodles and red cabbage, cheese fondue for two, and beef Stroganoff. But don't overlook the excellent fresh fish and steaks. Be sure to leave room for the scrumptious dessert cakes or pastries. This is a good choice for family dining; complete children's dinners are about $5 to $8.

Open Tuesday through Sunday from 5pm. Closed Monday off-season. Reservations suggested.

As the name suggests, **The Greenhouse,** 4140 Cedar Ave., near Stateline (tel. 916/541-5800), abounds in hanging plants and has plush grass-green carpeting. It's quite a charming place, with Tudor-style beamed walls, a floor-to-ceiling brick fireplace, and many antique German and English stained-glass hangings. Tables are candlelit, with white linen cloths and white napkins elegantly wound in the glasses. You might begin a meal here with escargots in fine herb butter; select an entree of roast prime rib au jus, chicken chasseur, sautéed scallops on rice, or veal marsala for $14 to $26; and finish up with an English trifle. All entrees come with fresh sautéed vegetables and rice pilaf or potatoes. A good wine list is available.

Just a short walk from casino action, The Greenhouse is open for dinner nightly from 5:30 to 10pm. Reservations essential. The Greenhouse bar, by the way, is a popular nighttime hangout.

A New England seafood restaurant serving fresh Maine lobster (you can select your own from a tank) is the last thing you'd expect to find in the Tahoe mountains. But here it is—**The Dory's Oar,** 1041 Fremont Ave., off U.S. 50 (tel. 916/541-6603), looking ever so much like a quaint Nantucket eatery and serving seafood flown in daily from the East Coast. The ambience is New England nautical, the pretty blue-and-white-papered and barnwood-paneled walls hung with bronze-plated plaques describing ships, ship lights, and maps. There are white ruffled curtains on the windows; gaslight lamps and dried flowers grace every table. Upstairs is a comfortable, pine-paneled ski-lodge bar with a unique fireplace. Dinners include bread, butter, salad-bar offerings, and rice pilaf, or a baked potato. House specialties include the above-mentioned lobster, baked stuffed baby salmon, jumbo shrimp cooked in spiced beer, and Pacific swordfish, for $13 to $30. For the steak lover, there is filet mignon, Porterhouse, and New York steak ($14 to $17).

The Dory's Oar is open for dinner nightly from 5 to 10pm.

Chez Villaret, 900 Emerald Bay Rd. (Calif. 89) (tel. 916/541-7868), is a cozy French country inn, its ambience enhanced at night by candlelight and taped classical music. Neat and pretty, it has tables covered in crisp white linen, curtained windows, and a few paintings and art prints on the walls. The menu features French nouvelle cuisine and changes daily according to what is available; there's a classic onion soup au gratin, as well as appetizers like steamed scallops and hearts of palm with raspberry vinaigrette. Entrees may include filet of veal with cream and wild mushrooms, filet of beef with three-peppercorn sauce, and Dover sole with butter, lemon, and parsley, all for $16 to $26. Tableside preparation is a specialty here, as are flambé desserts like crêpes Suzette ($8 for two). An impressive wine list comes bound in leather.

Chez Villaret is open daily from 6 to 11pm. Reservations are advised.

Friendly and casual, **Cantina Los Tres Hombres,** on Calif. 89, at 10th Street (tel. 916/544-1233), is a popular Tahoe hangout. It consists of several dining areas and a cozy cocktail lounge/bar, all filled with lots of live plants, rattan matting, pottery, a happy collection of piñatas—a zebra, a parrot, a giraffe, a peacock, and an elephant. There's even a desert room with planters of cacti. Somehow it all combines to create an appropriately south-of-the-border ambience. There's usually a wait for tables at dinner (they don't take reservations), during which time you can sit in the lounge and sip margaritas and listen to music or watch major sporting events. One menu is offered throughout the day, with simple entrees, combination plates, carnitas, fajitas, and specials of the day (Friday it's fresh fish), all in the $8 to $14 range.

Open daily from 11:30am to 10:30pm.

SOUTH ALONG THE SHORE

The tourist who flies from San Francisco to Los Angeles misses a lot. The stretch between Monterey and Santa Barbara is a delight. Throughout, the Pacific Coast scenery—and particularly along the spectacular Coast Hwy. 1 (Calif. 1)—varies from picture-postcard-pretty to breathtaking (emphasis on the latter), with nary an eyesore along the way.

We'll begin in Steinbeck country, Monterey. Adjacent to it is the charmingly quaint village of Carmel, formerly starring Clint Eastwood as mayor. No one could be so jaded as not to find the rugged Big Sur coastline a thrill—and speaking of being jaded, there's Hearst Castle at San Simeon coming up. At the end of this stretch, you finally enter Southern California—although it seems more like a well-to-do Mexico—in the beautiful seaside resort of Santa Barbara. Santa Barbara's mission is the most idyllic of them all—set on a hillside, it looks like a little piece of heaven, though our basis for comparison has yet to come.

1. Monterey

Portuguese navigator Juan Rodríguez Cabrillo was the first to sight Monterey, while sailing to Spain in 1542. The home of the Ohlone Indians for several thousand years, Monterey was a specific goal of the Spanish Crown in its conquest of the New

World. In 1602 Sebastián Vizcaíno followed in search of a suitable harbor for Manila galleons sailing back from the Philippines. He named the area Monterey in honor of the Count of Monterey, Viceroy of Spain.

But many years passed before the area was colonized. It was well over 200 years after Cabrillo's discovery that the place Richard Henry Dana called "the pleasantest and most civilized place in California" was settled, when Father Serra established the second of his now-famous chain of missions there. His landing site is now a state historic monument, although the original mission has been moved to nearby Carmel.

After the city of Monterey was established by the Spanish Crown in 1770, it became the capital of upper California and the port for galleons returning from Manila. Its presence also served to ward off Russian advances from the north.

Monterey was under Mexican rule from 1821 to 1846, and even today there are many architectural echoes—whitewashed adobe houses and pueblos—of this period. About a dozen such buildings have been preserved as historic monuments, among them the **Custom House**, across from the entrance to Fisherman's Wharf, where Commodore John Drake Sloat first officially raised the United States flag on July 7, 1846. Monterey was the port of entry for all foreign shipping on the California coast under Spanish and Mexican rule. The Custom House was the government's site for collection of duties. It is the oldest government building in California and was built under the Mexican regime.

Monterey adds an interesting footnote to naval history. How many cities have been captured by the United States Navy (in 1842 by Cmdr. Thomas Jones) and returned a few days later when it was discovered that there was no war and it was all a big mistake?

Monterey is also Steinbeck country. In the '40s Steinbeck wrote: "Cannery Row in Monterey . . . is a poem, a stink, a grating noise, a quality of light, a tone, a habit, a nostalgia, a dream." Returning in the '60s to the street he had given fame, he had this to say: "The beaches are clean where they once festered with fish guts and flies. The canneries which once put up a sickening stench are gone, their places filled with restaurants, antique shops, and the like. They fish for tourists, now, not pilchards, and that species they are not likely to wipe out."

It's true that **Cannery Row** is touristy. The entrepreneurs have moved in and upped the real estate value of the old waterside slum. They've planted sweet antique shoppes where Dora's girls once plied their profession and laden the shaky wooden wharf with direct-import gifts. But there's no reason you have to go as a tourist. You can skulk down there, sans camera and in wrinkled jeans, scuff barefoot along the rocky shoreline, and give one furtive glance toward Doc's house. Go down at dawn, at the "hour of the pearl," when the fishermen are just putting off from the docks, and you'll find that Cannery Row has not yet lost all its magic.

GETTING THERE

Monterey is easily reachable from points north or south (it's 330 miles north of Los Angeles, 130 miles south of San Francisco) via U.S. 101 and/or scenic Coast Hwy. 1 (Calif. 1). By air, American, Skywest, and United Airlines serve the Monterey Peninsula.

WHAT TO SEE AND DO

There's so much to see and do in beautiful Monterey, and in the vicinity, that it's a good idea to make your first stop at the **Monterey Peninsula Chamber of Commerce** and **Visitors and Convention Bureau,** 380 Alvarado St., between Franklin Street and Del Monte Avenue (tel. 408/649-1770). Here you can pick up maps and pamphlets, including several excellent free publications: *Monterey Peninsula Review, This Month on the Monterey Peninsula,* and guides to local restaurants and hotels, all chock-full of information about local attractions and facilities. Another free and comprehensive publication is *Key*—it's available at most hotels and shops.

In addition to exquisite natural beauty, the peninsula area offers a cornucopia of visitor attractions. Accommodations range from luxurious resorts to the charmingly quaint Carmel inns listed in a later section of this chapter.

The choice of fine restaurants is amazingly abundant—over 300 eateries serving Italian, Japanese, Mexican, German, Scandinavian, French, Filipino, Korean, Chinese, or whatever other cuisine your palate craves.

The sports-minded will find every kind of facility from golf and tennis to horseshoe throwing.

The Monterey Peninsula hosts the AT&T Pebble Beach National Pro-Am Golf Tournament in February, the Monterey Wine Festival in March, the Laguna Seca GT races in May, the Carmel Bach Festival in July, the oldest continuing Jazz Festival in September, and the Monterey Grand Prix Races in October.

And that's not to mention over a dozen movie theaters, parks, exciting annual events like rodeos and horse shows, flea markets, fish fries, exhibitions by kilt-clad bagpipers, Sierra Club hikes, lectures, demonstrations, and dozens of art galleries. And then there are the major Monterey historical sights, detailed below.

Path of History

The Path of History is a delightful walking tour that takes in many historic landmarks. Depending on the intensity of your historical fervor, you might want to take in all of them, or do an abbreviated tour of those grouped in the area called **Monterey State Historic Park.** The park's offices are at 525 Polk St. (tel. 408/649-7118). An admission of $3.50 for adults, $2 for children 6 to 17, allows you entrance to all state buildings for one day. There is a single-building admission of $1 for adults, 50¢ for children 6 to 17. Highlights of the latter tour include:

CUSTOM HOUSE When the area of Monterey was under Mexican rule, custom duties collected here from foreign shipping formed the principal revenue source for the government. After inspection and payment of custom duties, a ship was permitted to trade on the California coast. The Custom House, 1 Custom House Plaza, was the site where, on July 7, 1846, Commodore John Drake Sloat officially raised the United States flag. His action brought 600,000 square miles, including California, under the stewardship of the American government.

The north end of the Custom House, built about 1827, is the oldest part of the structure. In 1841 work was started to enlarge it, and by early 1846 it had been completed. The building was abandoned as a Custom House in about 1867 because, by then, San Francisco had become California's major port.

Hours are 10am to 5pm daily from March to October, to 4pm the rest of the year.

CASA DEL ORO This two-story adobe at the corner of Scott and Oliver streets was built when it was used as a warehouse, barracks, and hospital quarters for American seamen left at the port under consular care. In 1849 the building was leased to Joseph Boston and Company, a general store. The reason it's called Casa del Oro (house of gold) is that miners stored their treasures in an iron safe here in Gold Rush days—or so rumor has it.

Today it is owned by the state, operated by the Monterey History and Art Association, and preserved as a general store, stocked with burlap sacks full of coffee and beans, milk cans, ribbons, old tools, fabrics, dinnerware, and canisters of grains, noodles, etc. The building retains its original character and the merchandise is what could have been purchased in the mid-19th century.

Open Wednesday through Saturday from 10am to 5pm and on Sunday from noon to 5pm.

CALIFORNIA'S FIRST THEATER/JACK SWAN'S TAVERN Monterey owes its first theater to Jack Swan, an English sailor of Scottish ancestry who settled in Monterey in 1844.

Swan built the structure at the corner of Scott and Pacific streets in 1847–1848 as a boarding house and tavern. In 1847 the first stage performance was given by the soldiers of the New York Volunteer Regiment, using blankets as curtains, barrels and boards as benches. Among the first productions were scenes from *Romeo and Juliet.*

The building was given to the state for preservation in 1906, and the original structure remains, looking much the same today as in earlier times. The tavern is still operating and the theater is open for viewing Wednesday through Sunday from 11:30am to 5pm (it's open daily during the summer). The Troupers of the Gold Coast put on authentic 19th-century melodramas every Friday and Saturday night year-round (except Christmas week), adding Wednesday and Thursday performances in July and August. The curtain goes up at 8pm on all show nights.

The cost is $6 for adults, $5 for seniors (over 60) and teens, $4 for those younger. It's a great night out (tel. 408/375-5100 after 1pm Wednesday through Saturday).

COOPER-MOLERA ADOBE   The Cooper-Molera adobe, a 2½-acre complex at the corner of Polk and Munras streets, was built in the 1830s by John Rogers Cooper. It was willed to the National Trust for Historic Preservation by Cooper's granddaughter, Frances Molera. Captain John Rogers Cooper was a dealer in hides, tallow, sea otter pelts, and general merchandise. He was the half-brother of Thomas Larkin. As Cooper became increasingly wealthy from his trading operations, he expanded his one-story home to a two-story structure, erected large barns, and enclosed the complex with a high shingle-capped adobe wall. More than any of the other historic sites, the Cooper-Molera adobe typifies life in early California, from the live-in kitchen to the barnyard animals.

The adobe is open daily except Wednesday. From March to October, tours are given on the hour (except 1pm) from 10am to 5pm, to 4pm the rest of the year.

CASA SOBRANES   This adobe house at 336 Pacific St. was built during the 1840s by Don José Rafael Estrada, the warden of the Custom House, for his bride, Concepción Malarín. It's a Mediterranean-style house, with a cantilevered balcony and tile roof. The house is completely furnished, and decorated with an extensive collection of art by local artists.

It can be visited by tour only, offered on the hour daily except Thursday from 10am to 4pm (except 1pm) in winter, to 5pm from March to October.

LARKIN HOUSE   Built in 1835, this balconied two-story adobe at 510 calle Principal, at Jefferson Street, was the home of Thomas Oliver Larkin, who served as U.S. consul to Mexico from 1843 to 1846. The house also served as the consular office. Furnished in the style of the period with many original pieces, Larkin House is a museum of architecture and Monterey life. Next door is the house used by William Tecumseh Sherman; it now contains a museum depicting the roles of the two men in California history.

A 35-minute guided tour is offered throughout the day every hour on the hour (except noon) from 10am to 5pm, March to October; to 4pm the rest of the year; closed Tuesday. The last tour begins one hour before closing.

STEVENSON HOUSE   The original portion of this two-story home at 530 Houston St. dates to the late 1830s, when it was the home of Don Rafael Gonzáles, first administrator of customs of Alta California. In 1856 a French pioneer, Juan Giradin, and his wife became the owners. They made some additions and rented spare bedrooms to roomers, one of whom was Robert Louis Stevenson (he occupied a second-floor room during the autumn of 1879). He had come from Scotland to persuade Fanny Osbourne to marry him (she did). While here he wrote *The Old Pacific Capital,* an account of Monterey in the 1870s. Poor, unknown, and in frail health, he was cared for by Jules Simoneau, in whose restaurant he had his one full meal of the day.

The building has been restored to its period look, and several rooms are devoted to Stevenson memorabilia. It has been said that a ghostly spirit is sometimes seen in an upstairs children's bedroom, which makes for an additional point of interest.

Hours are 10am to 5pm from March to October, to 4pm the rest of the year; tours are offered every hour on the hour (except noon). The last tour begins one hour before closing. Closed Wednesday.

THE PACIFIC HOUSE Built in 1847 by David Wight for Thomas O. Larkin, Pacific House, at 10 Custom House Plaza, was first used for army offices and to store military supplies. Army horses were corralled behind the building, and this was a popular spot for Sunday bull and bear fights. Later it housed small stores and served as a public tavern, a courtroom, county clerk's office, newspaper office, law offices, a church—even a ballroom where a temperance society called the Dashaways held dances.

The Jacks family bought the property in 1880 and maintained the premises until 1954, when Miss Margaret Jacks made a gift of the historic building to the state. The first floor houses a museum of California history; the second floor has an extensive collection of Native American artifacts plus a few Mexican Indian and Eskimo pieces.

Hours are 10am to 5pm daily from March to October, to 4pm the rest of the year.

COLTON HALL Named for the Rev. Walter Colton, U.S. Navy chaplain who impaneled California's first jury, co-founded the state's first newspaper, and built its first public building, Colton Hall, 522 Pacific St., was planned as the town hall and public school. It was the scene of California's constitutional congress in 1849, when the constitution was written and the great seal of the state designed. There's a museum upstairs, and Old Monterey Jail adjoins, its grim cell walls still marked with prisoners' scribblings.

Open daily from 10am to 5pm.

VIZCAÍNO-SERRA LANDING SITE Just south of the Monterey Presidio on Pacific Street is the site where Sebastián Vizcaíno landed in 1602, and where, in 1770, Father Serra and Don Gaspar de Portolá founded Monterey, future capital and port of entry of California.

From here you're in a good position to proceed to—

Cannery Row

Entering Cannery Row, you still drive under the covered conveyor belts that once carried tinned fish from cannery to warehouse. But the corrugated-steel warehouses, vacated by factories, have been renovated and now house restaurants, boutiques, art galleries, antique shops, and other browsables. There's even free tasting of wine from the **Bargetto Winery,** 700 Cannery Row, Suite L (tel. 408/373-4053).

The best way to explore Cannery Row is simply to start at one end and meander along. There are a few complexes of shops, including some individual enterprises you should review.

Don't miss the **Bayside Trading Co.,** 225 Cannery Row (tel. 408/646-9944), just across from the Monterey Bay Inn and one block from the Coast Guard pier.

This exceptional shop is in a beautiful, big old cannery building (used at times by Hollywood), with high, beamed ceilings, taupe walls, and beige carpeting, all of which serve as excellent background for the variety of handsome objects displayed and sold here. Bayside selectively gathers attractive handmade goods of exceptional quality from around the world. There is nothing commonplace in its collection of colorful textiles, clothing, pottery, rugs, jewelry, glassware, carry-alls, desks, sideboards, train whistles, whatever. And to add to the attraction and beauty, prices are reasonable. Gift wrapping is complimentary and shipping can be arranged.

Bayside Trading is open daily: Monday through Thursday from 10:30am to 7:30pm, Friday to 8pm, on Saturday from 10am to 8pm, and on Sunday from 10am to 6:30pm. During the summer, the shop opens a bit earlier and closes a bit later.

At no. 625 is **Cannery Row Square** (three restaurants and about 15 shops). The Monterey Cannery at no. 700 houses the newest attraction, the **Spirit of Monterey Wax Museum.** It brings alive the people (all life-size) and places of the old Cannery Row—ladies of the night (the girls at Flora's), the drifters, fishermen, swindlers, Father Junípero Serra, legendary bandits—all much as John Steinbeck saw and wrote about them. Admission is $5 for adults, $4 for seniors and military, $3 for children 7 to 13, free for those 6 and under with an adult. The museum is open daily from 9am to 9pm.

Whatever else you may want to see in Monterey, don't miss the **Monterey Bay Aquarium,** at the west end of Cannery Row, 886 Cannery Row (tel. 408/648-4888). This is the largest exhibit aquarium in the nation. It is the $50-million creation financed by David and Lucile Packard at the behest of four local marine biologists, including his daughter, trained in the philosophies of Ed (Doc) Ricketts, the ecological marine biologist and prototype for "Doc" in Steinbeck's *Cannery Row.* The aquarium opened in October 1984.

Statistics alone simply do not do justice to this spectacular living gallery of the sea. The building is on the site of the old Hovden sardine cannery and houses an astounding display of more than 6,500 sea creatures that literally surround you. You step into an enchanted new world at the bottom of a three-story kelp forest housed in an acrylic-windowed tank holding over 300,000 gallons of sea water, with the seaweed waving gently as though moved by tidal surges. Sit down and quietly watch the hundreds of creatures slowly swimming back and forth—the greenlings, sand sharks, jacksmelts, rockfish—and you feel like a scuba diver in an underwater cathedral. And then there are the sea otters to see, the delightful clowns of the aquarium, all four orphans rescued by the staff. Feeding time for the otters is an acrobatic event you don't want to miss.

There are exhibits of coastal streams, tidal pools, a beach with seabirds that inhabit the salt marsh and sandy shore, and even touch pools where you can stroke a living bat ray or a sea star. You'll also have the opportunity to see orphaned sea otters being prepared for a return to the wild by staff members who swim with the pups, and help the young otters learn to find food and acquire other survival skills.

The Monterey Bay Aquarium is an ongoing changing exhibit of the sea world in Monterey Bay and off the California and Baja coast. The aquarium borders on the Monterey Canyon, one of the largest submarine canyons in the world—wider and deeper than the Grand Canyon. It is this canyon that provides the nutrients that support the richness of life in and around Monterey Bay, and that you will see, in part, at the aquarium. You may have already seen the kelp forest at its several levels or visited special temporary exhibits. A permanent exhibit now opens a new window into the deep as scientists beam live video broadcasts to the aquarium from an exploration vessel nearly 2,000 feet deep in Monterey Bay. The geography of the bay's 10,000-foot-deep canyon will be explored to discover new information about the animals that live there.

If you were any where near Monterey in 1990 and missed the exhibit Living Treasures of the Pacific, which showcased the living art and incredible beauty of jellyfish and other marine creatures of the Pacific, more's the pity. But you will have another opportunity to view a remarkable exhibit in 1991, one certainly quite different in its own beauty—Sharks. More than a dozen species of these sometimes fierce,

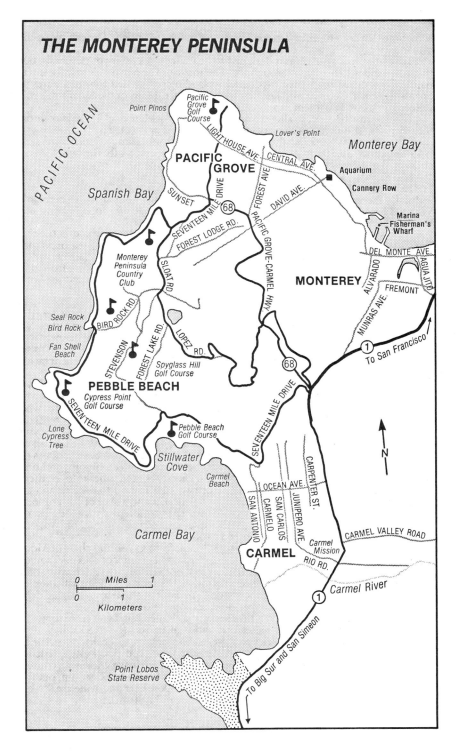

THE MONTEREY PENINSULA

PACIFIC OCEAN

Point Pinos

Pacific Grove Golf Course

Lover's Point

PACIFIC GROVE

Monterey Bay

Aquarium

LIGHTHOUSE AVE.

CENTRAL AVE.

Spanish Bay

SUNSET

FOREST AVE.

DAVID AVE.

Cannery Row

Marina

Fisherman's Wharf

SEVENTEEN MILE DRIVE

FOREST LODGE RD.

68

PACIFIC GROVE-CARMEL HWY.

DEL MONTE AVE.

AGUA JITO

SLOAT RD.

Monterey Peninsula Country Club

MONTEREY

ALVARADO

FREMONT

MUNRAS AVE.

Seal Rock
Bird Rock

BIRD ROCK RD.

LOPEZ RD.

1

To San Francisco

Fan Shell Beach

STEVENSON

FOREST LAKE RD.

Spyglass Hill Golf Course

68

PEBBLE BEACH

Cypress Point Golf Course

SEVENTEEN MILE DRIVE

Lone Cypress Tree

SEVENTEEN MILE DRIVE

Pebble Beach Golf Course

N

Stillwater Cove

Carmel Beach

OCEAN AVE.

CARPENTER ST.

Carmel Bay

SAN ANTONIO

CARMELO

SAN CARLOS

JUNIPERO AVE.

CARMEL VALLEY ROAD

Carmel Mission

CARMEL

RIO RD.

Miles   1
Kilometers   1

0   1

1

Carmel River

Point Lobos State Reserve

To Big Sur and San Simeon

sometimes shy, often misunderstood creatures will be included. The exhibit opens on January 13, 1991, and continues through October 21, 1991.

The nonprofit aquarium is designed to be visited on a do-it-yourself basis, but there are guides to help you throughout. The aquarium also makes it easy for international visitors to enjoy their experience, providing self-guided tour brochures in Spanish, French, German, and Japanese at the entrance. Many of the aquarium's volunteer guides are also fluent in a foreign language.

There's much to see, so allow two to three hours for your visit. There is a café on the premises for lunch, since you cannot bring in food or beverages.

The aquarium is open daily (except Christmas) from 10am to 6pm. Admission is $9 for adults, $6.50 for seniors over 65 and students, and $4 for the disabled and children 3 to 12 years. Children under 3 are admitted free.

Fisherman's Wharf

Like San Francisco, Monterey has not only a Cannery but also a Fisherman's Wharf. This one, near the old Custom House, is lined with craft shops, boating and fishing operations, fish markets, and seafood restaurants.

I've yet to find a time when Fisherman's Wharf was not busy, whatever the season. But one delightful advantage during the very crowded tourist season is that restaurants along the Wharf dole out free samples of their delicious clam chowder, rich with clams, carrots, and potatoes. You can just about fill up strolling from one end of the Wharf to the other. At the far end are very vocal seagulls and sea lions begging for breakfast, lunch, dinner, and all meals in between.

WHARF DINING If you get hungry for more than a sample of clam chowder, the choice ranges from a cup of fresh shrimp to a full restaurant meal. All in all, there's a gaggle of places to eat on the Wharf. In addition to the three described below, there are **Rappa's Restaurant,** located at the far end; **Domenico's Oyster Bar,** with fresh pasta and fresh fish cooked over an open hearth; and **Cafe Fina,** with excellent ravioli, pizza, and mesquite-barbecued fish. And these are just a few.

Strolling toward the bay end of the Wharf, midway on the right is the **Cove Restaurant,** no. 46 (tel. 408/373-6969), easily spotted by its small blue-gray awning and large bay window facing the walk. The Cove is ready for the early riser who enjoys a walk near the waterfront. The restaurant serves breakfast from 6 (6:30 on weekends) to 11:30am. You can get the usual accompaniments with eggs, or you may prefer your eggs with a hamburger, or Italian sausage, or squid, or fish, all of which arrive with potatoes and toast ($5 to $6). The Cove serves seven varieties of omelets ($5 to $7), most prepared with two cheeses and sautéed onions, and one exceptional combination of shrimp and cheddar cheese. For the pancake lover, there are short and tall stacks, alone or with one or two eggs ($3.50 to $4.25), and an incredible pancake sandwich composed of two pancakes and a slice of ham topped with an egg ($5.25). If you feel the need of further nutrition, there's a long list of side orders. For the cowards among us, the restaurant serves one egg, or two, but you can't dodge the potatoes and toast ($3 to $3.30).

Lunch, served daily from 11:30am to 3:30pm, features fish and chips of Monterey Bay rock cod ($5.50), as well as the Lucky Fisherman platter of rock cod, squid, prawns, and scallops, with one lonely oyster ($9); both dishes are served with soup or salad and french fries. The selection of sandwiches includes the usual complement, plus squid and fish. Among the seafood specialties ($5.50 to $7.50) are delicious deep-fried Pacific oysters, snapper, sole, scallops, and squid filets.

As you might expect, seafood is the specialty at dinner, but if you yearn for steak or prawns, there are good choices. All seafood and steak entrees ($8 to $15) include a choice of soup or salad, potato or rice pilaf, vegetables, and bread. Seafood specialties provide a wide choice: fish and chips, a tasty baked rock cod (local catch), Pacific oysters lightly breaded and quickly fried (a favorite of mine), or an enormous combination plate for the famished. There's a top sirloin steak, or teriyaki sirloin, but for those of two minds, steak with prawns may hit the spot. Beer and wine are served (house policy is not to serve alcoholic beverages before 11:30am).

The Cove Restaurant is open daily: Sunday through Tuesday from 6am to 5:30pm, the rest of the week from 6:30am to 9pm. *Note:* The Cove does not accept credit cards.

A bit farther down is the **Wharfside Restaurant and Lounge,** no. 60 (tel. 408/375-3956), in whose downstairs dining room you can enjoy a great view overlooking the end of the Wharf and the marina. You can have lunch or dinner at one of the tables or at a small but efficient and industrious bar. A glass partition discreetly serves as a divider between the bar and the serious-eating area. The pub menu offers great clam chowder and the expected selection of sandwiches, as well as a delicious hot crab sandwich for $6.50 and grilled squid at $5.50. Pizzas range from $6.75 to $11 without extras.

Upstairs is the dining room, which offers a somewhat more formal (though decidedly seaside) look, with sea-gray post-and-beam construction finished with maroon trim. It's a spot you won't want to leave—the view up there is worth any time spent in just sitting and watching the constant activity in the marina. In addition to its visual pleasures, the Wharfside dining room offers a complete range of seafood, moderately priced from $9 to $16. Daily specials may include fresh seasonal fish, beef, pasta, or calamari. A good selection of beers and California wines are offered as well as the services of the full bar.

The Wharfside is open daily from 11am to 9:30pm.

Now and then, if you're lucky, you'll happen upon a restaurant where the owners concentrate on the freshest food, deliciously prepared, and where the decor is basic and unaffected. That's the way it is at the **Abalonetti Restaurant,** near the bay end of Fisherman's Wharf (tel. 408/373-1851 or 375-5941). Abalonetti, in fact, is about as unpretentious as you can get—simple decor and furnishings, wood floors, no chandeliers, no full bar (though there are wine and beer). What they do feature is some of the freshest seafood you've ever eaten: whether it's squid, sole, Monterey rock cod, prawns, clams, scallops, oysters, crab, or excellent cioppino (San Francisco's version of bouillabaisse). And their homemade chowder is delicious. Seasonal delicacies include such choice entrees as Monterey Bay salmon and Pacific swordfish steak. In addition to nonseafood pasta, you'll also find steak and chicken on Abalonetti's menu. And for lunch there's also a good selection of salads and sandwiches.

Lunch will cost from $5.25 for pasta dishes to $8.50 for varied choices such as a steak sandwich, crab lunch, prawns, a crab Louie salad, and a combination seafood plate. Dinner ranges from $8.50 for deep-fried squid rings served with fries to $14.95 for the delicious combination cioppino, or steak and prawns, and includes chowder or tossed green salad plus French bread. Abalonetti has a satisfactory selection of wine by the bottle or glass, plus beer.

Lunch is served weekdays, except Tuesday, from 11am to 3pm, dinner from 5 to 9pm. Saturday and Sunday, Abalonetti is open from 11am to 9pm.

FISHING/BOAT TRIPS If you want to do more than just stroll, **Princess Monterey Cruises,** at the end of the Wharf (tel. 408/372-2628), runs 35- to 45-minute pleasure cruises on fishing-party boats (no fishing on these trips). The boats depart daily during the summer, on the hour from noon to 6pm. Adults pay $5; children under 12, $2.50.

In winter, there are 1½- to 2-hour narrated whale-watching cruises (best times are December to February) at $15 per person. Weekdays, boats depart on the hour from 10am to 4pm; weekends, from 9am to 4pm. It's suggested that you wear soft-soled shoes, since the decks are often wet; warm clothing, especially a windbreaker and hat; and sun glasses and sun screen. Reservations are recommended and check-in is 45 minutes prior to your departure time. Trips may sometimes be cancelled because of weather and sea conditions, so it's wise to call ahead.

If, on the other hand, you'd like to do some angling, **Monterey Sport Fishing,** no. 96 (tel. 408/372-2203, 24 hours), offers limited-passenger deep-sea-fishing trips. And if you didn't pack your rod or tackle, Monterey Sport Fishing has them to rent. They'll also sell you the required one-day fishing license; bait is free. Box lunches are available, as is a snack bar. Weekdays, the total package, including rod, tackle, license, and fish sack (I am forever optimistic), is $34.25. If you come fully equipped, the fare is $21. Weekends, the total package is $48.25; or the fare alone is $35. Be sure to make reservations. Weekdays, check-in time is 6:45am; weekends, it's 6am. Monterey Sport Fishing also has half-day or full-day charters by appointment.

Chris' Fishing Trips, no. 48 on the Wharf (tel. 408/375-5951, 24 hours), has the biggest party boats in Monterey—all diesel-powered and equipped with fish finders, radar, ship-to-shore, and deck lounges. The main business is cod trips, all during the year (weekdays for $21, weekends and holidays for $24). They also have (Chinook) salmon trips leaving at 6am (weekdays, weekends, and holidays for $35), and fall outings for albacore ($70 any day) with a departure time of 5am. Chris' will rent rods and tackle, and fishing licenses can be purchased at the shop; box lunches are available on order. Here, too, reservations are necessary. Charter boats are available.

Sam's Fishing Fleet, no. 84 on the Wharf (tel. 408/372-0577), has four fishing boats available, and they've been serving Monterey fisherfolk since 1914. Diesel-powered fishing boats depart weekdays at 7:30am (check-in time is 6:45am), weekends at 6:30am (check-in at 6am). Adults pay $21; children under 12, $14; weekends and holidays it's $24 and $15, respectively. Tackle can be rented and bait is free. Bring lunch and make reservations. Sam's also has group charters.

Note: While I have mentioned it above, it bears repeating—any time you plan a trip on the the water, be it for whale-watching, sightseeing, or fishing, it can get cool and often downright cold. It's wise to take a windbreaker and whatever else in the way of clothing it takes to keep you warm. You can always shed sweaters, heavy shirts, caps, jackets, or whatever, but if your clothing isn't up to holding in the warmth, it can be a very unpleasant trip.

Guided Tours

One of the easiest and most enjoyable ways to see Monterey is to be taken around. **Steinbeck Country Tours** (tel. 408/625-5107) without a doubt provides one of the most popular tours of the area. The tour encompasses the entire Monterey Peninsula and takes three to four hours. You are picked up at your local hotel (in Monterey, Pebble Beach, Carmel, or Pacific Grove) and taken on an enjoyable, informative trip around the peninsula, including the original 17-Mile Drive, Cannery Row, Pacific Grove, and Carmel.

Steinbeck Country Tours also has regularly scheduled tours from the Monterey Peninsula to Hearst Castle. The castle tour via Big Sur is an all-day affair leaving at 8am, returning at 6:30pm, and including a wine tasting at a local vineyard.

For reservations with Steinbeck Country Tours, call two to three days in advance or ask the guest representative at your hotel to make reservations. The cost of the Monterey Tour is $25, and it's well worth the price. The Hearst Castle Tour is $50, including the entrance fee.

The 17-Mile Drive

The whole Carmel–Pacific Grove–Monterey area, not to mention the breathtaking coast along Calif. 1, is so very scenic that the 17-Mile Drive may seem superfluous. But if you can't get enough of a good thing—and I can't—don't miss it. The 17-Mile Drive is situated in the Del Monte Forest, and costs $6 per car. This private road, famous for magnificent landscapes and seascapes, can be entered from any of three gates. Most convenient from town is the Calif. 1 Gate (take Munras Avenue to Calif. 1). When you pay your toll, you'll be given a map that points out 26 highlights along the way, including several picnic areas, six golf courses, the famous **Lone Pine,** and **Seal and Bird Rocks,** where you can see countless gulls, cormorants, and other offshore birds, as well as offshore herds of seals and sea lions.

If you don't want to pay the tab for the 17-Mile Drive, or don't feel that you have the time, there's a spectacular alternative. Start at Ocean View Boulevard (it follows after Cannery Row) and continue around to Asilomar Avenue. There are several places to stop and gape, for the views along the way are nothing short of spectacular. During the winter months a furious sea rages and bounds against the rocks. It's an awesome sight of a less than peaceful Pacific in all its arrogant beauty that residents—cormorants, seals, gulls—appear to regard quite casually.

At the end of your ride along Ocean View (in Pacific Grove) is the Fishwife Restaurant. If it's not a Tuesday, the Fishwife is a fine place for lunch or dinner (described below under "Where to Dine").

Golf Around the Peninsula

Monterey is also the gateway to the excitingly beautiful Monterey Peninsula—Northern California's playland for golfers. In the area surrounding the city, there are sea views and scenic drives, ghostly cypress trees, and Seal Rocks. But most of all, there are golf courses. The famed **Pebble Beach Golf Links** is here, on which the AT&T National Pro-Amateur Golf Tourney is held every February.

If you drool at the thought of playing at Pebble Beach Golf Links, but can't quite swing the price, there's an inexpensive alternative (not the same, but still a challenge). Head over to the **Pacific Grove Municipal Golf Course,** 77 Asilomar Ave. (tel. 408/375-3456 or 373-3063). The last nine holes overlook the sea and give you the joy(?) and challenge of coping with all the winds you need or want for a links course. It's not all that long (5,553 yards), but there's enough here to keep you busy. The fairways and greens are beautifully maintained, better than most municipal or even semiprivate courses. The course has a restaurant, pro shop, and driving range. Greens fees are $13 weekdays, $15 weekends; carts are $17. The course does not accept charge cards, nor are there senior discounts.

Of the many golf courses on the Monterey Peninsula and nearby areas, four are open to the public: **Laguna Seca, Pacific Grove** (described above), **Rancho Canada,** and **Del Monte.** Greens fees range from about $13 to $30 (plus cart) for 18 holes.

WHERE TO STAY

While the Monterey Bay Aquarium heads Cannery Row, a genteel gloved hand opens the door to the new and very grand **Monterey Plaza Hotel,** a Trusthouse Forte Hotel, at the opposite end, 400 Cannery Row, Monterey, CA 93940 (tel. 408/646-1700, or toll free 800/631-1339, 800/334-3999 in California). The hotel overlooks Monterey Bay and the Pacific and is just a short picturesque stroll from the aquarium. This is a $69-million resort with 290 luxury-size rooms and suites that showcase the surrounding sea. Beds are not king-size but emperor-size. Rooms are furnished in natural-wood tones, dark leathers, and designer fabrics in tones that vary from room to room. An armoire conceals each TV, desk, and drawers. As you might expect, bathrooms each have telephones, his and hers bathrobes, extra-thick towels. Terraces overlook the bay and its spectacular sunsets. The hotel provides a full-service staff, as well as a concierge, and can arrange entry to several local golf clubs, tennis courts, sightseeing, and transportation.

The hotel's restaurant, Delfino's, features northern Italian cuisine, of the Emilia-Romagna region. Delfino's conveys a feeling of old-world elegance: the wide polished ceiling beams, cloth-covered banquettes with dolphin prints, linen at lunch. The menu is à la carte, and dinner entrees range from $13 to $26 for such delectables as homemade pastas and magnificent medallions of veal. With salad, and perhaps wine, dinner for two will probably be between $80 and $120. Let's just say that the food is as superior as the service, and all is graced by the sweeping view of the bay and its inhabitants. Delfino's is open daily from 7 to 11am for breakfast; 11:30am to 2pm for lunch; and 6 to 10pm (to 10:30pm on Friday and Saturday) for dinner. On Sunday, Delfino's has a superb champagne buffet brunch from 10:30am to 2:30pm for $19.50. Reservations are always advised for dinner.

Singles and doubles are $130 to $295; suites, $300 to $600; $25 for each extra person.

Monterey Bay Inn, 242 Cannery Row, Monterey, CA 93940 (tel. 408/373-6242, or toll free 800/424-6242 in California), is directly on Monterey Bay. It has 47 spacious rooms surrounding an atrium. Each is elegantly decorated in light-toned woods and in coral, bone, and seafoam-green fabrics. Photographs of the area decorate the walls to give the rooms a feeling of the sea and a bit of Monterey history. Apart from the usual amenities, each room also has a dry bar and refrigerator, handy full-length mirrors on the sliding closet doors, and luxurious terrycloth robes (not for the taking). A hot tub is conveniently located at the atrium terrace on the fourth floor. An additional hot tub is located on the rooftop terrace, which boasts a spectacular view of Monterey Bay. There's a sauna in the workout room. The adjacent park affords access to the beach, and there are special facilities for scuba divers.

Single and double rooms range from $110 to $180, depending on the view; suites run $185 to $205. All rates include Continental breakfast and use of the health club. Parking is conveniently located beneath the inn.

The **Steinbeck Gardens Inn** is at 443 Wave St. (which parallels Cannery Row), Monterey, CA 93940 (tel. 408/372-1800, or toll free 800/248-8442), between Fisherman's Wharf and the Monterey Bay Aquarium. The inn is a small group of light sea-gray, very contemporary board-and-batten buildings. The entryway looks like the opening to a sumptuous greenhouse: paned glass, light, greenery, and palms in reed baskets. The lobby is cozy-plush. Window seats are in subtle tones of rose, blue, pink, plum, and green, and high ceilings add to the airiness of the room. And as you might expect, hanging in a position of dominance is a large photo of John Steinbeck. A handsome two-level courtyard with white patio furniture is a comfortable place for rest and relaxation after a day of sightseeing, as is the spa (hot tub), now secluded in the gazebo adjoining the inn. The inn's attractive library is large enough for a small conference and the perfect size for a small reception after your next wedding.

The rooms are spacious and airy with spreads and drapes done in delicate floral colors: subtle tones of pink, rose, gray, white, and mauve. Of course there is color TV (hidden in the chest) with remote control and HBO, plus a phone. Baths have plump, fluffy towels, all the necessary facilities, and lighting to suit the makeup artists among us.

Steinbeck Gardens Inn is a tribute to good looks and reasonable rates. Single or double occupancy is $70 to $110, "executive king" rooms are $90 to $135, and there are excellent weekly rates. Rates include complimentary breakfast and late-afternoon wine and cheese.

An alternative luxury accommodation in Monterey is the **Old Monterey Inn,** 500 Martin St. (off Pacific), Monterey, CA 93940 (tel. 408/375-8284). Ann and Gene Swett have turned their old family home into a country inn, and they've done a masterful job of it. The 10 rooms have lyrical names like Dovecote, Serengeti, and Tattershall. All have garden views, private baths, and beds with goose-down comforters and pillows. They're charmingly furnished, each in unique fashion, and special touches include fresh flowers, a sachet under your pillow, good soaps, and books and magazines to read. You can even get a picnic basket for a trip to Point Lobos or Big Sur. Eight of the rooms have wood-burning fireplaces, and one has a private patio. The baths are supplied with deodorants, toothpaste, shampoo, bath oil, even electric hair dryers and curlers. The newest accommodation is the elegant three-room Ashford Suite, the sitting room of which has marvelous bay windows with a wisteria border, a wood-burning fireplace, and a good-looking carved pine day bed.

At 5pm daily, guests can relax in the cozy living room before a blazing fireplace and partake of complimentary sherry, cheese, and crackers. An impressive breakfast (home-baked breads, perhaps a soufflé or Belgian waffles) is included in the rates, and is served in a delightful dining room, although you can also have it in your room or in the garden (weather permitting). On sunny days guests can loll about in hammocks, exercising away the breakfast repast, and look forward to enjoying tea and cookies in the afternoon.

If you'd like to stay at the Old Monterey Inn, reserve far in advance. Rates are $140 to $200 for single or double occupancy. The secluded Garden Cottage and Ashford Suite are $200.

In a class by itself on 17-Mile Drive is the luxurious **Lodge at Pebble Beach,** Pebble Beach, CA 93953 (tel. 408/624-3811), of which Pebble Beach Golf Links Spyglass Hill Golf Course is part. Though a long stay here could wreak havoc on your budget, you might want to spend a few nights at these posh digs while seeing the Carmel/Monterey area. But plan well ahead. (The 1992 U.S. Open Championship will be held here.)

In addition to the golf course, there's a beach, a heated swimming pool and sauna, fishing, 14 tennis courts, horseback-riding facilities, and 34 miles of bridle and hiking paths. Of course, the rooms are fitted out with every possible amenity; many even have wood-burning fireplaces.

About the famous Pebble Beach Golf Links—if you're a guest at the lodge and want to play 18, you're given priority in booking tee time. The cost of a round is $125 daily (including cart) for guests, $175 (including cart) for others.

If you can't stay, you might at least want to dine at the lodge's posh French restaurant, Club XIX (tel. 408/625-8519). It's extremely elegant, with oak-paneled walls, burgundy and forest-green carpeting and tablecloths, and fresh flowers in silver vases at every table. During the day you'll enjoy views of the golf course and bay; at night it's candlelit and romantic. A dinner at Club XIX might begin with an appetizer of foie gras with truffles or a Caesar salad for two, followed perhaps by a soup called veloute Bongo-Bongo—a creamy blend of oysters, spinach, herbs, and cognac. For an entree you might select stuffed quail in a potato nest with brandy sauce, or poached Monterey salmon, and finish off the feast with a soufflé Grand Marnier. If you're averse to spending $18 to $33 for an entree, come at lunch when lighter dishes are a more reasonable $8 to $14. Club XIX is open daily for lunch from 11:30am to 4:30pm and for dinner from 6:30 to 10pm. Reservations are advised.

There are several other excellent dining options at the lodge. The Cypress Room—with beautiful views of the 18th green and the bay—has many traditional favorites for breakfast, lunch, and dinner, when you may opt for a New York steak from the broiler, roast squab, or abalone ($19 to $32). The Tap Room is patterned after an English pub and loaded with golfing memorabilia. The menu changes daily: you might find prime rib, wienerschnitzel with spaetzle, thick-crust pizza, a chili platter, or grilled salmon filet ($8 to $19). The Gallery restaurant and bar overlooks the first tee and is open only for breakfast and lunch. It serves eggs in a multitude of forms and combinations, burgers and hot dogs, light lunches, fresh fruits, sandwiches, and a great German carrot cake.

Single or double accommodations cost $250 to $385; suites, $700 to $875.

In the fall of 1987 the lodge opened the **Inn at Spanish Bay,** off the 17-Mile Drive and just at the edge of the Del Monte Forest, about 300 yards from the Pacific (tel. 408/647-7500, or toll free 800/654-9300). Surrounded by the Links at Spanish Bay—a golf course designed by Tom Watson and Robert Trent Jones, Jr.—the inn is a three- and four-level hotel with 270 luxurious rooms and suites set on 236 acres. Approximately half the rooms face the ocean, the remainder having lovely forest views. Each room has its own fireplace; custom-made plush furnishings, including a living room furniture grouping and four-poster beds topped with down comforters; a separate dressing area; and either an outdoor deck or a patio. Baths are finished in Italian marble. As you might expect, there is 24-hour room service.

The Clubhouse overlooks the first tee of the Links at Spanish Bay. That's where you'll find the golf and pro shops, locker rooms, a complete fitness center, and a heated swimming pool. You can have breakfast or lunch at the Clubhouse Bar and Grill, which overlooks the first fairway. Greens fees for inn guests are $75, plus the mandatory golf cart ($18 per rider). There are a domed tennis pavilion and eight championship courts, two of them lighted for nighttime play, as well as a stadium court designed for tournaments.

The inn has three excellent restaurants to accommodate all tastes. The Dunes serves breakfast, lunch, and dinner on a seafront terrace or in the windowed salon, as the weather dictates. The menu is California cuisine, with entrees such as grilled filet mignon, roast rack of lamb, seared salmon with crème fraîche ($15 to $22), and exceptional pastas ($10 to $13). For more formal dining, there is the intimate, gracious Bay Club, open only for dinner. The room is done in muted earth tones, green accents complementing the Mediterranean cuisine. Your entree ($22 to $29) might be salmon in parmesan crust with tomato and basil sauce, or veal with prosciutto, sage, tomato, and marsala, possibly preceded by pancetta-wrapped grilled prawns. Casual dining is at Traps and the Lobby Lounge—sandwiches, salads, pizzas, oysters on the half shell, etc., as well as a fine selection of premium wines by the glass.

Rates are $200 to $250 for a room forest view, $300 for one with an ocean view, and $500 to $1,200 for the suites.

There is no question that bargains are few and far between in a popular haven for tourists, but one or two can be found in Monterey if you plan in advance and don't pick weekends such as that of the September Monterey Jazz Festival or the October Grand Prix.

Truly luxurious accommodations at a reasonable rate are what you'll find at the **Way Station,** 1200 Olmsted Rd., Monterey, CA 93940 (tel. 408/372-2945), just off Calif. 68. This attractive redwood motel, set among beautifully landscaped pines and well-groomed grounds, is conveniently situated near the Monterey airport, but not a sound of air traffic interferes with your comfort. The guest rooms convey the feeling of a town house rather than a motel. Rooms are done in tones of brown or blue, and the carpeting is plush with an inset of beige. Handsome historical prints give a decorator touch. High ceilings add to the luxurious feeling of spaciousness. At one corner of the room is a circular table, and above, a conveniently placed chandelier. Comfortable leather chairs are on wheels. Several rooms have balconies with sliding doors and screens, comfortable for lounging; others have bay windows facing the beautiful landscaping.

Adjoining is the Way Station Restaurant. Entry is past the bar into a handsomely proportioned room with high, beamed ceilings, ceiling fans, huge potted plants, and carpeting to match the landscape. Booths are separated by frosted-glass panels with designs of the stagecoach of early California. Service is friendly and attentive. Touches like the thin slice of lemon in the glass of water reflect the thought given to the preparation and presentation of the food. Breakfast is served all day and includes such toothsome dishes as carabaccia (poached eggs with vegetables) at $6.50 or pancakes covered with fresh fruit at $4.50. The salad bar has an exceptionally large number of choices and offers hot baguettes or sourdough bread, all for $6. But save yourself for dinner. Specialties of the house are veal and pasta. Seafood specials change daily. If you have a taste for Italian, try the chicken breast parmigiana baked and topped with mozzarella at $13, or the tortellini with Alfredo sauce for $13.25. The daily pasta special is worth asking your server about. If the dinner hasn't yet left you breathless, top it off with the homemade cheesecake, a caloric joy, with blueberry or strawberry sauce. There is a fine selection of California and Italian wines, some by the glass. Now there's a piano bar on weekends. The restaurant is open daily from 7am to 11pm.

Rates are $77 for singles, $88 for doubles, $116 for the luxury suites. Each additional person pays $10. The Way Station does not have room service or 24-hour phone service, but consider these as modest inconveniences in light of the above rates and quality of the accommodations.

Need I remind you of **Motel 6,** 2124 Fremont St., Monterey, CA 93940 (tel. 408/646-8585), where rates are $35 per person. Each additional adult is $6. TV is included; local calls are free. Reservations for summer months should be made at least six months in advance.

WHERE TO DINE

There are any number of places for dining in Monterey itself, not the least of which are **Delfino's** in the Monterey Plaza Hotel, **Club XIX** or the **Tap Room** at

Pebble Beach, and the **Way Station Restaurant** at the Way Station (much more moderate in price). Each is described above.

On Cannery Row, a good dining choice is the **Whaling Station Inn,** 763 Wave St., between Prescott and Irving Avenue (tel. 408/373-3778). It's entered via a rustic, wicker-furnished cocktail area, with barnwood walls and potted ferns. The interior is in the same motif as the cocktail lounge, but an added elegance is achieved by white taper candles in wrought-iron holders and white linen tablecloths. The entire effect is warm and homey.

All entrees include artichoke vinaigrette. Choices are à la carte and range from prime rib, pastas, and shellfish, to a variety of fresh fish broiled over mesquite charcoal, for $15 to $25. Desserts prepared by the pastry chef are displayed in all their tempting splendor; try a homemade cannoli.

The Whaling Station is open daily from 5 to 10pm, and there is free parking. Reservations advised.

---

2. Pacific Grove

The best-kept secret on the Monterey Peninsula is the little town of Pacific Grove. It occupies the northwest corner of the peninsula, between Monterey and Pebble Beach. The town got its start in the 1870s as a seaside resort for the Methodist Retreat Association of San Francisco. Tents would spring up in the summer, and church meetings would be held under the pines that gave the town its name. Before long, people started to settle in permanently; Pacific Grove has lots of houses that date from the late 19th century.

This quaint little town is nicknamed "Butterfly Town, U.S.A." The name comes from the **monarch butterflies** that congregate by the thousands in groves of Monterey pines every winter. They come from as far away as Alaska to cling to the trees. One spot in town famous for its "butterfly trees" is George Washington Park, at Pine Avenue and Alder Street. Pacific Grove's Butterfly Parade every October welcomes the monarchs; the town even imposes a $500 fine on anyone caught "molesting butterflies."

WHAT TO SEE AND DO

Pacific Grove has other draws besides the butterflies. The oldest working lighthouse on the West Coast is here—**Point Pinos Lighthouse,** at the northwest point of the peninsula on Ocean View Boulevard. It dates from 1855, when Pacific Grove was little more than a pine forest.

Then there's **Marine Gardens Park,** a stretch of shoreline along Ocean View Boulevard on Monterey Bay and the Pacific. It's renowned not only for its gorgeous flowers but also for its tidepool seaweed beds.

If the urge for discount shopping hits, a good place to begin is the **American Tin Cannery** outlet center, 125 Ocean View Blvd. (tel. 408/372-1442). It's just one block beyond the aquarium facing Monterey Bay. The American Tin Cannery houses an excellent collection of brand-name outlets—boutiques and specialty shops such as Van Heusen, Joan & David, Bass shoes, Banister shoes, Carter's children's wear, Royal Doulton china, Maidenform, Oneida stainless and silver-plated flatware, and Harvé Benard, just to name a few. And should hunger strike while shopping, there are several good restaurants within the American Tin Cannery, including an excellent first choice for breakfast, the First Watch, which I've discussed in detail below under "Where to Dine."

American Tin Cannery shops are open daily: Monday through Wednesday and on Saturday from 10am to 6pm, on Thursday and Friday to 9pm, and on Sunday from 11am to 5pm. Shops are closed Easter, Thanksgiving, Christmas, and New Year's. Restaurant days and hours vary.

Your next stop should be the **Pacific Grove Chamber of Commerce,** at the corner of Forest and Central avenues (P.O. Box 167), Pacific Grove, CA 93950 (tel.

408/373-3304). The friendly folks there can give you lots of information on Pacific Grove and its points of interest.

WHERE TO STAY

If you want to live, and not just see, the Victorian charm of Pacific Grove and the Monterey Peninsula, then don't miss the **Gosby House,** 643 Lighthouse Ave. (three blocks from Forest Avenue), Pacific Grove, CA 93950 (tel. 408/375-1287). It's one of the older houses in town, built by cobbler J. F. Gosby in the 1880s as a boarding house for Methodist ministers who came to town every summer for the Christian conferences.

It's a delightful place, with its dining room and parlor where a multitude of teddy bears reside and where guests congregate for breakfast in the morning and wine in the evening, getting a chance to relax and chat with strangers who rapidly become friends. The rooms—22 of them—are charmingly and individually decorated, with floral-print wallpapers, lacy pillows, and antique furnishings. Twelve of the rooms have fireplaces; all but two have private bathrooms with tub or shower, and phones. There are no TVs here to break your peace and quiet, but you'll find that you don't miss them at all.

Breakfast every morning is included in the price of your room. There's always lots to choose from—fresh hot muffins and breads, egg dishes, cereals, yogurt, granola, fruits and juices, coffee and tea. Each evening you can join other guests for a glass of wine or sherry and a nibble or two before you go off to enjoy one of the Monterey Peninsula's fine restaurants. And for late-night snackers, there are cookies before bedtime.

Rooms at the Gosby House cost $85 to $130, single or double. No smoking, please.

The Gosby House has a sister inn in Pacific Grove owned by the same chain— the **Green Gables Inn,** 104 Fifth Ave. (off Ocean Boulevard), Pacific Grove, CA 93950 (tel. 408/375-2095, or toll free 800/841-5252). Until a few years back it was the home of innkeepers/owners Roger and Sally Post, who opened their little gem to visitors in summer. Now it's a full-fledged inn, with 11 rooms. There are some rooms in the carriage houses out back, all with private baths. In the main house, a dainty Queen Anne, there's a suite with private bath; the other rooms share two immaculate bathrooms. Each of the rooms is individually decorated, and each is charming. The Green Gables' parlor is a delight; there's even an antique carousel horse on display. As at the Gosby House, there's a large breakfast spread every morning and wine in the afternoon.

Rooms at the Green Gables cost $100 to $155, single or double, including breakfast, afternoon wine, tea, and hors d'oeuvres. The Green Gables requests that their guests not smoke in the house.

Among the architectural charms of Pacific Grove is a stately and beautifully renovated 1904 mansion, the **Pacific Grove Inn,** 581 Pine Ave. (at Forest), Pacific Grove, CA 93950 (tel. 408/375-2825). This handsome structure is just two blocks from historic Main Street and five blocks from the beach. The inn has 10 elegant and charming accommodations, all quite light and airy (with heavier Victorian touches), including two suites. All have contemporary amenities: private baths, TVs, phones, queen- or king-size beds. The proprietors are most helpful and gracious, and can supply you with a wealth of local architectural and historical data.

Room rates vary seasonally from $55 to $130 for singles, $60 to $150 for doubles, $85 to $195 for suites. A full homemade buffet breakfast is $5.50.

WHERE TO DINE

The **First Watch,** in the American Tin Cannery, 125 Ocean View Blvd. (tel. 408/372-1125), is a great place for breakfast (perfect for the early riser), brunch, or lunch. (The closest entrance to the First Watch is off Eardley rather than Ocean View.) As part of what once was a factory, the ceiling of the First Watch is sky high (well, almost). One entire outside wall is of windows that, with a huge skylight, flood the room with light. And there are lots of ficus trees, hanging plants, and palms, plus a ceiling fan (at normal height) to enhance the good looks of the room.

The First Watch (like mother) believes that breakfast is the most important meal of the day, and they treat it as such. You can avail yourself of a traditional breakfast, but it would be a shame to pass by some of the delicious options. There are Crêpeggs, wherein a thin, sweet crêpe is anointed with whipped eggs and any number of other goodies you may choose ($5.50 to $7). Then there are 11 varieties of omelets ($5.25 to $6.50), other inviting egg creations such as the "Caps Etc." (sautéed mushroom caps draped with bubbly cheese and eggs). Of course, there is always the "Health Department," serving combinations of granola, raisins, nuts, and fruit, with or without yogurt; or simply a bowl of the season's freshest fruits ($2.25 to $3). Even the pancakes come in six varieties ($3.25 to $4.50), including wheat germ, raisin-walnut, or plain for the purist. I won't spell out the details of their exquisite french toast; suffice it to say that they begin with raisin bread. Of course, First Watch coffee is fresh-ground.

At lunch there's a fine choice of salads: mixed veggies, sautéed veggies, spinach with mixed greens and bean sprouts plus chopped egg and bacon, or a delicious taco salad with ground beef and chorizo ($4.50 to $7). The list of sandwiches is long and presents all sorts of delectables, from the vegetarian through a classic Reuben to pepper beef, Hawaiian, and my favorite, Al B. Core—a combination of white albacore tuna, water chestnuts, celery, and other goodies on whole-wheat bread. All sandwiches ($4.50 to $6) are served with potatoes, fruit, and a small salad. Service is first-rate—attentive, prompt, friendly, helpful. Even the background music is a pleasantly comfortable accompaniment to a fine meal.

First Watch is open daily from 7am to 2:30pm.

What more can you ask of a restaurant than good food, a well-appointed bar, good service, moderate prices, daily hours, a handsome setting, and a delightful view? **The Tinnery,** 631 Ocean View Blvd. (tel. 408/646-1040), has them all. The contemporary interior decor is sea gray with wood paneling, a perfect complement to the bay. Large black-and-white photographs of cannery operations are attractive reminders of one segment of Monterey's past. Indirect track and recessed lighting, banks of white mums dividing the dining rooms, ceiling fans, ficus trees, light-wood chairs, and a large fireplace all add to the welcome feeling of warmth in the Tinnery. A large expanse of window affords a broad view of Lovers Point Park and Monterey Bay. The roomy restaurant lounge, set apart from the main dining room, affords a comfortable spot for cocktails before dinner, and also has a limited menu for late dining until 1am. There is live entertainment nightly until 1am.

The Tinnery serves breakfast, and the crêpes Normandy—French pancakes with apples, cream, and brandy—while not your usual morning fare, are delicious. Lunch choices range from a delicious selection of sandwiches and burgers, salads, and soups, at $5 to $9, to somewhat grander fare such as teriyaki beef kebab or Monterey Bay snapper for $11. Dinner entrees are sufficiently varied to satisfy whatever your tastes may be. The Tinnery serves a superior prime rib for $17, and the Chinese chicken with snow peas and ginger sauce at $10 is a delicious change from the usual. All dinners are served with salad, vegetables, garnishes, and fresh-baked bread. It's one of the best buys in town. And to add to the pleasure of your meal, there's a good selection of California wines. The Tinnery also has a children's menu for breakfast ($3.50), lunch ($4.50), and dinner ($4.50).

Breakfast is served daily from 8 to 11am, lunch from 11am to 5pm, and dinner from 5 to 11pm.

And when you leave the Tinnery after breakfast or lunch, turn left and walk down (or drive if you must) about 100 feet. Bring your camera. Directly below the narrow park bordering Ocean View Boulevard you'll see dozens of harbor seals perched on the rocks being viewed by you and by the black cormorants inhabiting the bayfront.

For another terrific dinner in Pacific Grove, try **Fandango,** 223 17th St., off Lighthouse Avenue (tel. 408/373-0588), just a short walk from the Gosby House.

The restaurant is located in a long, thin building perpendicular to the street. Inside are several rooms, all slightly different, all very pleasant, whether you choose to be seated in the dining room with fresh flowers and fireside dining, or in the terrace room with its delicate fragrances from the wood grill. The restaurant features a new menu with an excellent selection of provincial Mediterranean specialties. Appetizers can be ordered à la carte, beginning with a plate of assorted tapas for $4.25. Two very popular entrees you don't want to overlook are the seafood paella, long a specialty of the house, and the authentic North African couscous. The recipe for the couscous has been in the Bain family (the very gracious owners/operators) for 150 years, and they import the spices to maintain the authenticity of the dish. Among the other excellent Mediterranean dishes are the cassoulet maison, the canneloni niçoise, and the Greek-style lamb shank. There is also a good choice of pasta, mesquite-grilled rack of lamb, or fresh seafood dishes. Fandango has a very nice international wine list from which to choose, and their desserts are out of this world. The list begins with a lovely caramel custard or chocolate mousse and graduates in calorie count up to a spectacular Grand Marnier soufflé served with fresh raspberry purée sauce and profiteroles.

Dinner entrees range from $14 to $20. A prix-fixe dinner for $20 includes tapas, a choice of the day's seafood selection, canneloni, grilled chicken, or cassoulet, plus dessert. The Fandango also serves lunch (light entrees and sandwiches for $5 to $10) and Sunday brunch.

The restaurant is open Monday through Saturday from 11am to 2pm and 5:30 to 10pm, on Sunday from 10am to 2:30pm. There's plenty of free parking (a real plus). Reservations are advised.

Whether you're about to start on the 17-Mile Drive or have already completed the loop and are beginning to have hunger pangs, you will be near what is possibly the best seafood restaurant in the area. The **Fishwife Restaurant,** 1996 Sunset Dr., at Asilomar Avenue in Pacific Grove (tel. 408/375-7107), justifiably popular with locals, is a real treat for tourists. The heritage of the restaurant's name dates back to the 1830s and an enterprising lady named Mercy Graham, who, while awaiting the return of her husband from Boston (which required sailing around Cape Horn to Monterey, then the capital of Mexican California), organized a small market to reprovision ships. She began to sell her Boston clam chowder and prepare local seafood, and became known affectionately as "the fishwife" (her husband died at sea). Today's Fishwife Restaurant still serves the Boston clam chowder its namesake served back then.

The Fishwife Restaurant is a pleasant place to be, with lots of wood, copper and brass, and colorful prints of fish and parrots. Track lighting is unobtrusive, as are the slit skylights. A rear dining room is sedately set away from the bar area. Daily specials featuring the fresh seasonal fish are listed with their prices on a blackboard that is brought to the table. Sand dabs were one such special when I visited and were perfectly grilled. They came with black beans and rice, a vegetable, and homemade cherry tomato sauce. The Fishwife has marvelous sandwiches (delicious duck sausage, crab salad on whole wheat, and *hot* Cajun sausage) and pasta selections for lunch, the latter prepared with fresh fettuccine. There's the elegant and delicious Alfredo, with optional choices of added crab, scallops, prawns, or clams.

Dinner entrees offer 16 excellent and varied seafood selections (in addition to the specials), among which are grilled Pacific snapper fresh from local waters and Mississippi-grown catfish. Two of the bestsellers at dinner are the sautéed calamari steak, served abalone style with shallots, garlic, and white wine; and the prawns Belize, sautéed with red onions, tomatoes, fresh serrano chiles, jicama, lime juice, and cashews. For the family carnivore, there is the New York steak with cracked peppercorns and mushrooms duxelles. Entrees are served with fresh vegetables, French bread, and black beans and rice or air-fried potatoes. When it comes to dessert, if you still have room, try the parfaits—delicious, but definitely not slimming. The house also has espresso, caffe latte, and a caffe reale (cappuccino flavored with Kahlúa or Argueso sherry).

Luncheon dishes cost $5 to $7; dinner entrees are $7.25 to $11.25. Child's plates for lunch or dinner are $4.75 to $5.50. The Fishwife has a wine bar and serves imported and domestic beers, and house wine by the glass, the carafe, or the bottle.

Open Wednesday through Saturday from 11am to 10pm; for Sunday brunch —featuring a seafood eggs Benedict— from 10am.

3. Carmel

The serene beauty of Carmel, a forest village encircled by mountains and rolling hills, makes it a must on every California visitor's itinerary. White beaches, gnarled cypress trees, magnificent landscapes and seascapes are the background for a sleepy village of narrow streets, quaint storybook houses, charming hostelries, and cozy restaurants. It's hard to imagine a more romantic setting.

Since the turn of the century the town has been a haven for artists and writers (galleries abound), and aesthetic considerations carry so much weight in the community that you might have difficulty identifying gas stations under their wooden eaves. Most of the houses don't even have street numbers, and according to local regulations, large, gaudy, or illuminated retail signs in public places "shall not be suffered, permitted, allowed to be placed, erected, or maintained." Nor can a tree be removed without specific permission from the city council, which is often not granted: A gladdening sight are the old trees smack in the middle of roads and in other unlikely places.

This is also a village of shops—more than 600 of them, mostly little boutiques dispensing such wares as basketry, pottery, and imported goods.

A yearly attraction is the annual **Carmel Bach Festival** in July, which brings lovers of baroque music from far and wide. For ticket information (you must purchase in advance), contact the Carmel Bach Festival, P.O. Box 575, Carmel, CA 93921 (tel. 408/624-1521).

WHAT TO SEE AND DO

For more information on the festival and other Carmel happenings, stop by the **Carmel Business Association,** on the second floor of Vandervort Court, on San Carlos between Ocean and 7th (tel. 408/624-2522); pick up maps, brochures, and the free publications mentioned in the Monterey section. It's open weekdays from 9:30am to 4pm. At any newsstand you can also get a copy of the *Carmel Pine Cone,* a weekly newsletter that has been keeping Carmel residents informed about local events for well over half a century.

There's also a **Tourist Information Center** at Mission Patio, on Mission between 5th and 6th (P.O. Box 7430), Carmel, CA 93921 (tel. 408/624-1711), which can help you find accommodations. They're open Monday through Friday from 9am to 4pm.

Carmel's principal village attractions (apart from its former mayor, Clint "Make My Day" Eastwood) are along Ocean Avenue and its side streets between Junipero and San Antonio avenues. Begin your explorations on Ocean at Junipero at the multilevel mall complex of gourmet and cheese shops, craft stores, restaurants, etc., called **Carmel Plaza,** and continue meandering along Ocean, stopping at some of the many galleries and shops. And speaking of shops, the most unique of shopping complexes is—

The Barnyard

Opened at the end of 1976, the Barnyard, on Calif. 1, off Carmel Valley Road, is a cluster of 60 or so shops and restaurants housed in authentic early California barns in a landscaped setting. There's no major department store, but there are a windmill and a water tank; it's quaint Carmel's version of a shopping mall, an old-fashioned town where you can shop in fresh air rather than air-conditioned comfort.

Hub of the Barnyard is the **Thunderbird Bookshop** (tel. 408/624-1803), where you can browse through the 50,000 books for sale while you're eating—just be careful with the gravy. Lunch is $4 to $6; dinner, $7 to $14, featuring the chef's daily special, fish, and great popovers. Lunch is served daily from 11am to 3:30pm; dinner, Tuesday through Sunday from 5:30 to 8pm.

Biblical Garden

While you're in town, take a stroll through the Biblical Garden of the Church of the Wayfarer on Lincoln and Seventh avenues. It's the second-oldest church in Carmel, dating back to 1904. The garden contains plants and trees mentioned in the Bible and indigenous to the Holy Land. Stepping stones lead to various flora, all of which are labeled as to biblical context, beginning with the apple tree—the tree of knowledge of good and evil forbidden to Adam and Eve. An interesting note from the Garden Committee brochure: Some biblical authorities insist the forbidden fruit was actually the apricot!

Carmel Mission

Continuing on subjects spiritual, Carmel also houses the **Mission San Carlos Borromeo,** at Rio Road and Lasuen Drive. This mission is notable as the burial place of Father Junípero Serra, who founded it in 1770. The present stone church, with its gracefully curving walls, catenary arch, and Moorish bell tower, was begun in 1793. Its walls are covered with a lime plaster made of burnt seashells.

In the cemetery beside the church 3,000 Native Americans are buried, their graves decorated with seashells. Other interesting features include the old mission kitchen, the first library in California, the high altar, beautiful flower gardens, the sarcophagus depicting Father Serra recumbent in death, the cell where he died, and the silver altar service he used.

This is one of the largest and most interesting of the California missions. It's open to visitors Monday through Saturday from 9:30am to 4:30pm, on Sunday from 10:30am.

WHERE TO STAY

Carmel boasts one of the highest-rated resort hotels in the country, **Quail Lodge,** 8205 Valley Greens Dr. (off Carmel Valley Road), Carmel, CA 93923 (tel. 408/624-1581, or toll free 800/538-9516, 800/682-9303 in California). In a superb pastoral setting on 250 acres of sparkling lakes, woodlands, and meadows, Quail Lodge offers all the facilities of the prestigious Carmel Valley Golf and Country Club to its guests. In addition to the 18-hole golf course and clubhouse, facilities include four tennis courts, two swimming pools, bicycle rental, a sauna for men, and a redwood hot tub, as well as shops and a beauty salon.

There are 100 rooms, suites, and cottages, of which I prefer the ones upstairs with cathedral ceilings. All have color TVs, dressing rooms, and balconies; some have fireplaces and wet bars. The rooms are newly redecorated with a light and airy southwestern flair. There's complimentary fresh-ground coffee in every room, as well as afternoon tea from 3 to 5pm. Free newspapers are delivered daily.

The posh Covey Restaurant on the premises serves refined European cuisine nightly in warmly elegant surroundings (breakfast and lunch are served daily in the clubhouse). The interior is done in a terra-cotta tones with teal and lilac accents. Tables are beautifully appointed in Belgian linen, set with Sienna china, adorned with fresh flowers, and lit by gaslamps. A delightful fireplace bar/lounge in Mexican motif adjoins. You can begin your meal with an appetizer of half a dozen escargots. Entrees, served with potato and a fresh garden vegetable, include poulet à l'orange, fresh trout amandine, and a sizzling steak au poivre flambé in brandy, for $15 to $28. Specialties of the house are rack of lamb and fresh seafood. For dessert, I like the crêpes flambés au Grand Marnier. Jackets are required for men, and reservations are essential.

The cost of luxury living (February through November) at Quail Lodge is $175 to $195, single or double. Suites are $215 to $260. A third person in the room is

$25 extra. Holiday season rates are $135 to $155, single or double; suites, $165 to $210.

The next selections are all right in the heart of Carmel activity, and each has its own unique charm.

Normandy Inn, Ocean Avenue, between Monte Verde and Casanova avenues, Carmel, CA 93921 (tel. 408/624-3825), is a delightful provincial hostelry housed in a shingled Tudor building. The terrace poolside patio (the pool is heated) is lined with trees, shrubbery, and potted plants. Rooms are just lovely, although each is somewhat different: About a quarter of them have fireplaces and/or kitchen areas, all have color TVs, and most baths have tub/shower combinations. All have switchboard phones and are charmingly decorated in country motif, with ruffled bedspreads, maple furnishings, shuttered windows, and old-fashioned print wallpapers. Rates for single or double accommodations are $89 to $130. Cottages for two to eight people cost $150 to $239. Be sure to reserve far in advance, especially in summer, or it's unlikely you'll find a room at the inn. Rates include a complimentary Continental breakfast.

More quaint rooms are found at the **Pine Inn,** Ocean Avenue, between Lincoln and Monte Verde (P.O. Box 250), Carmel, CA 93921 (tel. 408/624-3851). At the risk of being repetitious, I once again advise early reservations. The Pine Inn has an opulent lobby/lounge complete with red-flocked wallpaper, a blazing fireplace, plush furnishings, and a big grandfather clock. Each room is individually designed, but all are in turn-of-the-century motif—shuttered windows, lovely wallpapers, and antique furnishings, including brass beds in some rooms. Every room has a remote-control color TV, direct-dial phone, and tub/shower bath.

The Pine Inn also boasts the beautiful *Garden Room* and the *Gazebo Restaurant* for breakfast (7 to 11am); lunch (11am to 2:30pm); Sunday brunch; early dinner (5:30 to 6:30pm), which is an inexpensive prix-fixe affair ($9.50) with a good selection of entrees; and dinner ($10 to $18). Friday is Epicurean Feast night—a seafood and roast beef buffet ($18.50) with an assortment of delightful desserts served, from 5:30pm.

Rooms at the Pine Inn cost $75 to $185 a night, single or double.

Some of the loveliest rooms in town are at the **Carriage House Inn,** on Junipero, between Seventh and Eighth avenues (P.O. Box 1900), Carmel, CA 93921 (tel. 408/625-2585, or toll free 800/433-4732). This country-style inn, located in a quiet Carmel setting, has 13 exquisitely decorated accommodations. Amenities include king-size beds with down comforters, wood-burning fireplaces, small refrigerators, cable color TVs with free Showtime movies, and direct-dial telephones. Most second-floor rooms have sunken baths and vaulted beam ceilings. You will be pampered with Continental breakfast, brought to you each morning on blue willow china along with the morning paper; wine and hors d'oeuvres in the library in the evening; and twice-daily maid service and fresh flowers in your room. It's a delight.

Rates for one or two people are $125 to $225.

The Village Inn, Ocean Avenue and Junipero Street (P.O. Box 5275), Carmel, CA 93921 (tel. 408/624-3864), is a pretty, well-run, centrally located, and reasonably priced motor lodge, its rooms arranged around a courtyard/parking lot lined with potted geraniums. Rooms feature a tasteful homey decor with French country furniture. Complimentary Continental breakfast is served to guests each morning in the lounge, along with the morning paper. All 32 rooms are equipped with direct-dial phones, baths/showers, refrigerators, and cable color TVs. Singles and doubles pay $89 to $130, and rooms accommodating three to four people are $115 to $180. Children are welcome. There is off-street parking for guests.

Finally, there's **San Antonio House,** on San Antonio between Ocean and Seventh avenues (P.O. Box 3683), Carmel, CA 93921 (tel. 408/624-4334). Once again you have a garden setting with charming two- and three-room suites furnished with antiques and a private art collection. Innkeeper Jewell Brown unobtrusively sees to the needs and comfort of guests. All rooms have TVs, small refrigerators, fireplaces, private bathrooms, patios or gardens, and private entrances. Guests are also pampered with cream sherry, fresh flowers, a morning newspaper, and a breakfast.

Rates are $110 to $140, single or double; an additional person pays $20.

WHERE TO DINE

L'Escargot, Mission Street and Fourth Avenue (tel. 408/624-4914), has both superb French cuisine and a delightful interior. Housed in typical Carmel style in a shingle-roofed, beamed stucco building, it is warm and cozy within. Banquettes and chairs are upholstered in a quaint French fabric, and other provincial touches include hanging copperware, arrangements of dried and fresh flowers, leaded-glass windows, a beamed ceiling, and shelves of decorative plates. Desserts, wines, and a big pot of flowers are displayed on an oak centerpiece.

You might begin with an appetizer of escargots de Bourgogne or the smoked salmon (cured and smoked by André). The choice is not an easy one. Among the offerings are also braised fresh artichoke bottoms with herbs and a lovely puff pastry with wild mushrooms. As for the entrees, priced from $15 to $23, the house classic chicken with cream, foie gras, and truffles is still a vibrant memory. But anything you order will be superb. Other choices include a specialty of the chef, aiguillette de canard (breast of duck roasted with a special sauce); fresh scallops sautéed with orange-lemon butter; and one of my favorites, sweetbreads with cream, madeira, and mushrooms. L'Escargot has an extensive list of French and California wines. And don't pass up the desserts, each a masterpiece—say, the chilled Grand Marnier soufflé, which has the consistency of a delicate light ice cream; the utterly delicious crème caramel; or the classic mousse au chocolat. Owner/chef André Françot takes infinite care in the preparation of every dish, and as his wine list is extensive and well chosen, it's not surprising that he is the winner of many a culinary award.

L'Escargot is open Monday through Saturday from 6 to 9:30pm. Reservations are advised.

Another award winner is **Raffaello,** on Mission between Ocean and Seventh avenues (tel. 408/624-1541). The Florentine ambience here is hushed and rather formal (men are required to wear jackets); the decor is elegant—tables clothed in white linen, low lighting, and walls adorned with Italian paintings and mirrors. Bowls of fresh flowers grace every table. The cuisine is Italian, and entrees ($17 to $23) are served with soup, salad, and vegetables. Veal with fontina cheese and truffles, fettuccine romano, sweetbreads with cream and wine sauce, and filet of sole poached in white wine and herbs, stuffed with shrimp, are among the choices. Although you might order assorted cheeses or a light strawberry mousse for dessert, you can always opt for the rich and creamy zabaglione.

Raffaello is open nightly except Tuesday from 6 to 10pm. Reservations are requested.

Belgian owners designed **Casanova,** on Fifth Avenue between San Carlos and Mission (tel. 408/625-0501), to look like the European farmhouses of their childhood memories. Located in an old picturesque cottage (it used to belong to Charlie Chaplin's cook), Casanova is cozy and provincial, with intimate dining areas arranged under a low beamed ceiling. Heated by a wood-burning stove, it has checkered curtains and quaint lampshades from France, flower-bedecked tables with Mediterranean-blue cloths, bentwood chairs, and antique ceramic tiles embedded into the walls. For outdoor dining, there's a heated area with a little fountain. French and Italian music play in the background.

The day might begin at 8am over breakfast ($3 to $6) with french toast Grand Marnier, Belgian waffles, eggs in many styles, or my ignore-the-calories favorite of cheese blintzes. The luncheon and dinner menus change seasonally. Lunch, served with soup or salad, may include homemade linguine with prawns, scallops in a white-wine velouté, parmesan cream sauce; or white veal braised with mushrooms, leeks, white-wine sauce, and polenta ($7 to $11). All dinners (which average $19 to $26) include an antipasto salad; a choice of homemade soup, mushrooms in butter and herbs, or gnocchi verde alla romana; and an entree such as rack of lamb grilled with a mild garlic and Merlot-wine sauce. A list of over 1,240 French and Italian wines is available, and desserts are all homemade.

Open Monday through Saturday for breakfast from 8 to 11am, for lunch from 11:30am to 3pm, and for dinner daily from 5:30 to 10:30pm. Sunday brunch is served from 10am to 3pm.

What more could you ask of a restaurant than great food and good looks? One that you will enjoy from the moment you walk in is the **Rio Grill,** 101 Crossroads Blvd., at Calif. 1 and Rio Road in the Crossroads group of shops (tel. 408/625-5436). While you are waiting to be seated in the modern, southwestern-style dining room or in one of the cozy dining alcoves, you can watch the action in the Rio Grill's lively lounge or look at the above-the-bar cartoons of such famous locals as Bing Crosby and Clint Eastwood. The scene is fun, but you really come for the food, which is as impressive, attractive, and deliciously casual as the decor. You might start with one of the homemade soups that the Rio Grill offers daily, or choose the richer quesadilla with almonds, cheeses, and smoked tomato salsa. Then it's on to entree (or sandwich) heaven: a half slab of barbecued baby back ribs from the wood-burning oven perhaps, fresh fish from the grill, or maybe a skirt steak with sesame, soy, and ginger marinade on grilled bread. A different pasta is offered each day, as are hamburgers and cheeseburgers, but consider the joy of a grilled eggplant sandwich with roasted red peppers, fontina cheese, and watercress. Leave room for dessert; I had trouble deciding between the caramel-apple bread pudding and the caramel custard with chopped almonds.

Prices are moderate. Entrees go for $10 to $17, with most in the $11 area. Appetizers, soups, salads, and sandwiches are in the $3 to $8 range. The most expensive item on the menu is a delectable Rio Grill sweatshirt for $19. Service is young, friendly, knowledgeable, and helpful. A good selection of wines, including some rare California vintages, covers a broad price range.

Rio Grill is open daily. The lounge serves food all day, Monday through Saturday from 11:30am to 10pm and on Sunday from 11am to 11pm. The dining room serves Sunday through Thursday from 11am to 10pm, on Friday and Saturday to 11pm; the dining room is closed from 4 to 5pm. And now there's an outdoor seating area that adds a fresh air flavor to great food.

Carmel has more than its fair share of charming village restaurants, but one of the most delightful is the **Tuck Box English Room,** on Dolores Street, near 7th Street (tel. 408/624-6365). In September of 1987 the Tuck Box was firebombed in the early hours of the morning. It's since been rebuilt to look exactly as it did before, with perhaps a few more tucks here and there, a new hardwood floor, and a light-gray interior with charcoal trim. It's still just about everybody's favorite place for breakfast, locals and visitors alike.

In this small, shingle-roofed cottage, you can have breakfast, lunch, or a traditional afternoon tea (complete with hot buttered scones and homemade marmalade). The dining area is tiny, with a beamed ceiling, table bases that match the beams, a stone fireplace, and red-and-white-checked curtains in the front window. You can also dine outside at a few tables on the patio. At breakfast you can have fresh-squeezed orange juice for $1.50, and fresh fruit, bacon and eggs, with homemade muffins or scones, for $4. Lunchtime, the menu lists a choice of two or three entrees —for example, shepherd's pie, which is served with salad, vegetable, muffin or scone, for $4.50. For dessert there's homemade pie or cake with real whipped cream. The Tuck Box is open from 8am to 4pm; closed Monday and Tuesday.

The interior of **La Bohème,** at Dolores and 7th streets (tel. 408/624-7500), is cleverly designed to look like a provincial French street, complete with a painted blue sky and shingled houses. Tables are set with floral-print cloths in gay colors, blue-burgundy-and-white hand-painted dinnerware, and colorful posies of fresh flowers. Gleaming copper pots are hung from the wall.

Dinner is a three-course prix-fixe affair consisting of a large salad, a tureen of soup, and an entree—perhaps duckling sauté with raspberry sauce, filet mignon au poivre, or even paella. The price of dinner is around $18. Luscious homemade desserts are the perfect capper to a meal.

La Bohème is open daily for dinner from 5:30 to 10pm.

A charming little tea room, the **Pâtisserie Boissière,** in Carmel Plaza on Mission, between Ocean and Seventh avenues (tel. 408/624-5008). Housed in a shingle-roofed stucco cottage, it boasts an entrance heralded by a real Parisian street sign reading "Rue Boissière." The decor is cozily provincial, with white stucco walls and a low beamed ceiling, antique maple sideboard, tiled fireplace, and Louis XV–style chairs; you can also dine in a skylight café with garden furnishings. It's the perfect place for a light meal, at $5 to $8—perhaps a ham or camembert sandwich on French bread or a quiche Lorraine and salad with a glass of wine, topped off by a delicious homemade pâtisserie (like a chocolate éclair, or chocolate butter cream with crisp meringue) and coffee. For a heartier meal, specialties include coquilles St-Jacques (scallops, shrimps, and fresh mushrooms in a cream-and-sherry sauce) and a provincial chicken dish with white-wine sauce, tomatoes, and olives, served with rice. Such entrees cost $10 to $14 at lunch, $14 to $17 at dinner.

Hours are 9am to 9pm Wednesday through Sunday, otherwise to 6pm. Reservations suggested.

Shabu-Shabu, in the Carmel Plaza Mall (tel. 408/625-2828), invites you to take off your shoes and refresh yourself with an oshibori (warm, moist towel). It's easy to relax over your sake in this lovely country inn–style Japanese restaurant. You can sit the Japanese way on cushions at low tables, or Western style at highly polished redwood tables. Redwood-paneled walls are adorned with colorful Japanese kites and other folk-art items, a fireplace adds a cozy note, and Japanese music is played in the background.

The specialty is, of course, shabu-shabu for two; the name means "swish-swish," which is the procedure for cooking the meat. It consists of thin ribbons of beef, soybean cake, mushrooms, and fresh seasonal vegetables cooked at your table in a broth in an earthenware pot and served with dipping sauces. Yosenabe, made with fresh clams, scallops, shrimp, rock cod, and vegetables, is also available for two. Other items include prawn (enormous ones) and vegetable tempura; teriyaki steak, 10 ounces of it; and teriyaki chicken. All dinners cost $14 to $24 and come with soup, spinach salad, tsukemono (Japanese pickle), an appetizer (perhaps sashimi or tempura), rice, and a pot of delicious genmai tea, which is steeped in toasted rice. Shabu-Shabu has a knockout dessert—the Japanese answer to the banana split and far superior: bananas deep-fried in tempura batter and topped with green-tea ice cream.

A marvelous and very popular lunch is served daily except Sunday. Called obento, it features a Japanese-style lunchbox with several delicious courses ($6 to $9.50). The Miyako lunch includes tempura, chicken teriyaki, a California roll, rice, and soup; the Shogun lunchbox includes tempura, tuna sashimi, beef teriyaki wrapped around green onion, rice, and miso soup. Lunches are also prepared to go. Shabu-Shabu is open daily for lunch from 11:30am to 2pm and for dinner from 5:30 to 10pm. Reservations are suggested.

Almost everyone knows that Clint Eastwood owns a restaurant in Carmel, its name parodying the quaintness of its many competitors. The **Hog's Breath Inn,** San Carlos Street, between Fifth and Sixth avenues (tel. 408/625-1044), is always mobbed, partly because it's a very comfortable hangout and partly because you never know when Clint Eastwood, the former mayor of Carmel, is likely to drop in. Entered via a brick walkway, it has several dining and drinking areas. You can sit outdoors on a stone patio in director's chairs pulled up to tree-trunk tables, and there are two brick fireplaces to keep you warm. The main restaurant is dark and rustic, with farm implements, dried flower arrangements, and celebrity photos hanging on the walls. Another structure on the property is an equally rustic, very small pub, with a brick fireplace in the corner and two wild boars' heads mounted on the wall; a TV over the bar broadcasts sporting events.

Lunch at Hog's Breath, which costs $4.50 to $13, might consist of the fresh catch of the day or a sirloin steak sandwich on whole-wheat toast, each of these served with the soup du jour. Dinner entrees—such as double cut of prime rib—come with soup or salad, baked potato or rice, and a vegetable for $12 to $23.

Open seven days, the Hog's Breath serves lunch from 11:30am to 3pm; dinner hours are 5 to 10pm, and the pub and patio stay open until 2am. Reservations are taken for large parties only.

And finally, if you'd rather picnic than dine, stop at the **Mediterranean Market,** at the corner of Ocean Avenue and Mission Street (tel. 408/624-2022). This is a bazaar of gourmet foods, delectables, wines, caviars, mustards, booze, salads, nova, salami, cheeses, and baskets for toting or decoration. They will prepare a picnic basket for you with four hours' advance notice. The market is open daily from 8am to 6pm.

---

4. Big Sur

Not a town, but rather a loose description of the famous 90-mile stretch of rugged coastline on Calif. 1 between Carmel and San Simeon, the dramatic Big Sur region is probably the only place in the world described by its chamber of commerce as a place "to slow down . . . to meditate . . . to catch up with your soul." Flanked on one side by the majestic Santa Lucia Mountain Range and on the other by the rocky Pacific coast, it is traveled via breathtakingly scenic Calif. 1. Drive through slowly, making frequent stops at viewing turnouts, and taking in the sea and cliffs.

Although the area attracts many tourists, its highly individualistic residents make few concessions to them, and in no way is Big Sur touristy or in danger of becoming so. There are few recreational distractions—no town, no cute boutiques and art galleries, no tennis, golf, horseback riding, boating, or even movie theaters. Just the tranquility of unparalleled natural beauty where you can hike through redwood forests along miles of trails, picnic, go camping, fish, or enjoy the beach at several points along the coast: **Pfeiffer–Big Sur State Beach** (tel. 408/667-2315 for the park), **Kirk Creek, Plasket Creek, Jade Beach,** and **Willow Creek Beach.** (The only beach accessible by car is Pfeiffer, via Sycamore Canyon Road.)

The River Inn, 29 miles south of Monterey on Calif. 1, is generally considered the starting point of Big Sur, with most of the area's accommodations, restaurants, and other facilities between it and Deetjen's Big Sur Inn about 6 miles south. You can visit Big Sur on a day trip from Monterey or Carmel, perhaps stopping for lunch at Ventana or Nepenthe (details below). If you'd like to stay a while, the following is a pretty complete rundown on the accommodations situation.

Note: If you're planning a drive all the way south to **Morro Bay** (120 miles) on Calif. 1, do it during periods of good and relatively dry weather. Not only is the view lovelier, but landslides have occurred during the rainy season. In any event, it requires time (allow a full day) and close attention to driving for the trip. If you have a fear of heights, avoid this route. Heavy fog can also make the trip trying rather than enjoyable, so check weather conditions before leaving.

WHAT TO SEE

The Henry Miller Memorial Library

Henry Miller was probably Big Sur's most famous resident. He came here in 1944 and watched the area grow from a wilderness to a well-known artists' colony. In fact, his writings—works like *Big Sur and the Oranges of Hieronymus Bosch*—were instrumental in making Big Sur famous. Henry Miller fans will want to drop by the Henry Miller Memorial Library, about a mile south of the Ventana Inn. Miller's longtime close friend, artist Emil White, now deceased (who moved to Big Sur just after Miller did), turned his home and personal Miller collection into this tribute to his friend. The small cluttery library has been remodeled and now contains all of Henry Miller's books for sale, both new and used, rare and out of print. In the back gallery room of the library, there is a video viewing area where all the film made about Henry Miller can be seen; the original naïf-style paintings of Emil White can also be seen here. There is a sculpture garden, plus tables on the lawn where visitors can rest and enjoy the surroundings.

The library's hours are informal; it's usually open daily from 10am to 5pm, unless the "Closed" sign is posted outside. Call 408/667-2574 for information.

The Coast Gallery

This beautifully situated gallery (tel. 408/667-2301), 8 miles south of the River Inn, is Big Sur's original, and only, art gallery. Uniquely rebuilt from redwood watertanks after a flood in 1973, it shows works of over 250 local and artists and craftspeople from around the country—pottery, woodcarving, macramé, painting, sculpture, jewelry, etc. In addition, candles are made on the premises. The folks who run it are awfully nice, and it makes for good browsing. And now to complete your enjoyment, there is a picnic deli–cum–wine cellar featuring locally produced fine wines.

Open daily from 9am to 5pm in winter, to 6:30pm in summer.

WHERE TO STAY

Accommodations are many and varied, but few attempt the luxury-hotel trappings you'd find on any other major highway going through an area with such a high tourism rate—room service, even phones and TVs (the latter considered Philistine in these parts) are rare. Nevertheless, they all run at close to full occupancy, especially in summer, so reserve early. To write to any of the places below, just address inquiries to the name of the establishment, Big Sur, CA 93920. The same goes for the chamber of commerce.

Least typical of Big Sur hostelries is **Ventana Inn,** on Calif. 1, 4¼ miles south of River Inn (tel. 408/667-2331, or toll free 800/628-6500), a luxurious wilderness resort on a 243-acre oceanfront ranch, high in the mountains overlooking the Pacific. Opened in 1975, it fulfills a long-standing need for accommodations worthy of the wild and magical Big Sur countryside. Among the notables who have flocked to pamper themselves at Ventana are Henry Winkler, Barbara Streisand and Jon Peters, Goldie Hawn, and Francis Ford Coppola, not to mention the prime minister of Finland. Debra Winger and Timothy Hutton were married here in 1986.

The resort's 59 guest rooms are housed in 12 contemporary natural-wood buildings with slanted roofs that blend with the landscape. The elegantly rustic but very comfortable interiors are decorated in blue or green color schemes coordinated to handmade patchwork-quilt bedspreads. Walls are a combination of white stucco and cedar paneling, furnishings are wicker, and most accommodations have wood-burning fireplaces; others, very high ceilings. All have dressing rooms, private terraces or balconies overlooking the ocean or forest (11 with their own hot tubs), phones, color TVs, VCRs, refrigerators, heating, air conditioning, and baths with tubs and showers and goodies like bath oils, shampoos, massage oils, and oversize towels.

There are two 90-foot heated outdoor swimming pools, each with its own bathhouse and Japanese hot bath (one with a full sauna) with multiple jets, where you can soak *au naturel*—one section for men, one for women, and one for the uninhibited mixed crowd.

Moving along now to culinary luxuries, complimentary breakfast (fresh-baked croissants, danish pastries, fresh-squeezed orange juice, homemade granola with yogurt and fresh fruit, and tea or coffee) is served in your room or in the guest lobby each morning. The restaurant on the premises is, like everything else, first-rate—it's had a Mobil four-star rating for eleven straight years. The airy raw-cedar interior, with heavy beams, two large stone fireplaces, and cedar tile floor, is furnished with redwood tables, cane and bentwood chairs, and rattan-shaded globe lamps overhead. Ferns, potted plants, and baskets of fruit are placed here and there. You can dine on any one of three levels, with vista-revealing windows everywhere, or on a large outdoor patio terrace 1,200 feet above the Pacific overlooking a dramatic expanse of ocean and 50 miles of the Big Sur coast.

Lunch fare ranges from $10 to $18 for entrees like smoked Big Sur trout or salad nicoise. For dinner you might order roast glazed duckling or roast rack of lamb, for $18 to $30. Desserts baked in the Ventana's own French bakery are temptingly displayed and best chosen visually. The restaurant is open weekdays from noon to 3pm and 6 to 9:30pm, weekends from 11am to 3pm and 6 to 9:30pm. Call for reservations. After you dine you can browse through the adjoining general store, which carries everything from imported buttons and bows to garden tools, robes, books, and gifts.

Rates for doubles begin at $155 and go up to $715 (the latter for a suite). If you can't afford to stay here, at least splurge at the restaurant and take a look around. If you do want to stay here, be sure to make reservations well in advance.

Traveling with the family? Best bet (unless you're camping, about which more shortly) is the **Big Sur Lodge**, located in Pfeiffer–Big Sur State Park, a little over 2 miles south of River Inn on Calif. 1 (tel. 408/667-2171). The lodge has 61 units beautifully situated on over 800 parkland acres of towering redwoods, sycamores, big-leaf maples, and other sheltering trees. The cabins are quite large, with high peaked cedar and redwood beamed ceilings and walnut-paneled walls. The rooms are quite clean and most presentable. All are heated and equipped with private baths and parking spaces. Most of the cabins have either fireplaces or kitchens, or both. All have porches or decks with views of the redwoods or the Santa Lucia Mountains.

A great advantage in staying here is that you can use all the facilities of the park: fishing, hiking, barbecue pits, picnic facilities, plus the lodge's own large outdoor heated swimming pool with adjoining sauna, a gift shop filled with unique items, two grocery stores, and laundry facilities.

The Big Sur Lodge dining room is open for breakfast and dinner from March through December. Full breakfasts are $4 to $7. Dinner entrees, at $9 to $15, are served with salad and baked potato or rice. The menu features fresh seafood, steaks, and pasta dishes. Be sure to try the homemade desserts made fresh daily. The dining room is very pretty, by the way, with an interior waterfall and with big windows all around providing glorious woodland views; if you want to be in the forest rather than looking at it through glass, there's lots of patio seating under umbrellaed tables overlooking the river.

The rate for cottages for one or two people is $70, ascending to $110. Fireplace units are $15 more, and those with kitchens are $10 over the base rates. Reservations are a necessity. For a summer weekend, call two months ahead for the best selection.

Camping

Once again, your best bet is the 40-acre campsite belonging to **Ventana,** off Calif. 1 just before the resort (tel. 408/667-2331). The 98 campsites, in a gorgeous redwood setting, are spaced well apart for privacy. Each has a picnic table and fireplace, and bathrooms with hot showers are conveniently located. You can swim at Pfeiffer–Big Sur State Beach, 3 miles away. Campsites are $18 for two people in a vehicle, $3 for each additional person, $2 per dog.

Fernwood, about 2 miles south of the River Inn (tel. 408/667-2422), has 63 sites on 23 beautiful woodland acres, each with electricity, water, and a fire pit. About half the sites overlook the river. Rates are $19 a night with electricity, $17 without, for two people; $5 for each additional person. There's a restaurant on the premises (open daily from 11:30am to midnight) where they serve burgers, ribs, etc., and live music is presented on weekends; an attractive bar/cocktail lounge and a wine and cheese shop have been added. Also on the premises are a grocery store, where you can get wood, ice, and beer and wine; a gas station; and a motel with 12 units, all with showers and toilets. Singles pay $55 for motel accommodations; four people pay $78.

Another good choice for camping is the **Big Sur Campground and Cabins,** two-tenths of a mile below the River Inn (tel. 408/667-2322). Open year-round, it has campsites, bathhouses with hot-water showers, laundry facilities, freshwater faucets within 25 feet of each site, a large river swimming area surrounded by towering redwoods, play area with swings, grocery store, etc., and a volleyball/basketball court. Each campsite has its own wood-burning fire pit and picnic table. Rates are $19 for two people in a car, $3 for each additional person. Electrical and water hookups are $2.

Three A-frame cabins on the premises, with fully equipped kitchens, fireplaces, private terraces, and shower baths, are $83 for double occupancy, $9 for each additional person. They're very attractive, with high peaked raw-fir ceilings, throw rugs on glossy wood floors, and homey furnishings that include a rocking chairs. They sleep up to six. Two new modular units, with fireplaces (and some wood supplied) but no kitchens, are $66 and suitable for two. Six additional modular units do have kitchens; these cost $83, $9 for each additional person. Tent cabins without baths are $36.

More well-equipped camping facilities are in **Pfeiffer–Big Sur State Park**—with three areas of campsites open year-round. There's a 10-day limit on stays; for information, write to the Department of Parks and Recreation, **P.O.** Box 942896, Sacramento, CA 94296.

WHERE TO DINE

In addition to the many dining facilities at the above-mentioned accommodations, be sure to experience Big Sur's **Nepenthe,** 5 miles south of the River Inn (tel. 408/667-2345). It stands on the site of the Log House, which was built in 1925, 808 feet above sea level. Housed in a redwood-and-stucco structure, the dining room is ski-lodgey, with a big wood-burning fireplace, director's chairs at heavy wood tables, redwood and pine ceilings, and lots of windows. But unless the weather is really bad, everyone sits outside on the ocean-view terrace enjoying one of the most awesomely magnificent vistas anywhere. It's a magical place to while away a lazy and delightful afternoon; stay long enough to catch the sunset. Usually there are a few musicians hanging out here, playing to a background of scores of gaily chirping birds, and in general it's a lively, unpredictable, idyllic, and fun place to be. Service is casual, in keeping with the casual style of the place, but no one really cares. A light lunch, with entrees averaging $7 to $9, might consist of a Continental cheese board served with fresh fruit and bread and a liter of wine; follow up with a pot of English tea and dessert—perhaps homemade pumpkin spice cake. You can also get hamburgers, salads, and sandwiches at lunch. Dinner fare includes steak dishes, broiled chicken, and fresh fish of the day ($8 to $20).

Open daily from 11:30am to midnight, although the closing time varies, so call ahead if you plan on a late dinner.

Just across the highway from the Glen Oaks Motel on Calif. 1 is Marilee and Forrest Childs' **Glen Oaks Restaurant** (tel. 408/667-2623), a lovely place with a beamed ceiling, flower-filled windows, a wood-burning copper-chimneyed fireplace in the corner, and fresh flowers on every white-clothed table. Marilee's superb watercolors grace the walls; Forrest's masterpieces are culinary. The food is fresh and excellent. Dinner costs $9 to $18 for entrees like gnocchi, cheese pillows in sage butter or fettuccine with scallops and lobster, bouillabaisse, New York steak, and Chinese vegetables sautéed and served on a bed of wild rice. There's also fresh charcoal-broiled seafood, served with a variety of sauces. Desserts are prepared daily on the premises, and a small collection of California wines is available. Taped classical music enhances the ambience.

It's open daily from 6 to 9:45pm. Reservations are recommended for dinner.

5. San Simeon

Ever wonder what you'd do if you had the really big bucks? Not just a million, but hundreds of millions?

In the verdant Santa Lucia Mountains of San Simeon, on a hill he called La Cuesta Encantada (The Enchanted Hill), William Randolph Hearst left an astounding monument to wealth, a veritable shrine worthy of kings and maharajahs, the ego trip par excellence—**Hearst Castle.** Located on Calif. 1, about 94 miles south of Monterey, it was given to the state as a memorial to the late publisher in 1958.

The history of Hearst Castle dates back to 1865, when 43-year-old George Hearst purchased a 40,000-acre Mexican land grant adjacent to San Simeon Bay. He built a comfortable ranch house on the property, ran large herds of cattle over its ranges and foothills, and also crossbred Arabian horses with Morgans on the premises. He often entertained at the ranch (it still stands today, incidentally), and his only son, William Randolph, developed a great liking for the informal life at "Camp Hill." As a young man, busy launching his newspaper career, W.R. would often steal off to the San Simeon property for a quiet retreat. In 1919, when George Hearst's widow, Phoebe Apperson Hearst, died and William Randolph came into possession of the ranch, the present castle was under way.

The focal point of the estate is the incredible **Casa Grande,** with over 100 rooms all filled with priceless art treasures. There are Flemish tapestries, 15th-century Gothic fireplaces, 16th-century Spanish and intricately carved 18th-century Italian ceilings, a 16th-century Florentine bedstead, Renaissance paintings, and here and there are such items as a third-century Etruscan jar and an ancient Egyptian statue created over 3,000 years ago. That barely skims the surface. The Doge's Suite of the house was reserved for the most important guests, among them Winston Churchill and President Calvin Coolidge and his wife. Five thousand volumes (including some rare books) are housed in the library, along with one of the world's greatest collections of Greek vases. Three opulent minicastle guesthouses also contain magnificent art treasures.

A lavish private theater was used to show first-run films twice nightly—once for employees and again for the guests and host. Guests could also play pool and billiards in a room that would make you feel as if you were shooting pool in the middle of the Louvre.

And there are two swimming pools—the Byzantine-inspired indoor pool with intricate mosaic work surrounded by the most famous statues of antiquity copied in Carrara marble (at night, light filtering through alabaster globes created the illusion of moonlight) and the Greco-Roman Neptune outdoor pool, flanked by Etruscan-style marble colonnades and surrounded by more Carrara statuary.

Which is not even to mention the magnificently landscaped grounds, where—in outlying areas—the world's largest private zoo once existed. Within a 2,000-acre enclosure, monkeys, cheetahs, giraffes, camels, elephants, bears, bison, llamas, zebras, deer, eagles, and other birds were kept. For riding, Hearst had over 30 Arabian horses. Today only a few elk, Barbary sheep, Himalayan goats, deer, and zebras roam.

If you can fit San Simeon into your itinerary, it will make for a very interesting and enjoyable day's outing—a glimpse into a life-style that barely exists today, and that few, if any, of us have come near experiencing. There are four tours that you can take of Hearst Castle and the grounds. Tour I is recommended for the first-time visitor (150 stair steps). It covers the gardens, a guesthouse, and the ground floor of the main house—including the movie theater, where you'll see Hearst "home movies." Tour II takes in the upper part of the main house, including Mr. Hearst's private suite, office, libraries, duplex guest room, kitchen, and pools (300 stair steps). Tour III visits the guest wing with its 36 bedrooms and sitting rooms, pools, and gardens, and deals with interior design changes over a 20-year period (300 stair steps). Tour IV (not offered in the winter) covers the grounds, offering an opportunity to see the conservation room, wine cellar, and lower floor of one of the guesthouses (300 stair steps).

The tours, each of which lasts 1¾ hours, are conducted daily, except Thanksgiving, Christmas, and New Year's Day, beginning at 8:20am. Two to six tours leave every hour, depending on the season. Allow two hours between starting times if you plan to take more than one tour. Mid-June evening tours begin daily at 7pm. Don't just arrive; make reservations for your tour by calling Mistix (tel. toll free 800/444-

7275). Arrive without reservations and you're guaranteed a long wait—or you may not get in at all. Tickets cost $10 for adults, $5 for children 6 to 12.

Visitors park their cars at the Visitors Center parking lot and are transported by bus to the castle. If you bring lunch, there are picnic tables; you'll also find a gift shop and snack bar at the parking lot. Wear comfortable shoes—you'll be walking about a half mile and climbing over 300 steps.

---

6. San Luis Obispo

What a pretty and delightful place is San Luis Obispo! Nestled in the Los Padres Mountains midway between Los Angeles and San Francisco, it's an easygoing, postcard-picturesque little college town that grew up around an 18th-century mission. Among its tourist attractions are many historic landmarks, quaint Victorian homes, shops, restaurants, and sporting facilities. This is the beginning of Southern California beach country—the first point south where you don't have to be a member of the Polar Bear Club to dare stick your big toe in the water.

Other attractions? Concerts—an annual **Mozart festival** (first week in August), jazz and bands, etc.—often outdoors and under the stars, are frequent events, interspersed with dance performances, poetry readings, theater productions, and diverse activities ranging from wine-tasting dinners (many wineries within driving distance) to tug-o-war competitions. And San Luis Obispo has the largest **farmers market** in California—every Thursday night from 6:30 to 9pm. It's *the* local event. There's entertainment, dancing, food, open-pit barbecues, more food, and all the stores are open to 9pm.

One of the other big events in town that are fun to attend is the **Mardi Gras Parade** each February. In true New Orleans style, residents parade through the streets in myriad costumes. Then each May the city salutes its Spanish heritage with a five-day celebration known as **La Fiesta.** Spanish-style parties go on around the city, with visitors and residents in Mexican costumes also participating in a parade, arts and crafts shows, and dancing.

It's an easy town to walk around—most places of interest can be reached on foot—but the best thing about San Luis Obispo is the friendly townspeople, who always seem to have time to help a tourist, converse, and pass the time of day. About 42 miles south of San Simeon on Calif. 1, San Luis Obispo is also a good base for visits to Hearst Castle.

WHAT TO SEE AND DO

Make your first stop in town the **San Luis Obispo Chamber of Commerce Visitors Center,** 1039 Chorro St., between Monterey and Higuera (tel. 805/543-1323). Open seven days a week, this is one of the best-run chambers of commerce I have ever come across, with a staff that is friendly, helpful, and extremely well informed. Drop in to ask questions and pick up maps, get a calendar of events, and all sorts of information on local sights. Hours are 8am to 5pm Tuesday through Friday, and 9am to 5pm Saturday through Monday.

The Path of History

Like Monterey, San Luis Obispo has an easy-to-follow path, here linking about 20 historic landmarks. Get a map and follow the green line on the street. Highlights include—

MISSION SAN LUIS OBISPO DE TOLOSA The focal point of Mission Plaza, the old mission at 782 Monterey St. (tel. 805/543-6850), constructed of adobe bricks by the

Chumash Indians and completed in 1776, is one of the most beautiful and interesting of the Franciscan chain. A 1793 statue of Saint Louis (San Luís) is above the altar, and the 14 Stations of the Cross in the main church date from 1812. The belfry houses three large bells that were cast in Peru in 1818.

Most interesting is the Mission Museum, which contains a wealth of mission artifacts, among them vestments, books, handmade knives, a wedding dress brought over from Spain in 1831, portraits and photos of mission workers, bisque dolls, samplers, a wine press, tallow-making pot, and corn sheller. Many Native American relics are also displayed here: flints, arrowheads, wampum beads, dolls, baskets, clothing, cooking pots, drums, and grinding stones for making flour.

Particularly lovely is the mission's garden setting, with winding brick paths and benches by a creek, a small hill blanketed in morning glories as a backdrop. All is peaceful here.

The mission itself is open daily beginning with the 7am mass. The museum and gift shop are open every day except for Christmas, New Year's Day, Easter Sunday, and Thanksgiving; hours are 9am to 5pm. A donation of $1 (or $2 per family) is requested.

SAN LUIS OBISPO COUNTY HISTORICAL MUSEUM A wonderful place to browse, this little museum, which is run by the San Luis Obispo County Historical Society, is housed in the early-20th-century Carnegie Library building at 696 Montgomery St. (tel. 805/543-0638). The emphasis here is—naturally enough—on San Luis Obispo County history. Special exhibits are displayed periodically. The museum houses an extensive research library and owns hundreds of historical photographs. Permanent exhibits include artifacts of the Chumash Indians and early pioneers.

The museum is open Wednesday through Sunday from 10am to 4pm; closed Christmas Eve, Christmas, New Year's Day, Easter Sunday, and Thanksgiving.

ST. STEPHEN'S EPISCOPAL CHURCH Dating back to 1867, this pine-and-redwood structure is one of the first Episcopal churches in the state. The original pipe organ was donated by Phoebe Apperson Hearst (Patty's great-grandmother).

THE AH LOUIS STORE Practically unchanged since it was opened in 1874, this century-old establishment at 800 Palm St. (tel. 805/543-4332) is still in the hands of the original Cantonese family. Ah Louis was lured to California by gold fever in 1856. Unsuccessful in this venture, he came to San Luis and took a job as a cook, but he soon began a lucrative trade as a labor contractor, hiring and organizing Chinese crews to build the railroad. In addition to the store, he also started the first brickyard in the county, created county roads, had a vegetable and flower seed business, bred race horses, and was the overseer of eight farms.

Today you can chat with his son, Howard, who runs the store, while you browse about a clutter of Oriental merchandise. Hours are irregular, since Howard often just closes up and goes fishing; however, it's usually open daily, except Sunday.

BULL AND BEAR PIT This Court Street landmark is the site of a cruel sport indulged in by early Californians, when a bull and bear were pitted against each other in deadly combat.

Mission Plaza

In addition to the historical attractions, Mission Plaza houses several restaurants, shops, and boutiques that sell sandals, handcrafted gifts and jewelry, leather goods, pottery, and other such quaint-little-town-artsy-craftsy paraphernalia.

Also in Mission Plaza is the **Network,** 778 Higuera, a shopping complex.

The Creamery

Californians just can't resist turning their old factories and whatnot into tourist attractions. The Creamery, located at 570 Higuera St., was originally the Golden State Creamery, built in 1906 and for the next 40 or so years one of the most important milk-producing centers in the state. After that, its importance began to decline, and in 1974 it was turned into a shopping and restaurant mall, centered around the old cooling tower. Old freezer doors, workhouse lights overhead, and milk-can lamps attest to the Creamery's original function. There's even an old nickelodeon (costs a dime) showing scenes of devastation from the 1906 quake.

California Polytechnic State University

It's not quite Berkeley, but it does have a beautiful 5,169-acre campus, much of it devoted to agricultural studies. Kids especially like to visit the feed mill, meat-processing plant, dairy operation, ornamental horticulture greenhouse, barns, and chicken coops. As well, there's some interesting experimental architecture to see (it's the largest architecture school in the country), and the student recreation center has everything from pinball to bowling.

Best time to visit is the last full weekend in April, when a country fair called the Poly Royal takes place. There are rodeos, barbecues, soapbox races, and more.

Get a map outlining a self-conducted tour from the information desk in the administration building, which you can reach by bus directly from City Hall.

Beaches

The three main beaches in the area are **Avila Beach,** about a 10-minute drive south; **Pismo Beach,** about a 15-minute drive south; and **Morro Bay,** about 15 minutes away going north on Calif. 1.

Avila Beach, a quaint seacoast village, offers chartered deep-sea fishing and scenic pleasure cruises from the Port St. Luis Marina. It's the best swimming beach in the area (the water is the warmest, although still not warm enough for me), and there are barbecue and picnic facilities.

Pismo offers a 23-mile stretch of beautiful sandy beach. A year-round favorite sport is exploring isolated dunes, cliff-sheltered tidepools, caves, and old pirate coves. There's fishing from the Pismo Beach Pier (other pier amusements include arcade games, bowling, billiards, etc.) It should be good, since the Spanish word *pismo* means "a place to fish." (On the other hand, this resort town may be named for the Chumash Indian word *pismu*, which means "the place where blobs of tar wash up on the beach.") You'll also find a wide variety of restaurants and shops in the area, and it's a good place for antiques hunting.

Stop by the **Pismo Beach Chamber of Commerce,** 581 Dolliver St., Pismo Beach, CA 93449 (tel. 805/773-4382, or toll free 800/443-7778 in California), and pick up information about local attractions. The office is open weekdays from 9:30am to 5pm, on Saturday from 10am to 4pm.

Equally beautiful is **Morro Bay,** site of Morro Rock, the last of a chain of long-extinct volcanoes, and a winter and fall sanctuary for thousands of birds—cormorants, pelicans, sandpipers, even the rare peregrine falcon. It's wonderful to watch them from the beach or a window table at one of the bay-view restaurants.

The hub of the community is the **Embarcadero,** with its numerous seafood-with-a-view eateries; commercial fishing boats often unload their catch right at the restaurants. There are also seafood markets, boat and pier fishing facilities, shops, and art galleries to explore, as well as a nearby aquarium.

Morro Bay has many, many visitor attractions, including a state park, golf

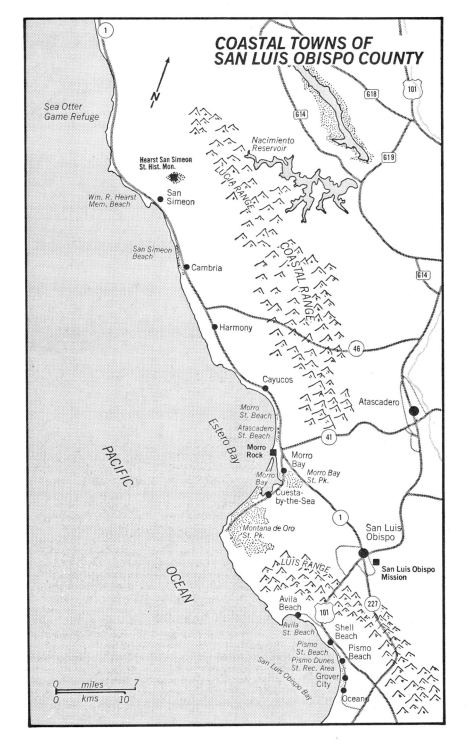

COASTAL TOWNS OF SAN LUIS OBISPO COUNTY

Sea Otter Game Refuge

Nacimiento Reservoir

Hearst San Simeon St. Hist. Mon.

Wm. R. Hearst Mem. Beach

San Simeon

San Simeon Beach

Cambria

Harmony

Cayucos

Morro St. Beach

Atascadero St. Beach

Morro Rock

Morro Bay

Morro Bay St. Pk.

Cuesta-by-the-Sea

Montana de Oro St. Pk.

Atascadero

Estero Bay

PACIFIC

OCEAN

SANTA LUCIA RANGE

COASTAL RANGE

SAN LUIS RANGE

San Luis Obispo

San Luis Obispo Mission

Avila Beach

Avila St. Beach

Pismo St. Beach

Pismo Dunes St. Rec. Area

Shell Beach

Pismo Beach

Grover City

Oceano

San Luis Obispo Bay

1

101

G18

G14

G19

G14

46

41

1

101

227

0   miles   7
0   kms   10

course, natural history museum, hiking trails, and of course, miles of beach. Morro Strand State Beach, just north of Morro Rock, is popular with surfers and fishermen.

Once again, head for the **Morro Bay Chamber of Commerce,** 895 Napa St., Morro Bay, CA 93442 (tel. 805/772-4467, or toll free 800/231-0592 in California), for information. They're open weekdays from 8am to 5pm, on Saturday from 9am.

Warning: At any beaches north of Santa Barbara (where California begins to live up to its sunny rep) you might be happier in a sweatshirt than a bikini.

WHERE TO STAY

The **Madonna Inn,** 100 Madonna Rd., San Luis Obispo, CA 93401 (tel. 805/543-3000), the unique, Disney-esque creation of Alex and Phyllis Madonna, is the most famous (or infamous) of the coast's hostelries. Nestled on 1,500 hillside acres, up a road lined with bubble-gum-pink streetlight posts, it's a fairyland castle with outdoor winding staircases, and a shingled roof topped with turrets and a weathervane. Each of the 109 rooms within is a uniquely eccentric thematic fantasy environment. Canary Cottage, for example, is all yellow, with birdcage light fixtures; several accommodations are posh rock-walled caves; and there's even one for height-mismatched mates, with a bed 5 feet long on one side and 6 feet on the other. You can choose Spanish, Italian, Irish, Alps, Currier and Ives, super-romantic, Native American, Swiss, or hunting decor.

When you enter the registration area, you can select the decor and theme of your room from a collection of hundreds of postcards. This doesn't mean you can just drop in and get a room—reserve as far in advance as possible; the place is always filled. Some favorite rooms—the results of careful perusal—are described below, and I suggest that you ask for one that sounds appealing to you (maybe even give a few alternatives) when you make reservations. When you arrive, if something you prefer is vacant, you can always change.

One of the most romantic is Love Nest, a honeymoon suite with a pink-carpeted winding stairway (all romantic-themed rooms lean very heavily to pink) leading to a cupola hideaway. In the same category is Morning Star, a two-room suite with a high, beamed cathedral ceiling, gold bed, gold tables, and gold-and-crystal chandelier. Carin, named for a Swiss word of endearment, is also a honeymoon favorite, with gold cherub chandeliers over the bed, a peaked slanted ceiling, love birds adorning the bath, and lots of guess what color. A little less of said color—here only the carpet, drapes, bathroom walls, and phone are pink—is in evidence in the delicate Anniversary Room, with flowery rose light fixtures and floral-print wallpaper.

The rock rooms are plush stone-walled caves, many of which have working fireplaces and/or rock-walled waterfall showers. Old World is one that has both of these features, and a predominantly red decor. Fireplaces but no cascading showers are in Yosemite Rock and Kona Rock, both furnished in lush green tones. On the other hand Cave Man, with leopard-skin bedspread and upholstery, has the waterfall but not the fireplace. This room connects to make a suite, if you so desire, with Daisy Mae, which has the most elaborate waterfall shower in the entire inn, plus several stained-glass windows depicting Daisy Mae herself. Another favorite rock room is Cabin Still (there's a still in the bath).

Additional choices, these for fairytale prettiness, are: Old Fashioned Honeymoon (ornately Victorian) and Victorian Gardens (ditto); Swiss Bell, Wilhelm Tell, Edelweiss, and Matterhorn (all with very charming Swiss decor); and finally the Safari Room (wild game theme) and Buffalo Room, this latter of special significance to the Madonnas, since the buffalo head mounted on the wall was once attached to their own buffalo, killed in an accident.

Each room has a color TV, direct-dial phone, and bath; you won't need a clock, since every hour is heralded by bells, Swiss yodels, and a musical passage on the Swiss alphorn. Should there be an extraordinary heat spell, the Old Mill is the only room with air conditioning.

Additional facilities in the main building include an enormous coffee shop, a dining room (rather pricey), and two cocktail lounges, all as outlandishly ornate and plushly pink as the rest.

The rate schedule is as follows: singles are $77, doubles run $82 to $140, and suites with fireplaces are $135 to $180.

More conventional accommodations are available at any of three conveniently located, well-run little motels, all at the junction of U.S. 101 and Calif. 1, within walking distance of each other and of town.

The **Apple Farm Inn,** 2015 Monterey St. (at the end of the Monterey exit off U.S. 101), San Luis Obispo, CA 93401 (tel. 805/544-2040, or toll free 800/255-2040 in California), sits sedately among the giant sycamores on the banks of San Luis Creek. The 68 pine-furnished rooms in this handsome turn-of-the-century Victorian structure are a delightful blend of country charm and traditional elegance. All have gas-log fireplaces. Some have four-poster or canopied beds; others, brass beds. There are cozy turreted areas with love seats, wing-back chairs, and window seats. Some rooms have bay windows with window seats and a view of San Luis Creek or the authentic mill house. The rooms also have all the amenities of a well-thought-out contemporary inn—oversize tubs, color TVs, turndown service, and phones. An outdoor heated pool, with a Jacuzzi, is open year-round; two specialty rooms above the mill house have decks overlooking this vista. And when was the last time you stayed at an inn or hotel where you received complimentary coffee or tea delivered to your door with your wakeup call? Other nice touches are a souvenir apple and gift card stationery. Adjacent to the inn is the Apple Farm Restaurant, described in delicious detail below.

Rates for single or double rooms are $85 to $150. Children under 18 stay free when sleeping in the same room with adults. The additional-person charge is $10.

The **Apple Farm Trellis Court,** 2121 Monterey St., San Luis Obispo, CA 93401 (tel. 805/544-2040, or toll free 800/255-2040 in California), adjoins the Apple Farm Inn and is structured like a motel, but that's where the similarity to most motels ends. The decor is cozy country, with gas fireplaces in all of the rooms. And guests can enjoy all the attractions of the Apple Farm Inn, including the pool area. Rooms have cable TVs, phones, and showers or combination baths. Rates for singles and doubles are in the range of $60 to $95.

At 1000 Olive St., San Luis Obispo, CA 93401, is the **Best Western Olive Tree** (tel. 805/544-2800), offering quality and pleasant accommodations. The Olive Tree has a restaurant on the premises, the Stuffed Olive, a reasonably priced coffee shop. There's also a sauna here along with the pool; all rooms have color TVs, direct-dial phones, and clocks. The most unique feature of the Olive Tree is its eight apartment suites, housed in an attractive shingled building, all with large terraces and big, fully equipped modern kitchens. Regular singles are $57 to $75; doubles and twins are $69 to $80. Once again, off-season rates are a few dollars less.

Another good choice is the friendly **Lamp Lighter Motel,** 1604 Monterey St. (at Grove), San Luis Obispo, CA 93401 (tel. 805/543-3709, or toll free 800/843-6882 in California), with 42 neat and clean motel rooms, a pool, and a heated whirl-pool. All have cable color TVs with free HBO movies, complimentary Continental breakfast, coffee makers, air conditioning, direct-dial phones, and tub/shower baths; clocks and irons are available on request. Rates are $37 to $65 for a single, $42 to $69 for a double.

The **Allstar Inn,** 1625 Calle Joaquin, San Luis Obispo, CA 93401 (tel. 805/541-6992), is located right off U.S. 101. The inn was finished in July 1988 and is hard to beat in terms of cost and attractiveness. It's a budget-saving beauty. Furnishings have natural-wood finish, pastels predominate even to the pattern of the comforters, and rooms are quite light. Of course, each has a color TV, a phone, air conditioning, and a tub/shower, plus oversize bath towels. As you might expect, there is a swimming pool. Singles are $28; for two it's $32.

Budget-minded travelers might also consider **Motel 6,** 1433 Calle Joaquin, San Luis Obispo, CA 93401 (tel. 805/549-9595), just off U.S. 101, with 87 units and a swimming pool. Best if you have a car, since otherwise it's just a mite out of the way. As with all Motel 6 facilities, the units are simple, clean, and with shower only. Singles are $28; each additional adult is $6. Color TV is free; all rooms have phones and local calls are free.

Camping

Facilities for camping abound in the San Luis area. For information about Pismo Beach and Morro Bay campsites, write to their respective chambers of commerce (addresses above). The San Luis chamber has a directory of about 40 local campgrounds included in their city map.

WHERE TO DINE

There are quite a few places in and around town, none of them dishing up unforgettable gourmet fare, but many offering good honest meals in very pleasant settings and hospitality you're not likely to forget. Such a one is **Linnaeas Café, 1110** Garden St., between Marsh and Higuera streets (tel. 805/541-5888).

The café, with its wooden counter, simple stools, and small circular tables, also serves as an art gallery; all the pictures on the wall are for sale. On a lovely patio in the back, you can enjoy the morning or evening with comfortable company.

The breakfast event begins at 7:30am. If you thought you've had eggs done in just about every conceivable way, order the egg burrito ($2.75) for a pleasant surprise: a flour tortilla lovingly enfolds fluffy scrambled eggs and a happy combination of chopped tomatoes, scallions, sliced black olives, and cheddar cheese, all topped off with a dollop of sour cream and guacamole. A somewhat lest zesty, but totally new and enjoyable, way to eat breakfast is old-fashioned rice pudding with steamed milk. After breakfast I couldn't resist the café au lait—one of the 12 available varieties of hot coffee. Linnaeas also serves eight types of iced coffee. If you're in a conservative mode, head for the granola table in the rear room, where you'll also find an overwhelming variety of yummies available to mix and match with your grains. Weekends, the café serves soufflés and other special delights.

If you thought breakfast couldn't be surpassed, just wait for the "SLO" rolls—you're in San Luis Obispo, remember—at lunch. An "SLO" roll is made of Armenian crackerbread and has various fillings, all with a cream cheese/mayo base. The Mexican variety is filled with cheese, tomatoes, chiles, and onions; the Italian version features zucchini, mushrooms, green olives, and jack cheese, with touches of parmesan and garlic. You buy the roll by the inch—$1.50 for each one-inch slice that looks much like a jelly-roll slice. In addition, choices of fresh-made soups and salads change daily: full-size salads are $4.75; smaller portions, $3. Soups are $2.50 per bowl, $1.50 per cup.

Linnaeas Café is not open for dinner, but wonderful things begin to happen about 6:30pm. Coffees from cappuccino to café au lait to Viennese are served with the desserts of the day—tortes, cranberry bread, carrot cake, Black Magic—all from $1.75 to $3.75 per portion. At about 8pm the live music begins. During the Mozart Festival the concerts are classical; other times, whatever suits the mood. And now there is a crafts gallery (local artisans) in the backyard to complement the fish ponds and the arbor covered with trumpet vine.

Breakfast is served 11am, lunch to 3pm, and coffee, dessert, and music go on until midnight. Bring your own conversation.

If you're fortunate enough to meet Linnaeas at the café—she's a joy—you'll begin to understand a lot more about the warmth and charm of San Luis Obispo.

Another fine eatery is **1865**, 1865 Monterey St., near Grand Avenue (tel. 805/544-1865), a ski-lodgey, redwood-paneled, candlelit restaurant with peaked 60-foot ceilings. Philodendrons 20 feet long hang from beams under the upstairs skylight, macramé hangings and color photographs adorn the walls, and one room has a corner fireplace with a large orange chimney. The bar is a comfortable hangout, and there's more seating outdoors, also around a fireplace. Tuesday through Saturday nights, jazz and other easy-listening music add to the friendly ambience. Steak and seafood entrees (like prime rib or fresh red snapper) are featured at dinner, all served with salad, rice pilaf or baked potato, and hot French bread. Prices range from $14 to $25. For dessert try the homemade chocolate mousse.

Open for lunch Monday through Friday (almost all entrees are under $8) from 11am to 2:30pm; for dinner, Monday through Thursday and Sunday from 5 to 9:30pm, on Friday and Saturday to 11pm. Reservations suggested.

F. McLintocks Saloon, 686 Higuera St., between Broad and Nipomo (tel. 805/541-0686), is right out of the Old West, complete with cowboy-and-Indian theme paintings (but a large oil of a nude over the bar), historic photos of the West, an elk-head trophy on one wall, turn-of-the-century lighting fixtures and bar. In addition, the food's great and the quantity is incredible. If there isn't room at the front or middle of the saloon, there's a patio with a few tables for outdoor dining, weather permitting.

Monday through Friday breakfasts are fairly typical fare—eggs, three-egg omelets, steak and eggs, waffles, oatmeal—but there are a few interesting exceptions like the scrambled eggs blended with spicy beef and pork and served with salsa. On weekends, try the huevos rancheros con tocino, two eggs on a corn tortilla topped with salsa and served with bacon, refried beans, and cheddar. For lunch, there is a good selection of hot and cold sandwiches and a variety of burgers, including a giant one-pounder built for two with a huge portion of fries; there's also a half-pound lean, tender buffalo burger on a sourdough roll. McLintocks thoughtfully has a kids' menu, with a choice of beef stew, grilled cheese sandwich, or a buffalo burger, which pretty well covers most 12-and-under appetites. As for dinner, there are steaks, chicken, chili, beef stew, salads, and some nightly specials served from 5pm as long as they last.

Breakfast ranges from $3 to $10, with most prices about $4.50. Lunch is $4.50 to $7; the one-pound burger for two is $7.50. Dinner will cost about $7 to $13; the kiddies' menu is $2 to $2.50.

F. McLintocks Saloon serves food weekdays from 6:30am to 8:30pm, on Saturday from 8:30am, and on Sunday from 8:30am to 4pm. Light late-night snacks are served Monday through Saturday from 9pm to midnight.

Down the road 12 miles south is the larger **McLintocks Saloon and Dining House,** in Shell Beach at 750 Mattie Rd. (tel. 805/773-1892); take U.S. 101 and get off at the Shell Beach Road exit. Housed in what once was a real ranch house, the restaurant still retains its western spirit and style: swinging saloon doors, walls lined with hunting trophies and cowboy paraphernalia, lantern-lit checker-board tablecloths, a blazing stone fireplace, and a craps table from speakeasy days. A real stuffed buffalo and a 1921 Model T Ford stakebed truck grace the lobby, and out back is "Hungry Horse Flats"—a covered, heated deck area crammed with antique farm implements, blacksmith memorabilia, and a collection of old license plates and branding boards. Tunes from a turn-of-the-century nickelodeon fill the air during good weather.

Dinners include a salad of either fresh spinach or greens, Trail Camp beans, salsa, garlic bread, onion rings, ranch-fried potatoes, and after-dinner liqueur or sherbet. All this, with an entree like hickory-smoked barbecued spareribs in pineapple-honey sauce, a 14-ounce top sirloin, or fresh abalone with drawn butter, will run you $18 to $27.

McLintocks Saloon and Dining House is open Monday through Friday from 11:30am to 3pm for lunch and 3 to 10:30pm for dinner; on Saturday and Sunday, dinner is served from 2pm. Early suppers are served weekdays from 3 to 5:30pm, on weekends from 2 to 4pm. *Big* western breakfasts are served every weekend: on Saturday from 8 to 11:30am and on Sunday from 9am to 1:30pm. Reservations are taken except for Friday and Saturday dinner.

The **Olde Port Inn** (tel. 805/595-2515) is superbly located at the end of the third pier on Avila Road right out on the boat-filled bay. Housed on two floors, it has windows everywhere providing wonderful views. There's lots of rustic nautical decor—columns made of pier pilings, oilcan bar stools, weathered wood ceilings and beams, and walls lined with photos of local fisherfolk. Hanging lamps with red-glass shades and candle lamps made from cut-tin clam-juice cans create a cozy glow. The bar bounces; upstairs it's quieter. And now there's an oyster bar.

The chef specializes in sautéing and charbroiling. Fish dinners simply do not come fresher; each day the chef goes down to the fishing boats and handpicks the catch for the evening. Similarly, the motto of the house is "Use the Freshest Produce Possible." These are clearly winning concepts: The restaurant has been under the same ownership for 18 years. Dinner entrees also include steak, pasta, and chicken, all served with chowder or spinach salad, a fresh vegetable, and new potatoes. Specialties of the house include prawns stuffed with jack cheese and wrapped with bacon, seafood pasta, a delicious cioppino, and a steamer special with crab claws, mussels, and clams in a butter and garlic sauce. Fresh fish entrees may include salmon, halibut, red snapper, petrale sole, mahi mahi, shark, and swordfish. Dinners cost $12 to $22.

The inn is open for dinner weekdays from 5:30 to 9pm, weekends to 10pm. There's nightly entertainment—rock, '40s swing, and sometimes jazz—in the downstairs cocktail area. Reservations are essential.

Originally built as a residence circa 1917, **This Old House,** Foothill Boulevard toward Los Osos Valley Road (tel. 805/543-2690), was named for the '50s pop song. It was turned into a restaurant of sorts, serving beer, whisky, and fried chicken and potatoes on paper plates. It was a rowdy cowboy hangout complete with shooting contests and an occasional horse in the bar. In an attempt to give the place some class, a model of Sputnik was put on the roof. These days it's a real restaurant where shootouts are frowned on, but still very western in feel. Bare oak floors, rodeo photos, and cowboy paraphernalia adorn the walls; there's a fireplace, a beamed barnlike ceiling, simulated gaslight chandeliers, and antique furnishings from country farms and ranches.

All entrees cost $12 to $27 and are served with salad, relish tray, ranch beans, Texas toast, salsa, potato, and sherbet. Straight from the oak pit are barbecued beef or spareribs, half a barbecued chicken, steak, and ribs; there's also a catch of the day barbecued over oak. Kids' plates are available.

Open for dinner nightly from 5:30 to 9:30pm. Reservations essential.

The Apple Farm, 2015 Monterey St., at the end of the Monterey exit from U.S. 101 (tel. 805/544-6100), an attractive and charming Victorian structure, originally got its name because the owners set out to collect "apple art." But that's only the start of it. When you go to the restaurant, be sure to allow time for going through the grist mill, antique bakery, and gift shop.

The Apple Farm is a tribute to the best of American country fare because virtually everything (with obvious exceptions) is homemade and delicious—soups created from scratch, chili, apple pies, and incredible dumplings made from fresh apples. Breakfast comes with hash-brown potatoes or fresh fruit, plus freshly baked muffins and biscuits. Lunch is accompanied by potato salad (homemade, of course) or fresh fruit, and there are three homemade soups daily to choose from. Dinner offers a simple but toothsome selection of chicken and dumplings, fish (including halibut, trout, and orange roughy), barbecued chicken and ribs, and prime rib, with baked or scalloped potatoes (when were you last offered scalloped potatoes?). Freshly baked cornbread (a specialty of the house) can be had with lunch or dinner. But save room for the famous hot apple dumplings, or one of the other luscious desserts. Breakfast or lunch will probably run $5 to $7; dinner, $9 to $14. All I can say is: *Go!* If you must wait for a bit, wait; or call ahead and get on the waiting list before heading off to the restaurant.

Open daily from 7am to 9pm.

At the Apple Farm Bakery you can watch apple dumplings and cinnamon rolls being made, and you can drool over a wide selection of pies, cookies, brownies, etc. Or visit the two-story gift shop, with a fascinating collection of decorative items. It got started when customers wanted to buy what they saw in the restaurant; now it offers models of California missions, wall hangings, books for all ages, toys, and cranberry glass, plus such goodies as apple butter and boysenberry spread. And you really should stop at the Old Mill House along San Luis Creek to see the authentic working water wheel and the covered footbridge, and to watch the apple cider press and grist mill in operation. Apple Farm–brand flour, coffee, butter, and ice cream are produced there using the power of an authentic 19th-century water wheel. And, oh yes, there's a marvelous place to spend the night—the Apple Farm Inn, mentioned above in the "Where to Stay" section.

7. Solvang

If you're traveling south from San Luis Obispo, most of the spectacular California coast is behind you; if you're on your way north, it's yet to come. Now is a good time to head inland to the charming Santa Ynez Valley.

GETTING THERE

You can take Calif. 246 into the valley from the north (it intersects with Calif. 1 at Lompoc, and U.S. 101 at Buellton), or Calif. 154 from Calif. 1/U.S. 101 at the south, near Santa Barbara. California 246 and 154 intersect east of the town of Santa Ynez.

The Santa Ynez Valley has only five small towns: the aforementioned Buellton and Santa Ynez, as well as Los Olivos, Ballard (the oldest, founded in 1860), and Solvang, the main attraction in the valley. Founded in 1911 by a group of Danish-Americans, Solvang (which means "sunny valley" in Danish) was much like any other rural California mission town until the end of World War II. Word of the quaint town spread, and as its popularity grew, the townfolk worked all the harder to preserve their heritage.

WHAT TO SEE AND DO

Make your first stop the **Solvang Chamber of Commerce Information Center,** 433 Alisal Rd., Solvang, CA 93463 (tel. 805/688-3317), for information. A convenient alternative is the **Visitor Information Booth** on Copenhagen Drive (there's only a mythical number of 1650) next to the Mid-State Bank. The Information Center on Alisal road is open daily from 9am to 5pm; the Information Booth is open weekdays from 10am to 4pm, weekends to 5pm.

Then set out to explore the town center, a cluster of little streets lined with quaint Scandinavian shops, inns, restaurants, and even windmills. You can wander about from shop to shop, or stop for a bite of Danish or Swedish food.

The oldest sight in Solvang is the **Mission Santa Ines,** 1760 Mission Dr. (Calif. 246). It was built in 1804, the 19th of Fr. Junípero Serra's series of 21 missions. Most of its buildings were destroyed by an earthquake in 1812 or ravaged by a fire in 1821, after which it was rebuilt. In the mid-19th century the mission was sold except for the church and living quarters. The rest deteriorated to ruins. It was restored to the Catholic church by Abraham Lincoln. Not until the early 20th century, however, did restoration work on the mission begin. In the winter of 1987, an extensive project restoring a large part of the convent and eight of the arches was begun; it was finally completed at the end of 1988.

Today Mission Santa Ines looks as it must have shortly after it was founded. It houses a museum of Indian and mission artifacts from the early days. The church, a chapel, the museum, and grounds are open daily for visitors: in summer, Monday through Saturday from 9am to 5pm and on Sunday from noon to 5pm; the rest of the year, Monday through Saturday from 9:30am to 4:30pm and on Sunday from noon to 4:30pm. The mission is closed Thanksgiving, Christmas, and New Year's Day. A donation of $1 is asked of adults.

The Santa Ynez Valley boasts a number of wineries that offer tastings and tours. You can visit the **Firestone Vineyard,** Zaca Station Road in Los Olivos (tel. 805/688-3940); **Vega Vineyards,** 9496 Santa Rosa Rd. in Buellton (tel. 805/688-

2415); and the **Ballard Canyon Winery,** 1825 Ballard Canyon Rd. in Solvang (tel. 805/688-7585). See the Solvang Chamber of Commerce for information on these and others, or call the wineries directly for visiting hours.

On your way out of Solvang going south on Calif. 154, you'll pass by one of the prettiest spots in the valley, the **Lake Cachuma Recreation Area** (tel. 805/688-4658). There are all sorts of activities year-round: camping, boating, fishing, picnicking, and horseback riding, to name a few.

Passing from the Santa Ynez Valley to Santa Barbara, Calif. 154 goes through the San Marcos Pass and up onto a ridge that affords a spectacular view of the valley and then—on the far side—the Pacific and the Channel Islands in the distance.

WHERE TO STAY

If you decide to stay in the Santa Ynez Valley, you'll like the **Sheraton Royal Scandinavian Inn,** 400 Alisal Rd. (P.O. Box 30), Solvang, CA 93464 (tel. 805/688-8000, or toll free 800/325-3535). It features 135 luxurious, air-conditioned rooms with cable color TVs and direct-dial phones; heated pool and spa; restaurant and cocktail lounge. Rates are $81 to $121, single or double.

There's also a **Motel 6** at 333 McMurray Rd., Buellton, CA 93427 (tel. 805/688-7797); it has 59 rooms and a pool. Rates are $27 for one person, $6 for each extra adult. Children under 18 stay free in the same room as their parents. All rooms now have phones and color TVs; local calls are free.

---

8. Santa Barbara

The best thing that ever happened to Santa Barbara was an earthquake! On June 29, 1925, a quake with a Richter magnitude of 6.3 virtually destroyed the entire business district, leaving the uninspired architecture of the town in shambles. An Architectural Board of Review was formed soon after to guide the rebuilding of the city, and a brilliant decision was made that has been in effect ever since. All new buildings had to be in similar Mediterranean style—basically the California adobe characterized by light-colored, sparkling stucco walls, low sloping terra-cotta–tile roofs, a glimpse here and there of lacy wrought-iron grillwork, and above all, a comfortable human scale. Although the buildings that sprang up here have many influences—Mediterranean, Spanish Colonial Revival, Mexican, Early California, Monterey, and even Moorish and Islamic—all are unified by the above standard, and all are in styles of architecture from areas with warm climates similar to Santa Barbara's.

Already blessed with the Santa Ynez Mountains as a magnificent backdrop, and a mostly gorgeous coastline, Santa Barbara has, with careful planning, become one of California's most beautiful cities. It is also (at least part time) the residence of some notable personages—one former president, a bevy of show-business personalities (Jane Russell, Karl Malden, Steve Martin, Robert Mitchum, Robert Preston, Jonathan Winters), and one remarkable chef, Julia Child.

The beauty of the Santa Barbara beach area cannot be disguised, even on an overcast day: Then the ocean and mountains to either side have the same blue haze often seen in Japanese paintings. The only blight on the scene is the oil rigs out on the ocean—difficult to ignore whether the sun is shining or not.

As you drive along State Street (a plaza boulevard, and the town's main drag) from U.S. 101, you'll first pass through the old section of town, which is in a continual state of redevelopment. But once you get into the heart of the city, life changes. The sidewalks are wide and landscaped, enhanced by flowering trees and planting beds, store signs are limited in size, mailboxes and newsstands are built into stucco walls, and at every pedestrian crossing is a living Christmas tree that serves as just a regular tree the rest of the year. Even billboards have been banned in this delightful city.

It would be a pleasure to while away an entire summer here, sunning oneself on the beach, taking long walks, visiting museums, dining in lovely restaurants, playing golf and tennis, horseback riding, bike riding, fishing, going to concerts, and luxuriating in the amazingly beautiful surroundings.

GETTING THERE

Just 92 miles north of Los Angeles and 332 south of San Francisco, Santa Barbara is reached by car via Calif. 1 or U.S. 101. Several airlines link both major cities with Santa Barbara, as do Greyhound buses and Amtrak.

PARKING

Assuming that you will probably be driving around the city, let me tell you now that on-street parking in the downtown area can be a real hassle. You can drive around forever (well, almost), day or evening, looking for a spot. Suffice it to say that the city has provided a sensible alternative: Municipal parking lots are conveniently located, with pedestrian walkways to State Street and the surrounding areas. Parking facilities are open 24 hours daily, and rates begin at 8am Monday through Saturday. In most lots, parking is free for the first 90 minutes (courtesy of the downtown businesses), 50¢ for the next hour, $1 for each additional hour, with a maximum of $8.50. *In certain lots, however, if you park before 9am, the rates can be steep—the first 90 minutes are still free, but thereafter it's $5 for each additional hour, or part, with a maximum of $25!* The purpose of this is to deter local employees from filling up the lots. The Visitor Information Center has a *Guide to Downtown Public Parking*, but be sure to ask which lots are involved.

WHAT TO SEE AND DO

Once again, there's so much to see and do in this lovely beach resort city that I advise you to visit the **Santa Barbara Visitor Information Center,** 1 Santa Barbara St., Santa Barbara, CA 93101 (tel. 805/965-3021), for maps, literature, and a calendar of the many and varied events taking place at all times. Among other things, they've planned out a scenic drive that takes in 15 major points of interest and a suggested walking tour of Santa Barbara's historical landmarks. It's especially important for you to have a map in Santa Barbara, particularly for evenings, when street signs are very difficult to see, much less read. Much of the city does not have street lights. The center sells a map of the city for $1, which is extremely useful in finding your way around. The Information Center is open Monday through Saturday from 9am to 5pm, on Sunday from 10am; however, it's still wise to call before you stop by.

Sights

STATE STREET If you have only a few days, however, you might start with State Street, which has one of the most interesting and attractive collections of shops and cafés west of the Hudson River—perfect for strolling, spending money, noshing, watching the passing parade, whatever. Starting toward the north end at Victoria Street, you'll enjoy every block of a slow stroll down to Ortega Street—about half a mile. Along the way, for those who tire easily, there are wood-and-stone benches on every block. If you've run out of places to shop along the way, try **La Arcada** between Anapamu and Figueroa (on the east side of State), a gathering of elegant boutiques for children's clothing, leather, art, jewelry, apparel (Pappagallo)—there's even a barbershop. The flowers, benches, and a fountain are there to help relax and refresh you. There's a cheese shop too, and the Acapulco restaurant at the end of the arcade.

Some of the historic highlights of Santa Barbara that you can see along the way are:

El Paseo, 814 State St., a picturesque shopping arcade with stone walkways, is reminiscent of an old street in Spain. Built around the 1827 original adobe home of Spanish-born Presidio Commandante José de la Guerra, El Paseo is lined with charming shops and art galleries. This is the hub of the city. Across the street is the **Plaza de la Guerra,** where the first City Council met in 1850, and where the first City Hall was erected in 1875.

Occupying a full city block on Anapamu Street, and set in a lush tropical garden, the **County Courthouse,** 1100 Anacapa St. (tel. 805/962-6464), is a supreme example of Santa Barbara nouveau-Spanish architecture—a tribute to bygone days when style and elegance outweighed more practical considerations. Few would guess that it was built as late as 1929. The architect, William Mooser, was aided by his son, who, having spent 17 years in Spain, was well versed in Spanish-Moorish design. Turrets and towers, graceful arches, unexpected windows, brilliant Tunisian tilework, winding staircases, intricately carved and stenciled ceilings, palacio tile floors, lacy iron grillwork, heavy carved-wood doors, and Spanish lanterns of hammered iron are among the impressive interior features. Magnificent historic murals by Dan Sayre Groesbeck, depicting memorable episodes in Santa Barbara history, are worth a visit in themselves. (The murals were done on cloth so that in case of a severe earthquake they could be removed.) An elevator whisks visitors up to **El Mirador,** the 85-foot-high deck of the clock tower, where there are sweeping views of the ocean, mountains, and terra-cotta–tile roofs of the city.

The courthouse is amazingly impressive and inspiring—don't miss it. It's open weekdays from 8am to 5pm, weekends and holidays (except Christmas) from 9am to 5pm. You can take a free guided tour on Wednesday and Friday at 10:30am and Tuesday through Saturday at 2pm.

Called the "Queen of the Missions" for its graceful beauty, the hilltop **Santa Barbara Mission,** at Laguna and Mission streets (tel. 805/682-4173 or 682-4175), overlooks the town—its gleaming white buildings surrounded by an expanse of lush green lawn, flowering trees and shrubs, a Moorish fountain under a pepper tree, and a misty backdrop of cloud-enshrouded mountains. It's the only California mission with twin bell towers, and it is regarded by many as the most beautiful. Established in 1786, the present mission is still used today by the parish of Santa Barbara. On display within are a typical missionary bedroom, tools, crafts and artifacts of the Chumash people, 18th- and 19th-century mission furnishings, paintings and statues from Mexico, and period kitchen utensils—grinding stones, baskets, and copper kettles.

You can take a self-guided tour Monday through Saturday from 9:30am to 5pm and on Sunday from 1 to 5pm. Adults are asked for a donation of $1; children under 16 go in free.

MUSEUMS Three privately maintained Santa Barbara museums are open to the public and charge no admission.

The **Santa Barbara Museum of Natural History,** beyond Old Mission Road, at 2559 Puesta de Sol Rd. (tel. 805/682-4711), is devoted to the display, study, and interpretation of Pacific Coast natural history—flora, fauna, and prehistoric life. Museum architecture, in typical Santa Barbara style, reflects early Spanish and Mexican influence, with ivy-colored stucco walls, graceful arches, arcades, a central patio, and lovely grounds. Exhibits range from diagrams and photographs of the life cycle of worms to Native American basketry, textiles, and a full-size replica of a Chumash canoe; from Native American art to fossil ferns to the complete skeleton of a blue whale. In addition to halls dealing with Native Americans, birds, mammals, the Paleolithic Age, minerals, and marine life, a planetarium offers shows on Saturday and Sunday.

Open Monday through Saturday from 9am to 5pm; on Sunday and Thanksgiving, Christmas, and New Year's Day from 10am to 5pm. Admission is $3 for adults, $2 for seniors and teens, $1 for children.

The **Santa Barbara Museum of Art,** 1130 State St., at Anapamu (tel. 805/963-4364, or TDD 963-2240 for the hearing impaired), houses an extraordinary

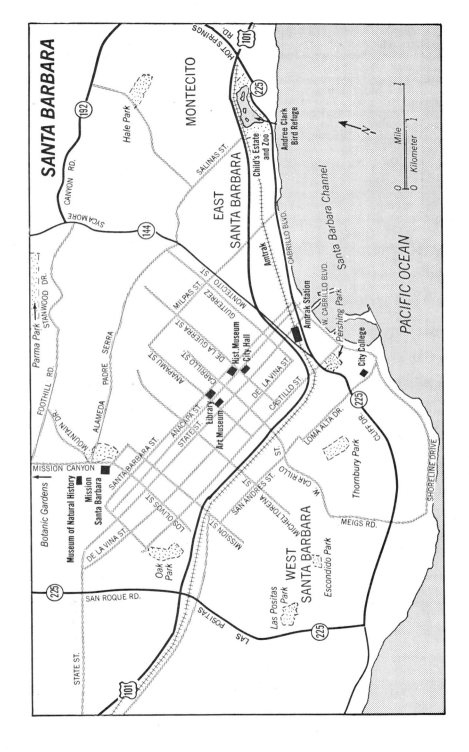

collection for a community its size. From an Egyptian New Kingdom relief to kinetic sculpture, there is something to interest almost everyone: Greek and Roman sculpture, painted vessels, and ancient glass; a European collection of impressionists like Monet and Pissarro, and early-20th-century European modernists like Chagall, Hoffmann, and Kandinsky; works of the Italian Renaissance and Flemish schools; a representative collection of American art by such artists as O'Keeffe, Eakins, Sargent, Hopper, and Grosz; Oriental sculpture, prints, ceramicware, scrolls, screens, and paintings; works on paper by such 17th- to 20th-century masters as Rembrandt, Canaletto, Fuseli, Ruskin, Degas, Picasso, and Miró; and a photography collection of over 1,500 images.

In 1985 the museum opened its expanded and renovated facility and currently houses over 14,000 works, which are exhibited on a rotating basis in new climate- and light-controlled galleries.

Some of the more recent special shows at the museum have included Regionalism: The California View; Kiyochika: Artist of Meiji Japan; Europe's Golden Age of Painting; Figurative Impulses: Five Contemporary Sculptors; Richard Misrach: Photographs of the American Desert; A Day with Toulouse-Lautrec; Dressed in Splendor: Japanese Costumes from 1700 to 1926; Painters of Light: American Impressionism; Nancy Graves: A Sculpture Retrospective; and Robert Capa: A Retrospective. In addition, there are regular concerts, lectures, performance art events, and film series.

The museum is open Tuesday through Saturday from 11am to 5pm (on Thursday to 9pm) and on Sunday from noon to 5pm. Admission is free. Focus tours of special exhibitions are conducted on Tuesday at 12:30pm and on Wednesday and Saturday at 1pm. Docent-led tours of the permanent collections and other exhibitions are given Tuesday through Sunday at 2pm.

The **Santa Barbara Historical Museum,** 136 E. De la Guerra St., at the corner of Santa Barbara Street (tel. 805/966-1601), deals with local lore. It's most interesting to take the free guided tour, given by a knowledgeable guide, on Wednesday, Saturday, and Sunday at 1:30pm. Exhibits include paintings of California missions by Edwin Deakin done between 1875 and 1890; a 16th-century carved Spanish coffer from Majorca, home of Padre Serra; objects of the thriving Chinese community of Santa Barbara, including a magnificent carved shrine from the turn of the century; Peruvian silver stirrups and a Spanish cope, both of the 17th century; oil portraits and artifacts of the De la Guerra family and other early notables of Santa Barbara history; many interesting pieces of correspondence; antique dolls; lots of period clothing; and many other relics, fine arts, and memorabilia that make the area's history come alive. The Gledhill Library for historical research is also located here.

Restoration and preservation of two important 19th-century Santa Barbara homes is a continuing project of the museum. The older of the two is the **Trussell-Winchester Adobe,** a State Historic Landmark located at 414 W. Montecito St. When Capt. Horatio Gates Trussell married Ramona Earys Burke (granddaughter of a mutineer of HMS *Bounty),* he built a home from much of the timber salvaged from the wreckage of the steamer *Winfield Scott.* The lines of the Trussell-Winchester Adobe are remarkably simple and uncluttered. The central portion of the home is of adobe brick, while the wings are of the timber wood. The result is an interesting and unique blending of Spanish and American styles. At 412 W. Montecito St. is the **Fernald House,** a fine example of the Victorian architecture style introduced to Santa Barbara in the late 1800s. The house was built by Judge Charles Fernald for his bride in the early 1860s. With many additions as his family grew, the house eventually contained 14 rooms and encompassed a square block. In 1959 the house was sectioned and moved to its present site. A considerable amount of work, money, and dedication went into the reconstruction and refurbishing of the Fernald house, so that it now serves as a perfect example of the pioneer American period home of the mid-1800s in Santa Barbara.

The Historical Museum is open Tuesday through Saturday from 10am to 5pm, on Sunday from noon to 5pm. The Gledhill Library is open Tuesday through Friday from 10am to 4pm. The Fernald House and Trussell-Winchester Adobe are open on Sunday from 2 to 4pm. There is no charge for admission to any of the above.

SANTA BARBARA BOTANIC GARDEN About 1½ miles north of the mission, the Santa Barbara Botanic Garden, 1212 Mission Canyon Rd. (tel. 805/682-4726), 65 acres of native trees, shrubs, cacti, and wildflowers, is also the site of a dam built by Native Americans in 1806. There are over 5 miles of nature trails to follow.

Open daily from 8am to sunset. Admission is $3 for adults, $2 for seniors and those aged 13 to 17 years, $1 for children 5 to 12, free for those under 5; the maximum fee per family is $8. Admission is free Tuesday and Wednesday. Free guided tours are conducted; however, I suggest that you call for the schedule, since it changes by the season of the year, the day of the week, and what you want to see.

MORETON BAY FIG TREE I'm not grasping for sightseeing attractions—this tree is really something! Native to Moreton Bay in eastern Australia, the *Figus macrophylla* is related to both the fig and rubber tree, although it produces neither figs nor rubber. The branch spread of this massive more-than-century-old (planted in 1877) example at Chapala and Montecito streets would cover half a football field—well over 10,000 people could stand in its shade at noon, and over an acre of ground covers its woody roots—and is hands-down the largest in the world! Once in danger of being leveled—for a proposed gas station, of all things—and later threatened by excavation for nearby U.S. 101, the revered tree has been fervently protected each time by its fans, who will no doubt go on protecting the fig tree's territorial rights for another century.

SANTA BARBARA ZOOLOGICAL GARDENS This is a good place to take the kids. At the zoo, 500 Ninos Dr., off Cabrillo Boulevard (tel. 805/962-6310 for recorded information, or 962-5339), over 400 exotic animals are displayed in open, naturalistic settings. In addition, there are beautiful botanic displays, a farmyard, picnic areas with barbecue pits, a gift shop, a snack bar, a miniature train ride, and a small carousel. It's all open every day except Thanksgiving and Christmas. During the summer (mid-June through Labor day) the hours are 9am to 6pm; other months, 10am to 5pm. Admission is $4 for everyone over 12, $2 for seniors and those 2 to 12; under 2, it's free.

ANDREE CLARK BIRD REFUGE Adjoining the Zoological Gardens, the refuge, at 1400 E. Cabrillo Blvd., is a lovely lagoon in a garden setting, where many varieties of freshwater fowl can be seen and fed. A foot and bike path skirt the lagoon, and it's so beautiful it doesn't even matter if you don't see birds. Serious birdwatchers can pick up a 50¢ eight-page pamphlet about local birds at the Museum of Natural History.

Activities

ANTIQUING, GALLERY BROWSING, AND SHOPPING There are close to 80 antique shops in Santa Barbara. **Brinkerhoff Avenue,** off Haley between Chapala and De La Vina streets, is where you'll find the greatest concentration, selling Early American furnishings, quilts, antique china, jewelry, Orientalia, and memorabilia, not to mention bric-a-brac and interesting junk. The free *Santa Barbara Visitor Press* lists the most notable, along with the town's many art galleries, boutiques, leather and handcraft shops, etc. You can get it at the Visitor Information Center, along with a brochure that lists antiques shops. In Santa Barbara you can buy everything from out-of-print books to mounted butterflies. Santa Barbara has 65 bookstores and 60 art galleries; and when you get hungry after shopping, there are over 300 restaurants to sustain your strength.

At 813 State St., a cluster of shops is located in an arcade called **Picadilly Square.** They range from a Native American art shop to a cheese store.

At the western end of State Street is **Stearns Wharf** (tel. 408/963-0611), Santa Barbara's answer to Fisherman's Wharf. Built on an 1872-vintage pier is a collection of shops, attractions, and restaurants, including the Harbor Restaurant (tel. 408/963-3311), a seafood eatery dating from 1941.

BOATING AND FISHING   **Sea Landing,** at the foot of Bath Street and Cabrillo Boulevard (tel. 805/963-3564), has three sportfishing boats and three sport diving boats. They offer a wide variety of fishing and diving trips, whale-watching cruises, as well as daily twilight and half-day cruises ($18 for adults, $16 for children under 12), three-quarter-day cruises ($30 for adults, $25 for children), and full-day cruises ($55 for adults, $40 for children). All boats are totally equipped with stocked galley (food and drink served on board), rental rods and tackle available; rates include bait. Fishing licenses can be obtained at the office. Reservations recommended.

In the summer months they also offer three-hour dinner and cocktail cruises with dancing to live music ($35 for steak dinner, $25 for cocktails only); departures are at 7pm. And you can take whale-watching cruises from February to the end of April ($18 for adults, $9 for children).

Forty power- and sailboats ranging from 13 to 50 feet are available for rent (by the day or hour) from **Sailing Center of Santa Barbara,** located at the Santa Barbara Breakwater (tel. 805/962-2826). Crewed or bare-boat charters are available. The center also offers sailing instruction for all levels of experience.

BICYCLING   This scenic and relatively flat area is marvelous for biking: along the 4-mile palm-lined coastal bikeway, through town, on miles of country roads, or to nearby Montecito. **Beach Rentals,** 8 W. Cabrillo Blvd., right at the beach (tel. 805/963-2524), has carefully maintained one-speed, tandem, and 10-speed bikes and roller skates for rent, and they'll suggest bicycle tours too. They also have single and double surrey-cycles: The single holds three adults and two children; the double holds four adults and two children. Surrey-cycles are for use along the bike paths. Open seven days a week. Bring an ID (driver's license or passport) to expedite your rental.

HORSEBACK RIDING   Several stables in the area rent horses and offer escorted rides along the many local trails. **San Ysidro Ranch Stables,** 900 San Ysidro Lane (tel. 805/969-5046, ext. 307), charges $23 for a one-hour guided trail ride; private lessons in western riding are $35 an hour, $20 per half hour. Reservations are essential.

HIKING   The **Sierra Club** (tel. 805/966-6622) is active in Santa Barbara. They can tell you about the many scenic trails in the Los Padres National Forest and other locations. The club does not have an office; any inquiries should be made by phone.

GOLF   There are four public golf courses to choose from in the Santa Barbara vicinity. The **Santa Barbara Golf Club** is located at 3500 McCaw Ave., at Las Positas Road (tel. 805/687-7087). The 18-hole course is 6,009 yards with a driving range. The pro shop and other nonplaying facilities were reconstructed and refurbished early in 1989. Weekday prices are $15; weekends you'll pay $16. For seniors the charge is $10 weekdays, $14 weekends. Carts are $18. Unlike many municipal courses, the Santa Barbara Community Course is well maintained and has been designed to present a good challenge for the average golfer.

The three remaining courses are located in nearby Goleta. The 18-hole, 7,000-yard **Sandpiper,** 7925 Hollister Ave. (tel. 805/968-1541), has a pro shop and driving range, plus a pleasant coffee shop. Weekday prices are $35, rising to $50 on the weekend. Carts are $22. The remaining two courses are both nine holes. **Ocean Meadows,** 6925 Whittier Dr. (tel. 805/968-6814), is 3,033 yards. Prices are $8 during the week, $9 on the weekend. Carts cost $8 weekdays, $9 weekends. The 1,450-yard **Twin Lakes,** 6034 Hollister Ave. (tel. 805/964-1414), charges $5.50 during the week, $6 on weekends. Hand carts are $1.

TENNIS   Public facilities include the **Municipal Courts** near Salinas Street and U.S. 101 (access off Old Coast Hwy.); the lighted **Las Positas Courts,** 1002 Las Positas

Rd.; and **Pershing Park** courts at Castillo Street and West Cabrillo Boulevard. In addition, there are several private tennis clubs and country-club courts, some of which allow guests. Check with the chamber of commerce.

You'll need a tennis permit to play on these public courts. Permits are available from the Recreation Department, 620 Laguna St. (tel. 805/564-5428 or 564-5517), or from the monitor at the facility. Adults pay $5 a day or $50 per year; children 17 or under play free.

Amusements

FIESTA The most exciting time to visit Santa Barbara is in early August during the **Old Spanish Days Fiesta,** since 1924 a yearly homage to the city's Spanish past, patterned after the community harvest festivals of Andalusia and Castile in Old Spain. This is no piddling little festival—it's a lavish five-day bash (beginning the first Wednesday in August) with colorful costumes, an opening ceremony of pageantry and traditional blessings on the steps of the Old Mission, equestrian events, rodeo, famous flamenco guitarists and dancers, variety shows, barbecues, big-name entertainers, a Spanish marketplace, a dazzling parade down palm-lined Cabrillo Boulevard with dozens of fancy floats, art shows, carnivals, outdoor dancing on the beach, symphony concerts, folk dancing, and much, much more. Many events are free.

Plan to arrive a little before Fiesta (make reservations as far in advance as possible—the town gets booked up 100%) and to stay till it's over. Even if you could get a room, you mightn't be able to get to it during Fiesta; you'd have to lug your suitcases through the crowded streets, many of which are blocked to traffic. The same problem pertains to getting out. Another reason to arrive early is to have time to pore over the schedules of events, get tickets when required, and enjoy the quiet of the beach and town before all the excitement begins.

NIGHTLIFE If you happen to be in town during the early part of October, there's the great **International Jazz Festival,** which began in 1989 and henceforth will be held annually. Don't miss it.

The **Lobero Theater,** 33 E. Canon Perdido St. (tel. 805/963-0761), dates back to 1872, when it was built by Giuseppi Lobero, an Italian who changed his name to José Lobero in deference to the Spanish traditions of Santa Barbara. When the theater went bankrupt in 1892, Lobero, faced with financial ruin and the failure of his dream, put a bullet through his head. By 1922 the building was closed and condemned.

The present Lobero Theater, built in 1924, stands on the same site, the locale of the original Opera House. Among those who have played here are Lionel Barrymore, Edward G. Robinson, Clark Gable, Robert Young, Boris Karloff, Betty Grable, and Anna May Wong (remember?). The Martha Graham troupe has also graced the stage, and concert luminaries have included Andrés Segovia, Arthur Rubinstein, Igor Stravinsky, and Leopold Stokowski.

A wide variety of productions are offered throughout the year—concerts, dance programs, recitals, operas, plays, travel films, and lectures. Call the theater to find out what's on during your stay.

The **Arlington Center for the Performing Arts,** 1317 State St., between Victoria and Sola (tel. 805/966-9382), derived its name from a hotel that occupied the same site from 1872 to 1925. It opened in 1931 in grand style, at the birth of the talking-picture era, presenting movies, vaudeville, and stage shows. The deluxe Arlington became Hollywood's testing ground for unreleased movies; big stars flocked to Santa Barbara to check audience reaction at Arlington sneak previews.

After World War II, when vaudeville had died, road shows began to book into the Arlington to supplement the movie fare. Mae West appeared here in *Diamond Lil* and was panned!

In 1976 the old theater was given a total facelift: reupholstered seats, new furnishings, facilities, and even exterior landscaping. And although film festival classic movies are shown occasionally (and even first-run popular movies), the theater features primarily big-name entertainers like Lily Tomlin, Wayne Newton, and Ray Charles; world-famous symphony orchestras like the Los Angeles Philharmonic; and many of the jazz greats.

In 1988 a new addition was made—the Arlington Court, a covered outdoor patio that features weekend art shows and a variety of special events throughout the year. Information on future events is available by calling 805/963-4408.

THE EARL WARREN SHOWGROUNDS Banquets, antiques shows, barbecues, rummage sales, famous flower shows, music festivals, horse shows, dances, cat shows, coin shows, the circus, a rodeo, or even a big-name entertainer is likely to be at the Earl Warren Showgrounds, Las Positas Road and U.S. 101 (tel. 805/687-0766). Check it out. .

WHERE TO STAY

So popular is Santa Barbara in summer that you simply must book in advance.

A Deluxe Trio

Some of the most elegant digs in town happen to be at one of the most prestigious hotels in California—**Four Seasons Biltmore,** 1260 Channel Dr., Santa Barbara, CA 93108 (tel. 805/969-2261, or toll free 800/336-3442), located on 21 acres of beautiful gardens and private ocean beach in the exclusive Montecito community. It's a refined resort hotel of the old school. When it opened in 1927 a concert orchestra played twice daily in the dining room, and separate quarters were available for personal servants accompanying guests. Although few people travel with servants these days, the Biltmore is still heavy on service.

The award-winning Spanish architecture (what else in Santa Barbara?) was the work of Reginald Johnson. He utilized Portuguese, Basque, Iberian, and Moorish design elements in a graceful combination of arcades, winding staircases, ramadas, patios, and artistic walkways, with lovely hand-painted Mexican tiles and grillwork throughout. The beauty of the estate is further enhanced by imposing views of the Pacific, the Santa Ynez Mountains, and the hotel's own palm-studded formal gardens. During 1988 the hotel underwent a $16-million facelift that would satisfy even the most discriminating client.

Each guest room or suite offers a view of either the Pacific, the Santa Ynez Mountains, a garden, or the Olympic-size pool. All accommodations are deluxe, with plush furnishings in Iberian style and mostly marble bathrooms. Many of the rooms have romantic Spanish balconies and/or fireplaces; some have private patios. All have remote-control color TVs, ceiling fans, and individual climate controls. Elegant touches include terrycloth robes, hairdryers, minibars, twice-daily maid service, overnight shoeshine, 24-hour room service, and full concierge service. And then there are cottages for those who desire the ultimate in luxurious privacy.

A collection of daily complimentary resort activities includes tennis clinics conducted by the tennis pro, toning exercises, arts and crafts, and special events for children. There are three lighted tennis courts, two swimming pools (including a 50-meter Olympic pool at the hotel's Coral Casino Beach and Cabana Club), a putting green, and shuffleboard and croquet courts. There are also beachfront cabanas and a sun deck.

As for the other basic necessities of life, the La Marina restaurant offers elegant evening dining from a select list of California-inspired specialties such as smoked rack of veal with a red-pepper flan, served with batter-fried golden beets, and seared sea scallops with wild rice and roasted peppers. Less formal but casually elegant is The Patio, a glass-enclosed atrium, which serves breakfast, lunch, dinner, and Sunday brunch. The La Sala lounge serves an afternoon high tea daily, with pastries made on the premises, as well as cocktails; La Sala also has live entertainment during the cocktail hour, and nightly except Sunday. The La Perla Dining Room affords poolside dining at the Coral Casino Beach and Cabana Club, or you might have a casual snack at The Raft.

For all this elegance, beauty, and comfort, singles or doubles and twins are

$290 to $375, depending on the view; cottages cost $325; cottage suites are $695 to $850.

Meanwhile, back at the ranch . . . back at the **San Ysidro Ranch,** that is, 900 San Ysidro Lane (off U.S. 101), Santa Barbara, CA 93108 (tel. 805/969-5046), another famous Montecito hostelry nestles in the Santa Ynez Mountains. Originally part of a Spanish land grant on which the padres raised cattle, and later a citrus orchard (there are still orange groves on the property, the produce of which is used for fresh-squeezed juice each morning), San Ysidro opened as a guest ranch in 1893. Over the years Winston Churchill, Sinclair Lewis, Rex Harrison, Groucho Marx, and Sidney Poitier have signed the register, and Jack and Jacqueline Kennedy spent their honeymoon here.

A quiet, beautifully landscaped 540-acre retreat, San Ysidro offers its guests tennis, a swimming pool, riding stables, badminton, croquet, miles of hiking and riding trails, and nearby golf. The Stonehouse restaurant, housed in the old citrus-packing house, is a charming candlelit establishment with a beamed ceiling, shuttered windows, antique furnishings, and paintings of local landmarks adorning the white sandstone walls. A delightful and airy glass-enclosed café area adjoins, the view of the grounds enhanced by many hanging plants inside.

Accommodations consist of 43 quaint cottages with charming country-inn antique furnishings. During the day a woodman makes the rounds with wood and kindling for your fireplace, and fresh flowers from the garden are left in your cottage. The cottages are all secluded in a random pattern among lush foliage and flowers, and most have porches so guests can sit outside and enjoy the view. All have direct-dial phones, modern baths, and TVs with complimentary movies. There also is an honor-system bar in the lounge. Thirteen cottages have Jacuzzis.

There are 12 doubles priced at $165 to $285; more luxurious cottage rooms, studios, and suites for two (some with private hot tubs) are $350 to $425. Additional persons in a room pay $15 each.

While you're staying at the San Ysidro Ranch, or having lunch at the Stonehouse, be sure to stop in at **The Adobe,** also at 900 San Ysidro Lane (tel. 805/969-5046), an extraordinary shop beautifully attended to by Mimi Forbes. (It's located directly across from the registration area for the ranch.) You'll find an attractive and very selective collection of elegant one-of-a-kind decorative and practical beauties, from the likes of a tall walking stick with a handsome carved head to one or two exceptional French impressionist paintings. Prices range from the modest to the less so, but whatever you choose will assuredly be unique. And should you want to have something shipped, they'll take care of it. The Adobe is open daily from 10am to 6pm.

El Encanto Hotel and Garden Villas, 1900 Lasuen Rd., Santa Barbara, CA 93103 (tel. 805/687-5000), was originally built in 1915 and subsequently restored to its grace and elegance. The property consists of 100 rooms, cottages, and villas nested on 10 woodland acres overlooking the city and Channel Islands (it's not easy to find, so be sure to ask directions). Beautiful landscaping has carefully tended gardens and brick walkways that contrast with areas of lush foliage, palm trees, and hibiscus. A lotus pond is surrounded by vine-covered old brick columns, and the music of thousands of birds permeates the atmosphere. Wandering the grounds is a delight.

The rooms and cottages are furnished in a combination of French country antique and tasteful modern. Most accommodations have patios, balconies, or verandas, about a third have kitchens, and half have wood-burning fireplaces. All are equipped with direct-dial phones, color TVs, and baths with tubs or showers.

On-premises facilities include an outdoor heated swimming pool and sun deck, a tennis court, a delightful outdoor terrace (perfect for sunsets and brunches) and a very beautiful restaurant, both with views of the hills and the Pacific. With windows all around, the view alone would suffice to make the El Encanto's beam-ceilinged dining room magnificent, but it's equally impressive within. Furnished with Louis XVI–style chairs, the room is papered in a delicate pattern; there are a few antiques, like an oak sideboard used to display decorative plates, some hanging plants, and lovely flower arrangements on every table. The fare is as fine as the setting, from the fresh croissants available at breakfast to the French nouvelle cuisine entrees served for dinner. The adjoining wicker-furnished lobby bar offers a beautiful view of Santa Barbara and the ocean below. There's dancing to live music here Tuesday through Sunday nights.

Accommodations are priced from $120 to $155 for the "small and cozy"; $180 to $235 for "spacious and special"; and $235 to $375 for "magnifique." El Encanto lives up to its name—"The Enchantment."

At the Beach

The blue-roofed cottages and buildings of the **Miramar Hotel-Resort,** 1555 S. Jameson Lane, in Montecito (P.O. Box 429), Santa Barbara, CA 93102 (take Calif. 101 to the San Ysidro turnoff; tel. 805/969-2203), have long been a famous Santa Barbara landmark. The hotel dates to 1887, when the Doulton family began to augment the meager income from their farm by taking in paying guests. When the railroad was constructed right on the property, Miramar became an important station and affluent guests began arriving in their own private railroad cars. As the popularity of beach and ocean vacations grew, it became a very chic place to go. Old registers are signed by many famous people, even royalty.

Today there are about 200 units set on 14 garden acres overlooking the Pacific. Facilities comprise two swimming pools, four tennis courts, a tennis clubhouse, a paddle-tennis court, 500 feet of private sandy beach, saunas and exercise rooms for men and women, a Jacuzzi, bike rental, and table tennis. Golf and horseback riding can be arranged. The Terrace Dining Room, filled with lush tropical plants and overlooking the pool, is open for breakfast, lunch, and dinner. Steak and seafood entrees are featured. There's live music Tuesday through Saturday nights in the adjoining cocktail lounge.

As for the accommodations, the furnishings are indifferent but the rooms are nevertheless comfortable; Miramar itself is so appealing that room decor doesn't seem all that important. Most attractive are the homey cottages (some with fully equipped kitchens) and the second-floor rooms with peaked raw-wood ceilings in the hotel's poolside section. All rooms are equipped with switchboard phones, color TVs, and tub and/or shower baths.

Rates for singles or doubles are $70 to $125. One-, two-, and three-bedroom suites are $100 to $385.

The **Franciscan Inn,** 109 Bath St. (at the corner of Mason), Santa Barbara, CA 93101 (tel. 805/963-8845), has to be one of the best buys for a stay in Santa Barbara due to its convenient location, reasonable price, attractive accommodations, and very pleasant personnel. The inn is situated just off Cabrillo Boulevard, one short block to the marina and beach. You can get there from U.S. 101 by exiting at the Castillo exit (going south) or the Cabrillo Boulevard exit (if going north).

There are 53 rooms at the Franciscan Inn and each is individually decorated in delicate pastels, and colors, and white. No two are alike, allowing considerable latitude in your choice. All are airy, comfortable, and spacious, and most have ceiling fans. Baths are furnished with the usual complements, plus fine, fat, fluffy towels. You'll have a phone with no charge for local telephone calls and a color TV of course, plus free HBO, and receive a complimentary copy of the morning's *Los Angeles Times.* Also included in the room rate is a complimentary Continental breakfast served in the comfortable lobby, where you'll find a friendly desk person (more like a helpful concierge) who dispenses suggestions on where to eat (there are several excellent restaurants within walking distance), sights to see, and things to do, and who can arrange for necessities such as transportation to the airport.

And of course, what would a California inn be without a pool? This one's heated and has an adjacent snack bar. If luxurious soaking is more your bag than swimming, there's also a hot whirlpool to help you relax after a hard day of sightseeing. There is also a coin-operated guest laundry on the premises.

Singles and suites range from $65 for one person (during the week and depending on the season) to $155 for a bilevel suite with a living room, a separate kitchen, and sleeping quarters upstairs and down that can accommodate up to four. A number of the rooms have fully equipped kitchenettes. The Honeymoon Suite has the added charm of a fireplace, even if you're not on your honeymoon. I suggest reservations well in advance of your trip if you're planning on traveling May through September.

Right in Santa Barbara is the newly renovated pink stucco **Tropicana Motel,** 223 Castillo St. (between Montecito and Yanonali), Santa Barbara, CA 93101 (tel. 805/966-2219), a 30-unit accommodation just a short walk from the beach. There are a heated pool and a Jacuzzi, both away from the street and very private, with lots of room for sunning. Rooms are homey and attractive. All are equipped with color TVs, AM/FM radios, phones, baths with tubs and/or showers, and refrigerators.

There are also suites available—an excellent buy if you like to do your own cooking. These have large eat-in kitchens, fully equipped right down to eggbeaters and potholders, not to mention ovens, full-size refrigerators, and toasters. The suites have a large bedroom and living rooms, sleep two to eight people, and must be rented for a minimum of three days.

Singles, which are hard to come by in summer, rent for $55 to $75, doubles and twins are $65 to $82, and three-room suites are $92 to $124 for two people; add $10 for each extra person.

Even closer to the beach is the **King's Inn,** 128 Castillo St. (between Yanonali and Mason), Santa Barbara, CA 93101 (tel. 805/963-4471), with 45 immaculate rooms in tip-top condition, a swimming pool with lots of sunning area, whirlpool, and sauna bath. The rooms are pleasantly furnished, and all have cable color TVs, direct-dial phones, air conditioning, tub/shower baths, and dressing rooms with big mirrors, and they're all quite lovely. Some second- and third-floor rooms have balconies. In summer, singles and doubles are $84 to $98. An additional person in your room is $6. Rates are slightly lower off-season (October to mid-May).

Budget visitors to Santa Barbara can seek refuge at Motel 6—there are two in Santa Barbara proper and one in nearby Carpinteria, about 10 minutes away by car. The **Motel 6** at 443 Corona del Mar, Santa Barbara, CA 93103 (tel. 805/564-1392), is located right near the beach. It offers basic, clean accommodations; rates are $36 for a single, $6 extra for each additional adult. It features a small pool, and there's no charge for local calls or for TV. Be sure to reserve far in advance, as this motel gets booked up quickly.

A second **Motel 6** is at 3505 State St. (between Las Positas and Hitchcock Way), Santa Barbara, CA 93105 (tel. 805/687-5400). Prices are the same as those above, and there is a large pool. No charge for local calls or TV.

The **Motel 6** in Carpinteria is, as I mentioned, about a 10-minute drive from Santa Barbara, at 4200 Via Real, Carpinteria, CA 93103 (tel. 805/684-6921). Prices here are $27 for a single, plus $6 for each additional adult. Carpinteria also has a pool, and there's no charge for local calls or TV.

In Town

Most people prefer to stay at the beach, but if you have a car you might consider the **Best Western Encina Lodge,** 2220 Bath St. (at Los Olivos), Santa Barbara, CA 93105 (tel. 805/682-7277). Set in a quiet residential area, a short walk from the mission and other attractions, it's a mere five-minute drive from the beach. All rooms are immaculate and tastefully decorated—furnishings, bedspreads, rugs, etc., all look spanking new. I especially like the rooms on the second floor of the oldest building, with beamed raw-pine ceilings. All rooms have color TVs, air conditioning, direct-dial phones, coffee makers, and clocks. Old-wing rooms have showers only; the rest have tub/shower combinations and dressing rooms. Apartments are also available.

Facilities include a pool, a whirlpool, sauna, a lobby shop, a beauty parlor and barbershop, and a very fine restaurant (open from 7:30am to 9:30pm), which you should try even if you don't stay here. An ever-changing lunch menu might feature sweet-and-sour chicken or barbecued ribs, each with soup or salad. I particularly recommend dinner here (5 to 9:30pm), when you can try the award-winning crab Mornay, served with soup or salad, saffron rice or au gratin potatoes, rolls and butter; meals go for $14 to $20. Don't miss the homemade pastries for dessert. The ambience, by the way, is quite nice: candlelight, hanging plants, red-clothed tables, oak paneling, and beamed stucco ceiling. There's also a full bar now.

Single rates are $84 to $112; doubles cost $88 to $116.

The oldest hotel in Santa Barbara (est. 1871), the **Upham,** 1404 De la Vina St. (at Sola), Santa Barbara, CA 93101 (tel. 805/962-0058), is also one of the most charming. Built by Amasa Lyman Lincoln, a Boston banker, the hotel is designed to look like an old-fashioned New England boarding house. A two-story clapboard structure, it has wide eaves and is topped by a glassed-in cupola and a widow's walk for viewing the sea. The original hotel changed hands several times over the years, once to a Cyrus Upham, whose name has remained.

Fronted by two immense ivy-entwined palms and entered via a large colonnaded porch, it is set in a well-tended garden with neat flowerbeds. The Upham was refurbished in 1983, and all 41 guest rooms now have antique armoires, brass or four-poster beds, and pillow shams; many have private porches and fireplaces. All the rooms have modern amenities—pushbutton phones, cable color TVs, and private baths. A complimentary Continental breakfast helps start the day, and in the afternoon, wine, cheese, and crackers are served in the lobby and in the garden. Louie's at the Upham is open for lunch, dinner, and Sunday brunch.

Room rates are $85 to $160, $220 for a master suite with fireplace, Jacuzzi, private yard, and king-size bedroom. The Upham is located in the heart of Santa Barbara, two blocks from State Street.

The **Bath Street Inn,** 1720 Bath St. (between Valerio and Mission), Santa Barbara, CA 93101 (tel. 805/682-9680), is a handsome Queen Anne Victorian built over a hundred years ago. This historic residence has two unusual features—a semicircular "eyelid" balcony and a hipped roof, unique even for Santa Barbara. And the century-old trees, the flower-filled patio with white wicker furniture, and the brick courtyard add to the inn's charm, as does the graciousness of the innkeepers.

In the expansion and reconstruction of the inn, great care was taken to incorporate modern safety features, yet to preserve the 1800s atmosphere of the original home. The living room is comfortable and inviting. The fireplace, Chinese rug, period prints, sideboard with attractively displayed crystal, ivory-and-white wallpaper, and fresh flowers create a pleasant warmth. The dining area has a traditional blue-and-white floral-print paper that complements the finely crafted woodwork and furnishings.

There are seven guest rooms in the Bath Street Inn, all with private baths. Each of the rooms has its own charm and uniqueness: one with a king-size canopied bed, another under the eaves with a superb sunset view from a balcony, others with mountain views or window seats with glimpses of the ocean.

Room rates, single or double, are $80 to $125 and include a full breakfast, evening refreshment, and the use of the inn's bicycles. Pets are not accepted.

WHERE TO DINE

A beautiful Santa Barbara restaurant is the **Epicurean Catering Co.,** 125 E. Carrillo St., between Santa Barbara and Anacapa (tel. 805/966-4789 or 962-6793). Fronted by a planter of lovely flowers (they change seasonally), it has an extremely pretty interior. An abundance of plants and flower arrangements complement French-reproduction floral-print wallpaper and cream-colored walls hung with framed botany prints. Carpeting is appropriately deep green. Decorative pewter and brass elk-shaped tureens adorn each candlelit table. There are three dining areas with skylights overhead, and a courtyard with latticework walls and a screened ceiling that rolls back in good weather for dining under the open sky. The whole effect is rather like a magic forest.

You might select an appetizer of bay shrimp, crab, and artichoke hearts, or a pâté of duck, veal, or pork with French bread. Soup comes with your entree—mushroom bisque with sherry or chilled borscht with sour cream—although you could opt for salad. As for the entrees, they range from $17 to $29, for steak and lobster, or filet of sole Epicurean with mushrooms, toasted almonds, and hollandaise. Everything is perfectly delicious, and the ambience, enhanced by taped classical music, is delightful. An extensive wine list is available.

Epicurean Catering Co. is open for lunch weekdays, except Wednesday, from 11:30am to 2:30pm. It's open for dinner Monday through Saturday from 5:30 to 9:30pm. Reservations are suggested.

The elegant **Casa de Sevilla,** 428 Chapala St., between Haley and Gutierrez (tel. 805/966-4370), has been a local favorite for over half a century. It's divided into several dining areas; I particularly like the front room with its wood-burning fireplace and sloped beamed ceiling. The ambience is warm and intimate, with shuttered windows, brass candle lamps on every table, and graceful chandeliers. Liberal use of sienna (drapes, walls, and carpeting) and antique bullfight posters provide a Spanish feel. In the evening, men are required to wear jackets.

The menu is the same at lunch (served from noon to 2pm) and dinner (from 6 to 10pm). You might begin with an appetizer of chili con queso, guacamole, or lobster cocktail. There are many barbecued entrees—salmon, filet mignon, and spareribs among them—for $14 to $23. A full Casa dinner, including Castilian soup (garbanzo purée), salad, relishes, chili con queso, rice or potato, dessert, and beverage, is priced according to entree at $16 to $30. The Kahlúa cheesecake is an excellent dessert. The restaurant is open Tuesday through Saturday.

Across the street from El Paseo is a restaurant that occupies a portion of Santa Barbara's old fortress, or presidio. It is the **Presidio Café,** 812 Anacapa St., between Canon Perdido and De la Guerra (tel. 805/966-2428). The café is a charming combination of the old and the new: A lovely outdoor area filled with lush plants and umbrella-covered tables surrounds a splashing fountain; one of the old presidio buildings—now with a glass wall—serves as a more elegant dining room (complete with white-clothed tables) overlooking the garden terrace; and the fortress's chapel (showing little trace of its original function) acts as a banquet room.

The service at the Presidio Café is as cheerful and friendly as its ambience. You can begin your day here with a hearty breakfast—perhaps an omelet or a croissant stuffed with fresh fruit or scrambled eggs, sausage, and cheese—for $6 to $8. Or you can enjoy a leisurely lunch of quiche, crêpes (such as turkey, broccoli, and mushroom with a light chicken sauce), a generous salad, sandwiches, or the café's specialty, tortilla soup. Luncheon dishes cost $6 to $8. Portions here are quite healthy, but you may want to save room for the rich and sinfully delicious chocolate mousse cake.

The dinner menu offers a marvelous group of choices. The "Start Here" segment lists appetizers (otherwise termed "grazings") that in combination could make a great light dinner. You might, for example, have the angel-hair pasta, with tomato, garlic, olive oil, and romano cheese, plus a minisalad—a small version of a Cobb, Chinese, or spinach salad. Dinner entrees include Spanish chicken, with the breast sautéed and beautifully seasoned with salsa Roja (a blend of garlic, cilantro, diced tomatoes, green onions, and white wine), and the bacon-wrapped shrimp stuffed with spiced filling and baked with garlic, butter, and white wine. Simpler tastes might simply go for the New York steak grilled with oyster mushrooms. Dinner entrees are served with sautéed vegetables, rice pilaf, and the Presidio's own special French bread. If the appetizer or grazing menu is too little and the dinner too much, Presisio solves the problem with some good à la carte choices that range from quiche to tacos to pizza. The Presidio offers the services and beverages of a full bar.

The Presidio Café is open for breakfast and lunch daily from 8am to 3pm; dinner is served Tuesday through Saturday from 5 to 9pm. Reservations are suggested for both lunch and dinner.

Mousse Odile is just a bit east of State Street at 18 E. Cota St. (tel. 805/962-5393). Breakfast and lunch are served on the Brasserie side of the restaurant, nicely done with oak flooring, red-and-blue-checked tablecloths, and fresh flowers. The Brasserie is not fancy, but has a pleasant, simple French provincial air. There's a bar along one wall, plus a refrigerated case and counter to the rear.

At breakfast, the French coffee was some of the most delicious I've ever had. As with all the "spécialités de la maison," my single egg arrived with fresh fruit—slices of banana, orange, and strawberries. Croissants can be ordered separately and are characteristically domestic, about three times the size of the Gallic variety. Apart from the usual egg preparations, Mousse Odile offers some exceptional choices, including a quiche du jour, waffles with crème anglaise (a delicious light custard sauce), and a variety of two- or three-egg omelets served with French bread, applesauce, and potatoes au gratin.

Luncheon choices are delicious: Cold plates include a marvelous pasta salad with smoked salmon and peas, and the céleri Victor with fresh cooked celery, egg slices, anchovies, capers, olives, and tomatoes. All cold plates are served with French bread and butter, and cost $5.75 to $6.75. Mousse Odile also offers Les Ficelles (12-inch-long Parisian sandwiches of roast lamb, chicken, or other meats), a great choice for picnicking with a bottle of wine or munching at the restaurant. The foregoing ($4.25 to $6.25) is finished with lettuce, tomato, pickles, and a Dijon sauce. If you happen to be in the mood for a hot lunch, there's a delicious white sausage made with pork and veal (boudin blanc), among other dishes, going from $7 to $9.75.

The main dining room for dinner adjoins the Brasserie. It, too, is very simple, but a bit more formal in its décor. Art deco lamps furnish soft lighting, and green plants against the walls and fresh flowers and candles on each table provide the finishing touches. Waiters with red bistro aprons over black trousers and white shirts attentively bustle about. For dinner, Mousse Odile offers such excellent choices as leg of lamb roasted with garlic and herbs (gigot provençal), several varieties of mushrooms served on a pastry shell (croûte aux champignons), and some truly exceptional specials that vary by the week, like Norwegian salmon poached in champagne and port wine. If you must have steak, there is filet mignon with pepper sauce and cognac. Entrees range from $13.25 to $17. Appetizers, from julienned celery root in mustard sauce to marinated mussels or warm smoked salmon with pasta, caviar, and chives, will add on another $4 to $6.25. A good selection of wines is available.

Mousse Odile is open Monday through Saturday for breakfast from 8 to 11:30am, for lunch from 11:30am to 2:30pm, and for dinner from 5:30 to 9pm.

For a pleasant spot to have breakfast, lunch, or an early dinner, try **Andersen's Danish Bakery and Restaurant,** 1106 State St., near Figueroa (tel. 805/962-5085). It's a small place, eminently suited to watching the passing parade or reading the day's paper. You'll spot it by the red-and-white Amstel umbrellas protecting the outside diners seated at the white tables on spanking-clean wrought-iron garden chairs. Even mid-November can be warm enough to eat out at 9am.

The food is delicious and nicely presented, portions are substantial, the coffee is outstanding, and the service is prompt and thoughtful. What more could one ask? Andersen's Goodmorning Breakfast ($3.95) includes bacon, eggs, cheese, fruit, jam (homemade), and bread baked on the premises. If you'd simply like fresh fruit, there's that too. Fresh strawberries with cream (when available) or a compote can be had for $2.95. The fresh fruit plate ($8.95) is enormous—certainly enough for two —and generally includes bananas, cheese, grapes, slices of orange and kiwis, bread, and a bit of ice cream.

For main meals, there's always the soup and sandwich of the day, as well as Andersen's quiche and liver pâté. Vegetarians can opt for an omelet with Danish Havarti cheese, a vegetable sandwich, a warm vegetable platter with a salad, or a cheese plate with fruit. For seafood lovers, there's the catch of the day—halibut, cod, trout—or the daily offering of Scottish smoked salmon with dill sauce ($8.95). A daily changing selection of European dishes may include Hungarian goulash, frikadeller (Danish meatballs), schnitzel, duckling, chicken with caper sauce, Danish meat loaf, and roast turkey with caramel sautéed potatoes. But if you yearn for smörgasbord, Andersen's is a first-rate choice. The mini-smörgasbord for two ($14) includes a collection of personal favorites, beginning with pickled herring, shrimp, smoked salmon, homemade liver pâté, cold cuts, and any number of warm surprises.

Luncheon and dinner choices range from $3.95 to $8.95, depending on the day's offerings. All orders can be prepared to go. Wine is available by the bottle or glass; beer is also served.

Andersen's is open daily: Monday through Saturday from 8am to 6pm, on Sunday from 9am.

You'll have to do a lot of searching up and down the coast to beat the first-class food served at **Brophy Bros. Clam Bar & Restaurant** in Santa Barbara, situated at the yacht basin and marina behind the breakwater off Harbor Way (tel. 805/966-4418). Heading west on Cabrillo Boulevard you'll pass the Castillo Street traffic light; then make a left at the *next* light, which is Harbor Way. A limited amount of parking is available next to the marina and yacht basin, but there's ample space in a lot on your left as you turn onto Harbor Way. Brophy Bros. is a short walk along the yacht basin, on the second floor of the small light-gray building ahead on your right.

Brophy Bros. serves fresh seafood plus two good meat selections, a Brophy Burger and a choice top sirloin. The seafood selection is first-rate, ranging from oysters and clams on the half shell, peel-and-eat shrimp, to oysters Rockefeller, to name just a few. Individual appetizers or clam-bar selections range from $5.50 to $9.50, with the exception of the oyster shooter at $1.30. As you might expect, there's also New England clam chowder or cioppino (California fish stew), plus an assortment of seafood salads and sandwiches.

For dinner, you might prefer half a fresh local lobster, stuffed and baked, then topped with hollandaise. On the other hand, scampi is one of the consistent favorites, sautéed with garlic, lemon, chablis, and a bit of tomato. The fish listed on the day's menu are always the best available from the day's fresh catch, perhaps albacore, swordfish, or thresher shark. The swordfish is, without exception, the best I have ever eaten in any restaurant in California—moist, beautifully seasoned, and delectably tender. If you prefer to try a bit of several choices, Brophy Bros. has a seafood platter as well as seafood skewers. Entrees cost $12 to $16 and are served with tossed green salad, coleslaw, and rice pilaf or fried potatoes. A good assortment of beers and wines is available.

Brophy Bros. is a fun, friendly, noisy, convivial scene of locals and tourists on almost any night (but not the place for a romantic, quiet dinner for two). The service is excellent and remarkably attentive in light of the crowd. And apart from the beauty of the food, it's hard to beat the view overlooking the fishing boats, sailboats, power launches—enough to turn any confirmed landlubber into a sea lover. If you want to avoid the rush, plan on eating either early (about 4pm) or late (after 9pm), especially on weekends, when you're competing with the locals for a table. On the other hand, you can eat seated at the bar—a good option during those hours when tables are at a premium. Brophy Bros. is one of the select California establishments I never miss when I'm in town. And in case you should wonder, dress is about as casual as you can get.

Brophy Bros. is open Sunday through Thursday from 11am to 10pm, on Friday and Saturday to 11pm. They don't take reservations, so expect at least an hour's wait during the usual dinner hours.

The **Palace Cafe**, 8 E. Cota, between State and Anacapa (tel. 805/966-3133), is simply stated a fine Cajun-Créole-Caribbean restaurant—busy, relaxed, and fun, but not for those who must have a quiet background for dining. Dress is casual whatever the hour. The café is divided into two rooms: As you enter, it's hot pink on the left and cool cream on the right. High ceilings, overhead fans, wood tables, bentwood chairs, posters, paintings, and murals sustain the Cajun look, with a French touch in the wine racks and streetlamps. While the standard restaurant table finish is often a few fresh flowers or a bottle of wine, the Palace Cafe features the ultimate symbol of Cajun cuisine—a huge bottle of McIlhenny Co. Tabasco. Service, like the clientele, is young—and very eager to please.

Before your first course or entree arrives, an assortment of delicious, hot, freshly baked muffins appears—molasses, jalapeño, etc. I have two favorite starters: the Cajun popcorn (Louisiana crawfish tails dipped in cornmeal buttermilk batter and flash-fried), served with creamy sherry wine sauce; and the Bahamian conch chowder, served with a pony of sherry. As for the main courses, emphasis is on seafood in its varied forms: Specialties of the house include the delicious Oysters Palace, baked in the half shell with a mixture of crawfish tails, mushrooms, green onions, and topped with a unique jalapeño beurre-blanc sauce; if "hot" is what you seek, the Louisiana Bar-B-Que shrimp, sautéed with the café's three-pepper butter sauce and served with white rice. But if you want meat, the Palace affords several good choices. You might try the blackened filet mignon served with a side of browned garlic butter, or the veal Acadiana (now and then it's rabbit), a pair of tender cutlets lightly floured, then flambéed with sherry and finished with an oyster-sherry cream sauce. The Palace also usually lists a pasta main course among the daily specials, and if there's a vegetarian in your party, the chef will prepare a unique vegetable platter to satisfy even the choosiest.

Should you still have space to accommodate dessert, the tart, tasty Key Lime pie is a good finish with coffee. On the other hand, if it happens to be on the night's menu, consider the Louisiana bread-pudding soufflé with whisky sauce, which must be ordered at the beginning of dinner to allow for adequate preparation time. It's a magnificent creation. The café has a good selection of California wines and several imports; beer is also available.

Starters cost $3.50 to $8.50; main courses, $12 to $22; desserts, $2.50 to $10. If you have a special place in mind for noshing or dinner, such as the beach, your boat, or a special rock, just telephone the Palace Cafe and they'll have your favorite dish ready in 15 minutes.

The restaurant is open nightly: Sunday through Thursday from 5:30 to 10pm for dinner, to 11pm for dessert and coffee; on Friday and Saturday to 11pm for dinner, to midnight for dessert and coffee. I suggest you make reservations, but if you do slip up, the restaurant will do its best to accommodate you. Dress is casual, whatever the hour.

Needless to say, in Spanish-style Santa Barbara, **Mexican eateries** abound. Many Santa Barbarans prefer the unpretentious Chicano haunts along State Street. They usually have a jukebox playing Spanish music, paintings on velvet of Mexican scenes, artificial flowers on the tables, and a warm, friendly, relaxed restaurant.

There are beautiful places to eat in Santa Barbara, elegant places, traditional places, some dripping with atmosphere, but there is one place where the food is head and shoulders above any of its kind between California and New York: **La Super-Rica Taqueria,** 622 N. Milpas St., between Cota and Ortega (tel. 805/963-4940). What makes it so? The cooking of the Gonzales family, and especially the incredible soft tacos. If you ever thought that a tortilla was a soft taco, you were wrong. La Super-Rica's soft tacos are as soft as a crêpe, about twice as thick (they have the texture of the blinis at the Russian Tea Room in Manhattan), and so delectable you could make a meal of these alone with the fresh salsa.

There's nothing grand about La Super-Rica except the food. The neighborhood was a barrio, before gentrification, and the restaurant remains unadorned, though the clientele is now a mix of the very affluent and the somewhat less so. (It has been reported that even Julia Child comes for the frijoles—a joyous mix of pintos, sausage, chiles, bacon, and herbs). The plates are paper, the cups Styrofoam, and the forks plastic, but the homemade soft corn tacos are thick enough to be leak-proof —just perfect for holding the delicious contents.

I had the taco de rajas—sautéed strips of chile pasilla with onions, melted cheese, and herbs on two soft tacos. Had I the appetite, I would also have ordered the alambre de pechuga, grilled chicken breast with bell peppers, onions, and mushrooms served on three corn tortillas. Those inclined to simpler fare might try the taco de costilla, tender strips of charbroiled top round served on two fresh homemade tortillas. Or if you're the type to go for it all, order the Super-Rica Especial, roasted chile pasilla stuffed with cheese and combined with charbroiled marinated pork, served with three soft tacos. For the vegetarian, the cordita de frijol fills thick corn tortillas with spicy ground beans. Prices range from $2 to $4.50. And to accompany the food, the assortment of Mexican beers is first-rate. Be sure to try the Chihuahua.

La Super-Rica Taqueria is open daily from 11am to 8:30pm. If you're thinking of going late, call first to check.

All right, so you want something a bit tonier and could go for some delicious New Mexican food. Head straight for the **Zia Café,** 421 N. Milpas St., at Reddick (tel. 805/962-5391), the culinary child of Douglas and Jane Scott of Santa Fe. Zia's New Mexican roots are immediately evident in the restaurant's sand-pink walls, light-wood chairs, chiles drying in the windows, desert prints—all very inviting and relaxed.

Zia's offers a wide variety of enchiladas, burritos, and tamales, served with red or green chile. The names may be familiar, but there's nothing commonplace about any of these house specialties. The chiles rellenos are prepared from two green-chile peppers stuffed with cheese and piñon nuts, dipped in batter, and deep-fried. And the green-chile enchilada, layered chicken and sour cream served with blue-corn tortillas, topped with sour cream and guacamole, is worthy of a three-page letter home. What's more, when you order a Zia specialty with chicken, you get a large portion of hot breast meat, enough to satisfy the appetite of the most voracious diner.

For breakfast, Zia's serves a flour tortilla with three scrambled eggs, covered with red or green chile, as well as huevos rancheros—blue-corn tortillas topped with two fried eggs and, again, your choice of red or green chile. I always opt for the green chile myself—Zia Café serves the best kind, that found along the southern Rio Grande. The New Mexican favorites range from $5.25 to $9; combination plates are $9 to $10.50. Beer and wine are available by the glass or the pitcher and liter, respectively. The service is as warm, friendly, and helpful as you would expect in a Santa Fe–style restaurant.

The Zia Café is open daily from 7:30am to 2:30pm and from 5 to 10pm.

Your Place, 22-A N. Milpas, near Mason (tel. 805/966-5151), has the look of a tourist restaurant, but a menu that belies its appearance. Though the restaurant has expanded to accommodate even more customers, it still holds a tank of exotic fish, carved screens, a serene Buddha, cloth butterflies, mirrored panels, and an impressive array of framed blowups of restaurant reviews.

Traditional Thai dishes, using distinctively fresh ingredients, are featured. The considerable menu includes appetizers, soups, salads, curries, vegetarian dishes, meat and poultry dishes, seafood entrees, noodle dishes, rice dishes—in fact, you may find the scope of the menu somewhat overwhelming (there are over 100 listings). If so, review the specialties of the house in the various categories. You might begin with Golden Wing, stuffed with ground chicken and bean thread, deep-fried and served with sweet plum sauce; or the Regal B.B.Q. spareribs marinated in a delicious "royal" sauce. Of the soup choices, I thoroughly enjoyed the tom kah kai—hot-and-sour chicken soup with coconut milk and mushrooms. You can order soup by the bowl or by the hot pot, which offers more than enough for two; however, if you're dining with food-sharing friends, order by the bowl and do some sampling. Among the meat and poultry dishes, the Siamese duckling, prepared with sautéed vegetables, mushrooms, and a ginger sauce, is difficult to resist. However, above all, the seafood specialties are a great treat. An excellent sizzling seafood platter arrives on a hot stove. Several of the dishes on the menu are spicy and may be ordered mild, medium, hot, or very hot.

Prices are moderate, entrees ranging from $5 to $12. The restaurant serves wine, sake, beer—including Thai beer and ale—plus such nonalcoholic drinks as hot ginger tea.

Your Place is open Tuesday through Thursday, as well as Sunday, from 11am to 10pm, on Friday and Saturday to 11pm.

Another spot you don't want to miss, especially if you yearn for barbecue, is **Woody's,** 229 W. Montecito St., at the beach side of U.S. 101 (tel. 805/963-9326). Woody's is woody all right—sort of "early cowpoke," with real wood paneling, post-and-beam construction, wood booths, and wood-plank floors. Jukeboxes over 25 years old play oldie classics such as "Stardust" with Artie Shaw's orchestra (you have to be over 55 to remember that one) and "Chattanooga Choo Choo" with Glen Miller. Woody's also has a touch of history as one of the gathering spots for the press who followed in the wake of the president from Santa Barbara.

When you enter, there's a counter ahead with all the menu items listed. Put in your order and you get a number; have a seat, your number is called, and you fetch the goodies. There are barbecued ribs (giant beef, meaty pork, or lean St. Louis style), baby back ribs, chicken, shrimp, ham, beef, turkey, duckling, a variety of burgers, and all sorts of combinations thereof, plus draft beer by the glass, jug, bucket, or the bottle. There's also chili by the bowl, plus fries, with or without a trip to a huge salad bar. If you're on a diet, but the rest of the family isn't, the lunch salad bar offers all you can eat for $3.75; at dinner it's $4.50. Kids get their own menu with items at kid prices. Also, Woody's will pack orders to go for a charge of 30¢ per order.

Lunch or dinner can cost anywhere from $3.50 to $12.50. A glass of draft beer ($1.50 for 16 ounces) comes in a Mason jar, the half-gallon frothy size shows up in a huge Kern jar ($4), and the bucket (over a gallon) is $8.50.

Woody's is open Monday through Saturday from 11am to 11pm, on Sunday to 10pm. There's another Woody's at 5112 Hollister Ave., near Patterson Ave. (tel. 805/967-3775). Both locations will deliver to Santa Barbara or Goleta for a $10 minimum order, plus $1 delivery charge.

Joe's Café, 536 State St., at Cota (tel. 805/966-4638), a Santa Barbara institution since 1928 (in a new location since 1984), offers good home-cooking, and people mob the place every night to dig in. The decor is as down-home as the food: red-and-white-checked tablecloths, captain's chairs, and mounted hunting trophies and photos of old Santa Barbara on the walls. Entrees, costing $7 to $15, and served with soup or salad, potato, pasta, or a vegetable, include rainbow mountain trout, home-style fried chicken, and a 12-ounce charbroiled sirloin steak. It's all prepared by chefs in big white hats working in an open kitchen. Sandwiches, pastas, and salads are also available (for $4 to $10), but there are no desserts. "We give them enough starch without it," explains the owner.

Joe's is open Monday through Thursday from 11am to 11:30pm, on Friday and Saturday to 12:30am, and on Sunday from 4 to 11:30pm. Reservations are suggested (no reservations on Saturday).

In the same category, but even more authentic and traditional, is **Arnoldi's Café**, 600 Olive St., off Cota (tel. 805/962-5394). Italian immigrants Joe and Hilda Arnoldi built the place themselves over 40 years ago. There's a mural in the back room of the mountains surrounding Lake Como, the Arnoldis' village in northern Italy, and a photo of the founding couple (also in Lake Como) over the mahogany bar. Candlelit tables are covered with red-and-white-checked cloths. A TV over the bar is always tuned to sporting events at a low-decibel level; there are three enclosed mahogany booths up front for intimate dining, and a bocce ball court out back where old-timers play on weekends. But most appealing is the wonderful jukebox of old Italian songs—Mario Lanza's "Be My Love," among other favorites.

And, of course, the food. All steaks are cut on the premises, ravioli and soups are homemade, and portions are huge. A 1½-pound T-bone, top sirloin, or New York steak is served with soup, salad, spaghetti or potatoes, and coffee for $15 to $18. Spaghetti or ravioli dinners, served with soup, salad, and coffee, run $9 to $12. For dessert there's vanilla ice cream or spumoni.

Arnoldi's is open daily except Wednesday from 5 to 11pm.

Piatti's Ristorante is an elegant country beauty to be found at 516 San Ysidro Rd., at East Valley Road in Montecito (tel. 805/969-7520), about a 10-minute drive from Santa Barbara.

As you walk up to the restaurant, there's an inviting patio neatly outfitted with white chairs, faux marble–topped tables, and handsome cream-colored umbrellas displaying the restaurant's name. All of which conveys the impression that dining will be a pleasant treat, and indeed it is.

The spacious interior has a polished country look. It's airy, comfortable, warm, relaxed. Everything from the small bar, on the left as you enter, to the exhibition kitchen will attract your eye. Minimurals, all in pastels, depict the things that make the restaurant and the region special—vegetables, sausages, pasta, beach scenes. Floors are of terra-cotta tile, and to one side a fireplace and pine sideboards add to the attractive rustic look. At the rear of the restaurant is another lovely patio (and garden), with overhead heating for outdoor dining.

Appetizers are exceptional, whether you are attracted to the eggplant rolled with goat cheese, the arugula and sun-dried tomatoes, the fresh sweetbreads with assorted mushrooms, or the homemade ravioli filled with white truffles and eggplant. For lunch you might consider one of the antipasti accompanied by a salad or the pizza of the day. But then review the entrees. There's a marvelous orecchiette Piatti—little pasta dumplings with cabbage, pancetta, Fontina cheese, garlic, and butter. Or the lasagna al pesto, with layers of fresh tomato pasta, pesto, grilled zucchini, sun-dried tomatoes, pinenuts, and cheeses—very rich, but very delicious. A specialty of the house is zuppa di pesce, seasonal fresh fish and shellfish cooked in a light tomato broth and served with grilled polenta. If pasta or fish is not to your taste, a tenderly grilled porterhouse steak served with Tuscan white beans may be more what you had in mind, or you can try the boneless breast of chicken prepared with fresh herbs.

Whether or not you have room for dessert, you should at least consider tiramisu—ladyfingers with mascarpone cheese, rum, and chocolate. For those counting every calorie, there is fresh seasonal fruit with or without gelato.

Entrees range from $8 to $18, but the average is about $12. Antipasto will add about $6 to the check, dessert about $4.

The restaurant has an excellent selection of wines—primarily California, plus a few Italian—and a full bar. The majority of wines are in the range of $18 to $32 per bottle. Select wines are available by the glass.

Piatti's is open Monday through Friday from 11:30am to 2:30pm for lunch and 5 to 10pm for dinner; Saturday and Sunday hours are noon straight through to 11pm. Reservations are advised.

IF YOU'RE HEADING NORTH . . .

If you're driving toward San Francisco from Los Angeles, or Santa Barbara and its environs, there simply is no alternative to the wild, crashing beauty of the ocean and the rugged cliffs along Calif. 1. And if you have the time, that's the way to go. But if precipitous views and the possibility of dirt or mud slides in the rainy season are not your cup of tea, U.S. 101 has its own sort of beauty. Between Goleta and Santa Maria, the countryside is probably what the Old West looked like if you ignore the utility poles, fences, and a few signs. Past San Luis Obispo, going north, are the voluptuous, gentle hills of California, muted beige with a soft matte finish, seductive in the warm sun. Then again, there are utility poles and signs staked out among the grazing cattle and free horses. A bit farther up, where the valley widens into another world, are the green metal dinosaurs bobbing up and down, draining the underground of its liquid resources. Whatever your point of view, and wherever you view it from, California is still among the virtuoso performances of creation.

9. Ojai Valley

It would be a shame to visit Santa Barbara and miss the nearby Ojai (pronounced "O-high") Valley, just 32 miles southeast along one of California's most gorgeous roads, Calif. 150. (It's also an easy day trip from Los Angeles.) The drive alone is scenic enough to justify the trip, but there's plenty to do in Ojai as well.

Traveling along 150 you'll pass **Lake Casitas,** a breathtakingly beautiful opalescent body of fresh water, with almost 100 miles of shoreline, that is a center for fishing (boats, bait, and such are available), boating, and camping (tel. 805/649-2233).

You can hike through the **Los Padres National Forest,** just north of town— over 500,000 acres of mountainous terrain, fields, valleys, and 140 miles of streams. There are hunting, camping, and picknicking throughout the forest.

There are more than 400 miles of riding and hiking trails in Ojai, not to mention an abundance of tennis and golf facilities. You can play tennis free at **Soule Park,** off Boardman Road (tel. 805/646-5633), and at **Libbey Park** in downtown Ojai across from the arcade. Golf is also offered at Soule Park's 18-hole, par-72 championship course; greens fees are $15 weekdays, $20 weekends and holidays; carts are $18.

Then there are antique shops, an art center, a historical museum, and many scenic drives, my favorite being to the spot where Ronald Colman viewed Shangri-la (it was Ojai Valley) in the movie *Lost Horizon* (go east on Ojai Avenue, then up the hill); a bench is provided, and there could be no more glorious spot for a picnic if you're so inclined.

You might also check out Ojai's shops. Most of the action is from Canada to Montgomery streets within an area extending one block south and two blocks north of quaint Ojai Avenue. It includes the Arcade on Ojai Avenue and two shopping centers, the **El Paseo Mall** and **Arcade Plaza.**

The **Ojai Valley Chamber of Commerce** is at 338 E. Ojai Ave. (P.O. Box 1134), Ojai, CA 93023, Calif. 150 (tel. 805/646-8126). It's open weekdays from 9:30am to 4:30pm, on Saturday from 10am to 5pm, and on Sunday to 4pm. Stop in for city maps, information, and a free copy of an informative booklet called *The Visitor's Guide to the Ojai Valley*, which lists scenic drives, galleries, and a calendar of events.

WHERE TO STAY

Ojai Valley Inn & Country Club, Country Club Road, Ojai, CA 93023 (tel. 805/646-5511, or toll free 800/422-6524), is the beauty of the valley, nestled in 200 acres of lush, green rolling hills, about 73 miles northwest of Los Angeles, 30 miles east of Santa Barbara, and 14 miles north of the ocean off Calif. 33. The Topa Topa mountain range, which surrounds the inn, was the setting for *Lost Horizon.*

The inn had a grand reopening in 1988; more than $35 million was spent to update the rooms, the facilities, the handsome adobe structures, and the 18-hole championship golf course (par 70). There are eight hard-surface tennis courts (four lit for night play), two pools (including a 60-foot lap pool), and a fitness center complete with exercise room, whirlpool, sauna, and steam room. Trails for joggers or bicycle riding (complimentary) connect the inn to the village. If you brought the kiddies, the inn considerately constructed a children's play area; during peak holiday periods, there are movies and western cookouts, plus a counselor to entertain them.

Today there are 218 lovely, spacious rooms and 15 suites, some with fireplaces, most with private terraces or balconies. The decor of the guest rooms is light and airy, with a southwestern flair in the colors and patterns of the spreads and drapes. Most rooms have sofas and all have writing desks. There are thoughtful touches like well-stocked minibars, coffee makers, plush terrycloth robes, hair dryers, and evening turndown service, as well as the usual color TVs (HBO), phones, etc. The terraces and patios open to expansive views of the 200 acres, the valley, and the magnificent Sierra Madre Mountains.

Dining facilities are first-rate, including the Vista Room, the Oak Grill and Terrace, the Club Bar, and terrace dining with a view of the mountains. New menus have been created for each of the restaurants to offer exceptional choices ranging from light fare, such as the coho salmon or gourmet vegetarian cuisine, to such heartier dishes as the grilled beef tenderloin served with a sun-dried-tomato béarnaise sauce. Also, 24-hour room service is available. For more details see the restaurant discussion following.

Room rates range from $180 to $240, single or double; one-bedroom suites, $295 to $350. Children of any age sharing the same room with their parents stay free. Maximum occupancy per room is four persons. For the golfers among you, there's a special three-day/two-night package that includes your room, two breakfasts, two dinners, plus unlimited golf-course play and free range balls during your stay (golf cart is extra). Otherwise, 18 holes (6,258 yards) will cost a guest $80, plus an additional per-player charge of $14 for a cart. For the use of tennis courts, guests pay $12 per hour. Other packages are also available.

Just up the road a bit farther is **Wheeler Hot Springs,** 16825 Maricopa Hwy. (that's Hwy. 33; P.O. Box 250), Ojai, CA 93023 (tel. 805/646-8131). It boasts not only the requisite mineral baths and massages expected at a spa (weekdays except Tuesday from 10am to 9pm, on Saturday from 9am to 10pm, and on Sunday from 9am to 9pm), but also has a terrific restaurant. After a tub and a rub, you can dig into a fine meal. The setting is rustic, with comfortable wood-and-wicker furniture and large fireplaces for the nippy days.

WHERE TO DINE

The emphasis all around is on health. The menu changes weekly to take advantage of fresh local herbs, fruits, nuts, seafood, and vegetables, but for dinner you might find fresh fettuccine with pine nuts and red pepper pesto; grilled local swordfish and leeks; or rosemary smoked lamb chops with an apricot port-wine sauce—priced at $13 to $19. Only wine and beer are served. The restaurant is open Thursday through Sunday for dinner, from 5 to 9:30pm, on Saturday and Sunday from 10am to 2pm for brunch. Be sure to reserve several days in advance for baths and meals.

One of Ojai's most beloved restaurants is the **Ranch House**, 102 Besant Rd., at South Lomita (tel. 805/646-2360). It was started by Alan and Helen Hooker, who came to Ojai in 1949, interested in the philosopher Krishnamurti. They rented an old ranch house, which they then turned into a boarding house. Within a year they had opened the restaurant. It's no longer in that first rented building, but in a beautiful location surrounded by an orchard, a bamboo thicket, and herb and flower gardens. It's a serene and tranquil place.

You can begin a meal here (now mostly à la carte) with an appetizer like chicken liver pâté, dig into a soup of curried mushrooms or Vietnamese chicken and crab, and then enjoy prime rib, crab voisin, chicken champagne, fresh fish, or a nut loaf. All entrees come with two fresh vegetables, and three kinds of fresh-baked breads, and cost $17 to $27. Be sure to leave room for one of the delicious desserts—rum trifle, applesauce cake, lime cheesecake, or ice cream with a choice of special Ranch House toppings: fudge, green ginger, pomegranate, fresh coconut.

If you can't get enough of the Ranch House while you're there, you can pick up a loaf of fresh-baked bread at the bakery or a copy of one of Alan Hooker's cookbooks. And the Ranch House has over 600 domestic and imported wines, for which they received the *Wine Spectator*'s Grand Award.

The Ranch House has dinner seatings Wednesday through Sunday at 6 and 8:30pm. Lunch is Wednesday through Saturday from 11:30am to 1:30pm and is served in the garden from May to September. Reservations requested.

Another charming eatery is **L'Auberge**, 314 El Paseo, at Rincon (tel. 805/646-2288). It occupies the ground floor of an old house; the dining room meanders through several small rooms and out to a delightful terrace with a lovely view. The decor is a pleasant lime and white. Owner Paul Franssen offers an array of crêpes (asparagus and mushroom, curried chicken) and omelets (cheese, mushroom, vegetable), along with salads and soups for brunch, all for under $10. Dinner can begin with an appetizer of snails in garlic butter, or smoked salmon. Entrees are varied from filet of sole amandine to frogs' legs to sweetbreads to a filet of beef with mushrooms, tomatoes, and madeira sauce. Entrees are all served with vegetables and bread, and cost $15 to $23. And for dessert there's white- or dark-chocolate mousse, cheesecake, or crème caramel.

L'Auberge is open for lunch on weekends from 11am to 2:30pm, and for dinner nightly except Tuesday from 5:30 to 9pm. Reservations are required for dinner.

Dining at the **Ojai Valley Inn & Country Club** (described above), on Country Club Road (tel. 805/646-5511), is a pleasant culinary adventure whether you choose to have a relaxed lunch or candlelit dinner in the Vista Dining Room or simply a casual bite in the Oak Grill or on the terrace.

The luncheon menu is varied enough to satisfy most any taste. There's an interesting selection of soups, sandwiches, and salads (such as the chicken with shiitake mushrooms accompanied by light noodles with sesame dressing), plus a choice of several burgers with interesting accompaniments, or a seafood dish such as delectably sautéed scallops, crab, and button mushrooms served in a light lobster sauce with buttered angel-hair pasta. At least one delicious vegetarian dish appears at lunch. Luncheon creations range from about $8.50 to $13.50.

Prix-fixe ($26) dinner at the Vista might start with baked mushroom caps stuffed with Cajun chicken, or the chilled crabmeat and chives vichyssoise. Choices from the entree list include an exceptional broiled Atlantic salmon filet with pesto hollandaise. Prime rib is accompanied by Yorkshire pudding; an outstanding alternative is the broiled mignonettes of beef tenderloin with peppercorn sauce.

As the Sunday buffet brunch ($25), the list of goodies is extensive: omelets, pasta, barbecue, all sorts of salads and desserts, plus an ice-cream sundae bar. To start, you might indulge yourself with a chicken-and-spinach terrine from a lengthy list of terrines and pâtés. Main events may include roast pork loin with raisins and apples, curried chicken breasts, or diced seafood and shrimp with lemon grass and ginger. Bring a hearty appetite.

Breakfast is served daily from 6 to 10:30am; lunch or brunch, from 11am to 2:30pm; dinner, from 6 to 10pm. Reservations are suggested for lunch and dinner.

LOS ANGELES

How can one define the enigma that is Los Angeles? It's an unrelated string of suburbs in search of a city; a megalopolis sprawl connected by 1,500 or so miles of slowing freeway; a promised land of sea, sand, and year-round sunshine filtering through the smog; once decadent playground of the rich; stamping ground of the stars; the most status-conscious city in the U.S.; a second home to New Yorkers who dismiss the rest of the country as "the flyovers"; headquarters for every kind of kook, cultist, and spiritual movement; a haven for the eccentric and yet a bastion of political middle-of-the-roadism. And finally, Los Angeles is about not caring what it's all about.

The variety of life-styles, activities, and places to see, and experience is mindboggling. Don't waste time trying to understand this pleasure-oriented paradox. Forget your preconceptions, relax, enjoy. Let L.A. work its magic on you, and soon you'll be right at home in fantasyland.

There's so much to do, your only problems might be having time to do it all, where to start, how to get there, and how long it will take.

You'll want to tour the studios—thrill to the feigned attack of King Kong and shake through a simulated major earthquake . . . see Johnny tape a "Tonight Show" . . . show off your new string bikini (or perfect unclothed body) on the beach . . . go shopping in chic Beverly Hills . . . gape at the homes of the stars . . . bring the kids to, or be a kid at, Disneyland, Magic Mountain, etc. . . . . eat homemade fudge, Belgin waffles, tacos, gourmet pizza, or shrimp Louie at the international stalls in Farmers Market . . . have a drink and a celebrity gawk at the Polo Lounge . . . match your footprints with those of over 200 stars at Mann's Chinese Theatre . . . see hit shows at the Music Center or big-name entertainment at the Hollywood Bowl.

That doesn't begin to skim the surface of visitor attractions that you'll be reading about in this chapter. They're seemingly endless, and they're scattered all over the place. First item on the agenda is to get a good map and orient yourself. Second is

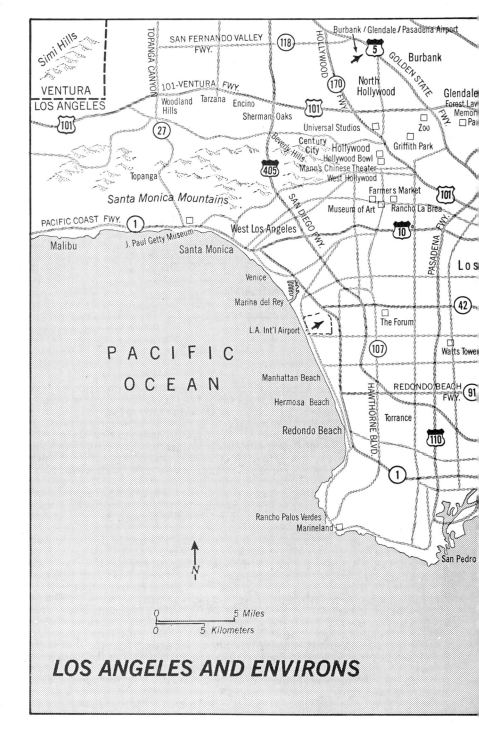

LOS ANGELES AND ENVIRONS

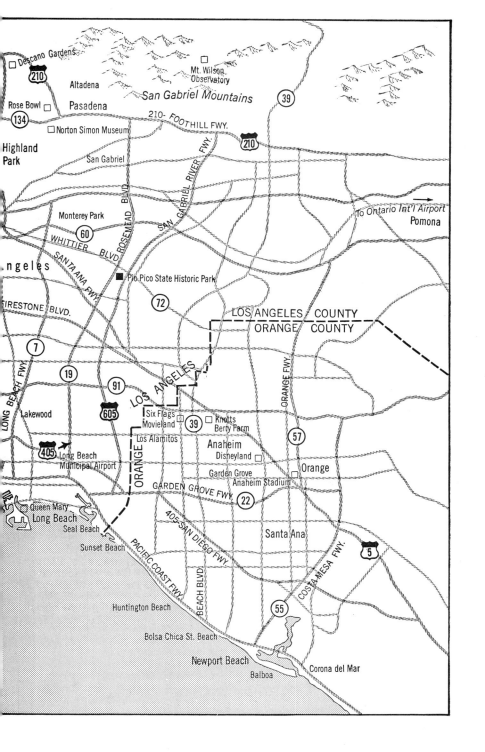

to get a copy of the Sunday edition of the *Los Angeles Times* and take out the "Calendar" section to see what's going on that week. And third, plan out your sightseeing priorities.

1. Getting There

AIRLINES

Some 36 international carriers, and all major domestic carriers, serve the Los Angeles International Airport (LAX)—third largest in the world in terms of traffic. Domestic carriers include **Alaska Airlines** (tel. 213/628-2100, or toll free 800/426-0333), **American Airlines** (tel. 213/935-6045, or toll free 800/433-7300), **Delta Air Lines** (tel. 213/386-5510), **Northwest Airlines** (tel. 213/380-1511, or toll free 800/225-2525, 800/252-2168 in California), **Piedmont Airlines** (tel. 213/977-4937, or toll free 800/251-5720), **Southwest Airlines** (tel. 213/485-1221, or toll free 800/531-5601), **Trans World Airlines** (tel. 213/484-2244, or toll free 800/221-2000), **United Airlines** (tel. 213/772-2121), and **USAir** (tel. 213/410-1732, or toll free 800/428-4322).

AIRPORTS

The **Los Angeles International Airport (LAX)** is situated at the far-western end of the city. If you're driving, two main roads will get you there: Century Boulevard, which runs east-west, and Sepulveda Boulevard, running north-south. The San Diego Freeway (I-5)—it's called that even in Los Angeles—and I-405 have exits to West Century Boulevard leading to the airport. Going north on Sepulveda Boulevard will take you directly to the airport; going south, you should turn right on 96th Street to get to the airport entrance. The city's RTD bus lines go to and from LAX; for the schedule and running times, call RTD airport information (tel. 213/646-8021). Free Blue, Green, and White shuttle buses ("Airline Connections") stop in front of each ticket building. Special handicapped-accessible minibuses are also available. If you need more information, call 213/646-8021.

Unless you plan to stay at one of the hotels near the airport, a taxi is *not* the preferred mode of transportation to your hotel or motel. Just about everything is miles away from the airport and the cost of taking a taxi can be more like a down payment on one. If you must take a taxi, confirm the price to your destination *before* getting in. Airport shuttles and commercial commuter vans provide direct airport service to most major hotels. Some smaller hotels also have private shuttles for their patrons; ask about transportation at the time you make your hotel or motel reservations.

Although LAX is the largest by far, in terms of size, service, and air traffic, Los Angeles is surrounded by airports. To the north is the **Burbank-Glendale-Pasadena Airport,** 2627 N. Hollywood Way, Burbank (tel. 818/840-8847); to the south are the **Long Beach Municipal Airport,** 4100 Donald Douglas Dr., Long Beach (tel. 213/421-8293), and the **John Wayne Airport,** 19051 Airport Way North, Anaheim (tel. 714/834-2400); and to the east is the **Ontario International Airport,** Terminal Way, Ontario (tel. 714/983-8282). Most of the smaller airports are for charters, commuter lines, or private planes.

Airport Buses

Don't just hop in a cab at the airport unless you don't mind spending a small fortune getting to your hotel. **Super Shuttle** (tel. 213/338-1111) has minivans that will take you from LAX to hotels or private residences within the L.A. area,

Beverly Hills, West L.A., etc. To hotels, the fare ranges from about $10 to $16; to private residences, it averages about $17 to $27. Give them the location and they'll give you a more specific price. To go to LAX on the Super Shuttle, you need a reservation at least one day in advance.

Airport Transportation (tel. 714/558-1411, or toll free 800/854-8171, 800/422-4267 in California) serves Orange County. The importance of Orange County is that, among other things, that's where Anaheim is, and Disneyland is in Anaheim. The fare to the Anaheim area is $12 per person from the airport. The fare to the Newport Beach area is $17.

Logo Express (tel. 213/641-0044) serves Pasadena and nearby areas. Their door-to-door rate is $15 per person, or $10 to a hotel.

Parking

Parking at LAX can be trying at best and utterly maddening on holidays with the added traffic and crowded lots. Parking in the terminal lot is $10 a day, which in a week or two runs up to a notable sum (but admittedly less than parking in a Manhattan garage). A thrifty alternative is **Auto Air Porter,** 2222 E. Imperial Hwy., between Douglas and Nash (tel. 213/640-1111, or toll free 800/752-3339 for about 50 miles around the airport). Rates are $5.50 per day for 10 days, $4.50 for each additional day. You are delivered by van from the facility to the terminal at LAX and picked up when you call on return. It's a 24-hour service. Auto Air Porter suggests that you arrive at their facility at least one hour before your departure time.

TRAINS

Amtrak service to and from San Diego in the south and Oakland and Seattle in the north, as well as points in between, operates out of the station at 800 N. Alameda (tel. 213/624-0171).

BUSES

The **Greyhound/Trailways Bus System** serves most cities in California. In Los Angeles, the main terminal is downtown at 208 E. 6th St., at Los Angeles Street (tel. 213/620-1200).

---

2. Getting Your Bearings

A glance at the map will show you that the so-called center of Los Angeles lies east of the Pacific Ocean (about 12 miles), on a direct line with the coastal town of Santa Monica. This is the **downtown** business and shopping center of the city. Greater Los Angeles radiates out from the downtown area in an ever-increasing number of suburbs. A vast network of freeways links the separate districts to each other and to downtown, and the city as a whole to the state.

Hollywood, which is on every tourist's itinerary, is just northwest of the downtown Civic Center via the Hollywood Freeway (U.S. 101). **Beverly Hills** adjoins Hollywood on the southwest. You can reach Beverly Hills by taking the Hollywood Freeway from the Civic Center and turning off Santa Monica Boulevard.

Connecting the downtown area and Beverly Hills, then continuing on through **Westwood** en route to the **Santa Monica** shoreline beaches, is **Wilshire Boulevard,** L.A.'s main drag. As Wilshire enters Beverly Hills, it intersects **La Cienega Boulevard.** The portion of La Cienega that stretches north from Wilshire to Santa Monica Boulevard is known (for obvious reasons) as **Restaurant Row.**

The next boulevard to the north of Santa Monica is **Sunset Boulevard** in Hollywood. The next section on Sunset between Laurel Canyon Boulevard and La Brea

Avenue is the famed **Sunset Strip.** Above that is equally famous **Hollywood Boulevard.**

Farther north via the Hollywood Freeway is the **San Fernando Valley.** Here you'll find **Universal City;** a right turn on the Ventura Freeway takes you to beautiful downtown **Burbank.**

Venice, the yacht-filled harbors of **Marina del Rey,** and the **Los Angeles International Airport** (LAX) are all south along the shore from Santa Monica.

3. Getting Around

It's a theory of mine that one of the reasons behind the great interest in things spiritual and mystical in L.A. is that if residents could only achieve astral projection, they could finally get somewhere without a car. Los Angeles is car city. Where else can you find drive-in churches where the traditional response of "Amen" has been replaced by "honk, honk"?

Although there is bus service, everything is so spread out you usually have to make three transfers to get where you're going and wait at least half an hour at each change. Whereas the elaborate network of freeways that connects this incredible urban sprawl will whisk you to your destination in a somewhat reasonable amount of time—unless, of course, it's rush hour, when streams of traffic can sit around for hours with nothing to do. Do your homework with a good map and you'll find getting around easy, if not always pleasant—the freeways are not what you'd call scenic routes. The most interesting things to look at are all the Rolls-Royces, Mercedeses, and Porsches driving along with you. If you haven't figured it out by now, always allow more time to get to your destination than you've been told it will take.

CAR RENTALS

The sights and restaurants are so far apart here, you'll probably do best to seek an unlimited-mileage arrangement, or at least one with sufficient free mileage to make your trip economical. On the freeways, those few "cents per mile" tend to mount rapidly into dollars. See the "Traveling Within California" section of Chapter I for some general advice about car rentals.

Car rentals of specific-size vehicles, including vans, are usually easier to obtain from the big car-rental companies. Each of the companies below has an office at Los Angeles International Airport, the Burbank and Long Beach airports, as well as throughout Greater Los Angeles: **Avis** (tel. toll free 800/331-1212), **Budget** (tel. toll free 800/527-0700), **Hertz** (tel. toll free 800/654-3131).

If you need something special to create a memorable impression, Budget Rent-A-Car has a subspecialty of renting out exotic cars. Budget has offices for rentals of these beauties in Beverly Hills (tel. 213/274-9173), Marina del Rey (tel. 213/821-8200), and on La Cienega Boulevard in Los Angeles (tel. 213/659-3473). Be aware that the cost per day may astound you and may require incredible credit-card deposits, but consider that you may be sitting where a "star" sat.

BUSES

If you don't have a car, you can reach most of the sightseeing centers in Greater Los Angeles by bus (take a good book along to while away ride time, something like *War and Peace*).

The network of local and express buses is operated by the Southern California Rapid Transit District (RTD). Their **ticket office** is at 419 S. Main St., Los Angeles, CA 90001 (tel. 213/626-4455), where you can obtain maps and schedules from the rack, or by writing or calling. You can also call them for detailed information on a given trip from point to point (for instance, "I'm in Burbank and I want to get to Wilshire and Santa Monica boulevards").

The office provides a pamphlet outlining about two dozen self-guided RTD tours, including visits to Universal Studios, Beverly Hills, and Disneyland.

There's also a convenient RTD office in ARCO Towers, 515 S. Flower St., adjacent to the Visitors and Convention Bureau.

The basic bus fare is $1.10 for all local lines. Express lines utilizing freeways have higher fares. Those visitors over age 65 (Medicare card must be shown to driver) qualify for a 55¢ fare during off-peak hours. Drivers carry no change; exact fare is required. In addition, for those riders who travel into counties other than Los Angeles (for instance, to Disneyland) there are extra charges.

If you're staying in Los Angeles for a period of time, you should consider the economical monthly passes: $42 to $102 (depending on the distance you're traveling) for unlimited riding on all local lines, $10 for the same privilege for senior citizens.

L.A.'s (Department of Transportation) minibuses run every 5 to 10 minutes in the downtown area of Los Angeles, covering such areas as Olvera Street, the Civic Center, Chinatown, Pershing Square, the garment district, and Occidental Center. Fare is 30¢ (exact change, please). Hop on, get off whenever you want to visit or shop, then catch another bus later, paying only another 30¢. There are marked minibus stops along the route.

TRAINS

In June 1990, the first of a network of commuter rail lines opened with **Blue Line** service from 7th and Flower Stations in downtown L.A. to 1st Street station in Long Beach. The trip takes 55 minutes with southbound trains leaving from L.A. from 5:35am to 8pm and northbound trains leaving from Long Beach from 5:30am to 6:55pm every 10 to 20 minutes. The regular fare is $1.10 for seniors and the disabled 55¢, and the blind and children under 5 free. For information, call 213/626-4455 or 639-6800.

TAXIS

You don't hop cabs as blithely in L.A. as you do in other cities—it seems the fare for any given ride is always at least $10. L.A. cabs charge $2 at flag drop (for the first two-tenths of a mile) and $1.50 a mile after that. Should you need one, call **Independent Cab Co.** (tel. 213/385-8294), **Checker Cab Co.** (tel. 213/624-2227), or **Yellow Cab Co.** (tel. 213/221-2331).

---

4. Los Angeles Fast Facts

For easy reference, here are some basic facts to help you orient yourself to the sprawling metropolis in the sun.

AREA CODES: Like "all Gaul," Los Angeles will be divided into three parts (by the telephone company) as of February 1, 1992. Area code **213** will continue to include most of downtown Los Angeles and surrounding communities such as Hollywood and Montebello. Area code **818** encompasses much of the San Fernando Valley and, as of this moment, Glendale and Pasadena. The new code **(310)** will include Los Angeles International Airport (LAX), plus the western, coastal, southern, and eastern portions of the county. Communities such as West Los Angeles, San Pedro, and Whittier will be part of the 310 area code. If you are in one area code and wish to call another, you must begin with the prefix "1", then dial the area code. All of which is attributed to the fact that Pacific Bell is running out of telephone numbers. Should you dial a number with the wrong area code, an operator will intervene and provide the correct code.

BABY-SITTERS: If you're staying at one of the larger hotels, the concierge can usually recommend organizations to call. Be sure to check on the hourly cost (which

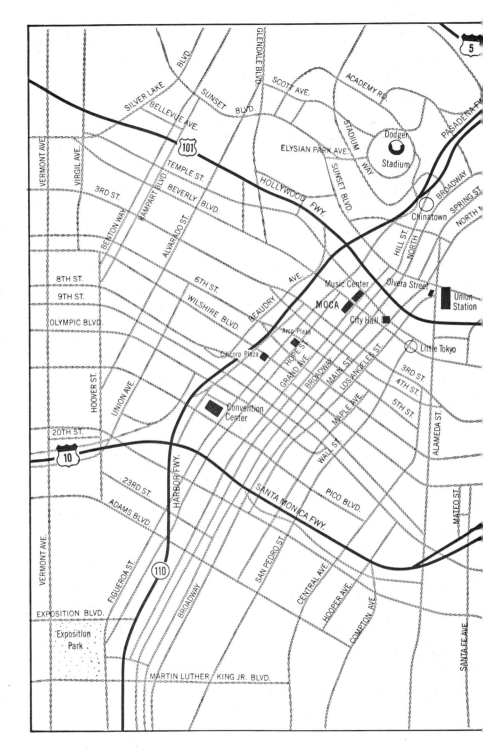

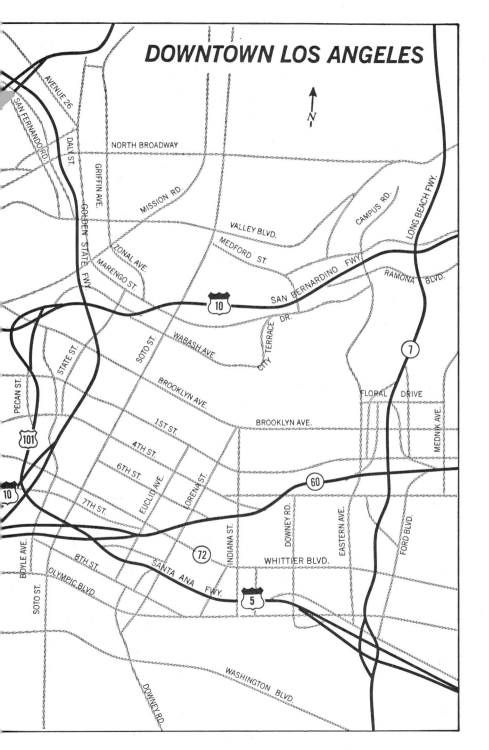

may vary depending on the day of the week and the time of day), as well as on any additional expenses such as transportation and meals for the sitter. You also might try the **Baby Sitters Guild**, P.O. Box 3418, 1622 Bank St., So Pasadena, CA 91031 (tel. 213/469-8246 from Los Angeles and west, or 818/441-4293 from the San Gabriel Valley); they've been in business since 1948. The Guild (licensed by the State of California) provides mature, bonded baby-sitters on call 24 hours.

BANKS: Banks are generally open Monday through Friday from 10am to 3pm, and some are open on Saturday to noon. However, if you need to cash a check, your hotel may be your best resource, depending on the amount involved.

CHARGE CARDS: Not all restaurants, stores, or shops in California accept all major credit cards, and some accept none. Therefore, check first if you expect to use plastic for a large expenditure—it can save annoyance and possibly some embarrassment. If you're visiting from another state, you may be surprised to discover that in California you can charge packaged liquor purchases.

CLIMATE: From May through October, weather in Los Angeles warrants light-weight summer clothing, with a sweater or lightweight jacket for the occasional cool evening or supercool restaurant. November through April, temperatures are cooler and generally require spring-weight clothing and a raincoat. However, even during the cooler months, it's not unusual to have a week or more of summerlike weather. (See the "Average Monthly Temperatures" chart on page 5.)

CRIME: As in all cities with a large influx of tourists from within the U.S. and abroad, crime is a problem. To avoid an unhappy incident or an end to what might have been an enjoyable trip, use discretion and common sense. Take traveler's checks and leave your valuables in the hotel safe. It would also be wise to review the "Crime" section of "California Fast Facts" in Chapter I for more safety tips.

CURRENCY EXCHANGE: Foreign-currency exchange services are provided by the **Bank of America** at 555 S. Flower St., third floor, (tel. 213/228-2721). **Deak International,** at 677 S. Figueroa (tel. 213/624-4240), also offers foreign-currency exchange services. Deak also has offices at the Hilton Hotel Center, 900 Wilshire Blvd. (tel. 213/624-4221).

DENTISTS: Hotels usually have a list of dentists should you need one. For other referrals, you can call the **Los Angeles Dental Society** (tel. 213/481-2133).

DOCTORS: Here, again, hotels usually have a list of doctors on call. For referrals, you can contact the **Los Angeles Medical Association** (tel. 213/483-6122).

DRIVING: I refer you to this heading under "California Fast Facts" in Chapter I. Navigating your automobile through the web of Los Angeles freeways can be a somewhat daunting experience, so I urge you to read this section.

EARTHQUAKES: Again, see the "California Fast Facts" section in Chapter I.

EMERGENCIES: For police, fire, highway patrol, or life-threatening medical emergencies, dial **911.**

EVENTS AND FESTIVALS: You can obtain a listing of special events in Los Angeles at the **Visitors Information Center,** downtown at 695 S. Figueroa St. (between Wilshire and 7th), Los Angeles, CA 90017 (tel. 213/689-8822), Monday through Saturday from 8am to 5pm; or in Hollywood at the Janes House, Janes House Square, 6541 Hollywood Blvd. (tel. 213/461-4213), Monday through Saturday from 9am to 5pm. The other option is to write to the downtown center at the above address.

For up-to-the-minute happenings, the Sunday edition of the *Los Angeles Times* has a "Calendar" section covering entertainment, the arts, studio gossip, museums, etc. (for Las Vegas and Laughlin as well as Los Angeles).

FOOD: There are lots of places to eat in L.A. for less than $5; the problem is that you can starve in the time it takes you to get from one to the other. On the other hand, you can spend as much as $75 per person for a meal, without wine or even valet parking. Los Angeles is a world with restaurants for everyone, more than you could believe would prosper—Chinese, Italian, Indian, American, Japanese, Moroccan, French, French-California, California-French, Japanese-French, elegant pizza, Greek, Czech, Jewish, Tuscan, vegetarian, Vietnamese, Lithuanian, Mexican, etc. And the food ranges from good to superb. I've tried to select some of the best in all price categories.

Not all restaurants are open daily. If you're planning an evening at one I haven't listed, call first and also ask if reservations are necessary. Check to see if they take plastic—not all the better restaurants do, and not all take every major credit card.

HAIR SALONS: If your hotel does not have a hair salon on the premises, they're usually glad to make a recommendation.

HOLIDAYS: Obvious holiday occasions and dates of major conventions are not the times to try for reservations on short notice. If you're not certain what events are in the offing, and you have specific vacation dates in mind, send for the annual list or call the Visitors Information Center—see "Events and Festivals," above.

HOSPITALS: To find a hospital near you, quickly turn to the Community Access pages at the front of the Pacific Bell *Yellow Pages*. There you will find a list of hospitals, with their locations superimposed on a map of the city. This is an especially useful reference in Los Angeles because the city is quite spread out and you probably won't know locations by address.

INFORMATION: The **Los Angeles Visitors Information Centers** are located in downtown Los Angeles and Hollywood. Addresses and phone numbers are given above under "Events and Festivals."

Beverly Hills has its own **Visitors and Convention Bureau** at 239 S. Beverly Dr. (tel. 213/271-8174, or toll free 800/345-2210).

LAUNDRY AND DRY CLEANING: Any one of the major hotels can take care of these services for you, but allow two days for the job.

LIQUOR LAWS: Liquor and grocery stores can sell packaged alcoholic beverages between 6am and 2am. Most restaurants, nightclubs, and bars are licensed to serve alcoholic beverages during the same hours. The legal age for purchase and consumption is 21, and proof of age is required. As I mentioned under "Charge Cards," above, in California you can purchase packaged liquor with your credit card; however, most stores usually have a minimum dollar amount for charging.

NEWSPAPERS: The *Los Angeles Times* is distributed throughout the county. Its Sunday edition has a "Calendar" section, which is an excellent and interesting guide to the entire world of entertainment in and around Los Angeles, the arts, what's doing, who's doing it, what's coming, and new restaurants, among other things.

RELIGIOUS SERVICES: Los Angeles has hundreds of churches and synagogues, and at least 100 denominations, formal and informal. Should you be seeking out a house of worship, your hotel desk person or bell captain can usually direct you to the nearest church of most any denomination. If not, the Pacific Bell *Yellow Pages* can usually provide the location and, frequently, the times of the services.

SPORTS (SPECTATOR):   Los Angeles has two major-league baseball teams— the **Los Angeles Dodgers** (tel. 213/224-1400) and the **California Angels** (tel. 714/937-6700); two NFL football teams—the **L.A. Raiders** (tel. 213/322-3451) and the **L.A. Rams** (tel. 714/937-6767); two NBA basketball teams—the **L.A. Lakers** (tel. 213/674-6000) and the **L.A. Clippers** (tel. 213/748-0500); and an ice hockey team, the **L.A. Kings** (tel. 213/419-3182). The Dodgers play at Dodger Stadium, located at 1000 Elysian Park, near Sunset Boulevard. The Angels and the Rams call Anaheim Stadium home at 2000 S. State College Blvd., near Katella Avenue in Anaheim. The Lakers and now the superb L.A. Kings hold court (or ice, as the case may be) in the Forum at 3900 W. Manchester Blvd., at Prairie Avenue in Inglewood. And these days the Raiders do their dirty work in the L.A. Memorial Coliseum, 3911 S. Figueroa, with the Clippers nearby in the L.A. Sports Arena, 3939 S. Figueroa.

And finally, there's the sport of kings. Lovely **Hollywood Park racetrack,** 1050 S. Prairie Ave. in Inglewood (tel. 213/419-1500), has thoroughbred racing from April through July and November through December. A computer-oriented screen offers a view of the back stretch and stop-action replays of photo finishes. There's also a children's play area with modern playground equipment and an electronic games area. Post time is 1:30pm Wednesday through Sunday. **Santa Anita racetrack,** 285 W. Huntington Dr. in Arcadia (tel. 818/574-7223), is one of the most beautiful tracks in the country and has thoroughbred racing from October through mid-November and December through late April. Weekdays, the public is invited to watch morning workouts from 7:30 to 9:30am. Santa Anita also has a children's playground. Post time is 1pm. Finally, there's **Los Alamitos Race Course,** 4961 Katella Ave. in Los Alamitos (tel. 213/431-1361 or 714/995-1234), featuring quarter-horse racing from mid-November through January and May through mid-August; harness racing is held from late February through April.

STORE HOURS: Stores are usually open Monday through Saturday from 10am to 6pm; closed on Sunday.

TAXES: California state sales tax is 7¼%; hotel tax is 12%.

USEFUL TELEPHONE NUMBERS: You can obtain **weather information** for Los Angeles at 213/554-1212, the **time** at 213/853-1212, and information on **local highway conditions** at 213/626-7231. For **nonemergency police matters,** phone 213/485-2121 or, in Beverly Hills, 213/550-4951.

Dial 411 for **directory assistance** and 800/555-1212 to obtain telephone numbers of establishments that have **toll-free service.**

---

5. Hotels

Generally, when you look for a hotel you try to choose one with a convenient location. In sprawling Los Angeles, however, a convenient location is a very limited concept. Nothing is convenient to everything and wherever you stay you can count on doing a lot of driving to somewhere else.

The most elegant digs are, for the most part, in Beverly Hills and Bel Air. Hollywood is probably the most central place to stay; downtown is convenient for businesspeople and offers proximity to many cultural attractions; Santa Monica and Marina del Rey are right on the beach; and families with kids might want to head straight to Anaheim or Buena Park.

I've listed more deluxe and upper-bracket hostelries here than in other chapters —there are simply more of them in star-studded L.A. than in other cities. Hotel listings are broken down by area, since L.A. communities are so far-flung, then further divided into the following categories: deluxe, upper bracket, moderately priced, and budget. All listings have been measured by the strict yardstick of value —the most for your money.

I'll lead off the hotel survey with glamorous—

BEVERLY HILLS

Deluxe

The **Regent Beverly Wilshire,** 9500 Wilshire Blvd. (at Rodeo Drive), Beverly Hills, CA 90210 (tel. 213/275-5200, or toll free 800/421-4354), the grande dame of Beverly Hills hotels, has cosseted international royalty, the rich, the incredibly rich, film and TV celebrities, stage personalities, U.S. presidents, corporate giants, and impresarios. It also houses Tiffany and Buccellati.

April 1990 celebrated the completion of a magnificently redone Regent Beverly Wilshire, which retains the very posh tone that has always been part of her beauty and charm. The spacious lobby reflects that elegance with its French Empire (or Directoire) furnishings, flooring of French and Italian marbles, restored bronze and crystal chandelier, hand-wrought sconces, and two paintings by Verhoven.

El Camino Real, the Beverly Wilshire's private street of cobblestones and gaslights which separates the Beverly and Wilshire wings, leads to your disembarking area. Following arrival, you're met by a guest-relations officer and personally escorted to your accommodations. No need to clutter up the lobby with luggage—it is recorded by computer and arrives by a separate lift.

Guest rooms, for the most part, are larger than those in the average hotel. Many Wilshire Wing rooms, in fact, have nearly doubled in size, while those on the Beverly side overlooking the pool are more compact but very comfortable with terraces at pool level and balconies above. All blend light and space with four lovely color themes—wheat, gentle rose, soft peach, and delicate celery green—and are beautifully appointed with a mix of period furniture. Each guest room has three phones, with a two-line phone on the desk, and there is cable color TV in every living room, bedroom, and bath. Special double-glazed windows ensure absolute quiet. As for the baths, they are the ultimate in luxury. All are lined in marble, with deep soaking tubs, separate glass-enclosed showers just about large enough for a small cocktail party, a large vanity, and lighting that totally surrounds you. Amenities include fresh flowers in each room, plush deep-pile white bathrobes, white scuffs, scales, hair dryers, and toiletries created for the hotel. There is steward service on every floor (a concept imported from Regent's Hong Kong property), as well as 24-hour concierge service.

There are three places to dine in the hotel. The Cafe, on the Wilshire and Rodeo Drive corner, specializes in classic down-to-earth meals. It's an elegant, updated version of the old-fashioned soda fountain, with black-and-white-striped marble floors and Roman shades; floor-to-ceiling windows make it a great spot for people-watching or simply collapsing after a hard day of shopping on Rodeo Drive. This is where you'll find Belgian waffles smothered in berries, lox and eggs, blintzes, a sampler of minisandwiches (including a hot dog, Reuben, and hamburger), several excellent salads, chili, and a choice of daily special entrees. The Cafe also has a superb fountain menu. Open from 6am to midnight.

The Lobby Lounge is an elegant European-style salon for tea (served from 3 to 5pm), light menus, late-night dinner fare, and cocktails—a place "to be seen." There's live entertainment in the evening.

The Dining Room is a beauty—done in Directoire style, with lush woods and soft fabrics. Luncheon offers a lengthy list of appetizers, soups, sandwiches, salads, and entrees, served from 11:30am to 3pm. For lunch my choices (in season) are the cold poached salmon and the Texas blue crab omelet with lobster sauce. For dinner, given a substantial appetite, I'd begin with the black mussel soup or angel-hair pasta with basil and tomato and move on to the grilled veal medallions with wild mushrooms and tarragon. Assuming that you have the zest for it all, dinner for two will range from $90 to $110, without wine. The Dining Room is open from 11:30am to 10:30pm. Reservations are suggested.

As for the other activities in and around the Beverly Wilshire, you might fling yourself into the fitness salon, where you can work out on all sorts of dynamic equipment while you watch the sensible folk relax in one of the two hot tubs (each with a different temperature) or lounge and snack in the sun by the Italian villa–style pool. Following your workout, you might opt for a stretch in the sauna or steam room, a massage, and for a final touch, a facial, manicure, and pedicure.

For single or double occupancy, the rate for superior rooms is $255; for deluxe rooms, $325; for one- and two-bedroom suites, $400 to $1,500; for the Presidential Suite, $3,000. There is no charge for children 14 years and under when they occupy existing bedding in the same room as their parents. Baby cribs are available at no charge. A chauffeured limousine or sedan one way from LAX is approximately $90, including tax and gratuity; scheduled airport van is $12 per person.

The **Beverly Hills Hotel and Bungalows,** 9641 Sunset Blvd. (at Rodeo Drive), Beverly Hills, CA 90210 (tel. 213/276-2251), is the stamping ground of millionaires and maharajas, jet-setters and movie stars. There are hundreds of anecdotes about this famous hotel and the world's most glamorous bar on its premises, the Polo Lounge. For years Howard Hughes maintained a complex of bungalows, suites, and rooms here, using some of the facilities for an elaborate electronic-communications security system and keeping a food-taster housed in one room! Perhaps this is the only hotel in the world that would provide him with such services as 23 kadota figs (24 would have been angrily returned) in the middle of the night. Years ago Katharine Hepburn did a flawless dive into the pool—fully clad in her tennis outfit, shoes and all; Dean Martin and Frank Sinatra once got into a big fistfight with other Polo Lounge residents. And in 1969 John Lennon and Yoko Ono checked into the most secluded bungalow under assumed names, then stationed so many armed guards around their little hideaway that discovery was inevitable. So it goes. The stories are endless and concern everyone from Charlie Chaplin to Madame Chiang Kai-shek.

What attracts them all? For one thing, each other. And of course you can't beat the service—not just the catering to such eccentricities as a preference for bear steak, but little things like being greeted by your name every time you pick up the phone. Further, the Beverly Hills Hotel is a beauty, its green and pink stucco buildings set on 12 carefully landscaped and lushly planted acres. Paths lined with giant palm trees wind throughout, and the privacy of each veranda and lanai is protected by flowering and leafy foliage. (It was the backdrop for Neil Simon's play *California Suite*.). Each of the 325 accommodations (which include 21 bungalows and garden suites) is custom-designed in the best Hollywood tradition, with tropical overtones—they're gorgeous. Of course, you can count on every amenity in your room.

In addition to the world-famous Polo Lounge, rendezvous headquarters of international society for almost 40 years, the Beverly Hills also has the Loggia and Patio (which adjoin the Polo Lounge) for breakfast and luncheon in a delightful garden ambience. And for gourmet dinners there's The Dining Room; you'll find this award-winning restaurant discussed under "The Top Restaurants" in Section 6 of this chapter.

The Pool and Cabana Club is centered around an Olympic-size turquoise pool, where hardly anyone ever swims but from which it is imperative, if one is *anyone*, to be paged to the telephone. The club is surrounded by colorful cabanas and also has two tennis courts. If you order lunch by the pool, it's not a hamburger on a paper plate—it's served up on fine china, and your little table is adorned with fresh-cut flowers.

An unusual facility is the Cinema Room, an intimate private screening room with the latest audiovisual equipment and beverage service available.

Now for the rates, which are determined by the size and location of your room: Singles range from $185 to $295; doubles, from $230 to $320; suites, from $395 to $1,100; and bungalows, from $495 to $3,100. If you can't afford to stay here for your entire L.A. trip, you might want to splurge for just a few nights to experience authentic Hollywood glamour at its best. If even that is out of the question, at least come by and have lunch or a drink in the Polo Lounge.

L'Ermitage, 9291 Burton Way (near Foothill Road), Beverly Hills, CA 90210 (tel. 213/278-3344, or toll free 800/424-4443), ranks with the finest hotels in the world. It has received the AAA's five diamonds and Mobil's four-star award.

Each of the 112 units is actually a small suite that includes a sunken living room, wet bar, dressing area, and powder room as well as a kitchenette. All townhouse suites have fully equipped kitchens. These suites are furnished in residential motif, like rooms in a fine home, and all have fireplaces. The rooms and hallways are hung with many paintings, but the most impressive are those in the Café Russe, L'Ermitage's exceptional restaurant for the exclusive use of hotel guests. Here there are originals by Renoir, Braque, and de la Peña!

Guests at L'Ermitage enjoy a morning paper at no charge. Luscious strawberries and brown sugar are delivered to each suite at 4pm, and complimentary caviar is served each afternoon in the elegant top-floor bar. Other thoughtful touches include overnight shoeshine and complimentary limousine service. There is a rooftop garden that features a mineral-water spa, heated pool, and private solarium.

All this luxury doesn't come cheap, but would you expect it to? One-bedroom executive suites are $225 to $295; one-bedroom town-house suites run $335 to $545, two-bedroom town-house suites are $455 to $625, and three-bedroom townhouse suites are $1,500.

Upper Bracket

The **Beverly Hilton,** 9876 Wilshire Blvd. (at Santa Monica Boulevard), Beverly Hills, CA 90210 (tel. 213/274-7777), is one of the poshest of the Hilton chain. The decor is luxurious, with each room individually decorated; amenities include in-room first-run movies and refrigerators. Most of the 592 rooms have balconies and overlook an Olympic-size pool and the surrounding hillsides. A miniature city (like most Hiltons), this one has every kind of shop and service desk, not to mention two heated swimming pools.

The Hilton's penthouse restaurant, L'Escoffier, combines gourmet cuisine with a panoramic view of the city. The plush decor utilizes such finery as lace tablecloths, gray-velvet drapes, and Louis XVI–style chairs. There is a prix-fixe dinner for $61; à la carte entrees cost $25 to $35. Open for lunch weekdays and for dinner Monday through Saturday, L'Escoffier also has music for dancing and a delightful parlor lounge for cocktails.

The award-winning Trader Vic's offers exotic international cuisine in an atmosphere of Polynesian splendor, a small red-lacquer bridge adding to the ambience. Celebrities can often be spotted here dining on unique dishes and sampling exotic drinks. À la carte entrees are $14 to $30.

Sunday champagne brunch ($25) and dinner buffets ($27), served nightly from 6 to 10:30pm, are most popular at Mr. H—another elegant Hilton eatery, this one with rich, muted decor, crystal chandeliers, and Jacobean chairs. A $14 buffet lunch is also served here.

Room rates at the Hilton depend on size and location, with stiffer tabs for rooms overlooking the pool or on higher floors. Singles range from $155 to $195; doubles, from $175 to $215. A plus is that there is no charge for children (even teenagers) staying in the same room as their parents; a third adult staying in a room pays $20.

Moderate

The 100-room **Beverly Rodeo,** 360 N. Rodeo Dr. (a block north of Wilshire Boulevard), Beverly Hills, CA 90210 (tel. 213/273-0300, or toll free 800/421-0545, 800/441-5050 in California), has in the last few years been completely redecorated in French provincial style. Owner Max Baril has packed a lot of luxury into this intimate, European-style hotel, beginning with the courteous attendant at the door.

Rooms are very pretty, with matching floral-print spreads and draperies, and baths have marble-topped sinks and extra phones. All rooms have color TVs, AM/FM radios, and air conditioning, and some have balconies and refrigerators.

The hotel's restaurant, the Café Rodeo (just great for people-watching along Rodeo Drive), is furnished in contemporary mode with natural woods and rattan. A charming outdoor courtyard—where breakfast and lunch are served—adjoins.

Rates for standard rooms at the Beverly Rodeo are $130 to $160; deluxe, $150 to $180; and executive rooms, from $160 to $190. Opulent suites cost $255 to $400. The one drawback here: no swimming pool.

The **Beverly Hillcrest,** Beverwill Drive (at Pico Boulevard), Beverly Hills, CA 90212 (tel. 213/277-2800, or toll free 800/421-3212, 800/252-0174 in California), is a multimillion-dollar luxury hostelry at the southern edge of Beverly Hills. Rooms are notably spacious and elegantly appointed in restrained and tasteful French provincial decor, many with half-canopied beds. Each has a refrigerator (with ice), remote-control color TV and radio, genuine marble bath with an extra phone, and a balcony. Facilities include a swimming pool with a palm-fringed terrace for sunning and refreshments and a parking garage.

A gleaming steel-and-glass outdoor elevator whisks you up 12 floors to the Top of the Hillcrest, a rooftop restaurant offering sweeping views of Beverly Hills, Hollywood, and the Pacific Ocean. Its lavish interior is done up in gold-flocked draperies, gold-leather upholstered chairs, and glittering crystal chandeliers. Most luncheon entrees are in the $10 to $14 range; dinners, including soup and salad, range from $17 to $27.50 for the likes of coq au vin or steak and lobster.

Breakfast, lunch (except Sunday), and dinner are also served daily at Portofino, a candlelit old-world Italian eatery with tufted red-leather booths, exposed brick and wood-paneled walls. Dinner entrees here include a salad, Italian bread, a cheese wedge, and a basket of fresh fruit. Scampi with rice, chicken cacciatore served with eggplant parmigiana, and fettuccine Alfredo are among the delicacies offered for $15 to $27. Cheesecake with warm cherries is a delicious dessert.

Single rooms at the Beverly Hillcrest are $125 to $135; doubles, $135 to $150; suites, $215 to $345. Special weekend rates are also available.

Not to be confused with the above is the 54-room **Beverly Crest Hotel,** 125 S. Spalding Dr. (just south of Wilshire Boulevard), Beverly Hills, CA 90212 (tel. 213/274-6801, or toll free 800/247-6432). Many of the rooms overlook a courtyard with a swimming pool surrounded by palm trees. Overlooking the pool is the Venetian Room Restaurant, serving breakfast, lunch, and dinner daily. And you can park your car in a spacious covered garage at no extra charge.

The guest rooms, which are on the small side, are each done in a pleasant shade of blue, peach, or orange. White- or black-lacquer furnishings give a contemporary look. Rooms here have good closet space, full-length mirrors, direct-dial phones, color TVs, air conditioning/heating, and tub/shower baths.

Single rooms are $98 to $110; doubles, $110 to $120.

HOLLYWOOD

Upper Bracket

The **Hyatt on Sunset,** 8401 Sunset Blvd. (two blocks east of La Cienega Boulevard), Hollywood, CA 90069 (tel. 213/656-1234, or toll free 800/233-1000), is popular with celebs (Gene Autry officially opened it and June Allyson cut the ribbon). It's a lively place, recently renovated, close to Restaurant Row on La Cienega Boulevard and to Sunset Strip nightlife. The 262 spacious bedrooms, housed on 13 floors, overlook the Los Angeles skyline and the Hollywood Hills. Rooms, decorated in subdued earth tones, have modern furnishings and dressing areas, plus all the conveniences: direct-dial phones, in-room movies on color TVs, and modern

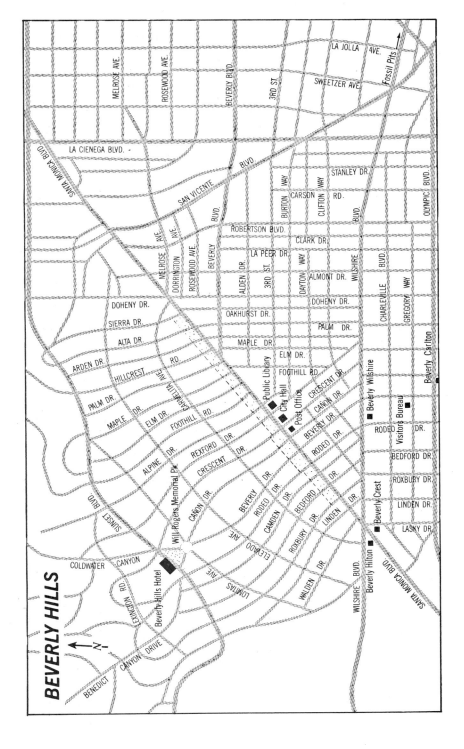

tub/shower baths. Most have private balconies. Facilities include a gift shop, rooftop swimming pool/sun deck, and valet or complimentary self-parking.

The Hyatt's restaurant, the Silver Screen, pays homage to the old days of Hollywood. Large blowups of oldtime scenes create a nostalgic atmosphere that is augumented by actual cameras, lights, and a director's chair. It's open daily from 7am to midnight. The Sunset Lounge on the premises features live jazz.

Singles cost $125 to $155, doubles are $145 to $175, and suites run $350 to $550. Special weekend rates are available.

There isn't enough space to list all the famous people who have resided at the **Château Marmont,** 8221 Sunset Blvd. (at Marmont Lane), Hollywood, CA 90046 (tel. 213/656-1010), a château-style apartment hotel lodged on a cliff just above Sunset Strip. Humphrey Bogart, Jeanne Moreau, Boris Karloff, Al Pacino, James Taylor, Richard Gere, Bianca Jagger, John and Yoko, Sophia Loren, Sidney Poitier, and Whoopi Goldberg have all been guests. Carol Channing met her husband here; Greta Garbo used to check in under the name Harriet Brown; and even Howard Hughes once maintained a suite.

Guests often gather in the great baronial living room, furnished with grandiose Hollywood antiques. (However, even if the hotel is full, the lobby may be empty). Otherwise, you'll find them lounging around the oval swimming pool amid semitropical trees and shrubbery.

All accommodations are furnished in tasteful English style, and all have color TVs, direct-dial phones, and daily maid service. Room service is available daily from 6:30am to 12:30am.

Regular rooms are $110, single or double. All the others have fully equipped kitchens and dens. Double rate in a studio with living room and bedroom is $140 a day; one-bedroom suites are $170 to $190, and two-bedroom suites run $235; a two-bedroom bungalow is $300, and penthouse suites are $235 to $450; cottages are $140 a night (they were added during the remodeling).

Moderate

Reliable standard accommodations can be found at the good old **Holiday Inn,** 1755 N. Highland Ave. (between Franklin and Hollywood Boulevard), Hollywood, CA 90028 (tel. 213/462-7181, or toll free 800/465-4329), a 22-story (they claim 23, but there's no 13th floor), 470-room hostelry in the heart of Old Hollywood. Rooms have been redecorated and are pleasant and comfortable. Every room is equipped with a remote-control color TV, clock radio, air conditioning, direct-dial phone, modern tub/shower bath, and a digital safe. For your convenience, there are three laundry rooms and ice and soda machines on every floor.

A revolving circular rooftop restaurant, Windows on Hollywood, features dancing and dining with a panoramic Hollywood view. Down on the second floor guests can lounge around a swimming pool/sun deck. The Show Biz Café, the hotel's rather plush coffee shop, serves breakfast, lunch, and dinner, and the Front Row Lounge, an intimate cocktail lounge, is open daily until 2am. A garage on the premises offers free parking.

Single rooms are $93 to $124, and doubles cost $110 to $141. An extra person in the room is $12; children 18 and under stay free in their parents' room.

Budget

One of the best of the budget category is the pleasant and centrally located **Hollywood Celebrity Hotel,** 1775 Orchid Ave. (near Hollywood Boulevard and Highland Avenue), Hollywood, CA 90028 (tel. 213/850-6464, or toll free 800/222-7017, 800/222-7090 in California). While you may be the only celebrity staying at the hotel, you still receive star treatment. The Hollywood Celebrity is a small hotel — 39 spacious and comfortable units, all with art deco treatment, and each with air conditioning, cable TV, radio, and phone. A complimentary Continental breakfast is served in your room is included in the rates, as is a bottle of wine upon arrival, the morning newspaper, and valet parking.

Singles are $65; doubles, $70 to $75. You can bring a pet in with you (of reasonable size), but that requires a $100 deposit. On the other hand, an extra person is only $8.

DOWNTOWN LOS ANGELES

Deluxe

California's most innovative hotel is the space-agey, 1,500-room **Westin Bonaventure, 404 S. Figueroa St.** (between 4th and 5th streets), Los Angeles, CA 90071 (tel. 213/624-1000, or toll free 800/228-3000), its five gleaming cylindrical towers downtown's most distinctive landmark. It's the creation of world-famous architect John Portman (he also did San Francisco's innovative Hyatt Regency). The beautiful six-story skylight lobby (a Portman trademark) contains a one-acre lake, trees, and gardens hanging from upper floors; the sound of splashing fountains penetrates the area. Twelve glass-bubble elevators rise from the reflecting pools, whisking guests up to the 23 upper floors while providing spectacular views of Los Angeles. The entire effect of this strong architectural statement is thrillingly sci-fi; you feel as though you've wandered into the 21st century.

Above the lobby is the Shopping Gallery with five levels of diversified shops and boutiques—men's and women's clothing stores, French gourmet food shop, photography center, hairdressers for men and women, you name it. You can rest from shopping in one of the circular seating areas, seemingly suspended in space, overlooking the bustling lobby activity.

Facilities include a large outdoor swimming pool and sun deck, with poolside dining; car-rental desks; tennis and health club facilities for men and women located just across one of the pedestrian bridges; 24-hour room service; and round-the-clock valet parking.

Then there are the cocktail areas and restaurants. The Sidewalk Café and adjoining Lobby Court, with tables under large fringed umbrellas, is the scene of nightly entertainment; it varies from jazz combos to mariachi bands. The Flower Street Bar, a rich mixture of marble, brass, and mahogany, is becoming the new downtown "hot spot" for cocktails. The rooftop Top of Five features gourmet Continental fare in the $22 to $30 range—for example, filet mignon and lobster tail with béarnaise sauce—and panoramic views, with a revolving cocktail lounge (the Bona Vista) below it on the 34th floor; the latter is a favorite pretheater rendezvous. The elegant Beaudry's, on the lobby floor, named for the famous 19th-century mayor, offers haute-cuisine fare in a stunning contemporary setting, with 18 intimate dining areas sheltered by shimmering gold-mesh curtains. Beaudry's offers such tempting dinner entrees as lobster ragoût in a puff pastry graced with an excellent Nantua sauce. Entrees at lunch cost $13 to $18; at dinner they range from $19 to $30. Inagiku, a first-rate Japanese restaurant patterned after a Japanese village with winding walkways, is composed of a steak house for teppanyaki cooking and a dining room with sushi and tempura bars as well as regular tables and tatami rooms.

As for the rooms, they're as modernistic and attractive as the rest of the hotel (no bedroom is more than six doors from an elevator); all are equipped with every luxury. The rooms are everything you'd expect from a first-class hotel—sophisticated and elegant, with floor-to-ceiling views of the city.

In short, there's nothing wanting at this exciting hotel—if you don't stay here, come by for a look around.

Single rooms are $150, doubles run $175 to $220, and suites begin at $300.

Contrasting with the Bonaventure's futuristic appeal is the **Biltmore**, 506 S. Grand Ave. (between 5th and 6th streets), Los Angeles, CA 90071 (tel. 213/624-1011, or toll free 800/421-8000, 800/252-0175 in California), a gracious old grande dame (built in 1923) among L.A.'s deluxe hotels. During the '30s and '40s the Academy Awards ceremonies were held here, including the year *Gone With the Wind* swept them all.

Always beautiful, the Biltmore today is looking better than ever following a $40-million facelift completed in 1987. The renovation enhanced the hotel's basic architectural structure while incorporating harmonious contemporary touches (such as the Jim Dine prints in the guest rooms) and updating to state-of-the-art its mechanical systems. The new entrance on Grand Avenue (formerly the back of the hotel) features a porte cochere where valet parking is available.

The lavishly appointed rooms are spacious and attractively decorated in pastel tones. Traditional French furniture houses the desk and TV. The rooms are, of course, equipped with every modern amenity, and the Biltmore offers such luxurious extras as 24-hour maid service and room service, hand-delivered messages, and a multilingual concierge staff. The Biltmore Health Club, featuring an elegant Roman spa–like pool, steam room, sauna, Jacuzzi, Nautilus equipment, and weights, is open daily for hotel guests and members.

Once the lobby of the hotel, the spectacular Rendezvous Court now serves as a lovely lounge where you can enjoy afternoon tea or evening cocktails. Overhead an ornate cathedral-like vaulted ceiling was hand-painted by (who else?) an Italian artist, Giovanni Smeraldi.

The Biltmore's dining facilities include the prestigious Bernard's, a luxurious environment—fluted columns, hand-painted beamed ceilings—in which to enjoy a combination classic French and regional American cuisine. At dinner, you might begin with an appetizer of Westcott Bay oysters. Entrees, priced at $23 to $35, include such specialties as grilled medallions of veal served with morels, and breast of chicken served with a fresh citrus sauce. Lunch is a bit less costly, with entree prices from $18 to $26. The hotel's Court Café is open for breakfast, lunch, and dinner and features regional American cuisine in a warm Mediterranean atmosphere. The Grand Avenue Bar offers a cold lunch buffet and in the evening show cases top-name jazz entertainment.

Rates for singles are $140 to $210; doubles, $160 to $240. Suites start at $390.

Returning once more to the dazzlingly ultramodern: the 487-room, 24-story **Hyatt Regency Los Angeles,** 711 S. Hope St. (at 7th Street), Los Angeles, CA 90017 (tel. 213/683-1234, or toll free 800/228-9000). It's part of Broadway Plaza, a 21st-century-style complex of shops, restaurants, offices, and galleries that includes a huge parking garage. The avant-garde tone is set by the two-story skylight-covered entrance lobby with a garden plaza, lounges, a sidewalk café, and boutiques. Wide escalators glide down to the lobby/reception area and gardens. Everything is a mélange of rich browns, reds, rusts, and golds, adorned with supergraphics and warmly enhanced by exposed brick, potted plants, trees, old-fashioned gaslight streetlamps, and overstuffed furniture.

Rooms at the Hyatt are innovative and attractive. Each has a full window wall offering surprisingly nice views for a downtown hotel, deep pile carpeting, oversize beds, dressing room, small sofa, color TV with in-room movies, etc. Strikingly futuristic in design and furnishings, they utilize the same bold textures and russet-gold color scheme prevalent throughout the building.

There's a revolving rooftop restaurant called Angel's Flight, offering a full-circle panoramic window tour of the city every hour, as well as gourmet lunches and dinners. The opulent Pavan (open for lunch and dinner Monday through Saturday) is the Hyatt's premier gourmet restaurant, the Lobby Bar its most congenial spot for cocktails. Also on the premises is the Sun Porch, a sidewalk café–coffee shop.

In addition, the Hyatt offers tennis and health-club facilities in conjunction with the nearby Los Angeles Racquet Club, and guests can use the pool at the Wilshire Hyatt. A concierge and nighttime maid service are luxurious extras.

Rates are $145 to $165 singles, $170 to $190 for doubles and twins; suites start at $275.

The 900-room **Los Angeles Hilton and Towers,** 930 Wilshire Blvd. (at Figueroa), Los Angeles, CA 90017 (tel. 213/629-4321), is centrally located near downtown attractions and offers easy access to major freeway entrances. Many rooms overlook the oval swimming pool, set in a hi-tech environment. The furnishings for this ultramodern building are contemporary in look and tone, done in mauve, seafoam green, gray, and camel. Every convenience and luxury is at hand, from 24-hour maid and room service to in-house movies, a writing desk, and double-panel glass windows to minimize outside noise. No-smoking rooms are available, as are those specially equipped for handicapped guests. And you can dine and drink by the hotel's outdoor swimming pool.

The premium Towers rooms (15th and 16th floors) have separate check-in facilities and a staff serving only Towers guests. The deluxe furnishings in these rooms include two-line telephones, morning newspaper delivery, and nightly turndown. The Towers lounge serves complimentary Continental breakfast and provides the latest Dow Jones reports (assuming you really want to know), as well as two TV sets, reading material, and games; later a daily cocktail hour is held here, with complimentary hors d'oeuvres and beverages.

If you find it a matter of importance on your vacation (and some people do), the Hilton now has a fitness center, located in the main lobby and offset from the pool.

The hotel's several restaurants include the 24-hour Gazebo coffee shop; the City Grill, with its California cuisine; and Miami of Tokyo, serving Japanese food nightly, as well as midday during the week. And the Lobby Bar serves cocktails and snacks and provides musical entertainment. But, above all, there is the ultra-contemporary, ultra-elegant Cardini's for superb northern Italian cuisine. The emphasis is on light pastas, with a good selection of fish and veal dishes. But there are such first-course beauties as bufala mozzarella garnished with sun-dried tomatoes, plus enticing entrees such as linguine with lobster, and swordfish with baby artichokes and calamata olives. At the end, pay attention to the pastry tray for just a few more gorgeous calories. Dinner for two, without wine, will be about $60 to $100. Lunch will run you somewhat less.

Room rates at the Hilton depend on placement and size. Singles are $150 to $175; double and twin-bedded rooms cost $170 to $195.

The **New Otani Hotel and Garden,** 120 S. Los Angeles St. (at 1st Street), Los Angeles, CA 90012 (tel. 213/629-1200, or toll free 800/421-8795, 800/252-0197 in California), is the city's only Japanese hotel, complete with a classical 16,000-square-foot Japanese garden for the exclusive use of guests. There's also a Japanese health club for men and women offering sauna, Japanese baths, and shiatsu massage in a garden setting. The 440 rooms are housed in a 21-story triangular tower. Facilities include four underground parking levels, a shopping arcade of over 30 shops, car-rental desk, etc., airport limousine service, and a choice of restaurants. Golf and tennis are available in conjunction with a nearby country club. A two-story shopping center adjoins the Otani.

The Canary Garden serves breakfast, lunch, and dinner (fresh-baked breads and pastries are a specialty). Commodore Perry's, named for the famous naval officer who forced Japan to open trade with the West, aptly features American and Continental specialties. And A Thousand Cranes is the evocative name of the Otani's lovely Japanese restaurant, which serves traditional breakfasts, lunches, and dinners (and a Japanese brunch on Sunday) in an authentic setting overlooking the waterfall and pond in the garden. It has both sushi and tempura bars. Tatami rooms are available.

The luxurious rooms are mostly Western in style; each has a refrigerator, oversize beds, shower bath with extension phone and radio, button-selector radio with city and hotel information channels in Japanese and English, direct-dial phones with message-alert light, alarm clock, color TV, smoke detector, air conditioning, and heating.

Rates for single rooms are $125 to $165; doubles are $145 to $185. I particularly like the Japanese suites with tatami-mat bedrooms, deep whirlpool baths, and balconies overlooking the garden—beginning at $375 a night.

One of the newer hotels in the downtown area is the **Sheraton Grande,** 333 S. Figueroa (between 3rd and 4th streets), Los Angeles, CA 90012 (tel. 213/617-1133, or toll free 800/325-3535), a splendid smoky-mirrored-glass structure. It's gorgeous and luxurious, starting in the large, open lobby and lounge, decorated with skylights and plants. There's daily piano entertainment here, and tea is served every afternoon.

The guest rooms—470 of them—are elegantly decorated in pastels with brilliant accents. Amenities include modern marble tub/shower baths, color TVs, direct-dial phones, butler service, and 24-hour room service.

The Sheraton Grande's restaurants include the Back Porch, an informal dining room overlooking the pool, serving three meals a day; and the gourmet room, Ravel, which serves California cuisine. Also on the premises are a new bar and eatery—Moody's; four movie theaters; a pool and sun deck; and a health club.

Rooms at the Sheraton Grande cost $180 to $210 for a single, $200 to $235 for a double, and $475 to $975 for a suite.

Budget

The **Hotel Stillwell,** 838 S. Grande Ave. (between 8th and 9th streets), Los Angeles, CA 90017 (tel. 213/627-1151), is conveniently situated in the downtown area. It's just a short distance to the Ahmanson Theater and Dorothy Chandler Pavilion in the Civic Center, which feature a variety of theatrical and musical events. It's also close to the Museum of Contemporary Art, Little Tokyo, Olvera Street, Union Station, and a variety of exceptional restaurants.

The hotel has 250 recently restored rooms (no-smoking rooms are available), including a variety of combinations to accommodate guests traveling alone or with children. Rooms are done very simply and comfortably in soft blue and gray tones. Each room has a shower/tub, a TV, a phone, and individually controlled air conditioning.

Adjoining the hotel is a restaurant serving Mexican food, but looking considerably more elegant and Continental than most. Also off the lobby is Hank's Bar and Grill, a cozy, friendly pub with all sorts of memorabilia. And to the rear of the hotel is Gill's Cuisine of India.

Single rooms range from $33 to $43; twin/doubles, $43 to $53; suites, $69 to $89. A note of caution regarding parking in front of the hotel: Despite loading-zone designations (for commercial plates only), it's wise not to leave the car unattended even briefly. You may come back to find a parking ticket under your windshield wiper.

EAST WILSHIRE

Upper Bracket

The **Hyatt Wilshire,** 3515 Wilshire Blvd. (at the corner of Normandie Avenue), Los Angeles, CA 90010 (tel. 213/381-7411, or toll free 800/233-1234), is a luxury hotel popular with businesspeople for its pushbutton comfort and convenient location. Its 400 rooms are housed on 12 floors; each is furnished in attractive modern style with one all-glass wall and, of course, all amenities, including first-run movies on your color TV and a clock radio. Facilities include a barbershop, car rental, and a heated outdoor swimming pool.

Breakfast, lunch, and dinner are served at Hugo's; at dinner you might order prime rib or grilled swordfish ($18), with various accompaniments.

Single rooms are in the $110 to $155 bracket; double and twin-bedded rooms are $125 to $175.

WEST WILSHIRE

Deluxe

Don't get confused about these Wilshire listings. The previous East Wilshire hotel is close to downtown. West Wilshire (it's a very long street) is slightly west of Beverly Hills, almost in Westwood.

Here we have a very special place, the **Beverly Hills Comstock,** 10300 Wilshire

Blvd. (off Comstock Street), Los Angeles, CA 90024 (tel. 213/275-5575, or toll free 800/343-2184), that caters to the carriage trade, offering mostly luxury suites. Quiet and peaceful, it offers an intimacy and privacy not possible at larger hotels and has a considerable celebrity clientele.

Rooms are large and decorated in either traditional or California modern motif. Of course, all have color TVs, direct-dial phones, tub/shower baths, etc. All the suites surround the courtyard pool area and have private balconies or patios. A restaurant on the premises, Le Petit Café, serves breakfast, lunch, and dinner and has a full-service bar.

Rates, which include parking, are $100 to $150 for a one-bedroom kitchen suite, $225 to $280 for a two-bedroom kitchen suite. Monthly rates are available.

WESTWOOD

Moderate

Wedged between Santa Monica and glamorous Beverly Hills, the student-dominated community (UCLA) of Westwood has over 400 shops, about 100 restaurants, and 15 first-run movie theaters. All of which combine to make it a convenient and pleasant place to stay.

The **Royal Palace Westwood Hotel**, 1052 Tiverton Ave., Los Angeles, CA 90024 (tel. 213/208-6677, or toll free 800/631-0100), is just north of Wilshire, right in the heart of Westwood Village. At the hub of surrounding communities—Beverly Hills, Century City, Santa Monica, West Los Angeles, and Bel Air—it's convenient to Hollywood, the beach, the airport, and the San Diego Freeway. The Royal Palace Westwood is also across from what will soon be the Dr. Armand Hammer Museum, which will house his complete $30-million art collection.

Each room has been redecorated, and all the bathrooms have marble vanities. All rooms have units with stoves, refrigerators, and stainless countertops. Some also have microwave ovens. You get color TV with three entertainment channels. Facilities include an exercise room and lounge.

Single rooms range from $57 to $84, doubles run $63 to $91, and suites are $110. Additional persons in a room pay $8 each.

Another Westwood choice, for fans of **Holiday Inn**, is a branch of said chain at 10740 Wilshire Blvd. (at Selby Avenue), Westwood, CA 90024 (tel. 213/475-8711, or toll free 800/472-8556, 800/235-7973 in California). This one offers 300 attractively furnished rooms—all twins with color TVs, direct-dial phones, tub/shower baths with marble sinks, minibars, and complimentary newspapers. Reflecting the English Tudor theme of the hotel's interior decor, there are hunting prints on the walls.

Facilities include a swimming pool, sun deck and Jacuzzi, and restaurant, the Café Le Dome, offering Continental cuisine. The Café Le Dome Cocktail Lounge here is popular with local basketball and football teams, many of whom stay at the hotel.

Singles are $105 to $115; doubles, $115 to $125; and suites, $170 to $400. Since kids 18 or under can stay free in your double room, this is a good choice for families.

WEST LOS ANGELES

West Los Angeles, as a glance at your L.A. map will show you, is just slightly south of Westwood, and within easy access of Beverly Hills, Century City, and Santa Monica.

Upper Bracket

The **Bel-Air Summit Hotel** (formerly the Bel-Air Sands), 11461 Sunset Blvd. (at the San Diego Freeway), Los Angeles, CA 90049 (tel. 213/476-6571, or toll free 800/421-6649, 800/352-6680 in California), is just minutes away from Beverly Hills, Westwood Village and UCLA, Century City, and 10 miles from LAX.

The 162 large, air-conditioned rooms and suites all feature large balconies or lanais and are decorated in subtle colors and understated European decor. All rooms have remote-control color TVs, VCRs, hair dryers, refrigerators, electronic security keys, radios, and direct-dial phones. There are two heated pools and a tennis court on the premises.

The hotel's dining room is Echo. Breakfast, lunch, dinner, and a fabulous Sunday brunch are served here, the last including champagne.

Rooms are $125 to $140 for singles, $140 to $185 for doubles; suites start at $270.

Moderate

The **Los Angeles West Travel Lodge,** 10740 Santa Monica Blvd. (at Overland Avenue), Los Angeles, CA 90025 (tel. 213/474-4576, or toll free 800/255-3050), is a clean and friendly 53-room establishment offering quite good value in this area. The pleasant modern rooms are equipped with direct-dial phones, tub or shower baths, clocks, color TVs, in-room coffee makers, and refrigerators. There's an enclosed private swimming pool with a sun deck, plus plenty of free parking.

Rates are reasonable, with single rooms at $56 to $70, and doubles at $63 to $85; $6 for an extra person.

CENTURY CITY

Deluxe

Built in 1966 on what was once the back lot of the Twentieth Century-Fox Corporation, the **Century Plaza,** Avenue of the Stars (off Santa Monica Boulevard), West Los Angeles, CA 90067 (tel. 213/277-2000, or toll free 800/228-3000), is a superstar in the galaxy of L.A. hotels. Designed by the celebrated Japanese architect Minoru Yamasaki, the 20-story hotel and 30-story tower—with a total of 1,072 rooms—occupy a commanding position adjoining Beverly Hills and right across the street from the ABC Entertainment Center, which houses an 1,850-seat Shubert legitimate theater and two ultramodern movie theaters. The tower's 30th floor is occupied by the 8,000-square-foot Plaza Suite. The Century Plaza is enormous—it appears roughly the size of New York's Grand Central Terminal—with its vaulted cathedral ceilings, two-story windows, and sunken lounge areas. It has the feel of a bustling city of tomorrow.

The $85-million tower (where former President Reagan stayed when in town) houses 322 rooms, with only 14 (exceptionally spacious) per floor. All have private balconies. In addition to the usual amenities, each has a wet bar and refrigerator, three conveniently located phones, an all-marble bathroom with separate soak tub and shower, double vanity and washbasins, and a heat lamp. As you might expect, the TV is contained in an armoire. Writing desks have travertine marble tops, and there's a live tree or lovely green plant in each room. All tower rooms receive a complimentary newspaper each morning, soft drinks and ice each afternoon, deluxe bath amenities such as robes and oversize bath towels, twice-daily maid service, and 24-hour room service featuring items from La Chaumière. There's also complimentary car service to and from Beverly Hills for shopping.

The 750 accommodations apart from the tower are furnished in garden motif with marble-topped oak furnishings and beautiful teal-blue or forest-green carpeting. Each has a balcony and is equipped with every imaginable amenity and luxury: color TV discreetly hidden in an oak armoire that doubles as a desk, three phones (bedside, tableside, and bath), refrigerator, AM/FM radio, clock, big closet, and tub/shower bath with marble sink, oversize towels, and scales. Extras range from the ultramodern—an elevator kitchen to keep food warm on its way to your room —to the homey practice of leaving a mint and a good-night note from the management on each guest's pillow when the beds are turned down for the night.

In addition to the Lobby Court (open from 11am to 2am), there are four major places to drink and dine. The newest restaurants are in the tower: La Chaumière, which blends California and Continental cuisine and presents it beautifully in a setting reminiscent of a fine European club; and the Terrace, for classic California dining. As with Yamato, a fine Japanese restaurant, there's more about this lovely restaurant in Section 6 of this chapter.

The lovely Garden Pavilion has floor-to-ceiling windows so that you can view the lush tropical gardens, reflecting pools, and fountains while you dine. It's open daily for breakfast, lunch, dinner, and Tuesday through Saturday for dancing to live music, and it is very popular with locals for Sunday brunch. The Café Plaza is a provincial-style coffee shop, its walls hung with French travel posters; open from 6am to 1am, it offers simple meals, sandwiches, and drinks.

Other Century Plaza facilities include two large outdoor heated pools, three Jacuzzis, a children's pool, and about 10 shops, airline desks, car-rental offices, ticket agencies, sightseeing and tour desks, and of course a concierge service. Guests can use the tennis courts and a health club just across the street.

Rates at the Century Plaza are $150 to $165 for a single, $175 to $190 for double; suites begin at $215. In the tower, singles are $215 to $230, doubles run $240 to $255, and suites begin at $950. The Plaza Suite is $3,500!

BEL-AIR

Deluxe

Neighborhoods just don't come more exclusive than Bel-Air, where every house is a mansion—and hotels don't exist that are more deluxe than the **Hotel Bel-Air,** 701 Stone Canyon Rd. (off Sunset Boulevard), Bel-Air, CA 90077 (tel. 213/472-1211), recipient of the Mobil five-star award. Set on exquisite tropical grounds and surrounded by the Santa Monica hills and Southern California's most prestigious estates, the Bel-Air is entered via a long awninged pathway. It's actually an arched stone bridge over a swan- and duck-filled pond, with small waterfalls here and there. Everywhere you look you see flowering trees and plants, banana palms, bamboo, orange and lemon trees. The architecture is Spanish, with arcades leading from one building to another. A large oval swimming pool is set amid the lush gardens and surrounded by a flagstone terrace. The public rooms are richly traditional, furnished in fine antiques, and a fire is kept burning in the entrance lounge.

There are 92 individually decorated rooms and garden suites, some with patios or terraces and some with wood-burning fireplaces, all with picture windows, two phones (one in the bath), and radios, and all redecorated by five different decorators.

Whether or not you stay here, come by for a drink in the bougainvillea court or a meal in the traditional and lovely dining room. At dinner, such entrees as Muscovy duck with tangerine-essenced sauce and loin of lamb Wellington baked in phyllo range from $20 to $35. Come by at lunch for cold dishes like lobster sausage with basil oil, as well as sandwiches, egg dishes, and full entrees—most of them Italian or seafood selections.

Single or double rooms are priced at $195 to $360; suites are $390 to $1,300.

SANTA MONICA

Upper Bracket

Sun worshippers who prefer a beach location will do well to choose a Santa Monica hotel. Not only do these offer proximity to the ocean, they also provide easy access to the airport, nearby Beverly Hills, and Westwood.

An elegant Santa Monica choice is the **Miramar-Sheraton Hotel,** 101 Wilshire Blvd. (between Ocean and 2nd), Santa Monica, CA 90401 (tel. 213/394-3731, or toll free 800/325-3535). Its name means "ocean view" and that's just what it has—it sits on a cliff overlooking the Santa Monica beach. The hotel was built in the 1920s, and the slow elegance of that era is evident in the public areas. In the courtyard there's a century-old fig tree that casts its shadow over the garden. The lobby is decorated with comfortable resortlike furniture, and the pool and surrounding garden beckon guests to swim and laze in the sun.

There are 305 guest rooms in the Miramar, in the older low buildings and the newer tower. Each is comfortable and luxurious, with a king-size bed or two double beds, color TV, direct-dial phone, in-room safe, and digital clock radio. Bathrooms are equally plush, with additional phones, honor bars, special soaps and shampoos, and oversize towels.

The hotel boasts several dining choices: the International Room, open for dinner; the Garden Room, overlooking the pool and garden, which serves breakfast and lunch; a coffee shop; and for entertainment and dancing, the Stateroom Lounge.

Rooms at the Miramar-Sheraton are $125 to $200 for a single, $145 to $220 for a double, and $250 to $600 for a suite.

Moderate

The **Pacific Shore Hotel,** 1819 Ocean Ave. (at Pico Boulevard), Santa Monica, CA 90401 (tel. 213/451-8711, or toll free 800/241-3848), has 168 air-conditioned rooms and suites with spectacular ocean or mountain views, color TVs, phones, AM/FM radios, and tub/shower baths. A large swimming pool, Jacuzzi, and saunas are surrounded by attractive tropical foliage. Other facilities include the Flamingo Lounge for cocktails, a gift shop, car-rental desk, beauty salon, and guest laundry. Soft-drink machines and ice machines are on every floor. Parking is free.

Rates for singles are $90 to $117; doubles, $94 to $127; suites, $225 to $375.

The **Radisson-Huntley Hotel,** 1111 2nd St. (at Wilshire Boulevard), Santa Monica, CA 90403 (tel. 213/394-5454, or toll free 800/556-4011, 800/556-4012 in California), offers 213 rooms and suites right near the beach. You can walk from the Huntley to the vicinity of the Santa Monica Pier, where you'll find over 300 shops, boutiques, and restaurants. There's no swimming pool on the premises, but the ocean is a stone's throw away. The rooms are large and attractive (all have ocean or mountain views) and are equipped with color TVs, AM/FM radios, direct-dial phones, and other modern amenities. Running up the front of the hotel is a glass elevator; the view on the way up (or down) is spectacular. Atop the hotel is a rooftop restaurant called Toppers, with magnificent views—be sure to see the sunset from here. Mexican cuisine is offered at lunch and dinner, but if you choose, there's always gringo-style pasta, as well as seafood, chicken, steak, and hamburgers. Toppers serves a Sunday champagne brunch from 11am to 3pm, and there is entertainment nightly from 8:30pm to 1:30am. In addition, there's a classy coffee shop called the Garden Café on the premises.

Single rooms at Huntley cost $115 to $125, and doubles run $125 to $135; suites rent for $155 to $260. Parking is free.

The **Holiday Inn Bay View Plaza,** 530 Pico Blvd. (at 6th Street, west of Lincoln), Santa Monica, CA 90405 (tel. 213/399-9344, or toll free 800/465-4329), has over 300 guest rooms with color TVs, minibars, direct-dial phones, air conditioning, private tub/shower bathrooms, and nice views of the ocean or city. The Bay View Café serves three meals a day, and there are a pool and free garage parking for guests.

Rates are $80 to $115 for a single, $85 to $130 for a double, $225 and up for a suite.

Budget

The **Santa Monica International AYH Hostel** has opened its doors at 1436 2nd St., P.O. Box 575, Santa Monica, CA 90406 (tel. 213/393-9913). Calls are answered personally between 7 and 11am and between 4pm and midnight; otherwise, you get recorded information. For an alternative source of information, call 213/831-8846 from noon to 5pm.

If you don't already know it, be advised that Santa Monica is one of Los Angeles's most popular beach communities. The Santa Monica hostel is just two blocks from the beach and Santa Monica Pier, about a mile from Venice beach. It's within walking distance of shops and restaurants and about two blocks from regional bus lines, including a direct bus to Los Angeles International Airport (about 7 miles). Buses to Los Angeles and its tourist attractions run regularly from stops near the hotel.

The Santa Monica hostel is one of the largest in this country and accommodates up to 200 guests, including groups and families on a space-available basis. Private family rooms have four beds. As with all hostels, showers and bathrooms are dormitory style. The hostel has guest kitchen facilities, a travel library, and a travel center.

Accommodations are $12 per night per person for members, $15 for nonmembers. Individual membership in the American Youth Hostel organization is $20 per year, which entitles you to stay at the local rate in any of the AYH hostels. If you are not a member, you can join at the hostel. Guests are limited to three-day stays; however, this can be extended to five nights with the approval of the manager.

Reservations are accepted *by mail only*, and are advised for visits during the summer months. Send the first night's fee for deposit.

MARINA DEL REY

Deluxe

Sandwiched between Santa Monica and the Los Angeles International Airport, Marina del Rey is a very popular waterfront resort, just two minutes from major freeways that connect with most L.A. attractions. There are over 6,000 boats in the water—making it the world's largest small-craft harbor.

One of the loveliest Marina del Rey hotels is the **Marina International,** 4200 Admiralty Way (at Palaway Way), Marina del Rey, CA 90292 (tel. 213/301-2000, or toll free 800/882-4000, 800/862-7462 in California). There are 127 lovely rooms and suites done in bright, light colors for a look of contemporary elegance. Of course, each room has color TV and bedside controls, direct-dial phone, and tub and/or shower bath. All junior suites have a phone in the bathroom. The 25 bungalows (originally called villas) were refurbished in 1988. These very spacious, luxuriously appointed accommodations have all been redone in warm, cozy, very contemporary California-casual style, with soft pastels of teal, rose, peach, and lavender and comfortable textured fabrics. Each has a sitting area, bedroom, bathroom, and lots of privacy. All the bungalows are located off a private courtyard.

The hotel's Crystal Fountain offers Continental cuisine in an indoor/outdoor garden setting. The restaurant is open for breakfast, lunch, dinner, and Sunday brunch. A unique service of the Crystal Fountain features selected appetizers, entrees, and desserts prepared tableside. And 24-hour room service is now available. Other facilities include a heated swimming pool and whirlpool (the beach is right across the street); golf and tennis can be arranged nearby. Free covered parking is available for guests. A bonus is free shuttle bus service to and from the airport.

Rates vary according to room location. Singles are $102 to $162; doubles and twins run $122 to $182. Suites and villas are $192 to $212 for a single, $232 to $315 for a double.

Under the same ownership is the **Marina del Rey Hotel,** 13534 Bali Way (at Admiralty Way), Marina del Rey, CA 90292 (tel. 213/301-1000, or toll free 800/882-4000, 800/862-7462 in California). Particularly lovely here are the rooms with balconies looking out over the boat-filled harbor, a view that all guests can enjoy from the beautifully landscaped swimming pool and sun-deck area. The hotel is on the marina's main channel and is surrounded by water. It's the only hotel on the waterfront.

Rooms are done in soothing blue-and-tan color schemes and fitted out with all modern conveniences, including color TVs, direct-dial phones, and AM/FM digital clock radios.

As at the International, tennis and golf can be arranged, the beach is a stone's throw away, and guests can utilize complimentary limousine airport service. The Dockside Café is the hotel's coffee shop, open daily for breakfast and lunch. The Crystal Seahorse features Continental fare at dinner from 6 to 11pm daily. The latter overlooks the marina, and mirrored tables, walls, and ceilings reflect the view.

Single rooms cost $125 to $170, doubles run $145 to $190, and suites are $375 to $450.

Upper Bracket

The **Marina del Rey Marriott,** 13480 Maxella Ave. (near the Marina del Rey Freeway and Lincoln Boulevard), Marina del Rey, CA 90292 (tel. 213/822-8555, or toll free 800/228-9290), is a delightful resortlike place. There are 283 air-conditioned rooms, all with color TVs (first-run movies are available), direct-dial phones, AM/FM clock radios, and tub/shower baths. The hotel's Maxfield's Restaurant and Lounge serves American-Continental fare in a cheery ambience. The Marriott is conveniently located next to the Villa Marina Center with its 30 shops. There are a swimming pool, spa pool, and pool bar, all in a landscaped courtyard complete with a rock waterfall, pond, and a bridge over a stream. The tropical theme extends to rooms (many with lanais), which have splashy floral-design spreads and drapes and are equipped with all the modern amenities.

Singles are $125 to $135; doubles and twins, $130 to $160; suites, $240 to $340. Airport transportation is complimentary.

STUDIO CITY

Moderate

A little bit west of Universal City is the **Sportsmen's Lodge,** 12825 Ventura Blvd. (at Coldwater Canyon Avenue), Los Angeles, CA 91604 (tel. 818/769-4700, or toll free 800/821-8511, 800/821-1625 in California). The hotel is nestled among redwood trees, with rustic wooden footbridges crossing freshwater ponds (the hotel's name derives from the fact that guests used to fish for trout in these ponds; nowadays they're home to swans and ducks), waterfalls, rock gardens, and lush tropical greenery. There are an Olympic-size swimming pool with lots of sundeck area, a variety of shops and service desks, bowling and golf nearby, and an airport limousine service.

A major asset is the next-door Sportsmen's Lodge Restaurant, 12833 Ventura Blvd. (tel. 818/984-0202). It's very attractive, with a glass-enclosed main dining room overlooking a pond and small waterfall. You might begin a meal here with an order of baked clams topped with bacon bits and pimento, then order an entree of veal piccata or duckling à l'orange with wild rice priced at $15 to $28. An early-dinner menu (served from 5:30 to 6:30pm) is cheaper. Cakes and rolls are fresh-baked daily. There's an extensive wine list, and an adjoining piano bar/lounge serves late suppers from 10pm. Open nightly and for Sunday brunches. Reservations are a good idea. There's also a coffee shop on the premises, serving breakfast, lunch, and dinner.

Rooms are large and comfortable and have been refurbished, but are not luxurious in any way; they do have color TVs, direct-dial phones, AM/FM radios, etc., and refrigerators are available. Many have balconies. The poolside executive studios ($146 for singles, $151 for doubles) are the most attractive accommodations. Regular rooms are $90 to $100 for singles, $100 to $110 for doubles.

PASADENA

Upper Bracket

The **Huntington Hotel,** 1401 S. Oak Knoll (three-quarters of a mile north of Huntington Drive), Pasadena, CA 91109 (tel. 818/792-0266, or toll free 800/

822-1777), set on 23 beautifully landscaped garden acres, sits nestled in the shadows of the San Gabriel Mountains overlooking the San Gabriel Valley. The grounds are famous, particularly the Japanese garden with its little wooden footbridge, and the wisteria-covered Picture Bridge adorned with Frank Moore's very charming paintings of early California scenes and accompanying verses of Don Blanding. The main hotel is closed. However, the Huntington is now being operated as a quaint country inn, renting rooms in a small, central building and handsome cottages on or about the grounds. One-bedroom accommodations range from $165 to $250. Cottages are available on a monthly basis only.

The **Pasadena Hilton,** 150 S. Los Robles Ave. (at the corner of Cordova Street), Pasadena, CA 91101 (tel. 818/577-1000), is a 13-story hostelry crowned by a rooftop restaurant. Fifteen minutes from downtown Los Angeles, it's only a block and a half south of Colorado Boulevard, famed for its Rose Parade. Rooms have been redecorated in soft earth tones. Some have beds with elaborate high headboards; all have spacious baths, refrigerators, and color TVs with in-room movies.

Singles range in price from $108 to $135, and doubles run $123 to $150. The higher figures are for accommodations with king-size beds and balconies. One-bedroom suites cost $250 to $375. You can dine in Skylights, overlooking the entire San Gabriel Valley or dance and enjoy live entertainment in the adjoining Slicks Night Club. Breakfast is served in the ground-level French-style Café Madagascar, and a lobby bar called Fanny's is a favorite rendezvous during happy hour. Other facilities include an outdoor swimming pool and parking; tennis and golf are nearby.

Moderate

The **Saga Motor Hotel,** 1633 E. Colorado Blvd. (between Allan and Sierra Bonita), Pasadena, CA 91106 (tel. 818/795-0431), is about a mile from the Huntington Library and reasonably close to Pasadena City College, Cal Tech, and the Jet Propulsion Lab. It's also well within striking distance of the Rose Bowl. But the bottom line is that the Saga has, by far, the most attractive rooms I've seen recently for the price, a fact suggested by the hotel's very inviting, sunlit, and spotlessly clean reception area.

The comfortable rooms are nicely decorated with brass beds, blue-and-white-checked spreads, and a blue-and-white tile baths with both showers and tubs. Amenities include cable color TVs and phones. A number of the rooms are located in a single-story building surrounding a pool; the remainder, in a small three-story building, overlook either the pool or a quiet street at the rear of the building. The pool is heated year-round and is surrounded by a wide sun deck with comfortable chaises.

A large suite available on the third floor is comfortably furnished with a couch and oversize cocktail table, a small frige, dining table for two, handsome upholstered club chairs, and a king-size brass bed. A small balcony holds enough furniture for relaxing and enjoying a midday or after-dinner libation.

Single rates are $55, and doubles cost $57; for one or two people with a king-size bed, $59, including a refrigerator. The suite, as described above, is $75. Complimentary coffee and doughnuts are included in the rates.

AIRPORT

Upper Bracket

The airport area has been developing in the last few years, and one of the newer additions is the 810-room **Sheraton Plaza La Reina,** 6101 W. Century Blvd. (near Sepulveda Boulevard), Los Angeles, CA 90045 (tel. 213/642-1111, or toll free 800/325-3535). The rooms have a quintessentially California look with rattan chairs and live plants; color-coordinated drapes and bedspreads are dark green and burgundy. All rooms are equipped with direct-dial phones; digital alarm clocks; color TVs with free sports, news, and movie channels; and AM/FM radios. All have carpeted baths with tub/shower combinations. A complimentary daily newspaper is delivered daily to your door.

On-premises facilities include a heated outdoor pool, shops and boutiques, a unisex beauty salon, car-rental counter, laundry and valet cleaning services, and complimentary use of an exercise room outfitted with Universal equipment. Free airport shuttle service is available.

Restaurants include the Plaza Brasserie, an airy, contemporary café open from 6am to midnight; and Landry's, open for lunch and dinner, where the focus is on steak, chops, and seafood, including a sushi bar. Drinks can be enjoyed in Zeno's (and some great hors d'oeuvres) or in the Plaza Lounge in the lobby. Room service is available around the clock.

Singles at the Plaza La Reina are $100 to $145, and doubles go for $120 to $165; suites begin at $300.

The **Los Angeles Airport Marriott,** Century and Airport boulevards, Los Angeles, CA 90045 (tel. 213/641-5700, or toll free 800/228-9290), is another good airport hotel choice. It offers 1,020 cheerfully decorated bedrooms with all luxury extras, including remote-control color TVs, AM/FM-stereo radios, alarm clocks, and even ironing boards, irons, and hair dryers if you like. There's also a guest laundry room—everything, in short, geared to the weary in-transit traveler.

There's a gigantic pool and garden sun deck, with a swim-up bar (the bar stools are actually in the pool), a whirlpool, and a cabana for refreshments. It's just one of the many eating and drinking facilities here, others including the Fairfield Inn, a coffee shop; the Lobby Bistro, serving buffet breakfasts, lunches, and dinners; and the Capriccio Room, for Continental cuisine and Mediterranean ambience. Cocktails and entertainment are offered in a luxurious lounge called Gammon's; you can also have cocktails in the lobby lounge.

Courtesy limousine service to and from the airport is provided, and there's parking space for over 1,000 cars.

Singles go for $110 to $160; doubles, $120 to $180. Suites begin at $275.

---

6. Restaurants

Los Angeles is one of the world's leading restaurant cities, almost as diverse in its range of ethnic eateries as New York. Its restaurants are exciting and utterly delightful, many of them taking advantage of the fine Southern California climate with outdoor seating, the rest creating unique and imaginative interiors (frequently with high noise levels) but with more aesthetic sophistication than gimmickry.

In the last decade or so Angelenos have become more knowledgeable about their food. They eat well and love to discuss restaurants and what appears to be a continually changing chef scene. Dining places are a major part of the star system and the status scene—you are where you eat, what you eat, and more important, you are where you're seated. Almost every plush dining establishment has its "A" tables and its social-outcast sections. Unless you're rich and famous, you might as well decide you're above such snobbery; after all, no matter where you sit the food's the same. And no matter where you go, if it's good—from sleazy-but-great hamburger joints to bastions of haute cuisine—you're likely to see the stars. Part of the fun of L.A. dining is star-gazing—it adds glamour, and glamour is a big element in L.A.'s dynamic dining experience.

The first section of restaurant recommendations is devoted to the most glamorous, fashionable—and usually expensive—gathering places of the rich and famous. They're chosen, however, more for culinary excellence than chic popularity. The remainder are broken down into expensive, moderately priced, and budget categories, then further subdivided as to nationality or type of cuisine. This being L.A., many of the following are "in" places too. Many of the restaurants recommended in the hotel section above are equally good—be sure to consider them as well. Reservations are advised at all Los Angeles restaurants, except Pink's Hot Dog Stand and similar places. Reservations are imperative at—

THE TOP RESTAURANTS

The creation of the late Jean Bertranou, **L'Ermitage,** 730 N. La Cienega Blvd., just north of Melrose Place, West Hollywood (tel. 213/652-5840), is one of L.A.'s most highly acclaimed restaurants. The owner, Dora Fourcade, has enhanced L'Ermitage's reputation for fine cuisine and lovely interior design. Since its inception, the restaurant has always maintained rigorous standards for the ingredients of its dishes. The wine list (all 12 pages) also reflects this pursuit of quality.

The delicate pastel-colored dining area is a masterpiece of understated elegance, reminiscent of private dining rooms in plush Paris homes. Tables are set with flowers, Christofle silver, and Villeroy and Boch china. Persian rugs on parquet floors and a wood-burning fireplace create a warm, sparkling atmosphere. A back patio with a fountain is enclosed by a domed glass skylight.

The menu changes seasonally. Since the incredibly light pastry at L'Ermitage is not to be believed, you would do well to begin with an hors d'oeuvre of puff pastry filled with a seasonal selection—perhaps tender stalks of young asparagus. The entrees might include roast squab on a bed of green cabbage and fresh foie gras; Maine lobster with green onions and julienne of mushrooms, served with potato purée; Viennoise of striped bass with mushrooms and fresh tomatoes, served with saffron angel-hair pasta.

Whatever you order, pace yourself to leave room for an unforgettable dessert, like poached pear in red wine and blackcurrant sauce with homemade vanilla ice cream in a delicate pastry shell, or a wonderful apple tart with a very thin and flaky crust. And as a reminder, L'Ermitage has one of the best cheese selections in Los Angeles. On the other hand, the ultimate treat would be one of the wonderful dessert soufflés, a choice of Grand Marnier or chocolate. Expect dinner to cost about $65 to $70 per person.

L'Ermitage is open Monday through Saturday, for dinner only, from 6:30 to 10pm. Reservations are suggested.

L'Orangerie, 903 N. La Cienega Blvd., two blocks south of Santa Monica Boulevard, in West Hollywood (tel. 213/652-9770), is not only one of this city's most renowned French restaurants but one of the most beautiful restaurants I've ever been in, and it features superb service. It reminds you of a French estate. It's light and airy thanks to multipaned arched floor-to-ceiling windows. Diners sit in Louis XVI–style chairs at tables elegantly set with Limoges china (made especially for the restaurant), Sheffield flatware, and long candles in elegant glass holders. The candlelight is gorgeous. Two murals depict L'Orangerie in the 17th century, and here and there throughout the restaurant are potted ferns and stunning floral displays. There's a stone-floored garden dining area under an awning complete with a fountain and vines climbing the latticework. The blue-and-white Portuguese-tile bar area is also inviting.

As you peruse the menu, you may want to sip L'Orangerie's special drink, a divine raspberry-champagne concoction. Appetizers include eggs scrambled with caviar, put back in the shells, and served in egg cups. The entrees are delectable (and expensive, at $60 to $80 table d'hôte—but worth every penny); you might try the veal medallions in a three-mustard sauce. Chicken-in-the-pot is hardly what you would expect to find listed on the menu at L'Orangerie, but there it is—half of a free-range beauty cooked in chicken stock and graced with simple herbs. The poached poulet, looking totally delectable, is surrounded by baby red potatoes and bits of carrots and turnips, eminently suitable for a centerfold spread and worth every bite of the $27.50. For dessert, don't miss the hot apple tarte or coussin au chocolat with vanilla sauce.

Dinner is served nightly from 6:30 to 11pm. Reservations are required, as are jackets for men.

Jimmy Murphy—for over a decade maître d' at the elite Bistro—struck out on his own several years ago with **Jimmy's,** 201 Moreno Dr., near Santa Monica Boulevard in Beverly Hills (tel. 213/879-2394). Backed by part owners Johnny Carson and Bob Newhart, Jimmy's was described as "a million-dollar-plus gamble that if you build a better VIP mousse trap, Los Angeles's top dining-out brigade will stand in line to be counted "in." Jimmy's is *the* place to be seen.

Such has proved to be the case, and with good reason. Jimmy has attracted personnel—waiters, bartenders, captains, etc.—from the best restaurants. He's also created one of the prettiest and most comfortable restaurants in town. The predominant color in the decor is the mossy gray-green of the lush carpeting and upholstery, set off by delicate blue-green accents. The walls are covered with exquisite wallpaper and fabric, and Baccarat crystal chandeliers are suspended from recessed ceilings painted to look like the sky. Tables are set with Limoges china, crystal glasses, and fresh flowers. One wall of windows overlooks the terrace with its small garden, fountain, shade trees, and tables under white canvas umbrellas. From the Chinoiserie statues at the entrance to the considered placement of mirrors, plants, and floral arrangements, Jimmy's is perfectly lovely in every detail, including the posh bar/lounge where a pianist entertains nightly.

You could begin lunch or dinner with an hors d'oeuvre of assorted shellfish or pheasant pâté with truffles. Dinner entrees, which cost $22 to $35, include filet mignon with foie gras and truffles wrapped in a fluffy pastry shell, salmon mousse with tomato and saffron sauce, and filet of sole with orange butter. The desserts—gloriously displayed—are superb. At lunch you might opt for a very good seafood salad, cold salmon in aspic, white fish with limes, or glazed oysters cooked in champagne, for $15 to $22.

Jimmy's is open for lunch weekdays from 11:30am to 3pm, and for dinner Monday through Saturday from 5:30pm to midnight.

The movie set and other socially prominent citizens are oft seen at **The Bistro,** 246 N. Canon Dr., at Dayton Way, Beverly Hills (tel. 213/273-5633), a restaurant conceived about two decades ago by Billy Wilder and Kurt Niklas, previously maître d' at Romanoff's. The charming decor here is authentically and elegantly Parisian belle époque, with mirrored walls, hand-painted panels of classical motif, tables clothed in white linen and set with gleaming silver, soft pink lighting, fresh roses on every table and beautifully arranged in baskets and pots here and there.

Both service and cuisine are top-notch. You'll find such excellent rich soups as lobster bisque and cream of watercress, as well as an outstanding mussel soup. Two appetizer choices you don't want to overlook are the papillote of salmon and the pheasant pâté. Cold entrees might include a duck or quail salad, or you may find the delicious shrimps and scallops atop angel-hair pasta with caviar sauce on the menu. All the pasta is homemade and fresh. Entrees might include eastern lobster on a bed of tagliatelle noodles, grilled salmon, perhaps a rack of lamb. For dessert, a sumptuous chocolate soufflé is recommended. The gentle sounds of piano music accompany the fine cuisine at dinner. Typical dinner offerings are about $24 to $35.

Dinner is served Monday through Saturday from 6 to 10:30pm. Reservations are essential, as are jackets for dinner.

The **Bistro Garden,** 176 N. Canon Dr., off Wilshire Boulevard (tel. 213/550-3900), is a lovely, comfortable part of the L.A. VIP restaurant scene, headquarters for the "movers and shakers," adorned by the "beautiful people." During the summer you can dine under striped umbrellas amid trees and flowering plants in the lovely outside garden.

Lunch at the Bistro Garden features many cold dishes such as papaya filled with shrimp and a salad of cold lobster and vegetables; other choices are omelets, hamburgers, and broiled shrimps with mustard sauce. Entrees cost $15 to $24. Don't pass up those desserts on the piano. Variety is always the order of the day. Dinner might begin with an appetizer of pâté maison or marinated herring, and continue with an entree of linguine with clam sauce, paprika goulash, or roast rack of lamb for two, for $22 to $32 per person.

The Bistro Garden is open Monday through Saturday from 11:30am to 3:30pm for lunch, from 6:30 to 11pm for dinner. Dinner only is served on Sunday, from 6:30 to 11pm. Reservations are always essential. There's another, new Bistro

Garden, both bigger and brighter, at 12950 Ventura Blvd. in the Valley (tel. 818/501-0202).

The Beverly Hills Hotel has had a long-standing relationship with the world of entertainment, so it's no surprise that **The Dining Room,** the hotel's new restaurant, 9641 Sunset Blvd. (tel. 213/276-2251), has black-and-white photographs of celebrities around the room and their favorite dishes on the menu—choices such as Johnny Carson's Lake Superior white fish, Sophia Loren's vitello tonato, Elizabeth Taylor's chili, and Liza Minnelli's salade de Provence.

Done in soft pastels, with comfortable booths, banquettes, and armchairs, the Dining Room also offers the chef's style of California cuisine, with light sauces, California products, the freshest ingredients (including herbs from the hotel's own herb garden), grilled meats and fish. There is a lengthy list of cold appetizers, among which is a choice of hors d'oeuvres brought to your table by cart. Among the hot first courses: the very popular escargots baked in baby russet potatoes with hot garlic butter. The seafood is prepared in several styles—baked lobster, blackened swordfish, poached salmon, and sautéed sea bass—while meat specialties are from the broiler with your choice of sauce. Entrees range from $19 to $35, and dinner will average $50 to $60 per person without wine.

Complimentary after-dinner truffles accompanied by chocolate-dipped strawberries should not deter you from at least a glance at the dessert choices. There is, of course, Frank Sinatra's favorite cheesecake—a creamy New York style—but it is also worth asking about the soufflé maison. The Dining Room has an excellent selection of domestic and international wines, currently priced from $18 to $250. Particular emphasis is on the California chardonnays and cabernets. California wines by the glass are $4 to $6.50.

The Dining Room is open for dinner Monday through Saturday from 6:30 to 10pm, with unobtrusive piano music played throughout. In keeping with the tradition of the Beverly Hills Hotel, telephones are available at each table. Reservations are as necessary as jackets.

La Scala & Boutique Restaurant, 410 N. Canon Dr., between Santa Monica Boulevard and Brightwon Way (tel. 213/275-0579 or 550-8288), is a petite beauty. On the whim of a moment, more years ago than I would care to remember, Jean Leon created a charming gourmet boutique and restaurant in Beverly Hills. They fast became the celebrity-packed, truly chic dining spots in Beverly Hills. Since then, Jean Leon's La Scala and the Boutique have merged into one, but the people who go there are still just as fascinating and delicious as the cuisine. Somehow, regardless of style, most of the customers consistently have the look of people in The Business.

As for the restaurant itself, it is easily identified by the name La Scala on the spotless white bowed awnings. And inside, faux orange trees are centered in a setting of dark woods, red-leather booths, amber mirrors, soft spot lighting, and fresh flowers. To the rear, directly above a small bar, are a number of those Gerald Price caricatures of famous Hollywood faces. Wine bottles are strategically placed here and there around the booths to remind you of the excellent cellar. At noon the clientele arrive in suits, dresses, short-sleeve shirts, warm-up suits, whatever; for dinner they are less of an eclectic mix. Surprisingly, the noise level is minimal, allowing for easy conversation, even though the restaurant is relatively small. If you have a choice, however, seating to the rear is preferred to avoid those grouped at the entrance waiting for tables.

What to eat? For lunch you might begin with the delicious bean soup with aromatic virgin olive oil (fagioli alla toscana con olio santo). Follow that with the popular luncheon specialty, Leon's chopped salad. Two of the other good main dishes are the cannelloni Gigi and the grilled shrimp marinara. Sandwiches are on the menu, as is a selection of cold plates. A half carafe of the house wine and a piece of cheesecake, or some of the delicious homemade ice cream with berries or chocolate, might round out your meal. Entrees are in the $10 to $15 range; on the other hand, most salads and soups are in the vicinity of $7 to $10.

For dinner you might begin with the extraordinary marinated salmon with white truffle, or, less extravagantly, with prosciutto and melon. Pasta dishes are featured, one of the house specialties being spaghetti alla checca, with chopped tomatoes, virgin olive oil, garlic, and basil. Beautifully prepared main courses include the grilled shrimp or langostines with white wine, the duck sausage with Cannelli beans, and the spring chicken with rosemary and white wine. There are also nightly changing specials. Entrees range from $11 to $19. A soothing end to the meal is the tiramisu, although many simply have the cappuccino.

La Scala & Boutique Restaurant is open Monday through Saturday from 11:30am to 11:30pm. There are no reservations for lunch, unless you happen to be a group of six or more. Reservations are definitely needed for dinner.

Chasen's, 9039 Beverly Blvd., at Doheny Drive, Beverly Hills (tel. 213/271-2168), is a long-enduring favorite. The original Chasen's, a chili parlor, was financed by none other than *New Yorker* editor Harold Ross, and early patrons at this "Algonquin West" included Jimmy Durante and James Cagney. Once James Thurber spent hours drawing murals on the men's room wall—they were immediately removed by an unimpressed and overly industrious cleaning lady who was fired posthaste.

The main dining room is richly wood-paneled and softly lit, with beamed ceilings, brass reading lamps, and plush tufted red-leather booths.

The menu has come along way since chili (Elizabeth Taylor's favorite; she has it sent to her), but the Continental fare retains an American simplicity that I'm sure Harold Ross would have approved. Specialties include the very special hobo steak (not listed on the menu), veal bone chop, and rack of lamb, in the $29 to $30 range. Everything is à la carte. You can top off your meal with the house special—banana or strawberry shortcake.

Chasen's is open for dinner only from 6pm to 1am; closed Monday. (Chasen's now accepts only American Express.)

Housed in an Early California–style terra-cotta stucco building, **Le Restaurant,** 8475 Melrose Place, off La Cienega Boulevard, West Hollywood (tel. 213/651-5553), has a star clientele and was actually once owned by singer Patti Page. It's truly beautiful, with an ambience as fresh as country air. The front room has pale-mauve silk wallcoverings, pink tablecloths, deep-green velvet booths, and a fireplace. There's lots of oak paneling throughout, and tables are separated by etched-glass dividers.

The menu is classically French. Dinner should begin with an appetizer, of which there is a wide selection ranging from a salad of endive and hearts of palm to foie gras de Strasbourg. Entrees like steak tartare, noisette of lamb served on fresh artichoke bottoms, and whitefish stuffed with tarragon in a white wine sauce are expertly prepared; they cost $20 to $34. For dessert, try the pâtisseries du chef.

Dinner is served Monday through Saturday from 6 to 10:30pm.

One clue to the high quality of **The Windsor,** 3198 W. 7th St., at the corner of Catalina, East Wilshire (tel. 213/382-1261), is that the Los Angeles Gourmet Society throws its parties here. Another may be that it's had the same owner for almost 40 years. Not only is the cuisine excellent, the ambience—very English clubby—provides a genuine feeling of well-being. The walls, paneled in rich mahogany or papered in flocked wall covering, are hung with coats-of-arms and $50,000 worth of original oil paintings.

But it's not only the decor that's reassuring. The Windsor is the kind of place where a dedicated staff of 50 have been employed an average of 12 years.

When you sit down, you'll be presented with a lavish à la carte menu with loads of Continental-style selections and a wine list to match. You might begin with a smoked salmon hors d'oeuvre, a beautifully presented seafood platter, or marrow bordelaise. The specialties include steak Diane, veal chop Florentine en croûte, tournedos of beef, and a considerable list of pastas. Entrees range in price from $16 to $30. For dessert it's a hard choice among baked alaska, soufflé Grand Marnier, and one of the delectable pastries. In total, dinner for two averages about $80, without wine. However, a complete pretheater dinner is available for $25. And à la carte lunches are less expensive than dinner; a full meal can be had for $20. The de jour lunch is excellent at $17.50.

Lunch is served weekdays from 11:30am to 3:30pm; dinner, Monday through

Saturday from 4:30 to 11pm. The pretheater dinner is served from 5 to 7:30pm. Tuesday through Saturday evening, soft piano music adds to your dining pleasure. Reservations are a must.

EXPENSIVE RESTAURANTS

I must admit that there's a fine line differentiating the following restaurants from the preceding ones. The upcoming selections are an iota less celebrated and chic, possibly a trifle less expensive. And at lunch many are moderately priced. Reservations are, once again, advisable at these establishments.

American/Steaks/Ribs

Hy's, 10131 Constellation Blvd., across from the ABC Entertainment Center (tel. 213/553-6000), is among the most attractive restaurants in Los Angeles and is one of the city's best spots for dining and dancing. The restaurant is entered via a massive porte cochere. Inside, the arched balconies, alcoves, and cascading tiers of tiny lights create an intimate atmosphere in the two-level dining rooms. Large tables, set aside for privacy, are draped in crisp ivory linens accented with soft pastel touches.

If you've just about been California-cuisined to death, Hy's would be a superb choice for your next meal. The extensive menu showcases the excellent prime steak patrons have come to expect (aging, boning, and trimming of the dry-aged beef are done on the premises); that's a given. But the restaurant also features excellent fresh seafood flown in daily from Hawaii and around the world, specialty salads, innovative pasta dishes, and mouthwatering desserts. At lunch a good start would be the Norwegian smoked salmon or the soup du jour. Entrees afford a wide variety of choices, from the Mediterranean seafood salad to the fettuccine with veal and shiitake and oyster mushrooms. Luncheon entrees range from $11 to $17.

Dinner specialties of the house are steak (T-bone, filet mignon, New York strip, Delmonico), prime rib, rack of lamb, veal, fresh seafood, and Maine lobster. Hy's uses Hawaiian kiawe-wood charcoal to cook the beef. A fine start to dinner would be the delicious blackened Cajun prawns or Hy's Caesar salad. You might then proceed to the rack of lamb, steak au poivre, or grilled chicken with cilantro-pesto sauce. Hy's traditional basket of hot cheese and garlic bread accompanies all dinner entree selections. Dinner entrees range from $16 to $32.

There's great live entertainment in the lounge on Monday, Friday, and Saturday nights; live music for their happy hour Tuesday through Friday, and on weekends from 9:30pm till closing. The lounge features jazz every Monday night.

Hy's is open for lunch weekdays from 11:30am to 2:30pm, and for dinner Monday through Saturday from 6 to 9pm. A late-night Gourmet Teaser menu is served after 9pm until closing. Reservations are necessary.

The **Musso & Frank Grill,** 6667 Hollywood Blvd., several blocks west of Cahuenga (tel. 213/467-7788), bills itself as Hollywood's oldest restaurant (est. 1919). It's the kind of place people return to again and again for the comfortably substantial ambience, superb service, and consistently excellent food that they have been turning out for over half a century. It's where Faulkner and Hemingway hung out during their screenwriting days. Musso & Frank Grill is a favorite of Jonathan Winters, Merv Griffin, Raymond Burr, and Sean Penn, among countless others.

The setting is richly traditional—beamed oak ceilings, red-leather booths and banquettes, mahogany room dividers (the kind with coathooks)—and soft lighting emanating from wall sconces and chandeliers with tiny shades.

The menu is extensive, and everything—soups, salads, bread, vegetables, even sauces and dressings—is à la carte. Try the delicious seafood salads such as the chiffonade or shrimp Louie, perhaps along with some Camembert that comes with crusty bread and butter. Diners wishing heartier fare might consider the veal scalloppine marsala, roast spring lamb with mint jelly and baked potato, or broiled lobster. Entrees average $10 to $30. Sandwiches and omelets are also available. The back of the menu lists an extensive liquor and wine selection.

Open daily except Sunday from 11am to 11pm.

A family enterprise started in 1938, **Lawry's The Prime Rib,** 55 N. La Cienega Blvd., just north of Wilshire Boulevard, Beverly Hills (tel. 213/652-2827), enjoys an excellent Restaurant Row location. It is the unique creation of Lawrence Frank, along with his brother-in-law, Walter Van de Kamp. Frank set out to offer "the greatest meal in America," serving one entree—the hearty prime rib he had enjoyed every Sunday for dinner as a boy (his father was in the meat business)—and serving it gloriously with flair and elegance. In order to showcase his famous beef, Frank originally purchased three gleaming silver carts (each cost as much as a Cadillac!) and hired experts to carve tableside. He also invented his now famous seasoned salt as the perfect seasoning for prime rib.

The ambience at Lawry's is like an oversize English country estate or posh private club. You might start out in the homey cocktail lounge, where drinks are served from a pewter-topped wood-paneled bar. The dining room is richly decorated with valuable original oil paintings (including one of the Duke of Windsor at age 7), Persian-carpeted oak floors, plush burnt-orange-leather booths, high-backed chairs at tables decked out in orange-sherbet cloths, and graceful brass chandeliers overhead.

As noted previously, there's only one entree—award-winning prime ribs of beef—a choice of four cuts, priced from $16 to $25. With it you get Yorkshire pudding, salad, creamed corn, mashed potatoes, and creamed horseradish. You can also get side dishes like creamed spinach or buttered peas, and a good wine list is available. There are delicious desserts to end the "perfect meal." Always drawn by some mysterious force to the rich and creamy, I immediately gravitate to the chocolate pecan pie.

Open Monday through Thursday from 5 to 11pm, on Friday and Saturday to midnight, and on Sunday from 3 to 10pm. Reservations suggested.

R.J.'s The Rib Joint, 252 N. Beverly Dr., between Dayton Way and Wilshire Boulevard, Beverly Hills (tel. 213/274-7427), is always mobbed, but it's no hardship to sit at the friendly bar for a little while until your table is ready. The floors are covered with sawdust here too, and the walls are hung with historic photos of Beverly Hills and old-time actors and actresses. The room is dominated by the granddaddy of all salad bars, the "green grocery," as it is known, which includes such offerings as spinach salad, fresh mushrooms, dates, guacamole, real Roquefort dressing, herring in cream sauce, shrimp, hearts of palm, and much more. All this is included with dinner entrees, but if salad-bar fare is all you want, it's about $12.

Sourdough rolls and butter are also served with the entrees, which cost $15 to $30 and include steaks, hickory-smoked chicken, crispy duck, or a bucket of clams. But the reason most people go to R.J.'s is for the beef and pork ribs that are grilled over oakwood and mesquite charcoal. Servings are huge, and for dessert a piece of R.J.'s chocolate cake is large enough for four; ditto the chocolate-chip cookie topped with vanilla ice cream, hot fudge, and real whipped cream. If you're like most customers here, you'll stagger out carrying leftovers wrapped in foil, creatively formed into various shapes—the swan is my favorite. Lunch is also served, for a less expensive $10 to $15.

R.J.'s has a well-stocked bar (over 500 brands). Only premium liquors and fresh-squeezed juices are used in drinks; they carry over 50 varieties of beer from all over the world.

R.J.'s is open weekdays from 11:30am to 10pm, weekends to 11pm. Reservations are essential.

The **Pacific Dining Car,** 1310 W. 6th St., at Witmer Street (tel. 213/483-6000), is just a few short blocks from the center of downtown Los Angeles. The restaurant has been authentically decorated to evoke the golden age of rail travel. Walls are paneled in warm mahogany with brass luggage racks (complete with luggage) overhead. Old menus and prints from early railroading days line the walls, and brass wall lamps with parchment shades light some tables.

The atmosphere is warm and friendly, but the main reason for going to any restaurant is the food, and in this the Pacific Dining Car excels. Steaks are prime, aged on the premises, and cooked over a mesquite-charcoal fire. At dinner, top sirloin, a New York steak, fresh seafood, veal, and lamb are all served for $22 to $37. For starters the calamari is excellent, but weight-watchers might prefer the beefsteak tomato and onion salad. Prices at lunch are less, at $19 to $29, and the menu items are basically the same. On a recent visit I enjoyed a perfectly charbroiled boneless breast of chicken, with choice of potato or tomato. There's an outstanding wine list. Desserts are simple fare such as apple pie.

Open 24 hours a day, seven days a week. Reservations are definitely advised for lunch and dinner. There's also a breakfast menu (egg dishes, salads, steaks), available from 11pm to 11am; prices are about $9 to $19. Great food!

Otto Rothschilds Bar and Grill, on the ground floor of the Dorothy Chandler Pavilion (tel. 213/972-7322), celebrates the unparalleled visual history of the motion picture industry and its stars. Photographs of stage and screen celebrities, taken by Otto Rothschild over a period of 40 years, adorn the walls of this handsome eatery.

The restaurant opens at 7am and offers the traditional egg-plus-whatever repasts, as well as some very exceptional omelets (including one with crab, avocado, and mushrooms); or you might consider such delights as the carameled apple pancake filled with sliced apples and dusted with a hint of cinnamon. Breakfast tabs range from $6 to $10.

There's nothing commonplace about lunch, either. I tend to focus on the appetizers and light entrees such as the Szechuan grilled chicken tenderloins with two dipping sauces or the prime rib chili served with corn chips. Entrees such as the garden fettuccine with wild mushrooms, asparagus, sun-dried tomatoes, broccoli, and zucchini, and the pan-seared chicken breast served over wild mushrooms appear regularly. Light entrees average $8; regular entrees cost about $10.

The list of dinner entrees includes excellent choices of prime meats, seafood, and pastas. A herb-roasted prime rib is served with whipped horseradish sauce; the rack of lamb comes crusted with Dijon herb crumbs; or if you take your seafood spicy, try the Cajun broiled colossal shrimp. Dinner entrees range from $16 to $28. The after-theater menu ranges from light entrees (smoked ham and cheddar omelet, a Rothschild burger, a salad) to the more substantive (pasta, fresh fish, even the herb-roasted prime rib of beef)—all from $12 to $19.

The restaurant is open weekdays from 7:30am to 11pm, weekends from 11:30am to 10pm. Reservations are essential.

A smashing addition to the restaurant scene is the **West Beach Café,** 60 N. Venice Blvd., one block from the beach in Venice (tel. 213/823-5396). It's a trendy eatery that specializes in California nouvelle cuisine. The decor is cool, modern, and minimalist, with white cinder-block walls, track lighting, and simple black chairs and white-clothed tables. The walls of the café serve as a gallery for an ever-changing variety of works by local artists.

Featured at lunch are hamburgers, Caesar salad, pasta, seafood, warm salad, and chicken, as well as many specials, which change weekly. Prices at midday average $10 to $18. Dinner entrees are more elaborate: Among the favorites are grilled Spanish red shrimp in achiote oil with garlic, and ancho chili with steamed potatoes tossed with cilantro and a side plate of steamed spinach. The menu changes weekly. Dinner prices range from $18 to $32. A special brunch is served on weekends, and includes eggs Benedict, Belgian waffles, huevos rancheros, and do-it-yourself tacos (you pick the ingredients), for $12 to $20. There's a fine wine list with selections to complement any meal.

The West Beach Café is open daily: for breakfast ($6 to $10), weekdays from 8 to 11:30am and weekends from 10am; for lunch, from 11:30am to 2:30pm; for dinner, from 6 to 10:30pm; and for late-night pizzas (made with whatever's in the kitchen), from 11:30pm to 1:30am ($13 to $17).

Chinese

One of the most "in" spots in Santa Monica is **Chinois on Main,** 2709 Main St. (tel. 213/392-9025), a high-fashion restaurant owned and operated by Wolfgang Puck and Barbara Lazaroff of Spago. It's a stunning extravaganza, decorated in green and pink with black touches. There are special details too: a pair of large cloisonné cranes, a Buddha over the bar, a large window full of blossoms, and exotic flowers all around.

But on to the fabulous food. Rather than the typical Chinese menu, Chinois on Main presents a delicious combination of Oriental, California, and French moderne cuisines. The à la carte menu is changed seasonally to take advantage of the freshest foods available. You might begin your meal with stir-fried garlic chicken with marinated spinach on radicchio leaves, or sautéed goose liver with warm ginger vinaigrette. First "flavors" (courses) range from $6 to $13. Entrees might include a whole sizzling catfish stuffed with ginger; phoenix and dragon (pigeon and lobster sliced on watercress with mushrooms and whole shallots, roasted in cabernet sauce); or charcoal-grilled Szechuan beef, thinly sliced, with hot chili oil and cilantro sauce. Entrees cost $15 to $28. And for dessert, you can partake of a rice tart flavored with lichee wine or assorted sherbets and fresh fruits, among other choices.

Chinois is open seven nights a week for dinner from 6 to 10:30pm, and Wednesday through Friday for lunch from 11:30am to 2pm. Reservations are essential and should be made as far in advance as possible. *Note:* The party atmosphere and acoustical design of the restaurant cause quite a din, so if you're looking for peace and quiet, Chinois may not be your dish. On the other hand, if you can't resist (and you really shouldn't), the only option is to dine early.

Continental/French

La Chaumière, in the Century Plaza Hotel, Avenue of the Stars, off Santa Monica Boulevard in Century City (tel. 213/277-2000), is the lovely restaurant in the tower of the hotel. The decor is elegant country French, and the food is a blend of Continental and California cuisines. As you enter, you'll first notice the fine wood paneling, brass fixtures, and large French tapestry. La Chaumière thankfully has the peace and order of a private club; unlike in a number of popular restaurants, your normal speaking tone can actually be heard by your dining companion.

For dinner, you might begin your meal with a marvelously creamy avocado soup with white wine and chunks of king crab at $7, or the coquille of shrimp, scallops, and morels with a brandy crayfish sauce for $9. Several excellent entree choices include an exceptional eggplant pirogue (it's rather like an eggplant boat) filled with shrimp, mussels, and crab, graced with a superb crayfish sausage, and topped with a Créole mustard sauce, for $26. Or you might be seduced by the delicate poached filet of sole with smoked salmon in a creamy watercress sauce, at $22. If you yearn for meat, last but far from least are the flavorful and incredibly tender tournedos of veal with morels and Calvados, for $29. And then there's dessert—the white-chocolate mousse quenelles with orange sauce at $6 is positively immoral.

If the above prices are too rich, go for lunch when entrees start at $13.

La Chaumière is open for lunch Monday through Friday from 11:45am to 1:30pm, and for dinner nightly from 6 to 9pm. Reservations are necessary.

Gourmet Organic/Natural Foods

The **Inn of the Seventh Ray,** 128 Old Topanga Canyon Rd., Topanga Canyon (tel. 213/455-1311), 4 miles from the Coast Hwy. (Calif. 1), offers creekside dining under the shade of ancient trees in a tranquil canyon setting. The most orthodox, and the most beautiful, of L.A.'s natural-food restaurants, the inn was opened about 16 years ago by Ralph and Lucille Yaney as a place to practice and share their ideas about the relationship of food to energy. For this reason, entrees are listed in order of their "esoteric vibrational value"; the lightest and least dense (more purifying items) are listed first and are also less expensive. The back of the menu explains it all, as well as the quality of the food and drink and their preparation.

The good vibes you get from lovingly prepared food are further enhanced by the natural setting (about half of the seating is outdoors) and carefully selected music. Tables overlook the creek and much untamed foliage. There's indoor seating too, in a slope-roofed shingled-and-stucco building with one glass wall overlooking the verdant mountain scene.

All foods and baked goods are prepared on the premises, all soups are home-made, and the greatest care is taken to see that everything is fresh and natural, without chemicals or preservatives. Even the fish is caught in deep water far offshore and served the same day. The dinner menu contains 10 entrees, priced from $12 to $22, all served with soup or salad, complimentary hors d'oeuvres, steamed vegetables, baked potato or herbed brown rice, and stone-ground homemade bread. The lightest item is called Five Secret Rays: lightly steamed vegetables served with lemon-tahini and caraway cheese sauces; the densest, vibrationally speaking, is a 10-ounce New York steak cut from beef fed on natural grasses, charbroiled and served with two steak sauces. A glass of delicious fruit wine is suggested as an apéritif, and delicious desserts are also available.

At lunch options expand to include sandwiches such as avocado, cheese, and sprouts, a cheese and fruit board, and additional salads. Omelets, quiche, and waffles are offered at Sunday brunch. Lunch and brunch entrees are mostly priced from $7 to $11.

Open for lunch weekdays from 11:30am to 3pm, on Saturday from 10:30am and on Sunday for brunch from 9:30am. Dinner is nightly from 6 to 9:30pm. Whether you're into natural foods or not, all the dishes are excellent and you will enjoy the setting. Reservations are essential for dinner.

Irish

Tom Bergin's Tavern, 840 S. Fairfax Ave., just south of Wilshire Boulevard at Barrows Drive (tel. 213/936-7151), is headquarters for L.A.'s Irish community and, like many an Irish bar, a famous gathering place for sportswriters, athletes, and rabid fans. This was the first L.A. restaurant to charter buses to pro football games—they still do, and hold 230 seats to the games reserved five years in advance. I always thought this kind of place existed only in New York and Dublin, but Bergin's has been going strong since 1936. Actors Bing Crosby and Pat O'Brien were early friends of the house.

Irish coffee is a house specialty. For dinner a mesquite-charcoal-broiled New York steak with onion rings, garlic cheese toast, salad, and potato is served. More traditional Irish fare, served with soup or salad and garlic cheese toast, is Dublin-style corned beef and cabbage with a steamed potato, or chicken Erin, simmered in cream and cider sauce, with bacon, leeks, mushrooms, and rice pilaf. Entrees cost $13 to $19. Burgers and salads are also listed, and for dessert you can sample the pieman's wares—fresh fruit pies—or imbibe the Bailey's Irish Cream Cheesecake. Lunch or "pub grub" (served at the bar, from $6 to $10) is less expensive, with entrees like Irish pot roast served with soup or salad, potato, and garden vegetables ($9).

For the record, Bergin sold the tavern in 1973 to two trusted regulars, Mike Mandekic and T. K. Vodrey, both of whom he knew would stick to traditions.

Bergin's serves lunch weekdays from 11am to 4pm, and dinner daily from 4 to 11pm. The bar is open to 2am.

Italian

Emilio's, 6602 Melrose Ave., at Highland, in Hollywood (tel. 213/935-4922), is an award-winning restaurant that attracts a celebrity clientele with its true Italian cooking. The downstairs dining room centers around the "Fountain de Trevi," bathed in colored lights. The decor is unrestrainedly ornate, with marble columns from floor to lofty ceiling, brick archways, stained-glass windows, lots of gilt-framed oil paintings, and fresh flowers on every table. You can also dine in the wine room, but my favorite spot for tender evenings is the balcony, intimate and softly lit.

As for the regional Italian cuisine, forget your budget and your diet; plan to order lavishly and savor every bite. You might begin with the antipasti ($5 to $10) of mussels blessed with spicy tomato sauce and garlic, or the scallops with oil and garlic. For your second course ($10 to $24), the brodetto adriatico (it's like cioppino) is heartily recommended, as are any of the several veal entrees. However, there are magnificent pasta selections, all homemade and prepared with delectable sauces to expand your joy of life: It's hard to ignore the linguine with shrimp and lobster cream sauce, or the rondelli stuffed with ricotta, mortadella, and spinach and sautéed with mushrooms and cream. Should you choose to lessen the cream calories, try the homemade noodles with sun-dried tomatoes, baby corn, carrots, and peas. And then depending on the day, you may find roast suckling pig or osso bucco on the menu.

The other desserts here are probably wonderful, but I've never been able to resist the creamy-rich zabaglione ($14 for two). And *do not miss* Emilio's cappuccino —it's incredible!

Emilio's is open for lunch Thursday and Friday from 11:30am to 2:30pm; for dinner nightly, including a Sunday buffet, from 5pm to midnight.

Ristorante Chianti & Chianti Cucina, 7383 Melrose Ave., at Martel, in Hollywood (tel. 213/653-8333), was opened in 1938 by the famous New York restaurateur Romeo Salta. This charming northern Italian restaurant has a long history in Hollywood, going back to the days when the cast party for *Gone With the Wind* was held here. And the young Mario Lanza was discovered while singing at Chianti. It's still the prestigious winner of many awards (even the wine list has garnered awards), and it's certainly one of the most popular restaurants in town. Although operating as a single entity, it offers two completely different dining experiences and menus.

Ristorante Chianti is traditional Italian in its looks—quiet, intimate, complete with red-velvet seating and sepia-tone murals—but the food is tastefully contemporary. Hot and cold appetizers range from fresh handmade mozzarella and prosciutto to the lamb carpaccio with asparagus to my favorite—marinated grilled eggplant filled with goat cheese, arugula, and sun-dried tomatoes. As for entrees, the homemade pasta is exceptional (as you might expect) yet deliciously untraditional, from the black tortelloni filled with fresh salmon and blessed with lobster sauce to the giant ravioli filled with spinach, ricotta, quail eggs, and touched with shaved black truffle. Other entrees include fresh fish and prawns, poultry, and a fine selection of meat dishes.

On the other hand, Chianti Cucina is contemporary Italian—bright, bustling, attractive—and designed to allow patrons to feel that they're dining right in the kitchen, as honored guests are customarily allowed to do in restaurants in Italy. The Cucina menu changes frequently but consistently features exceptional antipasti, pastas, and an entree selection that is pleasing if somewhat more limited than Ristorante Chianti's. Among the first courses, my choice for the day was the smoked duck with pearls of mozzarella and steamed spinach, lightly touched with a Mediterranean dressing. Carpaccio lovers can indulge in the beef filet with alfalfa sprouts and a bit of parmesan. Of the pasta dishes, you might try the lobster-and-shrimp–filled tortelli, seasoned with saffron in a lovely cream sauce, or the simple pasta dumplings with roasted pepper sauce, basil, and parmesan. As for entrees, there is always seafood, including fresh fish of the day, or for the hearty eater the osso buco braised with vegetables and wine, or perhaps the roasted rabbit stuffed with lamb loin, rosemary, and garlic. Entrees at either restaurant average $13 to $19; antipasti, $6 to $8.

For dessert, on either menu, you can always have fresh berries in season or the elegant cannoli, but why pass up the magnificent tiramisu? All pastries are made daily in the restaurant's bakery. An award-winning wine list is an additional bonus; there is also a full bar.

Ristorante Chianti is open nightly from 5:30 to 11:30pm. Chianti Cucina is open Monday through Saturday from 11:30am to midnight, on Sunday from 5pm to midnight. Reservations are essential.

Harry's Bar & Grill, 2020 Ave. of the Stars, on the Plaza Level of the ABC Entertainment Center, Century City (tel. 213/277-2333), is almost a mirror image of its namesake in Florence. The bar is very European, with its high walnut counter and tall wooden stools. The intimate dining areas have the wonderful pink light characteristic of Florence. Owners Larry Mindel and Jerry Magnin (they also own Chianti) hand-picked the paintings, tapestries, and furnishings on trips to Florence. They even made a mold of the oak wainscoting so that it could be duplicated in L.A., commissioned artist Lazero Donati (who created an oil painting for the Florence

Harry's) to do a similar painting for their establishment. The *original* Harry's, by the way, is in Venice, not Florence; it was a hangout of the late Ernest Hemingway, who wrote about Harry's in his novel *Across the River and Into the Trees.*

As much attention has been paid to cuisine and service as to lore and decor. At dinner the food is authentic northern Italian, with such superb Venetian and Florentine specialties as homemade duck prosciutto, beef pasta with gorgonzola and pine nuts, and veal scaloppine with balsamic vinegar and mustard. As you might guess when you taste it, all pasta is homemade. And seafood lovers, look out for the special catch of the day. Entrees average $17 to $25. At lunch you might opt for a pasta salad, hamburger, steak sandwich, or even grilled double lamb chops for $10 to $24.

Harry's is open for lunch Monday through Friday from 11:30am to 3pm, for dinner Monday through Saturday from 5:30 to 10:30pm. Reservations are essential.

Another "in" L.A. restaurant is **Spago,** 8795 Sunset Blvd., with its entrance at 1114 Horn, in West Hollywood (tel. 213/652-4025). Owned by chef Wolfgang Puck and designer Barbara Lazaroff, it's simple and elegant, in white, pink, mauve, and peach, with lots of flowers. The restaurant has a huge picture window, so diners can gaze out at the expanse of the city below it. Out back is an enclosed garden patio. The kitchen staff works in an open kitchen along one side of the dining room.

Pizza is a specialty here, though it looks nothing like the product of a neighborhood parlor. Wood-burning ovens cook your meal in the dining room. The pizza here comes with exotic ingredients like duck sausage, shiitake mushrooms, leeks, artichokes, or even with lox and cream cheese! If you prefer pasta, there's black-pepper fettuccine with Louisiana shrimp, roasted garlic, and basil ratatouille; or angel-hair spaghetti with goat cheese and broccoli; or ravioli filled with lobster. And there are more substantial dishes still, such as roast Sonoma lamb with braised shallots and herb butter, or grilled chicken with garlic and parsley. Entrees range in price from $19.50 to $26. To finish off, you can select one of the 18 pastry varieties made daily by the pastry chef and displayed on the kitchen counter.

The food is superb, the place is noisy, the celebrities are many, and you'll enjoy every minute of it. Spago is open nightly from 6 to 11:30pm. Reservations are required and should be made *three to four weeks in advance.*

Japanese

I've already made mention of **Yamato,** in the Century Plaza Hotel, Century City (tel. 213/277-1840), in the hotel listings, but it merits a second placement here. It's one of L.A.'s most beautiful Japanese restaurants, adorned with valuable antiques from Japan. In the foyer two massive Buddhist temple dogs—at least four centuries old—stand as guardians against evil. The elaborately carved overhead beams, 350 years old, are from Kyoto, and the fusumas—made into decorative panels—are 250 years old.

You can dine Occidental style at tables with bamboo chairs, but I much prefer the privacy of one of the 12 shoji-screened tatami rooms (which should be reserved in advance), where you sit on cushions. These latter rooms are simply adorned with a flower arrangement and a Japanese painting or scroll. Shoes are checked, and your meal is served by a waitress in classic kimono. There's no problem sitting, as there's a well under the table—actually, you can change positions with much more freedom than at a regular table. Downstairs, a sushi bar is at the center of things. Another room has eight teppanyaki tables. Upstairs, tables and tatami rooms are in a Japanese garden setting.

The fare is authentic and artfully prepared, and where concessions are made to the Western palate, they're so innovative that they enhance rather than diminish the traditional cuisine. A five-course gourmet dinner "planned with the emperor in mind" might include such dishes as shrimp tempura and beef teriyaki. A combination multicourse family-style dinner for two can also be ordered. From the hibachi, you can savor a delight such as charcoal-grilled, basted sirloin teriyaki, or poached salmon with cucumber. Entrees are served with soup, rice, vegetables, and green tea. Desserts include mandarin orange sherbet and a lovely green-tea ice cream. Dinners range from $12 to $35.

Catering to the ABC Entertainment Center crowds from across the street, Yamato also offers very reasonable pretheater specials. Meals are also moderately priced at lunch, served weekdays only from 11:30am to 2:30pm. Dinner is served Monday through Saturday from 5 to 11pm, on Sunday from 4:30 to 10pm.

Among the most popular Japanese restaurants in L.A. is **Tokyo Kaikan**, 225 S. San Pedro St., between 2nd and 3rd, downtown in Little Tokyo (tel. 213/489-1333). It's designed to look like a traditional Japanese country inn, with colored globe lights overhead, barnwood, bamboo- and rattan-covered walls adorned with straw baskets and other provincial artifacts. In addition to the regular seating, there are three food bars—tempura, shabu-shabu, and sushi.

A la carte dinner entrees, priced at $10 to $17, served with soup and rice, include beef sukiyaki, shrimp and vegetable tempura, and chicken and beef teriyaki. Full dinners average $16 to $22. The lunch menu offers a combination plate among its selections, which costs $9. At either meal, green-tea or ginger ice cream is the perfect dessert.

Tokyo Kaikan is open for lunch weekdays from 11:30am to 2pm, for dinner Monday through Saturday from 5 to 10pm.

An excellent choice for Japanese fare is **Horikawa**, 111 S. San Pedro, off 1st Street, downtown (tel. 213/680-9355). At the entrance of this tranquil restaurant is a small fountain such as is found in traditional Japanese gardens. There's a separate Teppan Grill Room, its beamed white walls hung with reproductions of works by Japanese artist Shiko Munakata; their perusal alone makes a visit here worthwhile. The sushi bar is adorned with wooden signs naming famous wholesale fish markets in Tokyo. As for the main dining room, its walls are covered with brown-and-white photomurals of famous Kyoto gardens. More traditional in appearance is the cocktail bar, with decor featuring murals of plum trees in the Ogata Korin style. Ryotei Horikawa, a section of the restaurant built in authentic Sukiya style, features haute cuisine prepared by noted chefs from Japan.

You can begin your dinner at Horikawa with a sushi sampler or seafood teriyaki. Complete dinners, priced at $35 to $75, might include shrimp tempura, sashimi appetizer, dobin-mushi (a seafood and vegetable soup served in a minipot), kani (crab) salad, filet mignon tobanyaki (served on a sizzling minicooker), rice, tea, and ice cream or sherbet. You can also order à la carte. In the Teppan Grill Room you might opt for filet mignon and lobster tail served with fresh vegetables, in the $18 to $30 range; most luncheon entrees in either room are in the $10 to $15 range. Ryotei dinners (served tea-house style, usually 11 to 13 courses) are $110 per person. Courses are usually selected by the chef according to the tastes of the diners.

What really sets this restaurant apart are the kaiseki dinners—an extraordinary 10-course dining experience (5 courses for lunch); dinners require two days' notice. The courses and, therefore, prices vary and are best discussed in advance once you know the number in your group; ask to reserve one of the lovely tea-house rooms.

Horikawa is open for lunch weekdays only from 11:30am to 2pm; and for dinner Tuesday through Thursday from 6 to 10pm, on Friday to 10:30pm, on Saturday from 5:30 to 11pm, and on Sunday to 9:30pm. Reservations advised at dinner.

Moroccan

Pass through the immense and magnificent carved brass doors and you're in another world, the exotic Arab world of **Dar Maghreb**, 7651 Sunset Blvd., at Stanley Avenue, Hollywood (tel. 213/876-7651); the entrance is on Stanley Avenue. You enter into a Koranic patio, at the center of which is an exquisite fountain under an open skylight. The floor is marble, and the carved wood-and-plaster walls are decorated with handmade tiles in geometric designs. A kaftaned hostess greets you and leads you to either the Rabat Room or the Berber Room. The former features rich Rabat carpets on the floor, marquetry tables, and silk cushions with spun-gold-thread designs. The Berber Room is more rustic, with warm earth tones, rugs from the mountain areas, and brass tables and trays from Marrakech. In both rooms diners sit on low sofas against the wall and on goatskin poufs (cushions). Berber and Andalusian music is played in the background, and there is belly dancing nightly.

The meal is a multicourse feast, including a choice of chicken, lamb, rabbit, squab, quail, or shrimp, eaten with your hands and hunks of bread, and shared, from the same dish, with other members of your party. It begins when a waiter in traditional costume comes around and washes everyone's hands in rose-scented water. There are six possible dinners, priced at $19 to $28 per person. The Fassi Feast (from Fez) begins with three Moroccan salads of cold raw and cooked vegetables, including tomatoes, green peppers with cucumbers, eggplant, and carrots. You scoop it up with hunks of fresh-baked bread. Eat sparingly and slowly—there's a lot more to come.

Next is b'stilla, an appetizer of shredded chicken, eggs, almonds, and spices wrapped in a flaky pastry shell and topped with powdered sugar and cinnamon. Now comes a tajine of chicken cooked with pickled lemons, onions, and fresh coriander. By this time you're well into enjoying eating with your hands, and, hopefully, you've ordered some wine to drink each course down with. The next course is couscous with lamb and vegetables—squash, carrots, tomatoes, garbanzo beans, turnips, onions, eggplant, and raisins. All the feasts include another entree of lamb and honey.

Dessert is a basket of fresh and dried fruits and nuts, and Moroccan cookies. Now it's time for another hand-washing, with rose water, followed by the tea-pouring ceremony—a veritable performance, the mint tea poured with expertise from a height of several feet.

The emphasis is on relaxed and leisurely dining; you'll enjoy it most if you eat just a little of everything, and eat very slowly. Don't miss Dar Maghreb; it's a memorable experience.

Dinner is served nightly from 6pm. Reservations are recommended.

Polynesian

What once was the glory of Polynesian restaurants has since turned from island to sea. **Trader Vic's,** 9878 Wilshire Blvd., at Santa Monica Boulevard (tel. 213/274-7777), has created an interesting nautical look in the Beverly Hilton Hotel with ship models and tropical shells. The Captain's Cabin has been expanded to accommodate merchant seamen, and the dark bar is now a somewhat more sophisticated lounge. But don't despair; all has not been abandoned at sea. The pleasant rum drinks with the cute little umbrellas remain, and some interesting additions have been made to the list of edibles.

The puu puus (otherwise known as hors d'oeuvres) include absolutely delicious crisp calamari. The padang prawns saté are also worthy of serious consideration—gently sautéed, skewered, brushed with a saté-chile butter, then finished via a short trip to the broiler. Or you might begin your meal with an order of barbecued spareribs from the Chinese oven or a Cosmo salad of fresh mushrooms, celery, and artichoke with the special mustard dressing. Two excellent entrees are the barbecued squab and the Indonesian lamb roast, completely trimmed and marinated and served with a peach chutney. On the other hand, if matured beef is your passion, the restaurant offers a chateaubriand for two. For dessert, there's mud pie or the Aloha ice cream—vanilla in mango sauce topped with banana chips. Entrees are about $16 to $30; appetizers, about $7 to $12; and desserts, in the neighborhood of $5.

Trader Vic's is open daily from 5 p.m. to midnight.

The ambience and views at most Marina del Rey harborside restaurants are generally better than the food. Nonetheless, everyone occasionally likes to go there to eat, especially for "islands" food. **The Warehouse,** 4499 Admiralty Way, near Lincoln and Bali Way (tel. 213/823-5451), is the creation of photographer Burt Hixson, who traveled 23,000 miles, ostensibly in a quest to find the perfect decor for his dream restaurant. Remembering the exotic wharves he had seen, he erected a two-level dockside structure, where one now dines on casks and barrels, or inside wooden packing crates. Burlap coffee bags line the walls; netting, rope, and peacock chairs further enhance the setting. The place is entered via a tropical walkway of bamboo and palm that extends over a large fish pond. Hixson's photos line the walls in this unusual restaurant, which is not only colorful but surprisingly unfunky and elegant. Most of the tables have a view of the marina, and many are outside right on the water.

Lunches range from $8 to $13. Dinner costs $17 to $26, with entrees from the world over: Foulet Dijon, Malaysian shrimp, steak teriyaki. Drink it down with beer from whatever nation you wish, or with an exotic rum concoction. Throughout the afternoon and evening there's the oyster bar for snacks like garlic bread, nachos, or quesadillas, and lots of seafood selections (shrimp, oysters, clams, chowder). Is the Warehouse touristy? Certainly, but with good food and all that atmosphere, who cares?

Open for lunch Monday through Friday from 11:30am to 2:30pm, for brunch on Saturday from 11am to 2:30pm, and on Sunday from 10am to 3pm. Dinner is served Sunday through Thursday from 5 to 10pm, on Friday and Saturday from 5 to 11pm. No reservations, except for groups of 10 or more.

MODERATELY PRICED RESTAURANTS

The following kinder-to-your-wallet selections are in the price range most of us choose when dining out if there's no special occasion. But take note that many of the aforementioned expensive places are very affordable at lunch.

American

There's fancy seaside dining galore, and then there's the great and simple food at **Aunt Kizzy's Back Porch,** 4325 Glencove Ave., in the Villa Marina Shopping Center (tel. 213/578-1005), Marina del Rey, which lends credence to the notion that "all-American food is still *in.*" It's southern home-cooked food prepared from time-honed recipes (collected from relatives and friends) that will keep your soul, body, and pocketbook intact. The cook is from Cleveland, Mississippi, and she has prepared southern-style and Créole food for about 40 years.

Nothing is easy to find in the shopping center, but you'll locate Aunt Kizzy's Back Porch if you face Von's (on foot), turn right, cross the small driveway, and walk straight on toward a discreet red neon sign bearing the restaurant's name.

For lunch any day of the week you can have fried chicken, plus two vegetables, rice and gravy (or cornbread dressing and gravy), and cornbread muffins—all for $6. Other choices may include smothered steak, chicken and dumplings, and some of the best smothered pork chops you've ever tasted. Specialties of the house (served Sunday only) are baked chicken with cornbread dressing and pungent barbecued beef ribs. The daily dinner menu includes most of the lunch entrees, plus chicken Créole; chicken and sausage jambalaya; catfish with heavenly hush puppies (fried to order); Uncle Wade's baked beef short ribs, truly lean, meaty, and falling off the bone; red beans and rice and hot links; and for the nonmeat eaters, an all-vegetable plate. All are $11, except the delicious catfish ($12), the meatloaf ($10), the beans, rice, and hot links ($10), and the vegetable plate ($7). Dinner entrees include the same extras as lunch entrees. Old-Time Country Desserts are extra, but $2 will buy a soul-satisfying portion of Grandmother Zady's Peach Cobbler, Miss Flossie's Floating Sweet-Potato Pie, or Sock-It-to-Me Cake filled with walnuts and cinnamon, and served warm.

There's a down-home Sunday brunch for $11, served buffet style, that defies the capacity of most humans. How about some scrambled eggs with cheese or an omelet and choice of bacon, sausage, grits, or grilled potatoes, followed by smothered pork chops, barbecued beef ribs, or fried chicken (to name just three options) and a choice of five vegetables, topped off by peach cobbler or Sock-It-to-Me Cake. All this comes with dessert, fruit juice, tea, coffee, or milk. *Note:* There are no toting privileges.

Showtime at Aunt Kizzy's is the late-night supper on Friday and Saturday. The Uptown Menu, $4 to $9, ranges from the likes of a short-rib sandwich to a salmon-and-spinach roulade (lightly grilled salmon on a bed of seasoned spinach which is rolled, then topped with a poach egg and a basil-hollandaise sauce). The Downtown Menu Late Night Supper (otherwise known as a Southern-Style Breakfast) would take Aunt Kizzy's grandparents from the schoolbus to lunch or through a whole morning of farm chores: fried catfish filet, smothered steak or pork chops, and other meats to accompany the two eggs any style, and biscuits, toast, grits, or home fries. The single Downtown Menu price is $8.

Aunt Kizzy's doesn't offer beer or wine, but the ice-cold lemonade served in a Mason jar is just about the best possible complement for the down-home cooking.

Aunt Kizzy's is open for lunch Monday through Saturday from 11am to 4pm, on Sunday to 3pm; dinner is Sunday through Thursday from 4 to 10pm, on Friday and Saturday to 11pm. *Note:* At the above prices, you can understand that Aunt Kizzy's does not accept credit cards.

Chinese

Twin Dragon, 8597 W. Pico Blvd., at Holt Avenue, just south of Beverly Hills (tel. 213/657-7355), is the domain of owner/chef Mr. Yu-Fan Sun, a master of Shanghai culinary arts, and his brother, manager James Sun. Twin Dragon is a large and comfortable restaurant with Chinese instruments and shell paintings decorating the walls, colorful antique tasseled lamps overhead, a medallion of a dragon complete with red electric eyes, and a gorgeous saltwater fish tank over the bar.

The menu is extensive, in good Chinese-restaurant tradition. Highly recommended are the spicy diced chicken with peanuts, braised shrimp spiced with chili peppers, and the fresh asparagus with prawns. Entrees cost $9 to $17. Peking duck is $24 and requires one-day advance notice. It's a good idea to put yourself in the hands of the chef, who will prepare specialties not on the menu.

Hours are 11:30am to 10pm daily (to 11pm on Friday and Saturday nights). They take reservations for groups of more than five people, and often there's a wait at dinner.

Shanghai Winter Garden, 5651 Wilshire Blvd., corner of Hauser Boulevard (tel. 213/934-0505), is one of my favorite Los Angeles Chinese restaurants. An archway depicting a phoenix and dragon, set in an intricately carved teak wall, separates the dining areas; Chinese paintings and woodcarvings adorn the walls; and overhead are large tasseled Chinese lamps. It all combines to create a very elegant effect, and the ambience is enhanced by taped Chinese music.

The menu offers a wide selection—over 150 entrees to choose from. Among the specialties are diced fried chicken sautéed with spinach, shrimp with bamboo shoots and green peas in a delicious sauce with crisp sizzling rice, crispy duckling made with five spicy ingredients and served with Chinese bread, and crushed white meat of chicken sautéed with diced ham, pine nuts, and green peas. Entrees are priced at $10 to $25. As you can see, this is a place for culinary adventures. For dessert, fried banana or apple serves four. Shanghai Winter Garden also offers daily lunch specials—eggroll, fried rice, and entree—for about $10.

Shanghai Winter Garden is open for lunch Monday through Saturday from 11:30am to 3pm, for dinner nightly from 4 to 10:30pm. Reservations accepted.

Grand Star, 943 Sun Mun Way, off North Broadway between College and Bernard streets (tel. 213/626-2285), is owned by Frank and Wally Quon and their mother, Yiu Hai Quon (born in 1897), recently a TV personality. There are four complete meals priced at $10 to $16 per person. The latter is the gourmet selection, including spicy shrimp in a lettuce shell, wonton soup, spicy chicken wings, Mongolian beef with mushrooms, lobster Cantonese, barbecued pork with snow peas, fried rice, tea, and dessert. If there are four or five in the party, Mama Quon's chicken salad is added, plus larger portions of all else. You can also order à la carte items ranging from dumplings flamed in rum to lobster sautéed in ginger and green onion for $8 to $16. Steamed fish, priced according to size, is a specialty, as are the cashew chicken, Mongolian beef, and Chinese string beans.

On the street level the Grand Star looks more Italian than Chinese; it's dimly lit, with black-leather booths and big bunches of dried flowers here and there. I prefer to sit upstairs, where tables are covered with red cloths and the family's fine collection of Chinese embroideries adorns the walls. Entertainment, usually a female vocalist with piano accompaniment, is featured at cocktail time and on most evenings.

Hours for lunch and dinner are 11:30am to 10pm Monday through Wednesday, to 11pm on Thursday, to midnight on Friday; noon to midnight on Saturday, to 10pm on Sunday.

Desserts

If your sweet tooth is acting up, head over to the **Beverly Hills Cheesecake Factory,** 364 N. Beverly Dr., off Brighton Way (tel. 213/278-7270), or to the **Cheesecake Factory of Marina Del Rey,** at 4142 Via Marina (tel. 213/306-3344). They offer relief in the form of a profusion of delicious baked goods—every conceivable variation of cheesecake (over 40 concoctions, including the incredible white-chocolate/raspberry truffle, fresh strawberry, coffee/brownie chunk, and Kahlúa almond fudge). There are also chocolate fudge cake, carrot cake, and much, much more. Prices average $4 to $8 for a portion of sheer bliss.

The Cheesecake Factory is also a reasonably priced, casual, and friendly restaurant with a substantial list of delicious dishes, including mouthwatering barbecue-style chicken and ribs and such spicy specialties as cashew chicken and shrimp Jambalaya, Louisiana blackened fish, and blackened steak. You can also get a whole breast of chicken served in several styles—teriyaki, Dijon, and grilled lime. A few of the other equally tasty options are the moo shu with spicy chicken; grilled chicken breast (or steak) fajitas, with all kinds of garnishes; or, for the vegetarian, a combination of fresh vegetables sautéed with curry, wine, and spices and covered with melted Jack cheese, or prepared Oriental-style with a special sauce, spices, and nuts and served over rice. There are also more than 15 varieties of fresh pasta, wonderful hot sandwiches, great omelets, and burgers. Entrees range from $6 to $16.

The desserts are all on display up front, so you can fantasize while waiting for a table. No reservations are taken, but your patience will be rewarded, I assure you. The Cheesecake Factory also has a good selection of wines and beers.

The Beverly Hills Cheesecake Factory is open daily: Monday through Thursday from 11am to 11pm, on Friday and Saturday to 12:30am, and on Sunday from 10am to 10pm. There's another Cheesecake Factory in Marina del Rey, at 4142 Via Marina (tel. 213/306-3344), which has the same fabulous desserts and food, plus full bar service. Monday through Saturday, it's open from 11:30am to 11:30pm; on Sunday, from 10am to 11pm. Other Cheesecake Factory locations are at 605 N. Harbor Dr. in Redondo Beach (tel. 213/376-0466) and at 6324 Canoga Ave. in Woodland Hills (tel. 818/883-9900).

Italian

Little Joe's, 900 N. Broadway, at College Street (tel. 213/489-4900), is a vestige of a once-Italian neighborhood in now-touristy New Chinatown. Opened as a grocery in 1927, it has grown steadily over the years; it now has several bars and six dining rooms. It's a wonderfully cozy restaurant with sawdust on the floors, hand-painted oil murals of Rome and Venice, soft lighting, and seating in roomy leather booths.

A meal at Little Joe's ought to begin with a plate of the special hot hors d'oeuvres—fried cheese, zucchini, and homemade ravioli. A complete six-course meal, including soup, antipasto, salad, pasta, vegetable or potato, bread and butter, and dessert, is priced according to entree: $15 to $22 for the likes of veal scaloppine, scallops, or halibut steak. Full pasta dinners are even less, and you can also order à la carte, for $10 to $18. At lunch, entrees are less expensive, at $6 to $13 for dishes like eggplant parmigiana, sausage and peppers, rigatoni, a sausage sandwich. Little Joe's is the best Occidental restaurant in Chinatown.

It's open Monday through Saturday from 11am to 9pm. Reservations are taken.

Sarno's Caffè Dell'Opera, 1714 N. Vermont, in Hollywood (tel. 213/662-3403), is a delightful place that combines two naturals—Italian food and opera. Owner Alberto Sarno is a former opera student himself, so he combined the family business with his love of singing. The restaurant is dim and cluttered, with lots of small tables, heavy antique chandeliers, bronze statuary, and hanging grape clusters.

The food is good and hearty. You can dine on fresh river trout in white sauce, chicken cacciatore, veal parmigiana, or one of many pasta dishes, or—if you have a real appetite—a complete dinner that includes fresh vegetables, soup, salad, bread, pasta, an entree, dessert, and coffee, tea, or milk. Pasta dishes cost $8 to $10, full dinners range from $13 to $17, and à la carte meat dishes (which are served with salad, roll, and beverage) cost $10 to $12. And if you want a light meal, there are salads and sandwiches to choose from, at $6 to $9. Pizza is $10 to $12, depending on the toppings. Pastries and spumoni are excellent.

The fun at Sarno's begins at 7:30pm. At that time Alberto and members of the staff and customers take turns regaling the restaurant with their renditions of opera arias, show tunes, and old Italian favorites. It's fun for everyone, and a great place for people with a yen to sing for a crowd.

Sarno's is open Sunday through Thursday from 11am to 11pm, on Friday and Saturday till 1am.

Pizza in Beverly Hills? Yes, but a very special kind of pizza—at **Prego**, 362 N. Camden Dr., at Brighton Way, in Beverly Hills (tel. 213/277-7346). It's a lovely place, all brick, white, and wood, with unusual modern art on the walls and sprays of seasonal flowers to add a touch of cheer. Music from Italy plays softly in the background.

Prego is basically a trattoria. The food is prepared in an open kitchen by expert chefs. There are lots of antipasti to choose from, like focaccia al formaggio (layers of thin Italian bread and stracchino cheese) and insalata Prego (romaine lettuce, carrots, celery, bell pepper, mushrooms, and vinaigrette). For an entree you have a choice of homemade pasta, like ziti with fresh tomato and basil or lobster-filled pasta, or a grilled dish like fresh fish, lamb with sage, rosemary, and butter, or Italian sausage with spinach. And then there are the pizzas—gourmet creations like the Puttanesca (my favorite), with tomatoes, black olives, capers, mozzarella, artichokes, and oregano; and Dell'Adriatico, with prawns, tomatoes, mozzarella, garlic, and basil. Entrees range in price from $10 to $19. For dessert there are assorted fruits and cheeses, pastry, and a variety of ice cream dishes like semifreddo al caffè—white-chocolate ice cream with espresso and whipped cream.

Prego is open Monday through Saturday from 11:30am to midnight, on Sunday from 5pm to midnight.

Japanese

I like **Fuji Gardens**, 424 Wilshire Blvd., between 4th and 5th streets, Santa Monica (tel. 213/393-2118), a pretty little place with comfortable leather booths, bamboo-pattern wallpaper, blue flags hanging from a rooflike structure over one wall of tables, and tablecloths of the same Japanese-restaurant blue.

Combination dinners here are an excellent value, like the beef teriyaki and lobster-tail combo, which comes with salad, chilled noodles, sashimi or tempura, an appetizer, tsukemono, soup, rice, and green tea. Most of these dinners are in the $10 to $15 range; you can also order à la carte items like salmon teriyaki with vegetable salad and noodles.

Lunches are also a terrific buy. A Makunochi lunchbox with entree, soup, tsukemono, rice, and tea costs $8 to $11; pork cutlet with tongkatsu sauce comes with the same accompaniments. The food here is as excellent, by the way, as it is reasonably priced. For dessert at either meal, try the green-tea or ginger ice cream.

Fuji Gardens is open for lunch weekdays from 11:30am to 2:30pm; and for dinner weekdays from 5 to 10:30pm, on Saturday and Sunday from 3 to 10:30pm.

Miyako, 139 S. Los Robles Ave., between Green and Cordova streets in Pasadena, in the basement of the Livingstone Hotel (tel. 818/795-7005), offers fine Japanese cuisine in an attractive setting. It gives you a choice of both tatami-room and table service, and fresh flower arrangements are placed about discreetly. From the tatami room, you can enjoy a view of a small Japanese garden, while attended by waitresses traditionally attired in kimonos. Subtle understatement is the order of the day.

I like to begin with a sashimi appetizer of tuna slices. A full Imperial dinner offers a combination of shrimp tempura, chicken teriyaki, and sukiyaki. Dinners and à la carte entrees cost $10 to $23. Lunches are priced around $7 to $14. The Miyako is on the same street as the Hilton but has been around much longer—since 1959 under the same owner.

Miyako is open for lunch weekdays from 11:30am to 2pm; and for dinner Monday through Thursday from 5:30 to 9:30pm, on Friday and Saturday to 10pm, and on Sunday from 4 to 9pm.

Jewish Deli

So where do you get a good pastrami on rye in this town? **Nate & Al's,** 414 N. Beverly Dr., off Brighton Way, Beverly Hills (tel. 213/274-0101), has been slapping pastrami on fresh-baked rye since 1945, not to mention chopped liver and schmaltz, kosher franks, and hot corned beef. Seating is in comfortable booths, and lighting is pleasantly low. A big counter up front handles take-out orders (everything from halvah to brie). There's always a line waiting to get in (no reservations), and probably half are New Yorkers.

Rather than strictly kosher, it is kosher style, which means that the incredibly extensive menu can range around both meat and dairy items. There are pastrami and corned beef sandwiches (all sandwiches are one size—huge), chopped liver, and other traditional favorites like cream cheese and Nova Scotia salmon on a bagel and the famous Reuben. An appetizer of gefilte fish with horseradish or chicken soup with matzoh balls or kreplach is a good beginning for any meal. And then there are potato pancakes, and cheese, cherry, or blueberry blintzes with sour cream and apple sauce, and roast turkey with potatoes, cranberry sauce, and vegetables. All these goodies cost $8 to $13. Leave room for a homemade dessert, perhaps apple strudel or chocolate cream pie. Wine and beer are available.

Open Sunday through Friday from 7:30am to 8:45pm, on Saturday to 9:30pm.

A year after Nate & Al's came on the scene, **Zucky's** appeared on the boardwalk in Santa Monica, then moved to 431 Wilshire Blvd., at 5th Street (tel. 213/393-0551). It has typical modernistic Jewish-deli decor: orange-and-gold-leather booths, Formica tables, and glass cases filled with Jewish delicacies.

It's not a kosher deli; you can even get fried shrimp or an omelet of crab, bay shrimp, and whitefish for lunch. But it does offer all the traditional favorites like cheese blintzes with sour cream, a chopped liver on rye, and chicken in a pot with matzoh balls, kreplach, vegetables, soup, and noodles, at $9.50 for two. The menu offers something for everyone. Sandwiches, omelets, salads, and hamburgers are a reasonable $5 to $7, and full hot meals cost $7 to $10. There's a wide choice of desserts from apple strudel to chocolate mousse, and drinks range from Dr. Brown's cream soda or an egg cream to beer and wine.

Zucky's is open Sunday through Thursday from 6am to 2am, and 24 hours on Friday and Saturday. Reservations are accepted.

A year later—1947—yet another Jewish deli appeared in a different part of town: **Langer's,** 704 S. Alvarado, at 7th Street, downtown (tel. 213/483-8050), where the walls are lined with portraits of the Langer family and grandchildren. It's a big, roomy place with counter seating and brown tufted-leather booths. A corner location (two windowed walls) makes it light and airy.

Once more the fare is kosher style rather than kosher, which means you can order the likes of pastrami and Swiss cheese on rye. Stuffed kishka with soup or salad, vegetable, and potatoes, meat blintzes with gravy, and an interesting sandwich combination of cream cheese and cashews are among the available entrees, for $6 to $14.

Langer's is open daily from 6:30am to 11pm.

Mexican

There's "gringo food"—fiery, with lots of cheese, sour cream, refried beans, tamales—and then there's the subtle, delicate, and delicious Mexican cooking of **Antonio's,** 7472 Melrose, in West Hollywood (tel. 213/655-0480). Antonio's is the picture of the sedate and proper Mexican restaurant—no bright reds, yellows, and greens here, but rather the quiet tans and browns suggestive of an aristocratic

Spanish heritage. The health- and weight-conscious should note that, unlike its "gringo-style" counterpart, the true cuisine of Mexico City is delicious and perfectly seasoned while being high in protein, low in cholesterol, and lean on the calories (which may account for the number of celebrities and dignitaries who dine here). A variety of fresh seafood and meats with exotic vegetables are featured, and the majority of entrees are steamed rather than fried.

Dinner entrees ($13 to $19) are light and unusual, such as costillas de puerco en chiptole—flavorful spareribs served in a chile-and-herb sauce—and Antonio's chayote relleno, featuring the tasty chayote squash filled with lean ground beef, ricotta cheese, and spices in a light tomato sauce. The menu changes daily, but fresh fish is available at all times. Chicken is served for a variety of tastes—Guadalajara style in tamales stuffed with assorted fresh vegetables, or stewed in a delicate green sauce of tomatillos, green peppers, and exotic spices. The cabbage leaves stuffed with a mixture of ground beef, chorizo, and herbs graced with chipotle sauce might interest meat lovers. Half orders of evening specials are available for the undecided. All entrees are accompanied by green-corn tortillas.

All this is not to say that if you crave cheese enchiladas, a hamburger, tacos, or enchiladas with guacamole, you won't find them here, but the true beauty of dining at Antonio's rests with the restaurant's simple seafood, meat, and chicken dishes. A cozy wine room, lined with vintage bottles, is available for a small dinner party.

Antonio's serves lunch Tuesday through Friday from noon to 3pm; dinner is Tuesday through Friday from 5 to 11pm, and on Saturday and Sunday from 2 to 11pm. A second Antonio's has opened on Santa Monica's "restaurant row" at 1323 Montana Ave., at 14th Street (tel. 213/395-2815).

Natural Foods

The Source, 8301 W. Sunset Blvd., at Sweetzer Avenue, West Hollywood (tel. 213/656-6388), is where Woody Allen met Diane Keaton for a typical L.A. lunch in *Annie Hall*—part of his New York–oriented statement about Southern California. Inside it's cozy, with curtained windows, tables set with fresh flowers, and a plant-filled stone fireplace in one corner. Those who want fresh air with their health food shouldn't be in L.A., but they can gasp for what's available while dining outside at one of the umbrellaed tables.

A typical dinner (which costs $9 to $11) is the cheese-walnut loaf, served with homemade soup or salad, and a basket of whole-wheat rolls and butter. Salads and sandwiches are also available. Much of the fare is still vegetarian, but chicken and fish are also served. Portions are huge. Lighter fare—crêpes, sandwiches, salads, etc.—costs $5 to $7. For dessert there's a so-good-it's-hard-to-believe-it's-healthy homemade date-nut cheesecake. Drinks range from yogurt shakes to the Hi-Potency Drink (orange juice, banana, wheat germ, and honey; or with milk and molasses). Of course there's always beer or wine.

Open Monday through Friday from 8am to midnight, on Saturday and Sunday from 9am to midnight. For breakfast, how about hot cereal made from ground oats and wheat, topped with sunflower seeds, raisins, bananas, apples, and nuts?

Diagonally across from the Farmers Market is the **Golden Temple,** 7910 W. 3rd St., near Fairfax Avenue, Hollywood (tel. 213/655-1891), its large windows overlooking the busy intersection. Hanging plants and stained-glass panels add color to the interior, but you might prefer to dine on the small patio with a colorful landscape mural on one wall.

The chef prepares a special soup and entree each day. Regular menu items include light fare at $5 to $8, like Santa Fe enchiladas—two corn tortillas layered with natural cheese, onion, and a mild chili salsa; topped with guacamole and sour cream, and served with refried beans. Servings are large, and dinner—priced at $7 to $10 —includes soup or salad and homemade bread. If you're not too hungry, you could make a meal of a bowl of soup and a guacamole salad or Chinese spring rolls with sweet-and-sour sauce. A selection of fresh juices includes carrot, pippin apple, cucumber/celery, and orange. Homemade desserts are prepared daily and can be purchased to go. The lunch menu is similar, but prices are lower.

The Golden Temple is open Monday through Saturday from 11:30am to 4pm and 5:30 to 10pm weeknights, and on Saturday to midnight.

Omelets

The Egg and the Eye, 5814 Wilshire Blvd., right across from the La Brea Tar Pits between Stanley and Curson avenues (tel. 213/933-5596), is one of the most popular restaurants in town. As the name implies, the Egg stands for about 37 varieties of omelets featured upstairs in a pleasant and airy restaurant; the Eye symbolizes the visual arts and crafts (all for sale) found in the galleries on the first and third floors—works ranging from Moroccan handmade rugs to painted eggs to art deco jewelry to posters. If there's a line (a more than likely occurrence), you can browse around until your table is ready.

The reason for the lines is that the omelets are excellent, artfully prepared the French way and filled with all kinds of good things: caviar and sour cream; potatoes, sour cream, and chives; pâté de foie gras, truffles, and asparagus spears; etc. If you're dining with a friend, you might want to share an omelet (they're big) and a salade niçoise. Omelets range in price from $7 to $12. A basket of black raisin bread and butter comes with all meals, and although there are dessert omelets (shaved chocolate, powdered sugar with rum flambé), I prefer a more traditional homemade cheesecake with strawberry sauce.

Open Tuesday through Friday from 11am to 2:30pm, on Saturday and Sunday from 10am; closed Monday. Reservations essential.

BUDGET RESTAURANTS

With all the struggling young actors and actresses in this town, you'd better believe there are quite a few places where you can eat cheaply. The surprising thing is that some of the places below are actually quite chic, and you'll see the famous lining up to get in with the would-be famous.

American

Good old-fashioned value and quality is what **Philippe The Original,** 1001 N. Alameda St., at the corner of Ord Street (tel. 213/628-3781), is all about—as well as the best French-dip sandwiches (beef, pork, ham, turkey, and lamb) on the lightest, crunchiest French rolls you'll ever sink your teeth into (about $3). Philippe's has been around since 1908, and there's nothing stylish about the place. It's democracy in action: You stand in line while your French-dip sandwich is being assembled with whatever goodies you want on the side and you carry it to one of several long wooden tables where there are movable stools. In addition, at $1.20 to $2.35, Philippe's serves homemade beef stew, chili and beans, two different soups daily, and pickled pigs' feet (they prepare and serve close to 200 pounds a week)—I confess I love them. A variety of desserts include New York–style cheesecake, cream and fruit pies, puddings and custards, and their own baked apples. Everything Philippe offers is delicious, all the way through to the doughnuts and coffee. The only changes I've noticed in the 45 years since I first discovered the restaurant's gastronomic joys are a little less sawdust on the floor and shorter hours. But coffee is still a dime!

Philippe's is open daily for breakfast, lunch, and dinner from 6am to 10pm. They serve a hearty breakfast to 10:30am daily, including Philippe's special cinnamon-dipped French toast. All the egg dishes can be topped with their zesty homemade salsa. Beer and wine are available. Cash only. There's free parking in the rear and a lot across the street.

Proximity to CBS Studios alone would probably guarantee **Roscoe's House of Chicken 'n' Waffles,** 1514 N. Gower St., off Sunset Boulevard (tel. 213/466-7453), a celebrity clientele. Its devotees have included Jane Fonda, Stevie Wonder, Flip Wilson, Eddie Murphy, Alex Haley, and the Eagles. The setting is very simpático, with slanted cedar and white stucco walls, changing art exhibits, track lighting overhead, lots of plants, and good music in the background.

Only chicken and waffle dishes are served, for $4 to $8, though that includes eggs and chicken livers. A chicken-and-cheese omelet with french fries accompanied by an order of homemade biscuits makes for a unique and delicious breakfast at $7. A specialty is a quarter chicken smothered with gravy and onions, served with waffles or grits and biscuits. You can also get chicken salad and chicken sandwiches. Homemade cornbread, sweet-potato pie, homemade potato salad, greens, and corn on the cob are all available as side orders, and there's wine or beer to have with your meal.

Roscoe's is open Sunday through Thursday from 9am to 11pm, on Friday and Saturday to 3am. Cash only. There's another Roscoe's in Los Angeles (midcity), 4907 W. Washington Blvd., at La Brea (tel. 213/936-3730).

The Original Pantry Café, 877 S. Figueroa, at 9th Street, downtown (tel. 213/972-9279), has been open 24 hours a day for over 60 years. Never closed, they don't even have a key to the front door. Its well-worn decor consists of shiny cream-colored walls graced with old patinaed oil paintings and hanging globe lamps overhead; big stainless-steel water pitchers and bowls of celery, carrots, and radishes are placed on every Formica table. In addition to that bowl of raw veggies, you also get a whopping big portion of homemade creamy coleslaw and all the homemade sourdough bread and butter you want—a meal in itself before you've even ordered.

When you do order, you'll be amazed at the bountiful portions of delicious food set before you by waiters in long flowing aprons. A Pantry breakfast might consist of a huge stack of hotcakes, big slabs of sweet cured ham, home fries, and cup after cup of freshly made coffee, for under $5. A huge T-bone steak, home-fried pork chops, baked chicken, and macaroni and cheese are served later in the day for $6 to $10. The Pantry is an original—don't miss it.

The oldest restaurant (est. 1930) in downtown Los Angeles is **Vickman's**, 1228 E. 8th St., off Central Avenue in the produce market (tel. 213/622-3852), open at 3am. During Depression days Vickman's sold a beef tip sandwich for 10¢, less than today's tax on the same item. Nowadays, prices are of course considerably higher, though still low by current standards. Practically unchanged, however, is the decor (or lack thereof): creamy walls, linoleum tile floors, fluorescent lighting, big Formica tables, and wooden booths ranging the walls. For some reason there's a huge scale in one corner. The Vickmans managers are always on the scene making sure the service and food are up to snuff. It is, and their clientele is so loyal it amounts to a cult.

They come for hearty breakfasts, perhaps a Spanish omelet, fresh-baked danish pastries, or the market omelet with fresh mushrooms and shallots, for $6 to $8. Fresh-squeezed orange juice is also available. At lunch there are blackboard specials like cold poached salmon with caper sauce, stuffed pork chops, and boiled chicken. On the other hand, you could order a bagel with cream cheese and lox, a chopped-liver sandwich, or a bowl of chili and beans. Leave room for a big hunk of home-baked fresh-fruit (strawberry, peach, etc.) pie with gobs of real whipped cream. It's all cafeteria style with no table service.

Vickman's is open weekdays from 3am to 3pm, on Saturday and Sunday from 3am to 1pm. No dinner. No credit cards. No reservations.

Clifton's Brookdale Cafeteria, 648 S. Broadway, at 7th St. (tel. 213/627-1673), is one of a chain of economy cafeterias that has kept the less prosperous of Los Angeles nourished for five decades. Clifford Clinton—not Clifton—founded the business on what, today, would seem to be a very unique principle: "We pray our humble service be measured not by gold, but by the Golden Rule." During the Depression he kept thousands from starving by honoring an extraordinary policy: "No guest need go hungry. Pay what you wish, dine free unless delighted."

Those shopping or sightseeing downtown can enjoy a huge, economical meal that might consist of split-pea soup ($1.10), hand-carved roast turkey with dressing ($4), baked squash with brown sugar ($1.15), and Bavarian cream pie ($1.50)—not a bad meal for under $8. Entrees cost $3 to $7, vegetable side dishes and soup are under $2, and salad platters and sandwiches run $2.50 to $4. There are over 100 à la carte items at modest prices. However, since there is a charge for everything, including bread and butter, you must limit your choices to make your meal economical. It's all fresh, delicious, and homemade too; even the baking is done on the premises. Fresh bakery items are sold at the front counter.

Clifton's Brookdale is open Monday through Thursday from 6am to 7:30pm, Friday through Sunday to 8pm. There is another Clifton's, downtown at 515 W. 7th St. at Olive (tel. 213/485-1726), open Monday through Saturday from 7am to 3:30pm.

Chinese

Grandview Gardens, 944 N. Hill Street, between College and Bernard streets (tel. 213/624-6048), is especially famous for dim sum. You can order drinks in the cocktail lounge, which is guarded by a huge gold Buddha at the door. The long dining room has a peaked beamed ceiling and burnt-orange walls lined with Chinese paintings. Especially on weekends, its tables are crowded with Chinese families partaking of dim sum delicacies. Generally there are three items to a plate, and each plate is priced at about $1.50. Pastries filled with barbecued pork, curried beef turnovers, ribs in black-bean sauce, steamed buns with chicken and mushrooms, lotusbean pastry, stuffed duck feet, fried and steamed dumplings, and steamed noodle rolls are among the many offerings. In addition to dim sum there are about 150 à la carte listings, ranging from sweet-and-sour pork to lobster with ginger and onion, for $6 to $15. Low-priced family dinners are also served.

Grandview Gardens is open daily from 10am to 10pm; dim sum is served from 10am to 3pm. Major credit cards are accepted. There is validated parking.

Hot Dogs and Hamburgers

Everybody lines up for **Pink's Hot Dogs,** on the northwest corner of La Brea and Melrose avenues (tel. 213/931-4223), near the heart of old Hollywood. The walls are lined with photos of famous hot dog fans, all signed affectionately to Paul Pink. The big treat is the chili dog, loaded with chili and onions and served with infinite skill. It costs about $2. Some 4,000 of these delicious beef dogs are sold daily between the hours of 7am and 2:30am. Outdoor tables are placed at the corner, but most people eat standing up.

If you want a gourmet hot dog (where else but in L.A.?), try **The Wurst,** 10874 Kinross Ave., in Westwood (tel. 213/824-9597). Sausages and hot dogs are the order of the day here, for under $3.50. All are specially prepared—steamed, then grilled over mesquite charcoal and served in fresh French baguette rolls. A variety of gourmet condiments is offered, including wine kraut, three types of mustard, the Wurst relish, and grilled onions; and fresh-cut french fries cooked in peanut oil are a perfect accompaniment. There's a bar-style counter with seating, as well as a stand-up counter that accommodates about 20. Unusual for a restaurant of this type is the background music—classical.

The Wurst is open daily from 11am to 10pm.

The search for the perfect hamburger has ended. Just head on over to **Cassell's Patio Hamburgers,** 3266 W. 6th St., at New Hampshire St., East Wilshire (tel. 213/480-8668), where Alvin Cassel dedicated his life for 30 years to perfecting a gastronomic triumph—the compleat burger. The place changed hands a few years back, but the current owners haven't changed a thing.

They begin each creation with over a third of a pound of freshly ground USDA prime Colorado beef, grinding it personally each day after trimming off every bit of suet. Your burger is cooked to exact specification on a uniquely slanted range that griddles the bottom and broils the top. Then it's served on a five-inch bun—the most natural kind obtainable and always fresh. You can top it with what amounts almost to a buffet of all-you-can-eat fixin's: lettuce, homemade mayonnaise, homemade roquefort dressing, freshly sliced tomatoes, onions, pickles. You can also have all the peaches, pineapple slices, cottage cheese, and homemade potato salad you want. Even the produce is all carefully selected. These divine burgers (plus a variety of sandwiches) and all the trimmings cost about $5.

Open Monday through Saturday from 10:30am to 4pm.

7. Sights

There's more to do in L.A. than just laze around on sun-drenched beaches. Hollywood's movie studios long ago opened their doors to visitors, revealing their fascinating "special effects" to one and all. Needless to say, these people can put on quite a show—it's their business. And in Hollywood-influenced L.A., even non-showbiz attractions take on a dramatic quality. The natural history of the La Brea Tar Pits has the aura of a sci-fi horror movie with life-size replicas of ancient beasts struggling for their lives in a bubbling death pit right in the center of town. Even death is more dramatic here, as you'll see at Forest Lawn, the cemetary where funerals are "staged."

All of which makes sightseeing in Los Angeles very special fun. I'll begin in—

DOWNTOWN LOS ANGELES

This ever-expanding sprawl of a city did have a germination point, in and around the Old Plaza and Olvera Street. Later growth pushed the heart of the city about seven blocks west to **Pershing Square.** Opening onto the square (now tunneled with parking garages), the deluxe **Biltmore Hotel** was constructed, and elegant residences lined **Bunker Hill** in the late 19th century, the mansions on the hill connected to the flatlands by a cable car poetically named Angels' Flight.

Then came the earthquake scare, and buildings over 150 feet tall were prohibited by city-planning authorities. This limitation drove many companies out to Wilshire Boulevard and the outlying areas, and Los Angeles proper fell into relative disrepair, with beautiful town houses giving way to slums.

It wasn't until 1957 that the ban on tall structures was removed (ostensibly because new building techniques have lessened earthquake disaster potential). At any rate, the removal of the ban marked the beginning of a renaissance in the downtown area. The **Civic Center,** which had been expanding since the mid-'20s, culminated in the 28-story **City Hall.**

The shimmering $35-million **Music Center** went up in the '60s, making downtown a cultural center. New office and exhibition buildings were erected in great numbers; the **Los Angeles Convention & Exhibition Center,** occupying a 38-acre site at 1201 S. Figueroa St., was erected, and, more recently, the **Seventh Market Place** at 725 S. Figueroa Street. New hotels have sprung up and old ones have been given a facelift. While you're downtown, take a look at the architecturally innovative **Westin Bonaventure Hotel** (see the hotel section).

And now, in downtown Los Angeles, at the heart of California Plaza on Bunker Hill, you will find the magnificent **Museum of Contemporary Art (MOCA),** designed by Japanese architect Arata Isozaki. For details, see the separate section on this exciting museum, below.

Although much of downtown is still run-down and undeveloped, that state of affairs is rapidly changing. There's much here to draw the visitor.

A Walking Tour of Old Los Angeles

This is one of the few areas of L.A. that you can see without your wheels. It's the district around **El Pueblo de Los Angeles,** the birthplace of the city in 1781, now restored along with 42 surrounding acres as a historical park. Organized walking tours are conducted from the Los Angelitas Docent Office, 130 Paseo de la Plaza, next to the Old Plaza Firehouse at 501 N. Los Angeles (tel. 213/628-0605); there's no charge, and they leave Tuesday through Saturday at 10 and 11am, noon, and 1pm.

The tour begins at **Old Plaza,** near the site where Spanish governor Felipe de Neve purportedly founded the pueblo. The founding was part of Spain's plan to colonize California by establishing presidios, missions, and pueblos. Planting lands were given to the first 11 families who settled here, and five years later each settler received title to his house and lot. Nowadays concerts and religious festivities take place here.

Opening directly on the plaza is the **Plaza Church,** on which construction was started in 1818 and continued till 1822. Although much of the original structure is gone or restored, it is filled with paintings and ecclesiastical relics and open daily to visitors and worshipers.

Many of the area's attractions are along colorful **Olvera Street,** one of the oldest streets in Los Angeles. It was originally called Vine Street because of the vineyards growing along it. In 1930 it was established as a typical Mexican marketplace, paved with bricks and Spanish tile. It contains over 85 shops and stalls, open daily from about 10am to 8pm (to 10pm in summer), selling pottery, jewelry, leather goods, piñatas, and simple Mexican food. There's even a blacksmith.

Also on Olvera Street is the **Avila Adobe,** the oldest existing residence in the city, dating from 1818; it was damaged by an earthquake in 1971. It has been restored and is open free of charge to visitors weekdays except Monday from 10am to 3pm, weekends at 4:30pm.

Across the street is **Pelanconi House,** the finest of the early Los Angeles brick structures built in mid-19th century. It first served as living quarters and wine cellar for the original owner; Pelanconi did not purchase the place until 1865. Subsequently it became a warehouse for Chinese merchants, and today it houses three Mexican restaurants, including Casa La Golondrina. The Victorian **Sepulveda House** is also of interest.

The **Pico House,** completed in 1870 and the first three-story building in Los Angeles, was designed to be the finest hotel in the city at a then-astronomical cost of $82,000. Lighted with gas, and housing several bathtubs, it was considered the last word in luxury.

Just south of Pio Pico House is the first wooden-frame building erected in Los Angeles—the **Merced Theater,** undergoing restoration. It opened in 1870, with seating for about 400, and performances were advertised in Spanish. In later years it was used as a saloon, a Methodist church, and an armory.

The Museum of Contemporary Art

Thousands upon thousands of words have appeared in publications from New York to Los Angeles and from San Francisco to San Diego—some flattering, some not so—about the city's new Museum of Contemporary Art (MOCA). Among all the verbiage, the most important message might well be: "Don't miss visiting this museum." The only Los Angeles institution devoted exclusively to exhibiting art from 1940 through the present, MOCA, in the downtown L.A. business district, at the heart of California Plaza on Bunker Hill, 250 S. Grand Ave. (tel. 213/621-2766), formally opened in December 1986. No matter what's on exhibit at the time you're in Los Angeles or how much you like contemporary art, a visit to this magnificent jewel in its handsome setting of skyscrapers is worth your time.

MOCA is the first United States creation of Tokyo architect Arata Isozaki. The birth of this unique edifice involved the efforts of an incredible mix of financial, political, and creative personalities (with some overtones of *The Fountainhead*). MOCA is ultimately a tribute to the brilliance of its architect and the planning push of Los Angeles. The physical constraints of the new museum were considerable—MOCA had to be built above a parking garage, yet the height of the museum was not allowed to compete or interfere with adjoining structures to be developed by the partnership underwriting its cost. Because MOCA would eventually be dwarfed by the surrounding buildings, Isozaki needed to attract attention with its materials and shapes.

The building's warm red sandstone blocks were quarried by hand in India and refined in Japan. There is a great deal to marvel at—the copper roofs, dark-green aluminum panels cross-hatched with bright-pink joints, the pyramid skylights, and the magnificent outdoor spaces. Two long rectangular reflecting ponds flanked by benches and trees are a perfect focus for quiet meditation after visiting the museum.

Seven gallery spaces comprise the heart of the museum. Gallery A rises 58 feet to the top of a pyramidal skylight; the remaining gallery spaces are 15 to 20 feet high. Stark-white walls, unencumbered by moldings or baseboard, offer a pristine surface for the art.

MOCA's Ahmanson Auditorium is the site for the intimately scaled live performances offered throughout the year, as well as for film and video programs intended to further development in these forms—a mark of MOCA's commitment to contemporary art. For information and tickets, call the MOCA Box Office (tel. 213/626-6828).

A courtyard to the right of the museum ticket booth is the setting for the Il Panino café (after the popular Italian *paninoteca,* or sandwich bar). The café serves a marvelous selection of sandwiches, soups, salads, desserts, and beverages, soft and harder (beer and wine). As might be expected in this artistic milieu, the sandwiches are creative, from the Norvegese (smoked salmon and mascarpone cheese, garnished with onion, tomato, capers, and dressing) to the Milano (sliced turkey breast, goat cheese, avocado, sun-dried tomato, and arugula, served on Italian Ciabatta bread).

Museum hours are 11am to 6pm on Tuesday, Wednesday, Friday, Saturday, and Sunday; to 8pm on Thursday. Regular admission is $4; students and seniors pay $2; children under 12 go in for free. The museum store, featuring changing displays of artist-designed objects, exhibition posters, catalogs, art books, and contemporary jewelry, is open during regular museum hours. Parking (other than metered) is now available one block north of MOCA for visitors to the museum. For $4 and a MOCA validation you may park at the 5-Star lot at 1st and Hope Streets for four hours weekdays from 10am to 6pm.

The Music Center of Los Angeles County

This $35-million gleaming glass complex of buildings, located at 135 N. Grand Ave., at 1st Street (tel. 213/972-7211), houses three theaters: the 3,197-seat **Dorothy Chandler Pavilion,** for opera, recitals, musicals, and dance performances (home of the Los Angeles Philharmonic; on the fifth floor is the Pavilion Restaurant); the **Mark Taper Forum,** seating 750, for intimate drama and forums; and the 2,100-seat **Ahmanson Theatre,** for plays and musical dramas. The center's five resident companies—the Los Angeles Philharmonic, Center Theatre Group, Los Angeles Music Center Opera, the Joffrey Ballet LA/NY, and the Los Angeles Master Chorale—perform year-round.

In another part of the Pavilion building are Otto Rothschilds Bar and Grill and the Backstage Café.

Free tours of all three theaters are conducted year-round on Monday, Tuesday, Thursday, and Friday from 10am to 1:30pm, on Saturday from 10am to 12:30pm. For reservations, call 213/972-7483. For parking in the garage during weekdays, you pay a $10 deposit on entry. The cost is $1.50 for 20 minutes, with a $10 maximum until 5pm. If you enter after 5pm, or any time on weekends or holidays, it's $5 maximum. On matinee days after 11am, the cost is $1.50 for 20 minutes, $5 maximum. The garage is open until 11:45pm.

New Chinatown/Little Tokyo

Neither is as big a deal as its San Francisco counterpart, but both are enjoyable clusterings of ethnic shops and restaurants. **New Chinatown** is bounded by North Broadway, North Hill Street, Bernard Street, and Sunset Boulevard. Mandarin Plaza, 970 N. Broadway, is the center of the action.

Little Tokyo is between Alameda and Los Angeles streets and 1st and 3rd streets, close to City Hall; its central mall is Japanese Village Plaza.

An hour or two is sufficient to explore either of these areas.

Wells Fargo History Museum

This museum chronicles the history of the American West, focusing on Southern California and Wells Fargo. It's located in the Wells Fargo Center, at 333 S. Grand Ave., near 4th Street (tel. 213/683-7166). Among over 1,000 objects on display in this well-lit, pleasantly laid-out museum is a stagecoach under construction, along with the tools used to build it. There's also an authentic 19th-century Concord stagecoach, designed to carry nine people for long distances. You can sit inside a coach under construction and listen to a narrative tape read from the diary of a young Englishman who made the long, arduous coach trip to Los Angeles. Other items on exhibit include mining artifacts, Wells Fargo memorabilia, and a 2-pound gold nugget (76% pure) discovered in 1975!

The Wells Fargo Museum is open weekdays from 9am to 5pm; it's closed on bank holidays. Admission is free.

Los Angeles Children's Museum

This delightful museum at 310 N. Main St. (tel. 213/687-8800) is a place where children learn by doing. Everyday experiences are demystified in an interactive, playlike atmosphere; children are encouraged to imagine, invent, create, pretend, and work together. In the Art Studio they can make everything from Mylar rockets to finger puppets. There's a City Street where they can sit on a policeman's motorcycle, play at driving a bus or at being firemen. Kids can become "stars" in the recording or TV studio; learn about health in a doctor's and dentist's office and about x-rays in an emergency room; see their shadows frozen on walls in the Shadow Box; and play with giant foam-filled Velcro-edged building blocks in Sticky City.

In addition to the regular exhibits, there are all kinds of special activities and workshops, from cultural celebrations to T-shirt decorating and musical-instrument making. There is a 99-seat theater for children where live performances or special productions are scheduled every weekend. Call the museum for upcoming events.

The museum is open on Saturday and Sunday from 10am to 5pm, on Wednesday and Thursday from 2 to 4pm. Summer hours are 11:30am to 5pm Monday through Friday, and from 10am to 5pm on Saturday and Sunday. Admission is $4.50 per person; children under 2 years are admitted free.

Natural History Museum

Located in **Exposition Park,** this exciting museum, the largest of its kind in the West, houses seemingly endless exhibits of fossils, minerals, birds, mammals, and suchlike. Exhibits and displays chronicle the history of human beings and their environment going back some 300 million years before we appeared on the scene and up to present day. They range from the dinosaur age to Maya, Aztec, Inca, and pre-Inca arts and crafts from the period 2500 B.C. to A.D. 1500. Animals are shown in their natural habitats; there are halls detailing American history from 1660 to 1914, mineral halls, bird halls—even a few dinosaurs on hand. In the Cenozoic Hall you can see mammal fossils from 65 million years ago; also shown here is the complete evolution of the horse from a fox-terrier-size animal to today. Other permanent displays include the world's rarest shark, Megamouth; a walk-through vault containing priceless gems; and an extraordinary collection of Los Angeles–built automobiles. There's much more, all of it fascinating.

The Natural History Museum, 900 Exposition Blvd. (tel. 213/744-3466), is open Tuesday through Sunday from 10am to 5pm. Admission is $4 for adults; $2 for children 12 to 17, seniors, and students with ID; $1 for kids 5 to 12; kids under 5, free. The first Tuesday of every month, admission is free.

HOLLYWOOD

The legendary city where actresses once pranced with leashed leopards, and Louella Parsons daily chronicled everyone's most intimate doings, is certainly on everyone's must-see list. Unfortunately the glamour—what's left of it—is badly tarnished, and Hollywood Boulevard has been labeled "the Times Square of the West."

But Hollywood seems unaware of its own demise. For one thing, the **HOLLY-**

WOOD sign is still on the hill, and its price keeps going up. According to the *Los Angeles Times Magazine,* the cost of the original in 1922 was $21,000; the cost of building a new one in 1978 was $250,000. And for another, salaries in the never-aging movie industry are forever on the rise—in 1988 they totaled almost $6.5 billion.

And still, if you look down, you'll be thrilled to see the bronze medallions along Hollywood Boulevard's **Walk of Fame,** bearing the names of over 1,800 stars who have trod these sidewalks from nickelodeon days to the present TV stars.

Near the star-crossed intersection of Hollywood and Vine is the disc-shaped **Capitol Records Building,** the first circular office building in the world.

As much a Hollywood landmark as the famous intersection, **Mann's Chinese Theatre** (formerly Grauman's), 6925 Hollywood Blvd., is a combination of authentic and simulated Chinese decor. Original Chinese heaven doves top the façade, and two of the theater's columns are actually from a Ming Dynasty temple. An enclosure in the forecourt was created for the signatures and hand- and footprints of the stars, and countless visitors have matched their hands and feet with those of Elizabeth Taylor, Paul Newman, Ginger Rogers, Humphrey Bogart, Frank Sinatra, etc. It's not only hands and feet, though; Betty Grable made an impression, as always, with her shapely leg; Gene Autry with the hoofprints of Champion, his horse; and Jimmy Durante and Bob Hope used (what else?) their noses.

A few blocks north of Hollywood Boulevard is the **Hollywood Bowl,** 2301 N. Highland Ave. (tel. 213/850-2000), summer home of the Los Angeles Philharmonic Orchestra and the world's most famous outdoor amphitheater. Every year a predawn pilgrimage is made by Angelenos to the Bowl for Easter sunrise services, which are televised and broadcast across the nation (more about the Bowl in the nightlife section, coming up).

Dedicated movie buffs might want to visit the **Hollywood Memorial Park Cemetery,** 6000 Santa Monica Blvd., between Van Ness and Gower streets (tel. 213/469-1181). This is where the mysterious lady in black annually paid homage at the crypt of Valentino on the anniversary of his death. Peter Lorre is buried here, as are Douglas Fairbanks, Sr., Norma Talmadge, Tyrone Power, Cecil B. DeMille, and Marion Davies. Hours are 8am to 5pm daily.

The Hollywood Wax Museum

One block east of Mann's Chinese Theatre is Spoony Singh's Hollywood Wax Museum, 6767 Hollywood Blvd. (tel. 213/462-8860), a last holdout of movie-world glamour. Singh, a bona-fide turbaned and bearded Indian Sikh, took over the barnlike museum some 25 years ago when it was in a state of utter disrepair; Shirley Temple's head had shrunk to the size of a tennis ball and Mickey Rooney's arms had dropped off.

Spoony built up his wax collection to 185 famous figures of the past and present, the most famous of which is Marilyn Monroe in her dress-blowing scene from *The Seven Year Itch.* Although most of the figures are screen stars—Raquel Welch (whose bras, under a shimmering silver midriff, were stolen so often that Spoony finally left her braless), Danny Thomas, Bing Crosby, Barbra Streisand, Archie and Edith Bunker, Sylvester Stallone, Christopher Reeve, Steve McQueen, Jane Fonda, Goldie Hawn, Michael Jackson, Bruce Springsteen, etc.—there is also a Hall of Presidents, where first citizens from George Washington to George Bush are on display. Most popular of these is John F. Kennedy at the lectern.

You'll also see tableaux ranging from the Last Supper to a Chamber of Horrors filled with maniacal demons and torture machines.

An added attraction is the **Movie Awards Theatre,** presenting a film that spans more than 40 years of Academy Award history. The sound track is composed of a medley of award-winning hit songs, and the clips include Vivien Leigh in *Gone With the Wind,* Bing Crosby in *Going My Way,* Yul Brynner in *The King and I,* and other old favorites right up to *Chariots of Fire.*

The museum is open Sunday through Thursday from 10am to midnight, on

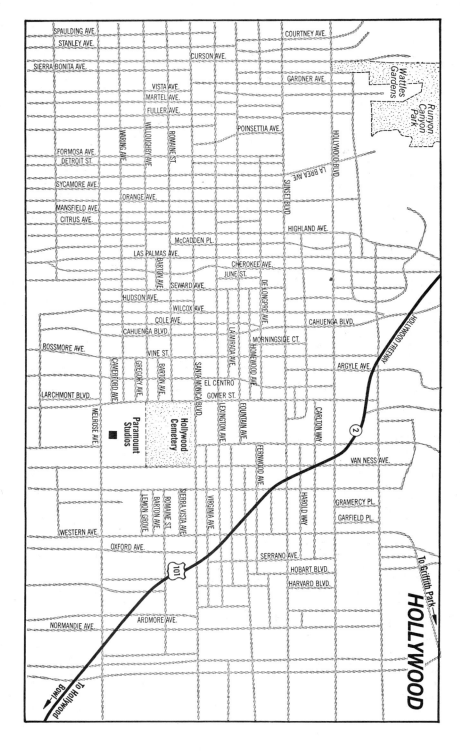

Friday and Saturday to 2am. Adult admission is $7; seniors, $5; children 6 to 12, $4 (under 6, free).

GRIFFITH PARK

To the northeast of Hollywood lies lovely, verdant Griffith Park, at 4,253 acres the largest park within the boundaries of any American city and the second-largest city-owned park in the world (the largest is in West Berlin). Home of the Los Angeles Zoo and the Observatory, it offers wide-ranging facilities, including golf courses, a large wilderness area, a bird sanctuary, tennis courts, a huge swimming pool, picnic areas, and even an old-fashioned merry-go-round. Other attractions are the **Gene Autry Western Heritage Museum,** the **Greek Theatre** (see the nightlife section), and **Travel Town Transportation Museum** (tel. 213/662-5874), where the kids can explore and climb all over retired railcars and airplanes and up into the cab of an old locomotive. Admission is free, and hours are 10am to 4pm weekdays, to 5pm weekends and holidays, from November 1 to April 30; to 5pm and 6pm, respectively, the balance of the year. There's a miniature train ride on weekdays from 10am to 4pm, on weekends to 5pm (adults pay $3; children 2 to 13, $2; those under 2 go in for free).

Major park entrances are at the northern tip of Western Boulevard (at the prettiest part of the park, **Ferndell,** where New Zealand horticulturists have created a lush setting of planting ferns from around the world); at the northern extremity of Vermont Avenue (leading into the part of the park containing the Greek Theater, the Observatory, bird sanctuary, and Mount Hollywood); and at the junction of Los Feliz Boulevard and Riverside Drive (leading to the municipal golf course, miniature trains, and children's zoo). At the junction of the Ventura and Golden State freeways is yet another entrance to the Los Angeles Zoo and Travel Town.

The Los Angeles Zoo

Only in Southern California would a zoo bill its offerings as a "cast of thousands." Here you'll see over 2,000 mammals, birds, and reptiles on a 113-acre "stage" divided into continental habitat areas: North America, South America, Africa, Eurasia, and Australia. Active in wildlife conservation, the zoo houses about 50 vanishing species. There's also an aviary with a walk-in flight cage, a reptile house, an aquatic section, and Adventure Island, the revamped children's zoo.

The original children's zoo, built in 1963, was demolished in 1988. In its place arose **Adventure Island,** a fascinating place with all sorts of interesting surprises. Adventure Island is a zoo that just wasn't intended to look like a zoo. Four distinct habitats were created to blend into one another in a space of about 2½ acres. There is the world of the mountain, meadow, desert, and shoreline. Adventure Island houses an aviary, tidepool, petting zoo, animal nursery, and outdoor theater for animal performances.

Children can pose in life-size fantasies at "photo spots" throughout Adventure Island, with a giant vulture or a snake, or even seeming to hang upside down like a bat. The zoo is open every day except Christmas from 10am to 5pm, in summer to 6pm. Admission to the zoo is $6 for adults, $5 for seniors, $2.50 for ages 2 to 12, and free for under-2s. Phone 213/666-4650 for more information.

Griffith Observatory and Planetarium

Atop the hill, closer to the heavens, is the Griffith Observatory and Planetarium, where the "great Zeiss projector" flashes five different shows a year across a 75-foot dome. Excursions into interplanetary space might range from a search for extraterrestrial life to a search of vital interest to locals—for the causes of earthquakes, moonquakes, and starquakes. One-hour shows are given daily except Monday (seven days in summer); for recorded show times, telephone 213/664-1191 (for a human, call 213/664-1181). Admission is $4 for adults, $3 for children 5 to 15. Those under 5 are admitted only to the children's programs at 1:30pm on Saturday.

At night the Planetarium is the setting for cosmic light-show/concerts under the stars. Powerful lasers produce dramatic effects covering the entire sky. Shows are presented Tuesday through Sunday; call 818/997-3624 for show times. Tickets cost $6 for adults, $5 for children 5 to 16.

Also here is the **Hall of Science**, with many fascinating exhibits on galaxies, meteorites, and other cosmic subjects. And the public can gaze through the Observatory telescope on any clear night except Monday until 10pm (nightly during the summer).

The Gene Autry Western Heritage Museum

The word "museum" always strikes me as a dull word for a place that is as exciting, interesting, educational, fascinating, and as much fun as the Gene Autry Western Heritage Museum, 4700 Zoo Dr. (tel. 213/667-2000). Don't miss it, with or without the kids!

Enter the California mission–style complex under a Hollywood-size arch and you are in a courtyard facing a life-size bronze of Gene Autry (once called "the singing cowboy" for those of you too young to know) and his horse Champion. To one side is an impressively tall bell tower. Off the courtyard are entrances to the museum and the theater, and straight on is the information center, where you can rent a recorded Acoustaguide tour ($3) described by Willie Nelson.

The museum, which opened its doors in November 1988, is a remarkable repository of the history of the American West, undoubtedly one of the most comprehensive in the world. The museum holds over 16,000 artifacts and art pieces, including 100 of Gene Autry's personal treasures. There are some superb bronze sculptures by Frederic Remington, including *The Bronc Buster* (1895) and *The Cheyenne* (1901), both donated by Mr. and Mrs. Autry. The museum is filled with artifacts that relate to the everyday lives and occupations of people who helped settle the West, but it also depicts the West of romance and imagination as created by artists, authors, filmmakers, TV, and radio. There are antique firearms, common tools, saddles (some intricately tooled), stagecoaches (including one that the kiddies can pile into, just one of many hands-on children's exhibits), equipment, clothing, toys, games, posters. There are marvelous displays on Wild West shows, including that of Buffalo Bill, but one of the most interesting is on the women of the Wild West shows, prototypes for today's woman—determined, self-reliant, and strong. The first women featured in these performances were sharpshooters, and the most famous of the group was Annie Oakley. By mid-1890 these women began to participate as bronc riders, trick riders, ropers, and bulldoggers. Many of the women's styles ultimately became part of the style of men's costumes: beadwork, fringe, feathers, quillwork, embroidery, painted designs—the beginnings of modern rodeo styles.

Toward the end of your visit the museum gently leads you from reality into the fascinating world of show biz, beginning with items from Buffalo Bill's Wild West Show, movie clips from the silent days, contemporary films, and memorabilia from TV western series. There's a Hollywood-type set with viewer-activated videos, including one on the stuntmen of westerns. The exhibits were capably designed by Walt Disney Imagineering.

The museum shop in itself is worth a tour that could easily take an hour. The irresistible temptations for large and small folk include cowboy hats, marvelous western posters, books, shirts, bolo ties, and silver and turquoise jewelry, just to name a few of the attractions.

One other note: The Gene Autry Western Heritage Museum is just across from the entrance to the zoo. Don't try to see the museum and the zoo in one day—there won't be time and you'll miss out on much of the fun. To simplify life, when pangs of hunger set in, the Golden Spur Café, open daily until 4:30pm, has a good selection of food (cafeteria style), reasonably priced. There are sandwiches including hot dogs ($2 to $3), soup ($2), salads ($3 to $4.50), desserts, and nonalcoholic beverages. The café also has light breakfast items (biscuits, fruit, fruit salad), served from 9:30 to 11 a.m.

The museum is open Tuesday through Sunday from 10am to 5pm; closed on Monday and Thanksgiving, Christmas, and New Year's Day. Admission to the museum is $5; $3.75 for seniors 60 and over, students 13 to 18, and college students with ID; $2.50 for children 2 to 12; under 2, free.

BEVERLY HILLS

As with the romance and beauty of Paris or the undiminished energy and sophistication of New York, the aura of Beverly Hills is unique. It's a curious mix of small-town neighborliness and a cosmopolitan attitude, all glossed over with a veneer of wealth. The power of the movies and moviemakers has stamped the city with its own brand of excitement. And the local industries of fashion, beauty, and finance have thrived on the world of entertainment.

Beverly Hills is, as everybody knows, the adopted hometown of many a motion-picture and TV star—George Burns, Warren Beatty, James Stewart, Kirk Douglas, Linda Evans, Harrison Ford, Jacqueline Bisset, Frank Sinatra, and Jack Nicholson, to name just a few. Its first mayor was the homespun philosopher/ comedian/star Will Rogers.

Douglas Fairbanks and Mary Pickford led the migration of stars to the area when they built their famous home, Pickfair, crowning the ridge at 1143 Summit Drive; today a drive through the glens, canyons, and hillsides of Beverly Hills will reveal one palatial home after another. And where else is there a city that would refurbish and redecorate a "convenience station" at a bus stop where its household employees wait?

It was once a big tourist trend to visit stars' homes, with bus tours and local visitors bureaus pointing the way. This activity is discouraged these days, celebs demanding privacy—at least in their own homes—from gaping and often inconsiderate crowds. You will see youngsters on the drive going into Beverly Hills hawking "Maps of Stars' Homes," but I don't vouch for their accuracy—many of the occupants pinpointed have not only moved, but have moved to Forest Lawn!

Within Beverly Hills are some of Southern California's most prestigious hotels, restaurants, high-fashion boutiques, and department stores—all used to catering to the whims of TV and film personalities and the very wealthy. Don't miss that remarkable assemblage of European-based and other super-upscale stores along Rodeo Drive. A shopping guide is available from the Beverly Hills Chamber of Commerce and Visitors Bureau (see below).

Beverly Hills is a part of town to drive around in, oohing and aahing and probably fantasizing that you, too, live here. Stop in at the Polo Lounge in the Beverly Hills Hotel for a drink, dine at one of its posh eateries like the Bistro, or buy a little something at one of the chic boutiques on Rodeo Drive—and absorb the glamour.

Tours

The **Beverly Hills Chamber of Commerce & Visitors Bureau,** 239 S. Beverly Dr., Beverly Hills, CA 90212 (tel. 213/271-8174, or toll free 800/345-2210), now offers a **Trolley Tour** at no charge. The trolley's unique charm and the knowledgable guides allow passengers to see Beverly Hills in style. The 30-minute tour leaves from the corner of Rodeo Drive and Dayton Way (you'll see a trolley sign there) and covers the posh downtown area as well as the exclusive residential neighborhoods. Tours are conducted Tuesday through Saturday from 10am to 6pm.

For a personalized look at Beverly Hills, you can book the Visitors Bureau's Ambassadear tour. The cost is $9 for members, $11 for nonmembers; and there's a four-hour minimum.

TOURING THE STUDIOS

Want to see what goes on behind the scenes at movie and TV studios? Universal Studios and NBC-TV have both arranged entertaining and informative tours, during which you might even get to see some of your favorite performers. If you have time for only one tour, Universal's is the more elaborate.

Universal Studios Hollywood

The largest and busiest movie studio in the world, Universal began offering tours to the public in 1964. It now attracts some five million visitors a year to the world of make-believe to see the where, why, and how of the studio that produced movies from *My Little Chickadee* to *E.T.*, *Jaws*, and *Conan the Barbarian*, and popular TV series from "Dragnet" to "Murder, She Wrote."

The guided tour of the studio's 420 acres aboard a tram takes about 1½ hours, after which you can stay for exciting live shows at the **Entertainment Center.** You'll pass stars' dressing rooms and countless departments involved in film production. And at Stage 32 you'll learn about special effects. You'll also see backlot sets like Six Point, Texas, the western town that has been used since the days of Tom Mix; that's not to mention the typical New York street (although it was devastated for *Earthquake*). The reason you don't recognize these streets from movie to movie is that they are constantly undergoing alterations in landscaping and exteriors to prevent audiences from becoming too familiar with them. Don't miss seeing the animal actors, including a star pig (sorry, no cats—they're too independent to train).

The tram encounters countless disasters along the way: an attack by the deadly 24-foot *Jaws* shark, a runaway train, a laser battle with Cyclon robots, an alpine avalanche, the complete collapse of a rickety wooden bridge you happen to be crossing, a flash flood, and more. There is a once-is-enough encounter with a 30-foot-tall King Kong. You're carried into a dark sound stage and suddenly you're on an elevated train in New York. You listen to newscasters warning about King Kong, then sirens, screams, and finally King Kong—raging, tearing, just 3 feet away. Universal's latest addition to the big scare is Earthquake—The Big One. This is a re-creation of a monster earthquake—an 8.3 on the Richter scale—that tears the ground right out from under you. It's an amazing, exciting, terrifying natural disaster. At the conclusion of this pleasantly scary journey (or before it), visitors can wander around the Entertainment Center, where several times each day skilled stuntmen fall off buildings, dodge knife blows, and ride trick horses. In addition, you can perform as a "guest star" in the Star Trek Adventure, in scenes that are filmed and intercut with actual footage with Leonard Nimoy and William Shatner. The "Miami Vice" action spectacular features more than 50 stunts and special effects packed into a 15-minute show.

Three new attractions were added in 1990—Steven Spielberg's fantasy adventure *An American Tail*, the *Back to the Future* Special Effects Stage, featuring live moviemaking techniques; and The Riot Act, a new action-packed stunt show.

An American Tail features all the stars of the animated film classic in the magical world of Fievel and his friends, including Dom Deluise's voice as Tiger the Cat. Guests are invited to play with the stars of the show in a re-created set adjacent to the production stage. Cinemagicians unfold a three-dimensional adventure in a mouse-size world of props and sets where children are able to slide on a banana peel, explore the inside of a bird cage, climb through a giant slice of Swiss cheese, cross a hot-dog bridge, and explore more than 40 larger-than-life cinematic effects.

The *Back to the Future* Special Effects Stage re-creates actual scenes depicting the ride on an outer-space freeway to the futuristic Hill Valley, as well as the climactic electrifying courthouse clock-tower scenes from *Back to the Future I* and *II*.

The Riot Act goes beyond a traditional stunt show to never-before-seen live movie stunts, including the blowing-up of a building, a dramatic high fall through floor planks, and the highest motion-pole balance ever attempted.

There are complete restaurants on the premises such as **Victoria Station** and Tony Roma's, plus a Famous Amos.

Universal Studios is located in Universal City, just off the Hollywood Freeway at the Lankershim Boulevard exit (tel. 818/508-9600). Tours are given daily, except Thanksgiving and Christmas, from 9am to 5pm in summer, and on holidays year-round (from 10am to 3:30pm the rest of the year; 9:30am to 3:30pm on weekends). Those over 12 pay $22; seniors, $16.50; children 3 to 11, $16.50; under 3, free. Parking is an extra $4.

You can see a television show being taped at Universal too. Call 818/508-9600 for information and schedules, or write in advance to Universal Studios, 100 Universal City Plaza, Universal City, CA 91608.

NBC Television Studios

The largest color studios in the U.S., NBC-TV's Burbank facilities are home for the "Tonight Show," Bob Hope specials, and many others. "Scrabble" and "Saved by the Bell" are taped here. A behind-the-camera glimpse at this complex will take you to the sets of the above shows; it's not guaranteed that you'll actually meet a star, but it's not impossible either—maybe Johnny Carson or one of his many guests or substitute hosts.

Aside from the glamour aspect, the tour is most interesting, including an inside look at scenery in production, wardrobe, props, special effects (where you can see yourself fly like Superman), the sound effects center, and rehearsal halls. The NBC Studios in Burbank are located at 3000 W. Alameda Ave., Burbank, CA 91523 (tel. 818/840-3537), easily accessible via the Hollywood or Ventura Freeway or by bus. No reservations are necessary for the one-hour tours, which run from 8:30am to 4pm weekdays, 10am to 4pm on Saturday, to 2pm on Sunday. The charge is $9 for adults, $8 for seniors, $6 for children 5 to 14, and free for children under 5. There's lots of free parking for tours and shows.

For tickets to any of the shows taped at NBC Studios (including the "Tonight Show"), you may write to the address above. You'll receive a "guest letter" in response to your request, which can be exchanged for tickets on your arrival in Los Angeles. The ticket office is open weekdays from 8am to 5pm, weekends 9:30am to 4pm. (*Note:* Tickets for the "Tonight Show" are available only on the day of the show; tickets for other shows may be picked up in advance. Minimum age limits vary from 8 to 18; it's 16 for the "Tonight Show.")

The Burbank Studios

Home of Warner Bros. and Columbia Pictures, the Burbank Studios, 4000 Warner Blvd. (tel. 818/954-1744), offer the most comprehensive and the least Disneyesque of studio tours. They call it the VIP tour, because it's created not for mass audiences but for small groups—no more than 12 people. It was, in fact, originally designed to introduce visiting VIPs to the workings of the studio and was later made available to film buffs.

The tours are very flexible, taking in whatever is being filmed at the time. Perhaps an orchestra is scoring a film or TV program—you'll get to see how it's done. Whenever possible, guests visit working sets to watch actors filming actual productions such as "Designing Women," "Murphy Brown," and "Night Court." You'll also tour set environments from jungles to Arctic tundra, from the Wild West to slum tenements. The wardrobe department and the mills where sets are made are also possible stops. It all depends what's going on the day of your tour.

Because you're seeing people at work, who mustn't be disturbed, there are only two tours a day (more during summer), weekdays at 10am and 2pm, and children under 10 are not admitted. Admission is $24 per person, and you must make reservations at least one week in advance.

BURBANK HISTORICAL SOCIETY

Burbank has been the butt of numerous jokes (thanks to Johnny Carson, who works there), but in fact it's a pleasant little town that's rapidly growing into a bustling city. It's headquarters to movie studios, TV stations, and record companies.

Burbank is proud of its heritage too. In 1871 Dr. David Burbank, a New England dentist, purchased the Rancho La Providencia Scott Tract and raised sheep. The Providencia Land Water and Development Company built the Burbank Villa Hotel in 1887 and so began the enterprising city of Burbank. The Burbank Historical Society has put together the **Gordon R. Howard Museum Complex,** 1015 W.

Olive Ave. (tel. 818/841-6333), which details the city's 100-year history, with dioramas of life in the early days, and some of its most famous residents—Lockheed, Moreland Bus, Disney Studios, and NBC. Gordon Howard displays a number of his antique motor vehicles at the museum, including a 1922 fire engine, a 1937 Mercedes, a 1937 Rolls-Royce, a 1939 Daimler, and the 1922 Moreland bus that Marilyn Monroe, Jack Lemmon, and Tony Curtis rode in the movie *Some Like It Hot.* Also on the grounds is one of the original houses built around the turn of the century to lure people to this new town in the valley. The Historical Society has done a good job of restoring and furnishing it.

The Gordon R. Howard Museum is open on Sunday only, from 1 to 4pm. While there is no charge for admission, the museum appreciates a donation—usually $1.

FOREST LAWN

There aren't many cities where a cemetery is on every tourist's sightseeing agenda, but then, there aren't many cemeteries like Forest Lawn. (Actually there are five Forest Lawns in L.A., but the most famous one is at 1712 S. Glendale Ave. at Los Feliz Road, Glendale; tel. 213/254-3131). Pick up a map at the Information Booth when you arrive. It lists the major points of interest. When you go to see the displays that have timed showings, be sure to arrive 10 minutes early. Gates close promptly.

Comic Lenny Bruce called it "Disneyland for the dead," and Evelyn Waugh wrote a satire, *The Loved One,* about it. But to founder Dr. Hubert Eaton, Forest Lawn was the cemetery of his dreams that would symbolize the joys of eternal life—"a great park, devoid of . . . customary signs of earthly death, but filled with towering trees, sweeping lawns, splashing fountains, singing birds, beautiful statuary, cheerful flowers . . . a place where lovers new and old shall love to stroll and watch the sunset's glow."

Highlights for the living include: Rosa Caselli Moretti's stained-glass re-creation of da Vinci's *The Last Supper* displayed in the Memorial Court of Honor of the Great Mausoleum. Moretti is the last member of a Perugia, Italy, family known for its secret process of making stained glass. Thousands of Southern Californians are entombed in the Great Mausoleum, among them Jean Harlow, Clark Gable, Carole Lombard, and W. C. Fields. The art terraces and the corridors are lined with reproductions of great works of Michelangelo and Donatello. In the Court of Honor are crypts that money cannot buy—they're reserved as final resting places for men and women whose service to humanity has been outstanding.

The big draw on the hill—next to the Forest Lawn Museum—is a special theater used for the presentation of two paintings, *The Crucifixion,* conceived by Paderewski and painted by Jan Styka, dramatically depicting the moment before Christ is placed on the cross (Pope John Paul II hailed it as "deeply inspiring"); and *The Resurrection,* by Robert Clark, which was conceived by Dr. Eaton. The paintings are shown every hour from 10am to 4pm daily.

Other attractions include Forest Lawn Museum's reproductions of Ghiberti's *Paradise Doors* and Michelangelo's *Sotterraneo;* the Court of David, housing a reproduction of Michelangelo's famous masterpiece; European cathedral stained glass from the 11th through the 15th century; churches like Wee Kirk o' the Heather, modeled after the 14th-century Scottish church where Annie Laurie worshiped; and the Church of the Recessional, a memorial to the sentiments expressed by Rudyard Kipling.

Forest Lawn isn't just for the dear departed. The churches have also been the setting for numerous christenings, services, ordinations, and some 60,000 or so weddings, including that of Ronald Reagan and Jane Wyman. It can be visited daily, admission free, from 9am to 5pm.

WILSHIRE BOULEVARD

L.A.'s main street might be called the city's Champs-Élysées (and then again, it might not)—but would that famed Parisian street ever have a section called the **Miracle Mile?** No, that's strictly Americana, and it refers to the portion of Wilshire between Highland and Fairfax. The boulevard passes through **MacArthur Park,** with its own lake, as well as **Lafayette Park.** Near the eastern edge of Miracle Mile, in **Hancock Park,** are the **La Brea Tar Pits.**

Los Angeles County Museum of Art

A complex of five modern buildings around a spacious central plaza, the Los Angeles County Museum of Art, 5905 Wilshire Blvd. (tel. 213/857-6000), in Hancock Park, is considered by some to be one of the finest art museums west of the Mississippi.

The **Ahmanson Building,** built around a central atrium, shelters the permanent collection, which encompasses prehistoric to conceptual art. The museum's holdings include Chinese and Korean art; pre-Columbian Mexican art; American and European painting, sculpture, and decorative arts; ancient and Islamic art; a unique glass collection from Roman times to the 19th century; the renowned Gilbert collection of mosaics and monumental silver; one of the nation's largest holdings of costumes and textiles; and an Indian and Southeast Asian art collection considered to be one of the most important in the world.

Major special loan exhibitions, as well as galleries for prints, drawings, and photographs, are in the Frances and Armand Hammer Building.

The **Robert O. Anderson Building** features 20th-century painting and sculpture, as well as special exhibits. The Leo S. Bing Center has a 600-seat theater, where lectures, films, and concerts are held, and the indoor/outdoor Plaza Café.

The **Pavilion for Japanese Art** was opened in September 1988. It was designed by the late Bruce Goff specifically to accommodate Japanese art, though certain elements of the museum are somewhat reminiscent of the Guggenheim Museum created by Frank Lloyd Wright—the curved rising ramp, the central treatment of light, the structure of the displays. An extraordinary touch by Goff was in the use of Kalwall (a translucent material) for the exterior walls to allow a soft, delicate entry of natural light much like that through shoji screens, at the same time performing the eminently practical function of screening out ultraviolet light. It is a serene touch that adds to the quiet beauty of the subjects. The pavilion may very well be the only public museum where Japanese art can be seen in this light.

The museum now houses the internationally renowned Shin'enkan collection of Edo Period (1615–1865) Japanese painting, rivaled only by the holdings of the former emperor of Japan. It also displays the museum's collections of Japanese sculpture, ceramics, and lacquerware.

The pavilion has on display the superb Raymond and Frances Bushell collection of netsuke (pronounced "net-ski") sculpture from the 18th through the 20th century, though most were produced during the Edo Period. You can see the amazingly detailed miniatures up close in their own gallery. These are figures carved from wood, ivory, and stag-antler materials and in all sorts of shapes of animals and people, real, mythical, and classic. The design and detail of netsukes are even more amazing in light of their use and the limitations of their shapes. The Japanese used inro (sectioned boxes) to hold money, tobacco, etc. A cord went from the top of the inro, under the kimono sash, and through the netsuke to keep the inro from falling. Netsukes needed to be compact and free of points that might catch on kimono sleeves, yet strong enough to support the weight of the inro. It's a rare collection that's sure to charm adults and children.

The museum offers a continuing program of outstanding special exhibitions (in 1990 there was the spectacular impressionist and postimpressionist collection of Walter H. Annenberg, in 1989 the magnificent Georgia O'Keeffe retrospective), films, lectures, guided tours, concerts, and a variety of educational events. Full admission (which admits visitors to specially priced exhibitions) is $5 for adults; $4 for senior citizens 62 and over and students with ID; $2 for children 6 to 17 years; free for children 5 and under. Free guided tours covering the highlights of the permanent collections are given daily.

There is a **Plaza Café,** as mentioned above, in the Leo S. Bing Center. It is open Tuesday through Friday from 10am to 4:30pm, on Saturday and Sunday to 5:30pm.

The museum is open Tuesday through Friday from 10am to 5pm, on Saturday and Sunday to 6pm. The second Tuesday of each month is free for all, except for admission to special exhibitions. The museum is closed every Monday, Thanksgiving, Christmas, and New Year's Day.

Parking at the visitors lot (turn north at the first block east of the Museum) is $1 for 20 minutes, $5 maximum on Saturday and Sunday, $8 maximum during the week.

Rancho La Brea Tar Pits/George C. Page Museum

Even today a bubbling, odorous, murky swamp of congealed oil, the tar pits are a primal sci-fi attraction right on the Miracle Mile. Part of Hancock Park, at 5801 Wilshire Blvd., the pits are the richest fossil site inherited from the Ice Age. They date back to prehistoric times (some 40,000 years back), when they formed a deceptively attractive drinking area for mammals, birds, amphibians, and even insects (many of which are now extinct), which crawled in to slake a thirst and stayed forever. Other animals, seeing them trapped, thought the victims easy prey and jumped into the mire to devour them. Although the existence of the pits was known as early as the 18th century, it wasn't until 1906 that scientists began a systematic removal and classification of the fossils. In subsequent years specimens brought up included ground sloths, huge vultures, mastodons (early elephants), camels, and prehistoric relatives of many of today's rodents, bears, lizards, and birds, as well as plants and freshwater shells. In one pit the skeleton of a Native American—dating, it is thought, from 9,000 years ago—was unearthed.

Over 100 pits, or excavations, have been made and over three million specimens removed in Hancock Park since the turn of the century. Currently there are six pits (places where asphalt seeps to the surface to form sticky pools) scattered throughout Hancock Park, including the Observation Pit and the Active Dig.

More than two dozen of the specimens have been mounted and placed for exhibition in the **Hancock Park George C. Page La Brea Discoveries Museum** at the east end of Hancock Park (tel. 213/936-2230). And replicas of the original trapped birds and animals stand fully life-size in their original setting, to spur your imagination. At the museum you can see a 15-minute documentary film and slides about the La Brea Tar Pits and test the adhesive quality of the death-trap asphalt for yourself. Over 30 exhibits include reconstructed skeletons of Ice Age animals.

The museum is open Tuesday through Sunday from 10am to 5pm. The Paleontology Laboratory, where scientists can be viewed cleaning, identifying, and cataloging fossils, is open Wednesday through Sunday. Museum tours are given Tuesday through Sunday (call for times). Admission is $5 for adults, $3 for seniors 62 and over and students, $1.50 for children ages 5 to 12; free for those 4 and under. Admission is free the second Tuesday of every month.

The Observation Pit, at the west end of Hancock Park behind the L.A. County Museum of Art, is open weekends only, from 10am to 5pm. Tours of the tar pits start from the Observation Pit and are conducted at 1pm on Saturday and Sunday.

The Pit 91 Viewing Station is open occasionally for visitors so that they can peer down into the "active" excavation where scientists continue to unearth and remove fossils.

WATTS TOWERS

A little-known American saga is the story of Simon Rodia, an Italian immigrant who came from one of the poorest districts in Rome, grew up in Watts, and worked as a tile setter. At the age of 40, he was impressed with the need to create something, to leave something behind in his adopted country. The result of this desire—after 33 years of work, with no encouragement, no help, and no equipment other than his tile-setting tools—is Watts Towers.

Ignoring the jeers and scorn of his neighbors, Rodia scavenged the city for bits and pieces of iron and tin, steel rods, seashells, broken tiles, old bottles (especially green ones), chips of flowered dishes, etc. With no blueprints, he turned this junk-yard of items into the Watts Towers, two of which soar 10 stories high (nearly 100 feet), the others averaging 40 feet. Outline designs have been made in the walls with hammers, horseshoes, and cookie cutters.

His task completed in 1954, Mr. Rodia suddenly and mysteriously left Watts. He was no longer there to guard his life's achievement, and in the years following the towers fell into disrepair, attacked for sport by vandals. As it turned out, though, the greatest danger to the towers was not from vandals but from the municipal building department, which ordered the towers to be leveled as "hazardous to the general public."

The issue became a nationwide cause célèbre. Art lovers from all over the world —including New York's Museum of Modern Art, which called them "works of great beauty and imagination"—protested vigorously. And a private Committee for Simon Rodia's Towers in Watts was formed for their protection, demanding that the towers be given a fair test. In front of national television cameras and newspaper reporters, the crucial experiment was performed—the towers were subjected to 10,000 pounds of pull by a derrick. Only one seashell toppled, and the city deemed them safe enough to stand. In 1963 the towers were designated a cultural monument by the City Cultural Heritage Board.

As for Rodia, he never returned to his towers. He was tracked down in 1959 in Martinez, California, but he seemed not to care about his amazing creation anymore. Some speculated that an artist has no further interest in his work after it is completed; others said he was broken by the criticism his work had engendered. Whatever the reason, he died with the secret in 1965, and a memorial service was held for him at the towers.

The towers are at 1765 E. 107th St., Watts, but they're still under renovation. The adjoining art center is open Tuesday through Saturday from 7am to 4pm (tel. 213/569-8181). At this writing, only group tours are conducted through the towers on weekdays; however, you can always call the art center to join any group touring the towers that day. On Saturday, from about 10am to 3pm, the staff at the art center does conduct tours through the towers for individuals, at a charge of $2 per person. To reach the towers, take the Harbor Freeway toward San Pedro, getting off and turning left at Century Boulevard. Go right on Central, left on 108th Street, then left onto Willowbrook to 107th Street.

HIGHLAND PARK

When you take the Pasadena Freeway to Avenue 43, you'll find yourself in the great Southwest; that is, at—

The Southwest Museum

Crowning a steep hill overlooking Arroyo Seco, the Southwest Museum is Los Angeles's oldest art treasury. The museum was founded in 1907 by amateur historian and Native American expert Charles F. Lummis, utilizing private funds. It contains one of the finest collections of Native American art and artifacts in the United States. Located at 234 Museum Dr., at Marmion Way (tel. 213/221-2163 for a recording, or 221-2164), it can be approached either via a winding drive up the hill or else through a tunnel at its foot, which opens onto an elevator that will carry you to the top.

Inside the two-story structure, the whole world of the original Americas opens onto a panoramic exhibition, complete with a Cheyenne summer tepee, rare paintings, weapons, moccasins, and other artifacts of Plains peoples' life. A two-level hall presents the culture of the native people of southeastern Alaska, Canada's west coast, and the northern United States. A major exhibition interprets 10,000 years of history of the people of the American Southwest, featuring art and artifacts of the native peoples of Arizona, New Mexico, Colorado, and Utah. The California Hall offers insights into the lifeways of the first Californians. The Caroline Boeing Poole Memorial Wing offers a changing display of more than 400 examples of native North American basketry from the museum's 11,000-plus collection.

The museum has an exceptionally interesting changing calendar of events and exhibitions throughout the year, such as the Native American Film Festival of documentaries and short subjects; lectures on the sacred art of the Huichols; Mexican song, dance, and costumes; and Mexican masks—to name just a few.

The Southwest Museum has undergone significant changes over the past eight years, and if you've never visited before or haven't been there recently, you'll find it fascinating and well worth your time. The museum is open Tuesday through Sunday from 11am to 5pm. Adults pay $4.50; seniors and students, $2.25; young people 7 to 18, $1; for those under 7, it's free.

And you can also visit the home of founder Charles F. Lummis, **El Alisal,** nearby at 200 E. Ave. 43 (tel. 213/222-0546). Lummis built this two-story "castle" himself, using rocks from a nearby arroyo and telephone poles purchased from the Santa Fe Railroad. His home was a cultural center for many famous personages in the literary, theatrical, political, and art worlds. It's open free to the public Thursday through Sunday from 1 to 4pm.

One of the very interesting aspects of El Alisal is the new and most attractive water-conserving garden. The primary plants are those that thrive in a Mediterranean climate. The experimental section, the yarrow meadow, is a substitute for a water-consuming lawn.

Yet a third attraction in the area is the **Casa de Adobe,** 4605 N. Figueroa St. (tel. 213/225-8653), a re-creation of an early-19th-century Mexican-Californian rancho. Latino art and artifacts are on exhibit from the Southwest Museum permanent collection, along with Spanish Colonial period furnishings. It's open Tuesday through Saturday from 11am to 5pm, on Sunday from 1pm. Admission is free (donations are accepted).

SIX FLAGS MAGIC MOUNTAIN

There's always a new and more spectacular thrill here. This time it's the Condor, which twirls you (and your stomach) at the top of a 112-foot pole. Or you can look forward to the incredible Tidal Wave, where you plunge 50 feet into a 20-foot wall of wild water—guaranteed as a hair-raising experience. Then there's the Z-Force, which will leave you hanging upside down from a swinging gondola so that a sheer drop of four stories seems certain. Or Roaring Rapids, a white-water rafting adventure complete with stair-step rapids and waterfalls (you will get wet). Those are just a few of about 100 rides and attractions—among them another thriller, the Great American Revolution—a huge roller coaster with a 360°, 90-foot-high vertical loop (that's right, you turn completely upside down). Aha! But wait until you try Ninja, the black belt of roller coasters—the first and only suspended coaster on the West Coast, which propels passengers from an overhead track through trees and along hills at angles of up to 110° and speeds of 50 mph. Or the screamer of them all, the Viper, described by Magic Mountain as pound for pound the most frightening roller coaster on earth. You're tossed into a loop, a corkscrew, and a 70-mph, 18-story drop from 188 feet above the ground and spiraled completely upside down seven times.

Attractions geared to tots are at Bugs Bunny World, with rides and creative play equipment specially designed for them. Bugs, who recently celebrated his 50th birthday here, personally greets his tiny guests, and the Animal Farm is right next door. And over at Spillikin Handcrafters Junction—an authentic 1800s crafts village—they can watch craftspeople (woodcarvers, weavers, etc.) at work.

In the Aquatic Stunt Arena, daily entertainment includes dolphin shows, high divers, and more. In summer the TDK Theater features big-name entertainers. And year-round, extravaganza variety shows, marching bands, magic acts, and local rock groups round out the bill.

You can pack a picnic lunch if you like, but there are many eateries in all price ranges, offering everything from chili to chicken yakitori. Not to mention countless stands selling pizza, hot dogs, burgers, tacos, corn on the cob, hot buttered popcorn, and other amusement park staples.

A one-price ticket admits visitors to all rides, amusements, and special attractions, including the big-name entertainment. Adults pay $23; seniors, $12; children under 48 inches, $12 (those 2 and under, free). Summer hours are 10am to 10pm weekdays, to midnight on Saturday and Sunday. Off-season hours (weekends and some holidays only) vary, so it's best to call ahead (tel. 805/255-4111 or 818/367-5965) for information. Parking is $5.

Magic Mountain is reached from U.S. 101 in Ventura by taking Calif. 126 through Fillmore to Castaic Junction, then turning south for about a mile at the junction of 126 and Interstate 5. From either direction, the park is two minutes west of the Golden State Freeway (I-5) at the Magic Mountain Parkway exit.

THE SPANISH MISSIONS

Throughout this book I've mentioned as sightseeing attractions many of the 21 missions created by Franciscan padre Junípero Serra (soon to be canonized). Built between 1769 and 1824, they reach from San Diego to Sonoma. In the Los Angeles area is one of the most visited of all the missions—

San Juan Capistrano

About 56 miles south of L.A. is the historic town of San Juan Capistrano, known for the swallows that return there each year and by the song "When the Swallows Come Back to Capistrano," written over 50 years ago. Though the swallows are getting fewer in number (and not exactly welcomed by many residents), they still return to the mission on St. Joseph's day, March 19. On October 23, the Day of San Juan, the swallows punctually leave for their home to the south, probably somewhere in South America.

The mission here dates from 1775. Recently it has become known more as an educational center than simply the focal point of swallow lore. A museum was added on to the mission 10 years ago and is now a repository of fascinating artifacts and murals depicting the mission era. The mission's great feature is the Serra Chapel, the oldest building in California still in use. The ruins of the Old Stone Church, the restored metal-working furnaces, and the adobe walls still in place—all contribute to the historic charm of the mission.

The mission may be visited daily from 7:30am to 5pm, and the admission charge is $2 for adults, $1 for youngsters under 12 if accompanied by their parents. For information, call 714/493-1424.

Mission San Fernando

Closer by, near the junction of the Golden State-Santa Ana (I-5) and San Diego Freeways (Hwy. 405) in San Fernando, the Mission San Fernando, 15151 Mission Blvd. (tel. 818/361-0186) has 7 acres of beautiful grounds as well as a convent. Dedicated in 1822, with an arcade of 21 classic arches and adobe walls 4 feet thick, it was a familiar stop for wayfarers along El Camino Real. The museum and the adjoining cemetery (where half a dozen padres and hundreds of Shoshone Indians are buried) are also of interest. Open daily from 9am to 4:30pm; $2 admission for adults, $1 for children 7 to 15.

Mission San Gabriel Archangel

Nine miles northeast of downtown L.A., San Gabriel, 537 W. Mission Dr. (tel. 818/282-5191), was formerly one of the best preserved of the missions, tracing its origins to 1771.

Due to the earthquake of October 1 and 4, 1987, it has been necessary to close the church, museum, and winery. Just when the mission will be able to open depends on how long it will take to raise the $3 million needed to repair and restore the buildings. The remainder of the grounds are still open to visitors.

In the church (with walls 5 feet thick to withstand the ravages of time) was an oval-faced, sad-eyed *Our Lady of Sorrows*—said to have converted the native peoples with its serenity. It has been stolen. The museum houses "aboriginal" American paintings on sail cloth depicting the 14 Stations of the Cross.

HUNTINGTON LIBRARY, ART COLLECTIONS, AND BOTANICAL GARDENS

At 1151 Oxford Rd. in San Marino (tel. 818/405-2141), the 207-acre former estate of industrialist Henry E. Huntington has been converted into an educational and cultural center housing rare books (including a copy of the Gutenberg Bible printed in 15th-century Mainz), original manuscripts, and great works of art.

His home is now one art gallery, where paintings, tapestries, furnishings, and other decorative arts are exhibited—chiefly English and French 18th-century works. The most celebrated is Gainsborough's *The Blue Boy,* but the art gallery also contains Rembrandt's *Lady with the Plume,* Sir Joshua Reynold's *Sarah Siddons as the Tragic Muse,* and a collection of Beauvais and Gobelins tapestries.

The Virginia Steele Scott Gallery for American art opened in 1984. Paintings range over a 200-year span from the 1730s to the 1930s. Some of the better known works are Gilbert Stuart's *George Washington,* John Singleton Copley's *Sarah Jackson,* George Caleb Bingham's *In a Quandary,* Mary Cassatt's *Breakfast in Bed,* and Fredric Church's *Chimborazo.*

The library's remarkable collection of English and American first editions, letters, and manuscripts includes the original manuscript of Thoreau's *Walden,* a 1410 copy of Chaucer's *Canterbury Tales,* and Benjamin Franklin's *Autobiography* in his own writing. All told, there are over two million manuscripts and 300,000 rare books ranging from the 11th century to the present.

If all that culture sets your mind aboggle, take a stroll in the magnificent Botanical Gardens, where you'll find a Desert Garden filled with many varieties of cactus, a Camellia Garden with 1,500 varieties, an Australian Garden, a Japanese Garden that includes a Japanese house, a Zen Garden and bonsai court, a Rose Garden, and a Shakespeare Garden of flowers and shrubs mentioned in plays by the Bard. Self-guided tour pamphlets of the gardens and the art gallery cost 25¢ at the bookstore.

The museum and grounds are open Tuesday through Sunday from 1 to 4:30pm (closed on major holidays). A donation of $2 per adult is suggested. *Note:* Sunday visitors must have advance reservations if they are residents of Los Angeles County.

THE NORTON SIMON MUSEUM OF ART

This important collection at Colorado Boulevard and Orange Grove, Pasadena (tel. 818/449-3730), sits among broad plazas, sculpture gardens, semitropical plantings, and a reflection pool.

Important areas covered here are old masters from the Italian, Dutch, Spanish, Flemish, and French schools, impressionist paintings, and 20th-century paintings and sculptures. Some highlights of the collections are works by Raphael, Rubens, Rembrandt, Rousseau, Courbet, Degas, Matisse, Picasso, Corot, Monet, and Van Gogh. A superb collection of Southeast Asian and Indian sculpture is also featured.

The museum is open Thursday through Sunday from noon to 6pm. Admission for adults is $4; students and senior citizens over 62 pay $2; under-12s are free when accompanied by an adult. The bookshop closes at 5:30pm.

DESCANSO GARDENS

E. Manchester Boddy began planting camellias in 1941 as a hobby. Today the Rancho del Descanso (Ranch of Rest) that he started contains thousands of camellias with over 600 varieties and over 100,000 plants—making it the world's largest camellia gardens. The County of Los Angeles purchased the gardens when Mr. Boddy retired in 1953, and over the years they have become an attraction that has delighted countless visitors.

In addition to the camellias, there is also a 4-acre rose garden, which includes some varieties dating from the time of Christ. A stream and many paths wind through a towering oak forest, and a chaparral nature trail is provided for those who wish to observe native vegetation. Each season different plants in the garden are featured: daffodils, azaleas, and lilacs in the spring; chrysanthemums in the fall; and so on. Within the gardens, monthly art exhibitions are held at the Hospitality House. Because the camellia originated in the Orient the Teahouse is located in the Camillia forest. Landscaped with money donated by the Japanese-American community, it features pools, waterfalls, and a rock garden, as well as a gift shop built in the style of a Japanese farmhouse. The Teahouse serves tea and cookies Tuesday through Sunday from 11am to 4pm. Other features include lunches served daily at the Café Court; docent-guided walking tours on Sunday at 1pm; and guided tram tours ($2) Tuesday through Friday at 1, 2, and 3pm, and on Saturday and Sunday at 11am.

Located at 1418 Descanso Dr. (at the junction of the Glendale and Foothill Freeways), La Canada (tel. 213/790-5571), the gardens are open daily from 9am to 4:30pm. Admission is $4 for adults, $2 for seniors, and $1 for children ages 5 to 12; persons under 13 must be accompanied by adults. Picnicking is allowed in specified areas. Parking is free.

ORGANIZED TOURS

If you're pressed for time and want to see a lot, or if you just feel like being lazy and leaving the driving to others, organized sightseeing may be for you. The largest selection of tours is available from **Gray Line Tours Company,** 6541 Hollywood Blvd., Los Angeles (tel. 213/481-2121). In air-conditioned coaches, with commentaries by guides, the individual tours include such attractions as Disneyland, Sunset Strip, the movie studios, Knott's Berry Farm (Buena Park), the Farmers Market, Hollywood, homes of the stars, San Diego, Catalina Island, Tijuana, the *Queen Mary* and *Spruce Goose* (Long Beach). Six Flags Magic Mountain, Beverly Hills, Universal Studios, and Movieland Wax Museum (Buena Park). All fares include admission to any attractions visited.

---

8. After Dark

The days when Los Angeles nightlife was one glamorous whirl under the scrutiny of gossip columnists is long gone, if indeed it ever really existed outside movie mags and columns. Basically, Los Angeles residents are suburban types whose idea of a good way to spend an evening is to have friends in for drinks, poolside barbecues, and hot-tubbing. When they do go out on the town, it's usually for dinner at some posh restaurant.

But that doesn't mean there's nothing to do. It's just that Angelenos, like New Yorkers, take their abundant nightlife for granted and only bother with it when they have out-of-town guests—then they have a great time and vow to "do this more often."

The entertainment business—film, TV, records, theater—is still the most important industry in Los Angeles. In and around L.A. there are over 150 active theaters, large and small, with plays, revues, concerts. There are over 60 jazz clubs. And in addition to all this, the Pacific Amphitheatre and the Universal Amphitheatre feature name performers, as do the Greek Theatre, the Hollywood Bowl (mostly classical), the Forum in Inglewood, and the Meadows Amphitheatre in Irvine.

If you'd like an idea of what's going on any given week (the schedule of events can change weekly), buy the Sunday *Los Angeles Times.* The "Calendar" section is what you want to save. "Outtakes" updates the lowdown; "Movies" hypes the new faces in films and new films in production. There's a parental film guide and a handy list of family attractions, a description of new movie openings and special programs (offbeat films) showing that week, plus all the museums, lectures, and exhibits you'd ever want to see. And if you have it in mind to make a side trip to Las Vegas, Laughlin, Reno, or Lake Tahoe, there are ads for many of the hotels, the headliners, and what's being offered that week in special rates. The "Calendar" also lists theaters, club acts, and what's opening or closing, including restaurants.

LIVE MUSIC

Gazzarri's on the Strip, 9039 Sunset Blvd., near Doheny Drive (tel. 213/273-6606), used to call itself "Hollywood's oldest disco." They've now changed to a live-music format, offering rock 'n' roll bands for dancing from 8pm to 2am Wednesday through Saturday. Admission is about $10 to $14, depending on the performers. The age group is early 20s; dress is casual. No credit cards. There's a two-drink minimum for those over 21, and you must be at least 18 to get in.

COMEDY

The **Comedy Store,** 8433 Sunset Blvd., one block east of La Cienega Boulevard, West Hollywood (tel. 213/656-6225), is the most important showcase for rising comedians in Los Angeles and probably in the entire United States. Owner Mitzi Shore has created a setting in which new comics can develop and established performers can work out the kinks in new material. It's always vastly entertaining.

There are three major parts to it. The **Mainroom,** which seats about 500, features an "open mike" (anyone can do three minutes of comedy) from 8:30 to 10pm on Monday, followed by professional stand-ups from 10pm to 1am. Admission is free, but there is a two-drink minimum. Other nights there's a continuous show of comedians, each doing about 15-minute stints. The talent here is always first-rate, ranging from people you've seen, or may see, on the "Tonight Show" and suchlike to really big names. Admission is $10 Tuesday through Thursday and $14 for the 9pm and 11:30pm shows on Friday and Saturday, with a two-drink minimum.

The original **Comedy Store,** open nightly with two shows on Saturday at 9 and 11pm, charges $12 for the early show, $14 for the late show, $9 on all other nights, and has a two-drink minimum. About 15 to 20 comedians perform. Monday night is amateur night when anyone with enough guts can take the stage for three to five minutes; there's no cover, but there is a two-drink minimum.

Finally, there's the **Belly Room,** with Thursday nights reserved for a singer showcase starting at 9pm; Friday through Wednesday is reserved for comediennes; there's a $3 cover and a two-drink minimum. Other nights you can enjoy music at the piano bar. There's no cover, but there is a one-drink minimum. Drinks are $3.50 to $7.

Improvisation, 8162 Melrose Ave., at Crescent Heights Boulevard, West Hollywood (tel. 213/651-2583), offers something different each night. The club's own television show, "Evening at the Improv," is now filmed at the Santa Monica location for national distribution. Although there used to be a fairly active music schedule, the Improv is mostly doing what it does best—showcasing comedy. Major stars often appear here—people like Jay Leno, Billy Crystal, and Robin Williams.

There is comedy nightly. Monday and Wednesday performances are at 8:30 and 11pm; on Tuesday, Thursday, and Sunday at 8 and 10:45pm; on Friday and Saturday at 7:30, 9:45, and 11:45pm. Sunday through Thursday, admission is $6.50 plus a two-drink minimum; on Friday and Saturday it's $8, $10, and $8, respectively, for the three performance times, plus the two-drink minimum.

The larger Improvisation is at 321 Santa Monica Blvd., near 4th Street, in Santa Monica (tel. 213/394-8664). Show times are the same as those at the Melrose location, with the addition of a Tuesday performance at 9pm, and an 8pm Monday-evening performance of the Bargain Basement Players. Admission prices and the two-drink minimum are the same.

Both locations have restaurants: Hell's Kitchen, serving Italian entrees at the West Hollywood club, and Tex-Mex cuisine at the Santa Monica spot.

CONCERTS—CLASSICAL, POP, ROCK, ETC.

To quote the *Los Angeles Times* "Calendar" section, "Why Does a $30 Ticket Become a $600 Ticket?" While there is a push to set limits on prices that (legitimate) ticket brokers can charge in California, as there is in New York, a big draw (e.g., Madonna) can currently effect a big price and affect lots of disgruntled fans. Or to sum it all up: At the moment, you may not be able to get tickets for big-name draws without a long wait in line (unbecoming a tourist) or a large hole in the pocket. The general prices given below are for nonscalping, nonbroker tickets.

The **Hollywood Bowl,** 2301 N. Highland Ave., at Odin Street (tel. 213/850-2000), is an outdoor amphitheater with perfect natural acoustics. It's the summer home of the Los Angeles Philharmonic Orchestra. The season begins July 1 and ends around mid-September.

Nowadays, internationally known conductors and soloists join the Los Angeles Philharmonic in classical programs on Tuesday and Thursday nights. The Philharmonic's Friday and Saturday concerts are more pop oriented. The season also includes a jazz series, a Virtuoso series, and a Sunday Sunset series. Several weekend concerts throughout the season feature fireworks, including the traditional July 4th Family Fireworks picnic concert.

Part of the Bowl ritual is to order a picnic basket from the Bowl caterers (call 213/851-3588 the day before the concert to order) or bring your own.

Seats for classical concerts start at $1 and ascend to $20 for bench seats, $20 to $66 for box seats. The box office opens in May, Monday through Saturday from 10am to 6pm; from July 2 and for the rest of the summer, it's open to 9pm and from noon to 6pm on Sunday. Parking space can be reserved for $10 (subject to availability), although at lots adjacent to the Bowl entrance, you can park for $6 and then take a shuttle. For evening performances be sure to bring a sweater or jacket—it gets chilly in those hills.

The **Greek Theatre,** 2700 N. Vermont Ave., Griffith Park (tel. 213/665-5857), is a place where the entertainment ranges from performances by the Dance Theatre of Harlem to artists like Barry Manilow, Ben Vereen, Joan Baez, Manhattan Transfer, Natalie Cole, Neil Diamond, and Tom Jones. The theater is patterned after the classic outdoor theaters of ancient Greece. Dance groups and national theater societies also perform here. The season runs from late May to early October. Tickets range in price from about $25 to $60. The ticket office is open weekdays only from 10am to 6pm.

The **Universal Amphitheatre,** 100 Universal City Plaza, just off the Hollywood Freeway, Lankershim Boulevard exit (tel. 818/980-9421 for a helpful human), is a 6,251-seat enclosed theater adjacent to the Visitors Entertainment Center at Universal Studios. It's well designed—no seat is more than 140 feet from the stage—and only top names perform here, usually for three to five days. Tickets are often sold out well before the concert dates, so haunt the box office in advance (hours vary; call the above number for information). Whom might you see here? Elton John, the Temptations, Bob Hope, Frank Sinatra, Gladys Knight and the Pips, Paul Simon, Linda Ronstadt, Herb Alpert, George Carlin, Robin Williams, George Burns, et al. Tickets are priced from about $25 to $75, depending on the performer.

THEATER

The **Music Center,** 135 N. Grand Ave., at 1st Street, downtown, is L.A.'s most prestigious performing arts facility. It consists of three theaters:

The **Dorothy Chandler Pavilion** (tel. 213/972-7211), home of the Los Angeles Philharmonic, is a 3,250-seat hall where concerts, recitals, opera, and dance performances are presented. Every year the L.A. Civic Light Opera has its summer season here. The American première of the London hit musical *Me and My Girl* was presented here.

The **Ahmanson Theatre,** a 2,100-seat legitimate playhouse, is (along with the Mark Taper Forum) home base of the Center Theater Group, which performs four plays here from mid-October to early May. Offerings have included Christopher Reeve in *Summer and Smoke,* Daniel J. Travanti in *I Never Sang for My Father,* and the West Coast premiere of Neil Simon's *Broadway Bound.* A variety of international dance companies and concert attractions round out the season.

Prices generally range from $20 to $50, but there are reductions available for students and senior citizens for specified performances. Phone the Music Center at 213/972-7211 for ticket information.

The **Mark Taper Forum** is a more intimate, circular theater with 750 seats. The emphasis here is on new and contemporary works, although you might catch something like Shakespeare's *The Tempest* as well. Productions have included *Green Card, Rat in the Skull, The Immigrant,* and *Ghetto.* Needless to say, with all this diversity, I can't begin to quote prices. There are reductions available to many performances for students and senior citizens. Phone 213/972-7373 for all ticket information.

The **James A. Doolittle Theatre** (formerly the Huntington Hartford Theatre), 1615 N. Vine St., near Hollywood Boulevard (tel. 213/462-6666), offers a wide spectrum of productions. For instance, they've had Kate Mulgrew in *Hedda Gabler,* as well as Michael Gross and Linda Purl in *The Real Thing.* Evening shows are at 8:30pm Tuesday through Saturday night and at 8pm on Sunday. Ticket prices generally range from $25 to $45.

The **Wilshire Theatre,** 8440 Wilshire Blvd., near La Cienega, Beverly Hills (tel. 213/410-1062), opened in 1980 with *The Oldest Living Graduate* starring Henry Fonda. More recent productions have ranged from musicals like *A Chorus Line* to *Aren't We All?* with Rex Harrison and Claudette Colbert. "In concert" offerings have included Shirley MacLaine, Charles Aznavour, Spandau Ballet, and the Eurythmics. Tickets are in the $25 to $50 range. There's parking for 1,200 cars.

The **Pantages Theatre,** 6233 Hollywood Blvd., near Vine Street (tel. 213/410-1062), is a Hollywood landmark dating from 1930. Built at a cost of $1.25 million (the equivalent of $10 million today), it was incredibly luxurious. For 10 years it was the setting for the presentation of the Academy Awards, including the first televised Oscar ceremony. It's been through several incarnations, including one as a fine movie house. In 1977 it began a new life as a leading legitimate theater with a production of *Bubbling Brown Sugar.* Recent productions have included *Me and My Girl* and *Starlight Express,* as well as the Julie Andrews/Carol Burnett TV special, the Grammy "Living Legend" Awards, and the Country/Western Music Awards. Ticket prices range from $25 to $60.

SOUTH OF THE BORDER

I'm not talking about flying down to Tijuana; there's festive Mexican entertainment offered at **Casa La Golondrina,** W-17 Olvera St., downtown (tel. 213/628-4349). Located on the city's oldest street, it's housed in the historic Pelanconi House (circa 1850). The café itself dates from 1924. You can sit by the fireplace, dine on Mexican fare, or just sip a huge margarita while enjoying strolling mariachi troubadours, flamenco guitarists, and the like. "Fiesta" entertainment is featured every Friday and Saturday night. There's no cover charge or minimum. Drinks and Mexican beer cost $3 to $4; a margarita, about $3 to $7. For dinner you can have a complete meal with two entrees (perhaps arroz con pollo and chile relleno), salad, Spanish rice, beans, coffee, and dessert, for under $17.50.

The café is open daily from 10am to 10pm.

MIXED BAGS

The **ABC Entertainment Center,** Century City, directly across from the Century Plaza Hotel, offers a variety of nightlife options. For openers, there's the **Shubert Theatre** (tel. toll free 800/233-3123), presenting big-time musicals—like *Cats* and *Les Misérables.* Evening prices range from about $30 to $65.

There are four plush first-run movie theaters in the complex (call 213/553-5307 to find out what's playing).

Then there's **Harry's Bar & Grill** (tel. 213/277-2333), which looks just like its namesake in Florence, for drinks and northern Italian dinners (see the "Restaurants" section for details).

The **Hollywood Palladium,** 6215 Sunset Blvd., near Vine Street (tel. 213/962-7600), provides a wide spectrum of entertainment. Traditionally it was the place for big bands, and they still play here on occasion—Ray Anthony, Tex Benecke, etc. And Lawrence Welk used to do his famous New Year's Eve from the Palladium. The Palladium more recently has offered rock groups like the Ramones. Latin music is also popular. Prices and hours vary with the attraction.

DISNEYLAND AND ENVIRONS

1. ANAHEIM/FULLERTON
2. BUENA PARK
3. IRVINE

Although physically Anaheim, Fullerton, Buena Park, and Irvine are among the most unprepossessing towns in California, they are also the ones that attract the most visitors. For if the natural surroundings are uninspiring and the streets lack any vestige of charm, the specially created attractions off the streets are enchanting—transformed by the magic wand of Walt Disney into a wonderful world of make-believe. And Disneyland is just one of the spectacular attractions in the area. There are also Knott's Berry Farm, the Movieland Wax Museum, and more. So take the kids—and if you don't have any kids, be a kid yourself.

1. Anaheim/Fullerton

Just 27 miles southeast of downtown Los Angeles, reached via the Santa Ana Freeway, Anaheim is Disneyland. Once a sleepy little town in the Valencia orange-grove belt, it offers excellent hotels and motels to handle the masses of visitors who come to visit the world-famed attraction. Disneyland is on everyone's must-see list.

GETTING THERE
If you're going by car, just get on the freeway heading south, and you'll be in Anaheim in about an hour. If you go by bus, take no. 460 from the RTD/Greyhound terminal downtown at 6th and Los Angeles streets. Fare is $2.50 each way.

WHAT TO SEE AND DO

Disneyland
This world of charm and magic is at 1313 Harbor Blvd. (tel. 714/999-4565), off the Santa Ana Freeway (I-5). Opened in 1955, the $307-million, 76-acre entertainment complex is "the happiest place on earth." Can you believe that in 1988 Mickey Mouse had his 60th birthday? Disneyland is split into seven themed lands, each with its own rides and attractions. You might start at the entrance and work clockwise, but the best plan of attack is to arrive at opening time and do all the most

popular rides first—Space Mountain, Big Thunder Mountain Railroad, Pirates of the Caribbean, etc. The themed lands are as follows:

Main Street U.S.A., the main drag of a small turn-of-the-century American town, is at the entrance to the park. This is a good area to save for the end of the day—particularly the Main Street Cinema, where you can rest your weary feet while enjoying silent film classics and cartoons. If you want to tour the entire park, trains (all 1890 or earlier vintage) of the Disneyland Railroad depart regularly from the Main Street Depot and completely encircle the park, with stops at Frontierland and Tomorrowland.

After sunset, there's a Main Street Electrical Parade spectacular—with fabulous whirling lights followed by Fantasy in the Sky fireworks.

Adventureland is inspired by exotic regions of Asia, Africa, and the South Pacific. Here electronically animated tropical birds, flowers, and tiki gods present a musical comedy in the Enchanted Tiki Room. Within a spear's throw, a jungle cruise is threatened by wild animals and hostile natives.

New Orleans Square re-creates the atmosphere of that city around the mid-1800s. Of course, you take a trip through the Haunted Mansion inhabited by 999 ghosts, always (heh! heh! heh!) in search of "Occupant 1,000." Pirates of the Caribbean takes you down a plunging waterfall through pirate caves, ending in a dynamite explosion set off by a "band of befuddled buccaneers."

Critter Country is inspired by the great outdoors. What better way to see this rugged country than in Davy Crockett Explorer Canoes? Best of all, between the Haunted Mansion and Country Bear Playhouse, you'll find Splash Mountain, the largest towering log-flume attraction in the world, the most elaborate and exciting ever created. Each log vehicle sends eight guests speeding through twisting waterways and scenic chutes. There's a chase through swamps, caves, and beehives of backwoods bayous, before a rise that leads to a 52-foot plunge into a briar-patch pond. Splash Mountain is a fantastic extravaganza, combining music, water, sudden falls, snapping alligators, harmonizing vultures, and angry bees; it also brings to life the escapades of Brer Rabbit, Brer Bear, and Brer Fox. You'll want to sing along when you hear "Zip-A-Dee-Doo-Dah" in the finale, an animal chorus celebrating Brer Rabbit's return to the briar patch.

Frontierland, with a log-walled stockade entrance, is America in the early 1800s—a land of dense forests and broad rivers inhabited by hearty pioneers. You can ride a raft to Tom Sawyer's Island, visit Big Thunder Ranch, and Big Thunder Mountain Railroad takes you in old ore cars through a deserted 1870s mine; during the trip the train is menaced by swarming bats, a waterfall rushing the tracks, an earthquake, falling rocks, etc.

Fantasyland has a storybook theme and rides—you can attend the Mad Hatter's wild Tea Party or fly over London to Never Never Land with Peter Pan and Tinker Bell. One of the park's most popular rides is in Fantasyland, the Matterhorn Bobsleds, a roller-coaster kind of ride past waterfalls and culminating in a big splash into glacier lakes at the bottom of the mountain. Bobsledders experience sudden drops in temperature as they race through chilling caverns, penetrate drifting fog banks, and encounter the Abominable Snowman.

Tomorrowland explores the world of the future. It has some of the most terrific Disneyland attractions, including Space Mountain, where you become an astronaut and experience a voyage through the cosmos. Other Tomorrowland attractions are the 3-D motion picture *Captain Eo*, a musical space adventure starring Michael Jackson performing his original score and a cast of merry, mythical space characters. The super-realism of the 3-D makes it seem as though the superstar were dancing off the screen and into the theater and as though lasers were firing overhead at hovering spaceships. Add to that the newer *Star Tours*, which puts you aboard a StarSpeeder as it takes off for the Moon of Endor, only to encounter a spaceload of misadventures. As you enter the Tomorrowland Spaceport, C-3PO and R2-D2 (the endearing and dynamic duo from *Star Wars*) are on hand to greet you. You board your own 40-passenger StarSpeeder, fasten your seat belts, and you are off on a remarkably real intergalactic adventure, with visual sensations and actual motion combining to create a thrill not to be believed until you've tried it. The Mission to Mars and the Submarine Voyage are two additional treats at Tomorrowland.

And don't forget to visit the **Wonders of China,** a marvelous morning tour of all the remarkably beautiful and historical wonders of that extraordinary land.

That, of course, is not the half of it. There are costumed Disney characters, penny arcades, restaurants and snack bars galore, fireworks (summer only), mariachi bands, ragtime pianists, parades, shops, marching bands, etc.

General admission to Disneyland is $27.50 for those 12 and older and $22.50 for children aged 3 to 11. Admission includes unlimited rides and all entertainment.

During the fall, winter, and spring seasons (mid-September through May), Disneyland is open Monday through Friday from 10am to 6pm, on weekends from 9am to midnight. In the summer season and on the Thanksgiving, Christmas, and Easter holidays, it's open every day from 8am to 1am. The parking lot ($4 charge) may be entered from Harbor Boulevard.

The Anaheim Convention Center

Yes, Virginia, there is something else in Anaheim. The Anaheim Convention Center, 800 W. Katella Ave. (tel. 714/999-8900), is a $60-million, 40-acre exhibit facility—the largest such complex on the West Coast—located directly opposite Disneyland. A variety of events are always going on here—they might include a Helen Reddy concert, a boxing match, an ice revue, an antique fair, a recreational-vehicles show, or even a circus performance. Check it out.

The Crystal Cathedral

It's worth a visit to see the church from which the Rev. Robert Schuller broadcasts every Sunday on TV; it's at 12141 Lewis St., Garden Grove (tel. 714/971-4000). The structure was designed by Philip Johnson, the world-famous architect, for the Garden Grove Community Church. The cathedral is an all-glass, star-shaped building towering 125 feet heavenward. The organ in the cathedral is magnificent and has over 13,000 pipes to generate an incredible richness of sound.

WHERE TO STAY

Families and Disney freaks might want to make Anaheim their Southern California base while taking in Disneyland and all the other nearby attractions.

Disneyland Hotel, 1150 W. Cerritos Ave., Anaheim, CA 92802 (tel. 714/778-6600), just adjacent to the park, is the only hotel on Disneyland's Monorail. Located on 60 attractively landscaped acres, it offers 1,132 guest rooms, six restaurants, five cocktail lounges, 35 shops and boutiques, every kind of service desk imaginable, an international artisans bazaar, a walk-under waterfall, three swimming pools, and 10 night-lit tennis courts. All the rooms are attractively furnished and equipped with every modern amenity.

Rates for singles are $150 to $198 a night, doubles and twins cost $165 to $219, and suites begin at $400.

The **Sheraton-Anaheim Hotel,** 1015 W. Ball Rd., Anaheim, CA 92802 (tel. 714/778-1700, or toll free 800/325-3535), features a unique English Tudor castle architecture. Public facilities include an award-winning dining room, a nightclub, a lounge, a heated outdoor swimming pool, and shuttle service to and from Disneyland and the airport. The hotel's 500 rooms are irreproachably modern, some with refrigerators; all have color TVs, radios, direct-dial phones, dressing rooms, tub/shower baths, and the like.

Singles range from $100 to $115, doubles run $105 to $125, and there's no charge for children 17 and under occupying the same room as their parents.

Very nice accommodations, too, at the **Anaheim Aloha TraveLodge,** 505 Katella Ave. (one block from Disneyland), Anaheim, CA 92805 (tel. 714/774-8710, or toll free 800/255-3050). The 50 rooms are pleasant standard motel units, all with color TVs and free cable movies, direct-dial phones, modern baths, and in-room coffee makers. There's a heated swimming pool with a slide.

Rates are seasonal but always include a Continental breakfast. May 15 to September 15, singles are $59; doubles and twins, $68. Off-season rates are lower. Children under 17 stay free in their parents' room the year round. In peak season, two-bedroom units that can accommodate six to eight people are $110.

There's a **Motel 6** at 921 S. Beach Blvd. (near Ball Road), Anaheim, CA 92804 (tel. 714/220-2866). There are 54 air-conditioned units, color TV is available, Motel 6 now has in-room phones (no charge for local calls), and there's a swimming pool on the premises. It's easy on the budget, clean, efficient, and comfortable. Singles are $30, plus $6 for each extra adult.

The ultimate in economy near Disneyland and Knott's Berry Farm is the **Fullerton Hacienda AYH Hostel,** 1700 N. Harbor Blvd., Fullerton, CA 92635 (tel. 714/738-3721), adjoining Anaheim. It's located on the site of an old dairy farm, surrounded by much greenery. As with all the AYH hostels I've been to, the accommodations are comfortable and the manager congenial and helpful. The hostel provides complete kitchen and bathroom facilities. It all operates under a self-help system: You're expected to clean up after yourself, leave the hostel tidy, and do small chores each morning as requested by the houseparents. The maximum stay is three consecutive days. If you travel much and can enjoy the very simple life, I suggest that it's worth joining the AYH—just ask for the application information. They welcome members of all ages. *Note:* No alcohol, drugs, or weapons are allowed on the premises, and smoking is not allowed in the building.

Rates are $10 for AYH/IYHF members and $13 for nonmembers.

WHERE TO DINE

Anaheim is not exactly one of the world's gourmet capitals. If you're just in town for the day, you'll probably eat at Disneyland, and if not, the Disneyland Hotel has a restaurant to suit every taste; most other hotels also have reasonable dining facilities.

If you should feel like a night out, however, try **Mr. Stox,** 1105 E. Katella Ave., between the Santa Ana Freeway and State College Boulevard (tel. 714/634-2994), offering hearty steak and fresh seafood dinners in an Early California setting. Hot entree specialties costing $12 to $22 include roast prime rib of beef au jus and mesquite-broiled fish, veal, and lamb; sandwiches and salads are also available, for $7 to $13. Homemade desserts, like the chocolate-mousse cake, are excellent. Mr. Stox has an enormous wine cellar as well. At night there's entertainment while you dine.

Open for lunch weekdays from 11am to 3pm (the menu is lower priced) and for dinner nightly from 5:30 to 10pm. Reservations suggested.

2. Buena Park

Just 5 miles from Anaheim is Buena Park, with a trio of major attractions: Knott's Berry Farm, the Movieland Wax Museum, and the tournament/banquet Medieval Times. Don't even think of doing them all in one day, much less combining them with Disneyland. If you want to see every attraction, it's advisable to stay in the area.

WHAT TO SEE AND DO

Knott's Berry Farm

In 1920, Walter and Cordelia Knott arrived in Buena Park in their old Model T and leased 10 acres of land. When times got hard during the Depression, Cordelia set up a roadside stand selling pies and preserves. As traffic increased, she added home-cooked chicken dinners to her offerings. The first day she sold 8, by the end of the year she was selling about 90 a day, and today the world-famous **Chicken Dinner**

Restaurant serves up over a million chicken meals a year! But even the first few years, lines were so long that Walter decided to create an Old West Ghost Town as a diversion for waiting customers. That's how it all began. The Knott family still owns the farm, and it has become the nation's third-best-attended family entertainment complex (the two Disney parks are before it). It's at 8039 Beach Blvd., Buena Park (tel. 714/220-5200), just south of the Santa Ana and Riverside/Artesia freeways. It's divided into five Old Time Adventures areas. They are:

Old West Ghost Town, the original attraction, a collection of authentic buildings, refurbished and relocated from actual deserted western ghost towns. Guests can immerse themselves in rip-roarin' Wild West lore—pan for gold, climb aboard the stagecoach, ride rickety train cars through the Calico Mine, get held up aboard the Denver and Rio Grande Calico Railroad, or hiss the villain at a melodrama in the Birdcage Theater.

Fiesta Village is a south-of-the-border environment of festive markets, strolling mariachis, wild rides like the Tampico Tumbler and Montezooma's Revenge—a loop roller coaster that not only turns you upside down but goes backward.

Roaring '20s Amusement Area contains the thrilling Sky Tower, a parachute jump that drops riders 20 stories (over 200 feet) at free-fall speeds. In addition to the 12 chutes, there's an observation car called the Sky Cabin, which revolves 360° while traveling up and down the tower. Thrill seekers will also want to try the XK-1, the ultimate participatory flight ride (or to put it another way, you pilot your aircraft using a control stick), as well as the Whirlpool. The Pacific Pavilion features *Splashdance,* with delightful dancing dolphins and sea lions. It's also the home of the 2,100-seat Good Time Theatre and the $7-million Kingdom of the Dinosaurs ride. Finally, there's the new Boomerang, a state-of-the-art coaster that turns riders upside down six times—three forward, three backward—in less than one minute. And if that doesn't shake your lunch around, nothing will.

Wild Water Wilderness is a $10-million, 3½-acre, turn-of-the-century California wilderness park with an exciting white-water ride, Bigfoot Rapids.

Camp Snoopy is Knott's themed area of the picturesque California High Sierra. It is a home for Charles Schulz's beloved beagle, Snoopy, and his pals, Charlie Brown and Lucy, who greet guests and pose for pictures. It's 6 rustic acres of fun for the young of all ages.

And now Knott's Berry Farm has opened the **Incredible Waterworks Show,** a sound, light, and water spectacular held on the park's Reflection Lake.

Knott's is open year-round except December 25. In summer it's open Sunday through Friday from 10am to midnight, on Saturday to 1am; winter hours are 10am to 6pm weekdays, to 10pm on Saturday, and to 7pm on Sunday.

Visiting Knott's costs $22 for adults, $16 for seniors over 60, $17 for children aged 3 to 11; those under 3 admitted free. There is unlimited access to all rides, shows, and attractions.

Movieland Wax Museum

Movieland (tel. 714/522-1155) features over 250 images of Hollywood's biggest movie and TV stars in over 100 authentic movie sets, including the latest additions: James Stewart, Bette Davis, Clint Eastwood, and Michael Jackson. Experience the thrill of stepping into supersets like the capsized ship in *The Poseidon Adventure,* snowbanks in the *Dr. Zhivago* set, and the bridge of the Starship *Enterprise.* In the Chamber of Horrors there are 15 sets and wax figures that re-create the special effects that made movies like *The Exorcist* and *Psycho* famous.

Unique gifts and movie memorabilia are available in our gift shops, and there is a large collection of mutoscopes and biographs.

The museum is open every day, rain or shine. Hours are 9am to 8pm. Once in, you can stay till 9:30pm. Lunch or dinner is available on the premises. Admission is $11 for adults, $9 for seniors, $7 for children 4 to 11 years; under 4, no charge. Parking is free. Movieland is located one block north of Knott's Berry Farm in Buena Park, Orange County. Take the Beach Boulevard exit South from the Santa Ana Freeway (I-5) and the Riverside Freeway (Calif. 91).

Medieval Times

Great fun at 7662 Beach Blvd., right near the Movieland Wax Museum in Buena Park (tel. 714/521-4740, or toll free 800/826-5358, 800/438-9911 in California). If you haven't already collapsed from the excitement of the rides, the walking, and the gawking, Medieval Times offers entertainment straight out of the 11th century (or thereabouts) in a castle setting. Here you can applaud tournaments, sword fights, jousts, and feats of skill performed by colorfully costumed knights on horseback—all this while being served dinner by serfs and costumed wenches.

Shows are Monday through Thursday at 7:30pm, on Friday and Saturday at 4, 6:30, and 9:15pm, and on Sunday at 1, 4:45, and 7:30pm. The price for adults is $27 to $32; for children 12 and under, it's $19 to $21. Medieval Times is an extremely popular year-round attraction so I suggest that if you plan to attend and cheer on your favorite knight, you make reservations at least two months in advance. A good time will be had by all.

WHERE TO STAY

If you're thinking of staying in Buena Park, you'll find that the **Farm de Ville,** 7800 and 7878 Crescent Ave. (at Calif. 39), Buena Park, CA 90620 (tel. 714/527-2201), has a lot to offer. It's located at the south entrance to Knott's Berry Farm, it's convenient to all nearby attractions, and buses to Disneyland (10 minutes away) stop right at the door. The 130 rooms are spacious, immaculate, and stylishly furnished; each has a color TV, radio, air conditioning, direct-dial phone, tub/shower bath, dressing area, and individually controlled heat and air conditioning. Facilities include two swimming pools with slides and diving boards, two wading pools for the little folk, two saunas, and a coin-op laundry; a Baker's Square restaurant, open from 6:30am to midnight, is on the premises.

Summer rates are $42 for a single, $44 to $52 for a double, with a charge of $4 for each additional person. Family units, accommodating four to six people, cost $80. The rest of the year, rates are about $2 less.

3. Irvine

Wild Rivers Waterpark is Orange County's newest family theme park, and its only waterpark. Located in Irvine off the San Diego Freeway (I-405) at 8770 Irvine Center Dr. (tel. 714/768-9453), Wild Rivers is a 20-minute drive from Disneyland.

Wild Rivers has more than 40 exciting rides and attractions in a tropical setting on 20 acres. Wild Rivers Mountain is over five stories high and has 19 thrilling rides. You can innertube down the side of the mountain, shoot through an underground tunnel, or slide down the length of a football field.

Thunder Cove features the only two side-by-side wave-action pools in the country, allowing for gentle body surfing or powerful bodyboarding—take your pick.

Explorers' Island is the perfect place for families with small children. It's there you'll find activity pools and scaled-down rides for little people.

Changing facilities and rental lockers are available, and there are food locations throughout the park. A picnic area is located just outside the main entrance for guests with personal food items.

Admission is $17 for those 10 and older, $13 for those 3 to 9 years; children under age 3 are admitted free. Seniors (55 and older) are $9, as is a spectator pass (which includes only dry activities). All adults and children admitted after 4pm pay $9. Parking is $4 per vehicle.

Wild Rivers' 1990 season runs from mid-May through the beginning of October. The waterpark is open weekends mid-May to June from 11am to 5pm, then daily to mid-June, when hours are extended to 10am to 5pm. The longer hours continue through Labor Day, when days open revert to weekends from 11am to 5pm.

PALM SPRINGS

Golf, tennis, and swimming pool capital of the world, Palm Springs has been the playground supreme of the rich—home to the Gabor sisters, Kirk Douglas, and Dean Martin, among many others. The honorary mayor, by the way, is Bob Hope, whereas the elected one is now Sonny Bono (formerly of Sonny and Cher).

The sun shines 350 days a year in Palm Springs (well, almost). Any number of golf tournaments are held in the area annually, including the Bob Hope Desert Classic and the Nabisco Dinah Shore Invitational. There are more than 300 tennis courts in the area, 42 golf courses (but only seven 18-hole courses are public, with average greens fees of $45), and as for those swimming pools, they number over 7,000—one for every five residents!

1. Getting There

Getting to Palm Springs is easy. It's 104 miles southeast of Los Angeles, about a two-hour drive via the San Bernadino Freeway (Interstate 10). You'll recognize it by the 1,336 windmills (a bit tall for Don Quixote, but enough to keep him busy). By plane (Delta, USAir, Continental, United, and American Airlines, among others) the trip takes 36 minutes from Los Angeles.

2. Getting Around

Once you're in Palm Springs, it's easy to get around via minibuses (tel. 619/343-3451). Typical of the luxurious life-style here, they're carpeted, air-con-

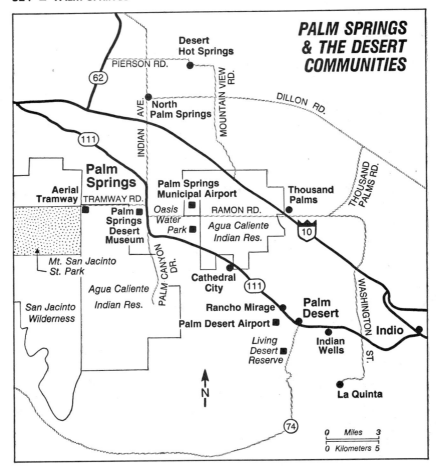

PALM SPRINGS & THE DESERT COMMUNITIES

ditioned, and equipped with stereophonic music. It's 50¢ to board and another 25¢ for each town you enter. The buses run from 6am to 9pm.

3. Hotels

Some of the most charming rooms in town are at **Ingleside Inn,** a hideaway estate at 200 W. Ramon Rd. (at Belardo), Palm Springs, CA 92262 (tel. 619/325-0046). Each of the 29 rooms and villas is uniquely decorated with antiques—perhaps a commode used by Mary Tudor, a canopied bed, or a 15th-century vestment chest will grace your room. Many rooms have wood-burning fireplaces; all have in-room whirlpools and steambaths, refrigerators stocked with complimentary light snacks and beverages, and whatever other luxuries you might crave, including a complimentary Continental breakfast. Once you pass the imposing wrought-iron gates (with the exception of my Toyota, most of the traffic passing through them are Rolls-Royces, Mercedeses, and the like), you leave the bustling world of the 20th century behind and enter an old-world era of luxurious relaxation and fine, remarkably friendly service. Facilities include croquet, shuffleboard, and a large swimming pool and Jacuzzi; golf, tennis, and horseback riding can be arranged.

Melvyn's, one of Palm Springs's most prestigious "in" spots, is on the premises. It was here that Frank and Barbara Sinatra hosted an "intimate" dinner for 66 close friends on the eve of their wedding. The food is excellent, the celebrity-watching first-rate, and the decor lovely—an 1895 carved oak-and-mahogany bar with beveled mirrors, lots of potted ferns, wicker and tapestry-upholstered furnishings, and white lace curtains. If you don't stay at the Ingleside Inn, at least come by for a meal at Melvyn's. At dinner you might begin with the goose liver pâté (with truffle) or the deep-fried brie with jalapeño jelly, and follow with an entree of veal chop grilled and accented with madeira wine, green peppercorns, and a wild French mushroom sauce. Your entree, ranging from $18 to $27, is served with soup or salad. The wine list is distinguished. The dessert selection changes daily but the chocolate-mousse pie, when available, is excellent. If that meal sounds a bit disastrous for your budget, come at lunch, when you can have a French dip sandwich, au jus with french fries, breast of chicken on sourdough bread, or one of the other hot entrees or cold plates, for $8 to $15. It's also popular for the Saturday and Sunday champagne brunch ($14 to $19), when you can choose from a variety of entrees, including eggs Florentine and their very popular prime-rib hash with poached eggs and mushroom sauce. All dishes are served with fresh fruit and unlimited Melvyn's champagne.

If you do decide to stay here, you'll join the ranks of Elizabeth Taylor, Howard Hughes, Mervyn Leroy, Ava Gardner, John Wayne, Bette Davis, Clare Booth Luce, Salvador Dali, Andre Kostelanetz, Gary Cooper, John Travolta, and Penny Marshall, all of whom have enjoyed the luxurious facilities at one time or another.

Singles or doubles and suites from October 1 to June 1 range from **$85 to $500**; rates are reduced in summer.

The **Palm Springs Hilton,** 400 E. Tahquitz Way (just two blocks west of Palm Canyon Drive), Palm Springs, CA 92262 (tel. 619/320-6868), one of Palm Springs's most glittering resorts, has an atmosphere more like that of a country club than a hotel. The three-story building blends into the natural environment and reflects the sand colors of the desert. The lobby, rooms, and restaurants are filled with original works of art, mostly contemporary serigraphs by David Weidman and sculptures by local artists.

The 263 rooms—built around a central garden and swimming pool and done in soft earth tones—are large and residential in feel, with sitting areas and large wooden shutters on the windows. All rooms have patios or balconies, large baths with thermostatically regulated showers and brass fixtures, color TVs, direct-dial phones, and individual temperature controls.

Recreational facilities, in addition to a swimming pool that is among the largest in the area, include two Jacuzzis, six tennis courts with a pro shop, exercise room, and children's game room. Golf can be arranged at nearby courses, and many resort shops are within easy walking distance.

The gourmet restaurant, the Tapestry, is located off the lobby and features Continental cuisine Tuesday through Saturday from 6 to 10:30pm. The Tapestry closes during the summer (June 1 to October 1). It is small and intimate, with Venetian crystal chandeliers and burl tables. The Terrace, also off the lobby, overlooks the swimming pool/garden area and is open daily for breakfast, lunch, and dinner. It offers coffee-shop fare, including low-fat, low-cholesterol dishes. There's also a poolside dining facility for snacks, and Harvey's, a piano bar/lounge.

Rates in season (December to May) are $115 to $195, single or double, depending on location; suites range from $205 to $685; rates are lower the rest of the year. Children under 17 stay free in a room with their parents.

There's an elegant, old-world charm about the **Villa Royale,** 1620 Indian Trail,

Palm Springs, CA 92262 (tel. 619/327-2314), true international beauty with the atmosphere of a European-style country inn, is one of those rare facilities where everything gets better with each passing year. This 3½-acre bed-and-breakfast resort is made up of a series of interior courtyards replete with statuesque pillars and antiques, shade trees and bougainvillea; in a fountain courtyard you can quietly listen to classical music. An attractive outdoor living room with a fireplace (really) and comfortable Italian wicker chairs affords luxurious relaxation to the pleasant sounds of a water garden.

Each of the 31 units reflects the character, colors, texture, and beauty of a particular country—Portugal, France, Italy, and England are just a few examples. The owners spent six years buying in Europe and sending their treasures back to Palm Springs; you'll find them in every room—carvings, sculptures, woven hangings, even custom-designed quilts and ruffled pillows. But there are some strictly American features as well: Several rooms have their own Jacuzzis on private patios, all rooms have color TVs and private phones, and room service is available for all meals. Two large swimming pools offer a modern complement to the more rustic pleasures of the Villa Royale.

Other pleasant touches: The *Los Angeles Times* is delivered to your door each morning; bicycles are available for your use at no charge; golf and tennis reservations can be made at nearby courts and courses. If you wish to have outside guests for dinner at the Villa Royale, this can be arranged in advance; however, outside guests cannot use other facilities, such as the pools.

As you might guess, dining facilities are attractive. There is a poolside breakfast room as well as a full-service dining room (the Europa room) for lunches and dinners. To enhance your dining enjoyment, the Villa Royale has put together—and is still accumulating—a collection of fine California and European wines and champagnes. Imported and domestic beers are also served. You can arrange (in advance) for a romantic, candlelit private dinner in your room or in the water-garden gazebo. Upon request, the kitchen will also pack a picnic lunch for you (with knapsack) to take on your excursions. A complimentary Continental breakfast is served daily at the Europa. The dining room is now open to the public. Luncheon or dinner ranges from $10 to $22, and the menu changes daily.

Standard guest rooms, single or double occupancy, are $49 to $65; with a Jacuzzi, $115 to $150. One-bedroom suites are $99 to $135. One-bedroom villas cost $125 to $150; with a Jacuzzi, $189 to $225. Two-bedroom villas (for up to four people) run $150 to $175. Two large private villas, each with its own pool (20 by 36 feet), patio, and enclosed yard, are $225 to $325. Both offer great privacy (no outside visibility). Extra-person occupancy is $25 per person. The lower prices are summer rates.

One of the more unique choices in Palm Springs is the **Spa Hotel & Mineral Springs,** 100 N. Indian Ave. (at Tahquitz Way), Palm Springs, CA 92262 (tel. 619/325-1461, or toll free 800/854-1279, 800/472-4371 in California). It is the only full-service "spa" resort in Palm Springs. Formerly the site was a shrine for the Cahuilla Indians, who claimed the springs had magical powers to cure illness. Today vacationers come here to "take the waters" and otherwise pamper body and soul. There are three pools on the premises, one of which is a conventional outdoor swimming pool with sun deck; the other two are filled from underground natural springs brimming with revitalizing minerals. In addition to the outdoor pools, there are 30 indoor sunken Roman swirlpools, also fed from the springs. And that's not all. There's also massage, complete gymnasium facilities, a eucalyptus vapor-inhalation room, and a rock steam room, where natural mineral waters are turned to three beneficial heat levels of steam. Guests can further enhance their healthy new appearances with facials, manicures, pedicures, and other beauty treatments. Facilities also include three night-lit tennis courts; golf is available to guests at a nearby country club.

The rooms are luxurious and elegantly appointed; all have refrigerators, direct-dial phones, color TVs, and baths with Travertine marble sinks. And the Continental cuisine served in Rennicks' Dining Room is excellent—along with their nutritious spa menu.

Rates for single or double rooms from mid-September to mid-December and May to June are $105 to $190, $20 for an additional person. From mid-December to late April, they are $145 to $215. During the summer, rates are much lower ($55 to $100).

Casa Cody Hotel, 175 S. Cahuilla Rd. (a half block south of Tahquitz Way), Palm Springs, CA 92262 (tel. 619/320-9346), is a newly restored and very attractive inn peacefully nestled in the heart of Palm Springs at the base of the mountain. Originally built by Harriet Cody, a relative of Wild Bill Cody, and once owned by Polly Bergen, the hotel now has 17 lovely, spacious ground-level accommodations, most with wood-burning fireplaces and private patios. There are elegant touches such as saltillo tile floors, dhurri rugs, and original art work displayed against a lovely background of gentle desert colors; furnishings are in a comfortable Santa Fe style. Ranging in size from studios to two-bedroom, two-bath suites, all accommodations have fully equipped kitchens (except for the "room" category, where there are small refrigerators), plus such expected touches as cable TVs and private phones.

And to add to life's joys, there are two swimming pools—one at the center of each of the two segments of the inn (you have your choice)—plus a tree-shaded whirlpool spa to relax when enjoyment overwhelms. There are complimentary poolside breakfasts and a Saturday-night wine-and-cheese party. Arrangements can be made for nearby tennis, golf, and access to a private health spa. Bicycles are available (complimentary) for leisurely exploration of surrounding elegant neighborhoods. And for those with an insurmountable supply of energy, the Carl Lyken desert trail up the mountain begins nearby. Indian canyons have been reopened and add to any hiking adventure.

The staff at Casa Cody is a remarkably helpful source of local information— places to go, what to do, etc. (The inn is close to the Desert Museum, the new Desert Fashion Plaza, and the total array of Palm Canyon Drive shops, restaurants, and galleries.) If you communicate more easily in French or Dutch, each is spoken by staff members.

Season rates range from $60 to $160; with rooms beginning at $60, studios at $75, one-bedroom accommodations at $105, and two-bedroom accommodations (for one to four persons) at $150. The charge for an extra person is $10. Rates are modestly higher during the winter (mid-December through April) and considerably lower from July through September. Should you require transportation from the airport, Casa Cody provides pickup.

In the style and tradition of a French Mediterranean auberge, **Le Petit Château,** 1491 Via Soledad, at Palmera, Palm Springs, CA 92264 (tel. 619/325-2686), is, as far as I know, the only clothes-optional B&B inn in the country. Le Petit Château is located in a very quiet, residential part of Palm Springs, about a mile from the downtown center. It's a charming separate environment, a "cocoon," as its owners Don and Mary Robidoux describe it, surrounded by bougainvillea-covered walls and hedges. Access is for guests only, so privacy and security are assured. The very pleasant aura of Le Petit Château is derived partly from the peace and solitude it affords; partly from the charm of its owners; partly from the tasteful French country style of each of the comfortable rooms, most with delightful brick patios; and partly from the option to enjoy the sun the way nature intended—"au naturel" poolside (or with clothing if you prefer). To enhance your tan, Le Petit Château also has a unique Mist Tanning System to keep you cool and your skin moist and soft. Don't worry about your age or your shape; guests range from their early 20s to late 60s, and most are world travelers with a love for an all-over tan.

Don and Mary Robidoux run Le Petit Château lovingly and casually. Breakfasts are an inviting combination of goodies to suit almost any appetite; Mary prepares a complete European-style repast with eggs, sausages, ham, muffins, sweet rolls, fresh-ground coffee, fresh fruit, and on and on. In the late afternoon, there's a buffet table with wines and a variety of fruits and cheeses.

There are only 10 rooms, so don't expect to call at the last minute and find accommodations (besides, the front gate is locked). But it's this very petite size that generates the comfortable social atmosphere. You can choose to be alone, but the great warmth and friendliness tend to draw one into the group. All rooms have TV, and there are three phones for common use by guests.

Rates are $110 for larger rooms (with kitchens) on Friday and Saturday, $92 Sunday through Thursday. For the smaller rooms (without kitchens), the cost is $103 on Friday and Saturday, $85 Sunday through Thursday. Prices are the same year-round. All rates are double occupancy, with European breakfast and afternoon wine and hors d'oeuvres included. Remember, prior reservations are necessary.

Among the more reasonable establishments in Palm Springs is the **Estrella Inn,** 415 S. Belardo, Palm Springs, CA 92262 (tel. 619/340-4117), located just a block from the center of town, but on a quiet, secluded street that seems to be miles from everywhere. The rooms here vary widely in size—from very small quarters to suites with lanai decks, wet bars, full kitchens, and fireplaces, to multiroom cottages. All rooms have air conditioning, direct-dial phones, and cable color TVs.

On the premises are two adult swimming pools, one children's pool, two spa pools, two Jacuzzis, and a lawn and court games area. There's no restaurant, but the inn serves a complimentary Continental breakfast every morning in the lobby lounge.

Rates at the Estrella Inn are $85 for a very small room, $125 for a room with two queen-size beds, and $195 for a two-bedroom cottage. Off-season rates are about 30% lower; weekly and monthly rates are also available off-season, monthly rates in-season. All prices are for single or double occupancy.

One of the best reasonably priced buys in Palm Springs is **El Rancho Lodge,** 1330 E. Palm Canyon Dr., Palm Springs, CA 92264 (tel. 619/327-1339). It has only 19 accommodations, which probably accounts for the congenial community feeling, plus the fact that most of the guests seem to be of the relaxed, over-50 generation. The accommodations are pleasantly furnished, roomy, and nicely maintained (quite possibly because the manager is also the owner). All are situated around a large heated pool and spa.

Those termed "hotel rooms" have one king-size bed or two twin beds, with the added luxury of small refrigerators and remote-control color TVs. Studios and two-room suites have the same sleeping arrangements and TVs as the above, but also have full kitchens; some of the two-room suites also provide two king-size beds. One of the special delights of these suites is that there are two full baths—a luxury rarely found even in pricey hotels.

A Continental breakfast, served poolside each morning, is included in the rates, which vary seasonally. Summer rates (June 1 through September 30) range from $40 for "hotel rooms" to $85 for two-room suites. Winter rates (October 1 through May 31) are $56 to $121. Monthly discount rates are available.

The **Westward Ho Hotel,** 701 E. Palm Canyon Dr., Palm Springs, CA 92264 (tel. 619/320-2700, or toll free 800/854-4345, 800/472-4313 in California), is pleasant, comfortable, and moderately priced. The motel (as I've already mentioned, they're all "hotels" in Palm Springs) has 208 rooms, all with a modified western look. Most have attractive Indian-print spreads, hanging cylinder lamps, upholstered chairs with casters (a distinct blessing), dark-wood bedsteads and furnishings, and warm brown carpeting. All the rooms have both tubs and showers. Those with two beds have separate sink facilities set apart from the bathrooms. There is a separate hanging closet space. Each room has individually controlled air conditioning, satellite color TV, and direct-dial phone. A heated "therapy" pool for guests is at the center of the complex, surrounded by comfortable lounges, and there is a small wading pool for children.

One of the conveniences of the motel is that it adjoins a Denny's Restaurant, open 24 hours. The food is consistently good and the prices are modest.

Rates at the Westward Ho Hotel are $60 to $75 from October through the third week of December, and $70 to $86 for the balance of the year. During holiday periods and special events there is a two-night minimum, and rates are slightly higher than above.

And forever there will be a Motel 6. In Palm Springs, however, it's **Hotel 6,** at

595 E. Palm Canyon Dr., Palm Springs, CA 92262 (tel. 619/325-6129). Advance planning is the key if you hope to stay here during the season—reservations should be made 12 months in advance. Singles are $29, plus $6 for each additional adult. It's clean, efficient, and convenient, and has a pool. All local calls are free, as is the TV. Need more be said?

In 1989 a new **Hotel 6** opened at 666 S. Palm Canyon Dr. (tel. 619/327-4200). There are 149 units and a pool. As with the Hotel 6 on East Palm Canyon Drive, all rooms have cable color TVs, are comfortably furnished, have individually controlled air conditioning, and are close to downtown Palm Springs as well as the golf courses and resort attractions. Singles are $32, plus $6 for each additional adult; no charge for color TV or local calls. To stay here, the key is to plan well in advance.

If Hotel 6 in Palm Springs can't accommodate you, try **Motel 6** at 78100 Varner Rd., Bermuda Dunes, CA 92201 (tel. 619/345-0550). It's about 15 driving minutes east of Palm Springs and has a smaller pool, but is just as clean and efficient, and costs a bit less per night. Singles are $26, plus $6 for each additional adult; no charge for color TV or local calls.

RANCHO MIRAGE

This rapidly developing southward expansion of Palm Springs is just 12 miles south via Calif. 111. It already has a restaurant row and many famous residents, among them Gerald and Betty Ford. It also contains one of the area's most luxurious accommodations, the Mobil four-star **Marriott's Rancho Las Palmas Resort,** 41000 Bob Hope Dr. (off Calif. 111), Rancho Mirage, CA 92270 (tel. 619/568-2727, or toll free 800/458-8786), set on 26½ beautifully tended garden acres. Opened in February 1979, the Marriott has 450 spacious rooms housed in two-story terra-cotta–roofed stucco buildings. Decorated in bright resort colors, the rooms are equipped with every luxury—oversize beds, color TVs with in-room movies, etc. As for the hotel's facilities, they include three restaurants decorated in Early California hacienda motif, plus a lounge and disco; two large outdoor swimming pools and Jacuzzis; the requisite shops; and hospitality, tour, and car-rental desks. Guests become automatic members of the Rancho Las Palmas Country Club down the road; it has 25 tennis courts (including 3 of red clay), a 27-hole championship golf course, pro shops for both sports, a driving range and putting green, a swimming pool, and a restaurant and snack bar. And anything not on the premises —from ballooning to horseback riding—can probably be arranged.

Rates for single or double occupancy are $260 to $280 from January through early May, $195 to $215 from May through early June, $110 to $130 from early June through the beginning of September, and $175 to $190 through late December. Extra adults pay $10 year-round; there's no charge for children under 18 occupying the same room as their parents. Be sure to ask about any special packages that might be available.

A more economical choice in Rancho Mirage is the **Allstar Inn,** 69-570 Calif. 111 (between Date Palm Drive and Frank Sinatra Drive), Rancho Mirage, CA 92270 (tel. 619/324-8475). As with all the Allstar Inns, the guest rooms are nicely furnished and spotlessly clean, plus they have full tubs and showers and free color TVs. At Rancho Mirage, there is a small pool and Jacuzzi. Singles are $33; doubles, $36. Summer rates are $6 lower. Reservations for the winter season (October through May) should be made well in advance.

---

4. Restaurants

There are many attractive restaurants in Palm Springs and more in the offing, but now and then the food doesn't quite measure up to the look. Some of the best restaurants in town are at the hotels already mentioned—**Melvyn's** at Ingleside Inn, **Rennicks'** at the Spa Hotel, etc. There are, however, other choices.

When you're in the mood for a truly fresh seafood dinner, the place to go is **Sorrentino's**, 1032 N. Palm Canyon Dr. (tel. 619/325-2944), undoubtedly the best seafood restaurant in town. As you may have guessed by the name, its origins are Italian-American, a fact reflected in the decor: green banquettes against red walls decked with oil paintings and wrought-iron–encased fixtures.

Virtually all the fish is fresh, and when it's "fresh frozen"—more often than not the case in Palm Springs—Sorrentino's tells you so. Some of the great choices on the extensive menu include a hearty seafood-and-chicken gumbo with andouille sausage and steamed rice, sautéed sand dabs (a particular favorite of mine), king crab legs, abalone steak, and of course, cioppino. While Sorrentino's is primarily a seafood house, the quality of the meat here is excellent. Some of the fine meat dishes include veal osso buco genovese, filet mignon, and a tender, moist roast rack of lamb. Sorrentino's also has a children's dinner (under 12) for $8.50 to $12.50, which offers a choice of four entrees. Entrees and specials for grownups range from $13 to $27. Sorrentino's has desserts one might expect to find in an Italian seafood restaurant—with one notable and surprising exception, English trifle.

Whether you're a party of one or eight, service is very attentive without being overbearing. The wine list, both domestic and imported, is limited but good. Sorrentino's has a huge bar adjacent to the main dining room, so if you have to wait for a few minutes, you'll be comfortable.

Open nightly from 5:30 to 10:30pm. Reservations are necessary.

Cedar Creek Inn, 1555 S. Palm Canyon Dr. (tel. 619/325-7300), is one of the most popular dining establishments in Palm Springs and with good reason. What more can you ask of a restaurant than fine food, comfortable and attractive surroundings, excellent service, and reasonable prices? The number of local residents who frequent the place is appropriate testimony to its quality.

Cedar Creek Inn has the tone of casual desert elegance, with its high ceilings, slate floors, ficus trees decorated with thousands of tiny lights, potted plants, floral wall patterns, and beamed ceilings. The entry area makes an attractive foyer for greeting guests. Above is an enormous decorative metal chandelier of leaves and flowers, and the reservations desk is graced with a lovely sculpted swan faced in gold. The bar area to the right of the entry has the look of a handsome pub with its unstructured seating arrangement and stone walls; it features live music Tuesday through Thursday from 7 to 11pm, on Friday and Saturday from 8pm to midnight.

Each of the dining rooms is decorated in a different spring tone—and decorative plates and plants add further color; overhead fans create quiet movement of the greenery. Polished wood booths along one wall are semi-enclosed—and the perfect choice for those who want an element of intimacy.

As testament to the quality of the food, the fish is usually fresh. (When it's "fresh frozen," the waitperson will advise you.) A special fresh chicken entree is offered each evening; the slowly roasted prime rib, served with horseradish sauce, is excellent; or consider the extraordinary Veal Swiss, seasoned with bread crumbs, sautéed, and topped with avocado, tomato, Swiss cheese and béarnaise sauce. Dinner entrees range from $15 for the special chicken entree to $18 for the New York steak or for the delicious scampi sautéed in lemon butter with lots of garlic, capers, bread crumbs, and parmesan. Dinners include a hearty house soup or the Cedar Creek's Greek salad, plus vegetables and homemade batter bread or garlic toast. Then there's a choice of baked potato, creamed corn, or rice pilaf.

For those of you not quite in the mood for dinner, Cedar Creek serves sandwiches all day, and what sandwiches! Consider the thinly sliced rare cold roast beef served open-faced on pumpernickel with brie cheese, butter lettuce, tomato, and Bermuda onion, with Dijon horseradish sauce on the side. All sandwiches are served with warm applesauce. If you'd rather opt for a salad, there's an exceptional Cobb salad or a Greek salad, but why not go for it with the inn's *spicy* chicken tostada salad? Sandwiches will cost $5.25 to $8.50; salads, $4.50 to $8. And for a happy end to it all (if you still have room), ask to see the dessert list with its dozen or so entries, all made fresh daily on the premises.

The Cedar Creek Inn is open daily for lunch and dinner from 11am to 9pm.

Dinner specialties are served from 4:30pm on. As I've indicated, there is a full bar. The wine list is not lengthy, but quite satisfactory.

The Otani, 266 Avenida Caballeros, at Tahquitz Way (tel. 619/327-6700), refers to itself as "a garden restaurant," and indeed this is the feeling you have when you enter. The decor is as lovely as Japanese architecture can be when blended with the best in contemporary design. There is an open airy atmosphere, with bamboo trees rising to what must certainly be a 50-foot ceiling. Rich dark woods, slate floors, marble counters, stylized fish sculptures, muted grass-green carpeting all mingle beautifully to create an aura of comfort. At the perimeter of the restaurant is a modest garden with a soft-spoken waterfall and brook.

There are four areas of preparation and dining, each with its own chef: teppanyaki, for grilled dishes; tempura, for delicately battered, deep-fried seafood and vegetables; yakitori, for grilled meats on skewers; and sushi/sashimi for seafood in its various modes. You can dine at a marble bar in any one of the four areas and watch the preparation and artful design of the food, or take the Occidental approach and be served at a table in the main dining area. Wherever you choose to sit, Otani offers selections from an à la carte or a set menu.

As you scan the menu, you will learn that sushi dates back to the theaters and "pleasure houses" of the Edo Period, when such bite-sized food was convenient; tempura was introduced to Japan by Portugese monks in the 16th century; and yakitori originated with the Dutch, who introduced falconry to the Japanese nobility (the falcon's catch was quickly grilled over charcoal in the field).

As you might expect, the meal is preceded by the presentation of a steamy hot towel. Next is the miso soup and a tiny taste of the chef's skill. Food at the bar is served on blue-and-white ware resting on deep-red laquered trays. Even the chopsticks are elegantly shaped, with bright little squares at one end.

The tempura set menu may include an assortment of shrimp, white fish, and seasonal vegetables; or you may choose 10 kinds of seasonal vegetables ($12 to $25). The à la carte selections range from delicious tempura garlic (that's what I said, *garlic*) to over 20 other choices, including Japanese eggplant, several varieties of mushrooms, oysters, lobster tail, etc. ($1.50 to $9).

As for yakitori, a special 12-skewer course ($23) features 10 different items and includes a particular favorite of mine—the bacon-wrapped quail egg. Those with a lesser appetite might consider the 8-skewer assortment, which includes an excellent asparagus-beef roll, among others.

If you're inclined to believe that sushi or sashimi should be the premier dish at a Japanese restaurant, you won't be disappointed at Otani. Over 25 seafood and vegetable variations on sushi range from tuna and sea urchin to freshwater eel and including a number of rolls. For those who've always thought that sushi was synonymous with raw fish, Otani is the place to review a number of outstanding cooked possibilities—the superb Manhattan roll with cooked tuna and daikon sprouts lovingly enclosed in a nori wrapper, for example.

Should you be fraught with indecision, Otani also offers a sampler menu, including a dish from each of the above categories plus dessert ($16 to $25).

If you have room for dessert, there's a first-rate cheesecake with various fruit sauces (strange as it may seem), as well as an apple sundae, fresh fruit, or one of several ice creams. At the end of my luncheon, I was presented with a work of art in the form of a cone-shape peeled orange with a strawberry perched on top and a cucumber-slice floral leaf. The service, I found, was attentive and helpful.

Otani is open for lunch Monday through Friday from 11am to 2pm; for dinner Sunday through Thursday from 5 to 10pm, on Friday and Saturday to 10:30pm.

The exterior of **Alfredo's,** 292 E. Palm Canyon Dr., at Via Entrada (tel. 619/320-1020), has always attracted me. It's simple, uncluttered, and inviting, with a forthright "Alfredo's" sign in neon script. The restaurant is just as handsome inside—dusty-rose and cream walls, with complementary maroon-and-cream furnishings, scenic lithographs, smoked mirrors, and frosted-glass art deco lamps overhead.

Appetizer prices start at $3.50 for Mama's fava beans or a Sicilian-style artichoke and go on up to $9 for the antipasto Alfredo. In the middle, at $6.50, is a favorite of mine, mozzarella marinara—deep-fried cheese cooked with the chef's special sauce. Interesting salads range from the house's dandelion salad at $4.50 to a cold seafood-and-linguine combination for $13.

Entrees range from veal marsala or filet mignon "Alfredo style" to pizza. And the spicy chicken wings have to be the best this side of Buffalo, N.Y. (Alfredo's hometown). They come in hot, medium, or mild, and are served in true Buffalo style—with celery sticks and blue-cheese dip ($5 for 10 pieces, $12 for 30 pieces, $16.50 for a bucket of 50 wings). If you thought that spaghetti and meatballs was hardly an inspired choice for dinner, at Alfredo's the homemade meatballs will prove you wrong. Not to be ignored either is a magnificent veal Alfredo—veal cutlets and eggplant in light batter, sautéed, separated with prosciutto, topped with mozzarella, then baked and finished with Alfredo's special sauce. And when was the last time you had steak and dandelions? Seafood entrees, including calamari, are served with Alfredo's pasta and artichoke sauce. Pasta specialties come with salad or soup.

Dinner entrees are $15 to $21 and include salad or soup, pasta, chef's vegetable, and fresh Italian bread. All recipes are cooked to order. There's a good selection of wines to accompany your meal.

Alfredo's is open nightly from 5 to 11pm. A small parking lot is located right behind the restaurant, off Via Entrada.

Lyon's English Grill, 233 E. Palm Canyon Dr., at Via Entrada (tel. 619/327-1551), has an almost theatrical woody English-pub ambience composed of stained-glass windows, old pub signs and maps, Tudor beamed walls, and heraldic banners suspended from the ceilings—not to mention waitresses in serving-wench costume. Even the menus were made in England, originally for a restaurant in Hampton Court. The most traditional thing to order is a prime rib dinner. Less expensive entrees are—in descending price order—roast duckling with wild rice, baked sea bass, and roast chicken. All entrees are priced from $13 to $19, and are served with soup or salad, a baked potato, and hot popovers.

Open daily from 5 to 11pm.

For hearty home cooking, a great selection, huge portions, and small-town ambience, head for **Billy Reed's**, 1800 N. Palm Canyon Dr., near Vista Chino (tel. 619/325-1946). Billy Reed's entry has the characteristic Palm Springs hacienda look—small fountain, foliage, and cool patio—but the Spanish resemblance ends there. Wicker furniture graces the outer lobby, and the interior is American/Victorian, with lace curtains and Tiffany stained-glass lamp shades. Somehow it all works. And though the place is huge, the low ceilings, breakfronts, and overhead pot-and-mug collections afford a feeling of warmth.

You can start your day here with a breakfast (priced under $7) such as sausage and eggs served with hash browns, toast, and butter. At lunch you might order the shrimp Louis, served with garlic toast or cornbread, a delicious chicken pot pie, or a bowl of chili with cubed sirloin and beans (from $7 to $14). Dinner entrees (for $12 to $20) include soup or salad, a fresh vegetable, and a baked potato or rice pilaf. Among the options are jumbo prawns, top sirloin, fried chicken, prime rib, or broiled scallops and shrimp en brochette with bacon, mushroom caps, and onions. Everything is truly delicious and, as I said before, portions are very large. Furthermore, instead of rolls, warm miniature loaves of bread are served.

Billy Reed's takes reservations only for very large parties, so you may have to wait a bit for a table, but the estimated time for seating is remarkably accurate and the food is really worth a bit of patience. Drink strenghts are as generous as food portions. Wine choices are limited, but good.

The entire menu is served all day, every day (except major holidays), from 7am to 11pm.

For good Italian fare, another place to go is **Perrina's,** 340 N. Palm Canyon Dr., between Amado and Alejo Roads (tel. 619/325-6544). Small, warm, and unpretentious, it's the hangout of the sports crowd, as well as the now-and-then choice of various celebrities, including a television game-show host, TV and film actors, and a well-endowed woman popular as a country singer. Larry Perrina's wife and daughter carry on the service. Larry used to play baseball in the minor leagues with Joe DiMaggio, and one wall of the restaurant is lined with photos of sports figures who were friends of his. The specialty is veal—piccata, scaloppine, marsala, etc.—served with soup or salad and fresh vegetables. But there's lots of pasta on the menu too: fettuccine Alfredo, manicotti, and linguine with garlic, olive oil, and anchovies. Meat dishes average $13 to $18; pasta runs $10 to $13, with baked mostaccioli ($13) a favorite with the "long-time" customers. A side order of pasta with a regular entree is $3. All dishes are prepared to order.

Perrina's serves dinner from 5 to 11pm Tuesday through Sunday; there's a piano bar from 7pm to 2am.

One of the really enjoyable eating experiences in Palm Springs is **Nate's Delicatessen and Restaurant** (also known as Mister Corned Beef of Palm Springs), 100 S. Indian Ave., at the corner of Tahquitz Way (tel. 619/325-3506). Unlike its New York, Los Angeles, or San Francisco deli counterparts, Nate's looks like a well-bred restaurant, but not to worry—it has all the great aromas of a super deli. Seating arrangements are very comfortable, and the modern, subdued decor is easy on the eyes. For entertainment, study the cartoons of character types on the walls—the maven, shiksa, feinshmacher; you're certain to find a few you know. The dining room is quiet even when crowded, and service is efficient, knowledgeable, and pleasant.

If you're a deli-lover, you'll want to eat your way through the entire menu. For breakfast, there are omelets in every conceivable combination—with salami, pastrami, corned beef, chopped liver, etc.—and then there are eggs with onions, with lox, with whitefish, even with grilled knackwurst. If you insist, there's always ham or bacon or sausage with eggs (no, this is not a kosher deli), french toast, or pancakes.

For lunch, there are sandwiches piled high with meats of your choice and served on Nate's hot rye bread (or whatever bread or roll you prefer) and a relish tray of kosher pickles and old-world sauerkraut. Corned beef, pastrami, chopped liver, tongue, salami, pepper beef, on down the list, are served in various combinations. You want a salad? They have eight varieties. You have a taste for blintzes, a cold gefilte fish plate, potato pancakes, a knish? Nate's has those too.

Save room for dinner. Nate's has a nine-course meal for $11, including the aforementioned relish tray and sauerkraut; an appetizer of juice or homemade chopped liver; soup or salad; entrees ranging from baked or fried chicken to corned beef, brisket, or seafood catch of the day; a vegetable; potato; hot rye bread; dessert; and coffee. Nate's also serves a daily dinner special for $8 from 4 to 8:30pm.

Breakfast prices range from $3.50 to about $9.50, though some of the more baroque special combinations—say, a plate of lox *and* whitefish *and* cod *plus* two eggs with bagel and cream cheese—will raise the rate to $17.50. Luncheon sandwiches are in the range of $6 to $9; salads cost about $9. Dinner is a bargain at $7 to $12. Beer and wine are available.

Nate's is open daily from 7:30am to 8:30pm.

The **Hamburger Hamlet** bar-grille, at 105 N. Palm Canyon Dr. (tel. 619/325-2321), is virtually the only place of its kind at the center of town, and its popularity rests on the exceptional quality and unique variety of its food as well as the singularly large portions of its drinks, nonalcoholic and alcoholic. Add to that the look of the interior: It's a bit like a well-groomed pub—comfortable, lots of wood, and with a working rotisserie in the center of the activity. During pleasant weather you can dine at the tables on the patio. And finally there is good service.

Hamburger Hamlet has an excellent variety of tasty choices for brunch, lunch, or dinner. There is a good selection of little dishes (grazings), soups including a lobster bisque for which they are famous, salads, spa salads (low-cal), big appetizers great for sharing, about 20 hamburgers (they do live up to their name) including one served in a pita pocket. There are lots of other sandwiches, but I particularly enjoy the Stella Special—a "halfer" sandwich with several options, plus soup and a green salad. Excellent chili dishes include a "prison chili" dinner with everything on it—sour cream, shredded lettuce, chopped red onion, and cheddar cheese, served with garlic toast. There are eggs and omelets galore, from huevos rancheros to a "hangover omelet" with jalapeño peppers. Several inspired vegetarian dishes include a casserole of double mushrooms with fresh leaf spinach covered with Jack and Muenster cheese. And the rotisserie provides chicken that's a specialty of the house. Lunch, brunch, or whatever will cost about $5 to $8. Dinner specialties are $9 to $11.

Last of all (or perhaps first, depending on the time of day), Hamburger Hamlet has a full bar that serves a frosted margarita, a red-eye special of part tomato juice and part Michelob beer, and an amaretto freeze with ice cream. All the establishment's drinks are quite generous in size. Premium varietal wines and champagne can be had by the bottle or the glass. Bass ale or Michelob is on tap and served by the mug or by the schooner (a two-hands container).

Hamburger Hamlet is open daily: Monday through Thursday from 11am to 9pm, on Friday to 10pm, on Saturday from 9am to 10pm, and on Sunday to 9pm.

Another pleasant restaurant in town is **Las Casuelas Terraza**, 222 S. Palm Canyon Dr. (tel. 619/325-2794). It's a charming Mexican place with white walls, archways, plants, and birds—some papier-mâché parrots and two real macaws. The waitresses wear Mexican peasant dresses, and a band plays in the bar. There are a number of separate dining areas, including two patios that look out on the action of Palm Canyon Drive. One has a gently splashing fountain.

The food is as pleasant as the ambience. You can nibble on guacamole or nachos and sip a margarita while you decide on your meal. There are lots of entrees to choose from, including a chimichanga; chicken with avocado, melted cheese, and ranchero sauce; whitefish filet with butter and toasted almonds; and a wide variety of combination platters served with rice and beans. They range in price from $13 to $20. Lunch is less expensive at $9 to $12. To finish off your meal there's an empañada apple pie, flan, and a variety of liqueur-laced coffees to choose from.

Las Casuelas Terraza's hours are 11am to 10pm daily for dinner (to midnight on Friday and Saturday for drinks). Reservations are advised. There are two other Las Casuelas in the Palm Springs area: the original, at 368 N. Palm Canyon Dr. (tel. 619/325-3213), and the more formal Las Casuelas Nuevas, at 70050 Calif. 111 in Rancho Mirage (tel. 619/328-8844). The last is larger than either of the other locations, with a lovely 200-seat formal Spanish garden.

A fine alternative to the better-known Mexican eateries in Palm Springs is **El Mirasol**, at 140 E. Palm Canyon Dr. (tel. 619/323-0721). It's a family restaurant —simply decorated with dark-wood chairs and tables, a beautiful desert mural on one wall, and potted plants—and serves classic Mexican combinations of tacos, enchiladas, chiles rellenos, tostadas, and burritos, and for the benefit of brunchers, egg dishes including huevos rancheros or chorizo and eggs. But the excellence of the menu is in the many *especialidades de la casa,* whether you choose the pork chile verde cooked with green chiles and tomatillos, or opt for the perfectly seasoned shrimp rancheros, a special treat prepared with bell peppers, onions, olives, and tomatoes.

The Mexican combinations ($5.25 to $10.25) are all served with rice and beans. Specialties of the house ($8 to $11) are accompanied by corn chips and salsa, rice, beans, and corn or flour tortillas. Beer and wine are available, as are other beverages.

El Mirasol is open Monday through Saturday for lunch from 11am to 3pm, for dinner from 5 to 9pm.

A real fixture on the Palm Springs eating scene is **Louise's Pantry,** 124 S. Palm Canyon Dr. (tel. 619/325-5124). It's a small place—just 47 seats—but it packs 'em in every day and night, and with good reason. It's hard to match Louise's quality and even harder to beat the price.

Home cooking is the order of the day. Louise's squeezes fresh orange juice daily, grinds its own beef, and bakes the sweet rolls, cornbread, pies, and cakes on the premises. There are three to six specials each evening, plus choices from a regular list of eight selections, like roast beef, grilled pork chops, New York steak, and deep-fried jumbo shrimp. Specials of the day may include lamb shanks, roast turkey, and pork tenderloin. And each of the above is served with a choice of soup or seafood cocktail, plus dinner salad, potato, fresh steamed vegetables, dessert, and beverage. Dinner selections cost $7.75 to $10.

Daily regulars on the lunch special list ($6 to $7) include baby beef liver, petrale sole, deep-fried shrimp, and roast beef. The changing choices may include chicken or beef pot pie, stuffed bell peppers, and sirloin tips with buttered noodles. Luncheon specials are served with soup or salad, fresh steamed vegetables, and homemade cornbread. There are also hot sandwiches, cold sandwiches, cold plates, salads, light lunches—all in the $4.75 to $7 range.

Louise's Pantry also serves breakfast with all sorts of accompaniments. If you're so inclined, you can even create your own omelet from a lengthy mix-and-match list of goodies. And then there are sundaes, shakes, fresh juices, and a Palm Springs Special—a supernutritious milkshake made with crushed dates.

You can order to take out. If it's a large order, call at least one hour prior to pickup. And in case you were wondering, Louise's Pantry does not serve beer or wine.

Louise's Pantry is open daily from 7am to 9:45pm; it's closed every year from about mid-July to mid-August. There's another Louise's Pantry (with the same menu) in Palm Desert, at 44–491 Town Center Way.

---

5. Sights

As elsewhere, make a stop at the **Palm Springs Desert Resorts Convention and Visitors Bureau,** 730 Hwy. 111, Suite 201, Rancho Mirage, CA 92270 (tel. 619/327-8411). They can answer all your questions and provide you with informative brochures and maps. Open weekdays only, from 8:30am to 5pm.

If you don't want to traipse out to Palm Springs Desert Resorts Convention and Visitors Bureau for information, the people at the **Palm Springs Chamber of Commerce** can be very helpful. The chamber is near the heart of town at 190 W. Amado Rd., at the corner of Belardo (tel. 619/325-1577), and is open Monday through Friday from 8am to 5pm, on Saturday and Sunday from 10am to 2pm.

For a fascinating tour of the Palm Springs area, the place to start is with **Palm Springs Celebrity Tours,** 333 N. Palm Canyon Dr., Suite 204A (tel. 619/325-2682). Celebrity Tours has been around since 1963. They take pride in their professional guides, who know all the ins and outs of Palm Springs and who will take you around in comfort. Groups are small and service is personalized. Their deluxe coaches are air-conditioned, seat up to 14, and afford very easy riding.

The one-hour tour is an inside view of Palm Springs, including the homes of movie stars and celebrities. The two-hour tour includes everything you'd see during the one-hour version plus the estates of Frank Sinatra and the very wealthy and well-connected Walter Annenberg, who has his own golf course. You'll also see the Tamarisk, Canyon, and Thunderbird country clubs, where the international elite meet to play. Then on to the Eisenhower Medical Center and beautiful date groves, with a brief stop for refreshments.

The one-hour tour meets at the office at the above address. For the two-hour tour, Celebrity Tours will pick you up at any hotel in Palm Springs. Rates for the one-hour tour are $10 for adults, $9 for seniors, $5 for children to 11 years. The two-hour tour costs $14 for adults, $12 for seniors, $7 for children to 11 years.

It's a good idea to make reservations (required) at least a day or two ahead for either of the tours. They fill up quickly, especially during the "high season." Tours go daily. For departure times, check when you make your reservations.

To gain a bird's-eye perspective, take a ride on the **Palm Springs Aerial Tramway,** which travels a distance of 2½ miles up the slopes of Mount San Jacinto. It takes you from the desert floor to cool alpine heights in less than 20 minutes; in winter the change is dramatic, from warm desert to deep snowdrifts. At the end of the ride is a restaurant, cocktail lounge, gift shop, game room, and picnic area, and also the starting point of 54 miles of hiking trails dotted with campgrounds. The tramway is located at Tramway Drive–Chino Canyon, off Calif. 111 north. Parking is free. It's open daily from 10am weekdays and from 8am weekends. The last tram up is at 8pm May 1 to Labor Day, and the last comes down at 9:45pm; the rest of the year the last cars are one hour earlier. Round-trip fare for adults is $14, and children 3 through 11 pay $9. You can also get a ride-'n'-dine combination for a sunset dinner at the Alpine Restaurant at the top. You can only buy the combination ticket at the bottom after 2:30pm; it's $18 for adults, $11.50 for children—a great bargain. No reservations. For further information, call 619/325-1391.

Not-to-be-missed Palm Springs attractions are the ancient Native American **Palm, Andreas,** and **Murray canyons** in a beautiful area of hiking trails, palm groves, even a waterfall with picnic tables nearby.

---

6. After Dark

Cecil's on Sunrise, in the Smoke Tree Shopping Center at Sunrise Way and East Palm Canyon Drive (tel. 619/320-4202), has classic rock 'n' roll of the '60s and '70s. There are live music, theme parties, and special events, plus comedy every Sunday night. Cecil's is open Thursday through Monday from 8pm to 2am. Cover charge is $5.

Zelda's, 169 N. Indian Ave. (tel. 619/325-2375), is nonstop action from 8pm to 2am. There are talent shows, fashion nights, theme parties, drinking, dancing, whatever. Depending on the night, Zelda's can appear to be a cross between a bunny club and a bodybuilder competition. To sum it up: If you're over 25, Zelda's is probably not your bag; under 25, it's hard to say. Admission is usually $3 weeknights, $5 weekends. During spring break, admission is $5 weeknights, $10 weekends.

Mary's Nightclub, 1700 N. Indian Ave. (tel. 619/322-6200), began life in 1990 under the auspices of Sonny Bono's wife. It's a late-night disco—the "in" spot—that showcases the newest sounds. The atmosphere is casual and relaxed, with an aura of understated elegance. The evening activities are nightly from 10pm to 2am.

FROM MALIBU TO NEWPORT BEACH

A visit to Southern California ideally includes a few day's retreat at one of the many beach resorts dotting the shore from Los Angeles to San Diego. But if you haven't the time for a relaxing seaside vacation, day trips to many of the areas listed below make for very pleasant excursions. You might want to explore the *Queen Mary* or *Spruce Goose*, both permanently docked in Long Beach, browse through the shops at San Pedro's quaint Ports O'Call Village, take a cruise to cove-fringed Catalina Island and see the marine forest from a glass-bottom boat, or just laze in the sunshine at any of the sandy coastal beaches described below.

1. Malibu

Just 25 miles from Los Angeles Civic Center, Malibu is the stretch of shoreline beginning at Topanga Canyon and extending westward along the Pacific Ocean (West Pacific Coast Hwy., or U.S. 101-A) to the Ventura County line. Once a privately owned rancho (purchased for 10¢ an acre), Malibu is now a popular resort city and acreage has become infinitely more expensive. During the '20s the emerging movie colony flocked here, and Malibu was famous for wild parties and extravagant *Great Gatsby* life-styles. There are still many famous residents, but they tend to keep a low profile.

WHAT TO SEE AND DO
Every year Malibu's beaches delight thousands of visitors, who engage in every activity from nude sunbathing to grunion hunting. Boating is also a popular activity.

J. Paul Getty Museum

The J. Paul Getty Museum, 17985 Pacific Coast Hwy. (tel. 213/458-2003), is a spectacular reconstruction of the Roman Villa dei Papiri, which was buried in volcanic mud when Mount Vesuvius erupted in A.D. 79, destroying Pompeii and Herculaneum. Completed in 1974, the present museum—the world's wealthiest—replaced the ranch house that Getty had opened to the public as a showplace for his collection. The museum is heralded by a colonnaded peristyle garden with a graceful reflecting pool and replicas of bronze statues unearthed at the site of the original villa. Reproductions of ancient frescoes adorn the garden walls, and over 40 different types of marble were used in the halls and colonnades. The museum's gardens include trees, flowers, shrubs, and herbs typical of those that might have been found at the villa.

Set on 10 acres, the museum houses the magnificent J. Paul Getty collection, which is fittingly strong on Greek and Roman antiquities. Notable works include a 4th-century B.C. Greek sculpture, *The Victorious Athlete* (known as the Getty bronze), possibly done by Lysippus, court sculptor to Alexander the Great.

In addition to the Greco-Roman pieces, the collection is also rich in Renaissance and baroque paintings and 18th-century French decorative arts, as well as medieval and Renaissance illuminated manuscripts, sculpture, and drawings (15th century to the end of the 19th), and 19th- and 20th-century European and American photographs. A recent addition to the manuscript collection is the *Prayer Book of Charles the Bold*, by Lievin van Lathem (1469). The painting galleries contain the only documented picture in the country by Masaccio, a Flemish baroque collection, and several important works by such French artists as Georges de la Tour, Nicolas Poussin, Jacques-Louis David, Jean-François Millet, and François Boucher.

In March 1990 the museum announced that it had acquired *Irises*, painted in 1889 by Vincent van Gogh. The Getty's greatest 19th-century painting, it is regarded as one of the most important works of art in the western United States. The *Irises* can be seen in the museum's second-floor galleries, together with a growing collection of important 19th-century paintings that includes Renoir's *La Promenade*, Édouard Manet's *Rue Mosnier with Flags*, Edvard Munch's *Starry Night*, and James Ensor's *Christ's Entry into Brussels in 1889*. Among other recent acquisitions is a watercolor by Honoré Daumier, *A Criminal Case*, illustrating one aspect of Daumier's fascination with the French judicial system. The museum also has major examples of styles of French silver that were fashionable in the late 17th and 18th centuries.

The Getty has adopted interactive video technology, allowing you to tailor your own tour. With this tool you can, for example, have the otherwise forbidden luxury of leafing through medieval and Renaissance manuscripts. It also offers demonstrations of techniques used in making manuscripts. Five of the museum's greatest manuscripts are presented in detail. Video discs feature much of the Getty's Greek vase and manuscript collections.

The museum's Garden Tea Room is in a lovely terraced setting of gardens, fountain, and sunshine (usually). Prices are moderate ($4 to $8) for sandwiches, salads, and snacks served cafeteria style. Wine and beer are available. Seating is inside or al fresco. Luncheon is served from 11am to 2:30pm; light refreshments, from 9:30am to 4:30pm. Picnics are not permitted on the premises.

Plans for a new home for a J. Paul Getty Center are under way. The site is on top of a cliff overlooking Brentwood and Bel Air. On completion of the project, the current museum will be devoted exclusively to ancient Greek and Roman art.

The Getty Museum is open Tuesday through Sunday from 10am to 5pm (the gate closes at 4:30pm), and there is no admission or parking charge. Docent orientation lectures are given at the ocean end of the main peristyle garden every 15 minutes between 9:30am and 3:15pm.

Note: Because there are limited parking facilities, if you plan to come bay car and park, *without exception* you must make a parking reservation 7 to 10 days in advance (by mail or by telephone). Visitors who do not have a car or who are unable to make parking reservations may enter the museum grounds by bicycle (racks are available), motorcycle, taxi, RTD bus 434 (request a museum pass from the driver), or by being dropped at the gatehouse by car. No walk-in traffic is permitted with the exception of RTD bus passengers.

WHERE TO STAY

For such a wealthy community, Malibu is singularly lacking in glamorous accommodations. The reason is simple: The residents are comfortably ensconced in their own gorgeous houses, and they don't want their quiet retreat turned into a bustling tourist resort. Local ordinances are designed to work against such a contingency.

Best bet is the **Casa Malibu,** 22752 Pacific Coast Hwy., Malibu, CA 90265 (tel. 213/456-2219), a hacienda-style accommodation built around a palm-studded inner courtyard with cuppa d'oro vines growing up the balcony and well-tended flowerbeds. The 21 rooms are cheerful and attractively furnished—all with private balconies. Each is equipped with a shower bath, phone, oversize beds, and color TV. Singles or doubles cost $120 to $130 overlooking the water, $85 to $95 if fronting the patio or coastal highway. Each extra person in a room pays $12 (over two); rooms with kitchens can be rented for an extra $12 per day (three-day minimum rental).

What once was the Tonga Lei Motel and Don the Beachcomber has been replaced by the lovely new **Malibu Beach Inn,** at 22878 Pacific Coast Hwy., Malibu, CA 90265 (tel. 213/456-6444, or toll free 800/462-5428), on the beach next to Malibu Pier. Malibu's first all-new beachfront motel in some 37 years rents its oceanfront and oceanview rooms with private balconies, color TVs, VCRs, phones, wet bars, coffee makers, etc., for $135 to $180, single or double occupancy, Continental breakfast included. Suites are available at $225 to $275.

WHERE TO DINE

Alice's, 23000 Pacific Coast Hwy. (tel. 213/456-6646), has an 18-year history as one of the liveliest restaurants in the area. Facing the Malibu Pier, the dining area is glassed in on three sides, and rear tables are on a raised platform so that everyone can view the ocean. It's light and airy, but most important the menu is mostly seafood —as always, beautifully fresh.

Among the tempting luncheon entrees are yellowtail with spinach, lemon, and tarragon butter; and the grilled chicken breast marinated in garlic, soy, and spices and served with a tomato-cilantro relish. But don't overlook the pasta choices, especially the spaghetti with hot Créole sausage, zucchini, and a sweet red-pepper sauce. Alice's also has a good selection of salads, warm and cold. Consider also the Malibu sausage burger with sautéed onions and peppers, and mustard dressing.

As for dinner, you might begin with the smoked Norwegian salmon served with caviar cream. Among the salads my choice is the hot roasted goat cheese salad with mixed greens, fresh herbs, walnuts, and a sherry vinaigrette. Some of the great entrees are Alice's grilled swordfish with herb butter and the stir-fried scallops with black-bean sauce and sweet peppers over pan-fried angel-hair pasta. But Alice's doesn't forget the meat lovers. Take your choice of a grilled New York–strip steak served with soy-glazed red onions, or the grilled veal rack chop with shiitake mushrooms, roast shallots, and cabernet sauce.

Luncheon salads, eggs, and sandwiches are $5.50 to $7.50; pastas, $7.50 to $9. Dinner entrees are $13.50 to $19; pastas, $8 to $11.50. Appetizers will add another $3.50 to $9.50. The list of delicious homemade desserts and pastries changes daily, so be sure to ask.

Alice's is open weekdays from 11:30am to 10pm, on Saturday from 11am, and on Sunday from 10:30am to 10pm. Reservations are advised.

Carlos and Pepe's, 22706 Pacific Coast Hwy. (tel. 213/456-3105), is a delightful weathered-wood seacoast structure. Inside you'll find a few touches from south of the border, including papier-mâché banana trees at the bar, complete with tropical birds. The interior is designed so that each table has an ocean view. An immense aquarium filled with tropical fish separates the bar and dining areas. The best place to sit is on the plant-filled, glass-enclosed deck directly overlooking the ocean.

The menu features a wide variety of Mexican dishes, including enchiladas, chimichangas (a burrito fried crisp), and Carlos' Wild Tostada. But the most popular ones here are fajitas, either steak or chicken, or a combination of both, arriving hot from a skillet containing peppers, onions, and tomatoes, served with flour tortillas, guacamole, salsa cruda, lettuce, and beans. And there are also such Gringo Specials as hamburgers, omelets, and steaks, for $5 to $15. Lunch will cost $7 to $9; dinner, $10 to $15. For dessert, you might try delicious mud pie (chocolate), the deep-fried ice cream, or one of the great (uncooked) ice-cream flavors; each costs $3. A wide selection of wines and imported beers is available, and there's a well-stocked liquor bar. But above all, Carlos and Pepe's is famous for their delicious 16-ounce margaritas, made with freshly squeezed juices.

Open daily from 11:30am to 2am, they serve appetizers until 1:30am. Meals are served till 11pm. Sunday through Thursday, till midnight on Friday and Saturday. No reservations.

La Scala Malibu, 3874 Cross Creek Rd., off Pacific Coast Hwy. (tel. 213/456-1979), is the venture of Jean Leon, whose ultrachic Beverly Hills restaurants are popular with the stars. This venture is different from its Beverly Hills counterpart. Solarium windows overlook the wilds of Malibu Creek out to the Pacific, creating a relaxed, casual atmosphere for friendly, leisurely dining.

Lunch at La Scala might begin with gazpacho, followed by fresh turkey salad with sliced tomato and hard-boiled egg, a cold plate of broiled chicken, or a hot entree such as veal and peppers, swordfish, or the daily fresh pasta, for $12 to $15. For dessert, try the homemade ice cream with fresh raspberries. Dinner begins with antipasti such as mozzarella marinara, seafood salad, carpaccio, or a Caesar salad, and continues with entrees such as baked sea bass, veal with pepperoni, or the nightly fresh pasta. Entrees cost $17 to $28.

La Scala Malibu is open for lunch weekdays from 11:30am to 2:30pm, and for dinner Monday through Thursday from 5:30 to 10:30pm, on Friday and Saturday to 11pm, and on Sunday to 10pm.

For leisurely breakfasts or lunches there's the **Sand Castle,** just off the pier at 28128 W. Pacific Coast Hwy. (tel. 213/457-2503). Housed in a gray shingled building, complete with weather vane and window's walk, it's right on the beach and has a wall of windows overlooking the ocean. The interior is rustic, with many nautical touches (ship-light chandeliers, rigging, etc.), and a big fireplace (ablaze at night) connects the restaurant and lounge. (The latter sees a lot of action on weekend nights.)

Breakfast can be a big order of steak and eggs with hash browns or homefries and hot buttered toast; an avocado, bacon, and Jack-cheese omelet; or buttermilk pancakes with bacon—each $6 to $10. Champagne brunch ($10), served from 9am to 4pm daily (till 2:30pm on Sunday), comes with a refillable glass of champagne and a choice of entrees—perhaps a seafood crêpe in mornay sauce served with a fresh fruit cup, or the steak and teriyaki chicken. Lunch fare runs the gamut from a Monte Cristo sandwich to scallops sautéed in white wine, for $8 to $18. An excellent buy are the sunset dinners, served from 5 to 7pm (4 to 7pm on Sunday). For about $8, these include soup or salad and a choice of entrees—London broil au jus with whipped potatoes, baked fresh fish with french fries, sautéed chicken piccata with rice pilaf, etc.

The Sand Castle is open daily for breakfast from 6am to noon, for lunch from 11am to 4pm, and for dinner from 5 to 10pm (to 11pm on Friday and Saturday). Reservations advised at dinner.

2. Redondo Beach

In the 1880s Redondo Beach was the largest shipping port between San Diego and San Francisco. With the decline of commercial shipping, it became—and still is—a modest beach resort, just a few minutes south of the Los Angeles International Airport.

WHAT TO SEE AND DO

For a complete rundown on Redondo Beach facilities, boating, sailing, and fishing trips, maps, brochures, etc., stop in at the **Redondo Beach Chamber of Commerce,** 1215 N. Catalina Ave. (tel. 213/376-6911).

At the **Fisherman's Wharf** pier you'll find a maze of architecturally attractive restaurants, over 50 shops, galleries, penny arcades, and fishing-equipment outlets. Although the restaurants concentrate on seafood, there is also Japanese, Polynesian, and Mexican cuisine available.

WHERE TO STAY

The **Portofino Inn,** 260 Portofino Way, Redondo Beach, CA 90277 (tel. 213/379-8481, or toll free 800/338-2993, 800/468-4292 in California), is beautifully situated at the middle of King Harbor so that each of the 169 rooms and two suites has a balcony overlooking either the yacht harbor or the ocean. The hotel completed an extensive renovation in 1989, and all the new accommodations are attractively furnished with bleached woods complemented by muted tones of pink, rose, and gray; color TVs; radios; honor minibars stocked with snacks and beverages; two-line direct-dial phones; and tub/shower baths. The inn provides a useful array of custom bath accessories (shampoo, soaps, hand and body lotions) and very plush bathrobes. Special touches include the complimentary morning newspaper and nightly turndown service. The hotel also has 20 totally furnished apartments available by the week or month, each with a living room, one or two bedrooms, a complete kitchen (including stove, range, microwave oven, and full-size refrigerator), and convenient maid service.

Dining and drinking facilities include the Marina Café (obviously with a marvelous view of the marina), the Marina Grill, and (you guessed it) the Marina Lounge. The café serves breakfast and lunch ($4 to $8.50) from 6am to 3pm. The grill serves dinner from 5 to 10pm; specialties of the house are beef, pasta, and chicken ($12 to $30). The lounge serves cocktails and hors d'oeuvres, and has live entertainment and dancing Wednesday through Sunday from 9pm to 12am. The Bayside "240," the inn's newest restaurant, features an excellent selection of seafood in its many forms, both hot and cold, and prepared with regional flair; don't miss it. The Bayside "240" is open for lunch and dinner daily and for Sunday brunch.

The Portofino Inn has a heated outdoor pool that overlooks the ocean, a Jacuzzi, and for somewhat more vigorous exercise, bicycles for guests' use. Complimentary health-club facilities are just a block away. The inn is within walking distance of some famous beaches, the historic Redondo Pier, a gaggle of major restaurants, shops, even sportfishing. It is 6 miles from Los Angeles International Airport (LAX). Complimentary shuttle service is available.

Rooms with a marina view cost $130 to $160, single or double; with an ocean view, $160 to $190. Suites are $240. Apartment rates (on request) vary depending on the length of your stay.

WHERE TO DINE

The Red Onion, 655 N. Harbor Dr. (tel. 213/376-8813), with its elaborate decor, is billed as a "Mexican Restaurant and Social Club." The ceiling is bamboo, an eclectic selection of chairs leans heavily to bamboo and rattan, ceiling fans whir slowly overhead, and photos of Mexico adorn the walls. Most tables afford a view of the harbor; there's an open brick-and-tile fireplace, attractive Persian carpeting, and ubiquitous foliage. A terrific bargain here is the happy hour, 4 to 8pm on weekdays. Order a drink and you can partake of an immense Mexican buffet—easily a full meal. However, if you should decide to dine at other hours, you'll find menu prices most reasonable, with hearty and delicious combination plates ranging from $10 to $14, and many, many à la carte items.

Open seven days from 11am to 2am. Food is served to 10pm.

3. San Pedro

Farther down the beach, picturesque San Pedro, the bustling port of Los Angeles, handles an estimated two million tons of cargo every month. It definitely merits a day's visit to see a little village-within-a-town created simply for tourists, which is nevertheless charming and fun.

PORTS O'CALL VILLAGE AND THE WHALER'S WHARF

To reach Ports O'Call, take the Harbor Freeway to the Harbor Boulevard off-ramp and turn right.

Combining the atmosphere of Old California with a 19th-century New Bedford whaling port, the wharf and village have over 80 international specialty shops and restaurants along winding cobblestoned streets. Part of the fun is watching the steady stream of yachts, luxury liners, tankers, freighters, schooners, and sailboats cruise past.

The village itself achieves an Early California motif with Spanish colonial–style architecture, archways, wrought-iron enclosed balconies, and an abundance of bougainvillea vines and banana palms. Across a graceful bridge the elm-shaded brick lanes of the wharf evoke New England with shingle-roofed buildings, lantern lights, multipaned windows, and tavern signs. Throughout, there are strolling entertainers and musicians (occasional band concerts in summer), and the very browsable shops provide a dazzling display of imported international merchandise ranging from Philippine jewelry to Japanese gun-powder tea.

Mardi Gras Cruises (tel. 213/548-1085) harbor tours leave daily at frequent intervals year-round and offer brunch, dinner, and afternoon cocktail cruises; from January to March **L.A. Harbor Sportfishing,** 1150 Nagoya Way, Berth 79 (tel. 213/547-9916), offers whale-watching cruises. Throughout the year they have half-day, three-quarter-day, and all-day sportfishing charters. If you'd like to know the kind and number of fish they caught the previous day, call 213/547-1318. In addition, **helicopter rides** leave Whaler's Wharf every few minutes for an aerial tour of the inner harbor area and Ports O'Call.

For meals, you can stop off at the **Ports O'Call Restaurant** at Berth 76 (tel. 213/833-3553); it's easy to spot because a red Chinese junk is moored in a pond near the footbridge to the entrance. The interior is nautical/Polynesian in motif. The menu features South Seas specialties like Java seafood curry and steak teriyaki, along with steak and seafood "mainland fare." Dinner entrees are priced at $14 to $22. Luncheon entrees are in the $10 to $14 range. The restaurant is open for lunch Monday through Saturday from 11am to 3pm; for dinner Monday through Thursday from 4 to 11pm, on Friday and Saturday to midnight; for Sunday brunch from 10 to 2:30pm and Sunday dinner from 4:30 to 10pm.

If, on the other hand, you're in a casual pub mood, head for **Whiskey Joe's** at Berth 75 (tel. 213/831-0181). Designed to look like a 19th-century waterside pub, it has a weathered clapboard-and-shingle façade and a quaint interior with several working fireplaces, curtained windows, and oil lamps on every table. Diners can sit indoors (most tables overlook the water) or outdoors on a brick terrace. Dinner offerings ($14 to $25) include steak, shrimp, mussels, clams, red-skin potatoes, and corn on the cob, plus burgers, chops, and chili.

Whiskey Joe's is open weekdays from 10am to 10pm, weekends to 11pm.

The admission-free village and wharf (at Berth 77) are open daily from 11am to 9pm in summer, to 7pm the rest of the year (tel. 213/831-0287).

4. Long Beach

Continuing south along the shore we come to Long Beach, the sixth-largest city in California, which does, in fact, offer a "long beach"—5½ miles of beckoning sand. It's also well equipped with tennis, golf, sailing, fishing, and boating facilities (departures from Pierpoint sportfishing landing and Belmont Pier), plus the picturesque **Seaport Village** shopping complex at the southeastern edge of the city.

WHAT TO SEE AND DO

The principal attraction of this resort town is the *Queen Mary* (tel. 213/435-3511), docked at the terminus of Pier J (at the southern end of the Long Beach Freeway, I-710) since the completion of her final 14,500-mile journey around South America in 1967.

She makes an imposing sight, her black hull and white superstructure a fifth of a mile long, and her three vermilion stacks jutting 150 feet into the air. Tourists can explore the ship's engine rooms, boilers, turbines, and machinery; the aft steering station (an emergency facility); the elegant three-deck-high Queen's Salon; re-creations of all classes of accommodations, and the contrasting GI quarters used when the *Queen Mary* transported 800,000 troops in World War II. Besides the extensive World War II display, there are a sound-and-light show, re-enacting a near-collision at sea, and a fine exhibit devoted to model-ship building (in the Hall of Maritime Heritage).

As in former days, there are about 25 specialty shops on board and a chapel for "at sea" weddings.

Next to the *Queen Mary,* under an aluminum dome, is Howard Hughes' famous World War II all-wood 200-ton seaplane, the **Spruce Goose.** It's the largest plane ever built—it had room for 750 troops—but flew only once. It's quite a big bird, with a wing-span (320 feet) that's longer than a football field.

A tour of the *Spruce Goose* affords you a look into the plane's cockpit and hold. You can also see a video of the plane's test flight. A special platform built adjacent to the *Goose* allows guests to see the cockpit, cargo area, and flight deck up close. Surrounding the mammoth plane are a variety of unique displays, as well as audiovisual presentations detailing the plane's construction, its one-and-only flight, and Howard Hughes' aviation career.

Tickets for the *Queen Mary* and the *Spruce Goose* combined cost $18 for adults, $10 for children 5 to 11 (under 5, free). The sights are open daily from 10am to 6pm; the ticket booth closes at 5:30pm. Parking is $4.

And while you're visiting the *Queen,* head ashore for the **Brighton Carnival.** It's an old-fashioned English fair with all kinds of fun, from rides on a Ferris wheel and double-tiered carousel to performances by jugglers, a one-man musical band, and death-defying high divers. There are also live musical revues, plus a 1939 auto show.

WHERE TO STAY

Want to spend the night? The ship has been turned into the 365-room **Queen Mary Hotel** (tel. 213/435-3511). Many of the luxurious original furnishings remain, although modern conveniences—phones, air conditioning, color TVs, etc. —have been added. Singles or doubles are $100 to $145; suities, $190 to $650. Parking is $4.

WHERE TO DINE

While you're in Long Beach you can dine at one of the three restaurants on board the *Queen Mary*—all with views of the city's skyline and small-boat harbor— serving both lunch and dinner (call 213/435-3511 for reservations). The Promenade Café also serves breakfast. The Chelsea specializes in fish and seafood. The Sir Winston, a beautifully appointed room filled with Churchill memorabilia and offering a panoramic harbor view, serves Continental cuisine (jackets and ties required for men).

---

5. Catalina Island

Relatively few tourists have seen this quaint, cove-fringed island just 22 miles off the Long Beach shoreline, yet Catalina offers scores of resort attractions. Crystal-clear water makes for excellent boating, fishing, swimming, scuba-diving, and snorkeling. There are miles of hiking and biking trails. The beautiful **Wrigley Memorial and Botanical Garden** is here. Camping, golf, tennis, and horseback-riding facilities abound. Big-band concerts in summer at the Catalina Casino, fabulous undersea gardens, and finally, the picturesque town of Avalon (the island's only city), named for a passage in Tennyson's *Idylls of the King*, round out the Catalina scene.

So different is Catalina from Los Angeles in every way that it seems almost like a different country, remote and unspoiled. Separated from the mainland over half a million years ago, it evolved to meet its environmental challenges, and even today there is unique plantlife. Archeology has revealed that at one time in history a race of giants lived here, and as late as the 1600s Spanish explorers found a Stone Age culture on the island. After Sebastián Vizcaíno visited the island in 1602 (searching for a pirate-free port for his treasure galleons), it was left in peace for about 150 years. But the sea otter, which was to play a large part in California history (see Chapter IV), was also to be the agent of the Catalina Indians' downfall when the animals were discovered in abundance in the area. In the early 1800s the island's native people and the sea otters were both wiped out by Russian fur hunters. It was, however, soon repopulated by pirates using its coves to store booty, plus cattle- and sheep-herders, and deported Asians who hid here until they could be smuggled back to the mainland. Then in the 1860s a mining boom hit the island and lasted until Union troops put an end to the "gold rush" during the Civil War.

After that, Catalina changed hands several times, finally beginning to take its present shape in 1892, when the Banning brothers bought it to develop as a fashionable pleasure resort. A fire wiped out the Bannings, however, and in 1915 they sold to William Wrigley, Jr., of chewing gum fame. During the '20s Wrigley brought the Chicago Cubs (he owned the team) to Catalina for spring training, and sportswriters helped publicize the island's romantic mystique. It became a favorite vacation spot of the wealthy and famous, with big-name bands playing in the Casino Ballroom (they still do) and yachts filling Avalon's harbor. This tourist boom was interrupted by World War II, when Catalina was an important military base.

Today Catalina is well enough known for all its hotels to be fully booked months in advance (reserve early), but it is untouristy, a genuinely tranquil and charming island retreat. Ownership of 86% of the island by the Santa Catalina Island Conservancy has helped to preserve the island's natural resources.

GETTING THERE

The *Catalina Express* (tel. 213/519-1212, or toll free 800/257-2227 in California), operates daily—year-round to Catalina from San Pedro and Long Beach, and in-season (about mid-June to Labor Day) from Redondo Beach. There are 19 daily departures; the trip takes about an hour. One-way fares from San Pedro are $14 for adults, $13 for seniors, $11 for children 2 to 11, 75¢ for infants. Long Beach/Redondo fares are about $2 higher for all except infants, who still are charged 75¢. The *Catalina Express* departs from the Sea/Air Terminal at Berth 95, Port of L.A. in San Pedro; in Long Beach, from the *Catalina Express* Port at the **Queen Mary;** and in Redondo, from the *Catalina Express* Port at 161 N. Harbor Dr. Reservations can be made by calling either of the above numbers.

Note: There are very specific baggage restrictions on the *Catalina Express*. Luggage is limited to 50 pounds per person. If you plan to camp, a camping permit can be obtained from L.A. County (tel. 213/510-0688) or Catalina Cover & Camp (tel. 213/510-0303). Reservations are necessary for bicycles, surfboards, dive tanks, etc. The U.S. Coast Guard prohibits carrying certain commodities on passenger vessels; if you have any questions about what you can take, call in advance. There are also restrictions on transporting domestic pets—again, ask.

Service to Catalina is also offered by **Catalina Cruises** (tel. 213/775-6111) in Long Beach and San Pedro at Berth 95, the **Catalina Flyer Catamaran** in Newport Beach at the Balboa Pavilion (tel. 714/673-5245), **California Cruisin'** from San Diego (tel. 619/235-8600), and the **Helitrans Helicopter Service** in San Pedro at Berth 95 (tel. 213/548-1314).

WHAT TO SEE AND DO

When your boat arrives in Avalon, as soon as you've finished oohing and aahing over the breathtaking view, head for the **Catalina Island Chamber of Commerce & Visitor's Bureau** on the Green Pleasure Pier for maps, brochures, and information on island activities. You can also call them (tel. 213/510-1520) for information and direct phone lines to airlines, hotels, boat transport, or sightseeing companies, or to find out about camping, hiking, fishing, boating, tennis, diving, golf, or horseback-riding facilities, or even to inquire about the weather. For an extremely useful free 48-page brochure, including a calendar of events, write to the Catalina Island Chamber of Commerce, Dept. DG, P.O. Box 217, Avalon, CA 90704.

The **Visitors' Information and Services Center,** on Crescent Avenue across from the Green Pleasure Pier (tel. 213/510-2000, or toll free 800/428-2566 in California), offers numerous island tours. (Ticket and information booths are also located at Island Plaza between Catalina and Summer, and at the Green Pleasure Pier.) They include the **Skyline Drive** (one hour and 45 minutes), costing $10.50 for adults, $9.50 for seniors, $7 for children 3 to 11; and the **Avalon Scenic Tour** (50 minutes), priced at $5 for adults, $4.50 for seniors, and $3.50 for children. The 3¾-hour, 30-mile **Inland Motor Tour** is one of the most interesting, much of it penetrating the 66 square miles of preserve owned by the Santa Catalina Island Conservancy. You'll see El Rancho Escondido, where pure-bred Arabian horses are raised, and likely view buffalo, deer, goats, and boars. Prices: $19.50 for adults, $18 for seniors, $12.50 for children. A 40-minute **Casino Tour** ($6 for adults, $5 for seniors, $4 for children) explores Catalina's most famous landmark.

Not to be missed is the 40-minute **Glass-Bottom Boat Trip** to view Catalina's exquisite undersea gardens and colorful fish. By day the trip is $5.25 for adults, $4.50 for seniors, and $3.50 for children; at night it's $6.25 for adults, $5.50 for seniors, and $4 for children. For the combination package of the Skyline Drive and Glass-Bottom Boat Trip, the prices are $14 for adults, $12.75 for seniors, and $9.50 for children. Then there are the 55-minute **Coastal Cruise** to Seal Rocks, where you'll see sea lions at play in their natural habitat ($5 for adults, $4.50 for seniors, $3.50 for children); and the one-hour **Flying Fish Boat Trip** ($6.25 for adults, $5.50 for seniors, $4 for children), during which an occasional flying fish even lands right on the boat!

There also are three lovely dining cruises. The **Sunset Buffet Cruise** (May through September) takes you aboard a historic paddle-wheeler along Catalina's coastline. Cocktails are served, plus a scrumptious buffet, and you'll dance to the music of the '50s and '60s. The **Twilight Dining at Two Harbors Cruise** (June through September) packages some of the nicest things about Catalina into one evening. The cruise makes its way along Catalina's coastline to a buffet dinner at Doug's Harbor Reef Restaurant, with complimentary wine or beer, music, and a flying-fish trip on the way home. The Sunset Buffet Cruise is on Wednesday, Friday, and Saturday; the Twilight Dining at Two Harbors Cruise is on Tuesday and Thursday. Both cruises are the same price: $35 for adults, $32.50 for seniors, and $20 for children.

And finally, should you wish to get about town on your own, you can rent a U-Drive (like a cross between a Jeep and a golf cart) or bicycle (the former for licensed drivers only, the latter for those with good leg muscles) at any of a number of rental agencies on the Crescent and throughout Avalon. You cannot, however, penetrate the island's interior with either of these vehicles. It's not allowed. Consider this about Catalina: If you live on the island, there's a 10-year waiting list for a permit to own a car, which may be one interesting solution to the air-pollution problem on the mainland.

WHERE TO STAY

In keeping with Catalina's untouristy image, the 30 or so hotels on the island, while all beautifully situated, maintain an almost pretentious unpretentiousness. Not only are there no big hotels of the Hyatt, Hilton, and Sheraton type—a factor I fully approve of—but the existing hostelries seem, regrettably, to go out of their way not to be quaint or charming. However, to carp about decor is petty, since there's nary an eyesore on the entire island, and perhaps the refusal to cater to tourism is the reason. Charming or not, as I said before, the hotels tend to be fully booked in season, so reserve early.

The little **Hotel MacRae,** 409 Crescent (P.O. Box 1517), Avalon, CA 90704 (tel. 213/510-0246), is a pleasant, two-story hostelry right across from the beach. It's decorated in bright, cheerful colors—parrot green, orange, yellow, red, and white. There are 23 rooms here, with a wide range of accommodations. Each room has a private bathroom, color TV, and heater for chilly nights. A complimentary Continental breakfast is offered every morning, and wine, cheese, and crackers are served in the evening. In the center of the hotel is a large, open courtyard, perfect for lounging or sunning.

Rates are $65 to $100 for a standard single or double room, $100 to $200 for a suite. Kitchen units are available.

At the **Island Inn,** 125 Metropole (just half a block from Crescent), P.O. Box 467 Avalon, CA 90704 (tel. 213/510-1623), innkeepers Martin and Bernadine Curtin have created the most attractive accommodations in town. The hotel's rooms are freshly painted pale blue-gray, accented in peach and set off by blue carpeting and blue-and-peach bedspreads. Shuttered windows and stained-glass lighting fixtures add further charm. All rooms have color TVs and private baths (some with tubs, all with showers); most also have AM/FM radios. The front desk will take phone messages; transportation is provided from the boat; complimentary coffee, juice, and a specialty bread are offered each morning; and there are ice and soda machines in the hall.

Rates for single or double occupancy are $80 to $160, $185 for a mini-suite, all May to September. October to May, rooms are $30 less, excluding holidays and weekends.

Also on the beach, **Hotel Villa Portofino,** 111 Crescent (P.O. Box 127), Avalon, CA 90704 (tel. 213/510-0555, or toll free 800/346-2326), has 34 rooms, all equipped with dressing areas, private baths (stall showers), and color TVs; none has a phone. The adjoining Ristorante Villa Portofino has been remodeled and features northern Italian cuisine. A buffet Sunday brunch is featured during the summer.

Accommodations at the Villa Portofino are $85 to $185 (higher rates on weekends), single or double; rates are much lower off-season.

The most superb views on the island are from the lofty **Zane Grey Pueblo Hotel,** off Chimes Tower Road (P.O. Box 216), Avalon, CA 90704 (tel. 213/510-0966). This Shangri-la mountain retreat is the former home of novelist Zane Grey, who spent his last 20 years in Avalon enjoying the isolation, the ocean view and harbor. He wrote many books here, including *Tales of Swordfish and Tuna,* which tells of his fishing adventures off Catalina Island. (The hotel has teak beams that the novelist brought from Tahiti on one of his fishing trips.) In another work, *What the Open Means to Me,* Grey described his ecstatic feelings about the island: "It is an environment that means enchantment to me. Sea and Mountain! Breeze and roar of Surf! Music of Birds! Solitude and Tranquility! A place for rest, dream, peace, sleep. I could write here and be at peace. . . . "

The hotel has a swimming pool/sun deck nestled in the mountains, with chairs overlooking Avalon and the ocean, and most of the rooms also have large windows and ocean or mountain views. There's also a patio with "the view," and a fireplace lounge wherein is a TV and piano. All the rooms are being renovated with new furniture, new carpeting, ceiling fans, and other touches to make life more pleasurable. All rooms have private baths (mostly with showers) but no phones or TVs. Coffee is served all day, and there's a courtesy bus to town.

In summer rooms cost $95 to $115 for one or two people, including Continental breakfast. Off-season rates are lower.

The **Catalina Canyon Hotel** (formerly the Paradise Island Inn), 888 Country Club Dr., Avalon, CA 90704 (tel. 213/510-0325, or toll free 800/253-9361), is set on beautifully landscaped grounds in the foothills of Avalon. There are 80 guest rooms, tastefully decorated and comfortably furnished. All include tub/shower baths, color TVs, AM/FM radios, phones, and balconies overlooking the outdoor pool and Jacuzzi. The Canyon Restaurant is on the premises for breakfast and lunch, and offers a Continental dinner menu. Room service is available. Cocktails may be enjoyed in the lounge or on the outdoor terrace overlooking the pool. The hotel is adjacent to a golf course and tennis courts. The hotel courtesy van meets guests at the air and sea terminals.

Rooms are $135 to $165, single or double, based on location and season; $10 for each additional person.

WHERE TO DINE

El Galleon, 411 Crescent (tel. 213/510-1188), is a large, warm, and woody nautical affair, complete with portholes, rigging, anchors, big wrought-iron chandeliers, oversize tufted-leather booths, and tables with red-leather-upholstered captain's chairs. There's additional balcony seating, plus outdoor café tables overlooking the ocean harbor. In summer the luncheon menu offers fresh seafood, burgers, steak, stews, salads, and sandwiches, at $6 to $12. The dinner menu features many seafood items, like cioppino, fresh swordfish steak, and broiled Catalina lobster tails in drawn butter. There are also a number of nonseafood entrees, ranging from country fried chicken and beef Stroganoff to broiled rack of lamb with mint jelly. Dinner prices range from $10 to $25.

Open daily for lunch from 11:30am to 2:30pm and for dinner from 5 to 10pm. The bar is open from 10am to 1:30am.

The Busy Bee, 306 Crescent, at the end of Metropole (tel. 213/510-1983), has been an Avalon institution for many years—since 1923, to be exact. In all those years it's undergone numerous changes, as witnessed by photos of its various incarnations on the wall of one dining area. The Busy Bee sits on the beach directly over the water. You can eat in several locations, including a lovely wrap-around patio (perfect for summer lunches) and an indoor room furnished with ceiling fans, plants, and tables. Even from here you have a terrific view of the bay through picture windows.

The fare is light—deli style. Breakfast, lunch, and dinner are served all day. The day starts with omelets, five variations on eggs Benedict, and other breakfast dishes for $5 to $10. Throughout the day there are over 80 items to choose from: hot and cold sandwiches, salads, Mexican specialties, pasta, burgers, etc. Some of the more popular items are the Chinese chicken salad, Buffalo burger, and a one-pound hamburger that almost defies consumption. The Busy Bee grinds its own beef daily and cuts its own potatoes for french fries; salad dressings are also made on the premises. The tab for these tasty dishes ranges from $7 to $17. All this, plus the irrefutable fact that the Busy Bee is Avalon's only waterfront bar with a harbor view.

The Busy Bee is open in summer from 8am to 10pm weekdays, to 11pm on weekends; winter hours are 8am to 8pm daily.

The **Sand Trap,** on Avalon Canyon Road, just past La Casitas on the way to the Memorial Gardens (tel. 213/510-1349), is a local favorite and a great place to escape from Front Street crowds. They serve breakfast, lunch, and snacks, any or all to be enjoyed while looking out over the golf course. The specialties of the house are delectable omelets served till noon and soft tacos served all day. The omelets ($5 to $5.50) contain such mouthwatering goodies as cheese and mushrooms, homemade chorizo, or (in the hearty machaca omelet) spicy shredded beef, cheddar, sour cream, and salsa. The soft tacos ($4.50 to $5.75) have a variety of fillings. The fare, from burgers to sandwiches and salads to chili ($2.50 to $6.25), is varied enough to satisfy most any appetite. Beverages range from the usual to the less so—cocoa-coffee, orange-spiced iced tea—to beer, wine, and wine coolers.

The Sand Trap is open daily from 7:30am to 3pm.

The **Dock Café** (tel. 213/510-2755) is directly across from the casino. You can sit on the deck, have breakfast, a snack, or a drink, and view the bay and boats that come up to the fuel dock.

The Dock Café serves a breakfast burrito (one of life's great start-the-day enjoyments), but you can stick with basic scrambled eggs served with corn tortillas and potatoes or refried beans. Or for the simple life, try granola with yogurt and sliced bananas. Lunch is served all day; there are salads and sandwiches, including a roasted chicken breast on grilled sourdough bread and a hot pastrami on a French roll. Specialties of the house include chicken guacamole tacos, fish tacos, a crispy tostada with chicken, and snack ribs, proclaimed messy and great.

Whether you're reviewing the breakfast, lunch, or snack menu, you'll find that most dishes will cost between $3 and $6. Top price on the menu goes to the tacos ($5.75 to $6.25). There are the usual beverages plus such interesting combinations as cocoa-coffee and "the blend," a mix of lemonade and iced tea. There are also beer, wine, coolers, and the Dock's own sangría.

The Dock Café is open from 8am to 7pm daily in summer, on weekends the rest of the year.

---

6. Newport Beach

Newport Beach is a world-famous recreational resort—kind of an American Riviera. Once cattle-ranch land above an uncharted estuary, Newport is now a busy harbor town that embraces the delightful peninsula/island town of **Balboa.** The phenomenal growth of hotel and restaurant facilities in the last few years indicates that Newport Beach is fast becoming the most popular of Southern California's coastal towns between L.A. and San Diego. Many tourists now use it as a vacation base from which to visit Anaheim, Buena Park, and other Orange County attractions.

Convenient bus tours are available—check at your hotel or at the **Newport Beach Chamber of Commerce,** 1470 Jamboree Rd. (at Santa Barbara Drive), Newport Beach, CA 92660 (tel. 714/644-8211); they're very helpful and some of the nicest people around.

WHAT TO SEE AND DO

A major focus of activity in the area for nearly a century has been a California historic landmark, the cupola-topped **Balboa Pavilion,** 400 Main St., which originally served as a bathhouse. Home of the **Tale of the Whale** seafood restaurant, the oldtime **Spouter Saloon,** and a country store, it is also the Newport departure point for boat service to Catalina, narrated cruises of Newport Harbor, whale-watching cruises, skiff rentals, and a large fleet of modern sportfishing boats. For cruise and charter information, call 714/673-5245; for sportfishing information, call 714/673-1434. At the pavilion you can take a ferry to **Balboa Island,** the ride costing 75¢ for cars, 30¢ for adult passengers.

The best way to see the bay is to buy a ticket for a narrated harbor cruise. In summer, the Catalina Passenger Service (tel. 714/673-5245) offers several trips daily leaving from the **Fun Zone Boat Co.** (tel. 714/673-0240) near the ferry landing. A 45-minute cruise costs $6 for adults, $5 for seniors, $1.50 for children under 12; under-5s, free.

You can also rent roller skates and bicycles here, right in front of the Balboa Inn. Newport Beach, in California tradition, also has a waterfront complex of **40** restaurants and shops. Called **Lido Marina Village,** it's located at Via Lido, just south of Pacific Coast Hwy. off Newport Boulevard. A unique feature of this complex: About eight of the establishments here sell yachts!

The **Newport Harbor Art Museum,** 850 San Clemente Rd., adjacent to Fashion Island and Newport Center, off Santa Barbara Drive (tel. 714/759-1122), merits a visit. The museum presents a varied schedule of exceptional exhibitions featuring 20th-century art from its collection of over 2,000 works, consisting predominantly of California paintings, sculpture, objets d'art, and photographs. The museum is open Tuesday through Sunday from 10am to 5pm; closed Monday. Admission is $4 for adults, $3 for seniors and students, $2 for children; Tuesday it's free for everybody.

WHERE TO STAY

Located on 26 landscaped acres, the **Hyatt Newporter,** 1107 Jamboree Rd. (near Backbay Drive), Newport Beach, CA 92660 (tel. 714/729-1234, or toll free 800/233-1234), is a resort complex par excellence, and an important hub of activity in this beach town. The John Wayne Tennis Club is on the premises, and guests can use its facilities for a reasonable fee; they include 16 championship courts (all lit for night play), spa equipment, steam/sauna, and a clubhouse. In addition, the hotel boasts three heated Olympic-size swimming pools, three whirlpools, and a children's pool, as well as a fitness room, volleyball court, shuffleboard, Ping-Pong, a nine-hole, par-three golf course, jogging trails, and much more. Several championship golf courses are located nearby. Three meals a day are offered in the Jamboree Café, and dinner is served in Ristorante Cantori and in the award-winning gourmet room, The Wine Cellar.

The 410 rooms, decorated in pastel tones, have contemporary furnishings. All have balconies or lanai terraces with a view of the Back Bay, gardens, or golf course, plus air conditioning, direct-dial phones, color TVs (with in-house movies), radios, and tub/shower baths.

Singles are $150 to $170; doubles, $170 to $190.

The 400-room **Newport Beach Marriott Hotel and Tennis Club,** 900 Newport Center Dr., Newport Beach, CA 92660 (tel. 714/640-4000, or toll free 800/228-9290), is a popular Newport Beach accommodation. Built around a nine-story atrium—of which a 19th-century Italian Renaissance–style fountain is the focal point—the hotel was designed so that over 85% of the guest rooms would offer ocean views. The rooms are strikingly decorated with cheerful drapes and bedspreads. Most have balconies overlooking the fountain courtyard hung with ivy and bougainvillea. Each is equipped with bedside remote-control color TV, radio, direct-dial phone, climate control, tub/shower bath, and a convenient amenity—an ironing board (iron on request). Two swimming and hydrotherapy pools are surrounded by a palm-lined sun deck. Eight tennis courts (all night-lit) are on the premises (along with a pro shop and snack bar), as well as a health club, and there's golf at the adjoining Newport Beach Country Club's 18-hole course.

The Marriott has two restaurants: Nicole's Grill, serving Continental and nouvelle cuisine in an elegant French provincial setting, and the cheerful indoor/outdoor J.W.'s Sea Grill, serving fresh seafood and American favorites.

Rates for single rooms are $159 to $179; twins and doubles are $175 to $195.

The **Sheraton Newport,** at 4545 MacArthur Blvd. (at Birch Street), Newport Beach, CA 92660 (tel. 714/833-0570, or toll free 800/325-3535), is conveniently located just half a mile south of the John Wayne/Orange County Airport. The 342 rooms and five beautifully appointed suites are centered around an atrium lobby, with ivy-draped balconies reaching upward to a skylight roof. Facilities include two night-lit tennis courts (no charge for courts), a heated swimming pool and Jacuzzi, and plenty of free parking. There are three restaurants: the Palm Garden, offering a steak-and-seafood menu at lunch and dinner; the Boardwalk Café, a garden-ambience eatery serving breakfast, lunch, and dinner; and the Palm Court, open for lunch only. The Reefwalker features live music for dancing Monday through Saturday nights.

Rooms are attractively color coordinated in three different schemes—mauve, teal, or lavender. Furnishings are of oak, with two leather armchairs in each room, and there is every modern amenity.

The Sheraton charges $110 to $145 for a single, $120 to $155 for a double, including full buffet breakfast daily and an evening cocktail party. Packages are also available.

WHERE TO DINE

For family dining (kids love it), consider the **Reuben E. Lee,** 151 E. Pacific Coast Hwy., near Bayside Drive (tel. 714/675-5790), a free-floating genuine replica of a famous 19th-century Mississippi riverboat, the *Robert E. Lee.* It's entered via canopied gangplanks, and the promenade decks are elegantly turn of the century. The restaurant specializes in fresh fish, shellfish, steaks, and prime rib, all prepared to perfection. A featured entree is the New Orleans bouillabaisse (a tasty concoction made with whole shrimps, lobsters, scallops, clams, fresh fish filet, and crabs' legs, all skillfully blended with tomato sauce and laced with wine). Steaks and prime rib come in all sizes and for all tastes. Dinner entrees cost $14 to $28. At lunch, sandwiches, salads, and hot entrees are in the $9 to $15 range. On Sunday the champagne brunch is not to be believed. There is a spectacular buffet: Whatever you enjoy or have ever wanted for brunch is probably there, plus all the champagne you'd like, and a glass of schnapps to boot. The spread is $18 for adults, $10 for children, and worth every penny.

The Sea Food Deck is open Monday through Saturday for lunch from 11:30am to 3pm, and Monday through Sunday for dinner from 4:30 to 10pm. Sunday brunch is from 10am to 3pm. Reservations are advised.

The Cannery, 3010 Lafayette Ave., at Lido Park Drive (tel. 714/675-5777), is housed in a remodeled 1934 fish cannery that used to turn out 5,000 cases of swordfish and mackerel a day. Now it's a historical landmark. The two-story restaurant is a favorite spot for locals and tourists alike—for good food, a colorful atmosphere, and friendly service. In the upper lounge, tables surround a corner platform where there's live entertainment every night from 8:30pm.

Fresh fish and local abalone are specialties here. At dinner there's always a superfresh chef's special catch of the day. Other good choices are eastern beef, chicken teriyaki, and rack of lamb. Dinner entrees cost $16 to $22. At lunch you might ask for the house special of the day, shrimp and fries, or sandwiches and salads for $5 to $9. Sunday champagne brunch is popular at $12 to $15, depending on the entree you select. The restaurant also serves a champagne buffet brunch while you cruise Newport Harbor aboard the Cannery's *Isla Mujeres;* the cost is $30. There's a Friday and Sunday champagne dinner cruise for $59.50.

Open Monday through Saturday for lunch from 11:30am to 3pm, on Sunday for brunch from 10am to 2:30pm, and for nightly dinner from 5 to 10pm. The seafood bar offers a limited menu until midnight. Reservations are advised.

Chanteclair, 18912 MacArthur Blvd., opposite the Airport Terminal between Campus Drive and Douglas (tel. 714/752-8001), is designed to be like a provincial French inn. A rambling stucco structure with a mansard roof, built around a central garden court, it houses several dining and drinking areas: a grand and petit salon, a boudoir, a *bibliothèque,* a garden area with a skylight roof, and a hunting lodge–like lounge. Furnished in antiques, it has five fireplaces.

The cuisine is Continental. At lunch you might order double-ribbed lamb chops, creamed chicken in pastry, or steak tartare, for $12 to $20. Dinner is an experience in fine dining—a worthwhile splurge, with entrees costing $19 to $30. You might begin with the game bird and pistachio pâté, or perhaps an order of beluga caviar with blinis and garniture (if you have to ask, you can't afford it). I'm also partial to the salads—say, a spinach salad flambé or hearts of palm. For an entree I recommend the rack of lamb served with a bouquetière of fresh vegetables and potatoes Dauphine. There's a considerable listing of domestic and imported wines to complement your meal; if you don't know what to select, the captain will be happy to help you choose. A soufflé Grand Marnier is the perfect dessert, which should be ordered ahead.

Chanteclair is open Sunday through Friday for lunch from 11:30am to 2:30pm, for nightly dinner from 6 to 10pm. Reservations are essential.

Marrakesh, 1100 W. Coast Hwy., near Dover Drive (tel. 714/645-8384), is a variation on the theme of Dar Maghreb, a previously described Moroccan restaurant in Los Angeles. The decor is exotic, with dining areas divided into intimate tents furnished with Persian carpets and authentic Moroccan pieces. Moroccan music enhances the exotic ambience. Seating is on low cushioned sofas, and the entire meal is eaten without silverware—you use your hands, and it's a remarkably sensual experience! It's something of a ritual feast, which begins, appropriately enough, when a server comes around to wash your hands. Everyone in your party shares the same meal—an eight- or nine-course feast priced at $18 to $26 per person. It consists of Moroccan soup, a tangy salad that is scooped up with hunks of fresh bread, b'stila (a chicken-filled pastry topped with cinnamon) or kotban (a lamb shish kebab marinated in olive oil, coriander, cumin, and garlic), a choice of four entrees (baked squab with rice and almonds, baked chicken with lemon and olives, baked fish in a piquant sauce, or rabbit in garlic sauce), lamb and vegetables with couscous, fresh fruits, tea, and Moroccan pastries.

Open daily for dinner from 5 to 11pm. Reservations suggested.

THE BOTTOM LINE: SAN DIEGO

California history began in San Diego with the arrival of Juan Cabrillo at Point Loma in 1542; later Fr. Junípero Serra established the first historic mission of El Camino Real here. The city's Spanish heritage is preserved in Old Town, a reconstruction of the first settlement, and the mission has been beautifully restored. Proximity to Mexico further enhances the Spanish flavor. But the most striking note in this coastal city is not its early California overtones. The predominant impression is water—seemingly endless vistas of the blue Pacific, of boat-filled harbors, quiet coves, and sparkling bays fringed with 70 miles of sandy shoreline beaches.

A couple of years ago San Diego was the third-largest city on the West Coast. But the numbers who came to look and decided to stay kept increasing, and today it's second in population. Now San Diegans (excluding the land developers) are beginning to wonder about the virtues of beauty.

San Diego is probably the best all-around vacation spot in the country, and it's blessed with the best climate. It's now the eighth-largest city in the U.S., though if you stood at its busiest corner you'd never know it. San Diego's secret is sunshine (most of the time), mild weather, soft winds, one of the most famous natural harbors in the world, and a very informal lifestyle. This adds up to sailing on Mission Bay or the Pacific; fishing, snorkeling, scuba-diving, and surfing (what else do you do with 70 miles of county waterfront?); lots of golf (there are over 60 courses) and tennis, biking, jogging, sunbathing, even hang-gliding. Or you can just go fly a kite any day.

Mission Bay Park alone has 4,600 acres for boating and beachcombing. However, to save San Diego from being totally overrun by visitors, the city has been blessed with an ocean cooled to a chilly average of 62°—not exactly bathtub temperature for swimming, but not bad for surfers who wear wet suits (and who cares if you're fishing?).

Then there's the surrounding territory. Within reasonable driving time you can be in the desert, the mountains, or even another country.

About 6,000 pleasure boats are moored in the San Diego Harbor and that's where the U.S. Navy berths the Pacific submarine fleet, along with an impressive collection of over 100 warships.

Many of San Diego's most popular attractions are discussed below; however, listings of entertainment happenings are best found in the Sunday edition of the *San Diego Union*, in the *La Jolla Light*, a weekly newspaper, and in the *Reader*, a weekly tabloid appearing every Thursday with more about San Diego and what's happening than you'll ever need to know.

---

1. Getting There

AIRLINES

Most of the major domestic carriers serve San Diego International Airport: **Alaska Airlines** (tel. toll free 800/426-0333), **American** (tel. toll free 800/433-7300), **Delta** (tel. 619/233-8040, or toll free 800/221-1212), **Northwest** (tel. toll free 800/225-2525), **Southwest** (tel. 619/232-1221), **Trans World Airlines** (tel. 619/295-7009), **United** (tel. 619/234-7171), and **USAir** (tel. 619/574-1234, or toll free 800/428-4322).

AIRPORTS

San Diego has one airport for commercial passenger service: **Lindbergh Field** (otherwise known as **San Diego International Airport)**, just west of the San Diego Freeway (I-5) at 3665 N. Harbor Dr. (tel. 619/231-7361). The airport is very convenient if you are staying west of I-5 (for example, the Pacific Beach area or La Jolla), if you're in the downtown area, or if you're situated not too far east of I-5 (near Hotel Circle, say). The taxi fare from somewhere as far as La Jolla is not unreasonable. To get to the airport going south on I-5, exit at Sassafras, continue south to Laurel, turn west on Laurel to Harbor Drive (stay in the right lane approaching Harbor Drive), and then turn north on Harbor Drive to the airport signs. To get to the airport going north on I-5, exit at Brant (Hawthorn), go north on Brant to Laurel, and west on Laurel as above. A number of the larger hotels have shuttle service to the airport.

TRAINS

Amtrak has service to and from Los Angeles, and from Los Angeles northward to Oakland, Seattle, and points in between. Amtrak also has daily service to Las Vegas, though there is a two-hour layover in Fullerton. The station in San Diego is at 1050 Kettner Blvd. (tel. toll free 800/872-7245), at the corner of Broadway.

BUSES

The **Greyhound/Trailways Bus System** serves most cities in California. In San Diego the main terminal is at 120 W. Broadway (tel. 619/239-9171).

---

2. Getting Around

Finding your way around San Diego requires only that you have some sort of map—almost any will do. Everything connects with everything else in a most sensible fashion. Then all that's required is a vehicle to transport you.

BUSES

Forget about the bus system. There's no question that the frequency of buses is satisfactory and the buses are neat and clean, but the time involved in getting from distant point A to point B (perhaps with a bag of golf clubs) may have you wondering whether you really wanted to spend your vacation time on a bus.

Consider the fact that the city of San Diego's area is approximately 70% as large as that of Los Angeles; and San Diego County's area is even larger than that of Los Angeles. If you're staying near Hotel Circle or downtown, the transport system will get you to Balboa Park, the zoo, Old Town, or Sea World in a reasonable amount of time, but generally the most convenient way to get around San Diego is by car. If you have no other way of getting around, pick up a map of the complete bus system downtown at the **Transit Store,** 449 Broadway at the corner of Fifth Avenue (tel. 619/234-1060). Maps for individual bus lines, indicating express and local stops, are also available there. The Transit Store is open Monday through Saturday from 8:30am to 5:30pm. Express bus fare is $1.25; local fare is $1. If you need detailed information and can't make the trip downtown, call **San Diego Transit** at 619/233-3004.

TROLLEY TOURS

But with or without a car, a great way to survey San Diego and Coronado (though not to the outer reaches of the county), and far and away the most fun (kids will love it), is on the **Old Town Trolley Tours of San Diego,** 4040 Twiggs St. (tel. 619/298-8687). The trackless trolley (a bus in disguise) looks like the old-time trolley, even to the red color. Though the total running time is 90 minutes, you can get off at any stop, then reboard another trolley for completion of the tour. The guide presents a fast-moving commentary that is entertaining and educational; areas covered are Old Town to downtown San Diego, Presidio Park to Balboa Park, and San Diego Bay to the Pacific. A schedule of stops and pickups can be had by calling the above number, writing the above address, or sending your request to P.O. Box 1237, Key West, FL 33041. Prices for the day, with as many on-and-offs as you choose, are $12 for adults, $10 for seniors on Mondays, $6 for youngsters 4 to 12 years, free for those under 4. The tours operate daily from 9am to dusk.

CAR RENTALS

Sights are so far apart in San Diego that you'll probably do best to find an unlimited-mileage arrangement, or at least one with sufficient free mileage to make your trip economical. On the freeways, those few "cents per mile" tend to mount rapidly into dollars.

As I pointed out in this discussion in Chapter I, my first words of advice are *plan ahead.* See the "Traveling Within California" section for other precautions to take.

Car rentals of specific-size vehicles, including vans, are usually easier to obtain from the big car–rental companies. Each of the companies below has an office at Lindbergh Field, as well as offices throughout Greater San Diego: **Avis** (tel. toll free 800/331-1212), **Budget** (tel. toll free 800/527-0700), and **Hertz** (tel. toll free 800/654-3131). However, one of the best buys I've found to date is **Alamo Rent A Car** (tel. toll free 800/327-9633). It has unlimited free mileage within the state and is just a stone's throw from the airport, at 3066 Kettner Blvd.; its shuttle service takes you from the baggage area at the airport to the office at Kettner Blvd.

---

3. San Diego Fast Facts

Although the city is by no means as difficult to negotiate as Los Angeles, San Diego presents its own set of confusions for the first-time—and repeat—visitor.

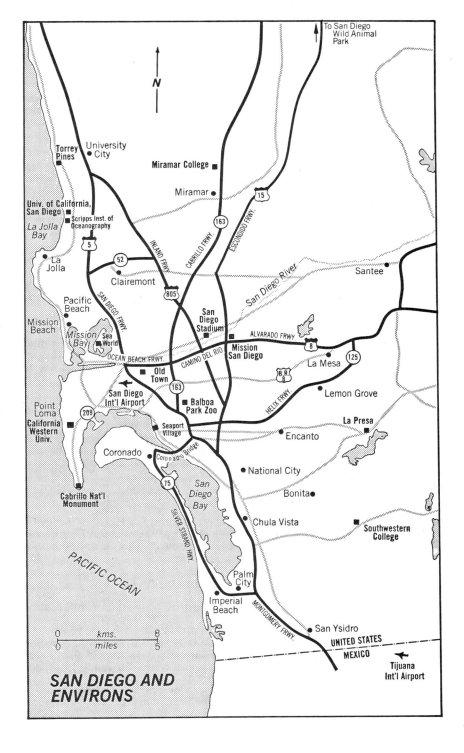

These alphabetically arranged entries are designed to help resolve some basic information needs.

AREA CODE: The area code for San Diego is **619,** as it also is for Palm Springs.

BABY-SITTERS: If you're staying at one of the larger hotels, the concierge can usually recommend organizations to call. Be sure to check on the hourly cost (which may vary depending on the day of the week and time of day), as well as on any additional expenses such as transportation and meals for the sitter.

BANKS: Banks are generally open Monday through Friday from 10am to 3pm, often from 9am to 4pm, and sometimes on Saturday. However, if you need to cash a check, your hotel may be your best resource, depending on the amount involved.

CHARGE CARDS: As I've said before, not all restaurants, stores, or shops in California accept all major credit cards, and some accept none. I suggest that you turn to Chapter I for details on this topic in the "California Fast Facts" section.

CLIMATE: A visit to San Diego warrants mostly summer-weight clothing from May through November, with a sweater or jacket for the occasional cool day, cool evenings, or supercool restaurant. December through April temperatures are quite a bit cooler—usually from the mid-50s to the mid-60s, and require somewhat warmer clothing. A raincoat, or at least an umbrella, can also be useful during these months.

CRIME: San Diego has a considerable influx of tourists from within the U.S. and abroad and, as with any such city, crime is always a problem. My best advice is simply to use discretion and common sense. Take traveler's checks, don't leave your luggage in plain sight in the car, and use the hotel safe for valuables. It would be wise to review the "Crime" section of "California Fast Facts" in Chapter I for more safety tips.

CURRENCY EXCHANGE: Foreign-currency exchange services are provided by **Deak International,** 177 Horton Plaza (tel. 619/235-0900).

DENTISTS: Hotels usually have a list of dentists, should you need one. For referrals, contact the **San Diego County Dental Society** (tel. 619/484-4795).

DOCTORS: Here, again, hotels usually have a list of doctors on call. For referrals, call the **San Diego County Medical Society** (tel. 619/565-8161).

DRIVING: I refer you to this heading under "California Fast Facts" in Chapter I. I might add that for some inexplicable reason, the freeway signs in San Diego, more often than in Los Angeles or San Francisco, indicate direction by the name of a town rather than the compass direction.

EARTHQUAKES: Again, see "California Fast Facts" in Chapter I.

EMERGENCIES: For police, fire, highway patrol, or life-threatening medical emergencies, dial **911.**

EVENTS AND FESTIVALS: The San Diego International Visitors Information Center, 11 Horton Plaza (First Avenue at F Street), San Diego, CA 92101 (tel. 619/236-1212), can supply you with a list of annual events. You can stop by (open daily from 8:30am to 5pm except holidays) or send the request, enclosing a self-addressed, stamped ($1 postage) business-size envelope. An alternative for information on what's going on in a given week is the Sunday edition of the *San Diego Union,* or on Thursday, the free weekly *Reader,* which covers virtually everything happening in the county, in detail. The *Reader* is rather spottily distributed to delis, liquor stores, and convenience stores, but it's worth searching out.

FOOD: San Diego has a good, though limited, selection of restaurants; with rare exceptions, however, few compare with the best of those in Los Angeles or San Francisco at any price level. Nevertheless, I've tried to select some places well worth a visit in all price categories.

Not all restaurants are open daily. If you're planning an evening at one not listed here, call first and ask if reservations are necessary. Check to see if they take plastic; not all of the restaurants do, and not all take every major credit card.

HOLIDAYS: Super Bowl dates or the week of the America's Cup races are definitely not the times to try for reservations on short notice. If you have specific vacation dates in mind, send for the annual list of events in town at that time or call the International Visitors Information Center—see the "Events and Festivals" entry, above.

HOSPITALS: To quickly locate a hospital near you for general and emergency care, turn to the "Community Access" pages at the front of the Pacific Bell *Yellow Pages.*

INFORMATION: The excellent **San Diego Convention and Visitors Bureau** and the **International Visitors Information Center,** 11 Horton Plaza, at First Avenue and F Street (tel. 619/236-1212), are open daily from 8:30am to 5pm. It offers visitors to San Diego a one-stop service center (staffed by multilingual attendants) for information on hotels (they'll even make reservations without charge), entertainment and sightseeing, fishing licenses, sporting activities, and boating permits, as well as information about excursions to Mexico. For a recorded message about local events, call 619/239-9696.

A similar helpful service is offered by the **Visitor Information Center,** 2688 E. Mission Bay Dr. (tel. 619/276-8200), off I-5 at the end of the Claremont–East Mission Bay Drive off-ramp. They're open Monday through Saturday from 9am to 6pm (sometimes 5:30pm), on Sunday to 4:30pm.

LIQUOR LAWS: Liquor and grocery stores can sell packaged alcoholic beverages between 6am and 2am. Most restaurants, nightclubs, and bars are licensed to serve alcoholic beverages during the same hours. The legal age for purchase and consumption is 21, and proof of age is required. In California some liquor stores accept credit cards for the purchase of package liquor; however, most have a minimum dollar amount for charging.

NEWSPAPERS: The *San Diego Union* (the morning paper) and the *San Diego Tribune* both have countywide distribution; however, the free weekly *Reader,* distributed each Thursday, gives comprehensive coverage on all special events (and some less than special) in greater detail. As noted in the "Events and Festivals" entry, distribution of the *Reader* is rather erratic; the paper is found primarily in delis, stationery stores, liquor stores, and convenience stores. It's definitely worth seeking out.

RELIGIOUS SERVICES: Places of worship are never in short supply in California, whatever the denomination. Should you be seeking out a house of worship, your hotel desk person or bell captain can usually direct you to the nearest church of almost any denomination. If not, the Pacific Bell *Yellow Pages* can usually provide the location and, frequently, the times of the services.

SPORTS (SPECTATOR): San Diego has a major-league baseball team, the **San Diego Padres** (tel. 619/280-4636); an NFL football team, the **San Diego Charg-**

ers (tel. 619/280-2111); and a professional soccer team, the **San Diego Sockers** (tel. 619/224-4625). The Padres and the Chargers play at Jack Murphy Stadium, 9449 Friars Rd., off Stadium Way and I-8; the Sockers play at the Sports Arena, 3500 Sports Arena Blvd., west of I-5.

For watching the sport of kings, there's the **Del Mar Race Track** (tel. 619/755-1141), at the Del Mar Fairgrounds west of I-5. The Del Mar racing season is for 60 days during the months of August and September.

STORE HOURS: Stores are usually open Monday through Saturday from 10am to 6pm. On Thursday they often stay open to 9pm; they're generally closed on Sunday.

TAXES: California state sales tax is 7¼%.

USEFUL TELEPHONE NUMBERS: You can obtain **weather information** for San Diego at 619/289-1212, **beach weather and surf reports** at 619/225-9492, the **time** at 619/853-1212, and information on **local highway conditions** at 619/293-3484. For **nonemergency police service,** call 619/531-2000. Dial 411 for **directory assistance** and 800/555-1212 to obtain telephone numbers of establishments that have **toll-free numbers.**

---

4. Hotels

The hotel setup in San Diego subdivides into several areas where hotels are clustered. They are as follows:

DOWNTOWN

The **Westgate,** 1055 Second Ave. (between Broadway and C Street), San Diego, CA 92101 (tel. 619/238-1818, or toll free 800/221-3802), is a luxury hostelry of the first order. The tone is obvious as soon as you set foot in the posh lobby, hung with Aubusson and Beauvais tapestries and furnished in priceless antiques. The pattern of the parquet floors is copied from that at Versailles, and the carpets are Kermin Oriental. Among the works of art, *The Prodigal Son* by Velázquez is valued at half a million dollars.

Each of the 225 spacious guest rooms is uniquely furnished, although the basic decor combines elements of the Louis XV, Louis XVI, Georgian, and English Regency periods. All rooms have two-line speaker phones, remote-control color TVs, minibars, private dressing areas, bathrobes, hairdryers, and even scales in the baths. The color TVs are discreetly hidden in elegant cabinets.

Le Fontaineblaeu, the Westgate's award-winning restaurant, has been called "the most elegant dining room built in this century." It should come as no surprise that the cuisine is Continental; the Westgate Dining Room (off the lobby), on the other hand, serves traditional American fare. The Fontainebleau is open weekdays for lunch from 11:45am to 2pm, for dinner from 6:30 to 10pm on Friday and Saturday from 6pm); dinner entrees run about $22 to $35. The Westgate Dining Room is open nightly for dinner from 6 to 11pm. Across from the Westgate Dining Room, the intimate Plaza Lounge is also open daily; it's a local gathering spot for many of San Diego's most talented performers.

Rates are $128 to $148 for singles, $138 to $158 for doubles. Suites range from $270 to $595.

HOTEL CIRCLE

Mission Valley is the most centrally located resort area in San Diego. Around its Hotel Circle are many restaurants, motels, hotels, and the largest shopping complex in the country, Fashion Valley Center. Recommended in Hotel Circle are:

Fabulous Inn, 2485 Hotel Circle Place, San Diego, CA 92108 (tel. 619/291-

7700, or toll free 800/824-0950, 800/647-1903 in California), is a moderately priced, modern four-story, 178-room complex at the extreme western end of the Hotel Circle. All rooms are large and attractively furnished. They have balconies, king- or queen-size beds, color TVs, air conditioning, baths with dressing areas, and direct-dial phones; some have refrigerators. A heated outdoor swimming pool and Jacuzzi are on the premises, and a restaurant adjoins. There are good tennis facilities just across the street, as well as an 11-hole golf course (that's what I said, 11 holes), and another restaurant.

The Fabulous Inn is almost at the intersection of two major freeways—I-8 and I-5—so you can reach almost any area of San Diego within a reasonable amount of time.

Singles are $55 to $72; doubles, $65 to $85.

Town & Country, 500 Hotel Circle North, San Diego, CA 92108 (tel. 619/291-7131, or toll free 800/854-2608, 800/542-6082 in California), with over 1,000 rooms one of the largest hotels in San Diego, is a "city within a city." There is seemingly every facility you could want or imagine—even a gas station. There are shops, car-rental, airline, and tour information desks, shuttle service to the airport and shopping, four swimming pools (one Olympic size), a therapy pool, sauna, four restaurants, two coffee shops, a disco, and two nightclubs. In addition, guests can use the Atlas Health Club across the street for a nominal fee. Club facilities include racquetball and tennis courts, weight and aerobics rooms, massage therapists, an outdoor lap pool, and an indoor whirlpool spa.

When it comes to good food and drink, the Town & Country offers a world of variety with its four restaurants, plus the Lanai Coffee Shop and Sunshine Deli. The Gourmet Room, featuring mouthwatering prime rib; Bonacci's, offering zesty Italian dishes; Kelly's Steak House, serving guess what; and Café Potpourri—all make dining a pleasure at Town & Country. Entertainment ranges from the unbounded energy of Crystal T's Live to the simplicity of the piano bar at Kelly's and the live bands and good-hearted imbibing in the Abilene Country Saloon and Le Pavillon Lounge.

Needless to say, the rooms are pleasantly decorated and have every amenity as well, including color TVs and weekday newspaper delivery.

Singles are $77 to $120, doubles and twins are $97 to $145, and parlor suites go for $195 to $385.

Under the same ownership is the 450-room **Hanalei Hotel,** 2270 Hotel Circle, San Diego, CA 92108 (tel. 619/297-1101, or toll free 800/854-2608). The hotel has an eight-story open atrium with waterfalls and ponds; glass elevators give you a splendid view on the way up to the 450 rooms. There's dining in the Polynesian Islands Dining Room, the Peacock, and the Oyster Bar. You can work out in the pool, relax in the Jacuzzi, or play golf or tennis. Guests can also use the Atlas Health Club for a nominal fee.

Single rooms are $83 to $120; doubles and twins, $93 to $130.

There's a convenient **Motel 6** at 2424 Hotel Circle North, San Diego, CA 92108 (tel. 619/296-1612). As with all Motel 6 locations, rooms are efficient, clean, and comfortable, and there's a small pool on the premises. Rooms have free television, air conditioning, and now phones—no charge for local calls.

The room rate is $34 for one person, $6 for each additional adult.

MISSION BAY

The **Bahia Resort Hotel,** 998 W. Mission Bay Dr., San Diego, CA 92109 (tel. 619/488-0551, or toll free 800/288-0770, 800/233-8172 in Canada), has a lovely situation on a peninsula surrounded by the waters of Mission Bay, with marine views in every direction. Sailboats and paddleboats are rentable at the Bahia dock, and there's an Olympic-size swimming pool, a therapy bath, and two tennis courts. One other unique offering of the Bahia is a pond containing four resident seals.

The rooms are pleasant and airy, furnished in modern motif. Each has a picture window (most with water views), color TV, direct-dial phone, and tub/shower bath with dressing area. About half the rooms have kitchens and balconies or patios.

Off the cozy fireplace lobby is a coffee shop serving breakfast, lunch, and dinner. The world's oldest Mercedes, built in 1902, sets the theme in the Continental dining room and Club Mercedes. Virtually a Mercedes museum, the restaurant features Mercedes-logo carpeting, plus Mercedes posters and drawings of antique models on the walls. Adjacent is the Club Mercedes, which offers live entertainment and the Comedy Isle, offering comedy acts Tuesday through Saturday.

Rates for one or two people during the summer are $100 to $225, single or double. They're less the rest of the year.

The **Catamaran**, 3999 Mission Blvd., San Diego, CA 92109 (tel. 619/488-1081, or toll free 800/288-6770, 800/233-8172 in Canada), is beautifully situated on Mission Bay, just a scenic, few-minute walk from the ocean. The hotel has 315 rooms, a new Atoll Restaurant, the Cannibal Lounge with live entertainment, and Moray's, a small piano bar. Rates are $130 to $185, single or double.

The **San Diego Princess**, a Princess Cruises resort (formerly Vacation Village), 1404 West Vacation Rd., San Diego, CA 92109 (tel. 619/274-4630, or toll free 800/344-2626), offers 449 modern rooms situated on 43 lushly landscaped tropical acres, with freshwater lagoons spanned by graceful bridges. Each of the modern rooms is equipped with every up-to-date amenity, plus a patio or lanai, dressing area, and in-room coffee maker.

Facilities include five swimming pools, eight tennis courts, a sailboat marina, a bicycle rental outlet, three restaurants—the Dockside Broiler (very good for steaks and seafood), the Pacific Princess (seafood specialties), and the Village Café (coffee shop)—a cocktail lounge, and a mile of white-sand beach.

Rates are $110 to $295 for singles, $125 to $395 for doubles.

A sternwheeler called the *Bahia Belle* cruises the bay, running hourly in summer (less often in winter) and stopping at the Bahia, the Catamaran, and the San Diego Princess. At night there's dancing to live music and cocktails aboard the *Belle;* fare is $7 per adult, $5 for children under 12 (tel. 619/488-0551).

HARBOR ISLAND AND SHELTER ISLAND

These two artificial peninsulas—just minutes from the airport and downtown —are a hub of San Diego hotel, nightlife, and restaurant activity.

The former contains the **Sheraton on Harbor Island** (tel. toll free 800/325-3535), actually a complex of two hotels; the **Sheraton Harbor Island East**, 1380 Harbor Island Dr., San Diego, CA 92113 (tel. 619/291-2900); and the **Sheraton Grand on Harbor Island**, 1590 Harbor Island Dr., San Diego, CA 92101 (tel. 619/291-6400). The properties boast a total of 1,100 handsomely furnished rooms, complete with color TVs, direct-dial phones, individual air conditioning, and one king-size bed or two double beds. All rooms have balconies and most have marine views.

The facilities at the Sheraton on Harbor Island are extensive: health club, five pools (two for kids), saunas, whirlpools, four night-lit tennis courts, jogging course, boat and bike rental, shops, and laundromat. There are a variety of dining choices too: Sheppard's (at the East), a gourmet restaurant; Spencers (at the Sheraton Grand), specializing in Black Angus beef; and the Café del Sol (in the East), a coffee shop. There's also Reflections (in the East), an elegant entertainment lounge.

Rooms at the Sheraton Grand on Harbor Island cost $130 to $175 for a single, $150 to $195 for a double. At the Sheraton Harbor Island East, singles are $120 to $165; doubles, $140 to $185.

A favorite accommodation, not just on Shelter Island but in all of San Diego, is **Humphrey's Half Moon Inn**, 2303 Shelter Island Dr., San Diego, CA 92106 (tel. 619/224-3411, or toll free 800/542-7400). It offers 183 rooms, all with water views and set amid lush tropical plantings. Not only are the views lovely, but the interior of each room is very attractive, with beamed pine ceilings (especially nice on upper floors where ceilings are sloped), bamboo and rattan furnishings, and blue seashell–motif bedspreads. Amenities include double sinks and makeup lights in the bath, direct-dial phones, color TVs, etc. Also included are free in-room coffee, 24-hour switchboard, complimentary movie channel, and free transportation to the airport or the Amtrak station. As for facilities, there are heated pools for adults and children, a Jacuzzi, table tennis, bicycles, and room for lawn games.

The adjacent restaurant, Humphrey's, has a very delightful garden decor and large windows providing views of the boat-filled marina. You can dine outdoors under white umbrellaed tables or inside where there's an abundance of plants and potted palms. Seafood is the specialty here. Humphrey's is also the setting for nightly entertainment, and a pianist plays during happy hour.

From April to October the hotel helps sponsor great jazz concerts with top-name performers in the park by the bay.

Rates are $95 to $115 for a single, $115 to $135 for a double. Suites are $140 and up. Children under 16 in a room with their parents are free.

CORONADO

The grande dame of San Diego's resort hotels, the **Hotel del Coronado,** 1500 Orange Ave., San Diego, CA 92118 (tel. 619/522-8000), opened its doors in 1888 and was designated a national historic landmark in 1977. The last of the extravagantly conceived seaside hotels, it is a monument to Victorian grandeur with its tall cupolas, turrets, and gingerbread trim. The register over the years has listed thousands of celebrity guests—12 U.S. presidents, and movie stars like Tony Curtis, Jack Lemmon, Robert Wagner, and Stefanie Powers are just a few. Former Secretary of the Interior Stewart Udall was moved to write a poem about the beauty of the early morning in Coronado during his visit, and rumor has it that Edward, Prince of Wales, met Wallis Simpson here.

The hotel's facilities include two swimming pools, six lighted championship tennis courts, a white-sand beach, and a health spa for men and women. The hotel also overlooks a championship 18-hole golf course and boat rental are nearby. There are four areas for dining and cocktails, including the majestic Crown/Coronet Rooms, magnificently unchanged since the turn of the century; the Prince of Wales, for gourmet dining; the Del Deli; and the Ocean Terrace Restaurant and Lounge.

And accommodations are fittingly exquisite, with custom-made furnishings and all conveniences.

Rates range from $145 for street-side standard rooms (single or double) and go up to between $275 and $300 for a deluxe lanai double with oceanfront or bay view (many options in between). Suites are $300 to $495. To stay here is a unique and memorable pleasure; if it's not in your budget, at least come by for a meal and stroll around the grounds.

---

5. Restaurants

What had been rated as the best restaurant in San Diego, Gustaf Anders, has left for Santa Ana in Orange County and it is missed. Nonetheless, there remains a large gathering of restaurants catering to all sorts of tastes and offering menus to match—gourmet French, ribs, dim sum, a great variety of seafood, more seafood, Mexican style ("gringo" and otherwise), Japanese (with and without sushi), hamburgers, etc.

In the section below are some favorite places chosen from the several hundred restaurants in San Diego (and more arriving each day).

Lubach's, 2101 N. Harbor Dr., at the corner of Hawthorn Street (tel. 619/232-5129), located on the Embarcadero, is an award-winning restaurant with a comfortably traditional decor. The wood-paneled walls are adorned with ship models, wagon-wheel chandeliers are suspended from the ceilings, the tablecloths create a sea of white linen, seating is in shiny red-leather banquettes, and a vase containing one or two rosebuds graces every table. A blazing fire in a brick fireplace adds a homey touch. The food is delicious—a combination of culinary art and the use of fresh fish and produce. A specialty is poached salmon in hollandaise sauce. Nonseafood entrees include veal chop sautéed with mushrooms and roast duck à l'orange. Dinner entrees cost $15 to $27.50. There's a selection of imported and California wines to complement your meal. For dessert you might sample one of the French pastries from the cart. Luncheon salads and sandwiches are $8 to $14.

Open for lunch weekdays from 11:30am to 4pm, for dinner Monday through Saturday from 4pm to midnight. Jackets are required for men at dinner. There is free valet parking. Reservations are advised.

Another Embarcadero seafood eatery of renown is the Ghio and Weber families' **Anthony's Star of the Sea Room,** 1360 Harbor Dr., at Ash Street (tel. 619/232-7408), next to the three-masted *Star of India*. Dramatically set overlooking the San Diego harbor, Anthony's interior is handsomely decorated, elegant, and comfortable. Specialties include the cioppino à la Catherine (Catherine is Anthony Ghio's mother) and oven-baked sole stuffed with lobster, shrimp, and crab. Dinner entrees cost $16 to $29.

It's open daily for dinner from 5:30 to 10:30pm. Reservations essential.

Adjoining is **Anthony's Fish Grotto** (tel. 619/232-5103), also run by the Ghio and Weber families. The decor is a shade less elegant, although you still have the panoramic harbor view, and prices are lower. Featured here are as many fish delicacies as the Oyster Bar in New York City offers. Reservations are not accepted—you just arrive. To continue the analogy, it's a bit like waiting for a train during rush hour in the home of the Oyster Bar, Grand Central Station, but don't let that discourage you—things move right along here. One of several house specialties is shellfish casserole à la Catherine (made with lobster meat, crab legs, shrimp, and scallops). But I suggest that if sand dabs are on the menu that day, order them; I've never tasted a more delectable, light, elegant fish. Most entrees are priced from $8 to $14 and the portions are large.

Hours are 11:30am to 8:30pm daily.

Across the street is **Anthony's Harborside** (tel. 619/232-6358). It also features seafood, and at night puts out a terrific salad bar. It's open for lunch weekdays from 11:30am to 4:30pm, for dinner nightly from 4:30 to 10:30pm. Reservations are essential.

Tom Ham's Lighthouse, 2150 Harbor Island Dr., Harbor Island (tel. 619/291-9110), is built at the west end of Harbor Island beneath a lighthouse (the official Coast Guard no. 9 beacon). You get not only good meals here, but can enjoy a museum as well. A collection of marine artifacts has been gathered from around the world, forming a nostalgic reminder of San Diego in the early 1800s. Featured on the dinner menu are such Lighthouse specialties as seafood Newburg, scampi, and scallops tomatillo. Dinner entrees range from $14 to $30. A buffet lunch includes an elaborate salad bar and three hot entrees, in addition to sandwiches, salads, and hot specialties ($7 to $14). But be sure to save room for dessert; the apple pie is scrumptious.

Tom Ham's Lighthouse is open for lunch weekdays from 11:15am to 3:30pm; a Sunday buffet brunch ($10) is served from 10am to 2pm.

Café Del Rey Moro is at 1549 El Prado in Balboa Park (tel. 619/234-8511). It would be a shame if you got lost, so let me point out that El Prado is the attractive extension of Laurel Street once it passes east of Sixth Avenue and enters Balboa Park. (Drive slowly and enjoy the sights.)

A San Diego landmark since 1914, when it was the Foreign Arts Building during the Panama California Exposition, Café Del Rey Moro is located in the historic House of Hospitality near the San Diego Museum of Art and close to the Old Globe Theatre. Set off from a central courtyard with all the trappings of a Spanish hacienda —central fountain, much greenery, small palms, wrought-iron benches—it's a perfect place to sit and relax on a warm summer day. The café rests serenely among gardens surrounded by high-flying eucalyptus and palm trees. You can dine outside on a brick terrace, with its white pillars, vine-covered trellises, and yellow-and-white striped awnings, overlooking a lower patio with a small fountain and lush gardens. Inside, the red-tile floors, the wall of glass doors, and the greenery hanging from a latticework ceiling give one the sense of still being outside on the terrace.

The fare is generally light—fresh fish and seafood simply prepared with a variety of local vegetables, herbs, delicate sauces, and a touch of Mexico's spices. The hearty bouillabaisse with fresh fish, king crab, shrimp, and clams simmered in a lovely fish stock is a superb meal. The brandy scallops are first-rate, served with oven-fresh sourdough bread for dipping. Among the meat dishes, one of my favorites is the loin of pork adobo—tender filets of pork loin marinated in a sauce of tomatoes, onion, garlic, and spices, then slowly braised. The selection of luncheon entrees is wide-ranging and sufficient to satisfy any appetite; there are great sandwiches, salads, omelets, soups mother never knew how to make, munchies, enchiladas, burritos, fajitas, etc. Dinners include salad, southwestern corn pudding, potatoes or rice pilaf, and sourdough bread. Lunches range from $5 to $7.25; dinners, from $8 to $15.

Topping off the menu is a luscious list of desserts and exotic coffees. Try the irresistible raspberry-macaroon torte, or if you feel stuffed or righteous, polish off your meal with one of the restaurant's good coffees. Margaritas are always available, as is sangría; Café Del Rey Moro has a well-stocked bar. They also offer a remarkably good selection of nonalcoholic beverages.

Luncheon is served daily from 11am to 4pm; dinner, Tuesday through Sunday from 5 to 8pm. Sunday champagne brunch is 10am to 3pm.

In Old Town, at 2836 Juan St., **La Piñata** (tel. 619/297-1631) is a cozy, friendly restaurant with a happy collection of the brightly colored Mexican toys that give it its name (donkeys, parrots, toros, rocket ships, elephants) hanging from the reed ceiling. It's just a bit out of the main stream of people traffic, which makes it a pleasant alternative to the larger, somewhat noisy tourist emporiums. And it has a small outdoor patio (with heaters, yet) where you can dine even on a coolish day and share your cheese quesadilla with the sparrows.

La Piñata is understandably popular among locals: It's attractive, the food is always good, prices are moderate, and service is pleasant and prompt. The restaurant prepares familiar dishes tastefully, be it fajitas, enchiladas, burritos, fajitadillas, tacos, tostados, or any combinations thereof. There's even a Mexican pizza—a flour tortilla covered with beans, beef, green chiles, tomatoes, onions, cheddar, guacamole, sour cream, and chopped olives. Caldo de albondigas con arroz y tortillas is a great, hearty homemade soup, cooked to order, and any one of the salads is a substantial accompaniment to an entree. For those who prefer very late breakfasts (after 11am), La Piñata has huevos rancheros, huevos with chorizo, and huevos with asada (charbroiled strips of sirloin).

Lunch or dinner at La Piñata costs about $3 to $8.50. A compliments-of-the-house cheese quesadilla always precedes your order. Don't overlook the delicious margaritas, offered in small, medium, or large (the large is about the size of a small bird bath). There's also a good selection of beer. If you decide to nosh on some of the marinated vegetables at your table, be forewarned—they're tonsil scorchers, especially those innocent-looking carrot slices.

La Piñata is open weekdays from 11am to 9pm, weekends to 9:30 or 10pm. *Note:* You can buy a piñata should you take a fancy to one.

The **Cotton Patch**, 2720 Midway Dr., near Rosecrans (tel. 223-7179), is my kind of place—a great down-to-earth restaurant that serves great down-to-earth food at reasonable prices. It's a bit out of the usual tourist route (a short distance east of I-5), but well worth the minor side trip.

Walk through an outdoor patio with a fireplace and you'll see a rustic restaurant with a log cabin–type interior: post-and-beam construction and deer heads competing for wall space with oil paintings and antique cooking and farming tools.

But to get down to basics: Everything comes in generous portions at the Cotton Patch—the drinks, the food, the quality, and the hospitality. When you sit down for dinner, you're promptly brought a pot of deliciously marinated red kidney beans (you could make a meal of these alone). As you peruse the menu, you're bound to notice that the specialty of the house is "meat," specifically a generous portion of prime rib of beef au jus, done to perfection and served with a creamy horseradish sauce that can bring tears to your eyes. But there are also the rack of lamb, porterhouse steak, New York steak, barbecued spareribs, southern fried chicken, plus veal and shrimp done in several delectable ways. Dinner entrees are served with soup or salad, your choice of potatoes (I challenge you to eat your way through the huge portion of fries), and some absolutely delicious hot cornbread. For dessert, try the pecan pie, cheesecake, or the ultrarich Mississippi mud pie.

The luncheon menu changes daily and is more limited, but still offers steaks reasonably priced. Prime rib is not served midday. Lunch costs $5.75 to $9. Dinner entrees range from $8 to $20, the top of the line being steak and Alaskan king crab; lobster is priced according to the market.

The Cotton Patch is open weekdays for lunch from 11am to 1pm, nightly for dinner from 4pm to midnight. If the parking lot in front is jammed when you arrive, don't despair; there's space in back—enter via the lane between the Cotton Patch and the adjacent fire-engine-red Boll Weevil.

Sandtrap Restaurant and Lounge, 2702 N. Mission Bay Dr. (tel. 619/274-3314), at Mission Bay Golf Course, south of Grand Street (turn right, and right again, just before the freeway entrance south). Just a mile north of the tourist information center on Mission Bay Drive lies one of San Diego's best-kept secrets for breakfast, the Sandtrap. It's a happy restaurant: It has a small counter, as well as a large publike dining room that overlooks a duck pond (with its waterfall) and the course's putting green. All that plus the lovely small terrace finished with umbrella-shaded tables and chairs, nicely suited to al fresco relaxing with refreshments from the restaurant.

The prices are right, the food's terrific, and the service is cheerful—especially hard to find at 7am. The three-egg omelets are delicious in whatever form you choose. For a real heart-warmer, there's a memorable Ortega-chile-and-cheese omelet. And that's just the beginning. There's always a big breakfast special, usually accompanied by cottage fries or fresh fruit, for a modest $4.50.

For breakfast, lunch, or dinner, the quantities served require a hearty appetite—even the salads are a full meal. For lunch, try one of the delicious daily specials or the sea legs suprême salad ($5 to $6.25). Two of the most popular lunchtime sandwiches at the Sandtrap are the 6-ounce sirloin steak at $5.75 and the half-pound hamburger, done exactly as ordered, for $4.25, both with fries and coleslaw or fruit. Homemade soups are a specialty of the house and with rolls and butter, a bargain at $2.75. Dinners range from $7.25 to $13 (the highest price is for the pepper steak or prime rib). There's also fresh fish daily for lunch and dinner. With your entree there's a choice of soup or salad. The dinner special changes daily. Monday through Thursday, it may be barbecued short ribs, carne asada, corned beef and cabbage, or old-fashioned pot roast (each $8.25). Weekends, it's prime rib for $10.25. The dinner specials are $1 less for early birds who dine between 4 and 6pm. You can't beat the quality, price, and the service. There's a full bar, and color TV to boot, and entertainment on Friday and Saturday nights.

The restaurant is open Sunday through Thursday, from 7am to 9pm, on Friday and Saturday to 10pm. If you want to try the Mission Bay 18-hole Executive Golf Course after breakfast or lunch, bring your clubs (or you can rent them in the pro shop).

6. Sights

In addition to the beach, a wealth of tourist attractions await the visitor to San Diego. We'll begin at the edge of downtown, at 1,400-acre—

BALBOA PARK

One of the nation's largest municipal parks, this one houses the San Diego Zoo and eight museums, including the Reuben H. Fleet Space Theater (about which more below). Inside the **California Building,** with its 100-bell carillon tower, is the **Museum of Man,** 1350 El Prado (tel. 619/239-2001), tracing the natural and cultural history of man; emphasis is on the native cultures of the Americas. Admission is $3 for adults, $1 for those 13 to 18, 25¢ for ages 6 to 12. It's open daily from 10am to 4:30pm.

The **International Aerospace Hall of Fame and San Diego Aerospace Museum,** 2001 Pan American Plaza (tel. 619/232-8322), is the home of the history of the great achievers of aviation and aerospace, and of a superb collection of historical aircraft and aviation and aerospace artifacts, including art, models, military accoutrements, dioramas, and filmstrip displays. The heroes honored range from the early experimenters to the astronauts, and the planes, from the early gliders to spacecraft. Admission is $4 for adults and $1 for children 6 to 17. Open daily from 10am to 4pm.

The **San Diego Natural History Museum,** 1788 El Prado, at the east end (tel. 619/232-3821), has a number of fascinating exhibits on desert and shore environments, endangered species, gems, and dinosaurs, plus a Discovery Lab where you can even touch a snake (while it's held by a museum worker). You can learn as much about the desert environment as you wish from the lifelike exhibits, and on a video screen that displays pictures of animals and provides information on animals of your choice. As part of the endangered-species exhibit, the museum has wildlife products and skins seized by authorities (you can even touch a tiger skin), along with exhibits that show wildlife in peril due to commercial exploitation and loss of habitat. Dinosaur and whale skeletons are on permanent display, including the only dinosaur ever excavated in San Diego County. (Dinosaurs may have vanished because the climate became less receptive to them, as it may become for us in the future.) And if you find earthquakes exciting, the museum also has a working, moving seismograph. The Sefton Hall of Shore Ecology displays an amazing collection of shells and a videodisc replica of the shore. There is also a gem and mineral exhibit that includes multicolored tourmaline, blue topaz, and orange garnets, all unearthed locally. Admission is $4.50 for adults and $1 for those 6 to 18; it's free for kids 5 and under. The museum is open daily from 10am to 4:30pm.

The **San Diego Museum of Art,** 1450 El Prado (tel. 619/232-7931), contains an impressive collection of painting and sculpture, as well as old masters; it also offers noteworthy traveling exhibits. Admission is $5 for adults; $4 for seniors, military, and students with ID; $2 for children 6 to 12; under 6, it's free. Admission is free the first Tuesday of each month. It's open Tuesday through Sunday from 10am to 4:30pm. Outside the gallery are a café and a small but beautifully designed sculpture garden, including works by Henry Moore and Jacques Lipchitz. Free docent tours are conducted Tuesday through Thursday at 10 and 11am, and Tuesday through Sunday at 1 and 2pm.

The **Timken Gallery** is right next to the San Diego Museum of Art, along the north side of El Prado (tel. 619/239-5548). The Timken is a private gallery that does not charge admission to see many of its masterful beauties. It houses works of many old masters, such as Boucher, Rembrandt, and Brueghel. The gallery also exhibits a rare collection of Russian icons and 19th-century American paintings. Admission is free. Open Tuesday through Saturday from 10am to 4:30pm, on Sunday from 1:30 to 4:30pm. The gallery is closed during September.

The **Hall of Champions,** 1649 El Prado in the Casa de Balboa (tel. 619/234-2544), honors San Diego athletes who have achieved national or world recognition in sports, among them Bill Walton and Maureen "Little Mo" Connolly. The theater runs sports films throughout the day. Admission is $3 for adults; $2 for seniors, students, and military with ID; 50¢ for children 6 to 17; under 6, free. Hours are 10am to 4:30pm Monday through Saturday and noon to 5pm on Sunday.

The **Reuben H. Fleet Space Theater,** located in Balboa Park two blocks from the zoo and just across from the Natural History Museum, is the largest theater/planetarium in the United States, and the first in the world to have a tilted hemisphere screen. It uses the most modern techniques, sophisticated effects, and equipment to give simulated journeys an incredible feeling of reality. In addition to space-tripping, the giant dome is the setting for thrilling travelogues and voyages under the sea and inside a volcano.

Several other such films have included *To The Limit,* and, at the Laserium, *Laserock* and *Lites Out Laserium.* (Children under 5 are not permitted in the laser shows.) One historic film shown here was *Hail Columbia!,* which traced the trip of the space shuttle *Columbia* from hangar to launch, through space, and back to earth at Edwards Air Force Base in California. It includes shots of earth from space and of astronauts working in zero gravity. The launch coverage is spectacular, as the camera is able to follow the craft farther into space than the human eye can see.

Adjoining the theater is the 8,000-square-foot **Science Center,** with more than 50 visitor-participation exhibits that beep, blink, float, whisper, and reveal, to make science come alive for visitors of all ages. This is no "hands-off" museum. Here you can match wits with a computerized teaching machine, compete in electronic tic-tac-toe, create designs with sand pendulums, and examine the iris and pupil of your own eye.

Admission to the Science Center is $2 for adults, $1 for juniors aged 5 to 15. Admission to the Space Theater/Laserium is $6.50 for adults and $3.50 for juniors. Children under 5 are not admitted to the laser shows. The building is open daily from 9:30am to 9:30pm. For recorded information on shows and times, call 619/238-1168; otherwise, 619/238-1233.

One of the most exotic collections of wild animals in the world—over 3,200 of them—lives at the **San Diego Zoo** in Balboa Park. Set in a lavishly planted 100-acre tropical garden, the zoo is famous for its rare and exotic species: cuddly koalas, long-billed kiwis, wild Przewalski's horses from Mongolia, pygmy chimps, and Galápagos tortoises. Of course, the usual lions, elephants, giraffes, and tigers are present too, not to mention a great number of tropical birds. Most of the animals are housed in barless moated enclosures that resemble their natural habitats. A simulated rain forest home has been added for the Sumatran tigers, and a new aviary is scheduled for completion early in 1991.

A 40-minute guided bus tour provides an overview ($3 for adults, $2.50 for kids 3 to 15). Alternatively, you can get an aerial perspective via the **Skyfari Tramway,** which is included in admission.

The **Children's Zoo** is scaled to a youngster's viewpoint. There are a nursery with baby animals and a petting area where kids can cuddle up to sheep, goats, etc.

Admission to the zoo is $11 for adults; children 3 to 15 pay $4. From July to Labor Day the hours are 9am to 5pm. Between Labor Day and the end of June the zoo closes at 4pm. For further information, call 619/234-3153 or 231-1515.

WILD ANIMAL PARK

A sister institution of the San Diego Zoo, Wild Animal Park, 30 miles north of downtown San Diego on I-15 and Via Rancho Parkway, is an 1,800-acre wildlife preserve dedicated to the preservation of endangered species. Some 1,500 animals from Asia, Latin America, Australia, and Africa roam freely in natural habitats, and about 1,000 birds are housed in two immense aviaries and other areas of the park. You can lead your own safari along the 1¼-mile **Kilimanjaro Hiking Trail,** which offers many good spots for photographing animals; or explore a jungle biome (a natural habitat complete with tropical plants) in **Tropical Asia.** Both of these attractions are in **Nairobi Village,** a 17-acre complex of native huts, with a Gorilla Grotto, waterfowl lagoon, petting area, gift shop, and animal shows. In addition, there's the 5-mile **Wgasa Bush Line Monorail Tour,** a "train" safari through sweeping savannas and veldts, with ample stops for viewing. There are also four amphitheaters where you can see animal shows, plus several restaurants, gift shops, and exotic botanical displays.

The Wild Animal Park is open daily from 9am to 6pm in summer, closing at various earlier hours (4 or 5pm) the rest of the year. An adult ticket package costs $15.50, $13.50 for seniors, and includes admission, shows, and the monorail tour; those aged 3 to 15 pay $8.50. Parking is $2. Call 619/480-0100 or 234-6541 for further information.

SEA WORLD

Mission Bay Park, north of downtown San Diego just west of I-5, is a multimillion-dollar aquatic playground with 4,600 acres of land and water area and facilities for every kind of water sport—sailing, boating, waterskiing, fishing, swimming, etc. But its main attraction is Sea World, 1720 S. Shores Rd. (tel. 619/222-6363, or 226-3901), a 135-acre marine zoological park and family entertainment center where the performers are dolphins, killer whales, otters, sea lions, even a performing walrus, and seals.

Six shows are presented continuously throughout the day, including a **killer whale show** featuring the Baby Shamu, born in 1988, and a 7,000-pound killer whale that does high jumps and back flips in the six-million-gallon aquarium at Shamu Stadium. Sea lions and otters star in the "Pirates of Pinniped"; high-flying dolphins and two species of small whales perform in "New Friends"; circus acrobats, singers, dancers, world-class skateboarders, and BMX bike riders do their thing in "City Streets."

Cap'n Kids World, a nautically themed playground, is for kids. Other exhibits range from a whale and dolphin petting pool (adults can participate) to one of the largest collections of waterfowl in the world. Rounding out the bill are shops, band performances, costumed characters (most are part of the Sea World show), rides, and a wide choice of eateries.

One price ($22 for adults, $18 for seniors, $16.50 for children 3 to 11, free for under-3s) admits you to all shows and exhibits. Sea World is open daily from 9am to dusk, with extended hours during summer and holiday periods, when there may be special entertainment, musical groups, or even a spectacular fireworks and laser display. Allow a full day (about eight hours) to see all the shows and exhibits; you'll enjoy it. Parking is free.

CABRILLO NATIONAL MONUMENT

Commemorating the discovery of the West Coast of the United States by European man in 1542 are a statue of Juan Rodríguez Cabrillo, an exhibit room, and audiovisual programs that tell his story, located in a park at the southern tip of Point Loma (take Calif. 209). Nearby is the restored **Old Point Loma Lighthouse.** From the tower, visitors have a sweeping vista of the ocean, bays, islands, mountains, valleys, and plains that comprise the area, and from mid-December to February it's a terrific vantage point for watching the migration of the gray whales (a tape-recorded message and audiovisual programs discuss the migrations). Also, stop at the visitor center (tel. 619/557-5450) on the premises to learn about Cabrillo whales, tidepools, and other aspects of the park. It's open daily from 9am to 5:15pm (to sunset in summer). Admission is $3 per private vehicle (if you have a senior 62 or over, there's no charge), or $1 per person in commercial vehicles.

MISSION SAN DIEGO DE ALCALA

While you're experiencing early California history, a visit to the first of Father Serra's missions, at 10818 San Diego Mission Rd. (tel. 619/281-8449), takes you back to 1769 with a museum of liturgical robes, books, and other relics. Open daily from 9am to 5pm. A $1 donation is requested.

OLD TOWN

The spirit of the founding of California is captured in the six-block area northwest of downtown San Diego called Old Town (reached from I-8 or I-5; take the Old Town Avenue exit off I-5 or the Taylor Street exit from I-8). Although Old Town was abandoned over a century ago for a more convenient business center near the bay, it has regained interest—this time as a state historic park. The park is bounded by Congress, Twiggs, Juan, and Wallace streets. Many of its buildings have been fully restored and are open to the public. In addition, there are shops, restaurants, art galleries, antiques and curio shops, and handcraft centers, including a complex called **Bazaar del Mundo,** on Juan Street, a modern version of a Mexican street market.

Among the historic buildings that have been reconstructed are the magnificent **Casa de Estudillo,** the **Machado/Stewart Adobe,** the *San Diego Union* newspaper office, the old one-room **Mason Street schoolhouse,** and the stables from which Alfred Seeley ran his San Diego–Los Angeles stagecoach line.

Just outside the boundary of the park is the "haunted" two-story **Whaley House,** once the focal point of high society.

There are two large parking areas at the entrance to the park, one near the **visitors information center,** 4002 Wallace St. (tel. 237-6770), open daily from 10am to 5pm. Here you can get maps and tour information. The State Historic Park offers free one-hour guided walking tours daily at 2pm.

Adjacent to Old Town is **Heritage Park,** where Victorian buildings built between 1850 and 1865 have been moved, restored, and preserved.

THE MARITIME MUSEUM

Located at 1492 N. Harbor Dr. (tel. 619/234-9153), this nautical museum consists of three restored historic vessels docked at the Embarcadero, downtown. They are the *Berkeley,* the first successful propeller-driven ferry on the Pacific coast, launched in 1898 (she participated in the evacuation of San Francisco following the great earthquake and fire of 1906); the *Medea,* a steam yacht built in Scotland in 1904 (she fought in both world wars); and the *Star of India,* the oldest square-rigged merchant vessel still afloat, launched in 1863.

You can purchase a boarding pass good for all three ships: $6 for adults, $5 for ages 13 to 17 and seniors, $1.50 for children 6 to 12. Open daily from 9am to 8pm, including a museum gift shop.

SEAPORT VILLAGE

One of San Diego's centers for shopping and dining is Seaport Village, 849 W. Harbor Dr., at Kettner Blvd. (tel. 619/235-4014). It is easily reached by following Harbor Drive south from the Maritime Museum. Seaport Village is connected to the new San Diego Convention Center by a waterfront boardwalk.

The 22-acre complex is beautifully landscaped, including an 8-acre public park, and has more than 50 shops. Galleries and boutiques sell handcrafted gifts, collectibles, and many imported items. Shops are open daily from 10am to 9pm. Two of my favorites are **Hug-A-Bear** (tel. 619/230-1362), with a selection of plush bears and woodland animals; and the **Seaport Kite Shop** (tel. 619/232-2268), with kites from around the world. I also enjoy the **Upstart Crow & Co.** (tel. 619/232-4855), a delightful combination bookstore and coffeehouse.

Adding to the charm of the area are the three plazas that re-create an eastern seaport village, Victorian San Francisco, and a traditional Mexican village.

A 10-acre expansion planned for 1992 will include even more retail shops, as well as a dozen new restaurant/bars for dining and late-night entertainment. An amphitheater area will feature special water events and other entertainment.

The restaurants in and near Seaport Village run the gamut from take-out stands to a Mexican bakery and more conventional facilities. The **Harbor House,** 831 W. Harbor Dr. (tel. 619/232-1141), offers good seafood with a pleasant view.

BOAT TRIPS

San Diego Harbor Excursions offers harbor cruises aboard sightseeing boats. One- and/or two-hour cruises depart daily from 1050 N. Harbor Dr., at the foot of Broadway. One-hour trips ($8.50) leave at 10 and 11:15am and 12:45 and 4:15pm; there is only one two-hour cruise ($12), at 2pm. Harbor Excursions also has a romantic dinner/dance harbor trip ($42) on Friday and Saturday aboard the sternwheeler *Monterey* from 7 to 9:30pm. For information, call 619/234-4111. On the other hand, if you'd just like a trip across the San Diego Bay to Coronado, the **San Diego Bay Ferry** will take you there any day, year-around, from the Broadway Pier on the San Diego side and from the Old Ferry Landing in Coronado. It runs every hour on the half hour, beginning at 7:30am. You can pick up tickets at the San Diego Harbor Excursions' ticket booth (with the blue awning). The fare is $1.50 each way (50¢ extra for bicycles) and $4 for an all-day pass (should you simply want to ride back and forth enjoying the bay).

7. Sports

Every sport and activity connected with water is popular in San Diego. Sportfishing in the ocean is among the finest on the Pacific coast. **H & M Landing, 2803 Emerson St.**, Point Loma (tel. 619/222-1144), offers the largest variety of fishing (they've been in the business since 1935) and whale-watching excursions. Their local fishing trips range from a half day at the Point Loma Kelp Beds to full-day fishing around the Coronado Islands. In summer and fall they will go out for albacore tuna; in winter and spring it's for rock cod. The really exciting trips are on the 88-foot *Spirit of Adventure* (sleeps 30) for 2- to 10-day fishing trips. H & M also has been watching gray whales since 1955 (Pacific Sea Fari Tours). This is also an opportunity to see sea lions, seabirds, and ocean life of all sorts. Expeditions described in Chapter XIV include stopovers at the Baja whale lagoons and the offshore islands.

Charter fishing boats also leave from **Islandia Sportfishing,** 1551 W. Mission Bay Dr. (tel. 619/222-1164), Mission Bay. January to March, Islandia also goes whale-watching. You can also fish (for no charge and with no license) off the **Ocean Beach Pier,** at the foot of Niagara Street in Ocean Beach (tel. 619/224-3359), and in the many city lakes (a daily recreation permit is required). For information on lake fishing, contact the **Lakes Recreation Section** of the San Diego Water Utilities Department (tel. 619/465-3474).

Sailing, scuba diving, surfing, swimming, and waterskiing are equally popular, as are nonwater sports from tennis (about 100 public courts, not to mention those at hotels and country clubs) and golf (there's a choice of 68 excellent courses) to sky-diving. Facilities are so abundant that I can't begin to list them here; see the "Information" entry in the "San Diego Fast Facts" section for some guidance.

8. La Jolla

"La Hoya" (that's how it's pronounced) is an oceanside residential portion of the coast, at the northern and western edge of San Diego. It successfully retains its "old-money" image, although adventurous young people are moving in on the coterie of millionaires, navy families, and retired citizens. For half a century the wealthy have been building beautiful retirement estates here, having selected the site for its lushness and rugged coastline, its beaches and cultural facilities. Along Prospect Avenue, running parallel to the coast, are about five blocks of boutiques, shops, restaurants, cafés, and art galleries. In all, it's a tasteful, restful, interesting place to visit.

WHAT TO SEE

The **Scripps Aquarium Museum,** 8602 La Jolla Shores Dr. (tel. 619/534-6933 for a recorded message with general information, or 534-3474), at the Scripps Institution of Oceanography, is world renowned for the research it does in the oceans. It invites visitors to view its aquarium of marine life and outdoor tidepool exhibit, with many of the specimens captured on scientific expeditions. The aquarium bookshop (tel. 619/534-4085) specializes in ocean-related books for students and scholars of all ages—preschool to postgraduate to "just interested." The aquarium is open daily from 9am to 5pm, with admission by donation. Nearby are excellent beach and picnic areas.

WHERE TO STAY

La Valencia, 1132 Prospect St. (at the corner of Herschel Avenue), La Jolla, CA 92037 (tel. 619/454-0771), is a gracious old Mediterranean-style resort that delights the senses at every turn. Dramatically situated on the ocean, it was designed in archetypical Early California Spanish style by architect Reginald Johnson back in 1926. From the colonnaded entrance with vine-covered trellis to the lush gardens that surround the large swimming pool to the exquisite mosaic tilework within, it's a beauty. Old-world charm, outstanding personal service, and an impressive scenic location have made it a frequent haven for celebrities and entertainers. At the back of the hotel, garden terraces open toward the ocean. Here, a free-form heated swimming pool is edged with lawn, flowering trees, shrubs, and a flagstone sunning deck. Other facilities include a sauna, a whirlpool, shuffleboard, and a mini health club.

La Valencia has 100 accommodations, including 10 suites. Guest rooms are decorated in subdued tones and with European antique reproductions. Pleasant amenities include terrycloth robes, oversize towels, bathroom telephones (bless them), Lancôme toiletries, nightly turndown service, and a daily complimentary newspaper. Select accommodations also have minibars, bathroom TVs, makeup mirrors, and safes. Most rooms have ocean views.

There are four delightful spots for dining. The elegant rooftop Sky Room serves lunch, including soup du jour or salad, and a superb prix-fixe dinner. The light French cuisine is enhanced by the spectacular beauty of the California coastline and the La Jolla Cove. The Mediterranean Room, with its adjoining patio for al fresco dining, offers a number of delicious choices: for lunch, an exceptionally large selection of salads, some fine sandwich plates, seafood, pasta, and several house specialties such as paella Valencia; for dinner, seafood, spring lamb and poultry, eastern beef, veal, and the specialties of the day. On the other hand, you might choose to have lunch or dinner at the Whaling Bar (done in New England nautical), one of the most popular watering holes in town, or at the Cafe La Rue. Both have the same menu of seafood selections, pasta, specialties of the day, and a goodly assortment of sandwich plates (my favorite is the Brooklyn steak sandwich) and salads.

I must make a separate statement about the extraordinary wine list. Whether or not you happen to be an oenophile, do look down the list of almost 600 individual choices of imported and domestic wines, including a 1961 Château Lafite Rothschild (Premier Grand Cru) and a 1961 Château Latour (Premier Grand Cru). To paraphrase a much-used quote, if you must ask the price of either of these 1961 gems, you can't afford them; but it is nice to look, and there are other fine choices that will accommodate just about every budget.

For evening relaxation, the La Sala Lounge has a pianist who entertains nightly.

Depending on location, rates for singles and doubles are $150 to $275; suites with a partial or full ocean view are $275 to $425.

The **Sheraton Grande Torrey Pines,** 10950 N. Torrey Pines Rd., La Jolla, CA 92037 (tel. 619/558-1500, or toll free 800/325-3535), which opened in 1989, looks every bit the $60-million luxury hotel. Though it has 400 rooms and four guest wings, its unique design disguises its true size. The Sheraton Grande Torrey Pines is one of those very rare hotels that offers the extraordinary combination of striking good looks, access to all sorts of excellent facilities, and a superb setting, plus services designed to cosset each guest.

As you pass under the porte cochere to enter the hotel, ahead of you beyond the lobby is a breathtaking view that sweeps from a brilliantly green fairway of the Torrey Pines Golf Course to the rugged blue-gray magnificence of the Pacific Ocean. The lobby spreads to either side to accommodate the beauty of the panorama. Overhead are massive chandeliers of metal leaves; inset carpeting is surrounded by slate and marble, and at the focal point of the lobby is an enormous display of fresh flowers. At one side is the Lobby Lounge, a lovely place for hors d'oeuvres and beverages in the evening. Below the lobby level, on the bluff, there is a massive oval pool with fountain, as well as a sunning deck, a heated whirlpool spa surrounded by Tuscan columns, and a snack bar.

Guest rooms are equally as impressive, their decks, patios, and balconies ranging in size from cozy to those large enough for a good-size cocktail party. Furnishings are of warm woods, and colors are restfully subdued—white, beige, brown, tan. All rooms have sitting areas, as well as dual-line phones, golf course and/or ocean views, self-service minibars, cable TVs, and 24-hour room service. Special in-room amenities include plush terrycloth robes and, in the bathrooms, supplies of excellent Caswell-Massey toiletries. There is butler service on every floor.

As for dining, the Torreyana Grille serves California cuisine, the centerpiece of the room being an exhibition grill where chefs prepare steaks, seafood, and poultry specialties. The setting is highlighted by water sculptures, lush plants, and stonework—and by live piano music that plays through lunch and dinner. Al fresco dining on the terrace is always a delightful option when the weather is perfect (as it frequently is). Breakfast choices include a variety of omelets, plus such nonegg choices as banana-nut french toast, plain or pecan waffles, or even berry pancakes. The luncheon menu offers something for everyone, from a burger with choice of toppings to a "grilled soup" with a rich chicken-broth base and your choice of additions such as smoked chicken, orzo shrimp, sautéed mushrooms, or a vegetable medley. At dinner your appetizer might be the crab cake with black-bean relish, or southwestern spring rolls with two dipping sauces. Grill items range from breast of chicken and New York sirloin with mango chutney to mahi mahi with sweet-onion confit. The evening fare also includes Signature Items—special creations such as the tenderloin medallions with cabernet demi-glace and sautéed shiitake mushrooms. Desserts change daily; all are prepared in the restaurant's own pastry kitchen. There is a fine wine list. Breakfast might cost $6 to $9, lunch $8 to $13, dinner $18 to $26 without appetizer, dessert, or wine. The Torreyana Grille is open daily for breakfast from 6:30am, for lunch from 11am to 2:30pm, and for dinner from 5:30 to 10:30pm.

On to activities. For the golfer, there are two attractive courses—the North and the South, both with spectacular views and inhabited by squirrels, bunnies, foxes, and other assorted wildlife (apart from the golfers). Then there are three lighted tennis courts, an exercise room, men's and women's saunas and showers, and the aforementioned pool for swimming your laps or simply lazing in the sun. Adjacent to the hotel is the Shiley Sports and Health Center of Scripps Clinic, which offers the use of their fitness center, health resource center, and sports medicine center. The fee to guests of the hotel is $7.50 per hour.

The Sheraton Grande Torrey Pines has complimentary limo service to the shops and restaurants of La Jolla. The village is charming and a delightful place to spend time browsing, shopping, and watching the passing parade.

Rates at the Sheraton Grande Torrey Pines are $185 to $275, single or double occupancy; suites start at $325; the Presidential Suite is $2,750.

Another elegant Old California accommodation is **Sea Lodge,** 8110 Camino del Oro (at the foot of Avenida de la Playa), La Jolla, CA 92037 (tel. 619/459-8271, or toll free 800/237-5211), overlooking the Pacific on a mile-long beach. Its 128 rooms are housed in a long and low stucco building with terra-cotta–tile roof, highlighted by fountains, beautiful landscaping and flowerbeds, open-air walkways, ceramic tilework, graceful arches, and Mexican antiques like the 200-year-old cathedral doors leading into the main dining room.

A centrally located swimming pool gleams jewel-like in the courtyard, where umbrellaed tables are set up for outdoor dining. Other facilities include tennis courts (no charge for use), a sauna, and complimentary underground parking. The Shores Restaurant (that's the above-mentioned main dining room) serves three meals a day, seven days a week, under a peaked beamed ceiling. The decor is richly Spanish and old-world, and all seats provide a panoramic view of the beach. Room service is also available. The Shores Lounge has a happy hour with daily specials.

As for the rooms, they're large and lovely, all with one barnwood wall (third-floor rooms—my favorites—have high sloped barnwood ceilings as well), and almost all have ocean views. Some rooms have air conditioning, all have the fresh ocean breeze. The rooms feature an ocean motif, and all are equipped with refrigerators, coffee makers, color TVs, phones, AM/FM radios, and modern amenities. All rooms have balconies or lanais, and some have kitchens.

Rates are seasonal: July through mid-September, singles cost $145 to $230; doubles, $155 to $240; oceanfront deluxe rooms and suites, $275 to $360. Rates are lower the balance of the year.

9. An Excursion to Tijuana

While you're this far south, you may as well go the extra 20 miles (via I-5 or 805) and cross the border to Tijuana, gateway to Mexico.

GETTING THERE
One of the easiest ways to get to the border is the **Tijuana (San Diego) Trolley** (tel. 619/233-3004). Big red trolleys (actual electric streetcars imported from Germany) depart from the corner of Kettner Boulevard and C Street, just across the street from the Amtrak station, every 15 minutes from 5am to 7pm, and every 30 minutes thereafter, with the last trolley returning from the border at 1am. Be sure to take the trolley that says "San Ysidro." The one-way trip to or from the border takes 45 minutes and costs $1.50 per person one way from Kettner Boulevard; have exact change in coins. There are 18 stops on the line, since it doubles as commuter transportation, but it's a comfortable, interesting, and inexpensive way to reach the border. Once at the border you'll need a taxi to get into town.

If you're driving into Mexico, you might prefer to park on the U.S. side and walk or take a bus or taxi into town (three-quarters of a mile). There are about half a dozen parking lots on either side of I-5, and by leaving your car on the U.S. side you avoid long waits when return traffic jams up at the border.

One way to avoid car problems is to take the **Mexicoach** (tel. 619/232-5049). Daily round-trip scheduled express buses go to downtown Tijuana, the Tijuana airport, the jai alai games, and bullfights ($11 round trip, $5.75 one way). Buses depart from the Amtrak terminal, 1050 Kettner Blvd., at Broadway, in San Diego, at 9, 10, and 11am, noon, then at 2, 4, and 6pm. The trip takes about 35 minutes going, 45 minutes to one hour returning (to pass through Immigration). The last bus returns at 6:45pm weekdays, 9pm weekends.

And of course, **Gray Line San Diego,** 1670 Kettner Blvd. (tel. 619/231-9922), has a full range of exciting San Diego and Tijuana tours, ranging from $22 to $46 for adults, $13 to $29 for children.

Warning: If you do drive in, be aware that *no U.S. insurance is valid in Mexico.* If you should be involved in an accident across the border, this can be troublesome at best. But you can buy special coverage near the border for a few dollars a day, or from AAA if you're a member. Whatever, *don't* go into Mexico without it. By the way, American citizens don't need a passport within 72 miles of the border (which includes Tijuana) for visits of less than 72 hours (foreigners should carry theirs), and you can shop with American dollars. However, it's wise to have identification (like a driver's license) with you.

WHAT TO SEE AND DO
If you'd like to do it yourself, stop by the **San Diego Convention & Visitors Bureau International Visitor Information Center** at 11 Horton Plaza, downtown at 1st Avenue and F Street (tel. 619/236-1212); they have information about Tijuana attractions. There is also a tourist information center at the border crossing.

In Tijuana you can see thoroughbred racing at **Agua Caliente** every Saturday and Sunday at noon in winter, at 1:15pm the rest of the year; greyhound racing is scheduled Wednesday through Monday nights.

Mexico's top matadors perform in two different **bullfight** rings every Sunday at 4pm between May and September.

And then there are jai alai games, often called the fastest sport in the world, played nightly except Thursday (starting at 8pm) at the **Frontón Palacio,** Avenida Revolución at Calle 7. Admission is $3 to $5. For information, call 619/260-0452.

You can also visit the **Tijuana Cultural Center,** located less than a mile from the border and across from the Plaza Río Shopping Center. It was designed to celebrate Mexico's heritage, and contains an Omnimax Space Theater, an anthropological museum, a bookstore, an arts and crafts center, and a performing arts center. Finally, you'll want to do some shopping at the duty-free stores along Tijuana's main street, Avenida Revolución.

WHERE TO DINE

You won't find the perfectly charming little south-of-the-border restaurant of your dreams here. Best bet is **La Costa,** Calle 7A no. 150, off Avenida Revolución (tel. 706/685-8494), a dimly lit, wood-paneled restaurant with big black tufted-leather booths that looks no more Mexican than many places in New Jersey. What it lacks in ambience, however, it makes up for in excellent fresh fish and seafood meals —so good, in fact, that they're worth the trip to Tijuana alone. A recent meal priced at about $12 consisted of two fish hors d'oeuvres, tomato salad, seafood soup, fresh-baked rolls and butter, broiled shrimp wrapped in bacon with rice, dessert, and coffee.

La Costa is open daily from 10am to midnight.

Just around the corner is **Pedrin's,** 1115 Avenida Revolución (tel. 706/685-4052). It's fancier than La Costa—all wood and white, with plants. On the bar there's an attractive seafood and wine display. On the second floor there's a terrace overlooking the street. The fare is seafood here too. For $5 to $11 you get the house hors d'oeuvres, a homemade soup, piping-hot bread, rice, an entree—fish, lobster, king crab, abalone, shrimp, oyster, almost anything you can think of—and dessert and coffee. It's a delightful place, a perfect spot to rest your feet after a long shopping spree.

Pedrin's hours are 11am to midnight daily.

LAS VEGAS

Las Vegas—Disneyland for the 21-and-over set . . . playground of the rich, the would-be-rich, the tourist from Albuquerque, the sophisticate from New York City. There's something here for everyone, and more often than not, everyone leaves a little something here. That's the rule of the game, and games are what Las Vegas is all about. Emotion runs high as money runs low, but there's always someplace to go to work off those lost-green blues.

Where else could you play tennis or work out at a health club 24 hours a day, seven days a week? Get to see Sinatra, Dolly, and Liza all in one week? Dine while watching a three-ring circus or charging knights on horseback?

The funny thing about Las Vegas is that it's never really been any different. From the start, the lure of Nevada was all glitter and gold. During the California Gold Rush it became a lucrative stopping-off place for prospectors. Gold, silver, and other precious metals were mined into the early 1900s, when the rich ore veins were finally picked clean.

The next boom came in on the tail of the Gold Rush, around 1905, when the Union Pacific Railroad built a depot in what immediately and henceforth became known as Las Vegas. As the iron horse flourished, so did Nevada property values. And always there was gambling—finally made legal in 1931—and big-time gamblers, who helped to make Las Vegas a legendary town while becoming legends themselves. Perhaps the most notorious of these was Nick the Greek, King of Gamblers from 1928 to 1949. In his time it's been said he won and lost more than $50 million—and managed to die broke.

Las Vegas is in a frenzy constructing "the biggest," "the most," "the finest," "the only"—with superlatives and hyperbole exploding daily. Hotels and resorts are rushing to build, to catch up, refurbishing rooms, expanding casinos, adding towers. (As in any business, a few of those in the status quo are slipping toward the auction block or into bankruptcy.)

Bugsy Siegel would never recognize the place. At the end of 1989, The Mirage opened in all its volcanic and waterfall splendor. Even the most jaded were forced to agree that Steve Wynn had created a uniquely spectacular environment for gaming, theater, dining, and relaxing. Seven months later, in June 1990, the Excalibur opened its 4,032-room, when-knighthood-was-in-flower resort at the southern edge of the Strip. It's another of the total-entertainment Circus Circus Enterprises. And with the advent of Excalibur, MGM Grand's Kirk Kerkorian gobbled up 115 acres across the street for what will reportedly become a movieland theme park with a 5,000-room hotel (they get bigger by the minute).

Las Vegas is on a roll. Growth and expansion have upped the projected hotel capacity to 85,000 rooms by the end of 1991. As of the moment, there's not an unemployed architect around. The town has graduated from stay-and-play to one of the country's fastest-growing metropolitan areas. It's become a town for families because of the success of the gaming industry, the appeal of the weather, the low cost of living, lots of jobs, and the great tax environment—there's neither a state income tax (gaming revenues satisfy 40% of the state budget) nor a corporation tax (companies are relocating to Las Vegas at the rate of two per month). Right now Las Vegas has a population of about 700,000; it's expected to double by 1994.

Whether or not you aspire to the big time, Las Vegas will welcome you with open casinos, and enough excitement and entertainment to keep you coming back again and again.

1. Getting There

AIRLINES

Nonstop flights connect Las Vegas with a number of cities in California: **Bakersfield** (Delta), **Burbank** (America West, USAir), **Fresno** (Delta), **Long Beach** (America West), **Los Angeles** (American, America West, Delta, USAir), **Ontario** (America West), **Orange County** (America West, Southwest Airlines, USAir), **San Francisco** (America West, United, USAir), **San Jose** (America West, Delta, USAir), **Santa Barbara** (Delta), and **Santa Maria** (American).

AIRPORT

Las Vegas has one main airport—**McCarran International Airport.** The $7.50 surcharge on your ticket to Las Vegas pays for this ultramodern airport, where you can begin gambling at the slots as soon as you disembark.

It takes about 15 minutes and $8 to $10 to get to the middle of the Strip by taxi. In addition to the base fare of $1.70 for the first seventh of a mile and 20¢ for each additional seventh of a mile, there is also a 20¢ tax per load for pickups at the airport and a 20¢ charge for each passenger over three. The limousine (or minibus) from the airport to Strip hotels costs $4 per person, $5.50 per person to downtown Las Vegas.

TRAINS

The **Amtrak** station is at 1 N. Main St., at the Union Plaza Hotel (tel. 702/386-6896, or toll free 800/872-7245).

BUSES

The **Greyhound/Trailways Bus System** (tel. 702/384-9561) serves Las Vegas from most cities in California and Nevada. The Greyhound/Trailways terminal is downtown at 200 S. Main. There are two dropoff/pickup stops on the Strip, at the Tropicana Hotel and at the Riviera. Tickets must be purchased at the downtown terminal before boarding. For general information and schedules, call your nearest ticket office.

2. Getting Around

Not only does Las Vegas have the distinction of being the oasis in an otherwise desert state mostly owned by the government (ours), it is also Nevada's largest city.

The sections that will interest you most as a tourist, however, are contained in a fairly compact area.

The **Strip,** more formally known as **Las Vegas Boulevard South,** and the **downtown Casino Center** provide the major entertainment and casino activity. The Strip runs from the Sahara Hotel south to the Hacienda Hotel, while the downtown Casino Center is concentrated on Fremont Street and the adjoining area.

Strip **buses** ply the route from the Hacienda to Fremont Street, stopping at all major hotels on the Strip. To return to the Strip from downtown, go to the corner of 3rd and Fremont streets. Bus fare is $1.10, and you'll need exact change. If you plan on using the bus several times, buy a 10-ride commuter card from the driver for $7.30. For transit information, call 702/384-3540. **Taxis** cost $1.70 for the first seventh of a mile, $1.40 for each mile after that. The **airport limo** from the airport to the Strip hotels costs $4 per person, $5.50 to downtown Las Vegas.

There's now a new/old mode of transport up and down the Strip. It's the **Las Vegas Strip Trolley** (tel. 702/382-1404), a classic trolley replica that stops at the main entrance of Strip hotels, as well as the Las Vegas Hilton and the Convention Center. The ride is climate-controlled and really quite pleasant. Trolleys run about every 30 minutes from 9:30am to 2am daily. You can't miss seeing them, because they do look like the old-fashioned trolleys. The fare is $1, and exact change is required.

CAR RENTALS

I've covered this topic under San Francisco, Los Angeles, and San Diego, but it still bears repeating because of its importance to all travelers, especially those who do not write it off as a business expense.

If you intend to do much traveling, let's say down to Laughlin and back, or to Boulder Dam, or covering much of the desert landscape, you might do best to find an unlimited-mileage arrangement, or at least one with sufficient free mileage to make your trip economical. On the highways, those few "cents per mile" tend to mount rapidly into dollars.

Whatever your destination, my advice is *plan ahead.* The general information given in the "Traveling Within California" section of Chapter I applies here too; you might want to refer to it.

Car rentals of specific-size vehicles, including vans, are usually easier to obtain from the big car-rental companies. Each of the companies below has an office at McCarran International Airport, as well as offices throughout Las Vegas: **Avis** (tel. toll free 800/331-1212), **Budget** (tel. toll free 800/527-0700), and **Hertz** (tel. toll free 800/654-3131).

Brooks Rent-a-Car, 3039 Las Vegas Blvd. South, at Convention Center Drive (tel. 702/735-3344), tries to maintain the lowest rates in Las Vegas, starting at $22 per day, with 100 miles free; or $40 per day, with unlimited mileage. Weekly rates begin at $140, with 700 miles free. Minivans are $50 a day, with 150 miles free. Charges over and above free mileage are at the rate of 25¢ per mile. All cars and minivans are late-model Fords. Brooks, open from 6am to 1am, can arrange for pickup and drop-off at the airport or your hotel until 11:30pm.

3. Las Vegas Fast Facts

As with the "Fast Facts" for all the major California cities, this section organizes, in alphabetical order, some basic information (and some not so basic) intended to help make your trip as enjoyable and hassle-free as possible.

AREA CODE: The area code for all of Nevada, including Las Vegas, is **702.**

BABY-SITTERS: If you're staying at one of the large hotels on the Strip or downtown, the concierge can make arrangements for you or recommend organizations to call. Be sure to check on the hourly cost (which may vary by day and time) as well as any additional expenses such as meals for the sitter.

The Las Vegas Hilton is unique in that it has a Youth Hotel on the premises for girls and boys aged 3 through 18. However, you must be a guest at the hotel to take advantage of these facilities.

BANKS: As with most cities, banks are generally open Monday through Friday from 10am to 3pm (some from 9am to 4pm). A few are open on Saturday from 9am to noon. However, if you need to cash a check, your hotel may be your best resource, depending on the amount involved. For a line of credit, see "Cash and Credit," below.

CASH AND CREDIT: As I've said above, cashing a check may be best accomplished at your hotel, depending on the amount. Also, you can readily cash traveler's checks at the cashier's cage in the casinos. If you intend to gamble, cash the checks first—they're not negotiable at the tables.

Establishing credit for a short-term stay in Las Vegas is accomplished more often through the casinos than through the banks. Bring credit cards, driver's licenses, and other identification, and you can usually be "cleared" within 24 hours to cash personal checks, etc., up to the limit you've arranged with the casino. Once you've established credit with a casino, it remains in effect for repeat visits to the city. It's also possible to write to a casino in advance and establish credit before you arrive.

CASINO PROTOCOL: You can wear, or not wear, almost anything at a casino. And at a craps table you can whoop and holler to your heart's content. Smoking is permitted at the majority of tables, but you may now notice some no-smoking tables. There is one strict prohibition in all casinos—no cameras are allowed.

CHIPS: Casino chips were once as good as cash anywhere in Las Vegas. Nowadays they are accepted only in the casinos where they're issued—and in church; some people still drop them into collection boxes, an old Las Vegas tradition. Reason for the change in use as currency: A rash of counterfeit chips began to show up. So cash in your chips before you leave any casino, unless you're planning to return there.

CLIMATE: It can be cold from December through March, frequently quite windy, with evening temperatures dropping to the mid-30s or 40s; daytime highs are around the 50s or low 60s, if that. So bring warm clothing if you plan to leave

A Closer Look at the Weather (in degrees Fahrenheit)

	High	Average	Low
January	55	44	33
February	62	50	39
March	69	57	44
April	79	66	53
May	88	74	60
June	99	84	68
July	105	91	76
August	103	88	74
September	96	81	65
October	82	67	53
November	67	54	41
December	58	47	36

your hotel at any time. April through October is summerwear time, but women might bring a lightweight sweater or stole. Many's the restaurant that has winter temperatures (especially those requiring jackets for men).

CRIME: In any city where as much money changes hands as in Las Vegas, you will also find crime. To avoid an unhappy incident, use discretion and common sense. If you're carrying a handbag, don't, for example, put it on the ledge just beneath the craps table where players rest their drinks. It's out of view and a tempting target. Always keep your handbag close to you and in plain sight. It would be wise to review the "Crime" section of the "California Fast Facts" section in Chapter I for more safety tips.

DENTISTS AND DOCTORS: Hotels usually have a list of dentists and doctors, should you need one; in addition, they are listed in the Centel *Yellow Pages.* For dentist referrals, call the **Clark County Dental Society** (tel. 702/435-7767); for a doctor, call the **Clark County Medical Society** (tel. 702/739-9989).

DRIVING: Any trip to Las Vegas from California involves desert driving. Take basic precautions at all times, but especially during the summer. Before leaving, check your tires, water, and oil. Take about 5 gallons of water in a clean container so that it can be used for drinking or for the radiator. Pay attention to those road signs suggesting when to turn off your car's air conditioner. Slow but continuous climbs through the mountains can cause overheating before you notice it on your gauge. And don't push your luck with gas. It may be 35 miles or more between gas stations, so fill up before you begin to run low.
 If your car overheats, *do not* remove the radiator cap until the engine has cooled, and then only very slowly. Add water to within an inch of the top of the radiator while the engine is running.

FESTIVALS AND EVENTS: The best and most comprehensive source for this information is the **Las Vegas Chamber of Commerce,** 2301 E. Sahara Ave., Las Vegas, NV 89104 (tel. 702/457-4664). The chamber is open weekdays from 8am to 5pm.
 You'll also find weekly information in the Friday edition of the *Las Vegas Review-Journal* and in *Today in Las Vegas;* see the "Information" entry below.
 While every day is "party day" in Las Vegas, the obvious holiday and special-event occasions are not the times to try for reservations on short notice; you might write ahead to the chamber of commerce for a list of the less-obvious big events. (Be advised that it's unwise to come without reservations, since you may not get a room, much less a seat at a $2 blackjack table.)

FOOD: Prices range from 89¢ to $70, with lots of choice in between. The bargain meals are usually breakfast and lunch; dinner tends to run higher. One of the city's main draws has always been its good food at moderate prices, calculated to bring in the gambling customers. Not only the downtown hotels but most of the Strip establishments have all kinds of gimmicks such as 89¢ breakfasts and eat-all-you-want buffet tables (which, for the most part, are no bargain). Scattered around town are plenty of nationally known franchise restaurants—pancake houses, taco stops, fish and chips, pizza parlors, and the so-called steakhouses.
 At the dinner shows at the larger hotels, the quality of the food is reasonable, and dinner plus a top-notch show for around $40 to $60 per person is not a bad buy—or at least it doesn't seem so in a city where visitors tend to let money flow like water.

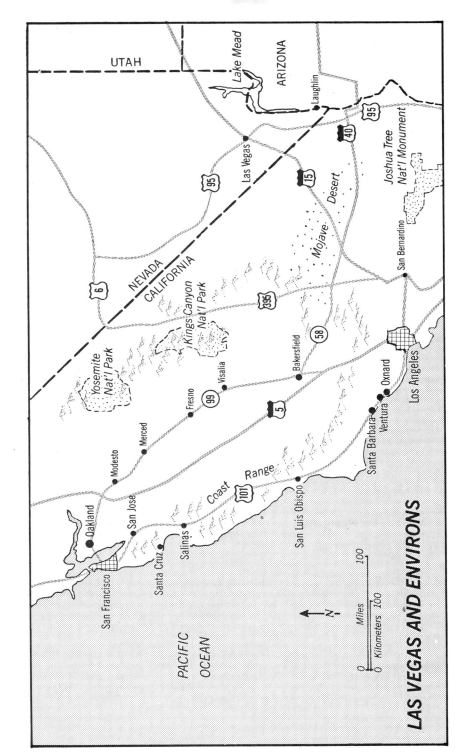

LAS VEGAS AND ENVIRONS

Unlike casinos, not all restaurants are open daily. If you have your heart set on a special place for dinner, be sure to check when it's open.

HAIR SALONS: First, ask at the hotel if there's a hair salon on the premises. If the hotel does not have one, ask for a recommendation. As a last measure, ask a blackjack dealer with a desirable hair style for a referral.

INFORMATION: For brochures, maps, information on accommodations, etc., stop at the **Las Vegas Chamber of Commerce,** a very helpful center for visitors. Their address, phone number, and hours are given above in the "Festivals and Events" entry.

For **Nevada tourism information,** including that for Las Vegas, call toll free 800/638-2328 (a 24-hour line).

For **Las Vegas reservations and show information,** call toll free 800/423-4745.

One of the best sources of information on what's doing in Las Vegas is *Today in Las Vegas,* a free weekly publication you'll find at almost any bell desk in a large hotel, as well as at the airport. It includes up-to-the-minute reviews and listings of all shows and events, as well as the performance times.

LIQUOR LAWS: There are no restrictions on the hours when liquor can be sold or served, but you must be 21 to buy or imbibe legally.

NEWSPAPERS: The *Las Vegas Sun* is the town's morning paper. The Friday edition of the afternoon paper, the *Las Vegas Review-Journal,* offers a rundown of the shows in town, as well as an overview of most other forms of entertainment, restaurants, and happenings in nearby resorts.

PETS: As in California, hotels and motels generally will not accept pets; ask before making the reservations. Motel 6 does accept a pet (within reason), but will not permit the animal to be left unattended.

If you travel via RV, motor home, or with trailer or van, and take pets with you, an ideal location next to the Strip is the Circusland RV Park, adjacent to the Circus Circus Hotel. Circusland has family and pet sections with dog runs.

POLICE: For **emergency** help, dial 911. The **nonemergency** police department number is 702/795-3111; that for the **Nevada Highway Patrol** is 702/486-4100. For **road conditions** call 702/486-3116.

RELIGIOUS SERVICES: The Las Vegas area has hundreds of churches and synagogues (at last count about 380) representing virtually every denomination. It's been said that on a per capita basis there are more houses of worship in Las Vegas than in any other metropolitan area in the nation, and we all know what everyone's praying for. The breakdown: 49% Protestant, 24% Roman Catholic, 23% Mormon, 3% Jewish.

The houses of worship listed below are located along the Strip and downtown (for other denominations and locations, consult the Centel *Yellow Pages*):

First Baptist, 300 S. 9th St., at Bridger Avenue, downtown (tel. 702/382-6177); **First Southern Baptist,** 700 E. St. Louis Ave., on the Strip (tel. 702/732-3100); **Guardian Angel Cathedral** (Roman Catholic), 302 E. Desert Inn Rd., on the Strip (tel. 702/735-5241); **St. Joan of Arc** (Roman Catholic), 315 S. Casino Center Blvd., downtown (tel. 702/382-9909); **Reformation Lutheran,** 580 E. St. Louis Ave., near the Strip (tel. 702/732-2052); **First United Methodist,** 231 S. 3rd St., downtown (tel. 702/382-9939); and **Temple Beth Sholom,** 1600 E. Oakey Blvd., near the Strip (tel. 702/384-5070).

STORE HOURS: Stores are usually open Monday through Friday from 10am to 9pm, on Saturday to 6pm, and on Sunday from 11am to 5pm.

TAXES: Sales tax in Las Vegas is 6%.

TIPPING: Those over 21 undoubtedly already know about tipping the usual 15% in restaurants. However, when you're at a table in a casino, be it craps, blackjack, roulette, baccarat, or whatever, a cocktail waitress will be around to ask if you want anything to drink. There is no charge for the drink, hard or soft, but it is appropriate for you to tip (or "toke") the waitress—$1 (or a comparable chip) is about right, more if you wish.

At the gaming tables, it's perfectly acceptable to tip the dealer or croupier in proportion to the service you've been getting and the size of your winnings.

When checking into a hotel with several bags, a tip of $5 is par for the course. Valet parking is a great convenience at any of the Las Vegas hotels. A tip of $1 is appropriate, and it's not much to pay for the service.

When you leave the hotel, a tip of $1 per day for the period of your stay, left with the maid or in the room, is a most reasonable amount and will be appreciated.

If you want a better-than-average seat at any one of the shows, tip the maître d'. The usual donation is $5, but if it's a "big name" show, you might up the ante to $20 for the seating *you* want, though the top of the range is optional.

USEFUL TELEPHONE NUMBERS: You can obtain **weather information for** Las Vegas at 702/736-6404 8am to 5pm, **information on highway conditions** at 702/486-3116, **the time of day** at 118 (a three-digit number, similar to **directory information,** 411).

---

4. Food, Fun, and Shelter in the Casino-Hotels

In previous chapters of this book, the questions of where to eat, where to stay, and what to do were separate categories, handled for the most part independently of one another. In Las Vegas, many of the top restaurants are right in the big hotels, ditto the casinos and the nightclubs. So I've organized things differently here, exploring the abundance of eating and entertainment facilities at each superhotel at the same time I'm discussing accommodations. As usual, I've begun with the most lavish Strip hotels and worked downward on the price scale (the last four casino-hotels, the Golden Nugget, the Union Plaza Park, and Union Plaza, are downtown). At the end of this chapter is a selection of good independent restaurants (not in a hotel) you won't want to pass up. There, too, I've begun with the most expensive and worked downward in price.

There are three major locations for big-hotel action in Vegas: along the **Strip,** in the **downtown** area on Fremont Street, and in a kind of P.S. to the Strip, along **Convention Center Drive,** which meets the Strip between the Riviera Hotel and the Desert Inn. In this chapter, these last are lumped in with the Strip hotels.

No matter how many hotels are contained in those areas, however (last count showed over 50,000 hotel and motel rooms for let—and I'm talking about doubles), a busy weekend still turns up one "No Vacancy" sign after another. Come weekends, convention time, any feeble excuse for a holiday or celebration, it's all full up. So *do not* come without a reservation.

THE LAS VEGAS STRIP HOTELS

The Mirage, 3400 Las Vegas Blvd. South, Las Vegas, NV 89125 (tel. 702/791-7111, or toll free 800/627-6667).

For all its neon and glitter, Las Vegas has finally come up with a real $630-million showstopper that halts traffic on the Strip without a spec of neon. Totally spectacular. After all, how can you possibly ignore a magnificent volcano that erupts every 15 minutes (it used to be every 5 minutes, but the rubberneckers caused too many traffic backups) in a setting of lush tropical landscaping and a five-story waterfall? (You can gape at the volcano in all its glory from 6pm to 1am.) And that's only for openers. Somehow you know that Steve Wynn, who began with the Golden Nugget downtown, has had a hand in creating this beauty with its brilliant white-and-gold-banded finish. His is a remarkable talent for crossing the flamboyant with the elegant to create what Las Vegas always strives to be.

Entrance to The Mirage is via a palm-lined causeway, over a lagoon, and up to a brilliantly white porte cochere. Here valet attendants move vehicles to parking areas via tunnels under the lagoon; baggage is unloaded and moved via an automated conveyor system. Should all this elegance and attention overwhelm you, a stop at the Lagoon Saloon, near the registration area, might be in order.

The Mirage resort forms a Y-shape complex on 100 acres (some of the most expensive real estate in the West). There are two natural habitats, other than those for the guests—one for the dolphins (to come soon) and another for one or two of the white tigers used in the Siegfried and Roy show. And behind the check-in area is a wall-length, 20,000-gallon aquarium with small sharks, rays, and over 30 varieties of tropical sea life. Once past the lobby—handsomely finished with bamboo, thatched ceilings, marble paving with inset carpeting, and rattan furnishings—and you're within a 90-foot-high, glass-enclosed atrium filled with palm and banana trees, tropical orchids, and waterfalls.

The Mirage has three 29-story towers with 3,049 accommodations, including one- and two-bedroom suites. The six ultra-elegant secluded lanai bungalows, each with its own private pool, have no price—they are reserved for names such as Michael Jackson. Throughout, bright tropical colors contrast with the restful mood created by the soft, neutral backgrounds and by the light, whitewashed natural rattan and caning of the furnishings. Floor-to-ceiling headboards of white louvered panels enhance the spaciousness of the rooms. Every room features either a pool, mountain, or Strip view. The top five floors are devoted exclusively to tower and penthouse suites accessible only by private elevators. Rooms equipped for the handicapped, as well as nonsmoking floors, are available on request.

Accommodations are $89 to $159 for deluxe rooms, $365 and up for suites.

There simply is nothing commonplace about The Mirage. The swimming area is a series of interconnected lagoons with tree-lined islands, waterfalls, grottos, and inlets. Nonswimming guests (like myself) can walk to the islands to bask gloriously in the sun. When hunger or thirst sets in, there is the Paradise Cafe or the Dolphin Bar for a lavish lunch or a cool drink. If swimming is not your preferred mode of exercise and relaxation, there will soon be six championship tennis courts. A fully equipped spa with an exercise room and sauna offers aerobics and massage to keep you in shape for the trials of the gaming tables. Needless to say, this paradise also includes a beauty salon and an elite collection of designer boutiques and shops.

And wait until you see the casino—magnificently designed to resemble a Polynesian village. The concept of putting gaming areas under wood canopies creates a unique feeling of intimacy. As for the gaming activities, there are those you would expect find everywhere else. But there are also $500 slots, baccarat tables with stakes from $5,000 to $15,000; and there is one private room where the smallest chip is worth $1,000.

And then there's the food. Naturally, The Mirage has 24-hour room service (rapidly disappearing in many hotels), with guaranteed 20-minute delivery. Outside of your guest room, there are restaurants specializing in steak and seafood and in Japanese, Italian, Chinese, and French cuisines; the California Pizza Kitchen; a coffee shop and buffet; and Coconuts Ice Cream Shop to satisfy your sweet tooth.

Kokomo's is situated within the tropical rain forest of the atrium and has its own interior lagoon. Kokomo's specialties are steak and seafood (the latter flown in daily). The hearty meat eater can always opt for Kokomo's 22-ounce T-bone steak or extrathick rib lamb chops from a select variety of steak, chop, and rib offerings ($14 to $28), while seafood choices range from Dungeness crab cakes to broiled lobster tail, with a lengthy list in between ($17 to $36). For lunch, if you've never had prime rib on a kaiser roll, this is where you'll find it, along with such tasty choices as a crock of chili, smoked trout filet, tostada salad, and seasonal fruits in the Caribbean fruit salad ($5 to $12). Desserts from the bake shop are calorically impressive—for chocolate lovers there's an outrageous chocolate-raspberry mousse cake. Kokomo's is open daily for lunch from 11am to 2:30pm, for dinner from 5:30 to 11:30pm.

With its placid streams, delicately formed gardens, and hand-painted murals, the **Mikado** has the quiet elegance of a private Japanese home. It offers dishes prepared in the teppanyaki style—thinly sliced New York steak, chicken, lobster, or vegetables—as well as a sushi bar. Dinners include a shrimp or scallop appetizer, miso or tori soup, Mikado salad, vegetables, tea, and dessert. Or you may decide on one of several combination dinners. Dinners range from $16 to $35; à la carte fare, served with rice and tea, costs $11 to $22. Sushi and sashimi, as well as a selection of rolls (California, tuna, etc.), are also available. For the indecisive, The Mikado also has an excellent udon pot—thick noodles with chicken, shellfish, and vegetables simmered in a delicious light broth ($20). The Mikado serves dinner nightly from 6 to 11:30pm.

The **Moongate** has the look of classical Chinese architecture surrounding an open courtyard. Sculpted panels form a backdrop for Oriental murals. Moongate serves the classic Cantonese and Szechuan cuisines, though desserts are deliciously Occidental creations of The Mirage chefs. Entrees include a variety of elegant poultry, meat, vegetable, and seafood dishes. The exceptional tea-smoked duck is marinated in Chinese spices and wine, slowly smoked, and cooked until crispy; or you might prefer the black-peppered beef, seasoned with crushed peppercorns and garlic, stir-fried, and served on a bed of crispy rice vermicelli. Among the seafood dishes is Maine lobster steamed or stir-fried with scallions and ginger, Szechwan style, or with black-bean sauce. Ah, but what a dessert is the crispy fried wonton filled with banana and white-chocolate chunks, dusted with brown sugar and cinnamon, and served with vanilla ice cream and walnuts! Definitely not for the dieter. The Moongate is open nightly from 5:30 to 11:30pm.

What would life be without an Italian restaurant? At The Mirage it is **Ristorante Riva,** offering northern Italian cuisine—the classic regional dishes—in a simple, elegant setting. If you have a taste for pasta, consider the homemade ravioli stuffed with ricotta cheese, spinach, and herbs and served with a fresh marjoram cream sauce. Or for seafood, there's always a fine cioppino—the zuppa di pesce with shrimp, scallops, lobster, mussels, and clams in a light tomato fish broth. Specialties of the day may include an elegantly simple broiled veal chop served with sautéed peppers. Need I add that hot and cold antipasti are on the menu at length. And then there are the desserts, from tiramisu to my favorite (and most un-Italian) crème brûlée. Entrees range from $11 to $27.

The **Bistro** conjures up carefree, romantic Montparnasse with handsome murals in the style of Lautrec and a touch of Degas here and there. Emphasis here is on Gallic specialties with delectable light sauces, not the weighty cream varieties. Entrees include elegant choices of poultry, veal, beef, lamb, and seafood. What do I mean by "elegant"? You may find the halibut filet topped with a shrimp mousse, baked and served with a vegetable sauce; the filet mignon broiled and served with beaujolais sauce; or the breast of duckling sautéed, sliced, and served with a peppercorn sauce. The appetizer list is fraught with temptation: Consider the wild seasonal mushrooms ("in crust"), sautéed with shallots, flamed with brandy, reduced with white wine and cream, flavored with fresh herbs, then lovingly folded into phyllo dough and baked. Entrees range from $19 to $30; appetizers add $8 to $13 to the total; desserts, including Sinful Chocolate, cost $4 to $6. The Bistro serves dinner nightly from 6 to 11:30pm.

The selection of restaurants is no less diverse for family dining. There are few restaurants where I've dined as often and as consistently well at a modest price as the **California Pizza Kitchen** in The Mirage. As you might guess, the Pizza Kitchen offers a lengthy list of individually sized wood-fired gourmet pizzas, beginning with the Original BBQ Chicken pizza and extending on through 23 more choices (including vegetarian and cheeseless). Delicious pasta is also available—for example, a broccoli fusilli blessed with garlic, sun-dried tomatoes, and parmesan—as well as salads. Desserts are as impressive as the entrees. Wine and a selection of 15 beers, including nonalcoholic, are also available. Pizzas range in price from $6 to $9; pasta dishes, from $7 to $9. And one other important factor: For those who don't want to leave the scene of the action, I should point out that the California Pizza Kitchen is handily situated right next to the race and sports book. The Pizza Kitchen is open weekdays from 11am to 11pm, weekends to 2am.

The **Bermuda Buffet** has the relaxed, airy look of the island's English gardens and offers an abundance of tempting all-you-can-eat choices (over 60 menu items each day) for breakfast (7 to 11am), lunch (11am to 3pm), and dinner (3 to 11pm), with dinner entrees ranging from $6 to $13. On Sunday there's a champagne brunch.

The **Caribe Cafe** is the bright and festive coffee shop of The Mirage. It's open 24 hours and offers a lengthy selection for the all-American breakfast, lunch, and dinner as you like them, and dishes for all hours in between.

For desserts, The Mirage delivers the goodies at **Coconuts Ice Cream Shop.** This light, bright ice-cream parlor serves *freshly made* ice creams, frozen yogurts, and sorbets daily from 10am to 10pm.

Not to be outdone in any respect, The Mirage presents outstanding entertainment. The 1,500-seat **Theatre Mirage** features a show starring the incredible illusionists **Siegfried and Roy.** Among the cast are those magnificent and extremely rare white tigers. It is one of the most expensive shows ever produced, with fabulous costumes and space-age staging and lighting. Siegfried and Roy perform the first three weeks of each month at 7:30 and 11pm, except Wednesdays. The cost is $56 plus tax, including two drinks and tips. International celebrities such as Cher, Kenny Rogers, Dolly Parton, and Johnny Mathis create their own magic the fourth week.

There is a new class of hotel moving into Las Vegas—the elegant, comfortable, nongaming establishment with quiet, laid-back class, lots of space, and lots of grass. For example, note the following selection.

Residence Inn by Marriott, 3225 Paradise Rd. (across from the Las Vegas Convention Center, near Desert Inn Road), Las Vegas, NV 89109 (tel. 702/796-9300, or toll free 800/331-3131).

Just as you thought you were finally getting used to bustling casino-hotel spectaculars, along comes the Residence Inn by Marriott, a breath of fresh air, with grass.

The Marriott is, as they say, a Residence Inn (nongaming), but it's really much more than an all-suite hotel. You have your own smartly designed and private living quarters, fully and comfortably furnished, and cleverly arranged with separate sleeping areas for nighttime privacy whether you're one, two, or four. Each of the accommodations is basically a beautifully decorated apartment with a breakfast bar and full kitchen—a full-size refrigerator, range and oven, microwave, coffee maker, dishware, dishwasher, glasses, and all. Marriott includes a complimentary shopping service for your groceries. Many of the living rooms have cozy wood-burning fireplaces; all have satellite color TVs and VCRs.

The penthouse suites are perfect for two or a family. They are on two levels with two bedrooms, two full bathrooms, two closets, even two TVs. All beds are queen-size.

And with a complimentary Continental breakfast there's also a complimentary daily newspaper. Maid service is weekdays (the Marriott feels that you should have weekends to yourself), and valet service and laundry facilities are available. There are, of course, a swimming pool and a heated whirlpool, adjacent to a Sports Court for racquetball. The inn also has a collection of board games for the use of the guests in their rooms. Thursday evenings from 5 to 6:30pm there's a complimentary barbecue, and hospitality hour is also weekdays from 5 to 6:30pm.

The 192 suites are grouped into small two-story structures set among beautiful landscaping. What's more, your private entrance is just steps away from the curbside parking—no vast parking lots or unreliable attendants. A handsome central building encloses the lobby and hearth room, where complimentary breakfast is served and where evening social hours are held. The helpful staff here will arrange transportation or recommend local activities and current attractions.

Rates for one to six nights in the studio suites (one bed) are $89 to $109 per night; the penthouse suites (two beds/two baths) are $129 to $149. For 7 to 29 nights the rates decrease by $10 per night. Pets are welcome.

Bally's—Las Vegas, 3645 Las Vegas Blvd. South, Las Vegas, NV 89109 (tel. 702/739-4111, or toll free 800/634-3434).

Bally's is more than a complete resort. It is, rather, like a self-contained suburb, or an entire town—and not a small one either. Tourists detour just to see it, and a guest could spend an entire vacation without venturing out. Everything is right here: a shopping arcade, a huge gambling casino, a comedy club, two nightclub theaters for big shows, six restaurants, four cocktail lounges, an Olympic-size swimming pool, a therapy pool that can seat 50 people at a time, 10 tennis courts (7 lit for night play), a youth center (adjacent to a Swensen's Ice Cream Parlor), and complete health clubs for men and women.

Within the rosy chandeliered casino there are about 1,000 slot machines, 11 craps tables, 84 blackjack tables, 9 roulette wheels, 2 baccarat games, 20 poker tables, 3 Big Six wheels, a keno lounge, and a race and sports book.

There are 2,832 guest rooms that range from $85 to $140, single or double, to $1,250 a night for sumptuous Royal Suites. Each air-conditioned room has a separate living-room area, color TV, direct-dial phone with message light (complimentary local calls), and an AM/FM clock radio; nightly turndown service is provided. Some rooms even have round beds and mirrored ceilings, and all are decorated with a jazzy flair. There's a metal star on every door, because Bally's management still feels that every guest is a star.

If the comfortably ensconced guest gets hungry, he or she can satisfy a variety of food cravings—to wit:

The **Café Gigi** serves haute-cuisine Continental fare in a Versailles-like setting. Some of the items of decor—like the ornate gold wall panels and mirrors, and the imposing door—are actually from the set of the movie *Marie Antoinette*. The menu proffers entrees (costing $27 to $40) like veal Oscar, filet mignon with foie gras and truffles, and steak Diane. You might precede your entree with an hors d'oeuvre of scampi or a wilted-spinach salad, and top it off with a dessert of crêpes Suzette. The café is open Wednesday through Sunday from 6 to 11pm.

Tracy's is named after Spencer Tracy, who was nominated 11 times for an Academy Award. He insisted that he was an "unromantic type" despite the fact that he appeared with nearly every top female star in Hollywood. The escalator ride to the restaurant takes you through a wonderland of beveled glass with reflections of a spectacular crystal chandelier glittering everywhere. The interior is done in soft shades of coral, with large gold pillars and two-story-high windows dominating the

---

Inflation Alert

It is hardly a secret that costs will rise regardless of the level of inflation. The author of this book has spent laborious hours attempting to ensure the accuracy of prices appearing in this guide. As we got to press, I believe we have obtained the most reliable data possible. Nonetheless, in the lifetime of this edition— particularly as it approaches 1992—the wise traveler will add 15% to 20% to the prices quoted throughout these pages.

---

room. Each round table is lit by a small white-shaded lamp and has comfortable chairs.

Dinner can begin with imported prosciutto and melon, creamy marinated herring, or perhaps Tracy's salad bowl with Belgian endive, artichokes, fresh mushrooms, and watercress. Entrees include mignonette of prime beef sauté with goose liver and truffle sauce, and broiled double-rib spring lamb chops with mint jelly, among others. All dinners are served with a choice of soup or salad, potatoes, and vegetables; entrees are $15 to $25. A large selection of desserts such as fresh strawberry shortcake and French pastries is available, and there's a good wine list.

If all this is not enough, there is a special Chinese menu as well. Appetizers include paper-wrapped chicken, rumaki with water chestnuts, and a combination plate with barbecued spareribs, eggroll, paper-wrapped chicken, fried prawns, and fried wonton. There's a spicy Szechuan chicken with sautéed Chinese vegetables, Mongolian beef, and fresh shrimps with sautéed vegetables. Entrees range in price from $13 to $20. Desserts include fresh pineapple, Chinese kumquats and lichee nuts, and homemade almond cookies.

Dinner at Tracy's is served Friday through Tuesday from 5 to 11pm.

At **Caruso's,** Italian specialties are served in an atmosphere of Venetian elegance. Cobblestone-motif carpeted floors, antique iron ovens, and classical statuary grace the room, and menus list pasta dishes (served with garlic bread, and a dessert of tortoni or spumoni) and lots of other entrees (served with pasta and garlic bread), including eggplant parmigiana, mountain brook trout sauté amandine, veal scaloppine, and chicken cacciatore, all for $15 to $25. For dessert there's a delicious Italian rum cake. Caruso's is open Friday through Tuesday from 6 to 11pm.

At **Barrymores',** copper and carved-oak accents create a warmly intimate ambience. Seafood is the specialty, with entrees like tempura shrimp island style. You can also get a prime-rib dinner served with Yorkshire pudding. Entrees range from $18 to $50. Barrymore's is open nightly from 6 to 11pm.

The **Deli** is a New York–style eatery. Its immense menu offers an astounding number of choices. Combination sandwiches include salami, Swiss cheese, turkey breast, coleslaw, and Russian dressing. And among the traditional favorites are cream cheese and Nova Scotia salmon on a bagel, pastrami on rye, a Reuben, matzoh-ball soup, and cheese blintzes, all for $5 to $12. For dessert try the deep-dish fruit pies with vanilla ice cream. The Deli is open daily from 8am to midnight.

The **Orleans Coffee House** is open around the clock and features a French Quarter decor. Most of the above-mentioned Deli fare is available here too, but you can also get hot entrees such as fried prawns with a choice of soup or salad, fresh vegetable, potato du jour, and rolls and butter.

The **Celebrity Room** features megastars—the likes of Frank Sinatra. Shows are about $30 to $50 (including two drinks), depending on the performer.

The **Ziegfeld Room** offers the musical superspectacular *Jubilee!* Cocktails and show in the Ziegfeld Room cost $27.50 weekdays and $30 weekends.

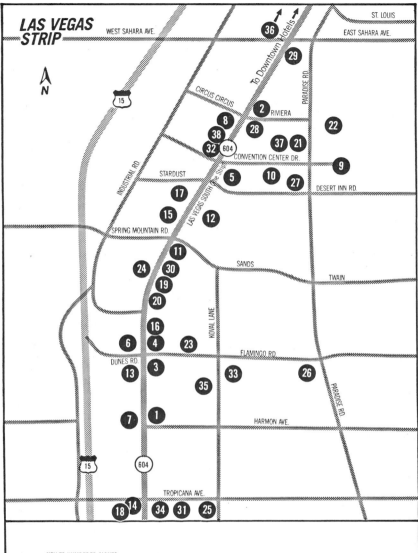

LAS VEGAS STRIP

N

KEY TO NUMBERED SIGHTS:

1. Aladdin
2. Algiers
3. Bally's
4. Barbary Coast
5. Brooks Rent-A-Car
6. Caesars Palace
7. Center Strip Inn
8. Circus Circus
9. Convention Center
10. Convention Center Lodge
11. Days Inn
12. Desert Inn
13. Dunes

14. Excalibur
15. Fashion Show Mall
16. Flamingo Hilton
17. Frontier
18. Hacienda
19. Holiday Casino/ Holiday Inn
20. Imperial Palace
21. Landmark
22. Las Vegas Hilton
23. Maxim
24. The Mirage
25. Motel
26. Quality Inn

27. Residence Inn Marriott
28. Riviera
29. Sahara
30. Sands
31. San Remo Ramada
32. Stardust
33. Super 8
34. Tropicana
25. Vagabond Inn
36. Vegas World
37. Villa Roma
38. Westward Ho

The **Celebrity Lounge,** close to the casino action, also offers live entertainment nightly. And **Bally's Theater** is the home of the Catch a Rising Star comedy club.

Caesars Palace, 3570 Las Vegas Blvd. South, Las Vegas, NV 89109 (tel. 702/731-7110, or toll free 800/634-6001, 800/634-6661 for reservations).

Arriving at Caesars Palace is like a giant step back in time to ancient Rome (well, almost), and, more specifically, to Caesar's palace. Lining the entranceway are double rows of cypress trees interspersed with magnificent fountains. Marble statues are scattered thither and yon. And you can't miss the People Mover, an automatic sidewalk originating from a Temple of Diana—or the newer People Mover leading to a geodesic dome that houses Omnimax. Omnimax is a tilted-dome theater with a wraparound screen with thrilling films and sensational audiovisual effects. At night, the hotel bathes itself in a blue-green light that glows and reflects over the entire couple of blocks that make up its façade. And the exterior of the Omnimax Theater is used for a light show. The main floor is also dotted with marble statues, the most imposing being the 18-foot-high replica of Michelangelo's *David.*

On the premises are seven restaurants, a giant 24-hour gambling casino, a nightclub featuring top entertainers, shops and service desks, eight tennis courts, golf nearby, two Olympic-size pools, and a fully equipped health club for men and women.

The private rooms are every bit as luxurious as the public ones. Rates are $125 to $170, single or double; add $15 for a third person in the room. Suites range from $230 to $800. The decor is last-days-of-Rome ornate, with mirrored walls, deep carpeting, and fancy arched dividers separating living area from sleeping area. Some of the rooms even have beds on raised platforms, with steps leading up. Of course, all the modern amenities are present and accounted for.

The newest culinary establishment at Caesars Palace is the **Empress Court,** where your palate is blessed with magnificent Chinese food prepared in the grand tradition by chefs from Hong Kong. This is definitely not your chow mein, sweet-and-sour whatever restaurant; if you had never eaten a bite, the stately columns and hand-rubbed woods would dispel that notion. Dishes are primarily Cantonese, but there is a good selection of other regional specialties, including some Szechuan dishes. To simplify life, assorted delights are included in a choice between two complete (prix-fixe) dinners: the Empress selection is about $55, and the Emperor, $40; dishes vary weekly.

If you prefer to pick and choose among the many dishes, your choice of appetizers ($7 to $14) might focus on the crispy crab claws or minced squab in crystal wrap. Your second course ($9 to $28) might include a rarity such as abalone and shark's-fin soup or bird's-nest soup with bamboo mushrooms. As to entrees ($22 to $46), every category is represented. There are abalone dishes, fresh fish, and other seafood, including exceptionally delicious gingered oysters prepared in a clay pot; vegetable and tofu dishes ($14 to $22); poultry, including golden crisp squab and the ultimate Imperial Peking duck (accompanied by a white-gloved waiter); selections of pork and beef; and fried rice unlike any you have ever eaten before, as well as noodles. Several of the truly exceptional desserts include Beijing glazed apples and banana, and the double-boiled bird's nest served in fresh coconut.

Need I say that dinner for two might easily approach $200, but it will be a spectacular event and one by which you will always remember Las Vegas. The Empress Court is open nightly. There are two seatings: 6 to 6:30pm and 9 to 9:30pm. Reservations are necessary and I suggest that you make them a few days in advance.

The **Bacchanal** continues in the style to which you quickly become accustomed at Caesars Palace. Done up in lavish Roman decor, complete with girls in harem outfits to pour your wine, it is open for a prix-fix dinner only, at about $60 per person for a banquet with appropriate wines included. Your evening repast will include tidbits, served with your apéritif, followed by more serious hors d'oeuvres, a variety of soups, fish, "a parade of gastronomical surprises," vegetables, desserts, cheeses, fruits, and coffee. The Bacchanal is open Wednesday through Sunday. There are two seatings: 6 to 6:30pm and 9 to 9:30pm.

Equally super-posh is the **Palace Court,** serving classic French cuisine in a minimuseum setting. It's reached via a round elevator with a crystal-and-bronze car. Works on display here include paintings of the 12 Caesars by the 17th-century Bolognese artist Camillo Procaccini. A weeping fig tree surrounded by chrysanthemums under a domed stained-glass skylight is the centerpiece. This is a place to go when you're willing to spend freely—it's easy to work up $70-per-person tabs. Dinner is served nightly, and specialties include fresh braised salmon Véronique, which you might precede with an appetizer of pike mousse. Entrees cost $25 to $55. A knowledgeable staff of sommeliers is on hand to help you select the proper wine. Dinner hours are 6:30 to 9:30pm nightly, with two seatings. Reservations are necessary.

Primavera, overlooking the Garden of the Gods swimming pool and spa, offers gourmet Italian cuisine with specialties from the north and south of Italy. For a first course, the antipasti cart presents an outstanding array of cold appetizers. Or you might defer to a house specialty such as the fried mozzarella or the elegant consommé garnished with egg flakes, spinach, and grated cheese.

The entree list begins with pasta, all homemade, including the chef's specialty of ravioli lightly filled with spinach and essence of veal, served with your choice of bolognese, marinara, or butter sauce. Several of the pasta entrees are also available as side dishes. The many veal entrees range from the veal marsala to a simple veal with prosciutto and fresh sage. One of the unusual poultry choices features thin slices of sautéed breast of chicken with kiwi fruit and lemon butter, finished with rich sherry wine. Prime sirloin steak is served sautéed and topped with a tomato sauce, or panfried with a touch of garlic. Maine lobster is served in a spicy marinara sauce. And look for the chef's specialty each evening.

Primavera offers a pastry cart of Italian specialties, as well as cheese with fresh fruit in season. Ice-cream desserts are meals in themselves—say, the cassata Caligula, with layers of pistachio, zabaglione, and chocolate ice cream.

Meat or seafood entrees cost $24 to $45, pasta dishes are $12 to $18, and appetizers run $7 to $17. To help sustain your appetite, you'll find a good selection of still and sparkling Italian wines. Primavera is open daily for breakfast from 7:30 to 11am, for luncheon from 11:30am to 2:30pm, and for dinner from 6 to 11:30pm.

La Piazza Food Court offers a vast selection of dishes from the most popular cuisines—Chinese, Italian, French, and Japanese. Your choices are mind-boggling—it's a market researcher's dream come true. La Piazza is open Sunday through Thursday from 8am to 10pm, on Friday and Saturday to midnight.

Other dining options include the **Ah-So Steak House,** serving table d'hôte Japanese teppanyaki dinners (about $45 per person) in an Oriental garden setting (open nightly from 6 to 11pm); **Spanish steps,** combining Moorish design with modernistic gleaming copper and brass decor and offering entrees ranging in price from $17 to $45 for arroz con pollo to steak and lobster (open nightly from 5:30 to 10:30pm); the **Falatium** for buffet-style meals for breakfast, lunch, and dinner; and the **Café Roma,** a 24-hour coffee shop.

For entertainment (in addition to the above-mentioned Omnimax) there's **Circus Maximus,** featuring acts like Tom Jones, the Pointer Sisters, Cher, Diana Ross, and Frank Sinatra. There are cocktail shows only—at 8:30pm and 11:30pm—priced at $25 to $50, depending on the performer and not including drinks. Closed Tuesday.

And rounding out the bill is **Cleopatra's Barge,** a replica of Cleopatra's trysting ship, complete with hydraulic mechanism to keep it in constant motion afloat on the "Nile." Open from 9:30pm to 4:30am, with a live band for dancing.

The Las Vegas Hilton, 3000 Paradise Rd. (adjacent to the Las Vegas Convention Center), Las Vegas, NV 89109 (tel. 702/732-5111, or toll free 800/732-7117).

Calling itself a vacation spa, the Las Vegas Hilton is one of the largest resort hotels in the world, with 3,174 rooms. It contains a corps of international restaurants, a grand casino, about 20 shops, and a landscaped 10-acre recreation deck on the third-floor roof with six night-lit tennis courts, an 18-hole putting course, shuffleboard, and a huge swimming pool. There's more. A complete 18-hole golf course is a mere step away, there are pagoda-style huts for cardplaying and snacking . . . well, you get the picture.

The extravagant lobby is hung with tier upon tier of glistening imported crystal chandeliers and boasts a 100-foot reception desk. Extravagance doesn't stop in the lobby. If anything, it is accentuated in the rooms, executed in a Continental decor, with one floor decorated in Spanish style, another in Oriental, another in French, and so on. The prevailing theme, whatever the floor, is luxury. Singles or doubles go for $80 to $165; suites, $350 to $1,100.

One particularly enticing feature for families is the "Youth Hotel." Supervised 24 hours a day, it even contains a supervised dorm for kids aged 3 through 18. Every conceivable kind of craft, sport, and activity is available to entertain the young while mom and dad are out on the town. Rates are about $5 an hour for each child. During the summer and on weekends and holidays throughout the year, kids can stay overnight for $30 (calculated from midnight to 8am).

Now, how about a meal? There are offerings from the delicate delights of Japan, the light pastas and veal dishes of Italy, the subtle and elegant cuisine of France, as well as the finest beef fare selected for Hilton steaks and prime ribs.

Le Montrachet, the pride of the Las Vegas Hilton, features Continental cuisine and a wine cellar with over 400 wines from around the world. Le Montrachet was created to achieve the utmost in elegant dining. The dark walls, plush banquettes, and flattering light create a rich, relaxed atmosphere, conducive to appreciation of the chef's superb creations.

Dinner at Le Montrachet was one of the finest I have had at any restaurant from New York to California. Ordering from the six-course, prix-fixe menu, I began my meal with chilled foie gras of duck on a checkerboard of miniature green beans. Then came poached oysters on the half-shell, topped with orange butter glaze, followed by a delicate sweet basil sorbet. Choice of entrees was between roast rack of lamb marinated with sweet basil, fresh dill, mint, shallots, and tarragon; or medallions of veal and morel mushrooms with Noilly cream sauce. A salad of lamb lettuce, endive, and watercress—tossed with walnuts, Dijon mustard, and lemon juice—was next, and all of the above was capped by a hot apple tart topped with caramel ice cream. The prix-fixe dinner is $55—about $20 less than if each course is ordered individually.

Should you decide to order à la carte, I suggest that you try something a bit different, and then wait for a very pleasant surprise. You might choose the medallions of venison on a bed of steamed red cabbage, or the poached filet of sole with mousse of lobster. A first or second course might be the raviolis of fresh crabmeat and morel mushrooms topped with caviar. Entrees also include seafood choices from Maine lobster to Dover sole, either grilled or boned and filled with mousse of lobster and served with truffle slices. The broiled veal chop stuffed with wild mushrooms and served with madeira sauce and truffles is excellent too, as is the broiled filet mignon served with a puff-pastry shell of wild mushrooms and a Pinot noir and Sandeman port-wine sauce.

Then by all means review the pastry cart. If by some quirk nothing catches your eye, scan the dessert list and consider the Swiss chocolate soufflé, crème anglaise with Cointreau, or the Painter's Palette with sorbets and fresh fruits of the season. Hors d'oeuvres range from $10 to $23; soup or salad, from $5 to $7. Entrees are about $23 to $38; desserts, $6 to $10. Le Montrachet is open daily from 6 to 11pm. Reservations are necessary, as are jacket and tie.

Most dramatic of the restaurants is **Benihana Village,** a complex of two Japanese restaurants for robata (barbecue) and hibachi dining. Four cocktail lounges set in a life-size Japanese village with lush gardens, running streams, and an imperial palace complete the picture. Guests are treated to periodic thunder and lightning storms and pouring rain (not on diners), electric fireworks displays, and dancing waters. Full dinners with appetizer, soup, salad, rice, vegetables, tea, and dessert cost $15 to $40. Dinner is served nightly from 6 to 11pm.

The **Hilton Steak House** serves immense Texas-style meals in a western setting. Entrees cost $18 to $30—served nightly from 6 to 11:30pm. The **Barronshire Prime Rib Room,** sporting a bibliothèque decor, offers full prime-rib dinners for $20 to $25 nightly from 6 to 11pm.

For light Italian fare, the lovely **Andiamo** features an open kitchen where guests can watch the chefs busily turning out delicious meals. The à la carte lunch and dinner menus both offer a remarkable selection. Lunch at Andiamo might begin with hot or cold antipasti, including such delectables as fresh asparagus with sweet-pepper sauce, and crisply fried squid with fresh tomato sauce. Pizzas are decidedly not those found at your local parlor—the porcini e salsiccia, for example, is composed of porcini mushrooms, Italian sausage, and tomato sauce with mozzarella, fontina, and provolone. Pasta? Try the ravioli Neri all' Aragosta with lobster, tarragon, and lobster sauce. An impressive list of entrees includes such selections as salmon, swordfish, a sirloin minute steak, and osso buco Andiamo. Your tab for lunch, without antipasti, wine, dessert, or coffee, will be about $10 to $16.

Andiamo's dinner menu is expansive, and the antipasti include one of my favorites, carpaccio di Manzo—wafer-thin slices of tenderloin of beef blessed with parmesan, olive oil, and lemon juice. Among the pasta entrees, you might choose the fettuccine verdi al pomodoro e melanzane—spinach egg noodles with eggplant, tomatoes, and sweet basil. Other entrees are exceptional too—a whole baby salmon sautéed in butter, a veal chop with morel mushrooms and marsala sauce, or a charcoal-broiled filet mignon with Barolo Riserva red-wine sauce. Pasta entrees run $12 to $20; seafood and meat courses will set you back $14 to $24. Should you still have space for dessert, and the patience to wait 30 minutes, the soufflés at $5 are heavenly—there's a choice of amaretto, Galliano, or lemon. Or you might consider the Venetian Dream of white espresso ice cream in a chocolate gondola for $9.

Andiamo is open daily for lunch from 11:30am to 2:30pm and for dinner from 6 to 11pm. Reservations are suggested.

The **Odyssey Buffet** is one of the best in town, displaying the Hilton's reputation for quality. The breakfast buffet ($6.50) is served from 7 to 9:30am; lunch ($7.75), from 11am to 2:30pm; dinner ($9.25), from 6 to 10pm. Saturday and Sunday, there is a champagne brunch ($9.25) from 8am to 2pm.

And finally there's **Mamchen's Deli,** western in decor with Mamchen's lettered in Hebrew-style characters. The menu is typical New York deli. Sandwiches, chicken soup with kreplach, chopped liver, etc., range from $7 to $10. Open daily from 11:30am to 10pm.

The 2,000-seat **Hilton Showroom** (Barbra Streisand was the first act when it opened) has featured a succession of superstars—Bill Cosby, Wayne Newton, Dionne Warwick, etc. The 8pm show costs about $25 to $50; the midnight show is $20 to $30, including two drinks. Closed Monday.

The **Casino Lounge** turns into a disco at night, offering live and taped music from 8pm to 3am. No cover or minimum.

Desert Inn, 3145 Las Vegas Blvd. South (directly opposite the Frontier Hotel), Las Vegas, NV 89109 (tel. 702/733-4444, or toll free 800/634-6906).

The handsomest façade of any hotel-casino on the Strip belongs to the Desert Inn, a 185-acre resort that, at the beginning of 1990, completed a multimillion-dollar redecoration and general improvement program. The beautifully landscaped grounds contain a lake, pond, and waterfall, as well as an Olympic-size swimming pool, large sun decks, 10 outdoor whirlpools, an 18-hole PGA-class championship golf course (greens fee for guests is $75 weekdays, $100 weekends; guests of guests pay $135), 10 tournament-class tennis courts (5 are lit for night play), and two shuffleboard courts. Other facilities include a gorgeous casino, five restaurants, three bars, a lounge, showroom, shopping arcade, auto rental, concierge, and beauty and barber shops.

There is also a luxurious health spa that is second to none as a pampering and fitness facility; it includes a gym, outdoor pool, hydrowhirls, saunas, massage, skin care, aerobics class, and other toning and relaxation programs.

The Desert Inn's 821 rooms, including 95 suites, are situated in several buildings. Guests now have a variety of room options to choose from, including private patios, hydrowhirl tubs, wet bars, refrigerators, bathroom phones, and more. Each room offers a spectacular view of either the Strip or the pool and the golf course, plus color TV climate control, and pushbutton phones.

Rooms at the Desert Inn are $90 to $180, single or double; one-bedroom suites are $250 to $550; two- to four-bedroom suites run $550 to $1,500. Prices vary with amenities and location.

As for dining, guests have a choice of the romantic **La Vie en Rose,** the Desert Inn's prized French gourmet restaurant (entrees, $26 to $45); the very posh **Portofino** (overlooking the casino) for northern Italian fare, with tableside cooking a specialty (entrees, $20 to $32); the elegant **HoWan,** for the finest delicacies from the provinces of China (entrees, $14 to $38); **La Promenade,** an elegant 24-hour dining alternative with poolside views; and the Country Club's sporty **Champions' Deli,** an informal and colorful dining spot looking out on the golf course and serving steaks, salads, sandwiches, and omelets daily from 8am to 5pm.

The showplace of the Desert Inn is the **Crystal Room,** featuring big-name entertainment like Rich Little, the Smothers Brothers, Lou Rawls, Marilyn McCoo, Roy Clark, among others. Shows usually cost $25 to $35, depending on the performer. There are no dinner shows. Shows are at 8 and 11pm on Tuesday, Wednesday, Friday, and Saturday; at 9pm on Thursday and Sunday.

Winners Choice Lounge also offers continuous top-talent musical presentations from 4pm to 3am daily.

The Tropicana Resort & Casino, 3801 Las Vegas Blvd. South, Las Vegas, NV 89109 (tel. 702/739-2222, or toll free 800/634-4000).

Located at the least flashy extremity of the Strip, the Tropicana replaces the glitter and razzle-dazzle that is the norm in Vegas with subtle (for this town) elegance. A major renovation a few years ago added a $25-million 600-room tower, a spectacular porte cochere entranceway; and a trilevel atrium with marble fountains, Aubusson carpets, and shop façades designed to look like those along the Champs-Élysées. Its art nouveau casino, under a stained-glass skylight ceiling, is exquisite. A second reconstruction completed in 1986 added another 22-story tower with 806 rooms (bringing the room count to 1,913), and a spectacular 5-acre water park and "island" with its own lagoons. The hotel also expanded the casino and redecorated several public rooms.

The hotel is set on lush tropical grounds, which make a nice background for what seems like the largest indoor/outdoor swimming pool in the world! Across from the hotel is an 18-hole, par-70 golf course with a clubhouse, pro shop, and locker rooms. The Tropicana Racquet Club offers 24-hour play on its four outdoor courts.

Rooms are done in light, airy, tropical decor and fitted out with all the modern amenities. Standard accommodations are priced at $79 to $135 a night; suites run $260 and up.

El Gaucho is the Tropicana's steak-and-chop house, done in Argentinian motif: beamed ceilings, hides on the walls, bits, branding irons, halters, cinches, stirrups, woven shawls. Beef is the specialty of the house—steaks, ribs, and combination plates. Entrees range from $15 to $27.50; the top end of the range is a steak-and-seafood platter. El Gaucho is open only for dinner, Friday through Tuesday from 6 to 11pm.

The **Rhapsody** offers an excellent selection of entrees for all tastes. Whether you're moved toward Long Island duckling, veal piccata, filet mignon, rack of spring lamb, scampi, rainbow trout, Columbia River salmon, cioppino (San Francisco), or broiled Australian lobster tails, the Rhapsody will delight your appetite. And the desserts are not to be ignored: There's peach Melba, baked Alaska, French pastries, chocolate mousse—many of those wonderful things you never seem to have enough room for.

Most entrees on the à la carte menu cost $16.50 to $27.50 per person, but some of the dishes are priced for two—for example, the chateaubriand for $39.50. The Rhapsody is open Wednesday through Sunday from 6 to 11pm; Sunday brunch is from 9am to 2pm.

The Tropics is just that—a Polynesian aura with beaded curtains, colorful banners, tiki figures, lighting glowing from large shells, and its own waterfall running through the center of the restaurant. The view to the outside is lovely. The restaurant has three tiers, glassed in, which overlook an "island" and all the activities and shows. The Tropics serves breakfast, lunch, and dinner Friday through Sunday from 7:30am. Other days it's to 2:30pm. Polynesian delights are the specialty of the house. Breakfast will cost $5 to $7.50; lunch, $7 to $13; and dinner, $12 to $21.

And there's a 24-hour coffee shop, the **Java Java Coffee Room,** as well as the **Island Buffet,** open 7am to 10pm, and **Mizuno's Teppan Dining.**

Then there's the **Tiffany Theater,** which is only incidentally a restaurant. It's primarily the setting for the lavish *Folies Bergère,* a dazzling musical extravaganza that has been delighting audiences since 1959 and is about to have a facelift. It's racy and funny and spectacular, with French cancan acts, live chimps, a horse, acrobats, comedians, magicians, and hundreds of semiclad and/or elaborately costumed lovelies. The 8pm dinner show is about $21 to $40, depending on your choice of entree; the 11pm show is $15 without food or drinks. There is no performance on Thursday.

Excalibur, 3850 Las Vegas Blvd. South, Las Vegas, NV 89119-1050 (tel. 702/597-7700, or toll free 800/937-7777).

Once-upon-a-time has come to life just across the Strip from the Tropicana. Opening date for Excalibur was June 1990—complete with towers, turrets, battlements, a moat and drawbridge, and a full staff of squires, ladies-in-waiting, troubadours, pages, and serfs, as befits the namesake of King Arthur's sword. For the moment at least, Excalibur holds the title of "the world's largest hotel/casino" with over 4,000 rooms. Built on a 117-acre site, it was brought into being by Circus Circus Enterprises at a cost of approximately $300 million. Suffice it to say that room count is a highly competitive business among Las Vegas hotels. It seems it's not how big you are but how many rooms you have, and one's king-of-the-mountain position is always being threatened.

As you might expect from Circus Circus Enterprises, Excalibur merges theater, festival, and casino into an extraordinary entertainment experience. A cobblestoned foyer leads visitors from the porte cochere into a 40-foot-high atrium with towering rock walls. Its centerpiece is a majestic fountain that rises three stories from the Fantasy Faire below to display a many-colored water-and-light show. The imposing granite registration desk is ornamented with murals depicting castle life and set off by authentic suits of armor.

Heraldic banners point you toward the entrance to the casino, its vast interior illuminated with row upon row of iron-and-gold chandeliers and surrounded by stained-glass windows inspired by tales of the Knights of the Round Table. The gaming area of more than 100,000 square feet has tables for blackjack, craps, and roulette, a keno lounge, a race and sports book, and 2,630 slot machines.

Among the many, many nongaming games offered are Sherwood Forest Archery, testing your aim with a crossbow, and William Tell Darts, where winning requires that you throw a jumbo dart into an apple (though not off the head of your child). As for total entertainment, theaters with Merlin's Magic Motion machines will physically move you to match fascinating visual effects you see on the screen in front of you (the first in North America). Combining the delights of food with the ultimate in entertainment, Excalibur has an 890-seat amphitheater with two dinner shows per evening. This is where you'll see Merlin, King Arthur, Queen Guinevere, and mounted knights in an extravaganza of medieval games and spectacular pyrotechnics.

Not to deny anyone of the joys of shopping, Excalibur has **The Royal Village** with its 23 shops and booths on the Fantasy Faire level. Shops include those featuring artisans and craftsmen—coin makers, glassblowers, candle makers, leathersmiths, etc. There is also a beauty salon for the repair of damsels.

Guest rooms are colorfully done in rich reds, forest green, and autumn gold set against a beige wall-covering that has the remarkable look of a stone finish. All the furnishings are quite comfortable, and the deluxe accommodations have a convenient sitting area. Each of the rooms has a full bath, phone, and color TV with in-room pay TV movies.

Accommodations are $45 to $65 for standard to deluxe oversize rooms, depending on the day and holiday (if any). Suites with Jacuzzis are $110. A charge of $7 per person is added for more than two persons per room. There is no charge for children under 12 in rooms with parents. Room rates (not including the suites) are generally reduced from late November through the first three weeks of December.

Seven themed restaurants grace the castle. There is **Lance-A-Lotta Pasta** for spaghetti, with an interior decor of whimsical treasures from places like Venice and Rome. Next door is **Oktoberfest,** a German beer garden (please don't ask if there was one in Camelot) complete with wooden trestle tables, beers from all nations, and Bavarian entertainment. On up Palace Lane is the **RoundTable Buffet,** a medieval fortress defined by barrel vaults and flying buttresses and decorated with paintings of the great knights of King Arthur's world. Past the 10-foot dragons that guard the castle gate is the **Sherwood Forest Cafe,** framed by a pair of friendly gargoyles; this is where you'll find a display of the king's cannons and armory. To top them all is **Sir Galahad's,** featuring prime roast beef carved tableside and served with Yorkshire pudding. And then there's **Robin Hood's Snack Bar,** a fascinating pavilion-type structure built around two large sycamore trees that extend through the roof. If the food doesn't hold your attention, the scene depicting the travels of Robin Hood is sure to. For intimate dining, the **Camelot Restaurant** is situated across from Excalibur's Canterbury Wedding Chapel. (The chapel is done in a rosy hue, and even has its own small apse for photography.)

Ramada Hotel San Remo and Casino, 115 E. Tropicana Ave., Las Vegas, NV 89109-7304 (tel. 702/739-9000, or toll free 800/522-7366).

For those who don't feel the need of a Strip location, the San Remo is a very handsome, comfortable place to stay, with new and beautifully redone accommodations and some of the most pleasant hotel personnel in town. It's just east of the Strip, right next to the Tropicana.

The San Remo is not in the how-many-rooms-are-there-today competition. There are 324 elegant and spacious accommodations in attractive classic Italian style —light walls and dark woods against dark leather (plus full-size baths with fluffy towels)—and all contain the expected amenities.

Room rates for a petit king, deluxe king, or the deluxe king with a pool view range from $50 to $60 Sunday through Thursday, $65 to $90 on Friday and Saturday, and $95 to $120 on holidays and during special events. Petite suites are $75 to $100, $130 on holidays; one- or two-bedroom suites are $150 to $400, $260 to $600 on holidays.

The gaming area offers all the usual options. One aspect of the casino I especially appreciate: It's roomier than most, and easier to get from one table to the next. What's more, it isn't necessary to elbow your way through the casino to get to the registration desk.

As with any proper Las Vegas hotel, there are a pool and a sunning area for total relaxation and tanning.

The San Remo has a lovely restaurant in **La Panache,** which offers fine Continental and American selections. Open Tuesday through Sunday from 5 to 11pm. The **Ristorante del Fiori** is the hotel's 24-hour casual-dining restaurant and buffet in a gardenlike setting. Breakfast buffet ($3) is served from 7 to 10am; luncheon buffet ($4), from 11am to 2pm; dinner ($5), from 5 to 9pm.

The Riviera Hotel, 2901 Las Vegas Blvd. South, Las Vegas, NV 89109 (tel. 702/734-5110, or toll free 800/634-6753).

The Riviera's lobby is tastefully arranged, with slot machines discreetly off to one side. Off the lobby is the hotel's promenade, lined with fashionable boutiques, shops, and airline offices. In addition to an immense and very popular casino, facilities include an Olympic-size pool surrounded by manicured lawns, and a palm-lined sun deck with piped-in music.

The addition of the Monaco Tower brought the Riviera's room capacity to 2,136. A third tower, under construction, will raise the room count to 3,720. At completion (scheduled for the end of 1990), there will also be a total of 10 restaurants, a deli, two pools, health clubs, and a jogging track.

The Monaco Tower is tastefully furnished, with bedroom and bath separated by a walk-through closet. Rooms cost $60 to $100 a night for double or single occupancy; suites run $130 to $600. All rooms have double or king-size beds.

The award-winning gourmet restaurant here is **Delmonico,** after the famous eatery once in the Wall Street district of New York City. It has been redecorated—rich pearl-gray walls are a backdrop for tables set with exquisite china, gleaming silver, and sparkling crystal. A well-stocked wine cellar is on the premises. A meal at Delmonico might begin with an appetizer of fresh pâté (created daily). Sumptuous entrees include sautéed medallions of veal with fresh melon and port wine. Complete prix-fixe dinners start at $27.50.

A wall-size mural in the **Ristorante Italiano** gives the diner a lovely view of a colorful Italian town. Entrees are priced from $16 to $34, and include osso buco, veal shank sautéed in olive oil with tomatoes, onions, and herbs; an accompanying order of broccoli in oil and garlic is a good idea.

Kristopher's is the Riviera's latest addition, a steak house located in the Monaco tower. It's a relaxed pastel environment with wicker chairs and ceiling fans, and there's also a lounge overlooking the pool area. The selection of entree choices on the prix-fixe menu includes prime rib, jumbo shrimp specially marinated, baby back ribs, T-bone steak, breast of turkey, blackened redfish, and swordfish (though the seafood choices change seasonally). The prix-fixe dinner, which includes everything from appetizer and wine to dessert, is $17 and is served from 5:30 to 11pm. The restaurant is open daily for breakfast (7 to 11am), lunch (noon to 4pm), and dinner (5:30 to 11pm). Breakfast will cost $3 to $10, and the buffet brunch, $9.

Of course, in this 24-hour town there's a 24-hour coffee shop, **Kady's Brasserie.** The Gourmet Buffet offers breakfast for $3, lunch for $4, and dinner for $5.

Currently running in the **Versailles Theater** is *Splash,* an aquacade spectacular. It's a great family show, with diving and swimming stars, mermaids, dancers, and showgirls. Shows are at 8pm ($23.50) and 11pm ($20.50). No nudity at the 8pm show. The theater is closed Wednesday.

At the **Mardi Gras Plaza** is a brilliant and long-running revue, *An Evening at La Cage,* starring a bevy of female impersonators—the best in town. It's clever, hilarious, and thoroughly enjoyable. The production is spectacular, with beautiful costuming and dance numbers. Shows are at 7, 9, and 11pm; admission is $11, which includes two drinks. Closed Tuesday.

Then there's **An Evening at the Improv,** arguably the most famous of all the stand-up comedy shops today. Shows are nightly at 8:30 and 10:30pm, and midnight. Admission is $13.50, which includes two drinks. *Crazy Girls—Fantasie de Paris* has shows at 8, 9:30, and 11pm. Admission is $11, which includes two drinks. There is no performance Thursday.

And now should you choose to enter the uncertain state of matrimony, it's all possible within the Riviera at the **Royale Wedding Chapel** (tel. 702/794-9494). What better place to take the gamble?

The Flamingo Hilton, 3555 Las Vegas Blvd. South, Las Vegas, NV 89109 (tel. 702/733-3111, or toll free 800/732-2111).

From its façade frieze of prismatic neon pink-and-orange flamingos to its tropical-resort-look palm-studded pool area, the Flamingo Hilton is an aesthetic tribute to its name. A renovation a few years back added a 28-story, 500-room tower; a modernistic casino with the familiar Hilton neon rainbow motif; a new restaurant; and a high-rise parking garage. And the Flamingo Hilton recently broke ground on what is to become a 28-story, 728-room luxury tower that will include an Italian restaurant, lounge, tour lobby, VIP lounge, outdoor plaza, and 20,000 square feet of additional casino space. The tower is scheduled for completion in early 1991.

Rooms here are pleasant. Those in the older building, which are convenient to the pool, are pretty and quaint, with homey furnishings and old-fashioned lamps and quilts. Accommodations in another 800-room tower (total room count is 2,920) offer views of the Strip or garden and are done in one of four color schemes (rust, green, beige/yellow, or peach) with coordinated wallpaper and drapes. They're large and equipped with every luxury, including closed-circuit gaming instructions on the color TV. The tower has a health club, tennis courts for day and night play, and a new gourmet restaurant, the Flamingo Room.

Rates are $70 to $118, single or double.

The **Flamingo Room** is a pleasant place to relax over breakfast, lunch, or dinner. The room is done in pastels and light woods, with soft recessed lighting and a large expanse of windows overlooking the pool. The salad bar for lunch has an appetizing array (one of the largest in town) of beautifully fresh choices, even including large shrimp. Dinner entrees offer a good selection of fresh fish, steaks, and rack of lamb for $15 to $28, though an average is about $18. Among the specialties of the house are a delicious mixed grill and the Flamingo barbecue. The Flamingo Room is open daily from 7am to 11am for breakfast, 11:30am to 2pm for lunch, and 5 to 11pm for dinner.

The innovative **Food Fantasy Restaurant** is a "buffeteria" with a sumptuous display of food (open from 6am to 9pm); the Old West–motif **Beef Barron** features (you guessed it) beef dinners, ribs, black-bean soup, and corn on the cob (a five-course steak dinner with wine is $46 for two); the **Peking Market** is designed to suggest a bustling Chinese marketplace and serves Cantonese fare; **Lindy's** is patterned after the famous New York deli; and the **Crown Room Buffet** serves breakfast and dinner buffets at very low prices.

The Flamingo's **Showroom** presents *City Lites,* a lavish ice spectacular, complete with gorgeous costumes, stunning sets, and all the rest. Dinner shows (at 7:45pm nightly) begin at $23; the 11pm show is $18, including two drinks.

There's also nightly entertainment in the **Casino Lounge**—singers and combos alternating with disco dancing.

Aladdin Hotel & Casino, 3667 Las Vegas Blvd. South, Las Vegas, NV 89109 (tel. 702/736-0111, or toll free 800/634-3424).

With all the bidders for the once-defunct Aladdin Hotel, including such heavy hitters as Wayne Newton and Johnny Carson, when the hands were finally played out, the winner for the hotel was a Korean-born resident of Japan with a very large wallet. The Japanese seem convinced of Las Vegas's success in the high-stakes contest for top billing as the gambling, entertainment, and convention center of the country. After all, Las Vegas is just a short jump from the La Costa Resort in Carlsbad—purchased by the Japanese in 1987 for $250 million. And La Costa, or any one of several Japanese-owned hotels in San Francisco, is little more than a five-hour hop from Japanese holdings in Hawaii.

The hotel has 1,100 modern, spacious rooms, totally redecorated and refurnished. The beige-and-gold furnishings convey a luxury theme, whether you choose to stay in one of the remodeled rooms or in a newly created duplex suite. Room rates are $70 to $130 per night, single or double occupancy. One- and two-bedroom suites are $375 to $600, and the duplex supersuite extravaganza is $2,500.

To keep you fit, comfortable, and relaxed, the Aladdin sports a rooftop recreation center with a pool, lighted tennis courts for night play, and a snack bar for the lounge lizards.

The Aladdin has three entertainment venues: the 700-seat **Bagdad Showroom,** the 100-seat **Sinbad Lounge,** and, topping all the hotels in Las Vegas, the 7,000-seat **Aladdin Theatre for the Performing Arts**—the largest theater in Las Vegas (apart from that at the university) and undoubtedly the one with the best acoustics. The theater has featured a remarkable range of performers from Rudolf Nureyev to Anita Baker, Fleetwood Mac, Tina Turner, and in a special charity reunion, the Doobie Brothers.

And what would a Las Vegas hotel be without its own version of a perpetual motion machine—the nonstop, 24-hour casino? Among the usual games, the Aladdin features a new poker room and a high-limit race and sports book.

The Aladdin has three excellent restaurants, a deli, and the usual 24-hour coffee shop so necessary to survival in Las Vegas. Most prestigious of the eateries is **The Florentine,** which offers French, Italian, and Continental cuisine prepared tableside. This elegant restaurant, as its name suggests, is graced with Florentine frosted-glass panels, as well as floral murals and crystal chandeliers. House specialties are veal marsala and sumptuous braised sweetbreads. Entrees on the à la carte menu are priced from $14 to $40. Wines from cellars all over the world are available here. Open Wednesday through Sunday from 6 to 11pm; reservations are suggested.

Another handsomely designed restaurant is **Wellington's,** an American version of an English pub—very masculine, with dark woods, brick floors, wrought-iron chandeliers, hunting prints, and, in the center of it all, a brass rotisserie. This beef house features certified Black Angus aged beef, as well as first-rate steaks and barbecued selections. Wellington's prepares excellent salads tableside and offers an extensive wine list. Entrees range from $9 to $17. Open nightly from 6pm to midnight. Reservations suggested.

Fisherman's Port has been a hit with diners from the day it opened. The restaurant features fresh seafood flown in from the East Coast. Despite the Cajun character of much of its cuisine, Fisherman's Port looks more New England than New Orleans, with its board floors, stanchions, captain's chairs, netting, and seascapes. The menu features soups, bisques, and bouillabaisse, and entrees range from orange roughy to Alaskan king crab, crayfish étouffé, and blackened red fish, all accompanied by hush puppies and black-eyed peas; the popular Cajun dishes are served spicy or mild, to suit your taste. Entree prices range from $11 to $40. There is a special wine list to complement the unique cuisine. The Fisherman's Port is open Wednesday through Sunday from 6pm to 11pm.

The Delicatessen looks like an old-time deli—dark-wood chairs with red cushions, red-and-black carpeting, and a counter that looks like an old-fashioned bar. You can watch the specialties of the house being prepared in an open kitchen—everything from scrambled eggs with lox and onions to cheese blintzes with sour cream or blueberries. Combination sandwiches, in an incredible variety, are served on three slices of thin corn rye and accompanied by potato salad, relish bowl, and garnish. For dinner, you can order the likes of boiled chicken in the pot, ot roast, or Ingine and clams or shrimp. Should you feel you have room for dessert, everything from cheesecake (five varities) to a banana split can be enjoyed while watching the keno board. Prices for luncheon or dinenr range from $5 to $12; for breakfast, from $3 to $6. The Delicatessen is open daily from 10am to midnight.

And last but by no means least is the **International Buffet.** Its style with Oriental dishes makes it one of the best buffets in town. This is where you'll find some of the better Chinese and Japanese dishes, plus an interesting array of other international offerings. The International Buffet serves breakfast ($5) from 7 to 10:30am, lunch ($6) from 11:30am to 2pm, and dinner ($8.25) from 4 to 10pm.

The Oasis, the Aladdin's 24-hour coffee shop, is ready whenever you are with sandwiches, salads, main dishes, desserts, and fountain selections. Prices go up to $10.

The Sands Hotel Casino, 3355 Las Vegas Blvd. South, Las Vegas, NV 89109 (tel. 702/733-5000, or toll free 800/446-4678).

The Sands, with its 18-story tower, 750 rooms and suites, and 10 garden buildings, lies in the middle of all the Strip action. The Interface Group, Inc., the owners of the Sands, has announced a $150-million improvement plan, including the addition of 1,200 rooms and 45,000 square feet to the casino. Currently facilities include two swimming pools, six night-lit tennis courts, shuffleboard, a nine-hole putting green, a beauty salon and barbershop, a tennis boutique, and the rest. Fully equipped women's and men's health clubs are staffed by professionals and feature heated whirlpools, saunas, and weightlifting and exercise equipment.

The spacious rooms are softly color coordinated in lovely hues. Fully equipped with all the amenities, they're quite spacious. Rates, single or double, run $70 to $105 for the outlying buildings and start at $150 for tower rooms.

The Sands' 30,000-square-foot casino contains a wide variety of the latest in hi-tech slot machines, keno, a complete race and sports book, craps, blackjack, roulette, baccarat, and Oriental games.

The Sands boasts a prestigious restaurant, the opulent **Regency Room,** which serves French/Continental cuisine. Among the fine array of specialties offered on the extensive menu are scampi provençal, filet of beef Wellington, quail, and roast duckling à l'orange, to name just a few. Entrees cost $16 to $37.50. There are also complete dinners from $16. The Regency Room is open Tuesday through Saturday from 6pm to midnight. Reservations are suggested.

The 24-hour **Garden Terrace** restaurant features everything from snacks and a soup-and-salad bar to full-course meals with daily menu specials, including "fish-by-the-ounce" from $5.75. The light, airy dining room overlooks a spacious outdoor pool and lush garden. Breakfast, served around the clock, offers a variety of omelets, scrambled eggs with nova and onions, eggs "your way," blintzes, griddle cakes, and the usual assortment of pastries, beverages, and fruit. For midday hunger pangs (whenever that might be), there is a fine selection of sandwiches, including "create your own" hamburgers. Dinner entrees may range from tenderloin of pork or prime rib to stuffed snapper. For the incurable steak lover, the Garden Terrace has sirloin or filet mignon. Prices range from $4 to $19.

The attractively appointed **House of Szechwan** offers an excellent menu of Chinese specialties with over 70 items to choose from, dishes ranging from $9 to $17. Chinese beer and wine are available. House of Szechwan is open Wednesday through Monday from 5pm to midnight. Reservations are suggested.

David-Papchen's Deli may be small in size, but assuredly makes Goliath-size sandwiches suitable for a Samson appetite. You'll know you're at the right spot by the dried sausages hanging from the ceiling, loaves of bread on display, and kaiser rolls set for stuffing. Everything is larger than life and absolutely delicious, from the super sandwiches to the succulent sausage platters and the many specials featured on the menu. Open daily from 7am to 10:30pm.

From opening day in 1952, the Sands has been a trendsetter in entertainment. The famous **Copa Room** (made famous by Frank Sinatra) has been home to brilliant stars and unique productions. Currently appearing is *Comedy Kings,* from the producers of *D.C. Follies.* Shows ($19) are at 8 and 10:30pm daily except Monday.

Nightly entertainment is also featured in the hotel's popular **Winner's Circle Cabaret** from 5pm to the wee hours. Talented groups satisfy everyone's musical taste with selections ranging from the Top 40 to country/western, and from Broadway hits to rock 'n' roll favorites from the '50s and '60s.

Dunes Hotel and Country Club, 3650 Las Vegas Blvd. South, Las Vegas, NV 89109 (tel. 702/737-4110, or toll free 800/634-6971).

The Dunes is another large Vegas hotel, with 1,285 rooms in two towers and a cluster of smaller buildings. Facilities include an 18-hole championship golf course and country club, health club for men and women, restaurants and bars, two immense pools (both Olympic size), many shops, and an opulent casino.

The private guest rooms are spacious and color coordinated. Each has running ice water, a separate theatrically lighted makeup area, and a table for in-room dining. Prices for singles or doubles range from $50 to $100 per night.

One of the major dining rooms is the exotic, palatial **Sultan's Table**. The motif comes from Kismet, a pleasure palace of the Far East. This one features lots of stained glass, a waterfall, and a tented entrance. The gourmet Continental menu features entrees (priced from $20 to $27.50) like breast of capon Kiev with wild rice. Open Wednesday to Sunday from 6 to 11pm. Jackets are required for men.

The **Dome of the Sea** is a seashell-shape seafood restaurant with a blonde mermaid playing the harp from a floating gondola. The basic color scheme is blue and green, with varicolored lights pouring through the domed ceiling. Among the specialties of the Dome are lobster thermidor in casserole, shrimp curry with rice pilaf, and bouillabaisse, for $25 to $35. Open Friday to Tuesday from 6 to 11pm.

Other choices include the **Chinese Kitchen** and a 24-hour coffee shop called the **Savoy**.

Currently the **Casino Theater** is dark.

Frontier Hotel, 3120 Las Vegas Blvd. South, Las Vegas, NV 89109 (tel. 702/794-8200, or toll free 800/634-6966).

The horseshoe-shape Frontier is heralded by a 200-foot-high sign. The hotel itself is surrounded by beautiful grounds, manicured lawns, fountains, and little rustic bridges over a reflecting pool. Within is an enormous and lavish casino, along with 600 guest rooms plus shops and services. A broad range of recreational facilities are on the premises: an Olympic-size swimming pool, three tennis courts (all lit for night play), and a putting green; golf is available nearby at the Desert Inn.

Rooms are decorated in bright mauves, teals, and blues. Rates are $35 Sunday through Thursday, $55 on Friday and Saturday, single or double.

Some 350 guest rooms and suites, plus the lobbies, casino, and sports book, have been redecorated, enlarged, and refurnished, and 636 rooms have been added in their new atrium tower. Frontier's restaurants have also been in a state of flux; hopefully they are settling in, because odds are they now have two real winners.

Justin's is Frontier's gourmet room, and a beauty it is, with reflections of its predecessor, Diamond Jim's. It's elegant and Victorian, styled with such touches as crystal chandeliers, red carpeting, and comfortably plush booths. Justin's specializes in tableside service with appropriate flourish. The list of house specialties has something for everyone: rack of lamb, veal Oscar, duck à l'orange, steaks, chops, and seafood. A different, full-course (prix-fixe) dinner is featured each night. Elegance notwithstanding, Justin's is friendly and the food is good. Dinner costs $19 to $49. Justin's is open nightly from 6 to 11:30pm. Reservations are suggested.

The new **Margarita's** is a warm, inviting, attractive Mexican restaurant done with touches of the Southwest: wrought iron, a cobblestoned floor, ceiling fans. Tortillas are made fresh on the premises and served with your meal with guacamole, bean dip, and salsa. You also can buy the tortillas to take out. While breakfast is more of a brunch, it still includes such excellent choices as scrambled eggs with Mexican sausage (huevos con chorizo), huevos rancheros to be sure, and Mexican variations on the omelet theme ($3 to $4). Specialties of the house include sizzling fajita platters ($6.50 to $9) and the cantina feast platter, a sampling for two of a quesadilla, beef burrito, chimichanga (a deep-fried burrito), and chicken enchilada ($10). The menu is loaded with other tasty choices ($2.50 to $6.50), from chicken, steak, and a swordfish dishes to the simpler tamale, enchilada, and chimichanga fare. For light nibblers, Margarita's also has a good selection of salads. The flambé ole! (for two) is the ultimate dessert ($6), prepared at your table with fresh strawberries, bananas, and kiwi sautéed with three different liquers and served over vanilla ice cream. Margarita's has a great selection of giant fresh-fruit margaritas. They also have Mexican beers, tequilas, and a respectable wine list. Service at Margarita's is attentive and friendly, a pleasant complement to the food. Open from 11am to 10:30pm.

Sahara Hotel and Casino, 2535 Las Vegas Blvd. South and Sahara Avenue, Las Vegas, NV 89109 (tel. 702/737-2111, or toll free 800/634-6666).

Situated at the north end of the Strip, the Sahara's three towers rise above a 20-acre complex that includes more than 1,500 guest rooms, five restaurants, a theater-showroom, two swimming pools, shops, and services. And, of course, there's an enormous casino with the usual accoutrements.

The rooms are spacious and bright, with modern decor and amenities. Singles and doubles rent for $55 to $125 per night.

Restaurant options range from deli meals to gourmet feasts. In the latter category is the classic gourmet **House of Lords,** done in regal red tones, with beamed ceilings, stained-glass fixtures, and polished dark woodwork. Specialties of the house are more Continental than English, however, running the gamut from scaloppine of veal marsala or française, to lamb chops, beef, and seafood, including abalone amandine, at $17 to $35. The House of Lords is open nightly from 6pm to midnight.

For an exotic dining adventure, South Seas fare is at the Sahara's **Don the Beachcomber** restaurant, lavishly done up in the expected exotic Polynesian decor. It's a comfortable restaurant where guests can enjoy any number of different tropical cocktails. As to food choices, Don the Beachcomber offers a menu of Polynesian favorites like boned Mandarin duck and lobster in rice wine sauce, as well as steak and other seafood, for $14 to $26. The restaurant is open Tuesday through Saturday from 5pm to 11pm.

As you might anticipate, the Sahara also has a 24-hour coffee shop, the **Caravan Room,** which turns out, among other things huge, heavenly banana splits. Then there's the **Garden Buffet,** offering an all-you-can-eat lineup of favorites for breakfast, lunch, or dinner. Items run the gamut of buffet food, including omelets, waffles, soups, salads, and carved meats, to name just a few; choices change through the day. The **Turf Club Deli** provides guests with great deli food, some of the best in town.

The **Congo Theater** has entertainment Thursday to Tuesday with shows at 8 and 11pm; the theater is closed Wednesday. Currently *Boylesque* ($11), the original Las Vegas female impersonation show, is on. The **Casbar Lounge** also features entertainment nightly from 7pm to 5am.

Stardust Hotel, 3000 Las Vegas Blvd. South, Las Vegas, NV 89109 (tel. 702/732-6111, or toll free 800/634-6757).

The Stardust is centrally located (right in the center of the Strip), and its immense casino is one of the liveliest in town. The sports and race book is of great size, with plenty of TV screens and comfortable seating. The hotel has 1,400 rooms located in six buildings and a tower. Facilities include an Olympic-size swimming pool, five restaurants, and a shopping arcade.

Accommodations run the gamut from motel-type rooms to penthouse. All rooms have every modern amenity. Rooms by the Garden are $30 to $45, single or double; in the Château area, $60 to $95; in the Tower, $80 to $95. Inquire about package plans, which include show tickets, etc.

Among the restaurants on the premises is **Tony Roma's** for ribs ($6 to $13), now open for lunch Thursday through Monday from 11am, and for dinner from 5 to 11pm.

Ralph's Diner is the Stardust's contribution to memories of places where some of us ate in the '50s and early '60s. There are a black-and-white-checkerboard tile floor, stainless-steel everything, an old jukebox, tiered booths, and a snack bar/soda fountain. About the only items missing are pictures of James Dean, Marilyn, and Elvis. Can you guess what, besides nostalgia, is served in Ralph's Diner? Hamburgers, fries, steaks, and those fountain drinks that somehow don't taste quite the same now. Meals cost $3.75 to $12. The diner is open daily from 7am to 10pm.

William B's is a toned-down version of a Texas steak house—dark, masculine, and woody. The prime attraction here is steak and more steak, with seafood running a strong second. Steaks range from the usual New York steak, filet, and rib-eye to prime rib, all of which are offered at $13 to $26. William B's is open daily from 5 to midnight.

Toucan Harry's is a 24-hour coffee shop serving everything from snacks (I'm partial to the hot chicken wings) to a lox and cream cheese platter, cold sandwiches, hot sandwiches, salads, seafood, steaks, vegetable plates, southern fried chicken, smoked pork chops, etc., from $4.50 to $12. And from 5pm to 2am, Toucan Harry's features Chinese cuisine, offering a lengthy list (over 40 choices) of appetizers, soups, entrees, and Szechuan-style dishes. Entrees from the Chinese menu cost $9 to $15.

The **Warehouse** is the Stardust's all-you-can-eat 450-seat buffet and one of the best in town. What's more, there are large comfortable booths and tables with plenty of elbow room. Breakfast is $5, lunch $6, dinner $8, and save room for dessert. It's open daily from 7am to 10pm, with dinner beginning at 4pm Saturday and Sunday, there's a champagne brunch from 7am to 3:30pm.

The big show takes place in the **Cafe Continental**—it's the lavish *Lido de Paris* revue, a Las Vegas tradition since 1958. Like the others of its ilk, it's great fun, with incredible sets and costumes, acrobats, and Bobby Berosini and his orangutans. There are two cocktail shows, at 7 and 11pm, priced at $26; closed Tuesday. The **Starlite Lounge** has entertainment nightly from 4pm to 3am.

Westward Ho Motel & Casino, 2900 Las Vegas Blvd. South, Las Vegas, NV 89109 (tel. 702/731-2900, or toll free 800/634-6803, 800/634-6651 in California).

Westward Ho has 1,000 attractive air-conditioned rooms and, believe it or not, seven swimming pools and whirlpools. In spite of its size, the staff is very friendly and helpful. The motel covers considerable acreage; fortunately, vans are provided to take you to your accommodations.

Every room has a color TV, phone, tub/shower bath, and dressing area, and all are spotlessly clean. Special rooms for the handicapped are available. And the location, right in the heart of Strip activities, couldn't be better. Singles and doubles are $39 to $42 Sunday through Thursday, $49 to $52 on Friday and Saturday. Also available are two-bedroom apartments that can sleep up to six, and cost $65 to $78 Sunday through Thursday, $75 to $88 on Friday and Saturday for four persons (there's a $2 per night charge for each extra person up to six). They're ideal for families or larger compatible groups traveling together.

The motel's casino has been expanded threefold and remodeled, with the lounge presenting free nightly entertainment. In addition to the usual automatic teller machines and other financial services offered at most casinos, Westward Ho also has a foreign-exchange desk.

La Cafe is Westward Ho's 24-hour eatery, decorated with latticed walls, a green lattice-pattern carpet, attractive tilework, ceiling fans, and lots and lots of ferns. Breakfast is served around the clock for $4 to $9. Lunch and dinner feature sandwiches and burgers, as well as hot food like barbecued ribs, fried chicken, and filet of sole, in the $7 to $16 range. A special New York steak or trout amandine, plus soup or salad, potato, rolls, and beverage, is $8. And if that's not enough of a bargain, there's a $4 luncheon buffet from 11am to 4pm, followed by a $5 dinner buffet until 10pm.

The Circus Circus Hotel, 2880 Las Vegas Blvd. South, Las Vegas, NV 89109 (tel. 702/734-0410, or toll free 800/634-3450, 800/634-6833 in Arizona, California, Idaho, and Utah).

The most unusual hotel on the Strip, Circus Circus has a building shaped like an enormous big-top tent, and its immense sign is clown-shaped. That's because inside there are world-famous circus acts going on every day (free) from 11am to midnight. The entire show—trapeze artists, acrobats, tightrope walkers, etc.—takes place in the world's largest permanent circus, on the mezzanine level, surrounded by an exciting arcade of midway games where kids (and adults) can play and watch the circus acts.

Other guest amenities include a shopping promenade, five restaurants, three snack bars, casinos, a race and sports book, and (can you believe it?) a wedding chapel.

The pleasantly decorated rooms (of which there are about 2,793, with 1,188 in the Circus Skyrise across the street), are priced from $29 to $45, single or double; rates change seasonally. Or you can park your camper in the Circusland RV Park for $12 a night, with all utility hookups.

For dining, you have your choice of the 24-hour **Pink Pony** coffee shop; the 24-hour **Skyrise Dining Room** (entrees about $7); the **Steak House,** a casual place for prime ribs, seafood, etc., ($12 to $28); the **Circus Circus Buffet,** for an all-you-can-eat buffet breakfast ($2.50) with over 40 items of all kinds, lunch ($2.75), and dinner ($4); the **Skyrise Snack Bar** and the **Snack Train,** for fast-food service; the **Delicatessen;** and the **Circus Pizzeria,** featuring—you guessed it—pizza (and pasta) at $7 to $14; and two snackbars.

For liquid refreshment you can visit the **Gilded Cage Lounge,** the **Skyrise Lounge,** or the revolving **Horse-A-Round Bar** with a view of the circus acts.

Fun things galore are tucked into the Circus Circus cornucopia of goodies. This is a sensational hotel-casino-circus that truly must be seen to be believed.

Vagabond Inn, Las Vegas, 4155 Koval Lane, Las Vegas, NV 89109 (tel. 702/731-2111, or toll free 800/634-6541).

The budget traveler should consider this pleasant 362-room hostelry right behind Bally's–Las Vegas. It has a swimming pool and sun deck, a Jacuzzi, a gift shop, and a small casino. There's also a restaurant and lounge near the registration desk. Rooms have color TVs, direct-dial phones, and air conditioning.

Rates are $39 to $50, single or double. An extra adult adds $6. There's ample free parking.

Super 8 Motel, 4250 Korval Lane, Las Vegas, NV 89109 (tel. 702/794-0888, or toll free 800/848-8888).

I simply can't remember the last time I stopped at a hotel or motel that had rooms with waterbeds. There are 10 such rooms at Super 8 Motel. Conveniently located one block from the Strip and newly redone, it adjoins the Ellis Island restaurant, open 24 hours daily. There is a pleasant, roomy lobby with sofas and chairs, and the comfortable rooms are nicely decorated with floral-pattern spreads in peaceful tones of beige and blue. All beds are queen-size, and all baths have tub/showers. Suites also have minifrigerators. Super 8, bless their hearts, also has laundry facilities. For the loungers and water sprites, there is a pool.

Weekday rates are $33 for one person, $38 to $40 for two. Weekend rates are $10 higher for singles or doubles, and there is a $2 charge for each additional person in a double. Suites are $64 weekdays, $74 weekends. Given a choice, I'd reserve a room on the second or third floor; it's quite a bit lighter than on the ground floor.

As for the adjacent **Ellis Island Restaurant,** the decor is pleasant and the menu selection excellent. Breakfast, lunch, dinner, and Sunday brunch are served, all at moderate prices.

Motel 6, 195 E. Tropicana Ave. (at Koval Lane), Las Vegas, NV 89109 (tel. 702/798-0728).

Just two blocks off the Strip, this branch of the amazingly low-priced and well-located Motel 6 chain has 890 units and is growing by the minute. All rooms have air conditioning and shower baths, as well as free color TVs and phones (no charge for local calls). There are even a swimming pool and a therapy pool.

Room rates are $28 for one person, $34 for two. Ask about the Family Plan if there are three or more of you. Be sure to reserve early and you'll not only enjoy very adequate accommodations, but save lots of money that will come in handy for shows and casinos.

THE DOWNTOWN LAS VEGAS HOTELS

Golden Nugget Hotel and Casino, 129 E. Fremont St. (at the corner of Casino Center Boulevard), Las Vegas, NV 89101 (tel. 702/385-7111, or toll free 800/634-3454).

When you consider accommodations in Las Vegas, among the best and most luxurious is the all-new Golden Nugget Hotel and Casino. Gone is the fantasy of the Wild West that once characterized the hotel. Today this extraordinary downtown establishment commands top rating among all casino-hotels. A hint of its interior elegance is presented by a new façade of pure-white Grecian marble, cut, hand-carved, and polished by old-world artisans, and by the white canopies, Tivoli lights, and beveled mirrors.

Oversize guest rooms have been decorated in soothing pastels, soft creams, and desert shades. All rooms are equipped with every modern amenity: direct-dial phones, AM/FM radios, color TVs, tub/shower baths, oversize terry towels, toilette articles, and more. Of course, the hotel affords the services of a concierge, 24-hour room service in addition to that of the coffee shop, same-day laundry and dry-cleaning srevice, car rental, valet parking, and other comfortable touches. The Golden Nugget prides itself on attention to detail, whether in the hotel's elegant appointments or in the extra effort extended by the staff to make a guest's stay enjoyable.

Rates for the hotel's rooms are $60 to $120, single or double; suites start at $220 and go up to $800. Children under 12 stay free in a room with their parents; extra adults pay $12 a night.

Set among beds of flowers and palm trees is an outdoor pool (open May through October) with a whirlpool spa, a snack bar, and a poolside lounge area. If relaxing in the desert sun is too much of a good thing, there's always the spa, a health emporium geared to body building, exercise, and aerobics. There are separate men's and women's facilities for massages, steam rooms, sauna, and whirlpool spas. A full-service beauty salon provides services for men and women.

The 30,000-square-foot casino is handsomely styled and designed, and well equipped for the total comfort of its customers. There are 42 blackjack tables, 8 craps layouts, 3 roulette wheels, 13 poker tables, a Big Six wheel, 3 baccarat tables, and a luxurious keno lounge. More than 700 video and traditional slot machines, all brass clad, add the finishing touch to the casino area.

Top-of-the-line restaurant at the Golden Nugget is **Elaine's**. It's located on the second level of the Spa Suite Tower. As you approach the ebony-black entry, you won't expect the classic French decor inside. The dining room is elegant, and the effect is rich. Your eye is caught by a superb Venetian crystal chandelier and the impressionist-style paintings. There's a feeling of privacy you rarely find in a dining room, undoubtedly effected by the curtained booths and well-spaced tables. The menu is à la carte. Among Elaine's excellent specialties are rack of lamb, chicken with wild mushrooms, bouillabaisse, and a fabulous quail with a mousse of veal. Entrees range from $24 to $37.50. The wine list is of the same fine quality as the food. Jackets are required for men, and reservations are suggested. Elaine's is open Thursday through Monday from 6 to 11pm.

Stefano's is the northern Italian restaurant in the Golden Nugget. As you enter, the feeling is that you're in an Italian garden. Stefano's has a varied menu with a wide range of choices among some dozen fresh pasta dishes, including an exceptional fettuccine with prosciutto, parmesan, and a silky cream sauce, as well as veal and fresh fish. A perennial search for the perfect veal piccata ended at Stefano's—delicate white veal, exquisitely tender, lightly touched with lemon, and served piping hot. It's the seemingly simple dishes that display the genius of the chef (this one is from Rome). If you've ever wanted to indulge a childlike urge to lick the plate, Stefano's will bring it on. Be sure to order the salad. It's light and so fresh there's sure to be a garden by the kitchen. And it's touched with just the right amount of delicate dressing. All this beauty and superb food isn't cheap, but it's worth the price. And the service is attentive. The menu is à la carte and dinner entrees range from $18 to $35. Stefano's is open daily for dinner from 6 to 11pm. Reservations are suggested.

Lillie Langtry's, named for the famed British actress who stole the heart of the infamous Judge Roy Bean, is a masterpiece of Victoriana. The walls are richly paneled in oak and mahogany, chairs plushly upholstered in a lovely floral velvet, tables handsomely set with wheat-colored linen. Flickering gaslamps, fine murals of the Old West, and pressed-tin ceilings are among the many other elements that help create this gorgeous setting. Like every other part of this fine hotel, it is done in perfect taste.

The dinner menu at Lillie's place is Cantonese. You might begin your meal with an order of golden-fried shrimp or crispy rumaki (broiled chicken liver and water chestnut wrapped in bacon). Suggested entrees include lemon chicken; shrimp Cantonese (jumbo shrimp with minced pork, onion, garlic, bean sauce, and other spices), and ginger beef cooked in oyster sauce and onion. Entrees, which range from $12 to $22, are served with oolong tea, rice, and fortune cookies. Two American entrees are listed; prime rib with baked potato, salad, and vegetable; and barbecued spareribs with corn on the cob and onion rings. Exotic drinks are also featured at Lillie's: the Rangoon Ruby (vodka and cranberry juice), the Oriental Devil (banana and rum), the Great Wall of China (coconut, rum, and vodka), etc. Lillie Langtry's is open nightly from 5 to 11pm.

And then there's the **Buffet,** which, as with everything else at the Golden Nugget, is done in style. It offers a beige-and-gold decor, individual booths, chandeliers, greenery, and pleasantly subdued lighting. The choice and quality of the food are excellent; the hot food is really hot, and the cold is cold. Breakfast is $5 and served from 7 to 10:30am, brunch is $7.50 and served from 10:30am to 3pm, and dinner is $8.75 and served from 4 to 11pm.

The **Carson Street Café** is open 24 hours and serves a steak for $2 from 11pm to 6am.

For your entertainment at the Golden Nugget there is a veritable roster of headliners who appear at the intimate, informal **Cabaret.** This is where you go to see the superstars light up the sky—David Brenner, Dolly Parton (her debut engagement was in the Cabaret), Kenny Rogers, Dionne Warwick, Harry Belafonte, Diahann Carroll, Vic Damone, Melissa Manchester, among others. There are two shows nightly, except Monday, at 8 and 11pm. The cost is $17 on up, depending on the performer, so it's best to call first.

California Hotel, 1st and Ogden Avenue, Las Vegas, NV 89125-0630 (tel. 702/385-1222, or toll free 800/634-6255).

For those seeking exceptional accommodations downtown, but would prefer rates somewhat lower than those of the Golden Nugget, there are two pleasant surprises. One is Sam Boyd's California Hotel, the other follows.

Rooms at the California are spacious, and neatly assembled in subdued floral colors. Those in the older of the two towers (totally remodeled) are especially light and airy, and furnishings are reminiscent of Hawaiian decor (undoubtedly influenced by the fact that a large concentration of the California's guests are from Hawaii). Rates are $40, single or double, Sunday through Thursday; $50 on Friday and Saturday; $60 on holidays. Maximum of four persons per room. There is an added $5 charge per night for an extra person, but no charge for children 12 and under staying in the same room with their parents. It's wise to do some advance planning for a stay at the California Hotel—they have 97% occupancy year-round.

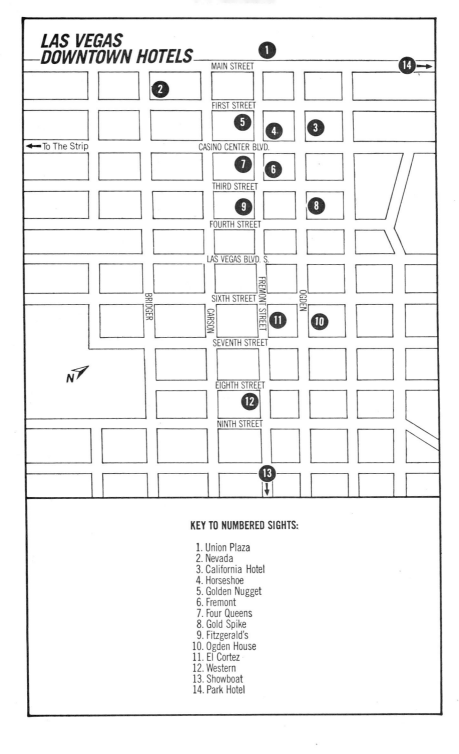

LAS VEGAS DOWNTOWN HOTELS

MAIN STREET

FIRST STREET

CASINO CENTER BLVD.

THIRD STREET

FOURTH STREET

LAS VEGAS BLVD. S.

SIXTH STREET

SEVENTH STREET

EIGHTH STREET

NINTH STREET

←To The Strip

BRIDGER

CARSON

FREMONT STREET

OGDEN

N

KEY TO NUMBERED SIGHTS:

1. Union Plaza
2. Nevada
3. California Hotel
4. Horseshoe
5. Golden Nugget
6. Fremont
7. Four Queens
8. Gold Spike
9. Fitzgerald's
10. Ogden House
11. El Cortez
12. Western
13. Showboat
14. Park Hotel

Gaming at the California offers about 1,000 slot machines and a daily slot tournament—enough to keep anyone busy for days. Or you might try your hand at blackjack, craps, roulette, keno, minibaccarat, or even Pai Gow poker. The sports book is open from 9am until the start of the last game, with betting available on all major sports and special events. For exercise other than picking up and putting down chips in the casino, there is an outdoor pool on the 13th floor, open during warm weather.

When hunger pangs strike, there's a lot to choose from. California's **Market Street Cafe** has a prime-rib dinner for less than $5; the **Redwood Bar and Grill** provides piano-bar entertainment, with or without an 18-ounce porterhouse, from 6pm to midnight; the **Pasta Pirate** features fresh pasta, seafood, and steaks; and the **Cal Club Snack Bar** has some great light meals. A note about this last: It's the only such eatery I've been in that offers chopsticks with other utensils, largely because it has some marvelous ultra-low-priced Oriental dishes, including the delicious Teri Bowl (teriyaki beef with rice) and shrimp tempura, as well as the usual hamburgers, hot dogs, etc.

Just steps from the California Hotel is California's RV facility—the only RV park downtown. There are 222 spaces having full hookups, plus 24-hour security, a seasonally heated pool open 24 hours, full laundry facilities, and a dog run.

Park Hotel & Casino, 300 N. Main St., Las Vegas, NV 89101 (tel. 702/387-5333, or toll free 800/782-9909).

The Park is another remarkably attractive buy in downtown accommodations. The spacious green–and–sand-pink lobby with its wicker chairs, greenery, and terra-cotta floors leads you to believe that the rooms would be airy, light, and attractively simple in their decor, as indeed they are. In the 435 rooms and suites, the basic tones of the lobby are set off by white lamps and light-cream wall covering. Baths are small, but the basins are set in the adjoining area. The entire hotel has a fresh, clean look.

Rooms at the Park, single or double, are $36 to $42 Sunday through Thursday; $52 to $60 on Friday and Saturday. Should you prefer a suite, those with one bedroom are $100 to $175; two bedroom suites are $175 to $225.

The 50,000-square-foot casino offers the continuous entertainment of 700 slot machines, black-jack, craps, and roulette, plus poker and keno games. You'll find live entertainment in the **Carousel Lounge**. And, of course, what would a self-respecting Las Vegas hotel be without a pool. At the Park, it has an attractive free-form shape so you never get bored with just paddling around.

For dining, there are the 24-hour **Garden Room**, the **Patio Buffet**, and **Shady Nook Snack Bar**.

Union Plaza Hotel and Casino, 1 Main St. (at Fremont Street), Las Vegas, NV 89101 (tel. 702/386-2110, or toll free 800/634-6575, 800/634-6821 in California).

This is another downtown choice. Its 1,037 rooms are complete with color TVs, direct-dial phones, tub/shower baths, and king or two queen-size beds. Rates are $30 to $60, single or double.

The hotel is connected to the Amtrak railroad station and adjoined by the Greyhound Depot. In addition to a large modern casino, facilities include several lounges and restaurants: the **Center Stage**, which serves dinner from a unique vantage point overlooking the lights of Fremont Street; **Kung Fu Plaza**, which serves Chinese-Thai food; and the 24-hour **Plaza Diner and Snack Bar.**

The **Sports Deck** features a heated pool, lighted tennis courts, and a quarter-mile jogging track.

The 650-seat **Plaza Theater Restaurant** features the *Nudes on Ice* review. There are two shows nightly (except Monday), at 8 and 11:30pm. The 8pm show costs $14 to $22 and includes dinner; the 11:30pm show is $9.50, with two cocktails.

The Union Plaza also offers entertainment from 3pm to 3am in the **Omaha Lounge,** off the casino.

---

5. More Restaurants

As I pointed out earlier, not all of the best restaurants are in the hotels. Here are some excellent choices, depending on your tastes and pocketbook. I've started with the most expensive and worked downward in price.

One last note: If you've never been to Las Vegas before or have eaten only in the hotels, you may find the seafood to be adequate but not exceptional. It's certainly not up to the standards of the Oyster Bar in Grand Central Station in New York City, for example. All this may change with the advent of the Mirage. It's the intention of the Golden Nugget hotel to have the finest seafood restaurant in the country. In the meantime, there are a number of good places to eat outside the hotels.

Whatever the length of your visit to Las Vegas, make the **Golden Steer,** 308 W. Sahara Ave., just west of the Strip (tel. 702/384-4470 or 387-9236), one of your required stops for dinner. (I wouldn't want you to miss it: From the Strip, turn west on Sahara, then turn into the lot after the Texaco sign on your right.)

The bar on your left as you enter has an Old West look and feel—red leather, steer horns, antique guns, western paintings, framed silver dollars, and red-velvet curtains. To one side there's a beautiful old glass-encased slot machine that's never gobbled up a single coin.

Among the excellent entrees offered, there are a number you would expect to find (and some you would not) in a restaurant called the Golden Steer. Choices range from half a broiled spring chicken at $12 to the prime rib (called a Diamond Lil or Diamond Jim) at $21 to $27.50. But then you may prefer either the moist and delicious rack of lamb or the chateaubriand for two at $24 per person. You can also enjoy a somewhat more unusual and sumptuous meal of the bobwhite quail—a pair for $25 per person. A beef and bird entree offers some of the best of both worlds, with quail and a petit filet mignon accompanied by wild rice for $22.50.

There is nothing commonplace about the veal or chicken specialties ($16.50 to $19.50), although you may have seen them listed on other restaurant menus. The quality is exceptional, whether you choose the veal française (dipped in egg batter and sautéed with mushrooms and lemon) or the Chicken of the Angels (a boneless breast sautéed with mushrooms and hearts of artichokes). As for the seafood, the highlight of the menu is an extra large imported Dover sole for $22, served à la carte with a baked potato. Other specialties from the sea include Australian lobster tail and Alaskan king crab legs priced according to market.

One of the pleasant surprises here: Without a doubt, the Golden Steer has the best baked potato I've ever eaten in any restaurant at any time; it's indicative of the quality you may expect, whatever you order. I also hear from a good source that the restaurant has the best Caesar salad, bar none. I simply did not have room to try it.

If you have room for dessert, there are several varieties of delicious cheesecake, or if you're a chocolate freak, the chocolate bombay ice cream may be just what it takes to hit the spot. Desserts range in price from $3 to $4.25.

The house offers a good selection of imported and domestic wines at reasonable prices. The Golden Steer menu identifies what it pours when you order your booze by its generic name—the quality, as you might expect, matches that of the food.

You don't want to join the crowd at the Golden Steer if you plan to eat and run back to the baccarat table. Service here is appropriately paced for dining, not gulping. Open daily from 5pm to midnight; closed on Thanksgiving and Christmas. Reservations are suggested.

Ask anyone living in Las Vegas for a list of the best restaurants and it will almost invariably include **The Tillerman,** 2245 E. Flamingo Rd., just west of Eastern Avenue (tel. 702/731-4036). It's all put forth in a handsome arboreal setting—a veritable forest of some six ficus trees reaching up to a cathedral-height ceiling and skylight. Trees, flowers, greenery are all live (no faux for the Tillerman). Banquettes are forest colors—deep green, rose, mauve—and floors are terra-cotta. Chairs in the main dining area have high backs, complementing the vertical lines of the room. Set apart from the central dining area are two cozy rooms perhaps designed for intimate chitchat over dinner.

In keeping with the air of the restaurant, tabletops are of highly polished wood, burgundy napkins are rolled into candle shapes, dinnerware is a classic blue and white. Though you might expect the waitpersons to be clad in forest green, as befits the elegant tone of the Tillerman, they are sprucely garbed in black trousers, white shirts, burgundy ties and braces.

Pending your order, you are first served deliciously crisp fresh crudités, accompanied by a salad. Then there are light, delicately flavored homemade baby loaves of bread (certainly the best I've ever tasted), from which one could make a complete meal. But on to the entrees. The specialty of the house is fresh ocean and freshwater seafood, flown in daily. And to quote the Tillerman, the beef is the finest available. I can attest to the seafood, but you simply can't believe the remarkable freshness of the accompanying vegetables.

Fish specials of the evening may range from trout to swordfish. Other seafood entrees, depending on the season: Dungeness crab, lobster, select Alaskan king crab legs (cracked at the table by your waitperson), seafood brochette. Whatever the choices are, I've yet to have one that was not exceptional. As to meat alternatives, you might opt for the pan-sautéed chicken breast or the full cut of the boned prime rib (when available). In the absence of the prime rib, you can't possibly go wrong with the filet mignon or New York strip steak. Entrees range from $15 to $34, the higher price being for the Alaskan king crab legs.

The Tillerman has a full bar—you may spend a bit of time waiting there for your table—but there is a consoling factor: Drinks are of very ample size, and even the house wine is above reproach.

The Tillerman does not take reservations. If you would rather not wait for a table, it's wise to come by 6:30pm, as the restaurant generally is full by 6:45pm. The Tillerman is open nightly from 5 to 11pm.

Step inside **Pamplemousse,** 400 E. Sahara Ave., one block east of the Strip (tel. 702/733-2066), and you're no longer in Vegas but on the Côte d'Azur. Pamplemousse is an intimate and elegant restaurant decorated in subtle shades of pink and wine, with candles and flowers and ceiling fans. Classical music or light jazz plays softly in the background. There's a wood-burning fireplace that's used on cool evenings, and an outdoor garden area under a bit of tenting. For small private parties, there's a dining area secluded from the main dining room. It's all extremely charming and un-Vegasy. The restaurant's name, by the way, which means grapefruit, was suggested by the late singer Bobby Darin; it just appealed to him for some reason. Darin was one of French owner Georges La Forge's numerous celebrity friends and patrons.

Pamplemousse has no fixed menu. The restaurants' talented chef prepares four entrees every evening from the freshest ingredients available. The house specialty is duck, served with one of four sauces—kiwi, orange, cherry, or banana rum. There are also fresh fish selections, and a beef or veal dish. But if there's something you're particularly craving, Pamplemousse will prepare a meal to order with 24 hour's notice. The $20 to $25 price of your entree includes fresh breads, fresh boiled eggs, and a basket of fresh raw vegetables served with a dip. And to accompany your meal, you can select from perhaps the most extensive wine list in Las Vegas, chosen personally by Georges La Forge with great care. Beer is available, but no hard liquor is served. And you can round out your meal with a delectable dessert—perhaps a tarte, a mousse, a crème caramel, homemade ice cream, or a flambé.

Pamplemousse is open Tuesday through Sunday from 6 to 11pm. Reservations are essential.

The **Savoia,** 455 E. Harmon, near Paradise Road and next to the St. Tropez Hotel (tel. 702/731-5446), is truly a beauty, and by no means a duplication of Georges La Forge's other success, Pamplemousse. The light, airy Savoia has an elegant out-of-doors look—a color scheme of pinks, rose, and cream, with much bleached wood and lots of greenery. It is divided into several interesting dining and drinking areas designed for different styles of dining, from the formal casual to a totally relaxed effect. In the main dining area, cream fabric booths, black faux-marble-topped tables, and bleached-wood chairs create an ambience of casual elegance. Table lamps touch everything with a soft, flattering glow. To one side of the main room, pillars surround a pizza oven, as does a semicircular counter, another choice for seating. Or you might prefer the lounge area for dining, a beauty in black with a spectacular ceiling that looks for all the world like the night sky. To the right and quite apart from the main room is a small, long, very light dining area. Recessed lighting here casts a lovely glow, and paintings throughout have touches of a desert spring.

Savoia offers a very diverse selection for light dining at midday. Choices from the Savoia Deli include some remarkable and plentiful platters from the assortment of smoked fish, cheese, and meats or from the vegetarian antipasti ($9 to $16). There are a number of fine pasta choices ($7 to $14), including an exceptional black lobster ravioli served with lobster-saffron sauce. Gourmet pizzas ($5.75 to $9.50) are a perfect size for most any appetite. The choice of hot appetizers ($4 to $7.25) includes several delicious seafood choices, plus escargots with garlic, Pernod, and parsley-butter garnish. Cold appetiers of carpaccio, roast peppers, and buffalo mozzarella are also served at midday, as are the soups and cold salads.

Evening entrees of veal, fowl, seafood, lamb, and beef present splendid and distinctive choices. If osso buco is a favorite of yours, you won't be disappointed. For the less intense appetites, medallions of veal can be ordered sautéed in a white wine-butter sauce with capers and fresh basil (San Remo). Among the fowl choices, I especially enjoy the braised quails Dodine, served on a bed of spaghetti squash (a delicious texture) and blessed with port wine. Among the seafood entrees, the salmon is perfectly poached or grilled. Noisettes of baby lamb are served with their natural juices and herbs. Beef choices include a petit filet mignon with sautéed shrimp scampi and a broiled New York sirloin steak. All specialty entrees ($10 to $20) are served with fresh vegetables and potato of the day.

The midday menu excludes evening entrees, but otherwise duplicates most of the offerings. Savoia also serves a famous and delicous French Riviera specialty, the pan bagnat—a round, crusty French bread abounding with albacore tuna, olives, and lettuce, layered with anchovies, hard-boiled eggs, and Savoia dressing.

However much you may order for the midday or evening meal, save space for dessert. The list is extraordinary and each dessert is a small spectacular ($2.50 to $4.25). To cite only one, there's the cappuccino cup—a fresh waffle cup edged with chocolate, garnished with Giandula ice cream, Frangelico, Chantilly, and assorted roasted candied nuts. As you might expect, Savoia has an excellent wine list, including a good selection of wines by the glass.

The Savoia is open daily from 10am to 11pm and always worth the short hop from the Strip.

The **Olive Garden Italian Restaurant,** 1545 Flamingo Rd., just east of Maryland Pkwy. (tel. 702/735-0082), is quite possibly the best modestly priced restaurant in Las Vegas (as the crowds there will testify). The interior is comfortable, casual, attractive; the quality of the food is first-rate; choices are varied and delicious; much is offered, including no-charge refills on the garden salad, the soup, and the breadsticks; service is attentive; and (bless their hearts) the very comfortable chairs at table have casters (which does help when you're backing away from the table or tucking in).

Taking it from the top, the choices of soup and salad for lunch ($2.75 to $6) include a nicely seasoned minestrone soup and a seafood pasta salad. Garden specialties ($4 to $5.75) present some toothsome pasta combinations, including a half cheese ravioli and half manicotti merger, spaghetti with truly tasty meatballs, and an excellent toasted ravioli ($3.50). If you opt for a sandwich ($ to $4.75), try the grilled chicken or the house's burger Italiano. The Olive Garden has a fine selection of single-person-size pizzas, including a classic four-cheese pizza for $4.25.

The Olive Garden has chicken, veal, steak, and seafood entrees ($7.75 to $12.50) to satisfy almost any appetite. There are also specials that change daily, all served with your choice of the daily vegetable or a pasta side dish, plus unlimited refills of garden salad and fresh-baked, hot garlic breadsticks (rather like slim baby loaves of garlic bread). Then there are the Olive Garden's combination platters, like the Northern Italian combination ($11.50), including veal piccata, Venetian grilled chicken, and fettucine Alfredo; or the southern Italian ($10.75), including veal parmigiana, lasagne, and manicotti. Let me mention that the Olive Gardens also has children's plates of spaghetti, lasagne, and ravioli ($2.75 to $3.25).

Desserts ($1.75 to $3.25) are luscious, like chocolate-mousse pie. And there is a full bar, not to mention a good selection of wines by the glass, the bottle, or the liter.

The Olive Garden is open daily: Sunday through Thursday from 11am to 10:30pm on Friday and Saturday to 11pm. The restaurant does not take reservations. If you eat early, you will have the advantage. I've noticed that they're frequently crowded for lunch by 12:15pm, and for dinner by 5:30pm, but it's worth the wait. One last note if you're off on a picnic or just touring about: Most menu items are available for take-out. Call ahead and your order will be waiting.

The **Famous Pacific Fish Co.**, 3925 Paradise Rd., between the Flamingo and the Sands (tel. 702/796-9676), is without a doubt one of the best seafood restaurants in Las Vegas. I counted at least seven fresh fish entrees on the menu—not "fresh frozen" or "frozen fresh," but *fresh-fresh,* and that's not easy to find in the desert.

From Paradise Road, the FPFC (Famous Pacific Fish Co.) has the look of a large, white, barnlike structure. The interior is a handsomely designed space with a high-pitched roof, white ceiling, white walls, dark woods, and much exposed piping and ductwork painted an unobtrusive battleship gray.

The FPFC has a fine selection of luncheon choices from a lengthy list of cold appetizers, salads, sandwiches, fish, and shellfish. The Dungeness crab cocktail with grapefruit mayonnaise is a great choice among the cold appetizers. As for the hot first courses, the tried-and-true oysters Rockefeller are excellent, but be sure to ask about the special soup of the day. The Fish Company marine salad, prepared with lobster, crab, shrimp, and scallops tossed with a homemade sour cream and cheese dressing, is really a treat. Sandwiches, available only at lunch, obviously include seafood combinations, but the FPFC also has other interesting choices such as the club-style croissant with smoked turkey and Monterey Jack cheese.

At lunch, fresh fish specials are served with a fresh garden salad or homemade coleslaw (the very best I've ever had), steamed vegetables, rice, and warm bread. During dinner a baked potato is an added option. Flights from both coasts bring in the fresh seafood, like Hawaiian ahi tuna, Louisiana catfish, or even East Coast monkfish. Among the shellfish choices, there's a delicious shrimp or scallop sizzling stir-fry with fresh vegetables. For the beef eater, there is the filet mignon from choice Iowa beef, mesquite-broiled and topped with sautéed mushrooms and onion rings.

Desserts change daily. The wine list is limited but good (most are from California wineries). There is also a nice selection by the glass.

Service is mixed, depending on the experience of the server. If you're the least bit fussy, simply indicate the amount of time you prefer to allow between courses.

Luncheon entrees cost $6 to $10, sandwiches and salads, $5 to $9. Dinner entrees are $13 to $20; salads, $7.50 to $9.50. Appetizers at lunch or dinner are $5 to $8.25. Alaskan king crab legs and lobster entrees are priced according to market.

The Famous Pacific Fish Co. is open Monday through Thursday from 11am to 10pm, on Friday and Saturday to 11pm, and on Sunday from noon to 10pm. Lunch is served daily to 4pm. It's always wise to make reservations.

As you pass through a simple granite courtyard, the small Japanese-style bridge on your left spans a pond that requires only a few koi (goldfish) to complete the tranquil introduction to **Oh No Tokyo**, 4455 W. Flamingo Rd., near Arville Street (tel. 702/876-4455). The entry prepares you for the lovely California/Japanese interior, vertical black blinds, shoji screens, and hanging half-curtains that divide the serving areas from the main rooms. You can choose to dine at a table or in one of several tatami rooms (assuming that everyone in your party has socks of whole cloth —remember, shoes are removed before you enter).

The last time I had Japanese food of comparable quality and diversity to that served at Oh No Tokyo was in New York City. The à la carte sushi menu is quite broad; it includes seaweed rolls and specialty rolls, among which is a superb Emperor's roll with shrimp tempura, scallops, green onion, and masago (smelt eggs). Prices are $4 to $5 for a two-piece order; quail eggs are 75¢ each. Plates of assorted sushi range from $8 to $25 and are served with soup. Other Japanese dinners, priced from $8 to $14, include such standards as shrimp and vegetable tempura, beef and chicken teriyaki, sukiyaki, and grilled mackerel, salmon, or the catch of the day. Special combination plates (teisuoku) offer a choice of one appetizer and two entrees, with soup, rice, tea, and ice cream, for the reasonable sum of $16. The lunch menu also offers a choice of delectable and light udon dishes (steaming noodle soup), with egg, chicken, or beef, at $4.25 to $7.

For more Occidental tastes, Oh No Tokyo adds charcoal-grilled dinners to the menu "in the tradition of Japanese boatmen." Entrees range from breast of chicken to steak and lobster, all served with soup, salad, vegetable kebab, and steamed rice. Prices begin at $9.50 and top at $26 for the steak and lobster.

Soft drinks are available, as are domestic and Japanese beers, Japanese draft beer, house wine by the glass or bottle, and plum wine by the glass.

Lunch is served weekdays from 11am to 2:30pm, and dinner Monday through Saturday from 5 to 10:45pm, when the last order is taken.

Should you call the **Café Santa Fe,** 1213 Las Vegas Blvd. South, Near Charleston (tel. 702/384-4444), you will first reach the adjacent Thunderbird Hotel. As a matter of fact, you can dine, nap, get married, and drink in the café's all-night bar (though not necessarily in that order) within the same enclave, since the hotel has a wedding chapel (the Mission of the Bells).

The Café Santa Fe is just a bit away from the main action on the Strip, but it's well worth the visit. It's a short stroll through the casino to the delicious food. The Karamanos family has tried, by way of its southwestern menu and handsome restaurant design, to capture the feeling of the true Southwest. The pink stucco walls, wooden pillars, beamed ceiling, Native American rugs, straight-backed Spanish chairs, cacti, and tiled floors all reflect the unique combination of Native American, Spanish, Mexican, and southwestern traditions found in the restaurant's cuisine.

If you arrive for breakfast, there are both the usual gringo offerings and those with a southwestern flair. Among the "Omelet Grande" choices are the Santa Fe Joe, with ground beef, pan-fried onions, mushrooms, spinach, and Swiss cheese; and the South of the Border, with shredded beef chili, onions, and Monterey Jack cheese. The caballero with a hearty appetite might also order three fresh eggs served with medallions of beef tenderloin, chile relleno, and casera potatoes. All egg orders come with casera potatoes, buttermilk biscuits, and preserves. Breakfast ranges from $3 to $5.75; the eggs with beef tenderloin is $8.

Highlights of the luncheon menu are two freshly made beef patties with chili and cheese, the barbecued sliced pork in a zesty sauce, and the New York–cut sandwich broiled and served open-faced with onion rings. The choices range from $4.75 to $5.75. Salads "from the pantry" include one with freshly cut greens topped with chili con carne, shredded cheese, diced tomato, sour cream, and guacamole; served with salsa and tostados. Salads, served with homemade squaw bread and butter, are $6 and $7.

Ah, but dinner's my favorite, and I simply could not resist the barbecued baby back ribs—absolutely delicious and served with frijoles covered with cheese and chunky french fries. What I could not finish I took home and it was just as good the next day. Conservative types might choose the boneless breast of plump chicken Mexicaine, marinated and topped with mushrooms, green-chile salsa, diced tomato, and Monterey Jack cheese.

Vegetarian customers will enjoy the café's beautifully fresh vegetables, steamed and served with spicy melted cheddar cheese. Guayamas jumbo shrimp, Veracruz filet of sole, and broiled halibut steak amandine comprise the seafood offerings. For beef lovers, the tournedos Taos—cooked the Zuñi way, with broiled tomato, banana fritters, and horseradish sauce—is a dish large enough to satisfy any appetite and then some, as are the broiled New York–cut sirloin with mushrooms and fried onions, and the steak Tampico, a skirt steak marinated, broiled, and served with Spanish rice, frijoles de la olla, salsa, and flour tortillas. Entrees, served with salad or soup, potato, vegetable, and squaw bread, range from $7 to $15.75 (for the New York–cut sirloin).

The Santa Fe's late-night menu combines a number of the specialties from breakfast and lunch with its South of the Border pot of chili. Prices range from $4 to $8.

Sweet Santa Fe desserts expand from deep-dish apple pie for $2.50 to rich chocolate cake with fudge frosting (big enough for two) for $5. The café offers a good selection of beers and wines with dinner, as well as the usual alcoholic beverages.

And all this is served with warmth, thoughtfulness, and attention to detail.

The Café Santa Fe and the bar are open 24 hours daily.

Art's Place, 532 E. Sahara Ave., near 6th Street (tel. 702/737-1466), is where you'll find the locals. There's nothing chichi about Art's Place; it's simply a great place to go for good food and conversation. Art's is an eatery almost every man will love—pleasant, relaxed, with lots of wood and hanging greenery, TV sets strategically placed for coverage of the sport of the moment, and walls decorated with pictures of athletes, fight posters, and many of Art's awards.

The food at Art's Place is first-rate, there's a lot of it, and the price is right. I couldn't finish the big bowl of chili I ordered, plus the fresh roll, but it made a great late-afternoon snack from the take-it-with-you container. Service is good and you'll even get a glass of water nicely presented with a thin slice of lemon. The kitchen may be a bit slower than you expect, but the food is all prepared from scratch and you won't regret the wait.

Art's Place serves the usual choices for breakfast ($2 to $6). Lunch offers delicious chili and great burgers served with fries ($3.25 to $5), a Philly steak sandwich ($6), and the specialty of the house. Art's famous chicken soup, by the cup, bowl, or take-home quart.

The list of appetizers ($4 to $5) is varied, including some delicious chicken wings, a shrimp basket, and a quesadilla that amounts to a whole meal. Regular dinner entrees ($5 to $12), served 24 hours, are half a barbecued chicken, delicious baby back ribs (full or half rack), and a combination of a half rack of ribs and half a barbecued chicken. The combination (top price) is served with your choice of baked beans, cole slaw, or corn on the cob; other dinners are accompanied by fries or a baked potato. And then there are some great specials served Monday, Wednesday, and Friday from 5 to 10pm, and on Sunday Art's has an all-you-can-eat fish and chips dinner for $5.95. On Tuesday from 5 to 10pm, Art's special is a 12-ounce prime rib served with potato and vegetable, also for $5.95. For an alcohol-laden dessert (or appetizer), check out the "Rebel A Rouser" for $4.75—a fascinating mix of Southern Comfort, amaretto, and brandy topped with chocolate truffle. Need I add that there is a full bar with a good assortment of beers, and wine by the glass.

Art's Place is open 24 hours daily.

I love **Chili's,** 2590 S. Maryland Pkwy., near Sahara (tel. 702/733-6402). What more can you ask of a restaurant than delicious food (every bite of it), fine presentation, friendly and prompt service, sizable drinks, and perfection in every little detail? And all of this in a relaxed, fun setting of family and nonfamily photos, and a collection of interesting odds and ends on a shelf that runs throughout the restaurant.

In a world fraught with mediocrity, at Chili's nothing is average. Let's say you order the marinated and grilled southwestern shrimp, as I did. First, the shrimp were done to perfection, served on a bed of rice deliciously seasoned with chopped scallions and bits of tomato, and accompanied by cole slaw you could eat by the bowlful, plus slices of cinnamon apple each in its own compact dish. Then the lemonade I ordered arrived in a large chilled glass mug with a slice of fresh lemon. Margaritas looked just as good and seemed to be among the most popular beverages in the house. Wine, beer, and a big selection of soft drinks are also available.

The menu is a delight because there's something for everyone. You don't want shrimp today? Then how about a full rack of charbroiled baby back ribs topped with Chili's own barbecue sauce, or fajitas, or Chili's strip steak. For those more in the mood for light noshes or serious snacking, there are homemade soups, chili, excellent salads, a variety of burgers, tacos, and sandwiches. Top price on the menu is $10 for the full rack of barbecued baby back ribs or the strip steak. Sandwiches, burgers, salads, etc., average $4 to $6. For kids 12 and under, there's a choice of burger, hot dog, or grilled-cheese sandwich for $2.

Chili's is open Monday through Thursday from 11am to 10pm, on Friday and Saturday to 11pm, and on Sunday from 11:30am to 10pm. The place doesn't take reservations, but things seem to move right along when you put your name on the list. You might even choose to eat in the bar and watch the Rebels on TV (given the right season).

The Vineyard, 3630 S. Maryland Pkwy., off Twain Avenue, in the Boulevard Mall (tel. 702/731-1606), is quite a production—a bustling indoor Italian street café with exposed brick and patinaed walls, terra-cotta tile floors, and shelves cluttered with wine barrels, etc. There's more seating (with similar decor) upstairs. The whole thing is quite charming, and the fare delicious. Fresh fruits and vegetables, homemade pasta, and fresh baked breads are served.

For openers, you can toddle up to the antipasto buffet and help yourself to all you want of its abundant offerings. They're included in the price of your dinner entree. You can also opt for the buffet bar as your entire meal: about $8 at dinner, $5 at lunch. When this fabulous smörgåsbord was last seen, it included meatballs, baked spaghetti, greens, a wide choice of fresh fruits, many salads, brussel sprouts, marinated mushrooms, big chunks of provolone cheese, pepperoni, artichoke hearts, real Roquefort, hard-boiled eggs, sausages, chickpeas, bean sprouts, fresh-baked breads, and more—all of it delicious.

Should you want an entree as well, dinner fare ranges from $10 to $16 for pasta dishes like manicotti, cannelloni, and lasagne, or steak or shrimp scampi; sandwiches and pizza are also available. Lunch fare is mostly under $6. Prices on some items are reduced for children under 10. On Sunday there's a Family Feast—all you can eat for $7.

The Vineyard is open Sunday through Thursday from 11am to 11pm, on Friday and Saturday to midnight.

Ricardo's, 2380 Tropicana Ave., at the corner of Tropicana and Eastern (tel. 702/798-4515), is a handsome hacienda-like building you might easily mistake for a new mission. As you enter, ahead is what appears to be a small Mexican plaza— pillars, tall cacti, a lovely fountain with a small balcony above, and a beamed ceiling so high it's not readily noticed. This is the main dining room. A skylight adds to the feeling of being outside. Booths and tables are well spaced. On your right is the Cantina, a large bar room with wooden booths and tables—mobbed, friendly. Two other dining rooms, and a garden dining area carry through the Mexican decor with wrought-metal chandeliers, upright leather-covered chairs, dark-brown wood tables —more austerely Spanish than Mexican in feeling.

Ricardo's serves what I've found to be the best Mexican food in Las Vegas. It's delicious and the portions are huge—bring a big appetite. Ricardo's has both meat and seafood dishes, and dinners range from $9.75 to $12. The carne Ortega is a generous portion of broiled top sirloin, thinly sliced, and smothered with steaming mild Ortega chiles and melted cheese. Those who enjoy seafood, a Ricardo's specialty, should try their enchilada à la Puerto Vallarta—a seafood enchilada consisting of a flour tortilla filled with shrimp, crab, and whitefish sautéed with onions, mild chiles, wine, and spices. Specialties of the house are served with cheese salad or soup, Mexican rice, and refried beans. The tostado entrees are truly an unforgettable experience—they're massive, delicious, and inexpensive, at $5.75 to $7.50. You can have all beef, or chicken, seafood, or diced pork. To wash all this down, Ricardo's has a good selection of beers, wines, margaritas (small, medium, large, and by the pitcher), fruit margaritas, sangría, and piña coladas.

Service is attentive and prompt. Two strolling guitarists look, sing, and play as though Mexico were their home—not Tante Elvira's flamenco, but gentle music to dine by.

Ricardo's is open Monday through Thursday from 11am to 11pm, on Friday and Saturday to midnight, and on Sunday from noon to 10pm. Reservations are essential for dinner, as the restaurant is usually full by 6:30pm, especially on weekends.

Marie Callender's, 600 E. Sahara Ave., at 6th Street (tel. 702/734-6572). The Callender family began making pies in 1948, when they sold their car for $700 and used the proceeds to start a small pie bakery. At first Marie baked about 10 pies a day, but after two years she was baking 200 a day. When the orders reached into the thousands, the family opened their first pie shop in Orange, California. Today there are some 150 Marie Callender restaurants in the West, three of them in Las Vegas. They serve not only pies but wholesome, home-style food.

The restaurant is open for breakfast with a heart-warming array of all-American favorites—ham and eggs, french toast, pancakes, as well as Belgian waffles with fruit and a delicious quiche Lorraine. Breakfast is served until 11am weekdays, to 1pm weekends.

Different soups—potato cheese, clam chowder, etc.—are featured each day by the bowl or tureen; they're accompanied by croissants or home-baked cornbread. Also available are selections from the salad bar, a Frisco burger (served on toasted sourdough bread and sprinkled with parmesan cheese), a tuna stack sandwich piled high with white albacore tuna salad, and an avocado and alfalfa-sprout creation sprinkled with walnuts. All these delights fall in the $6 to $8 price range.

The menu is in effect all day. Dinner (or lunch) favorites range from shrimp linguine (served with salad and bread) to a hamburger steak with a trip to the salad bar. The restaurant grinds its own meat and makes its own pasta. Prices range from $7 to $10.

Leave room for some pie. Apple, rhubarb, cream cheese, lemon, peanut butter, coconut, custard, banana, black bottom, etc., are all baked fresh daily, and all can be ordered with ice cream, whipped cream, or heavy cream.

Marie Callender's is open daily from 7am to midnight.

There are many things that make dining a delight at the **Peppermill,** 2985 Las Vegas Blvd. South, located directly across from the Stardust Hotel (tel. 702/735-4177). The interior is pleasant, attractive, and comfortable. The decor ranges from purple through rose, lavender, and black. Greenery is everywhere, and while you are aware that it's not from nature, it adds to the warmth of the room.

As for the food, everything is as it should be. The small loaves of bread arrive hot enough to melt the butter. And all is fresh as can be, from the tomatoes and vegetables in the soup to the spinach in the salad. Presentation of the food is exceptional, certainly more than I expected. Portions are enormous. The fresh-fruit salad was large enough for two, with some left over for Carmen Miranda.

The Peppermill serves breakfast, lunch, and dinner (as you might expect from a restaurant open 24 hours), plus all sorts of fountain specialties. The list of dishes is lengthy: omelets, pancakes, waffles, burgers, sandwiches, snacks, fruit plates, salads, pasta, steaks with shrimp or fettuccine and including a hearty T-Bone, ribs, chicken, or one of several varieties of seafood. In the sandwich department, I especially enjoy the breast of chicken Cordon Bleu—sautéed and layered with sliced ham, Swiss cheese, lettuce, and tomato, and served open-faced on a grilled roll.

Breakfast ranges from $4.50 to $8; sandwiches, $6.50 to $8; salads, $8 to $11; and entrees, $8.50 to $17. A cocktail lounge adjoining the dining area offers the services of a full bar and, of course, wine or beer. And should you manage room for dessert, be prepared to gorge on a work of art. Desserts cost $3 to $5. You simply won't believe the banana split.

The Peppermill also has a children's menu (under 12 years of age) for breakfast, lunch, and dinner ($3.25 to $5.50), as well as a choice of children's beverages ($1). The Peppermill, as I mentioned above, is open 24 hours daily.

The **Garden Eatery/Omelet House,** 2150 W. Charleston, near Rancho Drive (tel. 702/384-6868), has to be one of the best breakfast/lunch establishments in Las Vegas in terms of quality, quantity, and price. As you walk up to the restaurant, you may feel that you're about to enter the local betting parlor—no windows. The interior is very rustic, the bare ranch-house feeling: simple unpolished wooden booths and tables, wall lights, simple hanging lamps. But let's get down to the basics. You can just have eggs with the usual accompaniments, or you can have them with Vienna/Polish sausage. But why? There are 32 omelets and quiches to choose from ($2.75 to $5.75), including a real barn-burner, the Rio Grande Surfer, with chorizo sausage, onion, and cheddar cheese, plus 16 extras available to add on. Look for the Flatlanders Special, at a price compatible with its description.

You're a traditionalist? Try the old-fashioned buttermilk pancakes. You can even have them with apples, bananas, or blueberries and whipped cream (so much for tradition). For the superhearty eater, there's a "flap special" with two pieces of bacon or sausage, pancakes, and two eggs—all for $3.75.

On the other hand, if you arrive just in time for lunch, there's an assortment of absolutely delicious hamburgers served on fresh onion rolls (with spuds or a side of salad, pickle, and fruit garnish), salads, homemade soups, with pumpkin-nut bread or one of your choice, chicken fingers, or homemade chili. The "chile size" contains a third of a pound of lean ground chuck sprinkled with mixed cheeses and onions for $4.50, or there's a cup for $2. The Italian beef sandwich is a winner. Like everything else, it's big—tender roast beef chunks simmered in Italian sauce (gravy, to you purists) and served on Italian bread, then sprinkled with Jack cheese, for $5. The top price on the menu is $6. All drinks are of the "soft" variety, but for a great refresher, have their Freshen-Up, a delectable combination of orange juice, Fresca, and "special secret ingredients."

The Garden Eatery/Omelet House is open daily (except Thanksgiving and Christmas) from 7am to 3pm.

ALTERNATIVE AND SPECIAL-INTEREST TRAVEL

1. ADVENTURE/WILDERNESS TRAVEL

2. HEALTH AND FITNESS VACATIONS

3. PEOPLE-TO-PEOPLE VACATIONS

4. WOMEN-TO-WOMEN VACATIONS

5. PACK AND LEARN

More and more, the world of travel is being segmented into small packages, labeled not so much with destinations as with the activities (or inactivities) awaiting us when we arrive. That's what special-interest travel is all about; it encompasses everything from adventure/wilderness vacations to educational and study travel, health and fitness travel, political travel, and vacations for seniors.

The size of California is such that it affords many opportunities for adventure and wilderness travel. And on a per capita basis, California seems to offer more in the way of health and fitness vacations (mental and physical) via spas, yoga retreats, macrobiotic centers, or whatever, than any other state—or, in fact, than most other countries. (Meditate on the significance of that, if you will.) And the many older Americans who retire to or visit California are often afforded the opportunity here to do things outside of the usual.

Below I've covered a variety of special-interest vacations and activities offered throughout California, as well as a few in the Las Vegas area.

When it comes to considering alternative and special-interest travel, don't limit your vision. There's a great deal to do and to learn, many new interests to discover, whatever age you may be. One of the most interesting, useful, thought-provoking books about travel it's ever been my joy to read is *The New World of Travel,* by Arthur Frommer (published by Prentice Hall Travel). Read it—you'll see what I mean.

1. Adventure/Wilderness Travel

If running up and down Kilimanjaro or cross-country skiing 600 miles to the South Pole is your idea of a thrilling vacation, California may not be your cup of herbal tea. However, it can come close in terms of low- to medium-anxiety adventure, and can offer a lot of fun and excitement (even apart from that derived from driving the freeways).

SADDLE TRIPS

In the southeastern part of Yosemite National Park, high on the Sierra Nevada's west side, the **Minarets Pack Station** serves the Ansel Adams Wilderness Area in the Sierra National Forest. From the awesome heights of Banner Peak and Mount Ritter down to the roaring San Joaquin River, Minarets Pack Station can outfit you for an extraordinary vacation in the area of your choice. Whether you simply want to absorb the exceptional beauty of the Ansel Adams Wilderness or fish and hunt, Minarets supplies the surefooted animals and competent staff for your excursion.

For a spot trip, the Pack Station will pack you and your gear off to a campsite and pick you up for the return on a specified date—or if you wish, the packer and stock will remain with you; you provide the provisions and choose the itinerary.

Minarets can also plan and prepare a deluxe trip, providing you with camping gear, food, cook, packers, and stock for your entire wilderness stay. If you're the hardy type, on the other hand, you may prefer to backpack it—be packed up and sent out to ride or walk. In addition, Minarets Pack Station has a five-day hands-on, professionally taught packing course, with all meals and two-day pack trip included. Finally, special deluxe outfitted and guided hunts can be arranged.

Minarets Pack Station, in Miller Meadow, 95 miles northeast of Fresno, is open from June through October. Prices vary according to the area you'd like to visit, the number of people in the group, and the type of trip that appeals to your outdoor instincts. Write for details; you'll receive a very informative folder with a map of the areas covered by the Pack Station, plus rates, dates, etc. Before June 1, send your request to Larry Lovelace, Manager, Minarets Pack Station, 23620 Robertson Blvd., Chowchilla, CA 93610 (tel. 209/665-4106 or 665-3964).

June through September, **Yosemite Stables** has saddle trips to High Sierra camps. Because mules are used as opposed to horses, the rides are quite easy. The camps, about 8 miles apart, are equipped with tents containing beds with sheets, blankets, and mattresses; there's usually (though not always) at least one hot shower. Hot meals are provided for breakfast and dinner; midday there's a sack lunch. A four-day saddle trip (three nights and four days, each night at a different camp) costs about $400 per person, and a six-day trip (five nights and six days, each night at a different camp) runs each person about $600. Minimum age is 7; those under 12 must have previous riding experience. These trips are quite popular so it's a good idea to make your reservation early (the preceding December would be about right). For information, call the **High Sierra Reservations Desk** (tel. 209/252-3013) or write, detailing your interests, to **Yosemite Reservations,** 5410 E. Home Ave., Fresno, CA 93727.

If you're accustomed to being on horseback for prolonged periods of time, **Rock Creek Pack Station,** P.O. Box 248, Bishop, CA 93514 (tel. 619/935-4493 in summer, 619/872-8331 in winter), has a truly extraordinary vacation for you. This outfit schedules four-day mustang-tracking trips in the rarely visited Pizona area of the Inyo National Forest—the natural habitat of wild mustangs. You'll be accompanied by experienced tracker-guides who will share their knowledge of the social behavior of the horses and their environment. Rock Creek supplies everything except your bed roll, setting up tents at a new location each afternoon and serving meals chuck-wagon fashion. The cost is about $500 per person, all inclusive; write to the address above for details. This is not a ride for novices.

Rock Creek has five- and seven-day angler rides ($400 to $600), as well as wilderness trail rides ($450 to $625). There are also special four-day fall-color trail rides when fly-fishing is at its best.

For beginning riders, Rock Creek Pack Station has an ideal four-day trail ride into the John Muir Wilderness, offering an opportunity to explore the lakes and streams of the Mono Creek area. On layovers, participants can swim, fish, hike—or just relax and do nothing. The trip begins and ends at Rock Creek (cost is about $375).

All the Rock Creek trips are educational to some degree if you've never before been in the spectacular John Muir or Ansel Adams Wilderness. However, Rock Creek also has several trips specifically designed to expand your vision and insight into the wonders of this country. An eight-day horseback natural history expedition into the John Muir Wilderness (including the remarkable Bear Creek and French Canyon areas) is accompanied by a naturalist who shares his experience and knowledge of the wildlife, flora, glaciers, and history of the country. It's a great opportunity to fish for Golden trout and to photograph nature (cost is about $675).

The 12-day Sequoia–Kings Canyon National Park trail ride explores the majestic central section of the park with enough layover time to investigate many remote parts of Kings Canyon. The trip is limited to 10 guests, and the cost for the 13 days is about $1,100.

There are many variations on pack trips, and what's included in each, so it's a good idea to call or write first for brochures, then call for whatever added information you need. The decision won't be an easy one; consider taking one trip per year. If you'd rather put together your own private trail ride, the cost per person will generally range from $70 to $160 per day, depending on the number of people (minimum 3, maximum 20).

BACKPACKING, TREKKING, AND CAMPING

Backpack along what has been called "the finest mountain walk in western America" into the dramatic high country of Yosemite National Park, with its wildflowers, beautiful Tenaya Lake, and snowfields. Hikers' camps in the Yosemite backcountry provide shelter and meals for wilderness travelers. It's a great way for beginners to decide if backcountry hiking is their bag before investing in expensive wilderness-tripping accoutrements. Each of the five camps has a dining room for family-style meals and washrooms with hot showers (most of the time). You'll sleep in canvas tent-cabins, men separated from women. Camps are open late June through Labor Day, depending on the weather. Seven-day hikes with a naturalist cost about $450 per person. Backpackers who want to avoid the hassle of lugging food can arrange for breakfast and dinner at $25. For information, contact **High Sierra Reservations,** Yosemite Park and Curry Co., 5410 E. Home Ave., Fresno, CA 93727 (tel. 209/454-2002).

Another great group of backpacking trips is offered by **California Adventures,** the outdoor recreation program of the University of California at Berkeley. For eight years, California Adventures has provided a wide variety of fascinating outdoor trips. Though most are for three or four days, California Adventures also has backpacking trips for one or two weeks. You might hike around the lonely canyons, alluvial fans, and rugged hills of Death Valley, both on and off trail, on the way home enjoying a good long soak in a natural hot spring. Or you might head up to a hiking adventure in Sequoia–Kings Canyon National Park; Kings Canyon is the deepest chasm on earth, with a descent of over 7,000 feet from the rim of the canyon to the south fork of Kings River at the bottom. Prices for nonstudents of all ages and levels of experience range from $130 to $300 for most trips. The price of each trip includes van transportation, group equipment, and experienced leadership, but not food. For more information on the wide variety of activities offered, write to California Adventures, University of California, 2301 Bancroft, Berkeley, CA 94720 (tel. 415/642-4000).

Cooperative camping tours are becoming increasingly popular, and they certainly are among the least expensive modes of travel. Up to 14 people share a van, cruising by day and camping at night. The vehicle comes with camping equipment and the services of a professional tour escort. All you need to bring is a sleeping bag, a sense of adventure (though physical challenges are rarely involved), and some extra spending money for the occasional hotel stays or meals out included in the itinerary.

You decide on the type of tour, the departure date, and the tour length. The first day of the trip, a "food bank" is established (usually about $30 per person, per week). All members of the group take turns shopping for food along the way, and preparing meals at the camping ground. You are responsible for pitching your pop-up tent at night and packing it away in the morning. The driver's chore is driving. The largest and most successful cooperative camping organization is **Trek America,** P.O. Box 1338, Gardena, CA 90249 (tel. 213/323-5775, or toll free 800/221-0596). In 1972 they began offering young people (18 to 38) from the U.S. and all over the world an exciting, inexpensive, and fun way to experience America. Many of the smaller group camping tours, particularly of the West Coast, depart from Los Angeles and travel to Nevada and the Grand Canyon; some head north to San Francisco and Seattle; others go north, then down to San Diego. Prices range from $550 to $1,200 and are two to four weeks in length. TrekAmerica supplies all the camping equipment; all you need is a sleeping bag and a sense of adventure. You can get a free detailed color brochure by writing or calling TrekAmerica.

Without a doubt, one of the most unique approaches to touring is that of the **Green Tortoise** line, described as a "hostel on wheels." Take one large motorcoach, remove all the seats, replace same with a foam-rubber platform, and there you have it—room for a group of about 35 hardy souls to stretch out, recline, or sleep, as required. As per the Green Tortoise coach itself, each trip is a new adventure, with a flexible schedule, which allows all aboard the opportunity to explore, camp out, hike, whatever. Food costs are about $9 per day for breakfast and dinner; everyone helps in the preparation of meals—basically vegetarian—and with the cleaning up. Green Tortoise trips go everywhere (well, almost) and each varies in its destination and stops; in fact, the only guarantee you have is that you'll begin and end at a designated spot. For California, most trips begin at San Francisco and go north to Napa Valley; they may then go on to Lassen Volcanic National Park, Shasta National Forest, Trinity Alps, Redwoods National Park, and Fern Canyon, then back to San Francisco. The price of such a six-day Northern California loop is $180, plus the noted $9 per day for group cookouts; add to that the cost of a couple of restaurant meals. For detailed information, contact Green Tortoise, P.O. Box 24459, San Francisco, CA 94124 (tel. 415/821-0803, or toll free 800/227-4766 outside California).

ROCK CLIMBING

If you've ever harbored fantasies of joining the mountaineering set, you should know that Yosemite is world-renowned as a rock-climbing area. The **Yosemite Mountaineering School,** Yosemite, CA 95389 (tel. 209/372-1335), has a reputation for excellence in rock-climbing instruction. Multiday, multiskill classes are available (weather permitting) for all levels of expertise. Reservations and information are available at the Yosemite Mountaineering School at Tuolumne Meadows from June through late September, then at Curry Village in Yosemite Valley (tel. 209/372-1244).

For a rock-climbing comprehensive, **California Adventures,** University of California at Berkeley, 2301 Bancroft, Berkeley, CA 94720 (tel. 415/642-4000), offers introductory climbing trips to various locales, including selected sites in the Sierra. While all the rock-climbing trips are relatively short (at the most three days), you'll be packing a lot of fun and adventure into those days among some of the most magnificent landscapes in the West. Transportation is by car pool, and all group camping and climbing equipment is provided. The price to nonstudents is $78 to $145, depending upon the time (one day to three days).

Female staff members of California Adventures also offer the same course for an all-women's group at Yosemite. Women of all skill levels are encouraged to join.

California Adventures has private rock-climbing instruction for individuals or groups of up to three people, customized to personal abilities and goals. Whether your interest lies in advanced multipitch ascents or simply in working with and improving the skills you've acquired on your own, California Adventures will design a trip for you.

RAFTING

Also at Yosemite, you'll find one of the most popular rafting rivers, the Tuolumne, where miners once panned for gold. The river pours out of the national park and rushes down a thrilling and relentless series of rapids through a breathtakingly beautiful canyon. If you're game, the **American River Touring Association (ARTA),** a nonprofit organization, offers a three-day raft trip, departing in July and August, for $360. Or you may choose to ride the untamed Merced River, which booms down out of the Sierras and through Yosemite Valley from late April to early July; one- or two-day trips on the Merced are $85 to $190. ARTA offers other one- to three-day raft trips (to $360) from April through August. ARTA has a comprehensive booklet that covers everything you need to know in order to choose a trip: degree of difficulty, wilderness experience, good for families or first-timers, attractions, cost, etc. For information, contact ARTA, Star Route 73, Groveland, CA 95321 (tel. 209/962-7873, or toll free 800/323-2782).

Another organization offering white-water rafting down the Tuolumne River is **Sierra Max River Trips,** which has conducted excursions for thousands of people from 5 to 75 years of age. (When food celebrity Craig Claiborne went on one, he took along a good supply of California wines.) An excursion following the rapids of the main Tuolumne River lasts three days and two nights. The price, $380, covers the cost of guides (one for every four or five passengers), meals, equipment, and wet suits; sleeping gear can be rented for $20. Sierra Mac also offers white-water two-day trips down the main Tuolumne for $280. For further information, contact Sierra Max River Trips, P.O. Box 366, Sonora, CA 95370 (tel. 209/532-1327).

Mariah Wilderness Expeditions will take you white-water rafting and on other adventures from Southern California up to the Sierra rivers, the Colorado River in the Grand Canyon, the Rogue River in Oregon, and to some exciting spots outside the U.S. for rafting and sea kayaking. The majority of their California packages are one- or two-day excursions, but there is a great three-day run, with two nights of camping, along the Tuolumne River in Yosemite ($380). The trip is offered daily from April to October. There are any number of exciting two-day adventures, including family rafting trips with your own storyteller, and a beautiful package combining white-water rafting with hot-air bollooning. Mariah also offers all-women excursions that are challenging and fun (see "Women-to-Women Vacation," below).

For a remarkably detailed folder describing all the trips, the difficulty rating, and minimum ages, and including a calendar and price list, plus everything else you need to know, call or write to Mariah Wilderness Expeditions, P.O. Box 248, Point Richmond, CA 94807 (tel. 415/233-2303, or toll free 800/462-7424).

For all the fun and excitement to be found in Las Vegas, there's not much that can beat a five-day Colorado River trip with **O.A.R.S. (Outdoor Adventure River Specialists).** You fly from Las Vegas, arriving at the Bar 10 Ranch in time for lunch and an afternoon of such dude-ranch specialties as a mini-rodeo, trail rides, hiking, horseshoes—whatever you choose—followed by a first-class dinner. After breakfast the next morning, you'll be flown by helicopter into the Grand Canyon. Your four days of rafting begin at Mile 188, Whitmore Wash, and cover 90 miles to Pierce Ferry, just past the point where the Colorado River joins Lake Mead. This spectacular stretch of the river offers broad views of the Grand Canyon, and the modest rapids here give you the opportunity to decide if you'd like to try a little more white water some other time. You spend the nights ashore in tents and sleeping equipment supplied by O.A.R.S.

There are a limited number of dates for the five-day trips out of Las Vegas—six in all from mid-April through the end of August— so it's wise to call for reservations at least a month in advance. The $825 price includes transportation to and from Las Vegas, meals, use of the tents, and the overnight stay at Bar 10. O.A.R.S. also has 6-, 9-, and 13-day trips ($1,070 to $1,985) from mid-April to late October, meeting either in Flagstaff or Phantom Ranch. For detailed and helpful information on all trips, call or write O.A.R.S. Inc., P.O. Box 67, Angels Camp, CA 95222 (tel. 209/736-4677).

BICYCLING

Backroads Bicycle Touring, 1516 Fifth St., Suite Q427, Berkeley, CA 94710-1713 (tel. 415/527-1555, or toll free 800/533-2573 outside California), offers a number of five-day luxury tours in California through some of the state's most spectacular natural attractions—Wine Country (including sampling), the Redwood Empire, the Mendocino coast, Big Sur, and Death Valley. There's even a new five-day "singles only" trip through the Wine Country and Bodega Bay. The tours are leisurely, offering participants a choice of daily distances to match their cycling abilities, as well as a choice of bed-and-breadfast or camping accommodations. Each of the tours is accompanied by two professional tour leaders; a support van and trailer carry all gear, baggage, and provisions. You can bring your own bicycle or rent one of Backroads' custom-built bicycles. Groups are for all ages; if seniors find some trips a bit wearing, they can ride in the support van for part of the day. Most tours average $160 to $200 per day, with the camping tour a bit lower (about $100 per day). For further information and a copy of a free 63-page catalog, write or call Backroads Bicycle Touring.

Arrow to the Sun Bicycle Touring Company, P.O. Box 115, Taylorsville, CA 95983 (tel. 916/284-6263, or toll free 800/634-0942 outside California), has a great selection of tours ranging from 7 to 14 days, primarily in Northen California. The itinerary includes some of the most beautiful spots in the state—the Marble Mountains east of Eureka and west of Yreka, set aside as wilderness for generations, and the Sierra rim, including Lake Tahoe and Feather River country. There are a number of interesting "theme" tours: a hot springs and wine tour, a coastline bed-and-breadfast tour, a California Goldtrails tour, and a forest tour through the lush Indian Valley, to name a few. Tours through Baja California are also on the agenda. Groups, accompanied by a support van, usually consist of 15 or fewer. The tours accommodate varying levels of ability, from beginner or energetic beginner to intermediate to advanced; 30 to 50 miles are common distances traveled daily. The tours average $100 to $120 per day; prices include lodging, meals, and road snacks. Write or phone for further information or a copy of a detailed descriptive booklet.

If you're the adventurous type and don't need the luxury of a fine hotel or a superior B&B inn, consider the itineraries offered by the **American Youth Hostels.** You don't have to be under 18; some trips are designed to include people of all ages, while others are planned for specific age groups. Travelers stay primarily in hostels; every group is accompanied by a trained trip leader. One of the great advantages of American Youth Hostel adventure trips is cost. The organization has a 22-day California coast cycling trip, from San Francisco to San Diego. You may stay overnight in a genuine lighthouse hostel at Montara, tour Hearst Castle, visit Disneyland, and dig your toes into the sand at the beaches along the way—all for about $700, which includes lodging (tents, cooking utensils, and stoves when camping), group-prepared meals, a group activities budget, and the leadership costs. But American Youth Hostel trips are not limited to cycling. The group also offers hiking trips, motor trips, and other adventure trips. You can get a catalog of current offerings by writing or calling American Youth Hostels, Central California Council, P.O. Box 28148, San Jose, CA 95159 (tel. 408/298-0670).

HOUSEBOATING

For a special do-it-yourself vacation that includes fishing, sunbathing, swimming, hiking, sightseeing, and exploring, it's hard to beat a week or two on a houseboat. Houseboats give you the option of being with a congenial group or being alone, and afford you the choice of more activities than you ever thought you could squeeze into your trip. And they're easy to operate, even if you've never been at the helm before. Nearly everything you need to create your own fun is provided for you: fully equipped kitchen, a bathroom with shower, hot water, air conditioning, heating units, built-in beds, deck chairs, ice chests, and barbecue are usually standard. All you need to bring is food, your personal gear, and fishing tackle (and in some cases, bed linen).

Houseboats are relatively economical on a per-person basis. (When comparing costs among houseboat rentals, always check on the number of *adults* the houseboat will sleep, the supplies offered, and both the boarding and return times.) Houseboats that will sleep six adults generally range from $970 to $1,290 per week, depending on the season and location. Larger boats, accommodating as many as 10, are also available. One of the largest of the houseboat rental companies is **Seven Crown Resorts,** which has vacation packages on Nevada's Lake Mead, the wonder created by Hoover Dam, about 35 miles east of Las Vegas; and Lake Mohave, south of Lake Mead and just north of Laughlin, Nevada. The outfit also rents houseboats at Lake Shasta at Redding, California—about a three-hour drive north of San Francisco—and at the Sacramento River Delta, an endless and fascinating network of rivers and channels near Stockton, California. For information, call or write Seven Crown Resorts, P.O. Box 1409, Boulder City, NV 89005 (tel. toll free 800/752-9669).

WHALE-WATCHING

Few annual events attract as much attention and interest in California as the migration of the whales. Among the naturalists in this field and other guides offering trips to observe the migration and calving, **Biological Journeys,** 1696F Ocean Dr., McKinleyville, CA 95521 (tel. 707/839-0178 or 415/527-9622, or toll free 800/548-7555), is the largest. Using its own small cruise ships departing from San Diego, the organization takes amateur naturalists on its scientific journeys (February to about mid-March) along the coast of Baja California to the San Ignacio Lagoon, where you spend three days at this home of the graceful California gray whales. On the way to and from the lagoon, you will visit four of the remote and beautiful islands of Baja's west coast. Biological Journeys also offers a trip in March to watch the blue and fin whales in the Sea of Cortez, see them feeding and observe mothers with calves. You'll also snorkel, hike on the islands, and birdwatch. Another alternative is a cruise along the southernmost portion of the Gulf of California, where you find humpback whales in the waters of Cabo San Lucas and the Gorda Bank. Fifty or so humpbacks, among the acrobats of the whale world, spend their winters around the tip of Baja. There's time to snorkel at the Sea of Cortez's only coral reef and around the sea lion colony of Los Islotes. Trips take 9 to 12 days and accommodate 20 to 32 passengers—rather like a family-size group of guests who enjoy the discovery of fresh, uncluttered places. The cost is about $1,850 to $2,595 per person.

Other full-fledged, naturalist-led whale-watching expeditions are conducted by Sven-Olof Lindblad's **Special Expeditions,** 720 Fifth Avenue, New York, NY 10019 (tel. 212/765-7740, or toll free 800/762-0003). From January through March, Special Expeditions offers 12-day voyages aboard the 152-foot MV *Sea Lion* and the MV *Sea Bird*, each accommodating 70 passengers in 37 outside cabins. All staterooms have private facilities, lower beds, climate control, and large windows or port lights. Trips begin with a nonstop flight from Los Angeles to Loreto, then embark at San Carlos for Bahia Magdalena and points south, with stops to visit the spectacular islands and bays where the gray whales come to breed and give birth. Trips range from $2,800 to $4,000 per person, depending on the accommodations. Airfare is not included. Since Special Expeditions supports the concept of comfort, each ship has a spacious dining room, an observation lounge with a bar, and a sun deck. To afford access to almost anywhere, each ship also has a fleet of rubber landing crafts.

Pacific Sea Fari Tours, 2803 Emerson St., San Diego, CA 92106 (tel. 619/226-8224), in conjunction with **H & M Landing** (tel. 619/222-1144), has been conducting naturalist-led seagoing expeditions to Baja's most beautiful and remote islands for nearly 20 years. The smaller expedition group size minimizes the impact to the areas visited and adds to the enjoyment of those exploring the sea and land wilderness. Whale-watching trips are made to the Laguna San Ignacio, undoubtedly the most famous of the whaling lagoons, located midway down the Baja; to Laguna Ojo de Liebre, the northernmost of the Baja lagoons; and to the Sea of Cortez, home for many species of marine life, including blue and fin whales. Trips are 7 or 8 days to Laguna Ojo de Liebre (about $1,100 to $1,300), or 8 to 12 days for the more southern parts of the Baja (about $1,300 to $1,800). Accommodations are aboard vessels ranging in size from 75 to 88 feet, suitable for 12 to 30 passengers; all have air conditioning, large galleys, and lounge facilities, including color TVs, VCRs, and natural-history libraries.

Undoubtedly one of the most fascinating approaches to whale-watching is offered by **Mariah Wilderness Expeditions.** You journey 600 miles south of San Diego to Magdalena Bay for sea kayaking on the Pacific side of Baja. It's an exciting eight-day trip in March to the winter home of the California gray whale and of hundreds of sea lions and porpoises. The cost is $900 plus airfare. Call or write to Mariah Wilderness Expeditions, P.O. Box 248, Point Richmond, CA 94807 (tel. 415/233-2303, or toll free 800/462-7424).

---

2. Health and Fitness Vacations

A great many California time-off approaches to health and fitness, physical and mental, fall under this aegis, from the ultrachic to the simple yoga retreat.

SPAS

And so we start with the pampered, health- and fitness-inducing vacation. And where better to begin than at the totally renovated 1,000-acre **La Costa Hotel and Spa,** Costa del Mar Road, Carlsbad, CA 92009 (tel. 619/438-9111, or toll free 800/854-6564), a Southern California hotel and spa with 172 luxury guest units. Tennis courts, pools, golf courses, customized diets—there's much for everyone, including celebrity guests. But there's a price, of course: At the lower end of the scale, double rooms are $230 to $275; for double rooms on the golf course, the tab is $280; suites cost $350. The "Introduction to the Spa Plan" (three days/two nights, including sports and five treatments) is $280 per person per night for a double; $325 for a single. The "Original Spa Plan," including spa meals, a variety of health and beauty treatments, all sports, and much personal attention, is $450 per person, per night, for a double; $650 for a single.

You may have already guessed that La Costa is not for the relaxed, washed-jeans and beat-up-sneakers set; it is, rather, a "designer" spa, attracting sleek, well-coiffed guests who don fancy resortwear in the evening. It may be that the new Japanese owners, Sports Shinko, intend La Costa to be their first posh resort link to Hawaii. La Costa is about 1½ hours south of Los Angeles, just off I-5, between Carlsbad and Del Mar, and about a half hour north of San Diego.

A most attractive and beautifully groomed environment for fun and fitness, **Murrieta Hot Springs Resort & Health Spa,** 39405 Murrieta Hot Springs Rd., Murrieta, CA 92362 (tel. 714/677-7451, or toll free 800/322-4542, 800/458-4393 in California), is devoted somewhat more to your well-being than your coiffure. About a 1½-hour drive southeast of Los Angeles, or about a 1¼-hour drive north of San Diego, the hot mineral springs are on the site of what once was a Temecula village and were valued for their therapeutic properties. In 1987 a $3-million refurbishment program was begun remodeling the guest rooms and Stone Lodge.

Murrieta Hot Springs is spread over 47 acres of rolling hills. Three outdoor natural mineral pools of varying temperatures and sizes, from an Olympic pool to a bubbling Jacuzzi, are there to relax you. For the more energetic, there are 14 tennis courts, pathways for strolling or jogging, and a golf course at the adjacent Rancho California Country Club. As to the health part of the resort, you can soak away whatever may be making you stressful in a soothing hot mineral bath (with essential oils), followed by a body wrap; and the spa's mud bath is truly a balm for the body and spirit. An incredible variety of massages, European facials, and Finnish saunas will help refurbish the exterior. Mineral-bath prices, with various additions, range from $20 to $50; mud "experiences," massages, and facials begin at $30 and proceed up to $90 for the deluxe European facial.

As for the cuisine, meals are vegetarian or California cuisine, and delicious. Singles are $65 to $75; doubles, $75 to $95, for lodging only.

TOWARD PERSONAL GROWTH

At the other end of the spectrum, in terms of distance and direction (literal and otherwise), is the **Esalen Institute,** at Big Sur, CA 93920 (tel. 408/667-3000). Esalen was created in 1962, at the beginning of the upheaval years, as a center for encounter therapy. It has since evolved into a residential retreat center for personal-growth seminars. The Esalen catalog is the simplest way to find out what the institute offers. Call or write away for one.

Esalen seminars or workshops may be held over a weekend ($260 to $325) or a period of five days ($465 to $630); costs include room, board, and studies. Rates vary according to accommodations—bunk beds or doubles. For those new to Esalen, "Experiencing Esalen" is an orientation workshop that offers a great variety of subjects from which to choose.

Studies are conducted in some of the most relaxed surroundings imaginable: lush gardens, magnificent views, and natural hot springs, where you can soak as you watch the sun set into the ocean below. Should you prefer swimming, you can use the large pool, with or without swimsuit. Dress is casual for breakfast, lunch, dinner, and all hours in between (although not as casual as for swimming). The shared rooms are comfortable and simple, but lack telephones, TV sets, and radios—it is a retreat, after all. Some rooms have patios and ocean views, but you can hear the sound of the surf from any room. Meals are served buffet style in a friendly lodge dining room, and the food is absolutely delicious. It may also be some of the most wholesome you've had in years. At dinnertime there is a beer-and-wine bar.

Workshops and bed spaces fill up early during the summer, so it's important to plan in advance for Esalen. During the winter, when the 100 guest beds may not be fully booked, it is possible to stay at Esalen without enrolling in a seminar or workshop; you may simply want to meditate, write, or quietly relax. The cost would be in the range of $65 to $115 for a night in shared accommodations and a day, including dinner, breakfast, and lunch. For a complete weekend, without workshops or seminars, you can stay at Esalen for about $230, meals included, as space is available.

However much time you spend at Esalen, don't miss out on its famous massage —$60 for an hour of sheer bliss. Your body will reimburse you.

Esalen is located about 300 miles north of Los Angeles and 175 miles south of San Francisco, just south of Monterey and overlooking the spectacular surf.

YOGA RETREATS

About 60 miles northeast of Sacramento off I-80 (about 1½ hours driving) and up a dirt road, you'll find the **Sivananda Ashram Vrindavan Yoga Farm** at Grass Valley. (Come to think of it, it might be the place for a contemplative stop when returning from Reno.) This is undoubtedly the cheapest of the residential ashrams ($35 a night, $210 per week, $765 per month for a private room, including meals) and among the smallest, with space for only 30 guests. Shared rooms are $25 a night, $150 per week, $550 per month. Life at the ashram is rustic, simple, and quiet, consisting of a changeless routine of meditation and exercises. During your free time you can hike to a nearby hill and view the timeless beauty of the magnificent Sierras. They also offer a work-exchange program. For a very special vacation, write or phone Sivananda Ashram Vrindavan Yoga Farm, 14651 Ballantree Lane, Grass Valley, CA 95949 (tel. 916/272-9322).

Also near Grass Valley is **The Expanding Light,** close to Nevada City. This meditation retreat is located on the grounds of the Ananda World Brotherhood Village. Up to 125 visitors can engage in a retreat that includes classic yoga routines. There are morning and afternoon asanas (gentle stretching exercises), meditations, and classes on both Christian and Eastern themes. A week's stay is $280 in a shared room, and $385 in a private room, including three vegetarian meals a day and classes. Ananda is 17 miles from Nevada City and about 70 miles northeast of Sacramento. Write or call The Expanding Light, c/o Ananda World Brotherhood Village, 14618 Tyler Foote, Nevada City, CA 95959 (tel. 916/292-3494, or toll free 800/346-5350).

About 70 miles due north of Sacramento, just off Calif. 70, the **Vega Study Center** of Oroville, California, resides in a town of old Victorian homes and shops dating back to the early 1900s. The Vega Study Center is the teaching base for Cornellia and Herman Aihara, macrobiotic teachers and authors. Workshops and retreats run for one to two weeks. The cost, including full board, is $645 for one week, $1,195 for two weeks. Guests share rooms and sleep on pine beds with marvelous futon mattresses. Morning tea talks are by Cornelia and Herman Aihara. For a catalog or other information, write or call Vega Study Center, 1511 Robinson St., Oroville, CA 95965 (tel. 916/533-7702).

In the mountains of Santa Cruz, overlooking all of Monterey Bay, the Mount Madonna Center at Watsonville is a yoga-oriented conference and retreat facility used for discussions of some of the hottest (and coolest) psychological issues of the day. Over a long weekend or on a weeklong vacation, you might choose to focus on such broad issues as *Creativity and Success, Dying—Opportunity of a Lifetime,* or perhaps *Self-Hypnosis.* (Somehow, the fresh air and walks through the redwood forests always help to clarify the issues.)

A room and two vegetarian meals daily, plus snacks, ranges from $30 (dorms), to $35 (semiprivate rooms), to $60 (private rooms with baths); add about $95 for the weekend courses and seminars you'll doubtless select. Watsonville is about equidistant between Monterey and Santa Cruz (somewhat inland), and about 30 miles from San Jose. For detailed literature, contact **Mount Madonna Center,** 445 Summit Rd., Watsonville, CA 95076 (tel. 408/722-7175 or 847-0406).

---

3. People-to-People Vacations

A small but growing trend in vacations has been toward those that satisfy a desire for selfless involvement in other lives and in other modes of living.

POLITICAL

Habitat for Humanity asks for just such selfless involvement. Hundreds of Habitat volunteers spend retirement time (as did Jimmy and Rosalynn Carter) or vacation time at Habitat locations helping to build sturdy, low-cost houses side-by-side with the people in need. Volunteers pay for their own transportation and food, sometimes receiving only the most basic accommodations at the construction site. No prior construction experience is required, and almost anyone can be taught a useful skill.

Habitat for Humanity wants to make shelter a matter of conscience so that one day shacks will be gone, collapsing tenement houses will be no more, and there will be no homeless people sleeping on city streets.

For information on how you can devote your vacation to Habitat for Humanity and share in an experience that can change your life, contact Habitat for Humanity, Habitat and Church streets, Americus, GA 31709 (tel. 912/924-6935). Within California, there are Habitat for Humanity offices in San Jose, Santa Rosa, Pittsburg, Ventura, Stockton, Fresno, Sacramento, and San Diego; all need volunteer help.

PERSONAL

When it comes to the basic, people-to-people vacations, few get down to the rudiments quite like a country holiday spent on a farm or ranch. Some accommodate only a few guests in bunkhouses, with activities such as hiking, trail rides, campouts, fishing, and honest-to-goodness cattle drives for would-be cowboys. Other working cattle ranches, somewhat more citified, offer square dancing, steak fries, swimming in a heated pool, dinner theater, and private cabins. Invariably, they all offer good, wholesome food—all you can eat—and much of it home-grown.

Far and away, the best source of ranch and farm information nationwide, grouped by state, is a 224-page guidebook written by Pat Dickerman of New York and sold through the mails. The book has nine detailed descriptions of ranches in various locations throughout California and others in nearby Arizona and Utah. For a copy of the book, send $12 to **Farm/Ranch & Country Vacations,** 36 E. 57th St., New York, NY 10022 (tel. 212/355-6334, or toll free 800/252-7899).

---

4. Women-to-Women Vacations

There's a world of exciting trips for women of all ages to travel and learn together, see new places, explore, and learn new activities. Confidence grows by leaps and bounds when you discover the strengths and skills you already have by taking on new challenges with a strong support system behind you.

Woodswomen offers adventure travel for women of all ages. It's the most extensive adventure-travel organization for women in the world: They trek, climb, raft, bicycle, canoe, put together excursions. You can even set forth to spend a relaxing vacation learning about dog sledding.

Woodswomen has been around since 1977, when they began leading canoe expeditions for women in northern Minnesota. Since then they've been providing adventure and unique experiences for women—the excitement of new places, the freedom of the outdoors, and the fun of living out some of your dreams. And you may meet some of the most interesting, fun, bright women you've ever met. Most come alone, and ages range from 18 to 60 plus.

Wilderness travel is the basic element of the Woodswomen's program. Group sizes are small—15 or fewer, usually 6 to 8 women. The pace of the trips allows time for your eyes, head, and heart to enjoy nature—watch birds, see sunsets as you never have before, develop your own outdoor style, set out and learn. Woodswomen also offers programs in leadership and professional development.

Woodswomen has had excursions across the country—from exploring Cape Cod, Martha's Vineyard, and Provincetown; to sunbathing and paddling in Minnesota; to lazily exploring the beauties of Oregon's Rogue River, with an all-women string quartet adding to the music of the canyon; to kayaking through spectacular Alaskan fjords. International trips range from an Everest trek or trekking in Nepal to hiking in the Swiss Alps to scuba diving and snorkeling in Mexico, cruising to the Galápagos Islands, or climbing volcanoes in Ecuador.

In California, Woodswomen features rock-climbing instruction for beginners and intermediate-level climbers at the Joshua Tree National Monument. It's a week's adventure living in the spectacular beauty of the desert in spring. The rock-climbing program is the most comprehensive of its kind geared to your individual level. You'll learn the basics of getting off the ground, staying on the rock, and enjoying it all. You'll also be sampling fine Mexican cuisine, exploring the desert, and spending a relaxing evening at a spa.

The cost of the program is $575 for beginning and intermediate rock climbing, $625 for advanced climbing. Transportation is not included, though Woodswomen can provide you with information about transportation possibilities. Advance registration is required and I suggest that you register as early as possible. For detailed information, contact Woodswomen, 25 West Diamond Lake Rd., Minneapolis, MN 55419 (tel. 612/822-3809).

Among the many river trips available, all-women excursions, conducted by feminist tour operators, afford women wonderful opportunities to gain confidence and self-esteem, and to discover physical and inner strengths while trying something new, challenging, eminently satisfying—and fun. **Mariah Wilderness Expeditions** will take you white-water rafting and sea kayaking with other women, whether you're a beginner or an experienced hand.

Mariah offers three two-day/two-night trips, one (April through September) on the south fork of the American River (a great all-around river). This trip is designed for the novice and intermediate rafter ($180); in two days you travel down 21 miles of river and over 50 rapids. Another two-day/two-night excursion, also for the novice or intermediate, is on the Kings River (southeast of Fresno) deep in the Kings Canyon ($190). It's a thrilling, beautiful, fast-moving run on an uncrowded river. The group is limited to 50 women, and the campsite is right on the river, among pines and oak trees.

If you can only spare two days and one night, more's the pity, but Mariah offers a beauty in the trip down the Merced, a free-flowing river during most of May. The trip begins at the western entrance to Yosemite, where the current is swift and the rapids are mostly continuous. Wildflowers blanket large portions of the green hills in the area. The campsite, located deep in the canyon, is quite private. Limited to 25 women, the trip costs $205 per person. To go on this journey, one should have white-water experience or at least the fortitude for adventure. Mariah also offers a two-day/one-night trip on the Tuolumne River at Yosemite for $265 per person, limited to 20 women; here, too, white-water experience is needed.

Beyond California, Mariah Wilderness Expeditions has trips exclusively for women on Oregon's Rogue River (string quartet and all), on the main Salmon River in Idaho, and sea kayaking among the San Juan Islands in Washington State. Outside the U.S., there's kayaking and rafting in Costa Rica, and kayaking along the coastline of the Sea of Cortez in Baja California.

But certainly one of the most exciting trips Mariah offers has to be the all-women white-water rafting trip in the Soviet Union, where you'll join up with 10 Soviet women. It's guaranteed to change your view of the world. You should have white-water experience. The trip includes a total of 15 days and 14 nights, including 8 days on the magical Katun River in southwestern Siberia, where you'll visit Siberian villages, camp, raft, and share with the Soviet women. The cost of the trip (limited to 15 women) is $4,000, plus airfare of about $900 from Los Angeles to Moscow.

For details on these and other enticing tours, write or call Mariah Wilderness Expeditions, P.O. Box 248, Point Richmond, CA 94807 (tel. 415/233-2303, or toll free 800/462-7424).

---

5. Pack and Learn

FOR THE OVER-60 SET

There are some programs designed expressly for those over 60, one of which is described below. This is not to say that being over 60 precludes an interest in backpacking, white-water rafting, bicycling, fitness vacations, etc.; if you fall into that category and any of the previously described special vacations interests you, contact the source. Many are designed to include several age groups.

One of the most successful and lowest-cost vacation plans for persons aged 60 and older is that of **Elderhostel**. Short-term study tours—usually one- to three-week courses at colleges and universities in the U.S. and around the world—are the focus of the Elderhostel program. Elderhostel charges one fee, giving no guarantee of single or double rooms; housing is usually in university residence halls, sometimes dormitories, segregated by sex (except for couples). At the low end of the scale, for $250 a week (plus airfare) you receive room, board, and tuition (including classroom instruction each day). If you're concerned about being the only single woman in the group—no need to fret. Singles constitute about one-third of Elderhostel's volume, and two-thirds of these are women. For a catalog of current trips and study groups, call or write to Elderhostel, 80 Boylston St., Boston, MA 02116 (tel. 617/426-7788). The catalog is free for two years; thereafter, a $15 annual donation to the organization's Independence Fund will keep U.S. and foreign studies information flowing to you. (Participants in the programs continue to receive catalogs.)

AND FOR ALL AGES

Imagine for a moment a summer vacation that will enrich the rest of your life. The locale is 205 pine-clad acres tucked in among the San Jacinto Mountains where you can hike, fish, rock climb, and breathe. Hold that thought. Now visualize this as the setting for workshops that offer exceptional approaches to the study of music, dance, theater, and the visual and applied arts, including Mother Earth Father Sky workshops in Native American arts. Those are just a few of the joys of the **Idyllwild School of Music and the Arts (ISOMATA)**, P.O. Box 38, Idyllwild, CA 92349 (tel. 714/659-2171 or 213/622-0355). A catalog that details these workshops can be obtained without cost by writing or calling ISOMATA.

Classes for the public at large are conducted from June through September, and there is at least one class that each member of the family can enjoy for one or two weeks: wilderness photography, painting, drawing, collage, water media, visual-language development, study of mystical symbols, fiber-structure assemblage, papermaking, science-fiction writing, poetry, bookmaking as an exploration of shapes, photo etching, improvisational and assemblage sculpture.

Then there are the aforementioned Mother Earth Father Sky workshops: Navajo and Hopi weaving; Hopi, Acoma, and San Ildefonso potterymaking, taught by Blue Corn; Papago and Cahuilla basketmaking, among the highest forms of the art; Hopi sculpture carving, including kachinas; Kwakiutl-style mask carving; Hopi jewelrymaking with silver and stones; Casa Grande ceramics; Navajo weaving. The Mother Earth Father Sky workshops present a rare opportunity to gain both an understanding of the Native American artist's relationship to nature and a knowledge of the materials taken from our environment. Enrollment in these workshops is limited, and it is advisable to register early.

And what do we do with the kiddies for one or two weeks? ISOMATA children's center offers a multiarts program for youngsters aged 5 to 12 that gives them the opportunity to explore the elements of art, creative theater, movement, and music separately, and then as an integrated form. Specialized programs for children 9 to 12 focus on the expressive arts, from the magic of the theater itself to the creation and performance of an original play based on their own ideas. There are workshops in dance, painting, drawing, the construction of three-dimensional art, and the development of visual literacy. Children work with computers in producing individual publications and in creating animation with sound.

How to get to the Idyllwild School of Music and the Arts? The only way is to drive. It's about 2½ hours from either Los Angeles or San Diego. The ISOMATA catalog provides a map. While it may take you only an hour to where Hwy. 74 intersects with 215, it will take you another hour to pass through Hemet, head up into low-lying clouds and through what seems to be an endless series of left-right-left-right curves. But it's all worth it. If you're arriving at Palm Springs or the Ontario Airport and tell ISOMATA when your plane will arrive, they will send a van to meet you; the cost will be $50 each way.

Housing is available in comfortable rooms with private baths. For adults and adults with children, there are three types of housing. Campground housing with tent and trailer sites is based on one to four people for one week; the cost is $40 per week per tent site, $80 per week for a trailer site. Then there are residence halls with motel-like units that have twin beds and baths and accommodate one to three adults. Rates are $275 per person per week, including three meals; charges also include linens, which are changed weekly. Private rooms with meals are $375 per week;

availability is limited. Motels or homes can also be rented in the Idyllwild community. Costs obviously are exclusive of those for the various workshops.

As for the town of Idyllwild, it's a charming mountain village where you'll find B&Bs, eateries, a village market, bookstores, gift shops, a pizza palace, a Mexican restaurant (Senor Ruben's), the Forest Service, a service station, etc. All in all, it's rather like a small version of Woodstock, New York, less affected, a bit less artsy-craftsy, and a tad more rustic.

INDEX

GENERAL INFORMATION

DESTINATIONS

KEY TO ABBREVIATIONS: *B* = Budget; *B & B* = Bed-and-Breakfast; *CG* = Campgrounds; *CO* =
cottages; *D* = Deluxe; *E* = Expensive; *M* = Moderate.

NOW, SAVE MONEY ON ALL YOUR TRAVELS!
Join Frommer's™ Dollarwise® Travel Club

Saving money while traveling is never a simple matter, which is why the **Dollarwise Travel Club** was formed 31 years ago. Developed in response to requests from Frommer's Travel Guide readers, the Club provides cost-cutting travel strategies, up-to-date travel information, and a sense of community for value-conscious travelers from all over the world.

In keeping with the money-saving concept, the annual membership fee is low —$18 for U.S. residents or $20 for residents of Canada, Mexico, and other countries—and is immediately exceeded by the value of your benefits, which include:

1. Any TWO books listed on the following pages.
2. Plus any ONE Frommer's City Guide.
3. A subscription to our quarterly newspaper, *The Dollarwise Traveler*.
4. A membership card that entitles you to purchase through the Club all Frommer's publications for 33% to 50% off their retail price.

The eight-page **Dollarwise Traveler** tells you about the latest developments in good-value travel worldwide and includes the following columns: **Hospitality Exchange** (for those offering and seeking hospitality in cities all over the world); **Share-a-Trip** (for those looking for travel companions to share costs); and **Readers Ask . . . Readers Reply** (for those with travel questions that other members can answer).

Aside from the Frommer's Guides and the Gault Millau Guides, you can also choose from our Special Editions. These include such titles as **California with Kids** (a compendium of the best of California's accommodations, restaurants, and sightseeing attractions appropriate for those traveling with toddlers through teens); **Candy Apple: New York with Kids** (a spirited guide to the Big Apple by a savvy New York grandmother that's perfect for both visitors and residents); **Caribbean Hideaways** (the 100 most romantic places to stay in the Islands, all rated on ambience, food, sports opportunities, and price); **Honeymoon Destinations** (a guide to planning and choosing just the right destination from hundreds of possibilities in the U.S., Mexico, and the Caribbean); **Marilyn Wood's Wonderful Weekends** (a selection of the best mini-vacations within a 200-mile radius of New York City, including descriptions of country inns and other accommodations, restaurants, picnic spots, sights, and activities); and **Paris Rendez-Vous** (a delightful guide to the best places to meet in Paris whether for power breakfasts or dancing till dawn).

To join this Club, simply send the appropriate membership fee with your name and address to: Frommer's Dollarwise Travel Club, 15 Columbus Circle, New York, NY 10023. Remember to specify which single city guide and which two other guides you wish to receive in your initial package of member's benefits. Or tear out the next page, check off your choices, and send the page to us with your membership fee.

FROMMER BOOKS
PRENTICE HALL PRESS
15 COLUMBUS CIRCLE
NEW YORK, NY 10023
212/373-8125

Date_____

Friends:
Please send me the books checked below.

FROMMER'S™ GUIDES

(Guides to sightseeing and tourist accommodations and facilities from budget to deluxe, with emphasis on the medium-priced.)

☐ Alaska $14.95	☐ Germany $14.95
☐ Australia $14.95	☐ Italy. $14.95
☐ Austria & Hungary $14.95	☐ Japan & Hong Kong $14.95
☐ Belgium, Holland & Luxembourg $14.95	☐ Mid-Atlantic States $14.95
☐ Bermuda & The Bahamas. $14.95	☐ New England. $14.95
☐ Brazil $14.95	☐ New York State $14.95
☐ Canada $14.95	☐ Northwest $14.95
☐ Caribbean. $14.95	☐ Portugal, Madeira & the Azores $14.95
☐ Cruises (incl. Alaska, Carib, Mex, Hawaii,	☐ Skiing Europe $14.95
Panama, Canada & US) $14.95	☐ South Pacific. $14.95
☐ California & Las Vegas $14.95	☐ Southeast Asia $14.95
☐ Egypt. $14.95	☐ Southern Atlantic States. $14.95
☐ England & Scotland $14.95	☐ Southwest $14.95
☐ Florida $14.95	☐ Switzerland & Liechtenstein $14.95
☐ France $14.95	☐ USA. $15.95

FROMMER'S $-A-DAY® GUIDES

(In-depth guides to sightseeing and low-cost tourist accommodations and facilities.)

☐ Europe on $40 a Day $15.95	☐ New York on $60 a Day. $13.95
☐ Australia on $40 a Day $13.95	☐ New Zealand on $45 a Day $13.95
☐ Eastern Europe on $25 a Day $13.95	☐ Scandinavia on $60 a Day $13.95
☐ England on $50 a Day. $13.95	☐ Scotland & Wales on $40 a Day $13.95
☐ Greece on $35 a Day $13.95	☐ South America on $35 a Day $13.95
☐ Hawaii on $60 a Day. $13.95	☐ Spain & Morocco on $40 a Day $13.95
☐ India on $25 a Day $12.95	☐ Turkey on $30 a Day $13.95
☐ Ireland on $35 a Day. $13.95	☐ Washington, D.C. & Historic Va. on
☐ Israel on $40 a Day. $13.95	$40 a Day $13.95
☐ Mexico on $35 a Day $13.95	

FROMMER'S TOURING GUIDES

(Color illustrated guides that include walking tours, cultural and historic sites, and other vital travel information.)

☐ Amsterdam. $10.95	☐ New York $10.95
☐ Australia $9.95	☐ Paris $8.95
☐ Brazil. $10.95	☐ Rome. $10.95
☐ Egypt. $8.95	☐ Scotland. $9.95
☐ Florence. $8.95	☐ Thailand. $9.95
☐ Hong Kong $10.95	☐ Turkey $10.95
☐ London $8.95	☐ Venice $8.95

TURN PAGE FOR ADDITONAL BOOKS AND ORDER FORM

FROMMER'S CITY GUIDES

(Pocket-size guides to sightseeing and tourist accommodations and facilities in all price ranges.)

☐ Amsterdam/Holland $8.95	☐ Montréal/Québec City. $8.95
☐ Athens. $8.95	☐ New Orleans. $8.95
☐ Atlanta $8.95	☐ New York $8.95
☐ Atlantic City/Cape May $8.95	☐ Orlando $8.95
☐ Barcelona. $7.95	☐ Paris $8.95
☐ Belgium $7.95	☐ Philadelphia $8.95
☐ Boston. $8.95	☐ Rio $8.95
☐ Cancún/Cozumel/Yucatán. $8.95	☐ Rome. $8.95
☐ Chicago. $8.95	☐ Salt Lake City $8.95
☐ Denver/Boulder/Colorado Springs. $7.95	☐ San Diego. $8.95
☐ Dublin/Ireland $8.95	☐ San Francisco $8.95
☐ Hawaii. $8.95	☐ Santa Fe/Taos/Albuquerque. $8.95
☐ Hong Kong. $7.95	☐ Seattle/Portland $7.95
☐ Las Vegas. $8.95	☐ Sydney. $8.95
☐ Lisbon/Madrid/Costa del Sol $8.95	☐ Tampa/St. Petersburg $8.95
☐ London $8.95	☐ Tokyo. $7.95
☐ Los Angeles $8.95	☐ Toronto $8.95
☐ Mexico City/Acapulco. $8.95	☐ Vancouver/Victoria. $7.95
☐ Minneapolis/St. Paul $8.95	☐ Washington, D.C. $8.95

SPECIAL EDITIONS

☐ Beat the High Cost of Travel. $6.95	☐ Motorist's Phrase Book (Fr/Ger/Sp) $4.95
☐ Bed & Breakfast—N. America $11.95	☐ Paris Rendez-Vous $10.95
☐ California with Kids $14.95	☐ Swap and Go (Home Exchanging). . . .$10.95
☐ Caribbean Hideaways. $14.95	☐ The Candy Apple (NY with Kids). $12.95
☐ Honeymoon Destinations (US, Mex &	☐ Travel Diary and Record Book. $5.95
Carib). $14.95	☐ Where to Stay USA (From $3 to $30 a
☐ Manhattan's Outdoor Sculpture. $15.95	night). $10.95

☐ Marilyn Wood's Wonderful Weekends (CT, DE, MA, NH, NJ, NY, PA, RI, VT) $11.95
☐ The New World of Travel (Annual sourcebook by Arthur Frommer for savvy travelers) $16.95

GAULT MILLAU

(The only guides that distinguish the truly superlative from the merely overrated.)

☐ The Best of Chicago $15.95	☐ The Best of Los Angeles $16.95
☐ The Best of France $16.95	☐ The Best of New England $15.95
☐ The Best of Hong Kong. $16.95	☐ The Best of New York $16.95
☐ The Best of Italy. $16.95	☐ The Best of Paris $16.95
☐ The Best of London $16.95	☐ The Best of San Francisco $16.95

☐ The Best of Washington, D.C. $16.95

ORDER NOW!

In U.S. include $2 shipping UPS for 1st book; $1 ea. add'l book. Outside U.S. $3 and $1, respectively.
Allow four to six weeks for delivery in U.S., longer outside U.S.

Enclosed is my check or money order for $_____

NAME_____

ADDRESS_____

CITY_____ STATE_____ ZIP_____

0690